A PRISON DIARY

FROM HELL TO HEAVEN

By the same author

NOVELS

Not a Penny More, Not a Penny Less

Shall We Tell the President?

Kane and Abel

The Prodigal Daughter

First Among Equals

A Matter of Honour

As the Crow Flies

Honour Among Thieves

The Fourth Estate

The Eleventh Commandment

Sons of Fortune

SHORT STORIES

A Quiver Full of Arrows

A Twist in the Tale

Twelve Red Herrings

The Collected Short Stories

To Cut a Long Story Short

PLAYS

Beyond Reasonable Doubt

Exclusive

The Accused

FF8282

A PRISON DIARY

VOLUME ONE – BELMARSH: HELL

VOLUME TWO – WAYLAND: PURGATORY

VOLUME THREE – NORTH SEA CAMP: HEAVEN

MACMILLAN

A Prison Diary, Volume I – Belmarsh: Hell
First published 2002 by Macmillan

A Prison Diary, Volume II – Wayland: Purgatory
First published 2003 by Macmillan

A Prison Diary, Volume III – North Sea Camp: Heaven
First published 2004 by Macmillan

This omnibus edition first published 2005 by Macmillan
an imprint of Pan Macmillan Ltd
Pan Macmillan, 20 New Wharf Road, London N1 9RR
Basingstoke and Oxford
Associated companies throughout the world
www.panmacmillan.com

ISBN 1 4050 8851 6

A CIP catalogue record for this book is available from
the British Library.

Typeset by SetSystems Ltd, Saffron Walden, Essex
Printed and bound in Great Britain by
Mackays of Chatham plc, Chatham, Kent

CONTENTS

BELMARSH: HELL   1

WAYLAND: PURGATORY   267

NORTH SEA CAMP: HEAVEN   583

Permissions acknowledgements

A Prison Diary, Volume I – Belmarsh: Hell
The publishers gratefully acknowledge
Michael, Billy Little, Colin Kitto, Kenneth Chan and Derek Jones
for permission to reproduce copyright material.

A Prison Diary, Volume II – Wayland: Purgatory
'The Card Players', 1989, copyright © Fernando Botero,
courtesy, Marlborough Gallery, New York.

'Nature Notes on Osama Bin Laden as a poisonous mushroom'
copyright © Peter Brookes / *The Times*, London, 2001.

The author and publisher are grateful to George Carey
for permission to reproduce his letter on page 247, and
to Shaun for permission to reproduce original artwork
used in the plate section.

BELMARSH

HELL

TO

FOUL-WEATHER FRIENDS

INVICTUS

Out of the night that covers me,
Black as the Pit from pole to pole,
I thank whatever gods may be
For my unconquerable soul.

In the fell clutch of circumstance,
I have not winced or cried aloud;
Under the bludgeonings of chance
My head is bloody, but unbowed.

Beyond this place of wrath and tears
Looms but the Horror of the shade.
And yet the menace of the years
Finds, and shall find me, unafraid.

It matters not how strait the gate,
How charged with punishments the scroll,
I am the master of my fate:
I am the captain of my soul.

William Ernest Henley (1849–1903)

DAY 1   THURSDAY 19 JULY 2001

12.07 pm

'You are sentenced to four years.' Mr Justice Potts stares down from the bench, unable to hide his delight. He orders me to be taken down.

A Securicor man who was sitting beside me while the verdict was read out points towards a door on my left which has not been opened during the seven-week trial. I turn and glance at my wife Mary seated at the back of the court, head bowed, ashen-faced, a son on either side to comfort her.

I'm led downstairs to be met by a court official, and thus I begin an endless process of form-filling. Name? Archer. Age? 61. Weight? 178lbs, I tell him.

'What's that in stones?' the prison officer demands.

'12st 10lbs,' I reply. I only know because I weighed myself in the gym this morning.

'Thank you, sir,' he says, and asks me to sign on the bottom of the page.

Another Securicor man – known by the prisoners as water-rats – leads me down a long bleak cream-painted bricked corridor to I know not where.

'How long did he give you?' he asks, matter-of-factly.

'Four years,' I reply.

'Oh, not too bad, you'll be out in two,' he responds, as if discussing a fortnight on the Costa del Sol.

The officer comes to a halt, unlocks a vast steel door, and then ushers me into a cell. The room is about ten feet by five, the walls are still cream, and there is a wooden bench running along the far end. No clock, no sense of time, nothing to do except contemplate, nothing to read, except messages on the walls:

HARRY WAS HERE   FUCK ALL JUDGES
        JIM DEXTER Is INOCENT, OK!

A key is turning in the lock, and the heavy door swings open. The Securicor man has returned. 'You have a visit from your legals,' he announces. I am marched back down the long corridor, barred gates are unlocked and locked every few paces. Then I am ushered into a room only slightly larger than the cell to find my silk, Nicholas Purnell QC, and his junior, Alex Cameron, awaiting me.

Nick explains that four years means two, and Mr Justice Potts chose a custodial sentence aware that I would be unable to appeal to the Parole Board for early release. Of course they will appeal on my behalf, as they feel Potts has gone way over the top. Gilly Gray QC, an old friend, had warned me the previous evening that as the jury had been out for five days and I had not entered the witness box to defend myself, an appeal might not be received too favourably. Nick adds that in any case, my appeal will not be considered before Christmas, as only short sentences are dealt with quickly.

Nick goes on to tell me that Belmarsh Prison, in Woolwich, will be my first destination.

'At least it's a modern jail,' he comments, although he warns me that his abiding memory of the place was the constant noise, so he feared I wouldn't sleep for the first few nights. After a couple of weeks, he feels confident I will be transferred to a Category D prison – an open prison – probably Ford or the Isle of Sheppey.

Nick explains that he has to leave me and return to Court No. 7 to make an application for compassionate leave, so that I can attend my mother's funeral on Saturday. She died on the day the jury retired to consider their verdict, and I am only thankful that she never heard me sentenced.

I thank Nick and Alex for all they have done, and am then escorted back to my cell. The vast iron door is slammed shut. The prison officers don't have to lock it, only unlock it, as there is no handle on the inside. I sit on the wooden bench, to be reminded that *Jim Dexter is inocent, OK!* My mind is curiously blank as I try to take in what has happened and what will happen next.

The door is unlocked again – about fifteen minutes later as far as I can judge – and I'm taken to a signing-out room to fill in yet another set of forms. A large burly officer who only grunts takes away my money clip, £120 in cash, my credit card and a fountain pen. He places them in a plastic bag. They are sealed before he asks, 'Where would you like them sent?' I give the officer Mary's name and our home address. After I've signed two more forms in triplicate, I'm handcuffed to an overweight woman of around five foot three, a cigarette dangling from the corner of her mouth. They are obviously not anticipating any trouble. She is wearing the official uniform of the prison service: a white shirt, black tie, black trousers, black shoes and black socks.

She accompanies me out of the building and on to an

elongated white van, not unlike a single-decker bus, except that the windows are blacked out. I am placed in what I could only describe as a cubicle – known to the recidivists as a sweatbox – and although I can see outside, the waiting press cannot see me; in any case, they have no idea which cubicle I'm in. Cameras flash pointlessly in front of each window as we wait to move off. Another long wait, before I hear a prisoner shout, 'I think Archer's in this van.' Eventually the vehicle jerks forward and moves slowly out of the Old Bailey courtyard on the first leg of a long circuitous journey to HMP Belmarsh.

As we travel slowly through the streets of the City, I spot an *Evening Standard* billboard already in place: ARCHER SENT TO JAIL. It looks as if it was printed some time before the verdict.

I am well acquainted with the journey the van is taking through London, as Mary and I follow the same route home to Cambridge on Friday evenings. Except on this occasion we suddenly turn right off the main road and into a little backstreet, to be greeted by another bevy of pressmen. But like their colleagues at the Old Bailey, all they can get is a photograph of a large white van with ten small black windows. As we draw up to the entrance gate, I see a sign declaring BELMARSH PRISON. Some wag has put a line through the B and replaced it with an H. Not the most propitious of welcomes.

We drive through two high-barred gates that are electronically operated before the van comes to a halt in a courtyard surrounded by a thirty-foot red-brick wall, with razor wire looped along the top. I once read that this is the only top-security prison in Britain from which no one has ever escaped. I look up at the wall and recall that the world record for the pole vault is 20ft 2in.

The door of the van is opened and we are let out one by one before being led off to a reception area, and then herded into a large glass cell that holds about twenty people. The authorities can't risk putting that many prisoners in the same room without being able to see exactly what we're up to. This will often be the first time co-defendants have a chance to speak to each other since they were sentenced. I sit on a bench on the far side of the wall, and am joined by a tall, well-dressed, good-looking young Pakistani, who explains that he is not a prisoner, but on remand. I ask him what he's been charged with. 'GBH – grievous bodily harm. I beat up my wife when I found her in bed with another man, and now they've banged me up in Belmarsh because the trial can't begin until she gets back from Greece, where the two of them are on holiday.'

I recall Nick Purnell's parting words, 'Don't believe anything anyone tells you in prison, and never discuss your case or your appeal.'

'Archer,' yells a voice. I leave the glass cell and return to reception where I am told to fill out another form. 'Name, age, height, weight?' the prison officer behind the counter demands.

'Archer, 61, 5ft 10, 178lbs.'

'What's that in stones?' he asks.

'12st 10lbs,' I tell him, and he fills in yet another little square box.

'Right, go next door, Archer, where you'll find my colleague waiting for you.'

This time I am met by two officers. One standing, one sitting behind a desk. The one behind the desk asks me to stand under an arc light and strip. The two officers try to carry out the entire exercise as humanely as possible. First, I take off my jacket, then my tie, followed by my shirt. 'Aquascutum, Hilditch & Key, and YSL,' says the officer who is standing up, while the other writes this information down in the appropriate box. The first officer then asks me to raise my arms above my head and turn a complete circle, while a video camera attached to the wall whirrs away in the background. My shirt is returned, but they hold on to my House of Commons cufflinks. They hand back my jacket, but not my tie. I am then asked to slip off my shoes, socks, trousers and pants. 'Church's, Aquascutum and Calvin Klein,' he announces. I complete another circle, and this time the officer asks me to lift the soles of my feet for inspection. He explains that drugs are sometimes concealed under plasters. I tell them I've never taken a drug in my life. He shows no interest. They return my pants, trousers, socks and shoes but not my leather belt.

'Is this yours?' he asks, pointing to a yellow backpack on the table beside me.

'No, I've never seen it before,' I tell him.

He checks the label. 'William Archer,' he says.

'Sorry, it must be my son's.'

The officer pulls open the zip to reveal two shirts, two pairs of pants, a sweater, a pair of casual shoes and a washbag containing everything I will need. The washbag is immediately confiscated while the rest of the clothes are placed in a line on the counter. The officer then hands me a large plastic bag with HMP Belmarsh printed in dark blue letters, supported by a crown. Everything has a logo nowadays. While I transfer the possessions I am allowed to keep into the large plastic bag, the officer tells me that the yellow backpack will be returned to my son, at the government's expense. I thank him. He looks surprised. Another officer escorts me back to the glass cell, while I cling onto my plastic bag.

This time I sit next to a different prisoner, who tells me his name is Ashmil; he's from Kosovo, and still in the middle of his trial. 'What are you charged with?' I enquire.

'The illegal importing of immigrants,' he tells me, and before I can offer any comment he adds, 'They're all political prisoners who would be in jail, or worse, if they were still in their own country.' It sounds like a well-rehearsed line. 'What are you in for?' he asks.

'Archer,' rings out the same officious voice, and I leave him to return to the reception area.

'The doctor will see you now,' the desk officer says, pointing to a green door behind him.

I don't know why I'm surprised to encounter a fresh-faced young GP, who rises from behind his desk the moment I walk in.

'David Haskins,' he announces, and adds, 'I'm sorry we have to meet in these circumstances.' I take a seat on the other side of the desk while he opens a drawer and produces yet another form.

'Do you smoke?'

'No.'

'Drink?'

'No, unless you count the occasional glass of red wine at dinner.'

'Take any drugs?'

'No.'

'Do you have any history of mental illness?'

'No.'

'Have you ever tried to abuse yourself?'

'No.'

He continues through a series of questions as if he were doing no more than filling in details for an insurance policy, to which I continue to reply, no, no, no, no and no. He ticks every box.

DAY 1

'Although I don't think it's necessary,' he says, looking down at the form, 'I'm going to put you in the medical wing overnight before the Governor decides which block to put you on.'

I smile, as the medical wing sounds to me like a more pleasant option. He doesn't return the smile. We shake hands, and I go back to the glass cell. I only have to wait for a few more moments before a young lady in prison uniform asks me to accompany her to the medical wing. I grab my plastic bag and follow her.

We climb three floors of green iron steps before we reach our destination. As I walk down the long corridor my heart sinks. Every person I come across seems to be in an advanced state of depression or suffering from some sort of mental illness.

'Why have they put me in here?' I demand, but she doesn't reply. I later learn that most first-time offenders spend their first night in the medical centre because it is during your first twenty-four hours in prison that you are most likely to try and commit suicide.*

I'm not, as I thought I might be, placed in a hospital ward but in another cell. When the door slams behind me I begin to understand why one might contemplate suicide. The cell measures five paces by three, and this time the brick walls are painted a depressing mauve. In one corner is a single bed with a rock-hard mattress that could well be an army reject. Against the side wall, opposite the bed, is a small square steel table and a steel chair. On the far wall next to the inch-thick iron door is a steel washbasin and an open lavatory that has no lid and no flush. I

---

*73 people committed suicide in British prisons in 2001; 22 of them were first-time offenders. Over 1,500 prisoners attempted hanging, strangulation or suffocation in 2000, a rise of 50 per cent over the 1999 figures.

am determined not to use it.* On the wall behind the bed is a window encased with four thick iron bars, painted black, and caked in dirt. No curtains, no curtain rail. Stark, cold and unwelcoming would be a generous description of my temporary residence on the medical wing. No wonder the doctor didn't return my smile. I am left alone in this bleak abode for over an hour, by which time I'm beginning to experience a profound depression.

A key finally turns in the lock to allow another young woman to enter. She is dark-haired, short and slim, dressed in a smart striped suit. She shakes me warmly by the hand, sits on the end of the bed, and introduces herself as Ms Roberts, the Deputy Governor. She can't be a day over twenty-six.

'What am I doing here?' I ask. 'I'm not a mass murderer.'

'Most prisoners spend their first night on the medical wing,' she explains, 'and we can't make any exceptions, I'm afraid, and especially not for you.' I don't say anything – what is there to say? 'One more form to complete,' she tells me, 'that's if you still want to attend your mother's funeral on Saturday.'† I can sense that Ms Roberts is trying hard to be understanding and considerate, but I fear I am quite unable to hide my distress.

'You will be moved onto an induction block tomorrow,' she assures me, 'and just as soon as you've been categorized A, B, C, or D, we'll transfer you to another prison. I have no doubt you'll be Category D – no previous convictions, and no history of violence.' She rises from the end of the bed. Every officer carries

---

* There are no wooden items in the cell, as first-night prisoners often smash up everything.
† Nick Purnell QC asked Mr Justice Potts if I could be excused from the court to be with my mother. He refused our request. A second request was made at the beginning of the afternoon session, which he reluctantly agreed to. I reached my mother's bedside an hour before she died.

a large bunch of keys that jingle whenever they move. 'I'll see you again in the morning. Have you been able to make a phone call?' she asks as she bangs on the heavy door with the palm of her hand.

'No,' I reply as the cell door is opened by a large West Indian with an even larger smile.

'Then I'll see what I can do,' she promises before stepping out into the corridor and slamming the door closed behind her.

I sit on the end of the bed and rummage through my plastic bag to discover that my elder son, William, has included amongst my permitted items a copy of David Niven's *The Moon's a Balloon*. I flick open the cover to find a message:

> *Hope you never have to read this, Dad, but if you do, chin up,*
> *we love you and your appeal is on its way,*
> *William xx James xx*

Thank God for a family I adore, and who still seem to care about me. I'm not sure how I would have got through the last few weeks without them. They made so many sacrifices to be with me for every day of the seven-week trial.

There is a rap on the cell door, and a steel grille that resembles a large letter box is pulled up to reveal the grinning West Indian.

'I'm Lester,' he declares as he pushes through a pillow – rock hard; one pillow case – mauve; followed by one sheet – green; and one blanket – brown. I thank Lester and then take some considerable time making the bed. After all, there's nothing else to do.

When I've completed the task, I sit on the bed and start trying to read *The Moon's a Balloon*, but my mind continually wanders. I manage about fifty pages, often stopping to consider the jury's verdict, and although I feel tired, even exhausted, I can't begin to think about sleep. The promised phone call has not materialized, so I finally turn off the fluorescent light that shines above the bed, place my head on the rock-hard pillow and despite the agonizing cries of the patients from the cells on either side of me, I eventually fall asleep. An hour later I'm woken again when the fluorescent light is switched back on, the letter box reopens and two different eyes peer in at me – a procedure that is repeated every hour, on the hour – to make sure I haven't tried to take my own life. The suicide watch.

I eventually fall asleep again, and when I wake just after 4 am, I lie on my back in a straight line, because both my ears are aching after hours on the rock-hard pillow. I think about the verdict, and the fact that it had never crossed my mind even for a moment that the jury could find Francis innocent and me guilty of the same charge. How could we have conspired if one of us didn't realize a conspiracy was taking place? They also appeared to accept the word of my former secretary, Angie Peppiatt, a woman who stole thousands of pounds from me, while deceiving me and my family for years.

Eventually I turn my mind to the future. Determined not to waste an hour, I decide to write a daily diary of everything I experience while incarcerated.

At 6 am, I rise from my mean bed and rummage around in my plastic bag. Yes, what I need is there, and this time the authorities have not determined that it should be returned to sender. Thank God for a son who had the foresight to include, amongst other necessities, an A4 pad and six felt-tip pens.

Two hours later I have completed the first draft of everything that has happened to me since I was sent to jail.

DAY 2   FRIDAY 20 JULY 2001

8.00 am

I am woken officially – my little trapdoor is opened and I am greeted by the same warm West Indian grin, which turns to a look of surprise when he sees me sitting at the table writing. I've already been at work for nearly two hours.

'You'll be able to have a shower in a few minutes,' he announces. I've already worked out that in prison a few minutes can be anything up to an hour, so I go on writing. 'Anything you need?' he asks politely.

'Would it be possible to have some more writing paper?'

'Not something I'm often asked for,' he admits, 'but I'll see what I can do.'

Lester returns half an hour later and this time the grin has turned into a shy smile. He slips an A4 pad, not unlike the type I always use, through the little steel trap. In return he asks me for six autographs, only one to be personalized – for his daughter Michelle. Lester doesn't offer any explanation for why he needs the other five, all to be penned on separate sheets of paper. As no money can change hands in jail, we return to thirteenth-century England and rely on bartering.

I can't imagine what five Jeffrey Archer signatures are worth:

a packet of cigarettes, perhaps? But I am grateful for this trade, because I have a feeling that being allowed to write in this hellhole may turn out to be the one salvation that will keep me sane.

While I wait for Lester to return and escort me from my cell to a shower – even a walk down a long, drab corridor is something I am looking forward to – I continue writing. At last I hear a key turning and look up to see the heavy door swing open, which brings its own small sense of freedom. Lester hands me a thin green towel, a prison toothbrush and a tube of prison toothpaste before locking me back in. I clean my teeth, and my gums bleed for the first time in years. It must be some physical reaction to what I've been put through during the past twenty-four hours. I worry a little, because during my interrupted night I'd promised myself that I must remain physically and mentally fit. This, according to the prison handbook left in every cell, is nothing less than the management requires.*

After a night on the medical wing, one of my first impressions is how many of the staff, dressed in their smart, clean black uniforms, seem able to keep a smile on their face. I'm sitting on my bed wondering what to expect next, when my thoughts are interrupted by someone shouting from the other side of the block.

'Mornin', Jeff, bet you didn't expect to find yourself in 'ere.'

I look through my tiny window and across the yard to see a face staring at me from behind his own bars. Another grin. 'I'm Gordon,' he shouts. 'See you in the exercise yard in an hour or two.'

---

*They also emphasize in the same booklet that Belmarsh will not tolerate any form of bullying and they have a firm policy of no racial, ethnic or religious discrimination.

DAY 2

9.00 am

I'm let out of the cell and walk slowly down the corridor, to enjoy my new-found freedom, as Lester escorts me to the shower room. I feel I should let you know that in my apartment on the Albert Embankment, perhaps the facility of which I am most proud is the shower room. When I step out of it each morning, I feel a new man, ready to face the world. Belmarsh doesn't offer quite the same facilities or leave you with the same warm feeling. The large stone-floored room has three small press-button showers that issue a trickle of water which is at best lukewarm. The pressure lasts for about thirty seconds before you have to push the button again. This means a shower takes twice as long as usual but, as I am becoming aware, in prison time is the one commodity that is in abundance. Lester escorts me back to my cell, while I cling on to my small soaking towel. He tells me not to lose sight of it, because a towel has to last for seven days.

He slams the door closed.

10.00 am

I lie on my bed, staring up at the white ceiling, until my thoughts are once again interrupted by a key turning in the lock. I have no idea who it will be this time. It turns out to be a plump lady dressed in a prison uniform who has something in common with the West Indian barterer – a warm smile. She sits down on the end of my bed and hands me a form for the prison canteen. She explains that, if I can afford it, I am allowed to spend twelve pounds fifty pence a week. I must fill in the little boxes showing what I would like, and then she will see that the order is left in my cell sometime later today. I don't bother to enquire what 'sometime later' means. When she leaves, I study the canteen list meticulously, trying to identify what might be described as necessities.

I am horrified to discover that the first column on the list is dominated by several different types of tobacco, and the second column by batteries – think about it. I study the form for some considerable time, and even enjoy deciding how I will spend my twelve pounds fifty. (See pages 16–17.)

11.00 am

A bell rings, as if announcing the end of class. The cell door is opened to allow me to join the other inmates and spend forty-five minutes in the exercise yard. I'm sure you've seen this activity portrayed in many films – it's not quite the same experience when you have to participate yourself. Before going down to the yard, we all have to undergo another body search, not unlike one you might go through at an airport. We are then led down three flights of iron steps to an exercise yard at ground level.

I pace around the furlong square that is enclosed by a high red-brick wall, with a closely mown threadbare lawn in the centre. After a couple of rounds, I'm joined by Gordon, the voice who greeted me this morning from the window on the other side of the block. He turns out to be tall and slim, with the build of an athlete. He tells me without any prompting that he has already served eleven years of a fourteen-year sentence for murder. This is the fifth prison they've sent him to. Can't be for good behaviour, is my first reaction.* The author in me is curious to find out more about him, but I don't have to ask any questions because he

---

* It is not uncommon for a lifer to be moved from prison to prison, so that they can never settle or gain the upper hand.

PRISONERS NAME		NUMBER		WING AND CELL NUMBER		DATE :	
ARCHER		FE 828L		MEDICAL WING		JULY 20th	

TOBACCO	CODE	COST	QTY	TOTAL	CONFECTIONERY	CODE	COST	QTY	TOTAL
GOLDEN VIRGINIA (5g)	1	£ 1.25			FUDGE Bar Cadbury's		£ 0.15		
Red Bull Tobacco 12.5g		£ 1.42			FUSE BAR	45	£ 0.33		
H.M.P LIGHTER	2	£ 0.33			CADS F / N BAR 52g	46	£ 0.35		
	3				CADS CRUNCHIE	47	£ 0.35		
MATCHES	4	£ 0.10			CADS CHOC ECLAIRS	48	£ 0.65		
B & HEDGES SINGLES	5	£ 0.22			RIPPLE	49	£ 0.33		
B & HEDGES TWENTIES	6	£ 4.35			MALTESER: .	50	£ 0.35		
MARLBOROUGH TWENTIES	7	£ 4.35			TOFFO ASSORTED	51	£ 0.28		
SILK CUT KINGSIZE TWENTIES	8	£ 4.35			BOUNTY BAR	52	£ 0.33		
RONSON KINGSIZE 1x18	9	£ 3.20			MARS 65g	53	£ 0.30		
HAMLET CIGARS	10	£ 0.59			TWIX BAR 58g	54	£ 0.30		
CLAN AROMATIC	11	£ 3.39			TUNES	55	£ 0.42		
GOLDEN VIRGINIA 12.5g	12	£ 2.27			MILKY WAY	56	£ 0.16		
OLD HOLBORN 12.5g	13	£ 2.27			SNICKERS BAR	57	£ 0.32		
RIZALA RED / GREEN PAPERS	14	£ 0.20			MAYNARD; WINE GUMS	58	£ 0.32		
Red Bull or other brands Cig Paper	15	£ 0.12				59	£		
FILTERS	16	£ 0.52			YORKIES	60	£ 0.35		
					FRUIT PASTILLES	61	£ 0.30		
					EXTRA STRONG MINTS	62	£ 0.30		
BATTERIES					NUTS 50g / RAISINS	63	£ 0.45		
EVER READY R20S	19	£ 0.62			CRISPS READY SALTED	64	£ 0.28		
EVER READY R14S	20	£ 0.50			CRISPS CHEESE AND ONION	64	£ 0.28		
EVER READY R6S	21	£ 0.16			CRISPS SALT AND VINEGAR	64	£ 0.28		
ENERGISER LR20	23	£ 0.80			CRISPS OTHER (PLEASE STATE)	64	£ 0.28		
ENERGISER LR14	24	£ 0.52			PRINGLES READY SALTED	64	£ 0.55		
ENERGISER LR6	25	£ 0.28			PRINGLES SOUR CREAM	64	£ 0.55		
EVER READY PP9	26	£ 1.90			PRINGLES SALT AND VINEGAR	64	£ 0.55		
POSTAGE AND PHONECARDS					CHEWS ASSTD		£ 0.01		
1ST CLASS STAMPS (SINGLE UNIT)	241	£ 0.27			M & M PEANUTS	65	£ 0.36		
2ND CLASS STAMPS (SINGLE UNIT)	242	£ 0.19			POLO MINTS	66	£ 0.21		
STAMPS SPECIAL (SINGLE UNIT)	243	£ 0.08			KIT KAT 4 FINGER		£ 0.30		
					STARBURST		£ 0.33		
AEROGRAMMES (SINGLE UNIT)	244	£ 0.38			CAD FLAKE		£ 0.36		
PHONECARDS 1 X 20 UNITS	245	£ 2.00			TRACKER / LIONBAR		£ 0.32		
PHONECARDS 1 X 40 UNITS	246	£ 4.00			PICNIC		£ 0.37		
STATIONERY / ELECTRICAL					FREDO (SINGLE)		£	150	
A4. PADS	31	1.25			BOMBAY MIX		£ 0.42		
WRITING PADS	32	0.78			BEVERAGES AND SOFT DRINKS				
ENVELOPES	33	0.75			COFFEE PLASTIC JAR	162	£ 2.35		
BIC PENS	34	0.20			QUALITY TEABAGS	163	£ 0.62		
BMU COLOUR PENCILS	35	1.15			TWININGS HERBAL TEAS 1X20s		£1.17		
SKETCH PADS A.4	36	0.90			TWININGS HERBAL FRUITSTEAS 1X20s		£1.25	MIXED	
HELIX RULER 30cm	37	0.40			NESCAFE COFFEE SATCHETS	199	£ 0.09		
PLAYING CARDS	38		99p		CAPACHINO SATCHETS	196	£ 0.30		
All Radios etc Argos Catalogue Prices Plus 6%	150				OVALTINE	201	£ 1.57		
	152				NESTLE CONDENSED MILK LRG	171	£ 1.65		
FLASK SMALL (ENHANCED PRISONERS ONLY) 1x.05Ltr	281	6.13			DRINKING CHOCOLATE 250g	177	£ 1.36		
					MARVEL MILK POWDER	172	£ 1.89		
REPLACEMENT PRICE LISTS		£0.10			UHT WHOLE MILK/ SEMI SKIM 500m	76	£ 0.45		
					UHT SOYA MILK UNSWEETENED 500ml		£0.53		
					ROBINSONS APPLE / BLACK	70	£ 1.10		
	85	£0.38			ROBINSONS LEMON	71	£ 1.10		
PEANUTS SALTED	86	£0.42			ROBINSONS ORANGE	72	£ 1.10		
	87				LILT CAN OR 300ml	73	£ 0.50		
KIT KAT CHUNKEY		£0.33			COCA COLA OR DIET COKE 330ml	75	£ 0.50		
MONKEY NUTS		£0.50			S / SPRING BOTTLES	77	£ 0.49		
					T.D.Y. ORANGE JUICE	78	£ 0.68		
TODAYS SEEDLESS RAISINS 375g /SULTANAS		£0.90			WATER 1.5Ltr	79	£ 0.82		
SESAME SNAPS		£0.22			CANS 330ml FANTA	80	£ 0.50		
CRESPO BLACK OLIVES POUCH		£0.65			LUCOZADE	81	£ 2.15		
NESQUICK STRAWBERRY/CHOCOLATE 225g		£1.39			CRANBERRY JUICE		£1.16		

PRISONER'S NAME :		NUMBER :			WING & CELL NUMBER :		DATE :		

CARDS	CODE	COST	QTY	TOTAL	GROCERIES	CODE	COST	QTY	TOTAL
SMALL CARDS	83	£0.76			GRANULATED SUGAR 1Kg	160	£0.75		
LARGE CARDS	84	£1.16			T & L SUGAR GRAN 500g	161	£0.69		
XMAS CARDS LARGE	86				DEMERARA SUGAR 500g	164	£0.77		
XMAS CARDS SMALL	86				ROWSE HONEY 12 oz	176	£2.06		
XMAS CARDS BOX	87				ROBINSONS SQZY JAM		£1.26		
CARDS OTHER					FLORA MARGARINE	161	£0.69		
GIVE AS MUCH DETAIL AS POSSIBLE					DAIRYLEA PORTIONS	166	£0.70		
					MATURE CHEESE PORTIONS	174	£1.40		
- -					MINI CHEDDARS	158	£0.28		
- -					PEANUT BUTTER	198	~~£0.95~~	1.62	
TOILETRIES / HEALTH PRODUCTS					POT NOODLE CHIX / MUSH	168	£0.89		
					POT NOODLE CURRY	169	£0.89		
NIVEA CREAM 26ml	104	£1.24			POT NOODLE BEEF / TOM	170	£0.89		
E46 SKIN CREAM	110	£1.36	1.95		KOKA NOODLES 85g ASSTD		£0.32		
CHAP STICK / LIPSYL	100	£1.03			CUPPA SOUP	173	£0.22		
COCOA BUTTER NATURAL LOTION 500ml	102	£0.88			HEINZ SQZY MAYONNAISE		£1.76		
COCOA BUTTER PALMERS LOTION 260ml		£3.38			HEINZ SALAD CREAM	176	£2.00		
DAX POM green 100g	103	2.07			TOMATO KETCHUP 460g	182	£1.40		
VITAMINS 60s	106	£1.77			BROWN SAUCE	184	£1.86		
COD LIVER OIL CAPSULES	106	£1.90			OXO CUBES SINGLE	185	£0.09		
DP 90 VARIOUS	107	£6.90	5.90		KELLOGS CORNFLAKES 250g	178	£1.14		
GARLIC CAPSULES	108	£1.49			KELLOGS VARIETY 12s	179	£1.99		
	110	£0.95			KELLOGS RICE KRISPIES 250g	181	£1.14		
CAMAY CHIC - BLACK 100g	112	£0.45			ALPEN REGULAR	197	£1.36		
FAIRY SOAP WHITE EXTRA CARE 125g	113	£0.46			ALPEN ORIGNAL 760G		£2.60		
ZEST 125g		£0.52			WEETABIX 12s	180	£0.89		
WRIGHT COAL TAR SOAP BATH		£0.86			WEETABIX FAMILY	183	£1.67		
		£0.52			KELLOGS CRUNCHY NUT C/FLAKES		£1.89		
LUX HONEY MILK SOAP	116	£0.52			QUAKER SUGAR PUFFS 320g		£1.86		
PEARS TRANSPARENT	117	£1.06			KELLOGS FRUIT & FIBRE		£1.69		
COMFORT 1 Ltr	118	£1.27			QUAKER SHREDDED WHEAT 320G		£1.36		
FLANNEL FACE	119	£0.66			KELLOGS NUTRI BARS		£0.32		
IMPERIAL LEATHER SOAP 125g	120	£0.59			READY BREAK 250g		£0.87		
JOHNSONS Baby/lotion 200ml	121	£2.00			JACOBS CREAM CRACKERS	186	£0.50		
JOHNSONS BABY OIL 220ml	122	£2.24			T.D.Y. RICH TEA BISCUITS	187	£0.43		
SOFTKINS BABY OIL 260ml		£0.89			BOURBON CREAMS 200g	188	£0.46		
SOFTKINS BABY LOTION 260ml		£0.63			RITZ CHEESE 200g	189	£0.83		
VOSENE SHAMPOO	123	£1.76			SHORTCAKE 160g	190	£0.43		
SHAMPOO TIMOTEI 250ml	124	£1.96			CUSTARD CREAMS 200g	191	£0.46		
COLGATE TOOTH PASTE 50ml	125	£0.81			NICE 160g	192	£0.43		
EUCRYL TOOTH POWDER	126	£1.62			RYVITA	193	£0.69		
STERADENT TABLETS X 30	127	£1.36			McVITIES DIGESTIVE 250g	194	£0.68		
JORDAN TOOTH BRUSH MED	128	£1.18			McVITIES HOMEWHEAT MILK	196	£0.89		
SENSODYNE TOOTH PASTE	133	£2.06			T.D.Y. GINGER NUTS 200g	200	48?		
TOOTH PASTE ULTRA BRITE		£0.81				203	£0.98		
SHAMPOO NATURAL FAMILY 500ml		£0.87			McV HOB NOBS PLAIN 300g	204	£0.95		
NATURAL FREQ CONDITIONER 500ml		£0.78			McV HOB NOBS MILK/DARK CHOC		£1.14		
SHAMPOO B/FINE PRO VIT 250ml		£1.20			COCONUT RINGS		£0.48		
SHAMPOO B/FINE 400ml		£1.23			TDY FRUIT SHORT CAKE		£0.64		
WASH N GO SHAMPOO	114	£3.30			McV JAFFA CAKES		£0.83		
SHOWER GEL NATURAL 260ml	138	£0.80			McVITIES GINGER CAKE		£0.35		
HAIR GEL 226g	135	£0.60					£0.96		
DEODORANT DOVE SOLID STICK		£2.10			JOHN WEST TUNA OIL BRINE 200g		£0.99		
GILLETTE DEODORANT GEL STICK	111	£2.99			JOHN WEST CORNED BEEF 198g		£0.96		
GILLETTE AFTER SHAVE BALM	137	£4.73			GLENRYCKS PILCHARDS 155g		£0.64		
TOILET ROLLS TWIN	136	£0.99			PRINCESS HAM 200g		£0.97		
TDY MANS TISSUE	115	£0.76			HOTDOGS 400g		£0.60		
PRINCES PEAR HALVES SYRUP		£0.79			HEINZ COLESLAW SALAD		£0.92		
PRINCESS PEACHES SLICED		£0.72			HEINZ POTATO SALAD		£0.81		
PINEAPPLE CRUSH IN JUICE		£0.96			VALFRUTTA SWEETCORN		£0.64		
VALFRUTTA FRUIT COCKTAIL		£0.69							
BIRDS R.T.S CUSTARD 425g		£0.99							
AMBROSIA CREAMED RICE		£0.83							

INMATES SIGNATURE............... ....DATE.............

CHECKED BY.......................................POSTED BY........................

never stops talking, which I later discover is a common trait among lifers.

Gordon is due out in three years' time and, although dyslexic, has taken an Open University degree in English and is now studying for a law degree. He also claims to have written a book of poetry, which I seem to recall reading something about in the *Daily Mail.*

'Don't talk to me about the press,' he screeches like a tape recorder you can't switch off. 'They always get it wrong. They said I shot my lover's boyfriend when I found them in bed together, and that he was an Old Etonian.'

'And he wasn't an Old Etonian?' I probe innocently.

'Yeah, course he was,' says Gordon. 'But I didn't shoot him, did I? I stabbed him seventeen times.'

I feel sick at this matter-of-fact revelation, delivered with neither remorse nor irony. Gordon goes on to tell me that he was twenty at the time, and had run away from home at the age of fourteen, after being sexually abused. I shuddered, despite the sun beaming down on me. I wonder just how long it will be before I'm not sickened by such confessions. How long before I don't shudder? How long before it becomes matter-of-fact, commonplace?

As we continue our circumnavigation of the yard, he points out Ronnie Biggs, who's sitting on a bench in the far corner surrounded by geraniums.

'They've just planted those, Jeff,' says Gordon. 'They must have known you were comin'.' Again, he doesn't laugh. I glance across to see a sick old man with a tube coming out of his nose. A man who doesn't look as if he has long to live.

Another circuit, before I ask Gordon about a young West Indian who has his face turned to the wall, and hasn't moved an inch since I walked into the yard.

'He killed his wife and young daughter,' says Gordon. 'He's tried to commit suicide three times since they locked him up, and doesn't talk to no one.'

I felt strangely compassionate for this double murderer as we pass him for a third time. As we overtake another man who looks totally lost, Gordon whispers, 'That's Barry George, who's just been done for killing Jill Dando.' I don't tell him that Jill was an old friend and we both hail from Weston-super-Mare. For the first time in my life, I keep my counsel. 'No one in here believes he did it,' says Gordon, 'including the screws.' I still make no comment. However, George's and my trial ran concurrently at the Old Bailey, and I was surprised by how many senior lawyers and laymen told me they were disturbed by the verdict. 'I'll bet he gets off on appeal,'* Gordon adds as another bell rings to indicate that our forty-five minutes of 'freedom' is up.

Once again we are all searched before leaving the yard, which puzzles me; if we didn't have anything on us when we came in, how could we have acquired anything while we were walking around the yard? I feel sure there is a simple explanation. I ask Gordon.

'They've got to go through the whole procedure every time,' Gordon explains as we climb back up the steps. 'It's the regulations.'

When we reach the third floor, we go our separate ways.

'Goodbye,' says Gordon, and we never meet again.

I read three days later in the *Sun* that Ronald Biggs and I shook hands after Gordon had introduced us.

---

* On 2 July 2002, Barry George lost his appeal.

DAY 2

11.45 am

Locked back up in my cell, I continue to write, only to hear the key turning before I've completed a full page. It's Ms Roberts, the Deputy Governor. I stand and offer her my little steel chair. She smiles, waves a hand, and perches herself on the end of the bed. She confirms that the arrangements for my visit to the parish church in Grantchester to attend my mother's funeral have been sanctioned by the Governor. They have checked the police computer at Scotland Yard, and as I have no previous convictions, and no history of violence, I am automatically a Category D prisoner,* which she explains is important because it means that during the funeral service the prison officers accompanying me need not wear a uniform, and therefore I will not have to be handcuffed.

The press will be disappointed, I tell her.

'It won't stop them claiming you were,' she replies.

Ms Roberts goes on to tell me that I will be moved from the medical wing to Block Three sometime after lunch. There is no point in asking her when exactly.

I resolve to spend the time that I am locked up in my cell writing, sticking to a routine I have followed for the past twenty-five years – two hours on, two hours off – though never before in such surroundings. When I normally leave home for a writing session I go in search of somewhere that has a view of the ocean.

---

* There are four categories of prisoner, A, B, C, D. A-cat are violent and dangerous prisoners, with the possible resources, i.e. money, to escape; B are violent and dangerous, but not always murderers (i.e. GBH, ABH, manslaughter or rape); C, the vast majority, are repeat offenders or convicted of a serious, non-violent crime, e.g. drug-dealers; D are usually first offence, no history of violence, often with short sentences, and likely to conform to the system, as they wish to return to society as quickly as possible.

12 noon

I'm let out of my cell to join a queue for lunch. One look at what's on offer and I can't face it – overcooked meat, Heaven knows from which animal, mushy peas swimming in water, and potatoes that Oliver Twist would have rejected. I settle for a slice of bread and a tin cup of milk, not a cup of tinned milk. I sit at a nearby table, finish lunch in three minutes, and return to my cell.

I don't have to wait long before another woman officer appears to tell me that I'm being transferred to Cell Block Three, better known by the inmates as Beirut. I pack my plastic bag which takes another three minutes while she explains that Beirut is on the other side of the prison.

'Anything must be better than the medical wing,' I venture.

'Yes, I suppose it is a little better,' she says. She hesitates. 'But not that much better.'

She escorts me along several linking corridors, unlocking and locking even more barred gates, before we arrive in Beirut. My appearance is greeted by cheers from several inmates. I learn later that bets had been placed on which block I would end up in.

Each of the four blocks serves a different purpose, so it shouldn't have been difficult to work out that I would end up on Three – the induction block. You remain in 'induction' until they have assessed you, like a plane circling above an airport waiting to be told which runway you can finally land on. More of that later.

My new cell turns out to be slightly larger, by inches, and a little more humane, but, as the officer promised, only just. The walls are an easier-to-live-with shade of green, and this time the lavatory has a flush. No need to pee in the washbasin any more.

The view remains consistent. You just stare at another red-brick block, which also shields all human life from the sun. The long walk from the medical block across the prison to Block Three had itself served as a pleasant interlude, but I feel sick at the thought of this becoming a way of life.

A tea-boy or Listener* called James is waiting outside my cell to greet me. He has a kind face, and reminds me of a prefect welcoming a new boy on his first day at school, the only difference being that he's twenty years younger than I am. James tells me that if I need any questions answered I should not hesitate to ask. He advises me not to say anything to anyone – prisoners or officers – about my sentence or appeal, or to discuss any subject I don't want to see in a national newspaper the following day. He warns me that the other prisoners all believe they're going to make a fortune by phoning the *Sun* to let a journalist know what I had for lunch. I thank him for the advice my QC has already proffered. James passes over another rock-hard pillow with a green pillowcase, but this time I'm given two sheets and two blankets. He also hands me a plastic plate, a plastic bowl, a plastic mug and a plastic knife and fork. He then tells me the bad news, England were all out for 187. I frown.

'But Australia are 27 for two,' he adds with a grin. He's obviously heard about my love of cricket. 'Would you like a radio?' he asks. 'Then you can follow the ball-by-ball commentary.'

I cannot hide my delight at the thought, and he leaves me while I make up my new bed. He returns a few minutes later with a battered black radio, from I know not where.

---

* Selected prisoners are invited to become Listeners. They are then trained by the Samaritans so that they can assist fellow inmates who are finding prison hard to come to terms with, especially those contemplating suicide.

'I'll see you later,' he says and disappears again.

I take a considerable time balancing the radio on the tiny brick window sill with the aerial poking out between the bars before I am able to tune into the familiar voice of Christopher Martin-Jenkins on *Test Match Special.* He's telling Blowers that he needs a haircut. This is followed by the more serious news that Australia are now 92 for 2, and both the Waugh brothers look set in their ways. As it's an off-writing period, I lie down on the bed and listen to Graham Gooch's groan as two catches are dropped in quick succession. By the time a bell goes for supper, Australia are 207 for 4, and I suspect are on the way to another innings victory.

6.00 pm

Once again I reject the prison food, and wonder how long it will be before I have to give in.

I return to my cell to find my purchases from the canteen list have been left on the end of my bed. Someone has entered my cell and left without my knowing, is strangely my first reaction. I pour a cup of Buxton water into my plastic mug, and remove the lid from a tube of Pringles. I eat and drink very slowly.

7.00 pm

Three hours later another bell rings. All the cell doors are opened by prison officers and the inmates congregate on the ground floor for what is known as 'Association'. This is the period when you mix with the other prisoners for one hour. As I walk the longest route I can circumnavigate – walking is now a luxury – I discover what activities are on offer. Four black men wearing gold chains with crosses attached are sitting in one corner playing dominoes. I discover later that all four of them are in for murder. None of them appears particularly violent as they consider their next move. I walk on to see two more inmates playing pool, while others lounge around reading the *Sun* – by far the most popular paper in the prison if one is to judge on a simple head count. At the far end of the room is a long queue for the two phones. Each waiting caller has a £2 phonecard which they can use at any time during Association. I'm told I will receive one tomorrow. Everything is tomorrow. I wonder if in a Spanish jail everything is the day after tomorrow?

I stop and chat to someone who introduces himself as Paul. He tells me that he's in for VAT fraud (seven years), and is explaining how he got caught when we are joined by a prison officer. A long conversation follows during which the officer reveals that he also doesn't believe Barry George killed Jill Dando.

'Why not?' I ask.

'He's just too stupid,' the officer replies. 'And in any case, Dando was killed with one shot, which convinces me that the murder must have been carried out by a disciplined professional.' He goes on to tell us that he has been on the same spur as George for the past eighteen months and repeats, 'I can tell you he's just not up to it.'

Pat (murder, reduced to manslaughter, four years) joins us, and says he agrees. Pat recalls an incident that took place on 'prison sports day' last year, when Barry George – then on remand – was running in the one hundred yards and fell over at thirty. 'He's a bit of a pervert,' Pat adds, 'and perhaps he ought to be locked up, but he's no murderer.'

When I leave them to continue my walkabout, I observe that we are penned in at both ends of the room by a floor-to-ceiling steel-mesh sheet. Everyone nods and smiles as I pass, and some prisoners stop me and want to talk about their upcoming trials, while others who are sending out cards need to know how to spell Christine or Suzanne. Most of them are friendly and address me as Lord Jeff, yet another first. I try to look cheerful. When I remember that if my appeal fails the minimum time I will have to serve is two years, I can't imagine how anyone with a life sentence can possibly cope.

'It's just a way of life,' says Jack, a forty-eight-year-old who has spent the last twenty-two years in and out of different prisons. 'My problem,' he adds, 'is I'm no longer qualified to do anything when I get out.'

The last person who told me that was a Conservative Member of Parliament a few days before the last election. He lost.

Jack invites me to visit his cell on the ground floor. I'm surprised to find three beds in a room not much larger than mine. I thought he was about to comment on how lucky I was to have a single cell, but no, he simply indicates a large drawing attached to the wall.

'What do you think that is, Jeff?' he demands.

'No idea,' I reply. 'Does it tell you how many days, months or years you still have to go before you're released?'

'No,' Jack responds. He then points below the washbasin where a small army of ants are congregating. I'm a bit slow and still haven't put two and two together. 'Each night,' Jack goes on to explain, 'the three of us organize ant races, and that's the track. A sort of ants' Ascot,' he adds with a laugh.

'But what's the stake?' I enquire, aware that no one is allowed to have any money inside a prison.

'On Saturday night, the one who's won the most races during the week gets to choose which bed they'll sleep in for the next seven days.'

DAY 2

I stare at the three beds. On one side of the room, up against the wall, is a single bed while on the other side are bunk beds.

'Which does the winner choose?'

'You're fuckin'* dumb, Jeff. The top one, of course; that way you're farthest away from the ants, and can be sure of a night's sleep.'

'What do the ants get?' I ask.

'If they win, they stay alive until the next race.'

'And if they lose?'

'We put them into tomorrow's soup.' I think it was a joke.

Another bell sounds and the officers immediately corral us back into our cells and slam the doors shut. They will not be unlocked again until eight tomorrow morning.

A senior officer stops me as I am returning to my cell to tell me that the Governor wants a word. I follow him, but have to halt every few yards as he unlocks and locks countless iron-barred gates before I'm shown into a comfortable room with a sofa, two easy chairs and pictures on the wall.

Mr Peel, the Governor of Block Three, rises and shakes my hand before motioning me to an easy chair. He asks me how I am settling in. I assure him that the medical wing isn't something I'd want to experience ever again. Block Three, I admit, although dreadful, is a slight improvement.

Mr Peel nods, as if he's heard it all before. He then explains that there are five Governors at Belmarsh, and he's the one responsible for arranging my visit to Grantchester to attend my mother's funeral. He goes on to confirm that everything is in place, but I must be ready to leave at seven o'clock tomorrow morning. I'm about to ask why seven o'clock when the service

---

*I will only use foul language when it's reported in speech, which for most inmates is every sentence. Fuckin' is the only adjective they ever bother with.

isn't until eleven, and the journey to Grantchester usually takes about an hour, when he rises from his place and adds, 'I'll see you again just as soon as you've returned from Cambridge.'

Mr Peel says goodnight but doesn't shake hands a second time. I leave his office and try to find the way back to my cell. As I'm unescorted, I lose my way. An officer quickly comes to my rescue and guides me back on the straight and narrow, obviously confident that I wasn't trying to escape. I couldn't find my way in, let alone out, I want to tell him.

9.00 pm

Once locked back up in my tiny room, I return to *The Moon's a Balloon* and read about David Niven's first experience of sex, and laugh, yes laugh, for the first time in days. At eleven, I turn off my light. Two West Indians on the same floor are shouting through their cell windows, but I can neither follow nor understand what they are saying.* They go on hollering at each other like a married couple who ought to get divorced.

I have no idea what time it was when I fell asleep.

---

* This is a common experience in most jails, and can go on all night. They are known as 'window warriors'.

DAY 3   SATURDAY 21 JULY 2001

4.07 am

I wake a few minutes after four, but as I am not due to be picked up until seven I decide to write for a couple of hours. I find I'm writing more slowly now that there are so few distractions in my life.

6.00 am

An officer unlocks my cell door and introduces himself as George. He asks me if I would like to have a shower. My towel has been hanging over the end of my bed all night and is still damp, but at least they've supplied me with a Bic razor so that I can set about getting rid of two days' growth. I consider cutting my throat, but the thought of failure and the idea of having to return to the hospital wing is enough to put anyone off. The experience of that medical wing must deter most prisoners from harming themselves, because it's not the easy option. If you are sent back to the top floor you'd better be ill, or you will be by the time they've finished with you.

I go off to have my shower. I'm getting quite good at anticipating when to press the button so that the flow of water doesn't stop.

7.00 am

'Are you ready?' George asks politely.

'Yes,' I say, 'except that my black tie has been confiscated along with my cufflinks.'

George's fellow officer hands me a black tie, and a pair of cufflinks materialize. I can only assume that they had anticipated my problem. I point out to George that his black tie is smarter than mine.

'Possibly, but mine's a clip-on,' he says, 'otherwise I'd happily lend it to you.'

'A clip-on?' I repeat in mock disdain.

'Prison regulations,' he explains. 'No officer ever wears a tie as it puts him at risk of being strangled.'

I learn something new every few minutes.

The two of them escort me to the front hall, but not before we've passed through seven double-bolted floor-to-ceiling barred gates. When we reach the reception area, I am once again strip-searched. The officers carry out this exercise as humanely as possible, though it's still humiliating.

I am then taken out into the yard to find a white Transit van awaiting me. Once inside, I'm asked to sit in the seat farthest from the door. George sits next to the door, while his colleague slips into the spare seat directly behind him. The tiny windows are covered with bars and blacked out; I can see out, though no one can see in. I tell George that the press are going to be very frustrated.

'There were a lot of them hanging round earlier this morning waiting for you,' he tells me, 'but a high-security van left about an hour ago at full speed and they all chased after it. They'll be halfway to Nottingham before they realize you're not inside.'

The electric gates slide open once again, this time to let me out. I know the journey to Cambridge like the clichéd 'back of my hand' because I've made it once, sometimes twice, a week for the past twenty years. But this time I am taken on a route that I never knew existed, and presume it can only be for security reasons. I once remember John Major's driver telling me that he knew twenty-two different routes from Chequers to No. 10, and another twenty back to Huntingdon, and none of them was the most direct.

I find it a little stifling in the back of the van. There is no contact with the driver in the front, or the policeman sitting beside him, because they are sealed off, almost as if they're in a separate vehicle. I sense that George and his colleague are a little nervous – I can't imagine why, because I have no intention of trying to escape, as I abhor any form of violence. I learn later they are nervous because should anything go wrong they'll be blamed for it – and something does go wrong.

When we reach the M11, the van remains at a steady fifty on the inside lane, and I begin to feel sick cooped up in that armour-plated compartment on wheels. Our first destination is the Cambridge Crematorium, which is situated on the north side of the city, so when we come off the motorway at exit thirteen, I'm surprised to find that the driver turns left, and starts going in the wrong direction. We travel for a couple of miles towards Royston, before pulling into a large car park attached to the Siemens Building.

George explains that Siemens is where they have agreed to liaise with the local police before travelling on to the crematorium. One enterprising black-leather-clad motorcyclist (journalist) who spotted the van coming off the roundabout at exit thirteen has followed us to the Siemens Building. He skids to a halt, and immediately taps out some numbers on his mobile phone. The policeman seated in the front makes it clear that he wants to be on the move before any of the biker's colleagues join him. But as we have to wait for the local police before we can proceed, we're stuck.

It is of course unusual to have a cremation before the church service, but the crematorium was free at 10 am and the church not until midday. The following day the press come up with a dozen reasons as to why the funeral had been conducted in this order – from the police demanding it, through to me wanting to fool them. Not one of them published the correct reason.

Within minutes, the police escort arrives and we are on our way.

When we drive into the crematorium, there are over a hundred journalists and photographers waiting for us behind a barrier that has been erected by the police. They must have been disappointed to see the white van disappear behind the back of the building, where they slipped me in through the entrance usually reserved for the clergy.

Peter Walker, an old friend and the former Bishop of Ely, is waiting to greet us. He guides me through to a little room, where he will put on his robes and I will change into a new suit, which my son William is bringing over from the Old Vicarage. I will be only too happy to be rid of the clothes I've been wearing for the past few days. The smell of prison is a perfume that even Nicole Kidman couldn't make fashionable.

The Bishop takes me through the cremation service, which, he says, will only last for about fifteen minutes. He confirms that the main funeral service will be conducted in the Parish Church of St Andrew and St Mary in Grantchester at twelve o'clock.

A few minutes later, my immediate family arrive via the front door and have to face the clicking cameras and the shouted questions. Mary is wearing an elegant black dress with a simple brooch that my mother left her in her will. She is ashen-faced, which was my last memory of her before I left the dock. I begin to accept that this terrible ordeal may be even more taxing for my family who are trying so hard to carry on their daily lives while not letting the world know how they really feel.

When Mary comes through to join me in the back, I hold on to her for some time. I then change into my new suit, and go through to the chapel and join the rest of the family. I greet each one of them before taking my place in the front row, seated between William and Mary. I try hard to concentrate on the fact that we are all gathered together in memory of my mother, Lola, but it's hard to forget I'm a convict, who in a few hours' time will be back in prison.

10.30 am

The Bishop conducts the service with calm and quiet dignity, and when the curtains are finally drawn around my mother's coffin, Mary and I walk forward and place a posy of heather next to the wreath.

Mary leaves by the front door, while I return to the back room where I am greeted by another old friend. The two prison officers are surprised when Inspector Howell from the local constabulary says, 'Hello, Jeffrey, sorry to see you in these circumstances.'

I explain to them that when I was Chairman of Cambridge Rugby Club, David was the 1st XV skipper, and the best scrum-half in the county.

'How do you want to play it?' I ask.

David checks his watch. 'The service at Grantchester isn't for another hour, so I suggest we park up at Cantalupe Farm, and wait at the Old Vicarage, until it's time to leave for the church.'

I glance at George to see if this meets with his approval. 'I'm happy to fall in with whatever the local constabulary advise,' he says.

I'm then driven away to Cantalupe Farm in my armoured van, where the owner, Antony Pemberton, has kindly allowed us to park. Mary and the boys travel separately in the family car. We then all make our way by foot over to the Old Vicarage accompanied by only a couple of photographers as the rest of the press are massed outside St Andrew's; they have all assumed that we would be travelling directly to the parish church.

We all wait around in the kitchen for a few moments, while Mary Anne, our housekeeper, makes some tea, pours a large glass of milk and cuts me a slice of chocolate cake. I then ask George if I might be allowed to walk around the garden.

The Old Vicarage at Grantchester (circa 1680) was, at the beginning of the last century, the home of Rupert Brooke. The beautiful garden has been tended for the past fifteen years by my wife and Rachael, the gardener. Between them they've turned it from a jungle into a haven. The trees and flowerbeds are exquisite and the walks to and from the river quite magnificent. George and his colleague, though never more than a few paces away, remain out of earshot, so Mary and I are able to discuss my appeal. She reveals an amazing piece of new evidence concerning Mr Justice Potts that, if substantiated, could cause there to be a retrial.

Mary then goes over the mistakes she thinks the judge made during the trial. She is convinced that the appeal judges will at least reduce my four-year sentence.

'You don't seem pleased,' she adds as we walk along the bank of the River Cam.

'For the first time in my life,' I tell her, 'I assume the worst, so that if anything good happens, I'll be pleasantly surprised.' I've become a pessimist overnight.

DAY 3

We return from the river bank, walk back towards the house and over a wooden bridge that spans Lake Oscar – in reality it's a large pond full of koi carp, named after one of my wife's favourite cats, who after five years of purring and pawing at the water's edge failed to catch a single fish. After feeding our Japanese and Israeli immigrants, we return to the house and prepare ourselves to face the press.

David Howell says that he doesn't want me driven to the church in a police car and suggests that I accompany Mary and the family on foot for the four-hundred-yard walk from the Old Vicarage to the parish church. The police and the prison officers are doing everything in their power to remember that the occasion is my mother's funeral.

11.35 am

We leave by the front door, to find a crowd of journalists, photographers and cameramen waiting outside the gates. I estimate their number to be about a hundred (George later tells the Governor over his mobile phone that it's nearer two hundred). My younger son, James, and his girlfriend Talita, lead the little party on the quarter-mile journey to the church. They are followed by William and my adopted sister, Liz, with Mary and myself bringing up the rear. The cameramen literally fall over each other as they try to get their shots while we make our way slowly up to the parish church. One ill-mannered lout shouts questions at us, so I turn and talk to Mary. He only gives up when he realizes none of us is going to grace him with a reply. I find myself feeling bitter for the first time in my life.

When we reach the church door I am greeted by my cousin Peter, who is handing out copies of the Order of Service, while his wife Pat guides us to a pew in the front row. I'm touched by how many of my mother's friends have travelled from all over the world to attend the little service – from America, Canada and even Australia – not to mention many friends from the West Country where she spent most of her life.

The Order of Service has been selected by Mary and reveals so much about the thought and preparation my wife puts into everything. She must have taken hours selecting the prayers, hymns, readings and music, and she hits just the right note. Bishop Walker once again officiates, and my stepbrother, David Watson, gives a moving address in which he recalls my mother's boundless energy, love of learning and wicked sense of humour.

I read the final lesson, Revelation XXI, verses 1–7, and as I face the congregation, wonder if I'll manage to get the words out. I'm relieved to discover that I don't have to spend those final moments with my mother accompanied by the press, as they at least have had the courtesy to remain outside.

The service lasts for fifty minutes, and is about the only time that day when I can concentrate on my mother and her memory. Not for the first time am I thankful that she didn't live to see me convicted, and my thoughts turn to the sacrifices she made to ensure I had a decent education, and was given as good a start as possible, remembering that my father died leaving debts of around five hundred pounds, and mother had to go out to work to make ends meet. I tried in the later years to make life a little easier for her, but I was never able to repay her properly.

The service ends with 'Jesu, Joy of Man's Desiring', and Mary and I follow the Bishop and the choir down the aisle. When we reach the vestry, George immediately joins us. A member of the press has called Belmarsh to ask why I was allowed to return to the Old Vicarage.

'You'll have to say your goodbyes here, I'm afraid,' he tells us. 'The Governor has phoned to say you can't go back to the house.' I spend the next few minutes shaking hands with every-one who has attended the service and am particularly touched by the presence of Donald and Diana Sinden, who my mother adored.

After thanking the Bishop, my family join me as we begin the long slow walk back to the prison van parked at Cantalupe Farm. I glance to my left as we pass the Old Vicarage. This time the press become even more frantic. They begin to holler out their questions like a repeater gun.

'Are you expecting to remain a lord?'

'Do you hope to win your appeal?'

'Do you want to say anything about your mother?'

'Do you consider yourself a criminal?'

After about a hundred yards or so they finally give up, so Mary and I chat about her forthcoming trip to Strathclyde University, where she will chair a summer school on solar energy. The date has been in her diary for some months, but she offers to cancel the trip and stay in London so she can visit me in Belmarsh. I won't hear of it, as I need her to carry on as normal a life as possible. She sighs. The truth is, I never want Mary to see me in Belmarsh.

When we reach the van, I turn back to look at the Old Vicarage, which I fear I won't be seeing again for some time. I then hug my family one by one, leaving Mary to last. I look across to see my driver David Crann in tears – the first time in fifteen years I've seen this former SAS warrior show any vul-nerability.

On the slow journey back to Belmarsh, I once again consider what the future holds for me, and remain convinced I must above all things keep my mind alert and my body fit. The writing of a day-to-day diary seems to be my best chance for the former, and a quick return to the gym the only hope for the latter.

3.07 pm

Within moments of arriving back at Belmarsh, I'm put through another strip-search before being escorted to my cell on Block Three. Once again, James the Listener is waiting for me. He has from somewhere, somehow, purloined a carton of milk, a new razor* and two, yes two, towels. He perches himself on the end of the bed and tells me there is a rumour that they are going to move me to another block on Monday, as Beirut is only the induction wing.

'What's the difference?' I ask.

'If you're going to be here for a couple of weeks, they have to decide which block to put you on while you're waiting to be transferred to a D-cat. I think you're going to Block One,' says James, 'so you'll be with the lifers.'

'Lifers?' I gasp. 'But doesn't that mean I'll be locked up all day and night?'

'No, no,' says James. 'The lifers have a much more relaxed regime than any other block, because they keep their heads down and don't want to be a nuisance. It's the young ones who are on remand or doing short sentences that cause most of the trouble and therefore have to be locked up first.'

It's fascinating to discover how much of prison life is the exact opposite to what you would expect.

James then gives me the bad news. He's going to be transferred to Whitemoor Prison tomorrow morning, so I won't be seeing him again, but he has already allocated another inmate called Kevin to be my Listener.

'Kevin's a good guy,' he assures me, 'even if he talks too much. So if he goes on a bit, just tell him to shut up.'

---

* You're allowed one Bic razor a day, and not until you hand in your old one will they supply you with a new one. It was several days before I discovered why.

Before James leaves, I can't resist asking him what he's in for.

'Smuggling drugs from Holland,' he replies matter-of-factly.

'And you were caught?'

'Red-handed.'

'How much were the drugs worth?'

'The police claimed a street value of £3.3 million. I can only imagine it must have been Harley Street,' adds James with a wry smile.

'How much did you receive for doing the job?'

'Five thousand pounds.'

'And your sentence?'

'Six years.'

'And Kevin?' I ask. 'What's he in for?'

'Oh, he was on that Dome jewellery caper, driving one of the getaway boats – trouble was he didn't get away.' James pauses. 'By the way,' he says, 'the staff tell me that you aren't eating.'

'Well, that's not quite accurate,' I reply. 'But I am living on a diet of bottled water, KitKat and Smith's crisps, but as I'm only allowed to spend twelve pounds fifty a week, I'm already running out of my meagre provisions.'

'Don't worry,' he says. 'You'll be allowed another canteen list once they've transferred you to a new wing, so fill yours in tonight and Kevin can hand it in first thing in the morning.'

I smile at the man's ingenuity and see why the prison officers have made him a Listener. They obviously, like LBJ,* feel it's better to have him pissing out of the tent, rather than pissing in.

James then changes the subject to the leadership of the Conservative Party. He wants Kenneth Clarke to be the next leader, and he's disappointed that Michael Portillo missed the cut by one vote, because he's never heard of Iain Duncan Smith.

---

* Lyndon Baines Johnson, the thirty-sixth President of the United States.

'Why Clarke?' I ask.

'His brother was the Governor of Holloway, and has the reputation of being a fair and decent man. Mr Clarke strikes me as the same sort of bloke.' I have to agree with James, feeling that he's summed up Ken rather well.

4.30 pm

James leaves when Mr Weedon appears by the door, impatient to lock me back in. I'm beginning to learn the names of the officers. I check my watch, it's just after four thirty. Mr Weedon explains that as it's a Saturday and they're short-staffed, they won't be opening the door again until nine o'clock the next morning. As the cell door slams shut, I reflect on the fact that for the next seventeen hours I will be left alone in a room nine feet by six.

6.00 pm

I feel very low. This is the worst period of the day. You think of your family and what you might be doing at this time on a Saturday evening – James and I would have been watching the Open Golf from Lytham & St Anne's, hoping against hope that Colin Montgomerie would at last win a major. William might be reading a book by some obscure author I'd never heard of. Mary would probably be in the folly at the bottom of the garden working on volume two of her book, *Molecular to Global Photosynthesis*, and around seven I would drive across to Saffron Walden to visit my mother, and discuss with her who should lead the Tory Party.

My mother is dead. James is in London with his girlfriend.

DAY 3

William is on his way back to New York. Mary is at the Old Vicarage alone, and I'm locked up in jail.

10.00 pm

It's dark outside – no curtains to cover my little cell window. I'm exhausted. I pick up one of my new towels, fold it, and place it across my pillow. I lower my head onto the towel and sleep, disturbed only by what I assume is a fire-alarm test at 3 am.

DAY 4   SUNDAY 22 JULY 2001

5.43 am

I wake to find my tiny cell filled with sunlight. I place my feet on the floor and can smell my own body. I decide that the first thing I must do is have a long shave before even thinking about a writing session. As soon as they unlock the door, I'll make a dash for the showers.

There's no plug in the basin so I decide to improvise, and fill my plastic soup bowl with warm water and turn it into a shaving bowl.* The prison have supplied a stick of shaving soap, an old-fashioned shaving brush – I don't think it's badger hair – and a plastic Bic razor, not unlike the one you're given when travelling on British Airways (economy). It takes me some time to build up any lather. Above the basin is a steel-plated mirror measuring four inches square which reflects a blurred image of a tired, bristly man. After my shave in lukewarm water, I feel a lot better, even though I've cut myself several times.

I return to my chair behind the little square table, and with my back to the window begin writing. The sun is shining through the four panes of glass, reproducing a shadow of the

---

*I discovered later that you can buy a plug from the canteen for 25p, but if you leave your cell door open for more than a minute, it disappears.

bars on the wall in front of me – just in case I should forget where I am.

9.01 am

The key turns in the lock and my cell door is pushed open. I look up at an officer who has a puzzled expression on his face.

'What's happened to your cell card?' he asks. He's referring to a white card* attached to my cell door stating my name – Archer, D-cat, release date July 19th, 2005.

'It's been removed,' I explain. 'I've had six of them in the past two days. I think you'll find they've become something of a collector's item.'

Despite the absence of my card, the officer allows me to go off to the shower room, where I join a group of noisy prisoners who are looking forward to an afternoon visit from their families. One of them, a black guy called Pat, carries a clean, freshly-ironed white shirt on a hanger. I'm full of admiration and ask how he managed it, explaining that my children are coming to see me in a couple of days and I'd like to look my best.

'I'll send round my man to see you, your Lordship,' Pat says with a grin. 'He'll take care of you.'

I thank Pat, not quite sure if he's teasing me. Once I've completed another press-button shower – I've almost mastered it – and dried myself, I return to my cell to have breakfast. Breakfast was handed to me last night in a plastic bag, only moments after I'd rejected the evening meal. I extract a very hard-boiled egg from the bag, before disposing of the rest of its

---

* White cards denote Church of England, red cards Roman Catholic, yellow, Muslim, and green, Jewish. This is to show any dietary needs, and if you are attending a service when you should be locked up.

contents in the plastic bucket under the sink. While eating the egg – white only, avoiding the yolk – I stare out of my window and watch the planes as they descend at regular, sixty-second intervals into City Airport. A pigeon joins me on the ledge, but he's on the outside. I retrieve a piece of stale bread from the bucket under the washbasin, break it into small crumbs and drop them on the sill. He rejects my offering, coos and flies away.

9.30 am

The cell is unlocked again, this time for Association, and the duty officer asks me if I want to attend a church service. Not being utterly convinced there is a God I rarely go to church in Grantchester, despite the fact that my wife was for many years the choir-mistress. However, on this occasion it will mean a long walk and forty-five minutes in a far larger room than my cell, so without hesitation I thank God and say yes.

'RC or Church of England?' the officer enquires.

'C of E,' I reply.

'Then you'll be on the second shift. I'll call you around 10.30 straight after Association.'

10.00 am

During Association, prison officers watch to see if you become part of a clique or gang, and how you behave while in a group, or if you're simply a loner. I'm about to leave my cell, only to find a queue of prisoners waiting at my door. Most of them want autographs so they can prove to their partners or girlfriends that they were on the same block as the notorious Jeffrey Archer.

When I've finished what can only be described as a signing session not unlike the ones I usually carry out at Hatchard's, I'm joined by my new Listener, Kevin. He confirms that James was shipped out to Whitemoor early this morning.

'So what do you need, Jeffrey? Can I call you Jeffrey?'

'Of course. What do I need?' I repeat. 'How about a bowl of cornflakes with some real milk, two eggs, sunny side up, bacon, mushrooms and a cup of hot chocolate.'

Kevin laughs. 'I can sort out some Weetabix, skimmed milk, fresh bread. Anything else?'

'A decent razor, some shampoo, a bar of soap and a change of towels?'

'That may take a little longer,' he admits.

As everyone knows what I'm in for, I ask the inevitable question.

'I was part of the Dome jewellery raid, wasn't I,' he says as if everybody was.

What a sentence to deliver to an author. 'How did you become involved?' I ask.

'Debt,' he explains, 'and a measure of bad luck.'

Nick Purnell's words rang in my ears. *Don't believe anything you're told in prison, and never reveal to your fellow inmates any details of your own case.* 'Debt?' I repeat.

'Yeah, I owed a man thirteen hundred pounds, and although I hadn't spoken to him for over a year, he suddenly calls up out of the blue and demands to see me.' I don't interrupt the flow. 'We met up at a pub in Brighton where he told me he needed a speedboat and driver for a couple of hours and if I was willing to do it, I could forget the debt.'

'When did he expect you to carry out the job?' I ask.

'The next morning,' Kevin replied. 'I told him I couldn't consider it because I'd already got another job lined up.'

'What job?' I asked.

'Well, my dad and I've got a couple of boats that we fish off the coast, and they were both booked for the rest of the week. "Then I want my money," the man demanded, so I wasn't left with a lot of choice. You see, I was skint at the time, and anyway, he had a reputation as a bit of a hard man, and all he wanted me to do was transport four men from one side of the river to the other. The whole exercise wouldn't take more than ten minutes.'

'One thousand three hundred pounds for ten minutes' work? You must have realized that there was a catch?'

'I was suspicious, but had no idea what they were really up to.'

'So what happened next?'

'I took the boat as instructed up to Bow Creek, moored it near the jetty a few hundred yards from the Dome and waited. Suddenly all hell broke loose. Three police boats converged on me, and within minutes I was surrounded by a dozen armed officers shouting at me to lie down on the deck with my hands above my head. One of them said, "Blimey it's not him," and I later discovered that I'd been brought in at the last minute to replace someone who had let the gang down.'

'But by then you must have known what they were up to?'

'Nope,' he replied, 'I'm thirty-five years old, and this is my first offence. I'm not a criminal, and after what my family and I have been put through, I can tell you I won't be coming back to prison again.'

I can't explain why I wanted to believe him. It might have been his courteous manner, or the way he talked about his wife and fourteen-year-old son. And he was certainly going to pay dearly for a foolish mistake; one that he would regret for the rest of his life.*

---

* Kevin Meredith was tried and convicted at the Old Bailey on 18 February 2002 for conspiracy to steal, and sentenced to five years' imprisonment.

51

DAY 4

'Archer, Collins, Davies, Edwards,' booms the voice of Mr King, an officer not given to subtlety as he continues to bellow out names until he comes to Watts, before adding, 'C of E, now.'

'I think we'll have to continue this conversation at some other time,' I suggest. 'Our Lord calls and if he doesn't, Mr King certainly does.' I then join the other prisoners who are waiting on the middle landing to be escorted to the morning service.

11.00 am

A crocodile of prisoners proceeds slowly along the polished linoleum floor until we're stopped for another body search before entering the chapel. Why would they search us before going into a place of worship? We file into a large hall where each worshipper is handed a Bible. I take my place in the second row next to a young black man who has his head bowed. I glance around at what appears to be a full house.

The Chaplain, David (his name is written in bold letters on a label attached to his well-worn jacket), takes his place at the front of the chapel and calls for silence. He is a man of about forty-five, stockily built, with a pronounced limp and a stern smile. He stares down at his congregation of murderers, rapists, burglars and wife-beaters. Not surprisingly, it takes him a couple of minutes to bring such a flock to order.

While he goes about his task, I continue to look around the room. It's square in shape, and I would guess measures about twenty paces by twenty. The outer walls are red brick and the room holds about two hundred plastic chairs, in rows of twenty. On the four walls there are paintings of Christ and his Disciples, Christ being carried to the tomb after being taken down from the Cross, the Virgin Mother with an angel, the Raising of Lazarus, and Christ calming the storm.

Directly behind the Chaplain is a rock band – their leader is a pretty, dark-haired girl who has a guitar slung over her shoulder. She is accompanied by five Gospel singers, all of whom have tiny microphones pinned to their lapels. In front of the group is a man seated with his back to the congregation. He is working a slide projector that flashes up on a white sheet hung in front of him the words of the first hymn.

When the Chaplain finally gains silence – achieved only after a threat that anyone caught talking would immediately be escorted back to their cell – he begins the service by delivering three prayers, all unsubtly spelling out the simple message of doing good by your neighbour. He then turns to the girl with the guitar and gives her a slight bow. Her gentle voice rings out the melody of the first hymn, more of a Gospel message, which is accompanied heartily by the black prisoners who make up well over half the congregation, while the rest of us are a little more reserved. The group's backing singers are all white, and give as good as they get, even when the clapping begins. After the last verse has rung out, we are all ready for the sermon, and what a sermon it turns out to be.

The Chaplain's chosen theme is murder. He then invites us to pick up our Bibles – which he describes as the biggest bestseller of all time – and turn to the book of Genesis. He glances in my direction and winks.

'And it all began with Cain and Abel,' he tells us, 'because Cain was the first murderer. Envious of his brother's success, he gained revenge by killing him. But God saw him do it and punished him for the rest of his life.'

His next chosen example of a murderer was Moses, who, he told us, killed an Egyptian and also thought he'd got away with it, but he hadn't because God had seen him, so he too was punished for the rest of his life. I don't remember that bit, because I thought Moses died peacefully in his bed aged 130.

'Now I want you to turn to the Second Book of Samuel,' declares the Chaplain. 'Not the first book, the second book, where you'll find a king who was a murderer. King David. He killed Uriah the Hittite, because he fancied his wife Bathsheba. He had Uriah placed in the front line of the next battle to make sure he was killed so he could end up marrying Bathsheba. However, God also saw what he was up to, and punished him accordingly. Because God witnesses every murder, and will punish anyone who breaks his commandments.'

'Alleluia,' shout several of the congregation in the front three rows.

I later learnt from the Deputy Governor that at least half the congregation were murderers, so the Chaplain was well aware of the audience he was playing to.

After the sermon is over the Gospel singers sing a quiet reprise while the Chaplain asks if all those who are willing to put their trust in God might like to come forward and sign the pledge. A queue begins to form in front of David, and he blesses them one by one. Once they are back in their seats, we sing the last hymn before receiving the Chaplain's final blessing. As we file out, I thank the Reverend before being searched – but what could possibly change hands during the service, when they've already searched us before we came in? I find out a week later. We are then escorted back to our cells and locked up once again.

12 noon

At midday we're let out for Sunday lunch. There are four different dishes on offer – turkey, beef, ham and stew. As I am unable to tell which is which, I settle for some grated cheese and two slices of un-margarined bread, before returning to my cell to sit at my little table and slowly nibble my cheese sandwich.

Once I've finished lunch, which takes all of five minutes, I start writing again. I continue uninterrupted for a couple of hours until Kevin returns clutching a plastic bag of goodies – two Weetabix, a carton of milk, two small green apples, a bar of soap and – his biggest triumph to date – two packets of Cup a Soup, minestrone and mushroom. I don't leave him in any doubt how grateful I am before settling down to a plastic bowl of Weetabix soaked in milk. The same bowl I'd used to shave in earlier this morning.

4.20 pm

It's not until after four has struck that I am allowed to leave the cell again and join the other prisoners for forty-five minutes in the exercise yard. I quickly learn that you take any and every opportunity – from religion to work to exercise – to make sure you get out of your cell. Once again, we're searched before being allowed to go into the yard.

Most of the inmates don't bother to walk, but simply congregate in groups and sunbathe while lounging up against the fence. Just a few of us stride purposefully round. I walk briskly because I'm already missing my daily visit to the gym. I notice that several prisoners are wearing the latest Nike or Reebok trainers. It's the one fashion statement they are allowed to make. One of the inmates joins me and shyly offers ten pages of a manuscript and asks if I would be willing to read them. He tells me that he writes three pages a day and hopes to finish the work by the time he's released in December.

I read the ten pages as I walk. He is clearly quite well

educated as the sentences are grammatically correct and he has a good command of language. I congratulate him on the piece, wish him well, and even admit that I am carrying out the same exercise myself. One or two others join me to discuss their legal problems, but as I have little knowledge of the law, I am unable to answer any of their questions. I hear my name called out on the tannoy, and return to the officer at the gate.

'Mr Peel wants to see you,' the officer says without explanation, and this time doesn't bother to search me as I am escorted to a little office in the centre of the spur. Another form needs to be filled in, as James had phoned asking if he can visit me on Friday.

'Do you want to see him?' he asks.

'Of course I do,' I reply.

'They don't all want to,' Mr Peel remarks as he fills out the form. When he has completed the task, he asks how I am settling in.

'Not well,' I admit. 'Being locked up for seventeen hours ... but I'm sure you've heard it all before.'

Mr Peel begins to talk about his job and the problems the prison service is going through. He's been a prison officer for ten years, and his basic pay is still only £24,000, which with overtime at £13.20 an hour (maximum allowed, nine hours a week) he can push up to £31,000. I didn't tell him that it's less than I pay my secretary. He then explains that his partner is also a prison officer and she carries out her full overtime stint, which means they end up with £60,000 a year between them, but don't see a lot of each other. After getting his message across, he changes the subject back to Belmarsh.

'This is only a reception prison,' he explains. 'If you're convicted and not on remand, we move you to another prison as quickly as possible. But I'm sorry to say we see the same old faces returning again and again. They aren't all bad, you know, in fact if it wasn't for drugs, particularly heroin, sixty per cent of them wouldn't even be here.'

'Sixty per cent?' I repeat.

'Yes, most of them are in for petty theft to pay for their drug habit or are part of the drug culture.'

'And can they still get hold of drugs in prison?'

'Oh yes, you'll have noticed how rudimentary the searches are. That's because prison regulations don't permit us to do any more. We know where they're hiding the drugs and every method they use to bring them in, but because of the Human Rights Act we're not always allowed to carry out a thorough enough search. Some of them are even willing to swallow plastic packets full of heroin, they're so desperate.'

'But if the packet were to burst?'

'They'll die within hours,' he says. 'One prisoner died that way last month, but you'd be surprised how many of them are still willing to risk it. Did you hear the fire alarm go off last night?'

'Yes, it woke me,' I told him.

'It was a heroin addict who'd set fire to his cell. By the time I got there he was cutting his wrist with a razor, because he wanted to suffer even more pain to help take his mind off the craving. We whisked him off to the medical wing, but there wasn't much they could do except patch him up. He'll go through exactly the same trauma again tonight, so we'll just have to mount a suicide watch and check his cell every fifteen minutes.'

A horn sounds to announce that the exercise period is over. 'I suppose you'd better get back to your cell,' he says. 'If you weren't writing a book, I can't imagine what the authorities imagine will be gained by sending you here.'

DAY 4

5.00 pm

I return to my cell and continue writing until supper. When my door is unlocked again I go down to the hotplate on the ground floor. I settle for a Thermos of hot water, an apple and a plastic bag containing tomorrow's breakfast. Back in my cell I munch a packet of crisps and with the aid of half the hot water in the Thermos make a Cup a Soup – mushroom. The cell door is slammed shut at five thirty, and will not be opened again until nine thirty tomorrow morning, by which time I will have used the other half of the water from the Thermos to take a shave, in the same bowl as I eat the soup.

I spend the next couple of hours following the Open Golf on Radio 5 Live. David Duval, an American, wins his first Open, to see his name inscribed on the silver claret jug. Colin Montgomerie and Ian Woosnam put up a spirited fight, but are not around at the seventy-second hole.

I flick over to Radio 4 to hear Steve Norris (Vice-Chairman of the Conservative Party in charge of women's affairs) telling the world he always knew I was a bad man. In the election among Party members for candidate for Mayor of London, I defeated Mr Norris by 71 per cent to 29 per cent.

I turn the radio off and read a couple of chapters of *The Moon's a Balloon*, which takes Mr Niven to Sandhurst before being commissioned into the King's Own Highlanders. I rest my head on the rock-hard pillow, and, despite the prisoners shouting from cell to cell and loud rap music coming from every corner of the block, I somehow fall asleep.

DAY 5   MONDAY 23 JULY 2001

5.53 am

The sun is shining through the bars of my window on what must
be a glorious summer day. I've been incarcerated in a cell five
paces by three for twelve and a half hours, and will not be let out
again until midday; eighteen and a half hours of solitary confinement. There is a child of seventeen in the cell below me who has
been charged with shoplifting – his first offence, not even convicted – and he is being locked up for eighteen and a half hours,
unable to speak to anyone. This is Great Britain in the twenty-
first century, not Turkey, not Nigeria, not Kosovo, but Britain.

I can hear the right-wingers assuring us that it will be
character-building and teach the lad a lesson. What stupidity.
It's far more likely that he will become antagonistic towards
authority and once he's released, turn to a life of crime. This
same young man will now be spending at least a fortnight with
murderers, rapists, burglars and drug addicts. Are these the best
tutors he can learn from?

12 noon

I am visited by a charming lady who spotted me sitting in church
on Sunday. I end up asking her more questions than she asks

me. It turns out that she visits every prisoner who signs the pledge – I fear I didn't – and any inmate who attends chapel for the first time. She gives each prisoner a Bible and will sit and listen to their problems for hours. She kindly answers all my questions. When she leaves, I pick up my plastic tray, plastic bowl, plastic plate, plastic knife, fork and spoon, leave my cell to walk down to the hotplate for lunch.*

One look at what's on offer and once again I return to my cell empty-handed. An old lag on his way back to the top floor tells me that Belmarsh has the worst grub of any jail in Britain. As he's been a resident of seven prisons during the past twenty years, I take his word for it. An officer slams my cell door closed. It will not open again until two o'clock. I've had precisely twelve minutes of freedom during the last twenty and a half hours.

2.00 pm

After another two hours, I'm let out for Association. During this blessed release, I stop to glance at the TV in the centre of the room that's surrounded by a dozen prisoners. They're watching a cowboy film starring Ray Milland, who plays the sheriff. Normally I would flick to another channel but today it's the selection of the majority so I hang in there for ten minutes before finally giving up and moving on to the dominoes table.

An Irishman joins me and asks if I can spare him a minute. He's about five feet eight, with two scars etched across his face – one above his left eyebrow, short, the stitches still showing, and another down his right cheek, long and red. The latter I

---

*In prison, the morning meal, breakfast, is usually taken between 7.30 and 8.00, the midday meal is called dinner, and the evening meal tea. In Belmarsh, the following day's breakfast is given to you in a plastic bag when you go down to the hotplate for tea the night before.

suspect is the more recent. Despite this disfigurement, he has that soft lilt of his countrymen that I can never resist.

'I'm up in court next week,' he says.

'What for?' I ask.

'You'd rather not know,' he replies, 'but all I want to find out is, once I'm in court, am I allowed to defend myself?'

'Yes,' I tell him.

'But would it be better to give my side of the story to a barrister and then let him brief the jury?'

I consider this for a moment because during my seven-week trial I gained some experience of the legal profession. 'On balance,' I tell him, 'I would take advantage of any legal expertise on offer, rather than rely on your own cunning.' He nods and slips away. I dread meeting up with this sharp, intelligent Irishman at some later date to be told that his barrister was a fool.

I stroll back across the room to see how the film is progressing. Being a western, a gunfight to end all gunfights is just about to take place when the officer on duty shouts, 'Back to your cells.' A groan goes up, but to be fair to the duty officer, he's seated at the far end of the room and has no idea that the film only has another five minutes to run.

'The good guys win, Ray Milland gets the girl, and the baddies are all blown away,' I tell the audience assembled round the TV.

'You've seen it before?' asks one of the inmates.

'No, you stupid fucker,' says another. 'We always lose. Have you ever known it end any other way?'

Once locked back in my cell after the forty-five-minute break, I pour myself a glass of Buxton water, eat a packet of Smith's crisps and nibble away at an apple. Having finished my five-minute non-prison meal, I clean my teeth and settle down to another stint of writing.

I've written about a thousand words when I hear a key turning in the lock, always a welcome distraction because, as I've mentioned before, an open door gives you a feeling of freedom and the possibility that you might even be allowed to escape for a few minutes.

I'm greeted by a lady in civilian clothes who wears the inevitable badge – in her case, Librarian. 'Good afternoon,' I say as I rise from my place and smile. She looks surprised.

'If a prisoner asks you to sign a book, could you in future say no,' she says without bothering to introduce herself. I look puzzled; after all, I've been asked to sign books for the past twenty-five years. 'It's just that they are all library books,' she continues, 'and they're being stolen. They've now become like tobacco and phonecards, a trading item for drugs, and are worth double with your signature.'

I assure her I will not sign another library book. She nods and slams the door closed.

I continue writing, aware that the next opportunity for a break will come when we have the allocated forty-five minutes for afternoon exercise. I'm already becoming used to the routine of the door opening, lining up to be searched, and then being released into the yard. I've written about another two thousand words before the door opens again.

Having gone through the ritual, I stroll around the large square accompanied by Vincent (burglary) and another man called Mark (driving offence), who supports Arsenal. One circuit, and I discover that the only way to stop Mark boring me to death about his favourite football team is to agree with him that Arsenal, despite Manchester United's recent record, is the best team in England.

Desperate for a change of subject, I point to a sad figure

walking in front of us, the only prisoner in the yard who looks older than me.

'Poor old thing,' says Vincent. 'He shouldn't be here, but he's what's known as a bag man – nowhere to go, so he ends up in prison.'

'But what was his crime?' I ask.

'Nothing, if the truth be known. Every few weeks he throws a brick through a shop window and then hangs around until the police turn up to arrest him.'

'Why would he do that?' I ask.

'Because he's got nowhere to go and at least while he's inside the poor old sod is guaranteed a bed and three meals a day.'

'But surely the police have worked that out by now?' I suggest.

'Yes, of course they have, so they advise the magistrate to bind him over. But he's even found a way round that, because the moment the magistrate fails to sentence him, he shouts out at the top of his voice, "You're a stupid old fucker, and I'm going to throw a brick through your window tonight, so see you again tomorrow." That assures him at least another six weeks inside, which is exactly what he was hoping for in the first place. He's been sentenced seventy-three times in the past thirty years, but never for more than three months. The problem is that the system doesn't know what to do with him.'

A young black man runs past me, to the jeers of those lolling up against the perimeter fence. He is not put off, and if anything runs a little faster. He's lean and fit, and looks like a quarter-miler. I watch him, only to be reminded that my planned summer holiday at the World Athletics Championships in Edmonton with Michael Beloff has been exchanged for three weeks in Belmarsh.

'Let's get moving,' whispers Vincent. 'We want to avoid that one at any cost,' he adds, pointing to a lone prisoner walking a few paces ahead of us. Vincent doesn't speak again until we've overtaken him, and are out of earshot. He then answers my unasked question. 'He's a double murderer – his wife and her boyfriend.' Vincent goes on to describe how he killed them both. I found the details so horrific that I must confess I didn't feel able to include Vincent's words in this diary until six months after I'd left Belmarsh. If you're at all squeamish, avoid reading the next three paragraphs.

This is Vincent's verbatim description.

That bastard returned home unexpectedly in the middle of the day, to find his wife making love to another man. The man tried to escape out of the bedroom window, but was knocked out with one punch. He then tied the two of them next to each other on the bed, before going down to the kitchen. He returned a few minutes later holding a serrated carving knife with a seven-inch blade. During the next hour, he stabbed the lover eleven times making sure he was still alive before finally cutting off his balls.

Once the man had died, he climbed on the bed and raped his wife, who was still tied up next to her dead lover. At the last moment he came all over the dead man's face. He then climbed off the bed, and stared at his hysterical wife. He waited for some time before inserting the carving knife deep into her vagina. He then pulled the blade slowly up through her body.

During the trial, he told the jury that he'd killed her to prove how much he loved her. He was sentenced to life with no prospect of parole.

'Just remember to avoid him at any cost,' says Vincent. 'He'd slit your throat for a half-ounce of tobacco, and as he's going to spend the rest of his life in here, nothing can be added to his sentence whatever he gets up to.'

I feel sure he's just the sort of fellow Mr Justice Potts was hoping I'd bump into.

The hooter blasts out, the unsubtle indication that our forty-five minutes is up. We are called in, block by block, so that we can return to our individual cells in smaller groups. As I'm on Block Three, I have to hang around and wait to be called. When they call Two, I notice that the double murderer is striding purposefully towards me. I bow my head hoping he won't notice, but when I look up again, I see he's staring directly at me and still heading in my direction. I look towards the four officers standing by the gate who stiffen, while the group of black men up against the fence stare impassively on. The double murderer comes to a halt a few paces in front of me.

'Can I speak to you?' he asks.

'Yes, of course,' I reply, trying to sound as if we were casual acquaintances at a garden party.

'It's just that I would like to say how much I enjoy your books, particularly *The Prodigal Daughter*. I've been in here for eleven years and I've read everything you've written. I just wanted to let you know.' I'm speechless. 'And by the way,' he adds, 'if you want that bitch of a secretary bumped off, I'll be happy to arrange it for you.'

I really thought I was going to be sick as I watched him disappear through the gate. Thank God, into another block.

6.00 pm

I'm only locked up for an hour before the bell goes for supper. I pick up my tray and grab a tin of fruit that was donated by James – my first Listener – the night before he was transferred to Whitemoor. When I join the hotplate queue, I ask Vincent if he has a tin opener. He points to an opener attached to the wall on the far side of the room, 'But you're not allowed to open anything before you've collected your grub.' I notice that he's holding a tin of spam.

'I'll swap you half my tin of fruit for half your Spam.'

'Agreed,' he says. 'I'll bring it up to your cell as soon as I've collected my meal.'

Once again I can't find anything at the hotplate that looks even vaguely edible, and settle for a couple of potatoes.

'You ought to go for the vegetarian option,' says a voice.

I look round to see Pat. 'Mary won't be pleased when she finds out you're not eating, and let's face it, the vegetarian option is one of the few things they can't make a complete mess of.' I take Pat's advice and select a vegetable fritter. As we pass the end of the counter, another plastic bag containing tomorrow's breakfast is handed to me. 'By the way,' says Pat pointing to the man who has just served me, 'that's Peter the press, he'll wash and iron that shirt for you.'

'Thank you, Pat,' I say, and turning back to Peter add, 'My children are coming to visit tomorrow and I want to look my best for them.'

'I'll make you look as if you've just stepped out of Savile Row,' Peter says. 'I'll stop by your cell and pick up the shirt once I've finished serving breakfast.'

I move on and collect a Thermos flask of hot water from another prisoner, half for a Cup a Soup, half for shaving. As I climb the yellow iron steps back to Cell 29 on the second floor, I overhear Mark, the Arsenal supporter, having a word with Mr Tuck, the officer on duty. He's pointing out, very courteously, that there are no ethnic representatives among those selected to be Listeners, tea-boys or servers behind the hotplate, despite the fact that they make up over 50 per cent of the prison population. Mr Tuck, who strikes me as a fair man, nods his agreement, and says he'll have a word with the Governor. Whether he did or not, I have no way of knowing.*

When I arrive back on the second floor Vincent is already waiting for me. I pour half my fruit into his bowl, while he cuts his Spam into two, forking over the larger portion, which I place on the plate next to my vegetable fritter and two potatoes. He also gives me a white T-shirt, which I'm wearing as I write these words.

The cell doors are left open for about ten minutes during which time Peter the press arrives and takes away my dirty white shirt, a pair of pants and socks. 'I'll have them back to you first thing tomorrow, squire,' he promises, and is gone before I can thank him and ask what he would like in return.

My final visitor for the day is Kevin, my Listener, who tells me there's a rumour that I'm going to be moved to Block One tomorrow, where the regime is a little bit more relaxed and not quite as noisy. I'm sorry to learn this as I'm beginning to make a few friends – Kevin, James, Pat, Vincent, Peter and Mark – and am starting to get the hang of how Block Three works. Kevin sits on the end of the bed and chats as James had warned me he would; but I welcome the company, not to mention the fact that while a Listener is in the room, the door has to be left open.

Kevin had a visit this afternoon from his wife and children. He tells me his fourteen-year-old is now taller than he is, and his nine-year-old can't understand why he doesn't come home at night.

Mr Gilford, the duty officer, hovers at my cell door, a hint that even though Kevin is a Listener, it's perhaps time for him to

---

* The reason Mark feels so strongly is because tea-boys, Listeners and hotplate workers spend far longer out of their cells than the rest of us, so it's a real privilege.

move on. I ask Mr Gilford if I can empty the remains of my meal in the dustbin at the end of the landing – only one bite taken from the fritter. He nods. The moment I return, the cell door is slammed shut.

I sit on the end of the bed and begin to go through my letters. Just over a hundred in the first post, and not one of them condemning me. Amazing how the British people do not reflect the views of the press – I've kept every letter just in case my lawyers want to inspect them: three Members of Parliament, David Faber, John Gummer and Peter Lilley, and two members of the Lords, Bertie Denham and Robin Ferrers, are among those early writers. One former minister not only says how sorry he is to learn that I'm in jail, but adds that Mr Justice Potts's summing-up was a travesty of justice, and the sentence inexplicable.

I begin to make a mental list of my real friends.

DAY 6   TUESDAY 24 JULY 2001

5.44 am

I seem to have settled back into my usual sleep pattern. I wake around 5.30 am, rise at six, and begin my first two-hour writing session just as I would if I were in the tranquillity of my own home. I continue to write uninterrupted until eight.

I make extensive notes on what has taken place during the day, and then the following morning I pen the full script, which usually comes to about three thousand words. I also scribble a note whenever I overhear a casual remark, or a piece of information that might be forgotten only moments later.

I am just about to shave – a process I now take some considerable time over, not just because I have time, but also because I don't want to be cut to ribbons by my prison razor – when there is a bang on the cell door. My tiny window is flicked open and Ms Newsome shouts, 'Archer, you're being moved to House Block One, get your things ready.'

I should have realized by now that such a warning would be followed by at least a two-hour wait, but inexperience causes me to abandon any attempt to shave and quickly gather together my belongings. My only concern is that my children may be visiting me this afternoon and I wouldn't want them to see me unshaven.

DAY 6

I gather everything together and, as if I were returning home at the end of a holiday, I find I have far more possessions than I started out with. By the time I have stuffed everything into my large HM Prisons plastic bag, I begin to feel apprehensive about moving off Beirut to the lifers' wing.

10.07 am

My cell door is thrown open again, and I join a dozen or so prisoners who are also being transferred to Block One. I recognize one or two of them from the exercise yard. They can't resist a chorus of 'Good morning, Jeff', 'How was your breakfast, my Lord?', and 'We must be off to the posh block if you're coming with us.'

Kevin slips into the back of the line to tell me that my white shirt has been washed and pressed by Peter, and he'll have it sent over to Block One this afternoon, but I'll have to make out a new provisions list, as each house block has its own canteen.

The walk across to my new cell via several long corridors is accompanied by the usual opening and closing ceremony of double-barred gates every few yards, and when we finally arrive, we are herded into the inevitable waiting room. I've never been much good at waiting. We've only been standing around for a few minutes when a young officer, Mr Aveling, opens the door and says, 'Archer, Mr Loughnane wants to see you about real-location.' I've only just arrived.

'They're letting you out,' shouts one of the prisoners.

'Ask if I can share a cell with you, darling,' shouts another.

'Don't pay more than the going rate,' offers a third. Prison humour.

Mr Aveling escorts me across the corridor to a large, more comfortable room by the standards I've become used to during the past few days, and introduces me to Mr Loughnane and Mr Gates. I take a seat opposite them on the other side of the desk.

'More form-filling, I'm afraid,' says Mr Loughnane almost apologetically. 'How are you settling in?' he asks. I now accept this as the standard opening to any conversation with an officer I haven't met before.

'I'm fine, except for having to be locked up in such a confined space for so many hours.'

'Were you at public school?' Mr Gates asks.

'Yes,' I reply, wondering why he asked this non sequitur.

'It's just that we find public school boys settle in far more quickly than your average prisoner.' I don't know whether to laugh or cry. 'To be honest,' he continues, 'I've already filled in most of the boxes about whether you can read or write, if you're on any drugs and how often you've been to jail. I can also confirm that you have been allocated Category D status, and will therefore be moved to an open prison in the near future.' Like 'immediately', 'near future' has a different meaning in prison. Mr Loughnane explains that first they have to locate a prison that has a vacancy, and once that has been confirmed, there will be the added problem of transport. I raise an eyebrow.

'That's always one of our biggest headaches,' Mr Loughnane explains. 'Group 4 organize all the transport between prisons, and we have to fit in with their timetable.' He then asks, 'Do you know any Category D prisons you would like to be considered for?'

'The only open prison I've ever heard of is Ford,' I tell him, 'and the one piece of information I've picked up from a former prisoner is that they have a good library.'

'Yes, they do,' confirms Mr Gates checking the prisons handbook on the table in front of him, as if it were a Relais Chateaux guide. 'We'll give them a call later this morning and check if they have any spaces available.'

I thank them both before being escorted back to the waiting room.

'Have they fixed you up with the riverside suite?' asks one prisoner.

'No,' I reply, 'but they did promise I wouldn't have to share a cell with you.'

This feeble effort is greeted by clapping and cheers, which I later learn was because I'd stood up to a man who had blown his brother's head off. I'm glad I was told this later because, let me assure you, if I'd known at the time I would have kept my mouth shut.

The door is opened again, and this time Mr Aveling tells me that the senior officer on the block wants to see me. This is greeted by more jeers and applause. 'Be careful, Jeff, he thinks you're after his job.'

I'm led to an even more comfortable room, with chairs, a desk and even pictures on the walls, to be greeted by four officers, three men and one woman. Mr Marsland, the most senior officer present, two pips on his epaulettes,* confirms the rumour that as I won't be staying long he has put me on the lifers' spur. I am obviously unable to mask my horror at the very idea, because he quickly reassures me.

'You'll find it's the most settled wing in the prison, as most of the inmates have sentences ranging between twelve and twenty-five years, and all they want is an easy life. Otherwise they'll never be considered for transfer to a B- or C-cat, let alone parole.' Yet again, exactly the opposite of what one might imagine. 'And we also have a request,' says Mr Marsland looking

---

* One pip is a senior officer, two pips a principal officer.

down at a sheet of paper. 'Mrs Williamson is running a creative-writing course, and wonders if you would be willing to address her class?'

'Of course I will,' I said. 'How many normally attend?'

'Because it's you, we think they'll be record numbers,' says Mrs Williamson, 'so it could be as many as twelve.' I haven't addressed an audience of twelve since I was the GLC candidate for Romford thirty years ago.

'One problem has arisen,' continues Mr Marsland, 'I'm afraid there are no single cells available on the lifers' spur at the moment, so you'll have to share.' My heart sinks. Will I end up with a murderer, a rapist or a drug addict, or a combination of all three? 'But we'll try to find you a sensible cell-mate,' he concludes before standing to signal that the interview is over.

I return to the waiting room and only have to hang around for a few more minutes before we are taken off to our new cells. Once again I've been put on the top floor – I think this must be for security reasons. Cell 40 is a little larger than Cell 29, where I last resided, but far from double the size, remembering that it has to accommodate two prisoners. It measures seven paces by four, rather than five by three, and up against the far wall, directly in front of the lavatory, is a small bunk bed, which one would more normally associate with a nursery.

My room-mate turns out to be Terry. Terry the writer. He is the one who approached me in the yard and asked if I would read his manuscript. He's been selected to join me because he doesn't smoke, a rarity amongst inmates, and it's a prison regulation that if you don't smoke, they can't make you share a cell with someone who does. The authorities assumed I would be aware of this rule. I wasn't.

Terry, as I have already mentioned, is halfway through writing a novel and seems pleased to discover who his cell-mate will be. I find out later why, and it's not because he wants me to help him with his syntax.

Terry is outwardly courteous and friendly, and despite my continually asking him to call me Jeffrey, he goes on addressing me as Mr Archer. We agree that he will have the top bunk and I the bottom, on account of my advanced years. I quickly discover that he's very tidy, happy to make both beds, sweep the floor and regularly empty our little plastic bucket.

I begin to unpack my cellophane bag and store my possessions in the tiny cupboard above my bed. Once we've both finished unpacking, I explain to Terry that I write for six hours a day, and hope he will understand if I don't speak to him during those set two-hour periods. He seems delighted with this arrangement, explaining that he wants to get on with his own novel. I'm about to ask how it's progressing, when the door is opened and we're joined by a prison officer who has intercepted my freshly ironed white shirt. The officer begins by apologizing, before explaining that he will have to confiscate my white shirt, because if I were to wear it, I might be mistaken for a member of the prison staff. This is the white shirt that I'd had washed and ironed by Peter the press so that I could look smart for Will and James's visit. I'm now down to one blue shirt, and one T-shirt (borrowed). He places my white shirt in yet another plastic bag for which I have to sign yet another form. He assures me that it will be returned as soon as I have completed my sentence. On his way out, he tells me my visit has been postponed for a few days.

12 noon

After a second session of writing, the cell door is opened and we are let out for Association. I join the lifers on the ground floor, which has an identical layout to House Block Three. The lifers

(23 murderers plus a handful of ABH and GBH* to make up the numbers) range in age from nineteen to fifty, and view me with considerable suspicion. Not only because I'm a Conservative millionaire, but far worse, I will only be with them for a few days before I'm dispatched to an open prison. Something they won't experience for at least another ten years. It will take a far greater effort to break down the barriers with this particular group than the young fledgeling criminals of House Block Three.

As I stroll around, I stop to glance at the TV. A man of about my age is watching Errol Flynn and David Niven in the black-and-white version of *The Charge of the Light Brigade*. I take a seat next to him.

'I'm David,' he says. 'You haven't shaved today.'

I confess my sin, and explain that I was in the process of doing so when an officer told me I would be moving.

'Understood,' said David. 'But I have to tell you, Jeffrey, you're too old for designer stubble. All the lifers shave,' he tells me. 'You've got to cling on to whatever dignity you can in a hellhole like this,' he adds, 'and a warm shower and a good shave are probably the best way to start the day.' David goes on chatting during the film as if it was nothing more than background muzak. He apologizes for not having read any of my novels, assuring me that his wife has enjoyed all of them, but he only finds time to read whenever he's in jail. I resist asking the obvious question.

'What are you reading at the moment?' I enquire.

'Ackroyd's *Life of Dickens*,' he replies. And, as if he senses my incredulity, adds, 'Mr Micawber, what a character, bit like my father to be honest, always in debt. Now remind me, what was his Christian name?'

'Wilkins,' I reply.

---

* Actual Bodily Harm and Grievous Bodily Harm.

'Just testing, Jeffrey, just testing. Actually I tried to get one of your books out of the library the other day, but they've removed them all from the shelves. A diabolical liberty, that's what I'd call it. I told them I wanted to read it, not steal the bloody thing.' I begin to notice how few prisoners use bad language in front of me. One of the other inmates, who has been watching the TV, leans across and asks me if the story's true. I can just about recall Tennyson's poem of the gallant six hundred, and I'm fairly certain Errol Flynn didn't ride through the enemy lines, and thrust a sword into the heart of their leader.

'Of course he did,' says David, 'it was in his contract.'

On this occasion we do get to see the closing titles, because the duty officer has checked what time the film finishes. He prefers not to have thirty or forty disenchanted lifers on his hands.

At two we're invited to return to our cells for lock-up. This invitation takes the form of an officer bellowing at the top of his voice. On arrival, I find another 200 letters waiting for me on the bottom bunk. All of them have been opened, as per prison regulations, to check they do not contain any drugs, razor blades or money. Reading every one of them kills another couple of hours while you're 'banged up'. I'm beginning to think in prison jargon.

The public seems genuinely concerned about my plight. Many of them comment on the judge's summing-up and the harshness of the sentence, while others point out that bank robbers, paedophiles and even those charged with manslaughter often get off with a two- or three-year sentence. The recurring theme is 'What does Mr Justice Potts have against you?' I confess I don't know the answer to that question, but what cannot be denied is that I asked my barrister, Nick Purnell, on the third, fourth and seventh days of the trial to speak to the judge privately in chambers about his obvious prejudice, and request a retrial. However, my silk advised against this approach, on the grounds that it would only turn the whole trial into an all-out battle between the two of us. Lest you might think I am making this all up conveniently after the event, I also confided my fears to the Honourable Michael Beloff QC, Gilbert Gray QC and Johnnie Nutting QC during the trial.

It isn't until the second hour that I come across a letter demanding that I should apologize to all those I had let down. The next letter in the pile is from Mary. I read it again and again. She begins by remarking that she couldn't remember when she had last written to me. She reminds me that she is off to Strathclyde University this morning to chair the summer school on solar energy, accompanied by the world's press and my son Will. Thank God for Will. He's been a tower of strength. At the end of next week, she flies to Dresden to attend another conference, and has sent me a parcel which with any luck should arrive by the weekend. I miss her and the children, of course I do, but above anything I hope it won't be too long before the press become bored with me and allow Mary to carry on with her life.

When I come to the end of the letters, Terry helps me put them into four large brown envelopes so they can be sent on to Alison, my PA, in order that everyone who has taken the trouble to write receives a reply. While Terry is helping me, he begins to tell me his life story and how he ended up being in jail. He's not a lifer, which is perhaps another reason they asked him if he was willing to share a cell with me.

Terry has been in prison twice, graduating via Borstal and a remand centre. He began sniffing solvents as a child, before moving on to cannabis by the age of twelve. His first offence was robbing a local newsagent because he needed money for his drug habit. He was sentenced to two years and served one. His second charge was for robbing a jeweller's in Margate of £3,000 worth of goods for which he hoped to make around £800 from a London fence. The police caught him red-handed (his words), and he was sentenced to five years. He was twenty-two at the time, and served three and a half years of that sentence before being released.

Terry had only been out for seven months when he robbed an optician's – designer goods, Cartier, Calvin Klein and Christian Dior, stolen to order. This time he was paid £900 in cash, but arrested a week later. The fingerprints on the shop window he put his fist through matched his, leaving the police with only one suspect. The judge sentenced him to another five years.

Terry hopes to be released in December of this year. Prison, he claims, has weaned him off drugs and he's only thankful that he's never tried heroin. Terry is nobody's fool, and I only hope that when he gets out he will not return for a third time. He swears he won't, but a prison officer tells me that two-thirds of repeat offenders are back inside within twelve months.

'We have our regulars just like any Blackpool hotel, except we don't charge for bed and breakfast.'

Terry is telling me about his mother, when suddenly there is a wild commotion of screaming and shouting that reverberates throughout the entire block. It's the first time I'm glad that my cell door is locked. The prisoners in Block One are yelling at a man who is being escorted to the medical centre on the far side of the yard. I remember it well.

'What's all that about?' I ask as I stare out of our cell window.

'He's a nonce,' Terry explains.

'Nonce?'

'Prison slang for a nonsense merchant, a paedophile. If he'd been on this block we would have jugged him long ago.'

'Jugged him?'

'A jug of boiling hot water,' Terry explains, 'mixed with a bag of sugar to form a syrup. Two cons would hold him down while the liquid is poured slowly over his face.'

'My God, that must be horrific.'

'First the skin peels off your face and then the sugar dissolves, so you end up disfigured for the rest of your life – no more than he deserves,' Terry adds.

'Have you ever witnessed that?' I ask.

'Three times,' he replies matter-of-factly. 'One nonce, one drug dealer, and once over an argument about someone who hadn't returned a two-pound phonecard.' He pauses before adding, 'If they were to put him on this block, he'd be dead within twenty-four hours.'

I'm terrified, so I can only wonder what sort of fear they live in. The moment the prisoner disappears into the medical centre, the shouting and yelling stops.

4.00 pm

The cell door is at last unlocked and we are allowed out into the exercise yard. On my first circuit, about two hundred yards, I'm joined by a young prisoner – come to think of it, everyone is young except for me and David. His name is Nick, and if it weren't for his crooked front teeth and broken nose, he would be a good-looking man. He's been in prison for the past fourteen years, and he's only thirty-three, but he hopes to be out in four years' time as long as he can beat his latest rap.

'Your latest rap?' I repeat.

'Yeah, they've been trying to pin arson on me after what I got up to in Durham, but they've got no proof that I set fire to my cell, so they'll have to drop the charge.' He's joined by another lifer who has just completed four of his eighteen years.

79

There seems to be a completely different attitude among the lifers. They often say, 'Don't bother to count the first six years.' They acknowledge they won't be out next week, next month, or even next year, and have settled for a long spell of prison life. Most of them treat me with respect and don't indulge in clever or snide remarks.

On the next circuit I'm joined by Mike (armed robbery), who tells me that he listened to Ted Francis and Max Clifford on the radio last night, and adds that the boys just can't wait for one of them to be sent to prison. 'We don't like people who stitch up their mates – especially for money.' I stick assiduously to Nick Purnell's advice and make no comment.

When I return to the cell, Terry is about to go down for supper. I tell him I just can't face it, but he begs me to join him because tonight it's pineapple upside-down pudding, and that's his favourite. I join him and go through the ritual of selecting a couple of burnt mushrooms in order to lay my hands on an extra upside-down pudding.

By the time I get back to the cell, Terry is sweeping the room and cleaning the washbasin. I've been lucky to be shacked up with someone who is so tidy, and hates anything to be out of place. Terry sits on the bed munching his meal, while I read through what I've penned that day. Once Terry's finished, he washes his plate, knife, fork and spoon before stacking them neatly on the floor in the corner. I continue reading my script while he picks up a Bible. He turns to the Book of Hebrews, which I confess I have never read, and studies quietly for the next hour.

Once I've completed my work for the day, I return to reading *The Moon's a Balloon*, which I put down just after ten when war has been declared. The pillows are a little softer than those on Block Three, for which I am grateful.

DAY 7   WEDNESDAY 25 JULY 2001

5.17 am

'Fuck off,' cries a voice so loud it wakes me.

It's a few moments before I realize that it's Terry shouting in his sleep. He mumbles something else which I can't quite decipher, before he wakes with a start. He climbs out of bed, almost as if he's unaware there's someone in the bunk below him. I don't stir, but open my eyes and watch carefully. I'm not frightened; although Terry has a past record of violence, I've never seen any sign of it. In fact, despite the use of bad language in his novel, he never swears in front of me – at least not when he's awake.

Terry walks slowly over to the wall and places his head in the corner like a cat who thinks he's about to die. He doesn't move for some time, then turns, picks up a towel by the basin, sits down on the plastic chair and buries his head in the towel. Desperate and depressed. I try to imagine what must be going through his tortured mind. He slowly raises his head and stares at me, as if suddenly remembering that he's not alone.

'Sorry, Mr Archer,' he says. 'Did I wake you?'

'It's not important,' I reply. 'Do you want to talk about it?'

'It's a recurring nightmare,' he says, 'but for some unexplainable reason it's been worse for the past couple of weeks. When I was a kid,' he pauses, no doubt considering whether to confide in me, 'my stepfather used to beat me and my mum with a leather strap, and I've suddenly started having nightmares about it all these years later.'

'How old were you at the time?' I ask.

'About six, but it carried on until I was sixteen, when my mum died.'

'How did your mother die?' I ask. 'After all, she can't have been that old?'

'It's all a bit of a mystery,' Terry says quietly. 'All I know for certain is that they found her body in the front room by the grate, and then my stepfather buggered off to Brighton with my stepsister.' I have a feeling that Terry knows only too well what and who caused his mother's death, but he isn't yet willing to impart that information. After all, he's well aware I'm writing a daily diary.

'So what happened to you when he disappeared off to Brighton?'

'I was taken into care, followed by Borstal, remand home and finally jail – a different sort of education to yours.' How can those of us who have had a comparatively normal upbringing begin to understand what this young man has been through – is going through?

'Sorry,' he repeats, and then climbs back onto the top bunk, and is asleep again within minutes.

I climb out of bed, clean my teeth, rub a cold flannel over my face and then settle down to write for the first session of the day. At this early hour, all the other prisoners are asleep, or at least I assume they are, because not a sound is coming from the surrounding cells. Even the early-morning patrol of barking Alsatians doesn't distract me any longer.

In London I live near a railway track that winds its way into

Waterloo, but I am never woken by the late-night or early-morning trains. In prison, it's rap music, inmates hollering at each other, and Alsatians that don't disturb a lifer's dreams. Once I've completed my two-hour session, I begin the lengthy process of shaving.

Although my life is beginning to fall into a senseless routine, I hope to at least break it up today by going to the gym. I've put my name down for the 10 am to 11 am session this morning, as I'm already missing my daily exercise.

9.06 am

Just after nine, the cell door is opened and my weekly twelve pounds fifty pence worth of canteen provisions are passed over to me by a lady in a white coat. I thank her, but she doesn't respond. I sit on the end of my bed, unpack each item one by one. I settle down to enjoy a bowl of cornflakes swimming in fresh milk. This is the meal I would normally have in my kitchen at home, an hour before going to the gym. I'm used to a disciplined, well-ordered life, but it's no longer self-discipline because someone else is giving the orders.

10.00 am

I'm pacing up and down the cell waiting for the gym call when a voice bellows out from below, 'Gym is cancelled.' My heart sinks and I stare out of the barred window, wondering why. When the door is eventually opened for Association, Derek, known as Del Boy, who runs the hotplate and seems to have a free rein of the block, appears outside my door.

'Why was gym cancelled?' I ask.

'A con has got out onto the roof via a skylight in the gym,' he explains. Result – gym closed until further notice and will not open again until security has double-checked every possible exit and the authorities consider it a safe area again. He grins, enjoying his role as the prison oracle.

'Anything else I can help you with?' Del Boy enquires.

'Bottled water and an A4 writing pad,' I reply.

'They'll be with you before the hour has chimed, squire.'

I've already learnt not to ask what myriad of deals will have to be carried out to achieve this simple request. James had warned me on my first day about the prison term 'double-bubble', meaning certain favours have to be repaid twice over. During Association yesterday evening, I witnessed Derek cut a rolled-up cigarette in half and then pass it over to another prisoner. This was on a Tuesday, and the hapless inmate knew he wouldn't be able to repay the debt until today, when he would have his next canteen. But his craving was so great that he accepted, knowing that he would have to give Del Boy a whole cigarette in return, or he could never hope to strike up another bargain with him – or anyone else, for that matter.

11.10 am

It must have been a few minutes after eleven when my cell door is yanked open again to reveal Mr Loughnane. Just the sight of him lifts my spirits. He tells me that he has spoken to his opposite number at Ford Open Prison, who will have to refer the matter to the Governor, as he doesn't have the authority to make the final decision.

'How long do you expect that will take?' I ask.

'Couple of days at the most. He'll probably come back to me on Friday, and when he does, I'll be in touch with Group 4.' This simple transaction would take the average businessman a couple of hours at most. For the first time in years, I'm having to move at someone else's pace.

1.00 pm

We are all sent off to work. I'm down on the register under 'workshops' where I will have to pack breakfast bags that will eventually end up in other prisons. My salary will be 50p an hour. New Labour's minimum-wage policy hasn't quite trickled down to convicted felons. The truth is we're captive labour. I'm about to join the chain gang when another prison officer, Mr Young, asks me to wait behind until the others have left for the work area. He returns a few minutes later, to tell me that I've received so much registered mail they have decided to take me to it, rather than bring the stack to me.

Another long walk in a different direction, even more opening and closing of barred gates, by which time I have learnt that Mr Young has been in the prison service for eleven years, his annual basic pay is £24,000, and it's quite hard, if not impossible, to find somewhere to live in London on that salary.

When we arrive at reception, two other officers are standing behind a counter in front of rows and rows of cluttered wooden shelves. Mr Pearson removes thirty-two registered letters and parcels from a shelf behind him and places them on the counter. He starts to open them one by one in front of me – another prison regulation. The two officers then make a little pile of Bibles and books and another of gifts which they eventually place in a plastic bag, and once I've signed the requisite form, hand them all across to me.

'Peach,' says Mr Pearson, and another prisoner steps forward to have a parcel opened in front of him. It's a pair of the latest Nike trainers, which have been sent in by his girlfriend.

Both clutching onto our plastic bags, we accompany Mr Young back to Block One. On the way, I apologize to Peach – I never did find out his first name – for keeping him waiting.

'No problem,' he says. 'You kept me out of my cell for nearly an hour.'

Mr Young continues to tell us about some of the other problems the prison service is facing. We are onto staff benefits and shiftwork when an alarm goes off, and officers appear running towards us from every direction. Mr Young quickly unlocks the nearest waiting room and bundles Peach and myself inside, locking the door firmly behind us. We stare through the windows as officers continue rushing past us, but we have no way of finding out why. A few moments later, a prisoner, held down by three officers and surrounded by others, is dragged off past us in the opposite direction. One of the officers is pushing the prisoner's head down, while another keeps his legs bent so that when he passes us he leaves an impression of a marionette controlled by invisible strings. Peach tells me that it's known as being 'bent up' or 'twisted up', and is part of the process of 'control and restraint'.

'Control and restraint?'

'The prisoner will be dragged into a strip cell and held down while his clothes are cut off with a pair of scissors. He's then put in wrist locks, before they bend his legs behind his back. Finally they put a belt around his waist that has handcuffs on each side, making it impossible for him to move his arms or legs.'

'And then what?'

'They'll take him off to segregation,' Peach explains. 'He'll be put into a single cell that consists of a metal sink, metal table and metal chair all fixed to the wall, so he can't smash anything up.'

'How long will they leave him there?'

'About ten days,' Peach replies.

'Have you ever been in segregation?' I ask.

'No,' he says firmly, 'I want to get out of this place as quickly as possible, and that's the easiest way to be sure your sentence is lengthened.'

Once the commotion has died down, Mr Young returns to unlock the door and we continue our journey back to the cells as if nothing had happened.

Each block has four spurs, which run off from the centre like a Maltese cross. In the middle of the cross is an octangular glass office, known as the bubble, which is situated on the centre of the three floors. From this vantage point, the staff can control any problems that might arise. As we pass the bubble, I ask the duty officer what happened.

'One of the prisoners,' he explains, 'has used threatening and abusive language when addressing a woman officer.' He adds no further detail to this meagre piece of information.

Once back in my cell, Terry tells me that the prisoner will be put on report and be up in front of the Governor tomorrow morning. He also confirms that he'll probably end up with ten days in solitary.

'Have you ever been in segregation?' I ask him.

'Three times,' he admits. 'But I was younger then, and can tell you, I don't recommend it, even as an experience for your diary. By the way,' he adds, 'I've just phoned my dad. The *Daily Express* have been onto him offering a grand for a photo of me – *the con Jeffrey has to live with* – and they've offered him another thousand if he'll give them all the details of my past criminal record. He told them to bugger off, but he says they just won't go away. They sounded disappointed when he told them I wasn't a murderer.'

'You will be by the time the Sunday editions come out,' I promise him.

DAY 7

2.00 pm

Another officer opens the door to tell us that our afternoon Association will be cut short because the prison staff are holding a meeting. Terry tells the officer who passes on this information that any staff meeting should be held when we are banged up, not during Association. He makes a fair point, but all the officer says is, 'It's not my decision,' and slams the door.

2.02 pm

What is almost impossible to describe in its full horror is the time you spend *banged up*. So please do not consider this diary to be a running commentary, because I would only ask you to think about the endless hours in between. Heaven knows what that does to lifers who can see no end to their incarceration, and do not have the privilege of being able to occupy their time writing. In my particular case, there is Hope, a word you hear prisoners using all the time. They hope that they'll win their case, have their sentence cut, be let out on parole, or just be moved to a single cell. For me, as a Category D prisoner, I simply hope to be transferred to Ford Open Prison as soon as possible. But God knows what a lifer hopes for, and I resolve to try and find out during the next few days.

4.30 pm

Association. At last the cell door is opened for an extended period of time – forty-five minutes. When I walk down to join the other inmates on the ground floor, Paul (murder) hands me a book of first-class stamps, and asks for nothing in return. He either has no one to write to, or perhaps can't write. 'I hear you're having a postage problem,' is all he says, and walks away. I do not explain that my PA is dealing with all my letters, and therefore I have no postage problem, because it would only belittle such a thoughtful gesture.

During Association I notice that the high barred gates at the end of the room lead onto a larger outer area which has its own television, pool table, and more comfortable chairs. But I'm not permitted to enter this hallowed territory as you can only leave the restricted area if you're an *enhanced* prisoner.

There are three levels of prisoner: basic, standard and enhanced. Every inmate begins their sentence as standard – in the middle. This leaves you the chance to go up or down, and that decision depends solely on your behaviour. Someone who wishes to take on more responsibility, like being a Listener, a tea-boy or a cleaner, will quickly be promoted to enhanced status and enjoy the privileges that go with it. However, anyone who attacks a prison officer or is caught taking drugs will be downgraded to basic. And these things matter when it comes to your standard of living in prison, and later when the authorities consider your parole, and possible early release.

Terry, my cell-mate, hates authority and refuses to go along with the system, so spends his life bobbing up and down between basic and standard. Derek 'Del Boy' Bicknell, on the other hand, took advantage of the system and quickly became enhanced. But then he is bright, and well capable of taking on responsibility. He already has the free run of the ground floor and in fact never seems to be in his cell. I hope by now you have a picture in your mind of Del Boy, because he's a six-foot, twenty-stone West Indian who wears a thin gold chain around his neck, a thicker one around his right wrist, and sports the latest designer watch. He also wears a fashionable tracksuit and Nike shoes. Come to think of it, I'm the only prisoner who still wears a shirt, but if I were to remain here for any length of time, I would also end up wearing a tracksuit.

5.30 pm

Supper, called tea, is being served, so I return to my cell to collect my plastic tray and plate. Tonight it's egg and bacon and I'm just too hungry to say no. The egg has a solid yolk and the greasy bacon is fatty, curling and inedible. I drink a mug of Highland Spring water (a trade for two autographs on birthday cards) and finish the meal with a bowl of Cup a Soup (minestrone, 24p). At the next election no one will be able to accuse me of not knowing the price of goods in the supermarket, not to mention their true value.

Terry cleans our utensils before we return to Association on the ground floor, where I find Del Boy running a card school at the other end of the room. Why am I not surprised? He beckons me to join them. The game is made up of four lifers who are playing Kaluki. I watch a couple of hands while trying to keep an eye on the phone queue, as I'm hoping to speak to Mary. She should have returned from her day at Strathclyde University and be back in her hotel. By now you will have realized that she can't call me.

Paul (murder and stamps) announces he needs to phone his girlfriend and suggests I take over his hand while he joins the queue.

'Jeff's got to be an improvement on you,' says Derek as Paul rises to depart.

I lose the first hand badly, survive the second, and win the third. Thankfully, before Del Boy starts dealing the fourth, Paul returns.

'His Lordship's not bad,' says Derek, 'not bad at all.' I'm slowly being accepted.

The queue for the two phones doesn't seem to diminish, so I spend some time talking to a young lifer called Michael (murder). He's very pale-skinned, extremely thin, and covered in tattoos, with needle tracks up and down his arms. He invites me into his cell, and shows me a picture of his wife and child. By the time Michael is released from prison, his eight-month-old daughter will have left school, probably be married and have children of her own. In fact this twenty-two-year-old boy may well be a grandfather by the time he's released.

When I leave Michael's cell to rejoin the others I spot Ms Roberts, the Deputy Governor, who came to visit me when I was on the medical wing. She is surrounded by lifers. Ms Roberts has a real gift for putting these desperate men at ease.

I finally give up and join the phone queue, aware that we are fast approaching lock-up. When at last I make the one spare phone out of two a lifer who is on the other line leans over to warn me that any conversations made on these phones are tape-recorded by the police. I thank him, but can't imagine what they would find of interest eavesdropping on a chat with my wife. A hotel operator answers the call and puts me through to her room. The phone rings and rings.

7.00 pm

I return to my cell to be faced with another mountain of mail. Terry helps by taking them out of their envelopes before placing them in piles, cards on one side, letters on the other, while I continue to go over the script I've written that day. Terry asks if he can keep one or two of the cards as a memento. 'Only if they

91

have no address,' I tell him, 'as it's still my intention to reply to every one of them.'

Once I've finished correcting my daily script, I turn my attention to the letters. Like my life, they are falling into a pattern of their own, some offering condolences on my mother's death, others kindness and support. Many continue to comment on Mr Justice Potts's summing-up, and the harshness of the sentence. I am bound to admit they bring back one's faith in one's fellow men . . . and women.

Alison, my PA, has written to say that I am receiving even more correspondence by every post at home, and she confirms that they are also running at three hundred to one in support. I hand one of the letters up to Terry. It's from his cousin who's read in the papers that we're sharing a cell. Terry tells me that he's serving a life sentence in Parkhurst for murder. My cell-mate adds they haven't spoken to each other for years. And it was only a couple of hours ago I was feeling low because I haven't managed to speak to Mary today.

DAY 8   THURSDAY 26 JULY 2001

5.03 am

I've slept for seven hours. When I wake, I begin to think about my first week in prison. The longest week of my life. For the first time, I consider the future and what it holds for me. Will I have to follow the path of two of my heroes, Emma Hamilton and Oscar Wilde, and choose to live a secluded life abroad, unable to enjoy the society that has been so much a part of my very existence?

Will I be able to visit old haunts – the National Theatre, Lord's, Le Caprice, the Tate Gallery, the UGC Cinema in Fulham Road – or even walk down the street without people's only thought being 'There's the man who went to jail for perjury'? I can't explain to every one of them that I didn't get a fair trial. It's so unlike me to be introspective or pessimistic, but when you're locked up in a cell seven paces by four for hour upon hour every day, you begin to wonder if anyone out there even knows you're still alive.

10.00 am

Mr Highland, a young officer, unlocks my cell door and tells me I have a legal visit at ten thirty. I ask if I might be allowed to take a shower and wash my hair.

'No,' he says. 'Use the washbasin.' Only the second officer to be offhand since I've arrived. I explain that it's quite hard to have a shower in a washbasin. He tells me that I've got an 'attitude' problem, and says that if I go on like this, he'll have to put me on report. It feels like being back at school at the wrong end of your life.

I shave and clean myself up as best I can before being escorted to yet another part of the building so that I can meet up with my lawyers. I am deposited in a room about eight foot by eight, with windows in all four walls; even lawyers have been known to bring in drugs for their clients. There's a large oblong table in the centre of the room, with six chairs around it. A few moments later I'm joined by Nick Purnell QC and his junior Alex Cameron, who are accompanied by my solicitor, Ramona Mehta. Nick takes me slowly through the process of appeal against conviction and sentence. He's fairly pessimistic about conviction, despite there being a considerable amount of evidence of the judge's bias when summing up, but he says only those in the court room will remember the emphasis and exaggeration Potts put on certain words when he addressed the jury. The judge continually reminded the jurors that I hadn't given evidence, and, holding up Mrs Peppiatt's small diary not my large office diary, repeatedly remarked that 'no one has denied this is a real diary'. He didn't point out to the jury, however, that even if that diary had appeared in the original trial, it wouldn't have made any material difference.

On the subject of sentence, Nick Purnell is more confident, as several leading members of the Bar have made it clear that they consider four years to be not only harsh, but unjust. And the public seem to be universally in agreement with the professionals. Reduction of sentence can make a great difference, because any conviction of four years or more requires a decision by the Parole Board before you can be set free. Any sentence of less than four years, even by one day, means you are automatically released after serving half your sentence, assuming you've been a model prisoner. You're also eligible for tagging, which knocks off another two months, when you are restricted to your 'chosen place of residence' between the hours of seven pm and seven am the following morning.*

We go on to discuss whether this is the right time to issue a writ against Emma Nicholson for hinting that the millions of pounds I helped raise for the Kurds didn't reach them, with the twisted implication that some of the money must therefore have ended up in my pocket. Nick points out that Sir Nicholas Young, the Chief Executive of the Red Cross, has come to my defence, and even the *Evening Standard* is saying I have no case to answer. Alex tells me that several articles are now being written in support of my position, including one by Trevor Kavanagh in the *Sun*. He also points out that the *Daily Telegraph* had a tilt at Max Hastings.

I tell Nick that I want to issue a writ against Ted Francis to recover the £12,000 I loaned him, and for claiming that over twenty years ago he'd seen a Nigerian prostitute climbing out of my bedroom window. This is quite an achievement as Francis and I stayed at different hotels and my room was on the top floor. I do hope the poor girl was a member of the Lagos mountain rescue team.

My legal team understand my anger, but want to wait until the dust has settled. I reluctantly agree, but remain unconvinced. I can't help remembering that when I complained to Nick about

---

* For example, if my sentence was reduced by one year, from four to three, I would end up only serving sixteen months and be released on 19 November 2002; whereas with a four-year sentence, the earliest I could hope to be released would be 19 July 2003.

DAY 8

Mr Justice Potts's prejudiced attitude during the pre-trial hearings and the trial itself, he advised me against raising the matter with the judge in chambers, saying it would only exacerbate the problem.

On the hour I leave them to return to their world, while I am escorted back to mine.

12 noon

I take one look at what they're offering at the hotplate for lunch, and return to my cell with an empty plastic plate. I add a packet of crisps to my opened tin of Spam, before pouring myself a mug of cranberry juice topped up with Highland Spring. My supplies are already running low.

2.00 pm

Mr Weedon comes to my cell to let me know that I have a personal visit at three o'clock.

'Who?' I enquire.

He checks his list. 'William and James Archer.'

I am about to suggest it might have been more considerate of someone to warn me yesterday rather than tell me a few minutes before my sons are due to arrive. However, as Mr Highland has already threatened to place me on report for such insolence, I decide to keep my counsel.

3.00 pm

Over eighty prisoners from all four blocks are streaming towards the visitors' area. On the long walk to the other side of the building, I come across some inmates from my short stay on

House Block Three. It's rather like meeting up with old school chums. 'How are you?' 'What have you been up to?' 'Have you met up with . . .?' When we arrive in the waiting area, the search is far more rigorous than usual. Del Boy had already warned me that this is the one time the staff are nervous about the transfer of money, drugs, blades, knives, even guns, and anything else that might be passed from a relation or family friend on to a prisoner. I am pleased to discover that my own search is fairly cursory. After the search, I am asked to place a yellow sash over my shoulder so I look like a child about to go on a bike ride. This is to indicate that I'm a prisoner, so that I can't stroll out with my sons once the visit is over. I'm bound to say that I find this tiny act humiliating.

I'm then ushered into a room about the size of a large gymnasium. Chairs are set out in five long rows marked A to E. I report to a desk that is raised three or four feet above the ground, and another officer checks his list and then tells me to go to C11. All the prisoners sit on the right-hand side, opposite their visitors who sit on the left. There is a small, low table in between us which is screwed to the floor, and is meant to keep you apart. There is also a balcony above us that overlooks the whole room, with even more officers staring down on the proceedings to see if they can spot anything being passed across the tables below them. They are assisted by several CCTV cameras. A notice on the walls states that the tapes can be used as evidence for a further prosecution, and in capitals adds: THIS APPLIES TO BOTH PRISONERS AND THEIR VISITORS.

I walk down three rows to find William sitting on his own. He jumps up and gives me a big hug, and I'm reminded just how much I've missed him. James, he tells me, is at the canteen purchasing my favourite beverage. He appears a few minutes later, carrying a tray of Diet Cokes and several KitKats. The boys laugh when I pull all three Cokes towards my side of the table, and make no attempt to offer them even a stick of the KitKat.

Will begins by telling me about Mary's visit to Strathclyde University, where she made a short statement to the press before delivering her lecture. She began by remarking that it was the largest turnout she had ever managed for a lecture on quantum solar-energy conversion.

Will is not surprised to learn that I have received over a thousand letters and cards in the first few days at Belmarsh, and he tells me there are almost three times that number back at the flat. Support is coming in from every quarter, James adds, including thoughtful statements from John Major and George Carey.

'Alison has had a list typed up,' my younger son continues, 'but they wouldn't allow me to bring anything into the visits room, so I'll have it posted on to you tomorrow.'

This news gives me such a lift, and makes me feel guilty that I had ever doubted my friends would stand by me.

I alert the two boys to the fact that I am writing a day-to-day diary, and will need to see my agent, Jonathan Lloyd, my publisher, Victoria Barnsley, and my editor, Robert Lacey, fairly soon, but, as I am only allowed one personal visit every two weeks, I don't want to see anyone other than the family until I've been moved to an open prison.

Will tells me that he's already booked himself in for two weeks' time, but hopes I will have been transferred to somewhere like Ford long before then. Because I've not been reading any newspapers or listening to the news, as I'm heartily sick of inaccurate stories about myself and what I'm up to at Belmarsh, Jamie brings me up to date on the battle for the Tory Party leadership. He reports that the polls clearly indicate that the people who deserted the Conservatives at the last election want Ken Clarke, while the party membership favours Iain Duncan

Smith. I like and admire both men, though neither is a close friend. However, it doesn't take a massive intellect to work out that if we hope to win the next election, or at least make a large enough dent in the government's majority to ensure that opinion-formers believe we can win the following election, it might be wise to take some notice of the electorate's views as to who should be our leader.

I consider dropping Ken a note, but realize it may not help his cause.

Will goes on to tell me that Michael Beloff QC, Gilbert Gray QC and Johnnie Nutting QC are in regular touch with my legal team. Gilly wondered if Potts's animosity had been aimed at Nick Purnell, as it's the talk of the Bar that he lost his temper with Nick on several occasions during the pre-trial and trial itself, but never once in front of the jury.

'No,' I tell them, 'it was nothing to do with Nick. It was entirely personal.'

I'm momentarily distracted by an attractive young woman sitting directly in front of me in row B. A prisoner with his back to me is leaning across the table and kissing her. I remember being told by Kevin that this was the most common way of passing drugs. I watch more carefully and decide this is about sex, pure animal sex, and has nothing to do with drugs.

James tells me about the film he and Nod (Nadhim Zahawi, a Kurdish friend) enjoyed on Sunday evening, *Rush Hour 2*, which in normal circumstances I would have seen with them.

'Don't worry,' he adds. 'We're keeping a list of all the films you would have enjoyed, so that you can eventually see them on video.' I don't like the sound of the word 'eventually'.

I talk to Will about when he expects to return to America and continue with his work as a documentary cameraman. He tells me that he will remain in England while his mother is so unsettled and feels in such need of him. How lucky I am to be blessed with such a family.

An announcement is made over the tannoy to inform us that all visitors must now leave. Have we really had an hour together? All round the room a great deal of kissing commences before friends and family reluctantly depart. The prisoners have to remain in their places until the last visitor has been signed out and left the room. I spend my time glancing up and down the rows. The man whose kiss had been so overtly sexual now has his head bowed in his hands. I wonder just how long his sentence is, and what age he and his girlfriend will be by the time he's released from prison.

When the last visitor has left, we all file back out of the room; once again my search is fairly cursory. I never discover what the other prisoners are put through, though. Del Boy tells me later that if they've picked up anything suspicious on the video camera, it's a full strip-search, plus sniffer dogs.

On the way back to my cell, a Block Three prisoner tells me he will be going home next month, having completed his sentence. He adds that he had a visit from his wife who is sticking by him, but if he's ever sentenced again, she's made it clear that she'll leave him.

I'm only a few yards from my cell door when Mr Weedon tells me that the education officer wants to see me. I turn round and he escorts me up to the middle floor.

The education officer is dressed in a smart brown suit. He stands up when I enter the room and shakes me by the hand.

'My name's Peter Farrell,' he says. 'I see you've put yourself down for education.'

'Yes,' I confirm. 'I was rather hoping it would give me a chance to use the library.'

'Yes, it will,' says Mr Farrell. 'But I wonder if I could ask you to assist us with those prisoners who are learning to read and write, as I'm rather short-staffed at the moment?'

'Of course,' I reply.

'You'll get a pound an hour,' he adds with a grin.

We talk for some time about the fact that there are a number of bright people among the prisoners, especially the lifers, some of whom would be quite capable of sitting for an Open University degree. 'My biggest problem,' he explains, 'is that while the inmates can earn ten to twelve pounds a week in the workshops dropping teabags, jam and sugar into plastic containers, they only receive six pounds fifty a week if they sign up for education. So I often lose out on some potentially able students for the sake of tobacco money.'

My God, there are going to be some speeches I will have to make should I ever return to the House of Lords.

There is a knock on the door, and Mr Marsland, the senior officer, comes in to warn me that it's almost time for my talk to the lifers on creative writing.

4.30 pm

The lecture is set up in one of the waiting rooms and is attended by twelve prisoners serving life sentences plus two officers to keep an eye on proceedings. There are two types of life sentence, mandatory and discretionary, but all that matters to a lifer is the tariff that has been set by the judge at their trial.

I begin my talk by telling the lifers that I didn't take up writing until I was thirty-four, after leaving Parliament and facing bankruptcy; so I try to assure them that you can begin a new career at any age. Proust, I remind them, said we all end up doing the thing we're second best at.

Once I've finished my short talk, the first two questions fired at me are about writing a novel, but I quickly discover that the other inmates mostly want to know how I feel about life behind bars and what changes I would make.

'I've only been inside for eight days,' I keep reminding them.

I try valiantly to parry their questions, but Mr Marsland and his deputy soon have to come to my rescue when the subject changes to how the prison is run, and in particular their complaints about lock-up times, food, no ice and wages. These all seem to be fair questions, though nothing to do with writing. The officers try to answer their queries without prevarication and both have so obviously given considerable thought to inmates' problems. They often sympathize, but appear to have their hands tied by regulations, bureaucracy and lack of money.

One prisoner called Tony, who seems not only to be bright but to have a real grasp of figures, discusses the £27 million budget that Belmarsh enjoys, right down to how much it costs to feed a prisoner every day. I will never forget the answer to that question – £1.27 is allocated for three meals per prisoner per day.

'Then the caterers must be making a pound a day off every one of us,' Tony retorts.

The meeting goes on well beyond the scheduled hour, and it's some time before one of the prisoners, Billy Little who hails from Glasgow, actually asks another question about writing. Do I use my novels to expound any particular political prejudice? No, I reply firmly, otherwise I'd have very few readers. Billy is a left-winger by upbringing and persuasion and argues his case well. He finds a great deal of pleasure in giving me a hard time and making me feel ill at ease with the other prisoners. By the end of a heated exchange, he is at least listening to my point of view.

On the way back to the cells, Billy tells me he's written a short story and some poetry. He asks if I would be willing to read them and offer an opinion; a sentence I usually dread when I'm on the outside. He nips into his cell on the ground floor, extracts some sheets of paper from a file and passes them over to me. I leave him to find Derek 'Del Boy' Bicknell waiting for me outside. He warns me that Terry, my cell-mate, has been talking to the press, and to be wary of saying anything to him.

'Talking to the press?'

'Yeah, the screws caught him on the phone to the *Sun*. I'm told that the going rate for an exclusive with anyone who has shared a cell with you is five grand.'

I thank Derek and assure him I haven't discussed my case or anything of importance with Terry and never would.

When I return to my cell, I find Terry looking shamefaced. He confirms that he has spoken to the *Sun*, and they're keen to know when I'm being moved to Ford.

'You'll be on the front page tomorrow,' I warn him.

'No, no, I didn't tell them anything,' he insists.

I try not to laugh as I settle down to read through another three hundred letters that have been opened by the censor and left on the end of my bed. I can't believe he's had the time to read many, if any, of them.

When I've finished the last one, I lie back on my bed and reluctantly pick up Billy Little's twelve-page essay. I turn the first page. I cannot believe what I'm reading. He has such command of language, insight, and that rare gift of making the mundane interesting that I finish every word, before switching off the light a few minutes after ten. I have a feeling that you're going to hear a lot more about this man, and not just from me.

DAY 9   FRIDAY 27 JULY 2001

2.11 am

I am woken in the middle of the night by rap music blasting out from a cell on the other side of the block. I can't imagine what it must be like if you're trying to sleep in the next cell, or even worse in the bunk below. I'm told that rap music is the biggest single cause of fights breaking out in prison. I'm not surprised. I had to wait until it was turned off before I could get back to sleep. I didn't wake again until eight minutes past six. Amazingly, Terry can sleep through anything.

6.08 am

I write for two hours, and as soon as I've completed the first draft of what happened yesterday, I strip down to my under-pants, put a towel round my waist, and place another one on the end of the bed with a bar of soap and a bottle of shampoo next to it.

My cell door is opened at eight twenty-three. I'm out of the starting gate like a thoroughbred, sprint along the corridor and into the shower room. Three of the four showers are already occupied by faster men than I. However, I still manage to capture the fourth stall, and once I've taken a long press-button shower, I feel clean for the first time in days.

When I return to my cell, Terry is still fast asleep, and even a prison officer unlocking the door doesn't disturb him. The new officer introduces himself as Ray Marcus, and explains that he works in the censor's department and is the other half of June Stelfox, who took care of my correspondence on House Block Three. His job is to check every item of mail a prisoner is sent, to make sure that they're not receiving anything that is against the regulations: razor blades, drugs, money – or even food. To be fair, although the censors open every letter, they don't read them. Ray is carrying a registered package which he slits open in front of me, and extracts a Bible. The eleventh in nine days. Like the others, I donate it to the chapel. He then asks if he can help in any way with my mail problem. Ray, as he prefers to be called, is courteous and seems almost embarrassed by the fact that I'm not allowed to open my own post. I tell him not to worry, because I haven't opened my own post for years.

I hand over three large brown envelopes containing all the letters I've received the day before, plus the first week (70 pages) of my handwritten script, together with twelve first-class stamps. I ask if they can all be sent back to my PA, Alison, so that she can carry on as if I was on holiday or abroad. He readily agrees, but points out that as senior censor, he is entitled to read anything that I am sending out.

'That's fine by me,' I tell him.

'I'd rather wait until it's published,' he says with a grin. 'After all, I've read everything else you've written.'

When he leaves he doesn't close my door, as if he knows what a difference this simple gesture makes to a man who will be locked up for twenty-two hours every day. This privilege lasts

DAY 9

only for a few minutes before another officer strolling by slams it shut, but I am grateful nevertheless.

9.00 am

Breakfast. A bowl of cornflakes with UHT milk from a carton that has been open, and not seen a fridge, for the past twenty-four hours. Wonderful.

10.09 am

Another officer arrives to announce that the Chaplain would like to see me. Glorious escape. He escorts me to the chapel – no search this time – where David Powe is waiting for me. He is wearing the same pale beige jacket, grey flannel trousers and probably the same dog collar as he did when he conducted the service on Sunday. He is literally down at heel. We chat about how I'm settling in – doesn't everyone? – and then go on to discuss the fact that his sermon on Cain and Abel made it into *Private Eye*. He chuckles, obviously enjoying the notoriety.

David then talks about his wife, who's the headmistress of a local primary school, and has written two books for Harper-Collins on religion. They have two children, one aged thirteen and the other sixteen. When he talks about his parish – the other prisoners – it doesn't take me long to realize that he's a deeply committed Christian, despite his doubting and doubtful flock of murderers, rapists and drug addicts. However, he is delighted to hear that my cell-mate Terry reads the Bible every day. I confess to having never read Hebrews.

David asks me about my own religious commitment and I tell him that when I was the Conservative candidate for Mayor of London, I became aware of how many religions were being practised in the capital, and if there was a God, he had a lot of disparate groups representing him on Earth. He points out that in Belmarsh there are over a hundred Muslims, another hundred Roman Catholics, but that the majority of inmates are still C of E.

'What about the Jews?' I ask him.

'Only one or two that I know of,' he replies. 'Their family upbringing and sense of community is so strong that they rarely end up in the courts or prison.'

When the hour is up – everything seems to have an allocated time – he blesses me, and tells me that he hopes to see me back in church on Sunday.

As it's the biggest cell in the prison, he most certainly will.

11.10 am

Mr Weedon is waiting at the chapel door – sorry, barred gate – to escort me back to my cell. He says that Mr Marsland wants to see me again. Does this mean that they know when I'll be leaving Belmarsh and where I'll be going? I ask Mr Weedon but receive no response. When I arrive at Mr Marsland's office, Mr Loughnane and Mr Gates are also present. They all look grim. My heart sinks and I now understand why Mr Weedon felt unable to answer my question.

Mr Marsland says that Ford Open Prison have turned down my application because they feel they can't handle the press interest, so the whole matter has been moved to a higher level. For a moment I wonder if I will ever get out of this hellhole. He adds, hoping it will act as a sweetener, that he plans to move me into a single cell because Fossett (Terry) was caught phoning the *Sun*.

'I can see that you're disappointed about Ford,' he adds, 'but we'll let you know where you'll be going, and when, just as soon as they tell us.' I get up to leave.

'I wonder if you'd be willing to give another talk on creative writing?' asks Mr Marsland. 'After your last effort, several other prisoners have told us that they want to hear you speak.'

'Why don't I just do an eight-week course,' I reply, 'as it seems we're going to be stuck with each other for the foreseeable future?' I immediately feel guilty about my sarcasm. After all, it isn't their fault that the Governor of Ford hasn't got the guts to try and handle a tricky problem. Perhaps he or she should read the Human Rights Act, and learn that this is not a fair reason to turn down my request.

2.00 pm

A woman officer unlocks the cell door, a cigarette hanging from her mouth,* and tells Terry he has a visitor. Terry can't believe it and tries to think who it could be. His father rarely speaks to him, his mother is dead, his brother is dying of Aids, he's lost touch with his sister and his cousin's in jail for murder. He climbs down from the top bunk, smiles for the first time in days, and happily troops out into the corridor, while I'm locked back in. I take advantage of Terry's absence and begin writing the second draft of yesterday's diary.

3.07 pm

Terry returns to the cell an hour later, dejected. A mistake must have been made because there turned out to be no visitor. They

---

* The Director General of Prisons, Martin Narey, has since issued a directive that officers should not smoke when on duty.

left him in the waiting room for over an hour while the other prisoners enjoyed the company of their family or friends.

I sometimes forget how lucky I am.

4.00 pm

Association. As I leave my cell and walk along the top landing, Derek Jones, a young double-strike prisoner, says he wants to show me something, and invites me back to his cell. He is one of those inmates whose tariff is open-ended, and although his case comes up for review by the Parole Board in 2005, he isn't confident that they will release him.

'I hear you're writing a book,' he says. 'But are you interested in things they don't know about out there?' he asks, staring through his barred window. I nod. 'Then I'll tell you something they don't even know about in here.' He points to a large stereo in the corner of the room – probably the one that kept me awake last night. It resembles a spaceship. 'That's my most valuable possession in the world,' he says. I don't interrupt. 'But I've got a problem.' I still say nothing. 'It runs on batteries, 'cause I haven't got any ice.'

'Ice? Why would you need ice for a ghetto blaster?'

'In Cell Electricity,' he says laughing.

'Ah, I see.'

'Have you any idea how much batteries cost?'

'No,' I tell him.

'£6.40 a time, and then they're only good for twelve hours, so I wouldn't be able to afford any tobacco if I had to buy new batteries every week.' I still haven't worked out where all this is leading. 'But I never have to buy any batteries, do I?'

'Don't you?' I say.

'No,' he replies, and then goes to a shelf behind his bed, and extracts a biro. He flicks off the little cap on the bottom and pulls out the refill, which has a coil of thin wire wrapped around it. He continues. 'First, I make an earth by scraping off a little paint from the water pipe behind my bed, then I take off the plastic cover from the strip light on the ceiling and attach the other end of the wire to the little box inside the light.' Derek can tell that I'm just about following this cunning subterfuge, when he adds, 'Don't worry about the details, Jeff, I've drawn you a diagram. [See page 105.] That way,' he says, 'I get an uninterrupted supply of electricity at Her Majesty's expense.'

My immediate reaction is, why isn't he on the outside doing a proper job? I thank him and assure Derek the story will get a mention in my story.

'What do I get out of it?' he asks. 'Because when I leave this place, all I have to my name other than that stereo is the ninety quid discharge money they give you.'*

I assure Derek that my publishers will pay him a fee for the use of the diagram if it appears in the book. We shake on it.

5.05 pm

Mr Weedon returns to tell me that I am being moved to a single cell. Terry immediately becomes petulant and starts shouting that he'd been promised a single cell even before I'd arrived.

'And you would have got one, Fossett,' Mr Weedon replies, 'if you hadn't phoned the press and grassed on your cell-mate for a few quid.'

Terry continues to harangue the officer and I can only

---

*Inmates are given £90 when leaving prison if they are of NFA (no fixed abode), £45 if they have somewhere to live. They can go back on social security after a fortnight.

1) ADD PAPER CLIP TO WIRE THAT LEADS FROM STEREO TO INNER BROWN.

2) USE INNER PEN TO ATTACH WIRE TO ~~CIGERETTER~~ POWER INLET

3) ALWAYS ATTACH WIRE TO APE FIRST

4) ALWAYS MAKE SURE WIRE (1) DOESN'T TOUCH ANY OTHER METAL OR OTHER WIRE

5) MAKE SURE WIRE (3) DOESN'T TOUCH ANYTHING METAL OTHER THAN APE.

6) MAKE SURE WIRE (3) TOUCHES BARE METAL ON APE. (CLEAR PAINT)

7) USE OUTER PEN TO INSERT INTO ~~CIGER~~ POWER (3)(USB) BUTTON IS.

LIGHT →

TO CEL PIPE

TO LIGHT

Power Socket on Stereo

STEREO

LIGHT →

CELL PIPE

wonder how long he will last with such a short fuse once he returns to the outside world.

I gather up my possessions and move across from Cell 40 to 30 on the other side of the corridor. My fourth move in nine days. A six-foot four-inch Ghanaian who was convicted of murdering a man in Peckham despite claiming that he was in Brighton with his girlfriend at the time, returns to his old bunk in Cell 40. I feel bad about depriving him of his private cell, and it becomes yet another reason I want to move to a D-cat prison as soon as possible, so that he can have his single cell back.

I spend an hour filling up my cellophane bag, carrying it across the corridor, emptying it, then rearranging my belongings in Cell 30. I have just completed this task when my new cell door is opened, and I'm ordered to go down to the hotplate for supper.

6.00 pm

I once again settle for the vegetarian option, although Paul (murder and stamps), who ticks off each name on a clipboard at the hotplate, tells me that the chicken is passable. I risk it. He's wrong again. I won't give him a third chance.

During Association I spend half an hour with Billy Little (murder) in his cell, going over his work. He tells me he has at least another twenty years to serve as his tariff is open-ended, so I advise him to start writing a novel, even a trilogy. He looks doubtful. He's not a man who's ever put much faith in the word of a Conservative.

There's a knock on the cell door and a massive giant of a man ambles into the room looking like a second-row forward in search of a scrum. I noticed him on the first day as he stood alone in the far corner of the room, staring silently through me.

He was hard to miss at over six foot, weighing around twenty-one stone. He's never said a word to me since my arrival on the spur, and I confess to being a little apprehensive about him, even frightened. He's known as Fletch.

He's come to 'let me know' that Terry is no longer complaining about my being moved into a single cell because he accepts that by phoning the *Sun* he was 'out of order', but he has since been warned that one of the Sunday papers is going to run a story about him hitting a woman over the head with a snooker ball wrapped in a sock. One of the many things prisoners will not tolerate is anyone attacking a woman. Terry has told Fletch that he's terrified that some of the inmates will beat him up once the story is published.* Fletch is letting it be known that he doesn't want any trouble, 'even though he accepts that the lad was stupid to have talked to the press in the first place'. Fletch looks at me and says, 'I must be the only person on the spur who hasn't spoken to you, but then I hate everything you stand for. Don't take it personally,' he adds and then leaves without another word.

Billy tells me that Fletch is one of the most respected prisoners on the spur and, to my surprise, a Listener. 'Don't worry about him,' he adds, 'because I can tell you that one of the reasons we have so little trouble on this wing is because he was a bouncer for a London nightclub before he ended up in here. Last year he single-handedly stopped a riot over the state of the food. The screws could never have contained the problem on their own, and they know it.'

---

* Beatings up (hammerings) usually take place in the shower room, which is why some prisoners don't wash from one year to the next. The reason the shower room is the preferred place for retribution is because it's on the top floor at the end of a long corridor, more than four prisoners are allowed to congregate at any one time, and any excess noise is usually ignored as exuberance.

DAY 9

I leave Billy and return to Association to play a couple of hands of Kaluki with Del Boy (murder), Colin (GBH) and Paul (murder – seventy-five years between them). I win the first hand and lose the second by 124 points. It's been that sort of a day.

Just as I'm about to return to my cell for lock-up, Ms Roberts appears on the floor. Terry rushes across to her and begins an animated conversation. She does her best to calm him down. When he is placated enough to move on, I ask her if she's had a call from my solicitor.

'Yes,' she replies, 'and I'll have a word with you first thing in the morning. I hope you'll feel it's good news.' I don't press her for any details because several other prisoners have formed a queue as they also wish to speak to the Deputy Governor before lock-up.

9.00 pm

It has, as I have already stated, been an up and down sort of day, but I feel a little better after Ms Roberts' comments. What will she have to tell me tomorrow?

For the next couple of hours I go through another hundred letters that the censor has left on my bed. The pattern is now firmly set, but there is one letter in particular that amuses me – *I am writing to give you my full support, as I suspect that no one else is bothering to do so at the present time.* I smile because Ms Buxton of Northants reminds me just how fortunate I am to have so many people willing to fight my corner. I only have to think about Terry's phantom visitor to realize just how lucky I am.

DAY 10   SATURDAY 28 JULY 2001

5.42 am

I wake in a cold sweat, having had the strangest dream. I'm back at Oxford in the sixties, where I win the University cross-country trials, which would automatically ensure that I was awarded a Blue and a place in the team against Cambridge. As I ran the one hundred yards in my youth, this scenario seems somewhat unlikely. But it gets worse. I'm disqualified, and the race is awarded to the man who came second. When the cup is presented to him I lose my temper with the judges. The judges are David Coleman and the late Ron Pickering – two of the most decent men God ever put on Earth. They tell me they had to disqualify me because they just didn't believe I could possibly have won. No doubt the prison psychiatrist will have a theory.

6.11 am

I don't begin writing immediately as I consider the task I have set myself over the past few days: a close study of lifers.

DAY 10

On spur one, there are fifty-two men serving life sentences.* I've now held long conversations with about twenty of them, and have come to the conclusion that they fall roughly into two categories. This is of course an over-simplification, as each individual is both complex and unique. The first group consist of those who insist, 'It wasn't me, guv, it was all a stitch up. They didn't even find the murder weapon, but because of my previous record I fitted neatly into the required police profile.'

The other group hold their hands in the air and admit to a moment of madness, which they will eternally regret, and accept they must pay the penalty the law demands. One or two even add, 'It's no more than I deserve.'

My natural sense of justice makes me worry about the first group; are they all liars, or is there anyone on this spur serving a life sentence who is in fact innocent? But more of that later.

9.00 am

Saturdays differ from every other day of the week because you're not supplied with a plastic bag containing breakfast the night before when you queue for supper. At 9 am your cell door is opened and you go down to the canteen for a cooked breakfast – egg, beans and chips. I accept the egg and beans, and wonder how many Saturdays it will be before I'm willing to add the chips.

---

* On 30 June 1990, there were 1,725 inmates serving life sentences. On 30 June 2000 this figure had risen by 163 per cent to 4,540, 97 per cent of them male, of whom 3,405 were convicted murderers. It's important to remember that murderers are different to other criminals. For over 50 per cent it's a first offence, and when they are released, they never commit another crime. It's equally true to say that the other 50 per cent are professional criminals, who do not deserve a moment of your sympathy.

10.00 am

I'm given the choice of taking exercise in the yard, or remaining banged-up in my cell. I sign up for exercise.

On the first two circuits of the yard I'm joined by a group of drug dealers who ask me if I need anything, from marijuana to crack cocaine to heroin. It takes them some time to accept that I've never taken a drug in my life, and don't intend to start now.

'We do a lot of business with your lot,' one of them adds casually.

I would like to have replied, 'And I hope you rot in jail for the rest of your life,' but didn't have the guts.

The next inmate to join me is a hot-gospeller who hopes that while I'm in Belmarsh I'll discover Christ. I explain that I consider one's religion to be a personal and private matter, but thank him for his concern. He isn't quite that easy to shake off and sticks with me for five more circuits: unlike a visit from a Jehovah's Witness, there's no way of slamming the front door.

I hope to manage a few circuits on my own so I can think for a moment, but no such luck because I'm joined by a couple of East End tearaways who want my opinion on their upcoming court case. I warn them that my knowledge of the law is fairly sketchy, so perhaps I'm the wrong person to approach. One of them becomes abusive, and for the first time since arriving at Belmarsh, I'm frightened and fearful for my own safety. Paul has already warned me that there might well be the odd prisoner who would stick a knife in me just to get himself on the front pages and impress his girlfriend.

Within moments, Billy Little and Fletch are strolling a pace behind me, obviously having sensed the possible danger, and although the two young hooligans are not from our spur, one look at Fletch and they are unlikely to try anything. The tear-aways peel off, but I have a feeling they will hang around and bide their time. Perhaps it would be wise for me to avoid the exercise yard for a couple of days.

I'm finally joined by a charming young black prisoner, who wants to tell me about his drumming problem. It takes another couple of circuits before I realize that he doesn't play in a rock band; drumming is simply slang for burglary. I consider this particular experience a bit of a watershed. If you didn't know what 'drumming' was before you began reading this diary, you're probably as naive as I am. If you did, these scribblings may well be commonplace.

12 noon

Lunch. I am now a fully fledged vegetarian. Outside of prison I founded a club known as VAF and VOP, which many of my friends have become members of after sending a donation to the Brompton Hospital.* VAF is 'vegetarian at functions'. I have long believed that it is impossible, even in the best-run establishments, to prepare three hundred steaks as each customer would wish them cooked, so I always order the vegetarian alternative because I know it will have been individually prepared. VOP stands for 'vegetarian on planes'. I suspect many of you are already members of this club, and if you are, pay up and send your five pounds to the Brompton Hospital immediately. I am now adding VIP to my list, and can only hope that none of you ever qualify for membership.

---

* I am an admirer of the eminent heart surgeon, Sir Magdi Yacoub, and any donation you give will assist his current research.

2.00 pm

The cell door is opened and I am told that Ms Roberts wants to see me. I feel my heart pounding as I try to recall her exact words the previous evening.

When I join her in a room just off the bubble, she immediately confirms that my solicitors have been in touch, and she has told them that she wants me out of Belmarsh as quickly as possible. She adds that they moved Barry George (murder of Jill Dando) this morning, and I'm due out next. However, she has just received a phone call from a chief inspector in the Metropolitan Police, to warn her that they have received a letter from the Baroness Emma Nicholson, demanding an inquiry into what happened to the £57 million I raised for the Kurds.

I assure Ms Roberts that I was in no way involved with the receiving or distribution of any monies for the Kurds, as that was entirely the responsibility of the Red Cross. She nods.

'If the police confirm that they will not be following up Ms Nicholson's inquiry, then we should have you out of Belmarsh and off to a D-cat by the end of the week.'

As I have always in the past believed in justice, I assume that the police will quickly confirm that I was not involved in any way.

Ms Roberts goes on to confirm that Ford, my first choice, is unwilling to take me because of the publicity problem, but she hopes to discuss some alternatives with me on Monday.

Ms Roberts suggests that as my next lecture is coming up on Thursday, I should be released from my cell from nine in the morning until five in the afternoon, so I can prepare for the talk in the library where I will have access to reference books. She knows only too well that I can give this talk without a moment's preparation but, unlike the Baroness Nicholson, she is concerned about what I'm going through.

DAY 10

4.00 pm

Association. During the Saturday afternoon break, I go down to the ground floor, hoping to watch some cricket on the TV, but I have to settle for horse racing as a large number of prisoners are already sitting round the set intent on following the King George VI and Queen Elizabeth Stakes at Ascot. The sport of kings has never been one of those pastimes that I've taken a great deal of interest in. I've long accepted George Bernard Shaw's maxim on horse racing, that *it's nothing more than a plot between the upper classes and the lower classes to fleece the middle classes*. I turn away from the television and see a slight, rather anaemic-looking young man standing alone in the corner. He's wearing a raspberry-coloured tracksuit, the official garb of prisoners who do not have their own clothes. I've not come across him before, but he looks a most unlikely murderer. I stroll across to join Fletch, who I feel confident will know exactly who he is.

'He's got twenty-one days for shoplifting,' Fletch tells me, 'and has a mental age of about eleven.' He pauses. 'They should never have sent him to Belmarsh in the first place.'

'Then why put him on the lifers' wing?' I ask.

'For his own protection,' says Fletch. 'He was attacked in the yard during exercise this afternoon, and some other cons continued to bully him when he returned to Block Two. He's only got nine more days left to serve so they've put him in my cell.' Now I understand why there are two beds in Fletch's cell, as I suspect this is not an unusual solution for someone in distress.

One of the phones becomes free – a rare occurrence – so I take advantage of it and call Mary in Grantchester. She's full of news, including the fact that the former head of the prison service, Sir David Ramsbotham, has written to *The Times* saying it was inappropriate to send me to prison – community service would have been far more worthwhile. She tells me she also has a sackful of letters talking about the iniquity of the judge's summing-up – not to mention the sentence – and she's beginning to wonder if there might be the possibility of a retrial. I think not. Mr Justice Potts has retired, and the last thing the establishment would want to do is embarrass him.

After thirty-seven years of marriage I know Mary so well that I can hear the strain of the last few weeks in her voice. I recall Ms Roberts' words the first time we met: 'It can be just as traumatic for your immediate family on the outside, as it is for you on the inside.' My two-pound BT phonecard is about to run out, but not before I tell her that she's a veritable Portia and I am no Brutus.

The moment I put the phone down, I find another lifer, Colin (GBH), standing by my side. He wants to have a word about his application to do an external degree at Ruskin College, Oxford. I have already had several chats with Colin, and he makes an interesting case study. In his youth (he's now thirty-five), he was a complete wastrel and tearaway, which included a period of being a professional football hooligan. In fact, he has written a fascinating piece on the subject, in which he now admits that he is ashamed of what he got up to. Colin has been in and out of jail for most of his adult life, and even when he's inside, he feels it is nothing less than his duty to take the occasional swing at a prison officer. This always ends with a spell in segregation and time being added to his sentence. On one occasion he even lost a couple of teeth, which you can't miss whenever he grins.

'That's history,' he tells me, because he now has a purpose. He wants to leave prison with a degree, and qualifications that will ensure he gets a real job. There is no doubt about his ability. Colin is articulate and bright, and having read his essays and literary criticism, I have no doubt that if he wants to sit for a degree, it's well within his grasp. And this is a man who couldn't read or write before he entered prison. I have a real go at him, assuring him that he's clever enough to take a degree and to get on with it. I start pummelling him on the chest as if he was a punch bag. He beams over to the duty officer seated behind the desk at the far end of the room.

'Mr King, this prisoner is bullying me,' says Colin, in a plaintive voice.

The officer smiles. 'What have you been saying to him, Archer?'

I repeat the conversation word for word.

'Quite agree with you, Archer,' he says, and returns to reading the *Sun*.

6.00 pm

Supper. Vegetarian fingers, overcooked and greasy, peas that are glued together, and a plastic mug of Highland Spring (49p).

8.00 pm

I've just finished checking over my script for the day when my cell door is opened by an officer. Fletch is standing in the doorway and asks if he can join me for a moment, which I welcome. He takes a seat on the end of the bed, and I offer him a mug of blackcurrant juice. Fletch reminds me that he's a Listener, and adds that he's there if I need him.

He then begins to explain the role of Listeners and how they came into existence after a fifteen-year-old boy hanged himself in a Cardiff jail some ten years ago. He passes me a single sheet of paper that explains their guidelines. (See page 117.) Among

The Listeners

Who are they?
How do I contact them?
How do I know I can trust them?

Listeners are inmates, just as you are, who have been trained by the **Samaritans** in both suicide awareness and befriending skills.

You can talk to a Listener about anything in complete confidence, just as you would a Samaritan. **Everything you say is treated with confidentiality.**

Listeners are rarely shocked and **you don't have to be suicidal** to talk to one. If you have any worries or concerns, however great or small, **they are there for you.** If you have concerns about a friend or cellmate and feel unable to approach a member of the spur staff or healthcare team, then please tell a Listener in confidence. **It is not grassing and it may save a life.**

Listeners are easy to contact. Their names are displayed on orange cards on their cell doors and on most notice boards throughout the House-Blocks or ask any member of the spur staff.

Listeners are all bound by a code of **confidentiality** that doesn't only run from House-Block to House-Block but also through a great number of Prisons throughout the country. Any breach of that confidentiality would cause irreparable damage to the benefits achieved, and because of this code Listeners are now as firmly established as your cell door.

Fletch's responsibilities is to spot potential bullies and – perhaps more important – potential victims, as most victims are too frightened to give you a name because they fear revenge at a later date, either inside or outside of prison.

I ask him to share some examples with me. He tells me that there are two heroin addicts on the spur and although he won't name them, it's hard not to notice that a couple of the younger lifers on the ground floor have needle tracks up and down their arms. One of them is only nineteen and has tried to take his own life twice, first with an overdose, and then later when he attempted to cut his wrist with a razor.

'We got there just in time,' says Fletch. 'After that, the boy was billeted with me for five weeks.'

Fletch feels it's also vitally important to have a good working relationship with the prison staff – he doesn't call them screws or kangaroos – otherwise the system just can't work. He admits there will always be an impenetrable barrier, which he describes as the iron door, but he has done his best to break this down by forming a prison committee of three inmates and three officers who meet once a month to discuss each other's problems. He says with some considerable pride that there hasn't been a serious incident on *his* spur for the past eight months.

He then tells me a story about an occasion when he was released from prison some years ago for a previous offence. He decided to call into his bank and cash a cheque. He climbed the steps, stood outside the bank and waited for someone to open the door for him. He looks up from the end of the bed at the closed cell door. 'You see, it doesn't have a handle on our side, so you always have to wait for someone to open it. After so long in prison, I'd simply forgotten how to open a door.'

Fletch goes on to tell me that being a Listener gives him a

reason for getting up each day. But like all of us, he has his own problems. He's thirty-seven, and will be my age, sixty-one, when he is eventually released.

'The truth is that I'll never see the outside world again.' He pauses. 'I'll die in prison.' He pauses again. 'I just haven't decided when.'

Fletch has unwittingly made me his Listener.

DAY 11   SUNDAY 29 JULY 2001

6.27 am

Sundays are not a good day in prison because you spend so much time locked up in your cell. When you ask why, the officers simply say, 'It's because we're short-staffed.' I can at least use six of those hours writing.

Many of the lifers have long-term projects, some of which I have already mentioned. One is writing a book, another taking a degree, a third is a dedicated Listener. In fact, although I may have to spend most of today locked up in my cell, Fletch, Billy, Tony, Paul, Andy and Del Boy all have responsible jobs which allow them to roam around the block virtually unrestricted. This makes sense, because if a prisoner has a long sentence, they may feel they have nothing to lose by causing trouble, but once you've given them privileges – and not being locked up all day is unquestionably a privilege – they're unlikely to want to give up that freedom easily.

8.03 am

I shave using a Bic razor supplied by HMP. They give you a new razor every day, and it is a punishable offence to be found with two of them in your cell, so every evening, just before lock-up, you trade in your old one for a new one.

As soon as the cell door is opened, I make a dash for the shower, but four young West Indians get there before me. One of them, Dennis (GBH), has the largest bag of toiletries I have ever seen. It's filled with several types of deodorant and after-shave lotions. He is a tall, well-built, good-looking guy who rarely misses a gym session. When I tease him about the contents of his bag, Dennis simply replies, 'You've got to be locked up for a long time, Jeff, before you can build up such a collection on twelve-fifty a week.' Another of them eventually emerges from his shower stall and comments about my not having flipflops on my feet. 'Quickest way to get verrucas,' he warns me. 'Make sure Mary sends you in a pair as quickly as possible.'

Having repeatedly to push the button with the palm of one hand while you soap yourself with the other is a new skill I have nearly mastered. However, when it comes to washing your hair, you suddenly need three hands. I wish I were an octopus.

When I'm finally dry, my three small thin green prison towels are all soaking – I should only have one, but thanks to Del Boy ... I return to my cell, and because I'm so clean, I'm made painfully aware of the prison smell. If you've ever travelled on a train for twenty hours and then slept in a station waiting room for the next eight, you're halfway there. Once I've put back on yesterday's clothes, I pour myself another bowl of cornflakes. I think I can make the packet (£1.47) last for seven helpings before I'll need to order another one. I hear my name being bellowed out by an officer on the ground floor, but decide to finish my cornflakes before reporting to him – first signs of rebellion?

When I do report, Mr Bentley tells me that there's a parcel for me in reception. This time no one escorts me on the journey, or bothers to search me when I arrive. The parcel turns out to be a plastic bag full of clothes sent in by Mary: two shirts, five T-shirts, seven pairs of pants, seven pairs of socks, two pairs of gym shorts, a tracksuit, and two sweaters. The precise allocation that prison regulations permit. Once back in my cell I discard my two-day-old pants and socks to put on a fresh set of clothes, and now not only feel clean, but almost human.

I spend a considerable time arranging the rest of my clothes in the little cupboard above my bed and as it has no shelves this becomes something of a challenge. (See pages 124–125.)* Once I've completed the exercise, I sit on the end of the bed and wait to be called for church.

10.39 am

My name is among several others bellowed out by the officer at the front desk on the ground floor, followed by the single word 'church'. All those wishing to attend the service report to the middle landing and wait by the barred gate near the bubble. Waiting in prison for your next activity is not unlike hanging around for the next bus. It might come along in a few moments, or you may have to wait for half an hour. Usually the latter.

While I'm standing there, Fletch joins me on the second-floor landing to warn me that there's an article in the *News of the World* suggesting that I'm 'lording it' over the other prisoners. Apparently I roam around in the unrestricted areas in a white shirt, watching TV, while all the other prisoners are locked up. He says that although everyone on the spur knows it's a joke, the rest of the block (three other spurs) do not. Fletch advises

---

* This picture of my cell was drawn by Derek Jones. I was not allowed to take a photograph of it.

me to avoid the exercise yard today, as someone might want 'to make something of it'.

The more attentive readers will recall that my white shirt was taken away from me last week because I could be mistaken for an officer; my feeble attempt to watch cricket on TV ended in having to follow the progress of the King George VI and Queen Elizabeth Stakes; and by now all of you know how many hours I've been locked in my cell. How the *News of the World* can get every fact wrong surprises even me.

The heavy, barred gate on the middle floor is eventually opened, and I join prisoners from the other three spurs who wish to attend the morning service. Although everyone is searched, they now hardly bother with me. The process has become not unlike going through a customs check at Heathrow. There are two searchers on duty this morning, one male and one female officer. I notice the queue to be searched by the woman is longer than the one for the man. One of the lifers whispers, 'They can't add anything to your sentence for what you're thinking.'

When I enter the chapel I return to my place in the second row. This time the congregation is almost 80 per cent black, despite the population of the prison being around fifty–fifty. The service is conducted by a white officer from the Salvation Army, and his small band of singers are also all white. When I next see Mr Powe, I must remember to tell him how many churches, not so far away from Belmarsh, have magnificent black choirs and amazing preachers who encourage you to cry Alleluia. Something else I learnt when I was candidate for Mayor.

This week I notice that the congregation is roughly split in two, with a sort of demarcation zone about halfway back. The prisoners seated in the first eight rows have only one purpose – to follow every line in the Bible that the Chaplain refers to, to sing at the top of their voices and participate fully in the spirit of

By O Jones

the service. The back nine rows show scant interest in proceedings, and I observe that they have formed smaller groups of two,
three or four, their heads bowed deep in conversation. I assume
they're friends from different spurs and find the service one of
the few opportunities to meet up, chat, and pass on messages.
Quite possibly even drugs – if they are willing to go through a
fairly humiliating process.*

The Chaplain's text this Sunday comes from the Gospel of St
John, and concentrates in particular on the prodigal son. Last
week it was Cain and Abel. I can only assume that next week it
will be Honour Among Thieves.

The Chaplain tells his flock that he is only going to speak to
them for five minutes, and then addresses us for twelve, but to
be fair, he was quite regularly interrupted with cries of 'Alleluia',
and 'Bless us, Lord'. The Chaplain's theme is that if you leave the
bosom of your family, try to make it alone, and things go wrong,
it doesn't mean that your father won't welcome you back if you
are willing to admit you've made mistakes. Many of those in the
front four rows start jumping up and down and cheering.

After the service is over, and we have all been searched
again, I'm escorted back to House Block One, but not before
several inmates from Block Three come across to say hello.
Remember Mark, Kevin and Dave? I'm brought up to date with
all of their hopes and expectations as we slowly make our way
back to our separate blocks. No one moves quickly in prison,
because it's just another excuse to spend more time out of your
cell. As I pass the desk at the end of my spur, I spot a pile of
Sunday newspapers. The *News of the World* is by far the most

---

*Drugs are often packed into a condom and then pushed up the rectum.
Transferring them in the back pew of the chapel can't be a pleasant experience.

popular, followed by the *Sunday Mirror*, but there is also quite a large order for the *Sunday Times*.

When I return to my cell, I find my room has been swept and tidied, and my bed made up with clean sheets. I'm puzzled, because there was nothing in the prison handbook about room service. I find out later that the Ghanaian murderer wants to thank me for helping him write a letter to his mother. Returning favours is far more commonplace in prison than it is outside.

12 noon

Lunch: grated cheese, a tomato, a green apple and a mug of Highland Spring. I'm running out of water and will in future have to order more bottles of Highland Spring and less chocolate from the canteen.

After lunch I sit down to write the second draft of this morning's script, as I won't be let out again until four, and then only for sixty minutes. I clean my glasses and notice that without thinking, I've begun to split my double Kleenex tissue so that I can make the maximum use of both sheets.

4.00 pm

Association. During the hour break, I don't join the others in the yard for exercise because of the *News of the World* article, which means I'll be stuck inside all day. I can't remember the last time I remained indoors for twenty-four hours.

I join Fletch (murder) in his cell, along with Billy (murder) and Tony (marijuana only, escaped to Paris). They're discussing in great detail an article in the *Sunday Times* about paedophiles, and I find myself listening intently. Because on this subject, as in many others concerning what goes on in prison, I recall Lord

Longford's words, 'Don't assume all prisoners have fixed views.' I feel on safer ground when the discussion turns to the Tory Party leadership. Only Tony, who reads *The Times*, can be described as a committed liberalist. Most of the others, if they are anything, are New Labour.*

They all agree that Ken Clarke is a decent enough sort of bloke – pint at the local and all that, and not interested in his appearance, but they know very little about Iain Duncan Smith, other than he comes from the right wing of the Party and therefore has to be their enemy. I suggest that it's never quite that simple. IDS has clear views on most issues, and they shouldn't just label him in that clichéd way. He's a complex and thoughtful man – his father, I remind them, was a Second World War hero, flying Spitfires against the Germans and winning the DSO and Bar. They like that. I suspect if we were at war now, his son would be doing exactly the same thing.

'But he has the same instincts as Ann Widdecombe,' says Fletch. 'Bang 'em up and throw away the key.'

'That may well be the case, but don't forget Ann is supporting Ken Clarke, despite his views on Europe.'

'That doesn't add up,' says Billy.

'Politics is like prison,' I suggest. 'You mustn't assume anything, as the exact opposite often turns out to be the reality.'

5.00 pm

'Back to your cells,' bellows a voice.

I leave the lifers and return to my cell on the top floor to be incarcerated, supper excepted, until nine tomorrow morning –

---

* Convicted prisoners, Members of the House of Lords, and certified lunatics are ineligible to vote. I now qualify in two of the three categories.

sixteen hours. Think about it, sixteen hours. That's the length of time you will spend between rising in the morning and going to bed at night.

Just as I arrive at my door, another lifer (Doug) hands me an envelope. 'It's from a prisoner on Block Two,' he says. 'He evidently told you all about it yesterday when you were in the exercise yard.' I throw the envelope on the bed and switch on the radio, to be reminded that it's the hottest day of the year (92°). I open my little window to its furthest extent (six inches) to let in whatever breeze there is, but I still feel myself sweating as I sit at my desk checking over the day's script. I glance up at the cupboard behind my bed, grateful for the clean clothes that Mary sent in this morning.

6.00 pm

Supper. I can't face the hotplate, despite Tony's recommend-ation of Spam fritter, so I have another portion of grated cheese, open a small tin of coleslaw (41p) and – disaster – finish the last drop of my last bottle of Highland Spring. Thank heavens that it's canteen tomorrow and I'm allowed to spend another £12.50.

During the early evening, I go over my manuscript, and as there are no letters to deal with, I turn my attention to the envelope that was handed to Doug in the yard. It turns out to be a TV script for a thirty-minute pilot set in a women's prison. It's somehow been smuggled out of Holloway and into Belmarsh (no wonder it's easy to get hold of drugs). The writer has a good ear for prison language, and allows you an interesting insight into life in a women's prison, but I fear *Cell Block H* and *Bad Girls* have already done this theme to death. It's fascinating to spot the immediate differences in a women's prison to Belmarsh. Not least the searching procedure, the fact that lesbianism is far more prevalent in female prisons than homosexuality is in male establishments, and, if you can believe it, the level of violence is higher. They don't bother waiting until you're in the shower before they throw the first punch. Anywhere, at any time, will do.

It's a long hot evening, and I have visits from Del Boy, Paul, Fletch and finally Tony.

Tony (hotplate, marijuana only, escaped to Paris) started life as a B-cat prisoner, and was transferred after three and a half years to Ford Open (first offence, no history of violence). After eight blameless months they allowed him out on a town visit, so he happily set off for Bognor Regis. But after four visits to that seaside resort during the next four months, he became somewhat bored with the cold, deserted beach and the limited shopping centre. That's when he decided there were other towns he'd like to visit on his day off.

When they let him out the following month, he took the boat-train to Paris.

The prison authorities were not amused. It was only when he moved on to Spain, two years later, that they finally caught up with him and he was arrested. After spending sixteen months in a Spanish jail waiting to be deported (canteen, fifty pounds a week, and no bang-up until nine), they sent him back to the UK. Tony now resides in this high-security double A-Category prison, from where no one has ever escaped, and will remain put until he has completed his full sentence (twelve years). No time was added to his sentence, but there will be no remission (half off for good behaviour) and he certainly won't be considered for an open prison again. This fifty-four-year-old somehow keeps smiling and even manages to tell his story with self-deprecating humour.

Tony leaves me with a copy of the *Sunday Mirror*. Although it's not a paper I'm in the habit of reading, I am at least able to bring myself up to date on the county cricket scores, not to mention who among the fighting fit will find a place in the England team for the third Test against Australia on Thursday. My beloved Somerset are in second place in the county championship and doing well in their current fixture against Glamorgan. On the England front, the *Mirror*'s cricket correspondent is suggesting it's time to bring back Tufnell. I did an auction for Phil during his testimonial year, and although he's not always popular with the selectors, the packed banqueting hall at the Dorchester proved the regard in which he is held by the Middlesex supporters. It seems that Thorpe, Hussain, Vaughan and Croft are all injured and will not make the starting line while a reluctant Atherton will be called on once again to skipper the side. It doesn't seem to improve his batting.

Meanwhile, Australia fields the same team that so roundly defeated us at Lords. I always thought it was the visiting side that was meant to have injury problems.

I finally finish *The Moon's a Balloon*, which left me with the distinct feeling that Mr Niven must have lived a charmed life. I only met him once, and that was at a literary luncheon in Yorkshire, where he was on the circuit with *Bring on the Empty Horses*, the sequel to the book I've just finished reading. It was an occasion I shall never forget, because the other author was James Herriot of *It Shouldn't Happen to a Vet* fame. I was there to launch my first effort, *Not A Penny More, Not A Penny Less*, and was naturally delighted to be among such illustrious company. After the speeches had concluded, the authors were each escorted to a table, so that they could sign copies of their books.

Mr Niven's queue stretched across the dining-room floor and out of the front door, while Mr Herriot's fans were almost as legion. In my case, I didn't have a single customer. When the signing was over, Mr Niven graciously came across to my table,

DAY 11

purchased a copy of *Penny*, and told me he would read it on the flight back to Los Angeles the following day. He turned out to be one of the three people who paid for the book. A generous gesture, which many people have since told me was typical. But imagine my surprise when a few days later I received a hand-written letter from the Bel Air Hotel.

> *Dear Jeffrey,*
> *Much enjoyed Penny, have no doubt it will sell even more*
> *copies than Horses by the time you're my age.*
> > *Yours ever*
> > *David*

10.00 pm

Bang on ten, the rap music begins blasting out.

> Gunshot to the head, pussyboy gets dead
> Gunshot to the head, pussyboy gets dead
> Gunshot to the head, pussyboy gets dead
> Gunshot to the head, pussyboy gets dead
> Gunshot to the head, pussyboy gets dead
> Gunshot to the head, pussyboy gets dead . . .

Have you ever stopped at a traffic light to find yourself next to an open car with its radio full on? Do you then allow the offending driver to accelerate away? Imagine being in a cell with the music blasting out on both sides of you, but you can't accelerate away.

DAY 12   MONDAY 30 JULY 2001

6.03 am

Overslept, but then woken by the Alsatians off on their morning rounds. They are every bit as reliable as an alarm clock, but not as cheerful or optimistic as a cockerel. I put on a tracksuit, sit down at my desk and write for two hours.

8.10 am

A bowl of cornflakes with UHT milk, plus the added luxury of a banana which Del Boy has smuggled out of the canteen. I sit on the end of the bed and wait to see what fate has in store for me.

10.00 am

I'm told I must report to the workshops, despite putting my name down for education. Another long trek to a different part of the building. This time we're escorted into a large square room about the same size as the chapel, but with whitewashed, unadorned brick walls. The first person I recognize is Fletch, who is seated next to a prison officer behind a trestle table at the top of the room. He's obviously the works manager.

The work room has five rows of tables, each about thirty feet in length, with prisoners seated on both sides making up a chain gang. My group consists of four inmates whose purpose is to fill a small plastic bag with all the ingredients necessary to make a cup of tea. In the centre of the table placed between us are large plastic buckets heaped with small packets. At the bottom end of the table sits a silent Serb, who places four sachets of sugar in each bag and then pushes his contribution across the table to a Lebanese man who adds three sachets of milk. He then passes the bag on to an inmate from Essex who drops in three teabags, before it's passed over to me. My job is to seal up the bag and drop it in the large open bucket at my end of the table.

Every fifteen minutes or so another prisoner, whose name I never discover, comes and empties the bucket. This mind-numbing exercise continues for approximately two hours, for which I will be credited with two pounds in my canteen account.

The Serb (sugar) who sits at the other end of the table is, I would guess, around thirty. He's unwilling to discuss anything except the fate of ex-President Milošević, and the fact that he isn't cooperating with the European Court in the Hague. He will not talk about his crime or the length of his sentence.

Ali, the Lebanese man (powdered milk) who sits opposite me, is more forthcoming. He's been found guilty of 'breach of trust'. Ali tells me that he worked for a well-known credit-card company, and after several years was promoted to manager of a London branch. During that time he became infatuated with an American lady, who could best be described as high-maintenance, and used to the sort of lifestyle he couldn't afford. Ali began to borrow (his words) money from the company safe each night. He would then take her to a casino, where they would have a free meal, before he began working the tables. If he won, he would put the money back in the safe the next morning. If he lost, he would borrow even more the following evening. One night he won £5,000 and returned every penny the following day.

By the time his girlfriend had dumped him and flown back to the States, Ali had 'borrowed' £28,000. He decided to come clean and report the whole incident to his boss, assuring the company that it was his intention to repay every penny.

Ali then sold his house, cashed in his life-insurance policy, pawned a few valuables and reimbursed the company in full. He was later arrested, charged with breach of trust, and last Friday sent down for eighteen months. He will probably end up serving seven months and is due to be transferred to Ford (D-cat) next week. He is fifty-three, an intelligent and articulate man, who accepts that he will never be able to work in this country again. He plans to go to America or return to the Lebanon, where he hopes to begin a new life.

My former secretary, Angie Peppiatt, the Crown's main witness in my case, admitted to the same offence – breach of trust – while giving evidence at my trial. In her case she wasn't able to explain how thousands of pounds went missing, other than to smile at the judge and say, 'I have done things I am ashamed of, but it was the culture of the time.' I have recently asked my solicitor to place the full details in the hands of the police and see if she is subject to the same rigorous inquiry as I was. You may well know the answer by the time this book is published.

The Essex man (teabags) sitting next to Ali boasts to anyone who cares to listen that he is a professional gangster who specializes in robbing banks. The gang consists of his brother-in-law, a friend and himself. He tells me they make a very profitable living, but expect to spend at least half of their working lives in jail. He and Ali could not be more different.

The prisoner who turns up every fifteen minutes to empty

the large bucket at the end of the table doesn't hang around, so I can't discover much about him, other than he's twenty-three, this is his first offence, his case hasn't come before the court yet, and he's hoping to get off. If he doesn't, he tells me, he'll use the time to study for an Open University history degree. I don't think he realizes that he's just admitted that he's guilty.

A hooter blasts to indicate that the one hundred and twenty minutes are finally up, we are all escorted back to our separate spurs, and lunch.

12 noon

Lunch. What's on offer is so bad that I have to settle for a small tin of Heinz potato salad (61p) and three McVitie's biscuits (17p). As I return from the hotplate I see Andy leaning up against the fence that divides the spur from the canteen area. He pushes a bottle of Highland Spring through a triangle of wire mesh – the high point of my day.

2.00 pm

The Chaplain, David Powe, makes an unscheduled visit to my cell. He's wearing his dog collar, the same beige coat, the same dark grey trousers, and the same shoes as he has at the previous meetings. I can only conclude that he must be paid even less than the prison officers. He's kept his promise and got hold of some drawing paper for Derek Jones, who can't afford more than one pad a week.

The Chaplain goes on to tell me that he and his family will be off on holiday for the next three weeks, and just in case he doesn't see me again, he would like to wish me luck with my appeal, and hopes I'll be sent in the near future to somewhere a little less foreboding than Belmarsh. Before he leaves, I read to him my description of the service he conducted last week. He chuckles at the Cain and Abel reference – a man able to laugh at himself. He leaves me a few moments later to go in search of Derek, and hand over the drawing pads.

It was some hours later that I felt racked with guilt by the thought he must have paid for the paper out of his own pocket.

2.48 pm

My door is unlocked by Ms Taylor who enters the cell carrying what looks like a tuning fork. She goes over to my window and taps the four bars one by one.

'Just want to make sure you haven't loosened them, or tried to replace them,' she explains. 'Wouldn't want you to escape, would we?'

I'm puzzled by Ms Taylor's words because it's a sheer drop of some seventy feet from the third floor down to the exercise yard, and then you would still have to climb over a thirty-five-foot wall, topped with razor wire, to escape. Houdini would have been stretched to consider such a feat. I later learn that there's another thirty-five-foot wall beyond that, not to mention a few dozen Alsatians who don't respond to the command, 'Sit, Rover.'

I can only conclude it's in the prison manual under the heading, 'tasks to be carried out, once a day, once a week, once a year, once in a lifetime'.*

---

* I checked later. It *is* in the prison regulations, under 'Locks, Bolts and Bars'.

DAY 12

4.00 pm

I've put my name down for the gym again as I'm now desperate to get some exercise. When an officer hollers out, 'Gym,' I'm first in the queue that congregates on the middle floor. When the gate is opened, I'm informed by the duty Gym Instructor that only eight prisoners can participate from any one spur, and my name was the twelfth to be registered. The low point of my day.

I return to the ground floor and watch the first half of a Humphrey Bogart black-and-white movie, where Bogey is a sea dog who plays a major part in winning the war in the North Atlantic. However, we are all sent back to our cells at five, so I never discover if it was the Germans or the Americans who won the last War.

5.20 pm

I have an unscheduled visit from two senior officers, Mr Scanell and Mr Green. To be fair, most meetings in prison are unscheduled; after all, no one calls in advance to fix an appointment with your diary secretary. They are concerned that I am no longer going out into the yard during the afternoon to take advantage of forty-five minutes of fresh air and exercise. They've heard a rumour that on my last outing I was threatened by another prisoner, and for that reason I've remained in my cell. They ask me if this is true, and if so, am I able to supply them with any details of those who threatened me. I tell them exactly what took place in the yard, but add that I am unwilling to name or describe the young tearaway involved. They leave twenty minutes later with several pages of their report sheet left blank.

I ask Tony what would have happened if I'd told them the name of the two culprits.

'They would have been transferred to another prison later today,' Tony replied.

'Wouldn't it be easier for them to transfer me?' I suggest.

'Good heavens, no,' said Tony. 'That would demand a degree of lateral thinking, not to mention common sense.'

6.00 pm

Supper. Vegetable stew and a lollipop. The lollipop was superb.

6.43 pm

Fletch visits my cell and tries to convince me that it's my duty to name the cons who threatened me in the yard, because if I don't, it won't be long before they're doing exactly the same thing to someone less able to take care of themselves. He makes a fair point, but I suggest what the headlines would be the following day if I had given the officers the names: *Archer beaten up in yard; Archer demands extra protection; Under-staffed prison service doing overtime to protect Archer; Archer reports prisoner to screw.* No, thank you, I tell Fletch, I'd rather sit in my cell and write. He sighs, and before leaving, hands me his copy of the *Daily Telegraph*. It's a luxury to have a seventy-two-page paper, even if it is yesterday's. I devour every page.

The lead story is a poll conducted for the *Telegraph* by youGov.com showing that, although Iain Duncan Smith is running 40–60 behind Ken Clarke in the national polls, he is comfortably ahead with the Party membership. It seems to be a no-win situation for the Conservatives. The only person who must be laughing all the way to the voting booth is Tony Blair.

DAY 12

7.08 pm

I have a visit from Paul, a tea-boy – which is why he's allowed
to roam around while the rest of us are banged up. He says he
has something to tell me, so I pick up my pad, sit on the end of
the bed and listen.

Paul is about six foot one, a couple of hundred pounds and
looks as if he could take care of himself in a scrap. He begins by
telling me that he's just been released from a drug-rehabilitation
course at the Princess Diana centre in Norfolk. It's taken them
eight months to wean him off his heroin addiction. I immediately
enquire if he now considers himself cured. Paul just sits there in
silence and avoids answering my question. It's obviously not
what he came to talk to me about. He then explains that during
his rehab, he was made to write a long self-assessment piece and
asks if I will read it, but he insists that no one else on the spur
must find out its contents.

'I wouldn't bother you with it,' he adds, 'if it were not for the
fact that several prisoners on this spur have had similar experiences, and they're not necessarily the ones you might expect.'
He leaves without another word.

If you were to come across Paul at your local, you would
assume he was a middle-class successful businessman (he's in
jail for credit-card fraud). He's intelligent, articulate and charming. In fact he doesn't look any different to the rest of us, but
then why should he? He just doesn't want anyone to know
about his past, and I'm not talking about his 'criminal past'.

As soon as my cell door is closed, I begin to read the self-
assessment piece that is written in his own hand. He had a
happy upbringing until the age of six when his parents divorced.
Two years later his mother remarried. After that, he and his
brothers were regularly thrashed by their stepfather. The only

146

person he put any trust in was an uncle who befriended him and turned out to be a paedophile. His next revelation I would not consider for a plot in a novel, because it turns out that his uncle is now locked up on House Block Two, convicted of indecent assault on an underaged youth. The two men can see each other through the wire mesh across the yard during the afternoon exercise period. Paul doesn't know what he would do if he were ever to come face to face with his uncle. At no time in his exposition does he offer this as an excuse for his crime, but he points out that child abuse is a common symptom among those serving long-term sentences. I find this quite difficult to come to terms with, having had such a relaxed and carefree upbringing myself. But I decide to ask Fletch if Paul is a) telling the truth, b) correct in his overall assessment.

When I did eventually ask Fletch, I was shocked by his reply.*

10.00 pm

After I've read through Paul's piece a second time, I turn to the latest bunch of letters – just over a hundred – which keep my spirits up, until I switch on the nine o'clock news on Radio 4, to discover that there are still no plans to move me from this hellhole.

11.00 pm

I start to read John Grisham's *The Partner*, and manage seven chapters before turning the light off just after midnight. I can't believe it, no rap music.

---

* This sentence was added two weeks after I had written the original script.

147

DAY 13   TUESDAY 31 JULY 2001

5.55 am

Woke up before the Alsatians this morning. I've finally worked out why they make so much noise. It's because they are being fed on the same food as the prisoners. Write for two hours.

8.00 am

I finish the box of cornflakes and the last drop of UHT milk, hopeful that my canteen order will materialize at some time later today. I get dressed. I can move another notch up on my belt – I must have lost several pounds, but have no other way of confirming this.

9.00 am

When my cell door is opened, I don't join the other prisoners to go to the workshop as I have an appointment with the Education Assessor, Judy Fitt, known amongst the prisoners as 'Misfit' – a joke she must be heartily sick of.

When Ms Fitt arrives, the officer on the front desk calls for me, or to be more accurate, bellows out my name, as I'm on the top landing, and they never move from the ground floor unless they have to. I go down to meet her. Judy is a short – could lose a few pounds – blonde, of about forty with a happy, optimistic smile. I pick up two chairs from the pile by the TV and place them under the window at the end of the room. I think she's surprised that I insist on carrying her chair. Once seated, she takes me through all the education curriculum has to offer, from teaching reading and writing skills, through to taking a degree. Her enthusiasm leaves me in no doubt that Judy is another public servant dedicated to her job. She also suggests that in my case I could learn to cook, draw, or even, after all these years of avoiding it, discover how to use a computer. That would impress Mary.

I remind Judy that I'm only expecting to be at Belmarsh for a few more days, and would like to use my time to teach other prisoners to read and write. Judy considers this suggestion, but would prefer I gave a creative-writing course, as there are several inmates working on books, poems and essays who will have dozens of unanswered questions. I agree to her request and, aware of my escape plan, Judy suggests I ought to give my first lesson tomorrow morning. She pauses, looking a little embarrassed. 'But first I have to enrol you in the education department.' She passes me over yet more forms. 'Can you complete these tests and let me have them back later today so that I can process them in a matter of hours?'

'I'll try to have them completed by the end of the morning.'

She laughs. 'It won't take you that long.'

I return to my cell, and as I have nothing to do for the thirty minutes before lunch, begin to fill in the little boxes headed Education Test. I've selected some random examples:

1) English – spell these words correctly: wos, befor, wer, gril, migt, siad, affer.
2) Maths –
   a) 13+34, 125+386?
   b) how much change do you get from £5 if you spend £1.20?
3) what is 7.15pm on a twenty-four hour clock?
4) how much time is there between 4.30 and 6.15?
5) what is 25% of 300?
6) if 1 biscuit costs 25p, 6 are £1.38, 12 are £2.64, and 24 are £6, which is the better buy?

I complete the six pages of questions and return them to Ms Fitt, via Billy Little (murder), who has an education class this afternoon.

12 noon

Lunch. Provisions have not yet arrived from the canteen. Half a portion of macaroni cheese and a mug of Highland Spring. Have you noticed I'm beginning to eat prison food?

1.40 pm

My cell door is opened, and I'm told Ms Roberts wants to see me. I am accompanied to the Governor's office by Mr Weedon. I don't bother to ask him why, because he won't know, and even if he does, he wouldn't tell me. Only moments later I discover that Ms Roberts has nothing but bad news to impart and none of it caused by the staff at Belmarsh. My Category D status has been raised to C because the police say they have been left with no choice but to follow up Baroness Nicholson's allegations, and open a full inquiry into what happened to the money raised for the Kurds. As if that wasn't enough, the C-cat prison I've been allocated to is on the Isle of Wight. How much further away do they want me to be from my family?

The raising of my status, Ms Roberts explains, is based on the fear that while a further inquiry is going on I might try to escape. Scotland Yard obviously has a sense of humour. How far do they imagine I could get before someone spotted me?

Ms Roberts informs me that I can appeal against both decisions, and if I do, the authorities have agreed to make an assessment by Thursday. She points out that the Isle of Wight is a long way from my residence in Cambridge, and it's the responsibility of the Home Office to house a prisoner as close to his home as possible. If that's the case, I'm only surprised they're not sending me to the Shetland Isles. She promises to have a word with my solicitor and explain my rights to them. If it were not for Ms Roberts and Ramona Mehta, I would probably be locked up in perpetual solitary confinement.

I cannot express forcibly enough my anger at Emma Nicholson, especially after my years of work for the Kurds. One call to Sir Nicholas Young at the Red Cross and all her questions as to the role I played in the Simple Truth campaign could have been answered. She preferred to contact the press.

Ms Roberts points out that as my lawyers are due to visit me at two o'clock, perhaps I should be making a move. I thank her. Baroness Nicholson could learn a great deal from this twenty-six-year-old woman.

2.00 pm

I join Alex Cameron and Ramona Mehta in the visitors' area. This time we've been allocated a room not much bigger than my cell. But there is a difference – on three sides it has large windows. When you're behind bars day and night, you notice windows.

Before they go on to my appeal against conviction and sentence, I raise three other subjects on which I require legal advice. First, whether the Baroness has stepped over the mark. The lawyers fear she may have worded everything so carefully as to guarantee maximum publicity for herself, without actually accusing me of anything in particular. I point out that I am only too happy to cooperate with any police inquiry, and the sooner the better. The Simple Truth campaign was organized by the Red Cross, and the Treasurer at the time will confirm that I had no involvement whatsoever with the collecting or distributing of any monies. Ramona points out that several Red Cross officials, past and present, have already come out publicly confirming this.

I then tell my lawyers the story of Ali (£28,000 stolen and returned, but now doing an eighteen-month sentence for breach of trust). I ask that the police be reminded that Mrs Peppiatt admitted in the witness box to double-billing, stealing a car, taking her children on a free holiday to Corfu, buying presents for mistresses that didn't exist and claiming expenses for meals with phantom individuals. Can I hope that the CPS will treat her to the same rigorous inspection as Ali and I have been put through?

Third, I remind them that Ted Francis, the man who sold his story to the *News of the World* for fourteen thousand pounds, still owes me twelve thousand. I'd like it back.

The lawyers promise to follow up all these matters. However, they consider the reinstatement of my D-cat and making sure I don't have to go to the Isle of Wight their first priorities.

I ask Ramona to take the next five days of what I've written and hand the script over to Alison for typing up. Ramona leaves our little room to ask the duty officer if he will allow this. He turns down her request. Alex suggests I hold onto the script until I've been transferred to a less security-conscious prison. He also advises me that it would be unwise to think of publishing anything until after my appeal has been considered. I warn them that if I lose my appeal and continue to keep up my present output for the entire sentence, I'll end up writing a million words.

On the hour, an officer appears to warn us that our time is up. Ramona leaves, promising to deal with the problems of my D-cat and the Isle of Wight immediately.

While I'm waiting to be escorted back to Block One, I get into conversation with a Greek Cypriot called Nazraf who is on remand awaiting trial. He's been charged with 'detaining his wife in a motorcar' – I had no idea there was such a charge. I repeat his story here with the usual government health warning. Nazraf tells me that he locked his wife in the car for her own safety because he was at the time transferring a large sum of cash from his place of work to a local bank. He's in the restaurant business and for several years has been very successful, making an annual profit of around £200,000. He adds with some considerable passion that he still loves his wife, and would prefer a reconciliation, but she has already filed for divorce.

Nazraf comes across as a bright, intelligent man, so I have to ask him why he isn't out on bail. He explains that the court demanded a sum of £40,000 to be put up by at least four different people, and he didn't want his friends or business associates to know that he was in any trouble. He had always assumed that the moment he was sent to jail, his wife would come to her senses and drop the charges. That was five weeks ago and she hasn't budged. The trial takes place in mid-September...

This is all I could find out before we were released from the waiting room to continue on our separate paths – I to Block One, Nazraf to Block Four. His final destination also puzzles me, because Block Four usually houses terrorists or extremely high-security risks. I'd like to meet Nazraf again, but I have a feeling I never will.

6.00 pm

Supper. Provisions have arrived from the canteen and been left in a plastic bag on the end of my bed. I settle down to a plate of tinned Spam, a bar of Cadbury's Fruit and Nut, two McVitie's digestive biscuits and finally a mug of blackcurrant juice, topped up with Evian water. What more could a man ask for?

8.00 pm

Association. I am asked to join a group of 'more mature' prisoners – at sixty-one I am by far the oldest, if not the most mature – for their weekly committee meeting in Fletch's cell. Other attendees include Tony (marijuana only), Billy (murder), Colin (GBH) and Paul (murder).

Like any well-run board meeting, we have a chairman, Fletch, and an agenda. First we discuss the hours we are permitted to be out of our cells, and how Mr Marsland has made conditions more bearable since he became the senior officer. Fletch considers that relations between the two parties who live on different sides of 'the iron barrier' are far more tenable – even amicable – than at any time in the past. Colin is still complaining about a particular warder, who I haven't yet come across. According to Colin, he treats the prisoners like scum, and will put you on report if you as much as blink in front of him. He's evidently proud of the fact that he's put more people on report than any other officer, and that tells you all you need to know about him, Colin suggests.

I decide to observe this man from a distance and see if Colin's complaint is justified. Most of the officers make an effort 'to keep a lid on things', preferring a calm atmosphere, only too aware that lifers' moods swing from despair to hope and back to despair again in moments. This can, in the hands of an unthinking officer, lead to violence. Colin, I fear, is quick to wrath, and doesn't need to take another step backwards, just as things are going a little better for him.

The next subject the committee discuss is prison finance. Tony reports that the Governor, Hazel Banks, has been given a bonus of £24,000 for bringing Belmarsh Prison costs down by four hundred thousand. Hardly something a free enterprise merchant like myself could grumble about. However, Paul feels the money would have been better spent on inmates' education and putting electricity into the cells. I have no idea if these figures are accurate, but Tony confirms that he checked them in Sir David Ramsbotham's (head of the prison service) annual review.

When the meeting breaks up, Derek Del Boy Bicknell (murder) – interesting that he has not been invited to join the committee meeting – asks if he could have a private word with me. 'I've got something for you to read,' he says. I walk across the ground floor from Cell 9 to Cell 6. After he's offered me a selection of paperbacks, I discover the real reason he wishes to see me.

He wants to discuss his appeal, and produces a letter from his solicitor. The main grounds for his appeal appear to be that his former solicitor advised him not to go into the witness box when he wanted to. He subsequently sacked the solicitor and his QC. He has since appointed a new legal team to advise him, but he's not yet chosen a QC. Imagine my surprise when I

DAY 13

discover one of his grounds for appeal is that he is unable to read or write, and therefore never properly understood what his rights were. I look up at a shelf full of books above his bed.

'You can't read?'

'No, but don't tell anyone. You see, I've never really needed to as a car salesman.'

This is a prisoner who carries a great deal of responsibility on the spur. He's a Listener and number one on the hotplate. I earlier described him as a man who could run a private company and I have not changed my mind. Del Boy brings to mind Somerset Maugham's moving short story, 'The Bell Ringer'. However, it's still going to be a disadvantage for him not to be able to study his legal papers. I begin to wonder how many other prisoners fall into the same category, and worse, just won't admit it. I go over the grounds of appeal with Del Boy line by line. He listens intently, but can't make any notes.

8.45 pm

Lock-up is called so I return to my cell to face – delighted to face – another pile of letters left on my bed by Ray the censor. I realize the stack will be even greater tomorrow when the papers inform their readers that I will not be going to an open prison, after Emma Nicholson has dropped her 'I was only doing my duty' barb into an already boiling cauldron.

I've now fallen into a routine, much as I had in the outside world. The big difference is that I have little or no control over when I can and cannot write, so I fit my hours round the prison timetable. Immediately after evening lock-up is designated for reading letters, break, followed by going over my manuscript, break, reading the book of the week, break, undress, go to bed, break, try to ignore the inevitable rap music. Impossible.

Every time I finish the day's script, I wonder if there will be anything new to say tomorrow. However, I'm still on such a steep learning curve, I've nowhere near reached that dizzy height. But I confess I now want to leave Belmarsh for pastures new, and pastures is the key word. I long to walk in green fields and taste fresh air.

Billy (lifer, writer, scholar) tells me it will be better once I've settled somewhere, and don't have to spend my energy wondering when and where I will be for the rest of my sentence. He's been at Belmarsh for two years and seven months, and still doesn't know where he's destined for. Tony (marijuana only, escaped from open prison) warns me that, wherever I go, I'll be quickly bored if I don't have a project to work on. Thankfully, writing these diaries has solved that problem. But for how long?

DAY 14　　WEDNESDAY 1 AUGUST 2001

6.21 am

A long, hot, sleepless night. The rap music went on until about four in the morning, so I was only able to doze off for the odd few minutes. When it finally ceased, a row broke out between someone called Mitchell, who I think was in the cell above the music, and another prisoner called Vaz, who owned the stereo below. It didn't take long to learn what Mitchell planned to do to Vaz just as soon as his cell door was opened. Their language bore a faint resemblance to the dialogue in a Martin Amis novel, but without any of his style or panache.

8.37 am

Breakfast. Among my canteen selections is a packet of cereal called Variety, eight different cereals in little boxes. I start off with something called Coco Pops. Not bad, but it's still almost impossible to beat good old Kellogg's Cornflakes.

9.31 am

The morning papers are delivered to the duty officer. They're full of stories confirming that my status has been changed from D-cat to C-cat because of Emma Nicholson's accusations.

9.50 am

Ms Labersham arrives and actually knocks politely on my cell door, as if I were capable of opening it. She unlocks 'the iron barrier' and tells me that she has come to escort me to my creative-writing class.

I'm taken to a smoke-filled waiting room with no chairs, just a table. Well, that's one way of guaranteeing a standing ovation. Moments later a trickle of prisoners appear, each carrying his own plastic chair. Once the nine of them are settled, Ms Labersham reminds everyone that it's a two-hour session. She suggests that I should speak for about an hour and then open it up for a general discussion.

I've never spoken for an hour in my life; it's usually thirty minutes, forty at the most before I take questions. On this occasion I speak for just over forty minutes, explaining how I took up writing at the age of thirty-four after leaving Parliament, with debts of £427,000 and facing bankruptcy. The last time I gave this speech was at a conference in Las Vegas as the principal guest of a US hotel group. They flew me over first class, gave me a suite of rooms and sent me home with a cheque for $50,000.

Today, I'm addressing nine Belmarsh inmates, and Ms Labersham has confirmed that my prison account will be credited with £2 (a bottle of Highland Spring and a tube of toothpaste).

When I've finished my talk, I am surprised how lively the discussion is that follows. One of the prisoners, Michael (aged twenty-one, murder), wants to talk about becoming a song writer, a subject about which I know very little. I don't feel I can tell him that a lyricist is as different to a novelist as a brain surgeon is from a gynaecologist. Michael wants me to read out his latest effort. It's already forty verses in length. I offer you one:

> *No room, but to leave*
> *You call out, calling for me*
> *to come back*
> *but all you can hear is the sound of your own voice*
> *calling out my name*

Michael heard yesterday that the judge had given him a tariff of eighteen years.

'At least it's not telephone numbers,' he says.

'Telephone numbers?'

'Nine hundred and ninety-nine years,' he replies.

When I finish reading Michael's work, the group discuss it, before Terry (burglary, former cell-mate) reads three pages of his novel, which he hopes to have finished by the time they release him in December.

The group spend some time debating the use of bad language in a novel. Does it tell you anything about the character the author is writing about? Does it distract from the narrative? They go on to discuss the relative strengths and weaknesses of Terry's story. They don't pull any punches.

Tony (marijuana only) then tells the group that he is writing a textbook on quantum mechanics, which has been a hobby of his for many years. He explains that his efforts will add nothing to the genre – his word – but as a project it keeps him occupied for many hours.

The final rendering is one of Billy Little's poems. It's in a different class to anything we've heard up until then, and everyone in that room knows it.

Crash Bang Slam

Subject despised, committed wrong,
broken wounded, buffeted along,
concealed confined, isolated state,
parental tools, judicial hate.

Golden cuffs, silver chains,
reformed pretence, jewelled pains,
sapphire screams, diamond faults,
brick steel, storage vaults.

Uranium plutonium, nuclear chalice,
poison regimes, political malice,
confounded dark, loomin' sin,
atomised spirits, crushed within.

Seditious dissent, proletarian class,
duplicate religion, misleading mass,
ruinous poverty's, reducing rod,
whipping barbarous, bloodthirsty God.

Liberated justice, equality bound,
desecrating capitalists, unholy ground,
revolutionary concept, militant fire,
diligent radical, poetic desire.

Billy Little (BX7974)

During the last few minutes they begin to discuss when we'll get together again. The matter that most concerns the group is whether it should be during Association time or considered as an education class. On this they are equally divided, and I wonder if they will ever meet again.

12 noon

Lunch. I open a tin of ham (67p), extract half of it, to which I add two hard-boiled potatoes (prison issue). During the afternoon, I devour three digestive biscuits, and swig nearly a whole bottle of Evian. If I continue at this rate, I'll be out of water by Saturday, and like so many prisoners, facing the problem of double-bubble. Do you recall Del Boy cutting a cigarette in half, and expecting a whole one back the following day?

1.07 pm

My appeals against change of status and being sent to the Isle of Wight are brought round to my cell for signing. Ms Taylor says that the Deputy Governor wants the forms returned to her office as soon as possible. I read slowly through the two-page legal document, making only one small emendation. I sign on the dotted line, but remain convinced that the Home Office has already made up its mind, and there is nothing I can do about it. The golden rule seems to be: it mustn't look as if Archer's getting special treatment, even if he's being treated unjustly.

2.24 pm

My cell door is opened by Mr Bentley, who tells me that I must report to reception as there are several parcels for me to collect.

When I leave the spur, I am not searched for the first time and the duty officer simply points to the end of the corridor and says, 'My colleague will guide you.' It's taken them two weeks to feel confident that I have no interest in escaping or dealing in drugs. Actually if you tried to escape from Belmarsh – and the roof is the furthest anyone has managed – you'd need an architect's plan; the whole building is a maze. Even if you work here, I imagine it would take several weeks before you could confidently find your way around. Sometimes I wonder how the prison officers find their way out at night.

At the end of every corridor, a barred gate is opened and I am ushered through it. None of the gatekeepers seem to be surprised that I'm unaccompanied. I finally arrive outside the little cubbyhole called reception. The doors are pulled open to reveal Mr Pearson and Mr Leech.

'Good afternoon, sir,' Mr Pearson says, and then quickly corrects himself, 'Archer. I'm afraid we only have fourteen registered parcels for you this week.' He begins to remove them one by one from the shelves behind him. Half an hour later, I am the proud owner of four more Bibles, three copies of the New Testament, and a prayer book. I retain one copy of the New Testament, which is leather-bound, as I feel Terry would appreciate it. I suggest to Mr Leech that the rest should be sent to Mr Powe at the chapel. The other packages consist of three novels, two scripts and a proposal of marriage from a blonde woman of about fifty, who adds that if I don't fancy her, she has a daughter of twenty-four (photo enclosed).

I've considered printing her 'Dear Geoffrey,' (sic) letter and photograph, but my solicitors have advised against it.

When they've opened the final package on the shelf, I point to a box of tissues and ask, 'Are those also mine by any chance?'

Mr Pearson looks at Mr Leech, and says, 'I think they are.'

He passes across two boxes of tissues, making the whole expedition worthwhile.

Mr Pearson accompanies me – I say accompanies, because I didn't get the feeling of being escorted – back to my cell. En route he tells me that the prison was built ten years ago by a Canadian architect and it's all right-angles.

'It might have been more sensible,' he mutters, 'to have consulted serving prison officers, and then we could have pointed out the problems staff and inmates come up against every day.' Before I can offer an opinion, I find myself locked back in my cell.

2.57 pm

I've only been in my cell for a few minutes when Mr Weedon reappears bearing a slip of paper. It's a movement schedule, confirming my worst fears. I will be transferred to the Isle of Wight sometime during the week of 6 August 2001. (See opposite.) It is as I thought; the Home Office have made up their minds, and are unwilling to take any personal needs into consideration. I sink onto my bed, depressed. I am helpless, and there's nothing I can do about it.

3.14 pm

I'm writing the second draft of today's script, when the alarm bell goes off. I can hear running feet, raised voices and the scurrying of prison officers. I look out of my barred window but can see nothing but an empty yard. I gaze through the four-by-nine-inch slit in my door, and quickly realize that the commotion is not on our spur. I'll have to wait for Association before I can find out what happened.

4.00 pm

Association. Once again, I fail to get on the gym rota and suspect it's the same eight inmates who are pre-selected every day, and I haven't been a member of the club long enough to qualify. Let's hope they have a bigger gym on the Isle of Wight.

When I reach the ground floor, I see that Fletch is placed strategically in one corner, as he is at the beginning of every

NOTIFICATION OF TRANSFER

1-1-30.

N/ME... ARCHER....

NUMBER.. FF8282

Th s is to advise you that you are provisionally due to be transferred to
HMP..... CAMP HILL
Th s transfer will take place during the week beginning... 06-08-01

If you have relevant reasons that you feel you cannot be transferred, please discuss the
pro blem with your Houseblock Senior Officer.

Association, in case anyone needs to seek his help or advice. I slip across and have a word.

'What was all the noise about?' I ask.

'A fight broke out on Block Two.'

'Any details?'

'Yes, some con called Vaz has been playing rap music all night, and the man in the cell above him hasn't slept for three days.'

'He has my sympathy,' I tell Fletch.

'They didn't come face to face until this afternoon,' continues Fletch, 'when Mitchell, who was in the cell above, not only laid out Vaz with one punch, but set fire to his cell and ended up jumping on top of his stereo.' Fletch paused. 'It was one of those rare occasions when the prison staff took their time to reach the scene of the crime; after all, they'd received several complaints during the week from other prisoners concerning "the Vaz attitude problem".'

'What happened to the other guy?'

'Mitchell?' said Fletch. 'Officially banged up in segregation, but they'll be moving him to another wing tomorrow; after all, as I explained to Mr Marsland, he was doing no more than representing the views of the majority of inmates.' Another insight into how prison politics work, with Fletch acting as the residents' spokesman.

Billy Little (murder) asks me if I can join him in his cell to discuss a paper he's writing on globalization. He wants to discuss the BBC; its role and responsibility as a public broadcaster. He produces a graph to show how its viewing figures dropped by 4 per cent between 1990 and 1995, and another 4 per cent between 1995 and 2000. I tell Billy that I suspect Greg Dyke, the new Director General, having spent his working life in commercial television, will want to reverse that trend. The beneficiaries,

Billy goes on to tell me, giving detailed statistics, are Sky Digital and the other digital TV stations. Their graphs have a steady upward trend.

I ask Billy when he will have completed his degree course. He removes a sheet of paper from a file below the window. 'September,' he replies.

'And then what?' I ask.

'I may take your advice and write a novel. I've no idea if I can do it, but the judge certainly gave me enough time to find out.'

I can't always pick up every word this Glaswegian utters, but I'm deciphering a few more syllables each day. I've decided to ask Alison to send him a copy of Vikram Seth's *A Suitable Boy*. I consider it's exactly the type of work Billy would appreciate, especially as it was Mr Seth's first novel, so he'll discover what he's up against.

When I leave him, the pool table is occupied, the queue for the two telephones is perpetual, and the afternoon film is *Carry on Camping*. I return to my cell, door unlocked, and continue writing.

6.00 pm

Supper. I risk a vegetable fritter and two prison potatoes (three mistakes). I continue to drink my bottled water as if I have an endless supply (the temperature today is 91°). Double-bubble is fast looming, and I'll need to see Del Boy fairly soon if I am to survive. As I move down the hotplate, Andy (murder) slips two chocolate ice-creams onto my tray. 'Put one in your pocket,' he whispers. Now I discover what the word treat really means. Del Boy is standing at the other end of the counter in his role as number one hotplate man. An official title. As I pass the custard pie, I ask if we could meet up later. He nods. He can smell when someone's in trouble. As a Listener, Derek is allowed to visit any cell if another inmate needs to discuss a personal problem. And I have a personal problem. I'm running out of water.

7.00 pm

I settle down to go over my script for the day before turning to the post. The pattern continues unabated, but to my surprise, few mention the Kurds. Paul (credit-card fraud) told me when I was queuing up at the canteen that *The Times* had made it clear that I had no involvement with the collecting or distributing of any monies. That had been the responsibility of the Red Cross. However, there was one letter in the pile that didn't fall into any of the usual slots.

I have now been locked up in a Category A, high-security prison for two weeks, which I share with thirty-two murderers, and seventeen other lifers mainly convicted of attempted murder or manslaughter; I've lost my mother, who I adored; I've been incarcerated on the word of a man who colluded with the *News of the World* to set me up, and by a woman who is a self-confessed thief; and I'm about to be sent to the Isle of Wight, a C-cat prison, because of the word of Baroness Nicholson. So I confess I had to chuckle, a rare event recently, when I received the following missive. (See opposite.)

8.40 pm

My cell door is unlocked by an officer and Del Boy is allowed to join me. His smile is as wide as ever, as he strolls in looking like a rent collector visiting someone who doesn't always pay on time. He takes a seat on the end of the bed. For some time we

 Chan's Optometrist

Mr J Archer   Mr Kenneth Chan BSc. MCOptom.
Belmarsh House   90 High Street
Belmarsh   Lee-on-Solent
South East London   Hampshire
                                      PO13 9DA
                                      31/7/2001

Dear Mr. Archer

 I am sorry to trouble you. The reason I write to you is because one of
my patients like your spectacles (The rimless pair you wore when you went
to the funeral). I would be most grateful if you can let me know the brand, the
model number, the colour and the size of the frame. All these information
should be printed on the sides of the frame. Your reply will be appreciated.

 Thank you for your attention!

Yours Sincerely,

K. Chan.

discuss his upcoming appeal and the fact that he cannot read or write. It transpires that he can make out the odd word if he concentrates, but can only sign his name.

'I've never needed much more,' he explains. 'I'm a barrow boy, not a banker.'

He makes a fair point, because were you to close your eyes and listen to him speak, although he's quite unable to hide his cockney upbringing you certainly wouldn't know he was black. He promises to take reading lessons just as soon as I depart for the Isle of Wight. I'm not convinced he'll ever find out which floor the education department is on, until the curriculum includes 'double-bubble'.

'Now how can I help?' he asks. 'Because I'm the man.'

'Well, if you're the man, Derek, I'm running out of water, among other things.'

'No problem,' he replies, 'and what are the other things?'

'I'd like three bottles of Highland Spring, two packets of McVitie's chocolate biscuits and a tube of toothpaste.'

'No problem,' he repeats. 'They'll be delivered to your cell in the morning, squire.'

'And no double-bubble?'

'No double-bubble.' He hesitates. 'As long as you agree never to say anything because if anyone found out it wouldn't do my reputation any good.'

'No problem,' I hear myself saying.

On the outside, in that world I have vacated, a handful of people can make things happen. The secret is to know that handful of people. It's no different on the inside. Derek 'Del Boy' Bicknell is a natural Chief Whip, Fletch, the Leader of the Opposition, Billy, Secretary of State for Education, Tony, Chancellor of the Exchequer, Paul, Home Secretary, and Colin, Secretary of State for Defence. Wherever you are, in whatever circumstances, leadership will always emerge. Block One, spur one, houses thirty-two murderers, seventeen lifers, and, without realizing it, has formed an inmates' Cabinet. Nothing on paper, nothing official, but it works.

After Derek departs, I settle down on my bed to finish John Grisham's *The Partner*. It's too long, but what a storyteller.

10.07 pm

I put my head on the pillow. I can scarcely believe it, no more rap music. Well done, Mitchell.

DAY 15   THURSDAY 2 AUGUST 2001

5.51 am

A full night's sleep. For the first time I can hear the cars on the road in the distance. I write for two hours, interrupted only by the occasional bark of an Alsatian.

8.00 am

Breakfast. Frosties and long-life milk (second day).

9.00 am

Association. I remind Derek of my acute water-shortage problem. Now down to half a bottle. It's all under control, he claims.

I line up with the other prisoners for the gym.

Derek Jones (GBH, artist) spots me on the middle corridor and tells me that he did a spell at Camphill on the Isle of Wight. I quiz him, and discover that it has a fully equipped gym, one of the best in the country (by that he means in prisons), but he adds alarmingly that, 'It's full of shit-heads and scum. Young tearaways who think of themselves as gangsters because they've robbed some old lady. No one on the spur understands why you're being sent there.' I panic, desert the queue for the gym, run upstairs, grab my phonecard, rush back down and call Alison.

First I warn her (no time for pleasantries when you only have twenty units on your weekly card) that the next five days of the script are on their way, and to let Ramona know when they have arrived so she can confirm this on her next legal visit. I then ask to be put through to James. My younger son has assumed the role of joint head of the household in charge of finance, while William's responsibility is to take care of his mother. I don't lose a moment's sleep wondering if they're up to it. I quickly tell Jamie about the Isle of Wight and the loss of my D-cat status.

'Calm down, Dad,' he says. 'We've been working on little else for the past forty-eight hours. I know how you must feel being so out of touch, but we're on the case. Ramona spoke to the Home Office last night, and they're hinting that it's unlikely that there will even be an inquiry into the Kurdish matter. No one is taking Nicholson's accusations seriously, even the tabloids have ignored her.'

'Yes, but these things still take time; meanwhile I've been issued with a movement order.'

'The same source,' James continues, 'is hinting that you're more likely to end up in the home counties, but they're still working on it.'

I check my phonecard; I've already used six units. 'Anything else?' I ask. I want to save as many units as possible for Mary on Sunday.

'Yes, I need your authority to transfer some dollars into your sterling account. The pound has been off for the past couple of days.'

'That's fine by me,' I tell him.

DAY 15

'By the way,' he says, 'lots of people are talking about the judge's summing-up, so chin up. Bye, Dad.'

I put the phone down to find I have used seven of my twenty units. I leave James to worry about the currency market while I concentrate on trying to get my hands on a bottle of Highland Spring.

I check my watch. No point in returning to the gym queue, so I settle for a shower. You forget how dirty you are, until you discover how clean you can be.

11.00 am

The officer on the front desk bellows out, 'Exercise,' which once again I avoid. It's 92° out there in the yard, with no shade. I elect to sit in my cell, writing, with the tiny window as wide open as I can force it. When I've completed ten pages of script, I switch on the Test Match. The game is only an hour old, and England are 47 for 2.

12 noon

Lunch. I pick up my tray and walk down to the hotplate, but can't find a single item I would offer an emaciated dog. I leave with a piece of buttered bread and an apple. Back in my cell I tuck into the other half of my tin of Prince's ham, two more McVitie's digestive biscuits, and a mug of water. I try to convince myself that Del Boy is the man, and he will deliver – in the nick of time – because there's only two inches left in the bottle. Have you ever had to measure how much water is left in a bottle?

2.00 pm

An officer appears outside my cell door and orders me to report to the workshop, which I'm not enthusiastic about. After all, my application for education must surely have been processed by now. When I arrive at the bubble on the centre floor to join the other prisoners, I'm searched before having my name ticked off. We are then escorted down a long corridor to our different destinations – workshop and education. When we reach the end of the corridor, prisoners destined for the workshop turn left, those with higher things on their mind, right. I turn right.

When I arrive at education, I walk past a set of classrooms with about six or seven prisoners in each; a couple of prison officers are lounging around in one corner, while a lady sitting behind a desk on the landing crosses off the names of inmates before allocating them to different classrooms. I come to a halt in front of her.

'Archer,' I tell her.

She checks down the list, but can't find my name. She looks puzzled, picks up a phone and quickly discovers that I ought to be in the workshop.

'But Ms Fitt told me I would be processed for education immediately.'

'Strange word, immediately,' she says. 'I don't think anyone at Belmarsh has looked up its meaning in the dictionary, and until they do I'm afraid you'll have to report to the workshops.' I can't imagine what the words 'until they do' mean. I retrace my steps, walking as slowly as I can in the direction of the workshops, and find I am the last to arrive.

This time I'm put on the end of the chain gang – a punishment for being the last to turn up. My new, intellectually challenging job is to place two small packets of margarine, one

175

sachet of raspberry jam, and one of coffee into a plastic bag before it's sealed up and taken away for use in another prison. The young man opposite me who is sealing up the bags and then dropping them into a large cardboard box looks like a wrestler. He's about five foot ten, early twenties, wears a spotless white T-shirt and smart designer jeans. His heavily muscled arms are bronzed, so it's not difficult to work out that he hasn't been in Belmarsh that long. The answer to that question turns out to be three weeks. He tells me that his name is Peter. He's married with one child and runs his own company.

'What do you do?' I ask.

'I'm a builder.' When a prisoner say's 'I'm' something, and not 'I used to be' something, then you can almost be certain that their sentence is short or they're on remand. Peter goes on to tell me that he and his brother run a small building company that specializes in buying dilapidated houses in up-and-coming areas of Essex. They renovate the houses and then sell them on. Last year, between them, they were able to earn around two thousand pounds a week. But that was before Peter was arrested. He comes across as a hard-working, decent sort of man. So what's he doing in Belmarsh? I ask myself. Who can he possibly have murdered? His brother, perhaps? He answers that question without my having to enquire.

'I was caught driving my brother's van without a licence. My brother usually does the driving, but he was off sick for the day, so I took his building tools from the work site to my home and for that the judge sentenced me to six weeks in jail.'

Let me make it clear. I have no objection to the sentence, but it's madness to have sent this man to Belmarsh. I do hope that the Home Secretary, Mr Blunkett – who I know from personal dealings when John Major was Prime Minister to be a decent, caring man – will read the next page carefully.

'Are you in a cell on your own?' I enquire.

'No, I'm locked up with two other prisoners.'

'What are they in for?'

'One's on a charge of murder awaiting his trial, the other's a convicted drug dealer.'

'That can't be much fun,' I say, trying to make light of it.

Are you still with me, Home Secretary?

'It's hell,' Peter replies. 'I haven't slept for more than a few minutes since the night they sent me here. I just can't be sure what either of them might get up to. I can handle myself, but the two men I'm sharing a cell with are professional criminals.'

Are you still paying attention, Home Secretary?

'And worse,' he adds. 'One of them offered me a thousand pounds to beat up a witness before his trial begins.'

'Oh, my God,' I hear myself say.

'And he's putting more and more pressure on me each day. Of course I wouldn't consider such an idea, but I've still got another three days to go, and I'm beginning to fear that I might not be safe even when I get out.'

Home Secretary, this hard-working family man is fearful for his own safety. Is that what you're hoping to achieve for someone who's been caught driving without a licence?

I've received over a thousand letters of support since I arrived a Belmarsh and even at sixty-one I have found prison a difficult experience to come to terms with. Peter is twenty-three, with his whole life ahead of him. Hundreds of people are being sent to this Category A top-security prison who should never be here.

But what can I do about it? I can hear the Home Secretary asking one of his officials.

Classify anyone who is arrested as A, B, C or D before their trial begins, not after. Then, if they're D-cat – first-time offenders with no record of violence – they can, if convicted, be sent direct to an open prison. That way they won't have to share cells with murderers, drug dealers or professional criminals. And don't listen to officials when they tell you it can't be done. Sack them, and do it. I was allocated D-cat status within twenty-four hours because of my mother's funeral, so I know it can be done.

Home Secretary, you are doing irreparable damage to decent people's lives and you have no right to do so.

While I'm trying to take in Peter's plight, the pile of plastic bags has grown into a mountain in front of me. Another prisoner who I hadn't noticed before, obviously an old lag, slots quickly into the one position that ensures the chain moves back into full swing.

'This place is more about retribution than rehabilitation, wouldn't you say, Jeffrey?' What is it about the Irish that always makes you relax and feel you've known them all your life? I nod my agreement. He smiles, and introduces himself as William Keane.

Before I repeat what William told me during the next couple of hours, I must warn you that I haven't a clue how much of his tale can be authenticated, but if only half of it is true, God help the Prime Minister, the Home Secretary, the Secretary of State for Health and the Education Secretary.

William was born in Limerick, son of a prize fighter (Ireland must be the last country on earth that still has prize fighters) and a local beauty – William is a handsome man. Mrs Keane produced seven sons and five daughters.

Now William's accent is quite difficult to follow, so I often have to ask him to repeat whole sentences. His present home is a few hundred yards from the prison, so family visits are not a problem. It's the family that's the problem. One of them, the youngster, as William describes him, is on the far bench – marmalade and jam sachets – and at some point, William tells me, all seven brothers and one sister were in jail at the same time, serving sentences between them of one hundred and twelve years. I can only feel sorry for their mother.

William is completing a ten-year sentence for drug dealing, and has only twelve weeks left to serve. You notice he doesn't say three months, because three months would mean thirteen weeks.

He's actually quite fearful about how the world will have changed when in October he steps out of prison for the first time in a decade. He flatters me, a natural pastime for the Irish, by saying he's read all my books, as it seems half the leading criminals in England have.

During his time in six prisons (he's a post-graduate on such establishments), William has taken a degree, and read over four hundred books – I only point this out to make you aware that we are not dealing with a fool. He adds his condolences over my mother's death, and asks how the police and prison staff dealt with me when it came to the funeral. I tell him that they couldn't have been more thoughtful and considerate.

'Not like my brother's funeral,' he says. 'Not only were the whole family in handcuffs, but they had helicopters circling overhead. There were more police by the graveside than mourners.'

'But in my case,' I pointed out, 'no one thought I would try to escape.'

'Houdini couldn't have escaped from that bunch,' William retorts.

What puzzles me about William is that if the rest of the

family are as bright and charismatic as he is, why don't they combine their talents and energy and do something worthwhile, rather than settling for a life of crime?

'Drugs,' he replies, matter-of-factly. 'Once you're hooked, you can never earn enough to satisfy the craving, so you end up becoming either a thief or a pusher. And I have to admit,' William adds, 'I'm lazy.'

I've watched him carefully since he's joined the chain, and the one thing he is not, is lazy. He has filled more plastic bags than Peter and me put together. I point this out to him.

'Well, when I say lazy, Jeffrey, I mean lazy about settling down to a nine-to-five job, when you can pick up a couple of grand a week selling drugs.'

'So will you go back to the drug scene once you're released?'

'I don't want to,' he says. 'I'm thirty-five, and one thing's for certain, I don't need to come back inside.' He hesitates. 'But I just don't know if I'm strong-willed enough to stay away from drugs or the quick rewards that are guaranteed when you sell them.'

'How much are we talking about,' I ask, 'and which drugs in particular?'

'Heroin,' he says, 'is the biggest money-spinner. A joey' – even after an explanation, I'm still not quite sure what a joey is – 'has come down in price from one hundred pounds to forty since I've been in prison [ten years], which is a clear indication how the market has grown. And some people need as many as ten joeys a day. When I first came into prison,' William continues, 'cocaine was the designer drug. Today it's heroin, and it's often your lot who are on it,' he says, looking directly at me.

'But I've never taken a drug in my life,' I tell him, 'I don't even smoke.'

'I knew that the moment you walked in,' he said.

'How can you be so sure?'

'The first thing I check is the pallor of the skin – not bad for sixty-one,' he says, displaying that Irish charm again. 'Then I look at the nose, followed by the lips and finally the arms, and it's clear you're not a potential customer. But I'd be willing to bet there's something you need Del Boy to supply you with.'

'Bottled water, still, preferably Highland Spring.'

'How many bottles do you order from the canteen?'

'Four, maybe five a week.'

'Don't let the screws find out.'

'Why not? I pay for them.'

'Because while cannabis and cocaine remain in your bloodstream for a month, heroin can be flushed out in twenty-four hours. If it wasn't you, Jeffrey, the screws would assume you were a heroin addict trying to show up negative whenever you were called in for a Mandatory Drug Test, and it's all the fault of Ann Widdecombe.'

'How can it possibly be Ann Widdecombe's fault?'

'Because it was Widdecombe who first brought in the MDT. That single decision has turned some cannabis smokers into heroin addicts.'

'That's quite a quantum leap,' I suggest, 'and some accusation.'

'No,' says William, 'it was inevitable, and it only happened because Widdecombe knew nothing about the drug culture in prisons. How could she? Neither did you, before you were sent to Belmarsh. And worse, no one seems to have explained the problem to Blunkett either, because both are indirectly responsible for an unnecessary rise in heroin addicts, and even in some cases their deaths.'

'Hold on,' I say. 'That's accusing Blunkett and Widdecombe of manslaughter and cannot be either fair or accurate.'

'When you take an MDT, they test you for marijuana [cannabis], cocaine, crack cocaine and heroin,' continues William, ignoring my comment. 'It's a urine test, and your sample is sent to an independent laboratory and then returned to the prison a week later with the result.'

'I'm with you so far.'

'Marijuana can show up in urine for as long as twenty-eight days. You may well have smoked a joint three weeks ago, even forgotten about it, but it will still come up as positive on an MDT, which is not the case with heroin. Because if you drink pints of water immediately after taking the drug, you can clear any trace of heroin out of your system within twenty-four hours, which means you won't test positive.'

Pay attention, Home Secretary.

'If the test comes back positive for marijuana, the Governor can add twenty-eight days to your sentence and take away all your privileges. Twenty-eight days for one joint,' says William. 'So in prison some marijuana smokers who are on short sentences turn to heroin as an alternative because there's less chance of their sentence being lengthened. Result? They often leave prison as heroin addicts, having never touched a hard drug on the outside. Fact: a percentage of them die within weeks of being released. Why? Because the heroin in prison is considerably weaker compared with the gear you can get "on the out", which causes them to overdose when they inject the same amount. This is a direct result of government legislation.'

'So what would you do about it?' I ask.

'The Mandatory Drug Test should be for Class A and B drugs only [heroin, cocaine], not for marijuana.* This simple decision

---

* Since this was written, the Home Secretary has downgraded cannabis/marijuana to Class C classification.

182

would cut down the desire to experiment with heroin among twenty per cent of the prison population and would also save countless lives. If any your officials are stupid enough to suggest this isn't true, Home Secretary, tell them not to rely simply on statistics, but to spend a few weeks in prison where they'll quickly find out the truth.'

'I presume, however, it is true that drugs are the direct cause of our prisons being so overcrowded?'

'Yes, but it's a myth that heroin is the main cause of street crime. Crack cocaine is just as much of a problem for the police.' I don't interrupt. 'Crack cocaine,' William continues, 'is for crack-heads, and is far more dangerous than heroin. If you take cocaine you are immediately satisfied, and can be on a high after only one dose, and as you come off it, you may well fall asleep. If you take *crack* cocaine, once you've run out of your supply, you'll do anything to get your hands on some more to prolong the experience. It's the crack-cocaine addicts that rob old ladies of their handbags and young girls of their mobile phones, not heroin addicts; they're more likely to beg, borrow or shoplift. The problem the government hasn't acknowledged is that Britain is now the crack-cocaine capital of Europe, and if you want to set up an award for European drugs city of the year, you wouldn't have to look any further than Bradford. That city would win first prize, year in and year out.'

'Do you have a solution to the problem?' I ask.

'We should go down the Swiss route,' William suggests. 'They register addicts, who can report to a doctor and immediately become part of a detox programme and get their fix of methadone or subitrex. The Swiss recently held a referendum on the issue and the public voted overwhelmingly in favour of the registration of drug addicts and tackling the problem head-on. Result: street crime has fallen by 68 per cent.'

Well, what do you know, Mr Blunkett?

'Do you also want to learn about the National Health detox programme?' asks William. I nod. 'If you're a heroin addict "on the out" and report your addiction to a local GP, it will take you eight to ten weeks to get yourself registered. However, if you commit a crime and are sent to prison, you don't have to wait, because you'll be put on a detox programme the following morning.' William pauses. 'I've known addicts who've committed a crime simply to ensure they get themselves into prison and onto detox overnight.'

What about that, Home Secretary?

'And worse,' William continues, 'most of the addicts "on the out" who go as far as getting themselves registered, fail to turn up ten weeks later to begin the course, because by then they've either lost interest, or are too far gone to care.'

Enter the Secretary of State for Health.

William looks around the room at the fifty or so workers packing their little plastic bags. 'I can tell you every one in this room who's on drugs, even the gear they're on, and it often only takes a glance. And you'd be surprised how many of your friends "on the out", even one or two of those who have been condemning you recently, are among them.'

'Taking cannabis can hardly be described as a major crime,' I suggest. 'My bet is it will be decriminalized in the not too distant future.'

'I'm not talking about cannabis, Jeffrey. The biggest crisis the government is facing today is the rapid growth of heroin addicts. I can name three lords, two Members of Parliament, and two television personalities who are on Class A drugs. I know because a member of my family has been supplying them for years.' He names all of them. Two I already knew about, but the other five come as a surprise. 'In theory they should all be in jail along with you,' he adds. Check on all the young criminals coming into prison and you'll begin to understand it's a problem that few people, especially the politicians, seem willing to face up to. 'On your own spur alone,' he continues, 'five of the lifers are on heroin, and still getting the skag delivered to them every week.'

'How do they manage that?' I ask.

'Mainly during visits,' he says, 'mouth, backside, ears, even secreted in a woman's hair. Because of the Human Rights Act, prison searches are fairly cursory.'

'But this is a Double A Category high-security prison,' I remind him.

'That's not a problem if you're desperate enough, and there's nothing more desperate than a heroin addict, even when he's locked up in the segregation block.'

'But how?' I press him.

'Don't forget that most A-cats are also remand prisons, and so have prisoners coming in and out every day. If the new young criminals didn't already know, it wouldn't take them long to discover the economics of supply and demand, especially when such large sums of money are involved. A gram of heroin [a joey] may be worth forty pounds on the street, but in here it can be split up into five bags and sold for a couple of hundred. At those prices, some prisoners are willing to risk swallowing a bag of heroin just before they're taken down; then they simply have to wait to retrieve it; after all, there's a toilet in every cell. And,' he adds, 'my brother Rory can swallow a lump of heroin the size of a small eraser – five hundred pounds in value – hold it in his throat and still carry on a conversation. As soon as he's safely back in his cell, he coughs it up.'

'But despite your brother's unusual skill,' I point out, 'if, as you suggest, sixty per cent of inmates are on drugs, you'll need more than the odd prisoner who's willing to swallow a packet of heroin to satisfy the demand.'

'True,' said William, 'so stay alert during visits, Jeffrey, and you'll notice how much transferring of drugs is done by kissing. And whenever you see a baby dangling on its mother's knee, you can be sure the little offspring's nappy will be full of drugs. That's how the visitor gets it into prison. The kissing is how it's transferred from visitor to inmate. And there are still a dozen or more ways of getting the gear in, depending on which prison you're sent to. If you ever spot someone coming into jail wearing an Adidas tracksuit, look carefully at the three stripes. If you unstitch just one of them, you can fill it with five hundred pounds' worth of heroin.'

My only thought is that I have an Adidas tracksuit in my cell.

'My brother Michael,' continues William, 'discovered that in some prisons Waterstone's have the book franchise, so a friend of his would select an obscure title, fill the spine with drugs, and then ask Waterstone's to donate the book to the prison library. Once it had been placed on the shelf, Michael would take it out. Amazing how much heroin you can get into the spine of James Joyce's *Ulysses*. But in my last nick,' William continues, 'the *Sun*'s page-three girl was the most popular method of getting the skag in, until the screws caught on.'

'The page-three girl?'

'You do know what a page-three girl is, don't you, Jeffrey?' I nod. 'Most A- and B-cat prisons allow an inmate to order a morning paper from the local newsagent,' continues William, 'and because you're locked up for twenty-two hours a day, they even deliver them to your cell. One enterprising dealer "on the out" supplied the entire prison's needs, by sprinkling any orders all over the page-three girl in the *Sun*. He would then cut out another copy of the same photograph and seal it carefully over her twin, making a thin bag of heroin. He ended up supplying a grand's worth of heroin a day to one prison, with an officer unwittingly delivering his wares to the customer direct. He was making far more with his built-in customers than he could ever hope to make "on the out".'

'But how did he get paid?'

'Oh, Jeffrey, you're so green. On every spur, on every block, in every prison, you'll find a dealer who has a supplier on the outside and he'll know your needs within hours of your being locked up.'

'But that doesn't answer my question.'

'You make an order with your spur dealer,' continues William, 'say a gram of heroin a day. He then tells you the name and address of his supplier, and you select someone "on the out" to handle the payments. No standing orders, you understand, just cash. In your case you could have your supply delivered under the Scarfe cartoon in the *Sunday Times*.' I laugh. 'Or under the stamps on one of those large brown envelopes you receive every day. You'd be surprised how much cocaine you can deposit under four postage stamps. You watch the screws when the post arrives in the morning. They always run a thumb over the stamps, but you can get a lot more in via the envelope.'

'But they always slit the envelopes open and look inside.'

'I didn't say inside,' said William. 'You may have noticed that down the right-hand side of most brown envelopes there's a flap, which, if you lift carefully, you can fill with heroin and then seal back down again. I know a man who has *Motor Magazine* sent in every week, but it's under the flap of the brown envelope that he's getting his weekly fix.'

'As soon as the buzzer goes, I'm going to have to run back to my cell and write all this down,' I tell him.

'How do you write your books?' William enquires.

'With a felt-tip pen.'

'Lift the cap off the bottom and you can get about fifty pounds' worth of crack cocaine stuffed in there, which is why the screws make you buy any writing implements direct from the canteen.'

'Keep going,' I say, having long ago given up sealing any plastic bags, but somehow William manages to do that job for me as well.

'The most outrageous transfer I've ever seen was a twenty-seven-stone con who hid the drugs under the folds of his skin, because he knew no officer would want to check.'

'But they must have machines to do the checking for them?'

'Yes, they do, in fact vast sums have been spent on the most sophisticated machinery, but they only identify razor blades, guns, knives, even ammunition, but not organic substances. For that, they have to rely on dogs, and a nappy full of urine will put even the keenest bloodhound off the scent.'

'So visits are the most common way of bringing in drugs?'

'Yes, but don't assume that lawyers, priests or prison officers are above being carriers, because when they turn up for legal and religious visits, or in the case of officers, for work, they are rarely searched. In some cases lawyers are paid their fees from drugs delivered to their clients. And when it comes to letters, if they're legal documents, the envelope has to be opened in front of you, and the screws are not allowed to read the contents. And while you're standing in front of a screw, he's less likely to check under the stamps or the side flaps. By the way, there's a legal shop in Fleet Street that is innocently supplying envelopes with the words LEGAL DOCUMENT, *Strictly Private and Confidential* printed on the top left-hand corner. Several drug dealers have a monthly supply of such envelopes, and the only time they ever see a court is when they are standing in the dock.'

'You also mentioned priests?'

'Yes, I knew a Sikh giani [priest] at Gartree who used to give his blessing once a week in a prisoner's cell from where he supplied the entire Sikh community with drugs.'

'How did he manage that?'

'They were secreted in his turban. Did you know that a turban can be eighteen feet of material? You can tuck an awful lot of drugs in there.' William pauses. 'Though in his case, one of his flock grassed on him, and he ended up doing a seven-year bird.'

'And prison officers?'

'Screws are paid around three hundred pounds a week, and can pick up another thirteen pounds an hour overtime. Think about it. A half-dozen joeys of heroin and they can double their wages. I knew a member of the kitchen staff at my last prison who brought the stuff in once a week in his backpack.'

'But he would have been liable to a random search at any time?'

'True,' William replied, 'and they did regularly search his backpack, but not the shoulder straps.'

'But if they get caught?'

'They end up on the other side of the bars for a long stretch. We've got a couple in here right now, but they'll shift them out to D-cats before it becomes common knowledge.' He pauses. 'For their own safety. But the championship,' says William, like any good storyteller holding the best until last, 'goes to Harry, the amateur referee from Devon.' By now, William has a captive audience, as all the workers on our table have stopped depositing their wares into little plastic bags as they hang on his every word. 'Harry,' continues William, 'used to visit his local prison once a week to referee a football match. His contact was the goalkeeper, and at the end of each game, both men would return to the changing room, take off their boots and put on trainers. They would then leave carrying the other person's boots. There was enough heroin packed into the referee's hollow studs for him to buy a country cottage after only a couple of seasons. And remember, every match has to be played at home. There are no away fixtures for prisoners. However, the silly man got greedy and started filling up the football as well. He's currently serving a ten-year sentence in Bristol.'

'So where does the dealer get his supplies from?' I ask William as the hands of the clock edge nearer and nearer towards twelve, and I am fearful we may never meet again.

'They're picked up for him by mules.'

'Mules?'

'The dealer often recruits university students who are already hooked – probably by him. He'll then send them on an all-expenses-paid holiday to Thailand, Pakistan or even Colombia and give them an extra thousand pounds if they can smuggle a kilo of heroin through customs.'

'How big is a kilo?'

'A bag of sugar.'

'And what's it worth?'

'The dealer passes on that kilo for around £28,000–£35,000 to sellers, known as soldiers. The soldiers then add baking powder and brick dust until they have four kilos, which they sell on in grams or joeys* for forty pounds a time to their customers. A top soldier can make a profit of seventy to a hundred thousand pounds a month. And don't forget, Jeff, it's cash, so they won't

---

* A joey is about the size of two aspirins.

end up paying any tax, and with that kind of profit there are a lot of punters out there willing to take the risk. The heroin on sale at King's Cross or Piccadilly,' William continues, 'will usually be about four to seven per cent pure. The heroin that the mule brings back from an all-expenses-paid holiday could be as high as 92 per cent pure. By the way,' he adds, 'if the soldiers didn't dilute their wares – cut the smack – they'd kill off most of their customers within a week.'

'How many heroin addicts are there in this country?' I ask.

'Around a quarter of a million,' William replies, 'so it's big business.'

'And how many of those . . .'

A buzzer goes to alert the prison staff that the work period is over, and in a few moments we will be escorted back to our cells. William says, 'It's nice to have met you, Jeffrey. Give my regards to your wife – a truly remarkable woman. Sorry about the judge. Strange that he preferred to believe the word of someone who admitted in court to being a thief. But whatever you do, keep writing the books, because however long you live, there's always going to be a Keane in jail.'

William offers me one final piece of advice before we part. 'I know you've been attending chapel on Sundays, but try the RCs this week. Father Kevin preaches a fine sermon, and you'll like him.'

I walk back to my cell, delighted to have missed education, having spent two hours being educated.

On the route march back to my cell I'm joined by Ali (breach of trust, stole £28,000 from his employer, gave it all back), who has also received his movement order. He will be going to Springhill on Monday, a D-cat. He asks where I'm heading.

'I can't be sure,' I tell him. 'I'm down for the Isle of Wight sometime next week, but I've appealed against the move.'

'Can't blame you. By the way, did you notice how peaceful the workshop was this afternoon?' Ali asks.

'I didn't see any difference from the last time I was there.'

'No, the whole atmosphere changed the moment you walked into the room. The prison officers and even the inmates stop swearing, and a lot more work gets done.'

'I can't believe that.'

'Oh yes,' says Ali, 'they all know you're writing a book and you might mention them by name.'

'Not yours,' I remind him, 'you're still referred to as Ali. You're only the second person who wants their identity kept a secret.'

Once we reach the apex that divides Blocks One and Two, we go our separate ways. I wish him well.

As soon as I'm back in my cell, I grab a McVitie's biscuit and pour out my last mug of water, leaving only a dribble in the bottom of the bottle. I'm about to discover if Del Boy is the man.

I turn on the radio. England are all out for 185. I drown my sorrows in the last cup of water before starting on what I expect to be an extended writing session. I'm fearful of forgetting even a line of William Keane's monologue.

4.30 pm

I turn the radio back on to follow the cricket. Australia are 46 without loss, chasing a total of 185. Shall I continue writing, or be a masochist? I decide to go on listening for a few more minutes. In the next over, Slater is bowled, and by the time the cell door is opened for supper (vegetable pie and beans) Australia are 105 for 7, with only Gilchrist among the recognized batsmen still left at the crease.

7.00 pm

Association. I go in search of Del Boy like a helpless addict desperate for a fix. I find him sitting on his bed, head bowed, looking mournful. He bends down and slowly pulls out from under his bed a large brown-paper bag, and like a conjuror, produces three bottles of Highland Spring and two packets of McVitie's chocolate – I repeat, chocolate – biscuits. He is, unquestionably, the man.

I cuddle him. 'Get off me,' he says pushing me away. 'If anyone saw you doing that, I'd never be able to show my face in the East End again.'

I laugh, thank him, and carry off his spoils to my cell.

I pour myself a mug of water and am munching a chocolate biscuit when there's a knock on the cell door. I look up to see my next-door neighbour, Richard, standing in the doorway. I feel his eyes boring into me. 'The fuckin' *Mirror*,' he says almost in a shout, 'have been round to our fuckin' house and are pestering my fuckin' mum.'

'I'm sorry to hear that,' I say. 'But why are they doing that?'

'Just because I'm in the next fuckin' cell to you,' he says plaintively. I nod my understanding. 'They say you're going to describe me in your fuckin' book as a vicious criminal and they fear for your fuckin' safety. Do you think I'm fuckin' vicious?'

'You've given me no reason to believe so,' I reply.

'Well, now they're threatening my fuckin' mum, telling her that if she doesn't supply a fuckin' photo of me, they'll make it worse.'

'How?' I asked.

'By telling their fuckin' readers what I did.'

'I'm afraid you must phone your mother and explain to her that they'll do that in any case. By the way, what are you in for?'

'Murder,' he replies. 'But it wasn't my fuckin' fault.'

'Why, what happened?'

'I was out drinking with the boys at my fuckin' local, and when we left the fuckin' pub we came face to face with a bunch of fuckin' Aussie backpackers who accused us of stealing their fuckin' wallets. I promise you, Jeff, I'd never seen the fuckin' bastards before in my life.'

'So what happened next?'

'Well, one of 'em had a fuckin' knife, and when my mate punched him, he dropped the fuckin' thing on the pavement. I grabbed it and when another of them came for me, I fuckin' stabbed him. It was only fuckin' self-defence.'

'And he died from one stab?'

'Not exactly.' He hesitates. 'The coroner said there were seven stab wounds, but I was so fuckin' tanked up that I can't remember a fuckin' thing about it.' He pauses. 'So make sure you tell your fuckin' readers that I'm not a vicious criminal.'*

Once Richard returns to his cell, I go back over William Keane's words, before turning to the latest round of letters, still running at over a hundred a day. When I've finished them, I start reading a new book, *The Day after Tomorrow*, recommended by Del Boy – somewhat ironic. It's over seven hundred pages, a length that would normally put me off, but not in my present circumstances. I've only read a few pages, when there's a knock on the cell door. It's Paul (credit-card fraud). They're transferring him tomorrow morning back to the drug-rehab centre in Norfolk, so we may never meet again. He shakes hands as if we were business associates, and then leaves without another word.

---

* *Almost* all of the prisoners have stopped swearing in front of me.

I place my head on a pillow that no longer feels rock-hard, and reflect on the day. I can't help thinking that hurling red balls at Australians is, on balance, preferable to sticking knives into them.

DAY 16   FRIDAY 3 AUGUST 2001

6.07 am

Silent night. Woken by the Alsatians at 6 am. Should have been up in any case. Write for two hours.

8.00 am

Breakfast. Rice Krispies, long-life milk and an orange.

10.00 am

Avoid the workshop. It's not compulsory to do more than three sessions a week. Continue writing.

12 noon

Turn on cricket to hear CMJ telling me that Australia are all out for 190, giving them a lead of only five runs on the first innings. England are still in with a fighting chance.

12.15 pm

Lunch. The rule for lunch and supper – called dinner and tea –

is that you fill in a meal slip the day before and drop it in a plastic box on the ground floor. The menus for the week are posted on a board so you can always select in advance. If you fail to fill in the slip – as I regularly do – you're automatically given 'A'. 'A' is always the vegetarian option, 'B' today is pan-fried fish – that's spent more time swimming in oil than the sea, 'C' is steak and kidney pie – you can't see inside it, so avoid at all costs. Puddings: semolina or an apple. Perhaps this is the time to remind you that each prisoner has £1.27 spent on them for three meals a day. (See pages 192–194.)

When I leave my cell, plastic tray and plastic plate in hand, I join a queue of six prisoners at the hotplate. The next six inmates are not allowed to join the queue until the previous six have been served. This is to avoid a long queue and fighting breaking out over the food. At the right-hand end of the hotplate sits Paul (murder) who checks your name and announces Fossett, C., Pugh, B., Clarke, B., etc. When he ticks my name off, the six men behind the counter, who are all dressed in long white coats, white headgear and wear thin rubber gloves for handling the potatoes or bread, go into a huddle because they know by now there's a fifty–fifty chance I won't want anything and will return to my cell empty-handed.

Tony (marijuana only, escaped to Paris) has recently got into the habit of selecting my meal for me. Today he suggests the steak and kidney pie, slightly underdone, the cauliflower au gratin with duchesse potatoes, or, 'My Lord, you could settle for the creamy vegetable pie.' The server's humour has reached the stage of cutting one potato in quarters and placing a diced carrot on top and then depositing it in the centre of my plastic plate. Mind you, if there's chocolate ice-cream or a lollipop, Del Boy always makes sure I end up with two. I never ate puddings before I went to prison.

CHOICE	MONDAY	DIET
A	VEGETABLE SPRING ROLL	ALL DIETS (VEG)
B	BBQ CHICKEN	ORD/MOS/H
C	MIXED GRILL	ORD
	TUESDAY	
A	TOMATO AND ONION PASTA BAKE	ALL DIETS (VEG)
B	SPICY BEEF RIB	ORD/MOS
C	HAM AND CHEESE PASTA BAKE	ORD/H
	WEDNESDAY	
A	FRIED RICE AND VEGETABLES	ALL DIETS
B	POACHED EGG	ORD/MOS/H/VEG
C	FRIED EGG	ORD/MOS/VEG
	THURSDAY	
A	VEGETABLE PATTIE	ALL DIETS
B	ROAST PORK	ORD/H
C	ROAST BEEF	ORD/MOS/H
	FRIDAY	
A	VEGETABLE SAUSAGE ROLL	ALL DIETS
B	CHICKEN FRIED RICE	ORD/MOS/H
C	BAKED SAUSAGE ROLL	ORD
	SATURDAY	
A	CREAMY VEGETABLE PIE	ALL DIETS
B	COTTAGE PIE	ORD/MOS/H
C	—	
	SUNDAY	
A	SPICY VEGETABLE BAKE	ALL DIETS
B	ROAST BEEF e YORKSHIRE PUDDING	ORD/MOS
C	ROAST TURKEY e STUFFING	ORD/MOS/H

WEEK 1   LUNCH MENU

CHOICE	MONDAY	DIET
A	VEGETABLE FINGERS	ALL DIETS
B	FISH CAKES e TOMATO SAUCE	VEG/MOS/ORD
C	BEEF CHOW MEIN	MOS/ORD/H

	TUESDAY	
A	RATATOUILLE e MUSHROOMS	ALL DIETS
B	FISH IN TOMATO e BASIL SAUCE	VEG/MOS/ORD/H
C	LAMB STIFFADO	MOS/ORD

	WEDNESDAY	
A	SPICY VEGETABLE CURRY	ALL DIETS
B	CHICKEN TIKKA MASALA	MOS/ORD/H
C	PORK e APPLE SAUCE	ORD/H

	THURSDAY	
A	SWEET e SOUR VEGETABLES	ALL DIETS
B	CHICKEN STEAK IN BATTER	MOS/ORD/H
C	SWEET AND SOUR PORK	ORD/H

	FRIDAY	
A	VEGETABLE GRILL	ALL DIETS
B	OVEN BAKED FISH	VEG/MOS/ORD/H
C	CORNISH PASTIE	MOS/ORD

	SATURDAY	
A	VEGETABLE CUTLET	ALL DIETS
B	ROAST CHICKEN	MOS/ORD/H
C	—	

	SUNDAY	
A	CURRIED BEANS	ALL DIETS
B	CHEESE AND FRUIT	VEG/MOS/ORD/H
C	CHEESE AND CORNED BEEF	ORD

WEEK 5 LUNCH MENU

CHOICE	MONDAY	DIET
A	VEGETABLE CURRY	ORD|VG|V|MOS|H
B	CHICKEN STEAK	ORD|MOS|H
C	CURRIED LAMB	ORD|MOS
	TUESDAY	
A	SOYA BOLOGNAISE	ORD|VG|V|MOS|H
B	SAUSAGES IN ONION GRAVY	ORD|MOS
C	SPAGHETTI BOLOGNAISE	ORD|MOS|H
	WEDNESDAY	
A	GARLIC AND VEGTABLE STEAK	ORD|VG|V|MOS|H
B	PANE PORK CHOP	ORD
C	POACHED FISH IN PEPPER e TOM	ORD|VG|MOS|H
	THURSDAY	
A	JERK VEGETABLES RICE e COCUNUT	ORD|VG|V|MOS|H
B	CHEESE AND ONION FLAN	ORD|VG|MOS
C	JERK CHICKEN RICE e PEAS	ORD|MOS|H
	FRIDAY	
A	CREAMY VEGTABLE PIE	ORD|VG|V|MOS|H
B	PAN FRIED FISH	ORD|VG|MOS
C	STEAK AND KIDNEY PIE	ORD|MOS
	SATURDAY	
A	VEGETABLE BURGER AND ROLL	ORD|VG|V|MOS|H
B	BEEF BURGER AND ROLL	ORD|MOS
C	‐ ‐ ‐ ‐	
	SUNDAY	
A	BOMBAY POTATOES	ORD|VG|V|MOS
B	CHEESE AND FRUIT	ORD|VG|MOS|H
C	CORNED BEEF e CHEESE	ORD|MOS

ORD = ORDINARY   MOS = MOSLEM
V = VEGAN   H = HEALTHY OPTION
      VG = VEGETARIAN

But today, Tony tells me, there's a special on the menu: shepherd's pie. Now I am a world expert on shepherd's pie, as it has, for the past twenty years, been the main dish at my Christmas party. I've eaten shepherd's pie at the Ivy, the Savoy and even Club 21 in New York, but I have never seen anything like Belmarsh's version of that particular dish. The meat, if it is meat, is glued to the potato, and then deposited on your plastic plate in one large blob, resembling a Turner Prize entry. If submitted, I feel confident it would be shortlisted.

Tony adds, 'I do apologize, my Lord, but we're out of Krug. However, Belmarsh has a rare vintage tap water 2001, with added bromide.' I settle for creamy vegetable pie, an unripe apple and a glass of Highland Spring (49p).

3.18 pm

An officer comes to pick me up and escort me to the Deputy Governor's office. Once again, I feel like an errant schoolboy who is off to visit the headmaster. Once again the headmaster is half my age.

Mr Leader introduces himself and tells me he has some good news and some bad news. He begins by explaining that, because Emma Nicholson wrote to Scotland Yard demanding an inquiry into the collecting and distribution of funds raised for the Kurds, I will have to remain a C-cat prisoner, and will not be reinstated as a D-cat until the police have completed their investigation. On the word of one vengeful woman, I have to suffer further injustice.

The good news, he tells me, is that I will not be going to Camphill on the Isle of Wight, but will be sent to Elmer in Kent, and as soon as my D-cat has been reinstated, I will move on to Springhill. I complain bitterly about the first decision, but quickly come to realize that Mr Leader isn't going to budge. He even accuses me of 'having an attitude' when I attempt to enter a debate on the subject. He wouldn't last very long in the House of Commons.

'It wasn't my fault,' he claims. 'It was the police's decision to instigate an inquiry.'

4.00 pm

Association. David (life imprisonment, possession of a gun) is the only person watching the cricket on television. I pull up a chair and join him. It's raining, so they're showing the highlights of the first two innings. I almost forget my worries, despite the fact that if I was 'on the out', I wouldn't be watching the replay, I would be at the ground, sitting under an umbrella.

6.00 pm

I skip supper and continue writing, which causes a riot, or near riot. I didn't realize that Paul has to tick off every name from the four spurs, and if the ticks don't tally with the number of prisoners, the authorities assume someone has escaped. The truth is that I've only tried to escape supper.

Mr Weedon arrives outside my cell. I look up from my desk and put down my pen.

'You haven't had any supper, Archer,' he says.

'No, I just couldn't face it.'

'That's a reportable offence.'

'What, not eating?' I ask in disbelief.

'Yes, the Governor will want to know if you're on hunger strike.'

'I never thought of that,' I said. 'Will it get me out of here?'

'No, it will get you back on the hospital wing.'

'Anything but that. What do I have to do?'

'Eat something.'

I pick up my plastic plate and go downstairs. Paul and the whole hotplate team are waiting, and greet me with a round of applause with added cries of, 'Good evening, my Lord, your usual table.' I select one boiled potato, have my name ticked off, and return to my cell. The system feels safe again. The rebel has conformed.

7.00 pm

I have a visit from Tony (marijuana only, escaped to France) and he asks if I'd like to join him in his cell on the second floor, as if he were inviting a colleague to pop into his office for a chat about the latest sales figures.

When you enter a prisoner's cell, you immediately gain an impression of the type of person they are. Fletch has books and pamphlets strewn all over the place that will assist new prisoners to get through their first few days. Del Boy has tobacco, phone-cards and food, and only he knows what else under the bed, as he's the spur's 'insider dealer'. Billy's shelves are packed with academic books and files relating to his degree course. Paul has a wall covered in nude pictures, mostly Chinese, and Michael only has photos of his family, mainly of his wife and six-month-old child.

Tony is a mature man, fifty-four, and his shelves are littered with books on quantum mechanics, a lifelong hobby. On his bed is a copy of today's *Times*, which, when he has read it, will be passed on to Billy; reading a paper a day late when you have an eighteen-year sentence is somehow not that important. In a corner of the room is a large stack of old copies of the *Financial*

Times. I already have a feeling Tony's story is going to be a little different.

He tells me that he comes from a middle-class family, had a good upbringing, and a happy childhood. His father was a senior manager with a top life-assurance fund, and his mother a housewife. He attended the local grammar school, where he obtained twelve O-levels, four A-levels and an S-level, and was offered a place at London University, but his father wanted him to be an actuary. Within a year of qualifying he knew that wasn't how he wanted to spend his life, and decided to open a butcher's shop with an old school friend. He married his friend's sister, and they have two children (a daughter who recently took a first-class honours degree at Bristol, and a son who is sixteen and, as I write, boarding at a well-known public school).

By the age of thirty, Tony had become fed up with the hours a butcher has to endure; at the slaughterhouse by three every morning, and then not closing the shop until six at night. He sold out at the age of thirty-five and, having more than enough money, decided to retire. Within weeks he was bored, so he invested in a Jaguar dealership, and proceeded to make a second fortune during the Thatcher years. Once again, he sold out, once again determined to retire, because he was seeing so little of his family, and his wife was threatening to leave him. But it wasn't too long before he needed to find something to occupy his time, so he bought a rundown pub in the East End. Tony thought this would be a distracting hobby until he ended up with fourteen pubs, and a wife whom he hardly saw.

He sold out once more. Having parted from his wife, he found himself a new partner, a woman of thirty-seven who ran her own family business. Tony was forty-five at the time. He moved in with her and quickly discovered that the family business was drugs. The family concentrated on marijuana and wouldn't touch anything hard. There's more than a large enough market out there not to bother with hard drugs, he assures me. Tony made it clear from the start that he had no interest in drugs, and was wealthy enough not to have anything to do with the family business.

The problem of living with this lady, he explained, was that he quickly discovered how incompetently the family firm was being run, so he began to pass on to his partner some simple business maxims. As the months went by he found that he was becoming more and more embroiled, until he ended up as titular MD. The following year they tripled their profits.

'Meat, cars, pubs, Jeffrey,' he said, 'marijuana is no different. For me it was just another business that needed to be run properly. I shouldn't have become involved,' he admits, 'but I was bored, and annoyed by how incompetent her and her family were and to be fair, she was good in bed.'

Now here is the real rub. Tony was sentenced to twelve years for a crime he didn't commit. But he does admit quite openly that they could have nailed him for a similar crime several times over. He was apparently visiting a house he owned to collect the rent from a tenant who had failed to pay a penny for the past six months when the police burst in. They found a fifty-kilo package of marijuana hidden in a cupboard under the stairs, and charged him with being a supplier. He actually knew nothing about that particular stash, and was innocent of the charges laid against him, but guilty of several other similar offences. So he doesn't complain, and accepts his punishment. Very British.

After Tony had served three and a half years, they moved him to Ford Open, a D-cat prison, from where he visited Paris, as already recorded in this diary. He then moved on to Mijas in Spain, and found a job as an engineer, but a friend shafted him – a sort of Ted Francis, he says – 'so I was arrested and spent sixteen months in a Spanish jail, while my extradition papers were being sorted out. They finally sent me back to Belmarsh, where I will remain until I've completed my sentence.' He reminds me that no one has ever escaped from Belmarsh.

'But what happened to the girl?' I ask.

'She got the house, all my money and has never been charged with any offence.' He smiles, and doesn't appear to be bitter about it. 'I can always make money again,' he says. 'That won't be a problem, and I feel sure there will be other women.'

Tony is being considered for parole at the present time, but doesn't get on well with his probation officer. He claims she doesn't appreciate his sense of humour. He warns me to make sure I treat whoever they allocate to my case with respect, because this single individual can be the deciding factor as to whether you should be released or remain locked up in prison.

'So what will you do once you are released?' I ask.

He smiles and extracts a file secreted at the back of his cupboard. 'I'm going to sell agricultural equipment to the Senegalese.' He produces sheet after sheet of financial forecasts on Senegal's agricultural requirements, along with grants the British government will advance to help subsidize that particular industry.

'I wouldn't be surprised if you make a fourth fortune,' I tell him after studying the papers.

'Only women will stop me,' he says. 'I do love them so.'

'Lock-up,' is bellowed from the ground floor. I thank Tony for his company, leave his office, and return to my cell.

8.00 pm

I check over my script for the day and then spend a couple of hours reading my mail. If people go on sending me Bibles and prayer books, I'll be able to open a religious bookshop.

I try to find out the close-of-play cricket score, but have to settle for *Any Questions*. Ken Clarke is very forthright about the iniquity of my sentence, which is brave, remembering he's standing for the leadership of the Tory Party.

10.00 pm

Still no rap music, so for three nights running I can sleep soundly.

DAY 17   SATURDAY 4 AUGUST 2001

6.18 am

Woke several times during the night, not caused by any noise, but simply because I drank too much water yesterday. Cup a Soup (chicken, 22p), Oxo (9p) and a bottle of Highland Spring (69p). Still, I don't have to go that far for the lavatory.

The Alsatians wake me again just after six. Write for two hours.

8.30 am

On a Saturday morning, you are not only allowed to leave your cell, but you also get a cooked breakfast. Egg, beans and chips. I still avoid the chips. Tony selects two fried eggs and the most recently heated beans for me. They taste good.

9.00 am

Association. I seek out Fletch to check over the script I wrote yesterday on drugs. He verifies everything William Keane has told me, and then adds, 'Have you heard of China White?'

'No,' I reply, wondering if it's Wedgwood or Royal Doulton.

'China White was a shipment of pure heroin from the Golden Triangle that turned up in Glasgow a couple of years ago. It was so pure [97 per cent] that fifteen registered addicts died within days of injecting it, and then the stuff began to spread south, killing users right across the country. All prison governors sent out official warnings to inmates, telling them to weaken any dosage of heroin they had recently been supplied with. (See insert.) Come to my cell and I'll show you some literature on the subject.'

Back in his cell, Fletch checks through some papers in a file marked DRUGS. He then hands over several pamphlets and postcards that are given to all suspected drug takers the day they enter prison. It was the first time I'd seen any of this material. They include *The Detox Handbook, A User's Guide to Getting off Opiates* (second edition), *The Methadone Handbook* (fifth edition), *Cannabis* (ninth edition), a pamphlet on HIV, Hepatitis B and C, along with six coloured cards: Injecting and Infections (illustrated):

1) **Cannabis** – marijuana, puff, blow, draw, weed, shit, hash, spliff, tackle, wacky, ganja.
2) **Acid and magic mushrooms** – mushies, 'shrooms (LSD).
3) **Amphetamines** – speed, wizz, uppers, billy, amph, sulphate.
4) **Ecstasy** – E, doves, disco biscuits, echoes, hug drug, burgers, fantasy.
5) **Cocaine** – coke, charlie, snow, C.
6) **Heroin** – smack, gear, brown, horse, junk, scag, jack.

There are several slang names for each drug according to which part of the country you live in. The Misuse of Drugs Act divides illegal drugs into three classes, and provides for maximum penalties of between two and fourteen years.

	Drug type	Maximum penalties
Class A	**Amphetamines (Speed)** *if prepared for injection*	**Possession**: 7 years' prison and/or a fine
	Cocaine and Crack	**Possession with intent to supply, or supply:** life imprisonment and/or a fine
	Ecstasy (and drugs similar to ecstasy)	
	Heroin	
	LSD (Acid)	
	Magic Mushrooms *if prepared for use*	
Class B	**Amphetamines (Speed)** **Cannabis***	**Possession:** 5 years' prison and/or a fine
		Possession with intent to supply, or supply: 14 years' prison and/or a fine
Class C	**Anabolic Steroids**	**Possession:** 2 years' prison and/or a fine
	Benzodiazepines (e.g. temazepam, flunitrazepam, Valium)	**Possession with intent to supply, or supply:** 5 years' prison and/or a fine

Fletch tells me that we have our own heroin dealer on the spur, and he knows exactly who his customers are. There are fifty-eight prisoners on our spur and eleven of them are, or have been, on heroin and forty-one of them are currently taking drugs.

I'm about to leave when I see five roses on his window sill. Fletch is obviously a man who likes to have flowers in his room. I look at the little bunch more closely. He makes the petals out

---

* Recently downgraded to Class C.

HMP BELMARSH

GOVERNOR'S NOTICE TO INMATES NO: 64/2001

**POSSIBLE BATCH OF CONTAMINATED HEROIN
AT RISK OF CAUSING SEVERE SYSTEMIC SEPSIS
IN INJECTING DRUG USERS**

All inmates will be aware that possession, or use, of any controlled drug is an offence against prison discipline. However, any inmate who chooses to ignore this should be aware of possible health risks associated with injecting drugs.

It is possible that parts of a batch of heroin, which may have been responsible for a number of deaths in Scotland, Ireland and various parts of England last year, may be circulating on the drugs market again.

Any inmate who injects drugs is therefore placing himself at extreme risk.

GOVERNOR

of bread, and the raindrop effect on the red petals are grains of sugar. He paints them with a brush made up of hairs that have fallen out of a shaving brush. They are attached to the end of a pencil with the aid of a rubber band. He finally produces the colour by using a wet brush and applying it to the end of a red crayon. He's made six of these bread roses and planted them in a bread roll, as he's not allowed a flower pot because when broken it could be used as a weapon.

'Why won't they let you have a paintbox?' I ask.

'No boxes or tins are allowed in Belmarsh,' he explains, 'because they can also be turned into a weapon and weapons are a massive problem for the screws. They have to allow you a new Bic razor every day, otherwise all the cons would be unshaven. Last month a con glued two Bic razor blades to the end of a toothbrush, caught someone in the shower and left him with a scar across his face that no plastic surgeon will be able to disguise. Whenever you open a can of anything,' Fletch continues, 'you have to tip the contents out onto a plate, and pass the empty can back to an officer, as you could cut someone's throat with the serrated edge of the lid. However,' Fletch adds, 'there are still many other ways a determined prisoner can make himself a weapon.' I don't interrupt his flow.

'For example,' he continues, 'you could hit someone over the head with your steel Thermos flask. You could pour the hot water from your Thermos over another prisoner; you could remove one of the iron struts from under your bed and you'd have a crude knife; I've even seen someone's throat cut with a sharpened phonecard. Fletch picks up his plastic lavatory brush. 'One prisoner quite recently used his razor supply to shave down the handle [nine inches in length] so that he turned his bog brush into a sword, and then in the middle of the night stabbed his cell-mate to death.'

'But that would only ensure that he remained in prison for the rest of his life,' I reminded him.

'He already had a life sentence,' said Fletch without emotion. 'If a prisoner is determined to kill his cell-mate or even another prisoner, it's all too easy, because once you're banged up, the screws can't spend all night checking what's taking place on the other side of the iron door.'

Only two weeks ago I would have been appalled, horrified, disgusted by this matter-of-fact conversation. Am I already becoming anaesthetized, numbed by anything other than the most horrific?

When I leave Fletch's cell, Colin (football hooligan) is waiting to see me. He hands me a copy of his rewritten critique on Frank McCourt's latest book, *Tis*, as well as a poem that he's written. Colin offers me a banana, not my usual fee for editing, but a fair exchange in the circumstances.

I return to my cell and immediately commit to paper everything Fletch has told me.

12 noon

Lunch. Tony has selected a jacket potato covered in grated cheese. I eat his offering slowly while listening to the cricket on the radio. England have already collapsed, and were all out for 161 in their second innings, leaving Australia to chase a total of 156 to win the match and retain the Ashes. I leave the radio on, kidding myself that if Gough and Caddick make an early breakthrough, we could be in with a chance. Wrong again.

3.00 pm

Exercise. I haven't been out of the building for three days, and decide I must get some fresh air. After being searched, I step out into the yard, and immediately spot the two tearaways who threatened me the last time I took some exercise. They're perched up against the wire at the far end of the yard, skulking. I glance behind to find Billy and Colin are tracking me. Billy adds the helpful comment, 'You need a haircut, Jeffrey.' He's right.

I'm joined on the walk by Peter Fabri, who is all smiles. He's out on Monday, to be reunited with his wife and six-week-old child. As I have been writing about him this week, I check over my facts. 'You were offered a thousand pounds to beat up a witness, in a trial due to be heard at the Bailey in the near future?'

'Even that's changed since I last saw you,' said Peter. 'He's now offering me forty thousand to bump off the witness. He told me that he's made a profit of two hundred thousand on the crime for which he's been charged, so he reckons it's worth forty to have the only witness snuffed out. You know,' says Peter, 'I think if I was in this place for another fortnight, he'd be offering me a hundred grand.'

Home Secretary, I hope you're still paying attention.

Peter remains with me for three more circuits of the yard before he returns to his friends – three other prisoners with sentences of six weeks or less. I continue walking and notice that Billy and Colin have been replaced by Paul and Del Boy. I spot Fletch standing in the far corner. He likes corners, because from such a vantage point he can view his private domain. It becomes clear he has a protection rota working on my behalf, and I feel sure the officers loitering on the far side of the yard are only too aware of what he's up to.

I pass William Keane leaning against the wire fence chatting to his brother. He jumps up and runs across to join me. Paul and Del Boy immediately take a pace forward, and only relax when I put my arm round William's shoulder. After all, I haven't let anyone know which one of those sitting round the perimeter is the cause of problem.

Once again, I use the time to check the facts that William told me in the workshop. He corrects a couple of errors on the price of cocaine and once again explains how pure heroin is diluted/cut before becoming a joey or bags. When he has completed this explanation, I ask him what he intends to do when he's released in twelve weeks' time.

'Salvage,' he says.

'Salvage?' I repeat, thinking this must have something to do with shipping.

'Yes, I'm going to buy old cars, patch them up, see that they get their MOT certificate and then sell them on the estates round here.'

'Can you make an honest living doing that?' I ask.

'I hope so, Jeffrey,' he says, 'because I'm getting too old [thirty-five] for this game. In any case, there's enough of my family costing the government a thousand pounds a week without me adding to the taxpayers' burden. Mind you,' he adds, 'if they had let me out last week I might have ended up murdering someone.' I stop in my tracks and Paul and Del Boy almost collide into the back of me. 'My brother's just told me' – he points to the other side of the yard where a tall, dark-haired young man is leaning up against the fence – 'that my sister Brinie was kidnapped last week and repeatedly raped, and as most of the family are in jail, there's not a lot we can do about it.' I'm speechless. 'The bastard's been arrested, so we must hope that the judge gets it right this time.' He pauses. 'But for his sake let's hope he doesn't end up in the same prison as one of my brothers. Mind you,' he adds, 'don't bet on that, because the odds are quite short.'

As we turn the corner, he points up to a tower block in the distance. 'That's where another of my brothers, Patrick, fell to his death.' (Have you noticed that Mrs Keane has named all her sons after saints or kings?) 'You'll remember, that was the occasion when the whole family attended his funeral along with half the Metropolitan Police.' He pauses. 'They're now saying he might have been pushed. I'll find out more as soon as I get out of here, and if he was . . .' What hope has this man of remaining on the outside? I ask myself. I found out a few months later when I met up with yet another brother.*

When William slips off to rejoin his brother, I notice that Del Boy and Paul have been replaced by Tony and David. David (fifty-five, in possession of a gun) is overweight, out of shape and finding it difficult to keep up with me. The next person to join me is a young, bright, full-of-life West Indian, whose story I will not repeat, as it is the mirror image of Peter Fabri's. He too has no intention of even going through an amber light once they release him from Belmarsh. However, he admits that he's learnt a lot more about crime than he knew before he came into prison. He's also been introduced to drugs in the cell he shares with two other inmates.

'I'm clean, man,' he says rubbing his hands together. 'But one of the guys in my cell who's due out next week has tried heroin for the first time. He's hooked now, man, I tell you he's hooked.'

Are you still paying attention, Home Secretary?

I pass the tearaways, who haven't moved an inch for the past forty minutes and have to satisfy themselves with malevolent

---

* This sentence was added while I was editing Volume One, and had finally been transferred to a D-cat. As of today, 1 October 2002, William Keane is still 'on the out'.

stares. I feel confident that they aren't going to risk anything this time.

At four o'clock, we're called back in block by block. Several prisoners who are leaving next week including Peter (offered forty thousand to murder a witness), Denzil (come and see me when I'm a star), and Liam (do I need a barrister or should I represent myself?) come across to shake hands and wish me luck. I pray that they never see the inside of Belmarsh again.

4.00 pm

When I arrive back in my cell there's another stack of letters waiting for me on my bed, three stacks to be accurate. I start reading. It's turned out to be most helpful that the censor has to open every one. I'm particularly touched by a letter Freddie Forsyth sent to the *Daily Telegraph* about the length of my sentence, and the money I've raised for charity. The editor did not publish it.

5.49 pm

Last call for supper. Spur one is always let out first and called back last, because most of the inmates are lifers who will spend more time inside than anyone else on the block. It's prison logic and works because the turnover on the other three spurs is between 10 per cent and 20 per cent a week, so no one thinks of complaining.

I stroll down to the hotplate, but only so that my name can be ticked off, pick up a Thermos of hot water and return to my cell. I make myself a Cup a Soup (tomato, 22p) and eat a Mars Bar (31p) and a prison apple, as I continue to read today's letters.

DAY 17

6.30 pm

I pick up Colin's critique of Frank McCourt's *'Tis*. The improvement is marked since I read his first effort. He has now sorted out how much of the story he should reveal before he offers his critical opinion. This is obviously a man who once you tell him something is able to respond immediately. I then turn my attention to his poem.

Education Belmarsh

Open the labyrinths of time
blow out the cobwebs
and past life of crime
full of knowledge held within
the mind is truly a wonderful thing

It can be educated, it can be evolved
without education
can the problems be solved?

While locked away, there is plenty to see
they entrap the body
but your mind is still free
to wander the universe
and grow like a tree

So go to the library
and pick up a book
watch your mind grow
while other cons look

It's not down to them
to make you move
so go ahead read
and your mind will improve

Colin Kitto, May 2001
House Block 1, HMP Belmarsh

218

This poem reveals a lot about the man, where he's going, and where he's come from. I feel sure that before he completes his sentence, he will have that degree from Ruskin College. And don't forget, this is a man who couldn't read or write before he came into prison.

There is a polite knock on the door and I look up to see one of the officers peering through my little oblong window. He asks if I would be willing to sign autographs for his two daughters, Joanna and Stephanie. 'They both enjoy your books,' he explains, before adding, 'though I must admit I've never read one.'

He doesn't unlock the cell door, just pushes two pieces of paper underneath. This puzzles me. I later learn that an officer cannot unlock a cell door if he is not on duty. Once he has retrieved them, he adds, 'I'll be off for the first part of next week, so if I don't see you again, good luck with your appeal.'

7.30 pm

I begin reading a book of short stories that had been left on a table by the TV on the ground floor. It's titled *The Fallen* and the author, John MacKenna, is someone I've not read before. He's no storyteller, as so often the Irish are, but oh, don't I wish I could write as lyrically as he does.

9.50 pm

I finish reading John MacKenna in one sitting (on the end of the bed) – what assured, confident prose, with an intimate feel for his countrymen and his country. I conclude that God gave the Irish the gift of language and threw in some potatoes as an afterthought.

DAY 18　　　　SUNDAY 5 AUGUST 2001

6.00 am

Another good night's sleep.

Yesterday I wrote for six hours, three sessions of two, read for three – including my letters – and slept for eight. Out there where you are, five hours' sleep was always enough. In truth, the writing is an attempt to fill the day and night with nonstop activity. I feel sorry for the prisoners who have to occupy those same hours and cannot read or write.

8.00 am

Breakfast. A treat. Egg and beans on toast, two mornings in a row. I don't grumble. I've always liked egg and beans.

9.30 am

I hear the officer on duty holler up from his desk, 'RCs.'

I press the buzzer which switches on a red light outside my door – known as room service – to indicate that I wish to attend chapel. No one comes to unlock the door. When they yell a second time, I press the buzzer again, but still no one responds.

After they call a third time, I start banging on my door, but to no avail. Although I am not a Roman Catholic, after William Keane's recommendation I would have liked to hear Father Kevin preach.

10.03 am

Mr Cousins finally appears to explain that as I am not a Roman Catholic, the officer on duty assumed my name had been put on the wrong list, and transferred me back to C of E. I curse under my breath as I don't want to be put on report. A curse for me is damn or blast.

'You can always go next week,' he says. 'Just be sure you give us enough notice.'

'I was rather hoping that I won't be with you next week,' I tell him.

He smiles. I can see he accepts that his colleague has made a mistake, so I decide this might be a good opportunity to ask about the drug problem as seen from the other side of the iron barrier. To my surprise Mr Cousins is frank – almost enthusiastic – about passing on his views.

Mr Cousins doesn't try to pretend that there isn't a drug problem in prisons. Only a fool would. He also admits that because of the casual way officers have to conduct their searches, it's not that difficult to transfer drugs from spur to spur, block to block and even across a table during family visits.

'Not many officers,' he tells me, 'would relish the idea of having to use rubber gloves to search up prisoners' backsides three or four times a day. And even if we did go to that extreme, the inmates would simply swallow the drugs, which would only cause even more problems. But,' he continues, 'we still do everything in our power to prevent and cure, and we've even had a few successes.' He pauses. 'But not that many.'

When a prisoner enters Belmarsh he has an MDT. This takes the form of a urine sample which is all very well until it comes to heroin, a substance that can be flushed through the body within twenty-four hours. Most other drugs leave some signs in the blood or urine for at least four weeks. On the day they enter prison, 70 per cent of inmates show positive signs of being on drugs, and even with the twenty-four-hour proviso, 20 per cent indicate of heroin. If Mr Cousins had revealed these figures to me only three weeks ago, he would have left me staggered by the enormity of the problem. Already I have come to accept such revelations as part of everyday prison life.

'Our biggest success rate,' continues Mr Cousins, 'is among those prisoners coming up for parole, because towards the end of their sentence, they have to report regularly to the Voluntary Drug Testing Centre – there's one in every prison – to prove they are no longer dependent on drugs, which will be entered on their report, and can play a part in shortening their sentence. What we don't know,' he adds, 'is how many of them go straight back on drugs the moment they're released. But in recent years we've taken a more positive step to stamp out the problem.

'In 1994 we set up a Dedicated Search Team, known as the ghost-busters, who can move in at any time without warning and search individual cells, even whole spurs or blocks. This team of officers was specifically formed following the IRA escape from Whitemoor Prison in '93, but after all the terrorists were sent back to Ulster following the Good Friday Agreement, the unit switched their concentration from terrorism to the misuse of illegal substances. They've had remarkable success in uncovering large amounts of drugs and charging offenders. But,' he reflects, 'I have to admit the percentage of drug takers still hasn't fallen, and I speak as someone who was once a member of the DST. Mind you,' he adds, 'it's just possible that standing still is in itself an achievement.'

I hear the first bellow from downstairs for C of E, and thank Mr Cousins for his tutorial and his candour.

10.30 am

I report to the middle floor and join those prisoners who wish to attend the morning service. We line up and are put through the usual search before being escorted to the chapel. Malcolm (Salvation Army officer) is surprised to see me, as I had told him yesterday that I intended to go and hear Father Kevin preach. Before I take my seat in the second row, I give him the précised version of how I ended up back in his flock.

No backing group this week, just taped music, which makes Malcolm's job all the more difficult, especially when it comes to stopping the chattering in the back six rows. My eyes settle on a couple of Lebanese drug dealers sitting in the far corner at the back. They are deep in conversation. I know that they're from different spurs, so they obviously use this weekly get together to exchange information on their clients. Every time I turn to observe them, their heads are bowed, but not in prayer.

The sermon this week is taken from Luke. It's the one about the ninety-nine sheep who are safely locked up in the pen while the shepherd goes off in search of the one that's strayed. Malcolm faces a congregation of over two hundred that have strayed, and most of them have absolutely no intention of returning to the pen.

But he somehow battles on, working assiduously on the first six rows, with whom he is having some success. Towards the end of the service his wife reads a lesson, and after the blessing,

DAY 18

Malcolm asks his congregation if they would like to come forward and sign the pledge. At least forty prisoners rise from their places and begin to walk forward. They are individually blessed before signing the register.

They look to me like the same forty who offered themselves up for salvation last week, but I am still in no doubt that Malcolm and his wife are performing a worthwhile mission.

12 noon

Lunch. I settle for more beans on toast, an apple and a mug of water. I suppose I should have stated the obvious at some point, namely that alcohol is forbidden, which is no great loss to me as I rarely drink more than a glass of red wine in the evening.

4.00 pm

Association. I run downstairs, phonecard in hand, thirteen units left for Mary. A long queue has already formed behind the two payphones. One of the disadvantages of living on the top floor.

I turn my attention to the large TV in the middle of the room. Several prisoners are watching the Sunday afternoon film with Tom Hanks and Geena Davis. It's the story of a women's baseball team set up in 1942 when, because of the outbreak of the Second World War, the men's teams had to be disbanded.

I turn my head every few moments but the queue doesn't seem to diminish, so I go on watching the film. Several prisoners join me during the next half-hour.

Del Boy (murder) to tell me he's somehow purloined a copy of the weekly menu for my diary.

Fletch (murder) wants to come to my cell at six and read something to me. I ask if he could make it seven, as I'll still be writing at six. 'Suits me,' he says, 'I'm not going anywhere.' Prison humour.

Tony (marijauna only, escaped to Paris) then leans across and asks if the identification of one of his girlfriends could be removed from yesterday's script. I agree and make a note of her name.

I spot Billy (murder) and recommend the book of short stories by John MacKenna, but he walks on past me without a word. I suppose by now I shouldn't be surprised by anything.

Dennis (GBH, large bag of toiletries) taps me on the shoulder. He starts to tell me about the visit of his son on his first birthday, and how he can't wait to get out and be with his wife and children. Join the club.

Miah (murder) who's the spur hair cutter – known, not surprisingly, as Sweeny Todd – says he can fit me in at seven tomorrow evening. I thank him, explaining that I must have my hair cut before Mary and the boys come to visit me on Thursday. When I glance round, the queue for the phone is down to three. I leave Mr Hanks and Ms Davis and take my place at the back.

Just as I reach the front, another prisoner barges in front of me. As he's a double murderer and his right hand has HATE tattooed on his four fingers, I decide not to mention that I thought I was next in line. Ten minutes later he slams down the phone and walks away effing and blinding. I slowly dial the Cambridge number to be reminded that I only have thirteen units left on my card. Mary answers. She sounds cheerful and is full of news. The trip to Dresden went well, and while she was abroad she felt her life was getting back to normal. Perhaps because the German tabloids aren't quite that obsessed with my incarceration. William accompanied her, and was a tower of strength, while James stayed behind to manage the shop.

Ten units left.

Mary tells me that following Emma Nicholson's letter the police are hinting that they may not even carry out an inquiry. I explain that despite this I've been reassigned to C-cat status, and would like my D-cat back as quickly as possible. She assures me that Ramona and James are working on it.

Seven units left.

I tell her how many letters I have been receiving every day, and she counters by saying that she's getting so many at home and in London that there just aren't enough hours to answer them all. She's designed an all-purpose reply so that she can get on with her own work.

Five units left.

Mary adds that not only are my friends remaining constant, but she's had a dozen offers to join them on their yachts or in their holiday homes, and one even on safari. I've always known we had foul-weather friends, but both of us have been touched by the public's overwhelming support.

Three units left.

I let her know that I've already written over forty thousand words of the diary, but can't be sure what my regular readers will make of it. Mary says she's looking forward to reading an early draft, and will give me a candid view. She is incapable of doing anything else.

One unit left.

We begin our goodbyes, and she reminds me I will be seeing her and the boys on Thursday, something to look forward to.

'Do you know how much I . . .'

All units used up. I hear a click, and the phone goes dead.

As I walk away, I hear the words 'Lock-up' bellowed out from just behind me. As reliable as Big Ben, if not as melodious. It has to be five o'clock.

6.05 pm

Supper. I go down to the hotplate and have my name ticked off by Paul – prisoners do a seven-day week with no holidays or bank holidays – and pick up a Thermos flask of hot water and a chocolate ice cream. Back in my cell I make a Cup a Soup (mushroom, 22p), eat another Mars Bar (31p), and enjoy a chocolate ice-cream (prison rations).

7.00 pm

I'm washing my plastic plate in the basin when there's a knock on the door. The cell door is pulled open by an officer to reveal the massive frame of Fletch standing in the doorway. I had quite forgotten he was coming to read something to me.

I smile. 'Welcome,' I say, like the spider to the fly. The first thing I notice is that he's clutching a small green notebook, not unlike the type we used to write our essays in at school. After a brief chat about which prison I'm likely to be sent to, and his opinion of Mr Leader, the Deputy Governor, he turns to the real purpose of his visit.

'I wonder if I might be allowed to read something to you?' he asks.

'Of course,' I reply, not sure if it's to be an essay, a poem, or even the first chapter of a novel. I settle on the bed while Fletch sits in the plastic chair (prisoners are only allowed one chair per cell). He places the little lined book on my desk, opens it at the first page, and begins to read.

If I had the descriptive powers of Greene and the narrative drive of Hemingway, I still could not do justice to the emotions I went through during the next twenty minutes; revulsion, anger, sympathy, incredulity, and finally inadequacy. Fletch turns another page, tears welling up in his eyes, as he forces himself to resurrect the demons of his past. By the time he comes to the last page, this giant of a man is a quivering wreck, and of all the emotions I can summon up to express my true feelings, anger prevails. When Fletch closes the little green book, we both remain silent for some time.

Once I'm calm enough to speak, I thank him for the confidence he has shown in allowing me to share such a terrible secret.

'I've never allowed anyone in Belmarsh to read this,' he says, tapping the little green book. 'But perhaps now you can appreciate why I won't be appealing against my sentence. I don't need the whole world to know what I've been through,' he adds in a whisper, 'so it will go with me to my grave.' I nod my understanding and promise to keep his confidence.

10.00 pm

I can't sleep. What Fletch has read to me could not have been made up. It's so dreadful that it has to be true. I sleep for a few minutes and then wake again. Fletch has tried to put the past behind him by devoting his time and energy to being a Listener, helping others, by sharing his room with a bullied prisoner, a drug addict, or someone likely to be a victim of sexual abuse.

I fall asleep. I wake again. It's pitch black outside my little cell window and I begin to feel that Fletch could give an even greater service if his story were more widely known, and the truth exposed. Then people like me who have led such naive and sheltered lives could surely have the blinkers lifted from their eyes.

I decide as soon as they let me out of my cell, that I will tell him that I've changed my mind. I'm going to suggest that he could do far more good by revealing what actually happened to him than by remaining silent. In all, I think I've woken five or six times during the night, my thoughts always returning to Fletch. But one comment he made above all others burns in my mind, *Fifty per cent of prisoners in Belmarsh can tell you variations of the same story. Jeffrey, my case is not unique.*

I decide I must use whatever persuasive powers I possess to get him to agree to publish, without reservation, everything in that little green book.

DAY 19   MONDAY 6 AUGUST 2001

5.17 am

I've spent a sleepless night. I rise early and write for two hours. When I've finished, I pace around my cell, aware that if only I had held onto Fletch's little green notebook I could have spent the time considering his words in greater detail.

8.00 am

I know I've eaten a bowl of Corn Pops from my Variety pack, because I can see the little empty box in the waste-paper bin, but I can't remember when. I go on pacing.

9.00 am

An officer opens the cell door. I rush down to the ground floor, only to discover that Fletch is always let out at eight so that he can go straight to the workshops and have everything set up and ready before the other prisoners arrive. Because of the length of his sentence, it's a real job for him. He's the works manager, and can earn up to forty pounds a week. I could go along to the workshops, but with seventy or eighty other prisoners hanging around, I wouldn't be able to hold a private conversation with him. Tony tells me Fletch will be back for dinner at twelve, when he'll have an hour off before returning to the workshops at one. I'll have to wait.

When I return to my cell, I find a letter has been pushed under my door. It's from Billy Little (murder). He apologizes for being offhand with me during Association the previous evening. August is always a bad month for him, he explains, and he's not very good company for a number of reasons:

I last saw my son in August 1998, my favourite gran died in August, the heinous act of murder that I committed took place on August 22, 1998. As you can imagine, I have a lot on my mind.

I can't begin to imagine, which I admit when I reply to his letter. He continues ...

During this period, I tend to spend a long time inside myself. This could give an impression to those who don't know me of being ignorant and unapproachable. For this I apologise.

By this time tomorrow, you'll be sunning it up by the pool, or that's how Springhill will feel in comparison to Hellmarsh. In a way, you've been lucky to have spent only a short period here, a period in which you've brought the normal inertia of prison to life.

Over the last three weeks you will have felt the resentment of other prisoners who feel strongly that equality should be practised even in prisons. You no doubt recall the Gilbert and Sullivan quote from *The Gondoliers* – when everybody is some-body, then nobody is anybody.

I think what I'm trying to say is that your status, friend-liness and willingness to help and advise others has not gone unnoticed by those who are destined to spend a great deal longer incarcerated.

For this I thank you, and for your inspiration to press me to think more seriously about my writing. I would like to take you up on your offer to keep in touch, and in particular to check over my first novel.

I'll be resident here for another month or two, or three, before they move me onto a first stage lifer main centre [*Billy has been at Belmarsh for two years and seven months*] I'll let you know my address once I've settled. My number is at the bottom of this letter.

You are Primus Inter Pares

Yours,

Billy (BX7974)

I sit down at my table and reply immediately.

12 noon

When Fletch arrives back from the workshops, he finds me waiting by his cell door. He steps inside and invites me to join him.* I ask if I might be allowed to borrow his notebook so that I can consider more carefully the piece he read to me the previous evening. He hesitates for a moment, then goes to a shelf above his bed, burrows around and extracts the little green notebook. He hands it over without comment.

I grab an apple for lunch and return to my cell. Reading Fletch's story is no less painful. I go over it three times before pacing up and down. My problem will be getting him to agree to publish his words in this diary.

---

* You never enter someone else's cell unless invited to do so.

3.37 pm

Mr Bentley opens my cell door to let me know that the Deputy Governor wishes to see me. As I am escorted to Mr Leader's office, I can only wonder what bad news he will have to impart this time. Am I to be sent to Parkhurst or Brixton, or have they settled on Dartmoor? When the Deputy Governor's door is opened, I am greeted with a warm smile. Mr Leader's demeanour and manner are completely different from our last meeting. He is welcoming and friendly, which leads me to hope that he is the bearer of better news.

He tells me that he has just heard from the Home Office that I will not be going to Camphill on the Isle of Wight or Elmer in Kent, but Wayland. I frown. I've never heard of Wayland.

'It's in Norfolk,' he tells me. 'C-cat and very relaxed. I've already spoken to the Governor,' he adds, 'and only one other member of my staff is aware of your destination.' I take this as a broad hint that it might be wise not to tell anyone else on the spur of my destination, unless I want to be accompanied throughout the entire journey by the national press. I nod and realize why he has taken the unusual step of seeing me alone. I'm about to ask him a question, when he answers it.

'We plan to move you on Thursday.'

Only three more days at Hellmarsh, is my first reaction, and, after asking him several more questions, I thank him and return to my cell unescorted. I spend the next hour considering every word Mr Leader has said. I recall asking him which he would rather be going to, Wayland or the Isle of Wight. 'Wayland,' he'd replied without hesitation.

In prison it's necessary to fight each battle day by day if you're eventually going to win the war. First it was getting off the medical centre and onto Block Three. Then was escaping

DAY 19

Block Three (Beirut) and being moved to Block One to live among a more mature group of prisoners. Next was being transferred from Belmarsh to a C-cat prison. Now I shall be pressing to regain my D-cat status, so that I can leave Wayland as quickly as possible for an open prison. But that's tomorrow's battle. Several prisoners have 'Take each day as it comes' scrawled on their walls.

4.00 pm

I try to write, but so much has already happened today that I find it hard to concentrate. I munch a bar of Cadbury's Fruit and Nut (32p), and drink a mug of Evian (49p) topped up with Robinson's blackcurrant juice (97p).

6.00 pm

Supper. I catch Fletch in the queue for the hotplate, and he agrees to join me in my cell at seven. 'Miah [murder] is cutting my hair at seven,' I tell him, 'so could we make it seven fifteen? I can't afford to miss the appointment, as I'm still hoping for a visit from my wife on Thursday.'

7.00 pm

Association. I sit patiently in a chair on number 2 landing waiting for Miah. He doesn't turn up on time to cut my hair, so I return to my cell and wait for Fletch. He does arrive on time and takes a seat on the end of the bed. He doesn't bother with any preamble.

'You can include my piece in your book if you want to,' he says, 'and if you do, let's hope it does some good.'

I tell him that if a national newspaper serializes the diary, then his words will be read by millions of people, and the politicians will have to finally stop pretending that it isn't happening or they will simply be guilty by association.

We begin to go through the script line by line, filling in details such as names, times and places so that the casual reader can properly follow the sequence of events. Tony (marijuana only) joins us a few minutes later. It turns out that he's the only other person to have read the piece, and it also becomes clear that it was on his advice that Fletch decided not only to write about his experiences, but to allow a wider audience to read them.

There's a knock on the door. It's Miah (murder). He apologizes about missing his appointment to cut my hair, but he's only just finished his spell on the hotplate. He explains that he can't fit me in tomorrow, because of his work schedule, but he could cut my hair during Association on Wednesday. I warn him that if he fails to keep the appointment on Wednesday, I'll kill him, as my wife is coming to visit me on Thursday and I must look my best. Miah laughs, bows and leaves us. *I'll kill him.* I said it without thinking, and to a convicted murderer. Miah is 5ft 4in, and I doubt if he weighs ten stone; the man he murdered was 6ft 2in and weighed 220 pounds. Strange world I'm living in.

Fletch, Tony and I continue to go over the script, and when we've completed the task, Fletch stands up and shakes me by the hand to show the deal has been agreed.

8.00 pm

For the next two hours, I transcribe out Fletch's words, adding to the script only when he has given me specific details, background or names. By the time I've completed the last sentence, I'm even more angry than I was when he read the piece to me last night.

10.00 pm

I lie awake in my thin, hard prison bed, my head resting on my thinner, harder prison pillow, and wonder how decent normal people will react to Fletch's story. For here is a man of whom any one of us might say, there but for the grace of God go I.

These are the words of the prisoner known as Fletch (murder, life imprisonment, minimum sentence twenty-two years).

> My name is . . .* I am thirty-eight years old and serving a life sentence for a murder I did not commit, but I only wish I had.
>
> My whole life has been a fuck-up from the start. I was born in Morriston in Wales and although I loved my family, I have only had six real relationships in my life, or as real as I felt they could be. The sort of relationship you want to rush home to, and regret leaving in the morning when you return to work.
>
> I met my wife when I was seventeen, and even today would happily die for her. We had a twenty-year relationship, though both of us had other lovers during that time. Of the six relationships I've had, two have been with men, which is where the complication begins. Because of years of sexual abuse I suffered during my childhood, I have never really enjoyed sex, whether it be with a man or a woman.
>
> Even today, I detest sexual contact and accept that it is what has caused the break-up of my relationships. I was always able to perform, and perform it was, but in truth it was nothing more than a chore, and I gained no gratification from it.

_____

*I presented Fletch's original script to my publisher in full; names and places have been necessarily omitted from the final text.

I never felt able to tell my wife the truth about my past, despite the twenty years we'd shared together. It's so easy to claim you've been abused, and shift the blame onto someone else. It's so easy to claim you couldn't prevent it, and it's also virtually impossible to prove it.

The truth is that I had no idea that what I was experiencing wasn't the norm. Wasn't every child going through this? My childhood ended at the age of nine when I was sent to a home.

Overnight I became a plaything for those who were employed to care for me, those in power. They even managed to secure a place of safety order from a court so I couldn't be moved and *they* could carry on abusing me.

During the 1970s corporal punishment was common in children's homes. For some of the staff it was simply the way they got their kicks. First they caned little boys until they screamed, and then they buggered us until we were senseless; not until then did they stop. Nine other children from that home can confirm this statement; two are married with children of their own, two are gay, five are in jail.

Two of the five in jail are serving life sentences for murder.

After a time, the abuse becomes a form of love and affection, because if you didn't want to be caned, or belted with a strap, you give in and quickly accept the alternative, sexual abuse. By the age of twelve, I knew more about perversion and violence than any one of you reading this have ever read about, or even seen in films, let alone experienced.

By the age of twelve, I had been abused by the staff at my home in ——, local social workers, care staff and a probation officer. All of these professions attract paedophiles, and although they are in the minority (20%), they are well aware of each other, and they network together, and most frightening of all, they protect each other.

I know a child who was articulate enough by the age of fourteen to tell the authorities what he was being put through, so they just moved him around the country from home to home before anyone could begin an investigation, while other paedophiles carried on abusing him.

At the age of thirteen I ran away and made my way to —. When I reached —, I began sleeping rough in —. It was there that I first met a man called *****, who offered me somewhere to sleep. That night he got me drunk, not too difficult when you're only thirteen. He raped me, and after that began renting me out to like-minded men. Whenever you read in the tabloid press about rent boys for sale, don't assume that they do it by choice, or even that they're paid. They are often locked up, and controlled like any other prostitute, and have little or no say in what happens to their life.

***** controlled me for about six months, bringing to the flat judges, schoolmasters, police officers, politicians and other upstanding citizens who are the back-bone of our country (I can tell you of birthmarks, wounds and peculiarities for almost every one of these men).

One night in the West End when I was still thirteen, I was arrested by the police while ***** was trying to sell me to a customer. I was collected from the nick by a social worker, who took me to a children's home in —. The home was run by a magistrate, ******. For the next fourteen days, [he] buggered me night and day before issuing a court order that I should be returned to [my original children's home], where it was back to caning and systematic abuse.

After a couple of months, I was transferred to —, a hospital for emotionally disturbed children. Once again, the staff abused me and this time they had a more effective weapon than caning. They threatened to apply EST, electric shock treatment should I try to resist. I ran away again, returning to —, and have lived there ever since. I was only fourteen at the time, and ***** soon caught up with me. This time he installed me in the flat of a friend where seven or eight men would bugger me on a daily basis. One or two liked to whip me with a belt, while others punched me, this could be before, during or after having sex. When they eventually stopped, they occasionally left a small present (money or gift) on my pillow. This wasn't much use, because I never got out of the flat, unless I was accompanied by *****.

By the age of fifteen, I was sniffing glue, regularly getting drunk, and having sex with countless men. But it didn't hurt any more. I felt nothing, it was all just part of my daily life.

This life, if that's what you can call it, continued for another four years, during which time I was photographed for porn magazines, and appeared in porn films.

By the age of eighteen, I no longer served any purpose for these men, so I was thrown out onto the street and left to fend for myself. That was when I committed my first crime. Burglary of a department store, Lillywhites. I was arrested and sent to Borstal for six months. When I was released, I continued with a life of crime, I wasn't exactly trained for anything else.

By now I was six foot one and weighed 190 pounds, so didn't find it difficult to get a job in security, which is so often on the fringes of crime.

In 1980, at the age of eighteen, I met my future wife, who had no idea what my real job was, or that for twelve years I had been sexually abused. During the next five years, we had two sons, and twelve years later in 1997, we decided to get married.

I was already earning a good living as a criminal, and everything went well until I was arrested in 1997 for DSS fraud. I had been making false claims in several names for several years, to the tune of £2.8 million, for which I received a three year sentence, which caused my marriage to be put off.

During my time in jail, I began by letter and telephone, to let my wife know that I had for sometime been involved in a life of crime. But it wasn't until I was released that I revealed to her any details of the sexual abuse I had been put through. Her reaction was immediate and hostile. She was disgusted, and reviled, and said she couldn't understand why I hadn't reported these men to the authorities. What authorities were there for me to report to? 'I was only nine years old when it all began. After all it was the authorities who were buggering me,' I told her, 'and by the age of eighteen, when I was no longer of any use to them, they threw me out onto the streets.'

She couldn't come to terms with it. So I was rejected once again, and this time it was by someone I cared for, which made it far worse. She described me as a filthy person, who allowed dirty old men to rape me, because I wanted love and affection. There was no way I could begin to make her understand.

By being open and honest, I had lost the one person I truly loved. My life had been ruined by these evil men, and now they had even robbed me of my wife and two children.

All I now wanted was to kill the five monsters who were responsible, and then die in the hands of the police.

There were five paedophiles who had taken away my life, so I planned to take away theirs. I quickly discovered that two of them had already died, so there were only three left for me to deal with. Their names were ***, **** and *****.

I carefully planned how I would kill them, and then later die in the hands of the police.

I drove down to —and kidnapped *** and brought him back to —, leaving him at my flat with three friends, who agreed to guard him while I returned to the coast to pick up *****. I then planned to go onto — and collect **** and bring them both back to —.

I arrived back in — at one-thirty in the afternoon, when *****'s next door neighbour told me that I had just missed him. I phoned — to warn them that I would be late, because I couldn't risk grabbing him in broad daylight. It was then that they told me the news. They had already killed ***.

I was enraged. I've always been a cold person emotionally, but I cried on the journey back to London, because I had wanted to kill *** myself. I had needed to cleanse myself of these three evil men, and all I had now was a dead body on my hands and three terrified associates.

I drove back to —, breaking the speed limit most of the way. On arrival, I cleaned all the finger-prints from my flat and told the others that I would deal with ***** and **** in my own way. That was when the police burst in; twenty-four armed officers pinned the three of us to the ground, handcuffed and arrested me.

I discovered later that ***** had already phoned the police and told them he feared for his life. I gave my solicitor all the details, and he said that because I was in __ at the time of ***'s death, they wouldn't charge me with murder, but they could charge me with conspiracy to murder. They charged me with murder, and I was sentenced to a minimum of twenty-two years.

Yes, I am doing a twenty-two year sentence for a crime I didn't commit. I only wish I had, and I also wish I had killed **** and ***** at the same time.

I am now a Listener at Belmarsh and feel useful for the first time in my life. I know I've saved one life, and hopefully helped many others.

My demons still haunt me, of course they do, but I somehow keep them at bay. I won't complete my twenty-two year sentence, but I will choose the time and manner of my death.*

It's only shame that prevents me from contacting anyone I know. A feeling of worthlessness, a dirty little rent boy that allowed older men to use, beat and abuse him, because he needed to be loved, and no longer cared what happened to

---

* Fletch subsequently attempted to commit suicide on 7 January 2002.

him. How can I ever expect my wife, my children, or my family to understand?

I hope by telling this story, I may save someone else from the horror I've been put through, so that that person will never be visited by the same demons, and worse, will not end up in jail on a charge of murder.

11.23 pm

I go to bed asking myself should the man known as Fletch have to spend the rest of his life in jail? If the answer is yes, don't we perhaps have some responsibility to the next generation, to ensure that there aren't other children whose lives will end by the age of nine?

DAY 20   TUESDAY 7 AUGUST 2001

6.16 am

I have a better night's sleep. Perhaps Fletch's allowing his story to be committed to paper has helped. I write for two hours.

8.00 am

Breakfast. Frosties and the last dribble from the second carton of long-life milk. Not quite enough left to soak my cereal. Canteen provisions due in today, and as I'm leaving on Thursday I will be able to repay all my bubbles: Del Boy (water and biscuits), Tony (Mars Bar), and Colin (stamps, twelve first-class).

10.00 am

Association. I am strolling around the ground floor, when I notice that one of the prisoners, Joseph (murder), is playing pool. He's by far the best player on the spur and occasionally clears the table. This morning he's missing simple shots that even I would sink. I lean against the wall and watch him more carefully. He has that distant look on his face, so common among lifers.

When the match is over and the cues have been passed on

to waiting inmates, I comment on his standard of play. I think the word I select is rubbish.

'I've got something on my mind, Jeff,' he says, still distant.

'Anything I can help with?' I ask.

'No thanks, it's a family matter.'

11.00 am

I see that my name is chalked up on the board for a legal visit from my solicitor, Tony Morton-Hooper.

Over the years I have found that professional relationships fall into two categories. The ones that remain professional, and the ones when you become friends. Tony falls firmly into the second category. We have a mutual love of athletics – he has represented many track stars over the years – and despite a considerable age difference, we relax in each other's company.

We meet up in one of those small rooms where I come in from one side and am locked in, and moments later he enters by a door on the opposite side, and is also locked in. The first thing I notice is that Tony is wearing a thick yellow rubber band around his wrist; it will allow him to eventually escape, but for the next hour he is also incarcerated.

Tony begins by telling me that Wayland Prison is certain to be a far more relaxed regime than Belmarsh, and as good a place as any to be until I am reinstated as a Category D prisoner. I ask Tony what the latest is on that subject.

'It's all good news,' he tells me. 'The media have worked out that you have nothing to answer, and we've been through your files and they show the matter was raised in Parliament in 1991 when Lynda Chalker was Overseas Development Minister and she gave a robust reply. She also wrote you a long letter on the subject at the time.' He slides both the letter and the Parliamentary reply across the table.

'Was Ms Nicholson an MP then?' I ask.

'She most certainly was,' says Tony, 'and more importantly, a full investigation was carried out by the Foreign Office, so we're sending all the relevant papers to the police and pointing out that a second inquiry would be an irresponsible waste of public money.'

'So can I sue her for libel?' I ask.

'Not yet,' he replies. 'I talked to the police yesterday, and although they will not release a copy of the letter she sent to them, they made it clear that the accusations were such that they had no choice but to follow them up.'

'If we issue a writ, will she have to release that letter?'

'Yes. It would automatically become part of the evidence.'

'Then we must have grounds to sue her.'

'Not yet,' Tony repeats. 'Let's wait for the police to drop their inquiry before we take any further action. And that could be quite soon, as Radio 4's *Today Programme* have been in touch with Mary. Their research team are also convinced that you have no case to answer, and they want her to appear on the programme.'

'Of course they do,' I say, 'because all they'll want to talk to her about is my appeal.'

'As long as she doesn't discuss the case while an appeal is pending, I'm in favour of her doing the interview.'

'She could of course quote from Lynda Chalker's letter and the Parliamentary reply,' I suggest.

'Why not?' says Tony. 'But let's proceed slowly, step by step.'

'Not something I'm good at,' I admit. 'I prefer proceeding quickly, leap by leap.'

Tony then removes some papers from his briefcase, and tells

me that the appeal will be officially lodged tomorrow. I have to sign an agreement to appeal against sentence, and another against conviction.

Tony would give me a fifty–fifty chance of having the verdict overturned if it were not for the 'Archer' factor. 'If you weren't involved it would be thrown out without a second thought. There wouldn't even have been a trial in the first place.' He puts the odds even higher on getting the sentence reduced. Mr Justice Potts's comment that mine was the worst example of perjury he had ever known has been greeted by the legal profession with raised eyebrows.*

We then turn to the subject of the prison diary, of which I have now completed fifty thousand words, and I warn him that it's going to come as a shock to most of my regular readers. He asks how I'm getting the script through to Alison, remembering this is the tightest-security prison in Europe. I remind him that I am still receiving two to three hundred letters a day, and the censors allow me to turn them round and send them back to my office the following morning, so another ten handwritten pages aren't causing the censor any concern.

'Which reminds me,' I continue, 'could you ask James to wear a cheap watch the next time he visits me, and then I can exchange my Longines.' I hadn't for a moment imagined I would end up in prison, so I was wearing my favourite watch on the day of the verdict, and after twenty years I'd be sorry if it was stolen. James has hankered after it for some time and has already asked me to leave it to him in my will (mercenary brat). 'Will can have the rest of the estate as long as I can have the watch,' James insists. Longines have stopped making that particular slim

---

* Since the court case, Dr Susan Edwards, Associate Dean of Buckingham Law School, has researched every perjury case during the last ten years.

model. Nevertheless, William had agreed to the deal as he considers the overall arrangement very satisfactory.

'I think you'd better wait until you've left Belmarsh before you start swapping watches,' advises Tony. 'And then only when you can be sure that the regulations are a little more relaxed.'

We complete all legal matters, and as he can't escape until the hour is up, we turn our thoughts to the World Athletics Championships in Edmonton, where I had hoped to be spending my summer holiday with Michael Beloff.* Tony tells me the fantastic news that Jonathan Edwards has taken the gold in the triple jump.

'He won easily,' Tony adds, 'clearing nearly eighteen metres. He's so relaxed since his gold in Sydney that I doubt if he will be beaten before the next Olympics at Athens in 2004, and even Mr Justice Potts won't be able to stop you being there to witness that.'

When the prison officer returns to open the door on Tony's side of the room, I leave him in no doubt that the number one priority is sorting out the Kurdish debacle, so that my D-cat can be reinstated as quickly as possible. I also add that I do not require any lawyers to travel to Norfolk at vast expense. They can relay messages through Mary, who's as bright as any of them. Tony smiles, agrees and shakes hands. He has the hands of a heavyweight boxer, and I suspect he'd survive well in prison. They release him, but as I don't have a yellow band around my wrist, I slump back into the seat on the other side of the table and wait.

---

* Michael Beloff QC is an Olympic judge and is allowed to take a guest to the World Championships. His wife Judith has never shown much interest in watching half-naked men running around a track, so we've been a regular 'item' at such events for the past thirty years.

On the circuit we're known as Jack Lemmon and Walter Matthau.

DAY 20

12 noon

In the lunch queue – always a great place to catch up on the gossip – Fletch briefs me on Joseph's problem. I now understand why he couldn't pot a ball on the pool table this morning. When I reach the hotplate, Tony recommends the 'spaghetti veg-etarian', which is disguised to look like bolognaise.

'Au gratin?' I suggest.

'Of course, my Lord. Liam, fetch his lordship the grated Parmesan.' A small plastic packet of grated cheese is produced from under the hotplate, opened in front of the duty officer and sprinkled over my spaghetti. This is greeted with a huge round of applause from the prisoners and laughter from the officers. In a lifer's day, this is an event.

Back in my cell I enjoy the dish, but then it is my twentieth day on prison rations. I've been able to take another notch in on my belt. So I reckon I've lost about half a stone.

2.00 pm

When the cell door is opened again, I dash down to the middle level, already dressed in my gym kit, and keep running on the spot by the barred gate. This time I am ticked off the select list of eight from our spur. After a search followed by a route march to another part of the building I've never been to before we arrive in a changing room where we are all supplied with a light blue singlet and dark blue shorts. This, I assume, is just in case any prisoner has spent time at both Oxford and Cambridge.

The gym is divided into two sections. The larger room is the size of a basketball court, where twelve of the prisoners play six-a-side football. We currently have one former Arsenal and Brent-ford player residing at Belmarsh. There is also a weight-lifting room, about a third of the size of the basketball court, where forty-seven sweaty, tattooed, rippling muscled youths pump iron, so that when they get out of here they will be even more capable of causing grievous bodily harm.

The room is so packed that you can't move more than a few feet without bumping into someone. There are two running machines, two rowing machines and two step machines, in which the younger prisoners show scant interest. I do a six-minute warm-up on the running machine at five miles an hour, which affords me an excellent view of what's going on in the centre of the room. The forty-seven fit young men are pumping weights, not a pretty sight, especially as most of them are sim-ply on an ego trip to establish their status among the other prisoners on the block. I wonder how many of them have worked out that Fletch, Tony, Billy and Del Boy carry the most influence on our spur, and not one of them would be able to locate the gym.

Once I've completed 2,000 metres on the rower in nine minutes, I move on to some light weight-training, before doing another ten minutes on the running machine at eight miles an hour. While I'm running, I begin to notice that many of the lifers have a poor posture. Their backs are not straight, and they swing their shoulders when lifting heavy weights rather than use their arm muscles properly. The two officers in charge can't do much more than keep an eye on what's going on in both rooms. It would be far more sensible to have three sessions of gym each day, with fewer bodies present, then the coach would be able to fulfil a more worthwhile role than just acting as a babysitter. I put this suggestion to one of the officers, and once again they fall back on 'staff shortages'.

After ten minutes on the running machine, I return to the weights before ending on the step machine. When the officer bellows out, 'Last five minutes,' I move on to stretching exercises and complete in one hour exactly the same programme as I would have gone through in the basement gym of my London flat. The only difference is that there, there wouldn't be a murderer in sight.

Back in the changing room, I feel I've done well until Dennis (former Arsenal and Brentford player) joins me and reports that he's scored six goals. I congratulate him, and ask him if it's true that he's been selected to captain Belmarsh for the annual fixture against Holloway? This brings far more laughter and cheers than it deserves, although half the prisoners immediately volunteer to play in goal.

'No, thank you,' says Dennis. 'I've got enough women problems as it is.'

'But you told me that you'd had a good visit on Sunday when your wife and child came to see you?'

'One of my wives,' corrects Dennis. 'And one of my children.'

'How many others do you have?' I ask.

'Three of both,' he admits.

'But that's bigamy,' I say. 'Or possibly trigamy.'

'Get a life, Jeff, I'm not married to any of them. There are no fathers hanging around with shotguns nowadays. They're all partners, not wives. Like a company chairman, I have several shareholders. Thank God I'm banged up in here at the moment,' he adds, 'because if they called an AGM I wouldn't want to have to explain why they won't be getting a dividend this year.'

It's clear that none of the other prisoners listening to this conversation consider it at all unusual, let alone reprehensible. Heaven knows what Britain will be like in fifty years' time if everyone has three 'wives' but doesn't bother to actually marry any of them.

When I return to my cell, I find my canteen order waiting

for me on the bed. I drink mug after mug of water, followed by two KitKats, before going off to have a shower.

4.00 pm

Association. My first assignment is to return a bottle of water to Del Boy (Highland Spring) before searching out Tony to hand over a Mars Bar, followed by Colin (twelve first-class stamps). Having cleared my debts (bubbles) – no one charges me double bubble – I join the other prisoners seated around the television. They're watching the World Athletics Championships. An officer called Mr Hughes brings me up to date on progress so far. After the first day of the decathlon, Macey is leading by one point, and is preparing for his heat in the 110 metre hurdles, which is the first event of the second day. I tell Mr Hughes that Edmonton was where I had originally planned to spend my summer holiday.

'I see that there are a lot of empty seats in the stands,' says Mr Hughes, 'but I find it hard to believe that they're all now in prison.'

Just as Macey goes to his blocks, I spot Joseph standing in the corner – a man who prefers the centre of the room. I leave the World Athletics Championships for a moment to join him.

'Any news of your son?' I ask.

'No.' He looks surprised that I've found out about his problem. 'I've phoned his mother, who says that he's under arrest and she's trying to get in touch with the British Consul. They've got him banged up in a local jail. What are prisons like in Cyprus?' he asks.

'I've no idea,' I tell him. 'Until they sent me to Belmarsh, I didn't know what they were like in England. Just be thankful it's not Turkey. What's he been charged with?'

'Nothing. They found him asleep in a house where some locals had been smoking cannabis, but they've warned him he could end up with a seven-year sentence.'

'Not if he was asleep, surely,' I suggest. 'How old is he?'

'Eighteen, and what makes it worse, while I'm stuck in here I can't do anything about it. My wife says she'll phone the Governor the moment she hears anything.'

'Good luck,' I say, and return to the athletics.

Mr Hughes tells me I missed Macey. He came second in his heat, in a new personal best. 'You can't ask for more than a PB from any athlete,' says Roger Black, the BBC commentator, and adds, 'Stay with us, because it's going to be an exciting day here in Edmonton.'

'Lock-up,' shouts the officer behind the desk at the other end of the room.

I politely point out to the officer that Roger Black has told us we must stay with him.

'Mr Black is there, and I'm here,' comes back the immediate reply, 'so it's lock-up, Archer.'

6.00 pm

Supper. I am now in possession of two tins of Prince's ham (49p), so I take one down to the hotplate to have it opened. Tony adds two carefully selected potatoes, which makes a veritable feast when accompanied by a mug of blackcurrant juice.

After supper I return to work on my script, when suddenly the door is opened by an officer I have never seen before.

'Good evening,' he says. 'I know you'll be off soon, so I wonder if you'd be kind enough to sign this book for my wife. The bookshop told me that it was your latest.'

'I would be happy to do so,' I tell him, 'but it's not mine. It's been written by Geoffrey Archer. I spell my name with a J. It's a problem we've both had for years.'

He looks a little surprised, and then says, 'I'll take it back and get it changed. See you at the same time tomorrow.'

Once I've finished today's script, I read three letters Alison has handed over to Tony Morton-Hooper. One of them is from Victoria Barnsley, the Chairman of my publisher, HarperCollins, saying that she is looking forward to reading *In the Lap of the Gods*, and goes on to let me know that Adrian Bourne, who has taken care of me since Eddie Bell, the former Chairman, left the company, will be taking early retirement. I'll miss them both as they have played such an important role in my publishing career.

The second letter is from my young researcher, Johann Hari, to tell me that he's nearly ready to go over his notes for *In the Lap of the Gods*.* Though he points out that he still prefers the original title *Serendipity*.

The last letter is from Stephan Shakespeare, who was my chief of staff when I stood as Conservative candidate for Mayor of London. His loyalty since the day I resigned brings to mind that wonderful poem by Kipling, 'The Thousandth Man'. Among the many views Stephan expresses with confidence is that Iain Duncan Smith will win the election for Leader of the Conservative Party by a mile.

We won't have to wait much longer to find out if he's right.

---

* The novel has since been renamed *Sons of Fortune*, and I have since changed my publisher to Macmillan.

DAY 21   WEDNESDAY 8 AUGUST 2001

6.03 am

This will be my last full day at Belmarsh. I mustn't make it too obvious, otherwise the press will be waiting outside the gate, and then accompany us all the way to Norfolk. I sit down at my desk and write for two hours.

8.07 am

Breakfast. Shreddies, UHT milk, and an apple. I empty the box of Shreddies, just enough for two helpings.

9.00 am

I am standing in my gym kit, ready for my final session, when Ms Williamson unlocks my cell door and asks if I'm prepared to do another creative-writing class.

'When do you have it planned for?' I ask, not wanting her to know that this is my last day, and I've somehow managed to get myself on the gym rota.

She looks at her watch. 'In about half an hour,' she replies.

I curse under my breath, change out of my gym kit into

slacks and a rather becoming Tiger T-shirt which Will packed for me the day I was sentenced. On my way to the classroom, I pass Joseph at the pool table. He's potting everything in sight, and looking rather pleased with himself.

'Any more news about Justin?' I enquire.

He smiles. 'They've deported him.' He glances at his watch. 'He should be landing at Heathrow in about an hour.' He pots a red. 'His mother will be there to meet him, and I've told her to give him a good clip round the ear.' He sinks a yellow. 'She won't, of course,' he adds with a grin.

'That's good news,' I tell him, and continue my unescorted journey to the classroom.

When I arrive I find Mr Anders, the visiting teacher, waiting for me. He looks a bit put out, so I immediately ask him how he would like to play it.

'Had you anything planned?' he asks.

'Nothing in particular,' I tell him. 'Last week we agreed that the group would bring in something they had written to read to the class, and then we would all discuss it. But not if you had anything else in mind.'

'No, no, that sounds fine.'

This week, nine prisoners and three members of staff turn up. Four of them have remembered to bring along some written work: Colin reads his critique of Frank McCourt's latest book, Tony takes us through his essay on prison reform, which is part of the syllabus for Ruskin College, Oxford, Terry reads a chapter of his novel and we end with Billy's piece on his reaction to hearing that he'd been sentenced to life, and his innermost thoughts during the hours that followed. I choose Billy's work to end on, because as before it was in a different class to any other contribution. I end the session with a few words about the discipline of writing, aware that I would not be with them this time tomorrow. I'm confident that at least three of the group will continue with their projects after I've departed, and that in time Billy's efforts will be published. I will be the first in the queue for a signed copy.

On the way back to my cell, I bump into Liam, who, when he's on the hotplate, always tries to slip me a second ice-cream. He thrusts out his hand and says, 'I just wanted to say goodbye.' I turn red; I've not said a word to anybody following my meeting with Mr Leader, so how has Liam found out?

'Who told you?' I asked.

'The police,' he replied. 'They've agreed to bail, so I'm being released this morning. My solicitor says that probably means that they are going to drop all the charges.'

'I'm delighted,' I tell him. 'But how long have you been in jail?'

'Three and a half months.'

Three and a half months Liam has been locked up in Belmarsh waiting to find out that the police are probably going to drop all the charges. I wish him well before he moves on to shake another well-wisher by the hand. What was he charged with? Perverting the course of justice. A taped phone conversation was the main evidence, which the court has now ruled inadmissible.

Once I'm back on the spur, I phone Alison to let her know that ten more days of the diary are on their way. She tells me that the letters are still pouring in, and she'll forward on to Wayland those from close friends. I then warn her I'm running out of writing pads; could she send a dozen on to Wayland along with a couple of boxes of felt-tip pens? Interesting how I use the word dozen without thinking, despite the fact that decimalization has been with us for over thirty years. In another thirty years, will my grandchildren take the euro for granted and wonder what all the fuss was about?

12 noon

Lunch. Egg and beans, my favourite prison food, but this time I only get one egg because there's an officer sitting where Paul is usually placed. However, Tony still manages a few extra beans.

2.00 pm

I begin writing again, only to be interrupted by three officers marching into my cell: Mr Weedon, accompanied by Mr Abbott and Mr Cook, who are ominously wearing rubber gloves. Mr Weedon explains that this is a cell search – known by prisoners as a spin – and for obvious reasons it has to be carried out without any warning.

'What are you searching for?' I ask.

'Guns, knives, razor blades, drugs, and anything that is against prison regulations. I am the supervising officer,' says Mr Weedon, 'because Mr Cook and Mr Abbott are being tested for the National Vocational Qualification, and this search is part of that test. We will start with a strip-search,' he says, keeping a straight face.

I stand in the middle of my tiny cell, and remove my Tiger T-shirt. I then hold my hands high in the air before being asked to turn a complete circle. Mr Abbott then tells me to rub my hands vigorously through my hair, which I do – hidden drugs, just in case you haven't worked it out. This completed, I am allowed to put my T-shirt back on. Mr Cook then asks me to take off my shoes, socks, trousers and pants, all of which are carefully examined by the two junior officers wearing rubber gloves. Once again I am asked to turn a full circle before they invite me to lift the soles of my feet so they can check if I'm wearing any plasters that might be concealing drugs. There are no plasters, so they tell me to get dressed.

'I will now accompany you to a waiting room while your cell is being searched,' Mr Weedon says. 'But first I must ask if you are in possession of anything that belongs to another prisoner, such as guns, knives or drugs?'

'Yes, I have an essay written by Tony Croft, and a poem by Billy Little.' I rummage around in a drawer, and hand them over. They look quickly through them before passing them back. 'I am also in possession of a library book,' I say, trying not to smirk. They try hard not to rise, but they still turn the pages and shake the book about. (Drugs or money this time.)

'I see it's due back today, Archer, so make sure you return it by lock-up, because we wouldn't want you to be fined, would we.' Mr Weedon scores a point.

'How kind of you to forewarn me,' I say.

'Before we can begin a thorough search of your cell,' continues Mr Abbott, 'I have to ask, are you in possession of any legal papers that you do not wish us to read?'

'No,' I reply.

'Thank you,' says Mr Weedon. 'That completes this part of the exercise. Your cell will now be searched by two other officers.'

I was told later that this is done simply for their self-protection, so that should they come across anything illegal, with four officers involved, two sets of two, it becomes a lot more difficult for a prisoner to claim 'it's a set-up, guv' and that whatever was found had been planted.

'Burglars!' I hear shouted by someone at the top of their voice, sounding as if it had come from a nearby cell. I look a little surprised that the officers don't all disappear at speed.

Mr Weedon smiles. 'That's us,' he says. 'We've been spotted, and it's just another prisoner warning his mates that we're out on one of our searching expeditions, so they'll have enough time to dispose of anything incriminating. You'll hear several toilets being flushed during the next few minutes and see a few packages being thrown out of the window.'

Mr Abbott and Mr Cook leave me to be replaced by Ms Taylor and Ms Lynn, who begin to search my cell.

Mr Weedon escorts me to the waiting room on the other side of the spur and locks me in. Bored, I stroll over to the window on the far side of the room, and look down on a well-kept garden. A dozen or so prisoners are planting, cutting, and weeding for a pound an hour. The inmates are all wearing yellow Day-Glo jackets, while the one supervisor is dressed casually in blue jeans and an open-necked shirt. It's a neat, well-kept garden, but then so would anyone's be, if they had a dozen gardeners at a pound an hour.

I am amused to see that one of the prisoners is clipping a hedge with a large pair of shears, quite the most lethal weapon I've seen since arriving at Belmarsh. I do hope they search his cell regularly.

Twenty minutes later I'm let out, and escorted back to Cell 30. All my clothes are in neat piles, my waste-paper bin emptied, and I have never seen my cell looking so tidy. However, the officers have removed my second pillow and the lavatory bleach that Del Boy had so thoughtfully supplied on my first day on Block One.*

6.00 pm

Supper. I take down my second tin of ham (49p) to be opened by a helper on the hotplate. Tony adds two potatoes and a

---

*Bleaching powder can be added to pure heroin, diluting its strength, thus ensuring a larger profit for the dealer. It's against regulations to have two pillows.

spoonful of peas, not all of them stuck together. After I've eaten dinner, I wash my plastic dishes before returning downstairs to join my fellow inmates for Association. I decide to tell only Fletch, Tony and Billy that I'll be leaving in the morning. Fletch said that he was aware of my imminent departure, but didn't realize it was that imminent.

Sitting in his cell along with the others feels not unlike the last day of term at school, when, having packed your trunk, you hang around in the dorm, wondering how many of your contemporaries you will keep in touch with.

Fletch tells us that he's just spent an hour with Ms Roberts, and has decided to appeal against both his sentence and verdict. I am delighted, but can't help wondering if it will affect his decision to allow the contents of the little green book to be published.

'On the contrary,' he says. 'I want the whole world to know who these evil people are and what they've done.'

'But what if they ask you to name the judges, the schoolmasters, the policemen and the politician?'

'Then I shall name them,' he says.

'And what about the other nine children who were put through the same trauma? How do you expect them to react?' Tony asks. 'After all, they must now all be in their late thirties.'

Fletch pulls out a file from his shelf and removes a sheet of paper with the names typed in a single column. 'During the next few weeks I intend to write to everyone named on this list and ask if they are willing to be interviewed by my solicitor. A couple are married and may not even have told their wives or family, one or two will not be that easy to track down, but I'm confident that several of them will back me up, and want the truth to be known.'

'What about ***, **** and *****?'

'I shall name them in court,' Fletch says firmly. '*** of course is dead, but **** and ***** are very much alive.'

Tony starts to applaud while Billy, not given to showing much outward sign of emotion, nods vigorously.

'Lock-up,' hollers someone from the front desk. I shake hands with three men who I had no idea I would meet a month ago, and wonder if I will ever see again.* I return to my cell.

When I reach the top floor, I find Mr Weedon standing by my door.

'When you get out of here,' he says, 'be sure you write it as it is. Tell them about the problems both sides are facing, the inmates and the officers, and don't pull your punches.' I'm surprised by the passion in his voice. 'But let me tell you something you can't have picked up in the three weeks you've spent with us. The turnover of prison staff is now the service's biggest problem, and it's not just because of property prices in London. Last week I lost a first-class officer who left to take up a job as a tube driver. Same pay but far less hassle, was the reason he gave. Good luck, sir,' he says, and locks me in.

9.00 pm

I begin to prepare for my imminent departure. Fletch has already warned me that there will be no official warning, just a knock on my cell door around six-thirty and a 'You're on the move, Archer, so have your things ready.' 'There's only one thing I can guarantee,' he adds. 'Once you've been down to the reception area you will be kept hanging around for at least another hour while an officer completes the paperwork.'

---

* I have already decided, once I'm released I will visit Billy (14 more years) and Fletch (19 more years) if they will allow me to.

DAY 21

9.30 pm

I read through the latest pile of letters, including ones from Mary, Will, and another from Geordie Greig, the editor of *Tatler*, who ends with the words, *There's a table booked for lunch at Le Caprice just as soon as you're out.* No fair-weather friend he.

I then check over the day's script and decide on an early night.

10.14 pm

I turn out the light on Belmarsh for the last time.

DAY 22   THURSDAY 9 AUGUST 2001

4.40 am

I wake from a restless sleep, aware that I could be called at any time. I decide to get up and write for a couple of hours.

6.43 am

I check my watch. It's six forty-three, and there's still no sign of life out there in the silent dark corridors, so I make myself some breakfast. Sugar Puffs, the last selection in my Variety pack, long-life milk and an orange.

6.51 am

I shave, wash and get dressed. After some pacing around my five-by-three cell, I begin to pack. When I say pack, I must qualify that, because you are not allowed a suitcase or a holdall; everything has to be deposited into one of HM Prisons' plastic bags.

7.14 am

I've finished packing but there is still no sign of anyone stirring. Has my transfer been postponed, cancelled even? Am I to remain

DAY 22

at Belmarsh for the rest of my life? I count every minute as I pace up and down, waiting to make my official escape. What must it be like waiting to be hanged?

7.40 am

I empty the last drop of my UHT milk into a plastic mug, eat a McVitie's biscuit, and begin to wonder if there is anyone out there. I reread Mary's and Will's letters. They cheer me up.

8.15 am

My cell door is at last opened by a Mr Knowles.

'Good morning,' he says cheerfully. 'We'll be moving you just as soon as we've got all the remand prisoners off to the Bailey.' He checks his watch. 'So I'll be back around 9.30. If you'd like to take a shower, or if there's anything else you need to do, I'll leave your door open.'

Forgive the cliché, but I breathe a sigh of relief to have it confirmed that I really am leaving. I take a shower – I've now mastered the palm, press, soap, palm, press method.

During the next hour several prisoners drop by to say farewell as the news spreads around the spur that I'm departing. Del Boy relieves me of my last bottle of water, saying he could get used to it. Once he's left, I suggest to an officer that I would like to give my radio to one of the prisoners who never gets a visit. The officer tells me that it's against the regulations.

'To give something to someone in need is against the regulations?' I query.

'Yes,' he replies. 'You may be trying to bribe him, or repay him for a supply of drugs. If you were seen giving a radio to another prisoner, you would immediately be put on report

264

and your sentence might even be lengthened by twenty-eight days.'

My problem is that I just don't think like a criminal.

I wait until the officer is out of sight, then nip downstairs and leave the radio and a few other goodies on Fletch's bed. He'll know whose needs are the greatest.

9.36 am

Mr Knowles returns to escort me to the reception area where I first appeared just three long weeks ago. I am placed in a cubicle and strip-searched, just as I was on the day I arrived. Once I've put my clothes back on, they handcuff me – only for the second time – and then lead me out of the building and into what I would describe as a Transit van. Down the left-hand side are four single seats, one behind each other. On the right-hand side is a cubicle in which the prisoner is placed like some untamed lion. Once I'm locked in, I stare out of the little window for some time, until, without any warning, the vast electric barred gates slide slowly open.

As the black Transit van trundles out of Belmarsh, I have mixed feelings. Although I am delighted and relieved to be leaving, I'm also anxious and nervous about being cast into another world, having to start anew and form fresh relationships all over again.

It has taken me three weeks to pass through Hell. Am I about to arrive in Purgatory?

WAYLAND
PURGATORY

THE THOUSANDTH MAN

One man in a thousand, Solomon says,
Will stick more close than a brother.
And it's worth while seeking him half your days
If you find him before the other.
Nine hundred and ninety-nine depend
On what the world sees in you,
But the Thousandth Man will stand your friend
With the whole round world agin you.

'Tis neither promise nor prayer nor show
Will settle the finding for 'ee
Nine hundred and ninety-nine of 'em go
By your looks, or your acts, or your glory.
But if he finds you and you find him,
The rest of the world don't matter;
For the Thousandth Man will sink or swim
With you in any water.

You can use his purse with no more talk
Than he uses yours for his spendings,
And laugh and meet in your daily walk
As though there had been no lendings.
Nine hundred and ninety-nine of 'em call
For silver and gold in their dealings;
But the Thousandth Man he's worth 'em all,
Because you can show him your feelings.

His wrong's your wrong, and his right's your right,
In season or out of season.
Stand up and back it in all men's sight –
With *that* for your only reason!
Nine hundred and ninety-nine can't bide
The shame or mocking or laughter,
But the Thousandth Man will stand by your side
To the gallows-foot – and after!

Rudyard Kipling (1865–1936)

To Mary

The thousandth woman

DAY 22 THURSDAY 9 AUGUST 2001

10.21 am

It is a glorious day: a day for watching cricket, for drinking Pimm's, for building sandcastles, for mowing the lawn. Not a day to be travelling in a sweatbox for 120 miles.

Having served twenty-one days and fourteen hours in Belmarsh, I am about to be transported to HMP Wayland, a Category C prison in Norfolk. A Group 4 van is my chauffeur-driven transport, with two cubicles for two prisoners.* I remain locked in for fifteen minutes awaiting the arrival of a second prisoner. I hear him talking, but can't see him. Is he also going to Wayland?

At last the great electric gates of Belmarsh slide open and we begin our journey east. My temporary moving residence is a compartment four feet by three with a plastic seat. I feel nauseous within ten minutes, and am covered in sweat within fifteen.

The journey to Wayland prison in Norfolk takes just over

---

* As I explained in *Volume One* of these diaries, there are four categories of prisoner: A, B, C, D. A-cat are violent and dangerous prisoners, with the possible resources (i.e. money) to escape; B-cat are violent and dangerous, but not always murderers: they might be in for GBH, ABH, manslaughter or rape, or have already served five years in an A-cat; in C-cats, the vast majority are repeat offenders or convicted of a serious, non-violent crime (i.e. drug-dealing); D-cats are usually for first offenders with no history of violence, who are likely to conform to the system, as they wish to return to society as quickly as possible.

three hours. As I peer through my tiny window I recognize the occasional familiar landmark on the Cambridge leg of the trip. Once the university city is behind us, I have to satisfy myself with a glimpse at signposts whenever we slow down at roundabouts to pinpoint where we are: Newmarket, Bury St Edmunds, Thetford. So for this particular period of my life that very special lady, Gillian Shephard, will be my Member of Parliament.

The roads become narrower and the trees taller the further east we travel. When we finally arrive at Wayland it couldn't be in starker contrast to the entrance of Belmarsh with its foreboding high walls and electric gates. And – most pleasing of all – not a member of the press in sight. We drive into the yard and come to a halt outside the reception area. I sense immediately a different atmosphere and a more casual approach by prison officers. But then their daily tariff is not gangland murderers, IRA terrorists, rapists and drug barons.

The first officer I meet as I walk into reception is Mr Knowles. Once he has completed the paperwork, he signs me over to a Mr Brown, as if I were a registered parcel. Once again, I am strip-searched before the officer empties my HMP Belmarsh plastic bag onto the counter and rummages through my possessions. He removes my dressing gown, the two large blue towels William had so thoughtfully supplied and a blue tracksuit. He informs me that they will be returned to me as soon as I am enhanced.*

'How long will that take?' I ask.

'Usually about three months,' he replies casually, as if it were

---

* Every prisoner begins life as standard and then, according to his behaviour, moves up or down. There are three levels of status: basic, standard and enhanced – and in some prisons, super-enhanced. Enhanced prisoners are afforded extra privileges. They are allowed to wear their own clothes, have longer periods out of their cell, have two extra visits per month and another £5 a week added to their weekly canteen account. So it's well worth becoming enhanced as quickly as possible.

a few grains of sand passing through an hourglass. I don't think I'll mention to Mr Brown that I'm hoping to be moved within a few days, once the police enquiry into Baroness Nicholson's complaint concerning the Simple Truth appeal has been seen for what it is.*

Mr Brown then places my beige slacks and blue shirt on one side, explaining that I won't get those back until I've been released or transferred. He replaces them with a striped blue prison shirt and a pair of jeans. After signing over my personal possessions, my photograph is taken, holding up a little black-board with the chalk letters FF 8282 under my chin, just as you've seen in films.

I am escorted by another officer to what I would describe as the quartermaster's stores. There I am handed one towel (green), one toothbrush (red), one tube of toothpaste, one comb, two Bic razors and one plastic plate, plastic bowl and plastic cutlery.

Having placed my new prison property in the plastic bag along with the few possessions I am allowed to retain, I am escorted to the induction wing. Mr Thompson, the induction officer, invites me into his office. He begins by telling me that he has been in the Prison Service for ten years, and therefore hopes he will be able to answer any questions I might have.

'You begin your life on the induction wing,' he explains, 'where you'll share a cell with another prisoner.' My heart sinks as I recall my experience at Belmarsh. I warn him that whoever I

---

*The Baroness Nicholson had written to Scotland Yard asking them to make a full enquiry into what had happened to the £57 million raised for the Kurds by the Simple Truth campaign which I spearheaded in 1991. This resulted in my being moved to a C-cat closed prison from Belmarsh rather than a D-cat open prison as originally planned. She had insinuated that not all the money had reached the Kurds, hinting that some of it may have ended up in my pocket. My D-cat status will be reinstated once the enquiry has been completed. This must be the first example, in British legal history, of someone being presumed guilty, and sentenced, even before being interviewed by the police.

share a cell with will sell his story to the tabloids. Mr Thompson laughs. How quickly will he find out? Prison would be so much more bearable if you could share a cell with someone you know. I can think of a dozen people I'd be happy to share a cell with, and more than a dozen who ought to be in one.

When Mr Thompson finishes his introductory talk, he goes on to assure me that I will be moved into a single cell on another block once I've completed my induction.*

'How long will that take?' I ask.

'We're so overcrowded at the moment,' he admits, 'that it could take anything up to a month.' He pauses. 'But in your case I hope it will be only a few days.'

Mr Thompson then describes a typical day in the life of Wayland, making it clear that prisoners spend considerably less time locked in their cells than they do at Belmarsh, which is a slight relief. He then lists the work choices: education, gardening, kitchen, workshop or wing cleaner. But he warns me that it will take a few days before this can be sorted out. Nothing is ever done today in the Prison Service, and rarely even tomorrow. He describes how the canteen works, and confirms that I will be allowed to spend £12.50 per week there. I pray that the food will be an improvement on Belmarsh. Surely it can't be worse.

Mr Thompson ends his dissertation by telling me that he's selected a quiet room-mate, who shouldn't cause me any trouble. Finally, as I have no more questions, he accompanies me out of his little office down a crowded corridor packed with young men aged between eighteen to twenty-five, who just stand around and stare at me.

---

* There are four main blocks at Wayland – A, B, C, D. The induction wing is part of A block. There is also a separate block, E. However, this is designated for sex offenders only, and is at the far end of the prison on the other side of a high wire fence.

My heart sinks when he unlocks the door. The cell is filthy and would have been the subject of a court order by the RSPCA if any animal had been discovered locked inside. The window and window sill are caked in thick dirt – not dust, months of accumulated dirt – the lavatory and the wash basin are covered not with dirt, but shit. I need to get out of here as quickly as possible. It is clear that Mr Thompson doesn't see the dirt and is oblivious to the cell's filthy condition. He leaves me alone only for a few moments before my cell-mate strolls in. He tells me his name, but his Yorkshire accent is so broad that I can't make it out and resort to checking on the cell card attached to the door.

Chris* is about my height but more stocky. He goes on talking at me, but I can understand only about one word in three. When he finally stops talking he settles down on the top bunk to read a letter from his mother while I begin to make up my bed on the bunk below. He chuckles and reads out a sentence from her letter: 'If you don't get this letter, let me know and I'll send you another one.' By the time we are let out to collect our supper I have discovered that he is serving a five-year sentence for GBH (grievous bodily harm), having stabbed his victim with a Stanley knife. This is Mr Thompson's idea of someone who isn't going to cause me any trouble.

6.00 pm

All meals are served at a hotplate, situated on the floor below. I wait patiently in a long queue only to discover that the food is every bit as bad as Belmarsh. I return to my cell empty-handed,

---

*Where prisoners have requested not to have their real names included, I have respected their wishes.

grateful that canteen orders at Wayland are on a Friday
(tomorrow). I extract a box of Sugar Puffs from my plastic bag
and fill the bowl, adding long-life milk. I munch a Belmarsh
apple and silently thank Del Boy.*

6.30 pm

Exercise: there are several differences between Belmarsh and
Wayland that are immediately apparent when you walk out into
the exercise yard. First, you are not searched, second, the distance you can cover without retracing your steps can be multi-
plied by five – about a quarter of a mile – third, the ratio of
black to white prisoners is now 30/70 – compared to 70/30 at
Belmarsh – and fourth, my arrival in Norfolk causes even more
unsolicited pointing, sniggering and loutish remarks, which only
force me to curtail my walk fifteen minutes early. I wish Mr
Justice Potts could experience this for just one day.

On the first long circuit, the salesmen move in.

'Anything you need, Jeff? Drugs, tobacco, phonecards?'

They're all quite happy to receive payment on the outside
by cheque or cash.† I explain to them all firmly that I'm not
interested, but it's clearly going to take a few days before they
realize I mean it.

When the barrow boys and second-hand salesmen have
departed empty-handed, I'm joined by a lifer who tells me he's
also sixty-one, but the difference is that he's already served
twenty-seven years in prison and still doesn't know when, if ever,

---

* See *Volume One – Belmarsh: Hell*.
† Dealers inside a prison will nominate someone 'on the out' to whom you can
send a cheque if you want a regular supply, assuming a) you have the money,
b) someone outside is willing to join in this subterfuge. 90 per cent of such
transactions are for drugs. But more of that later.

he'll be released. When I ask him what he's in for, he admits to killing a policeman. I begin a conversation with a black man on the other side of me, and the lifer melts away.

Several of the more mature prisoners turn out to be in for 'white collar' crimes: fiddling the DSS, the DTI or HM Customs. One of them, David, joins me and immediately tells me that he's serving five years.

'What for?' I ask.

'Smuggling.'

'Drugs?'

'No, spirits,' he confesses.

'I didn't realize that was against the law. I thought you could pop across to Calais and . . .'

'Yeah, you can, but not sixty-five times in sixty-five days with a two-ton lorry, carrying twenty million quid's worth of whisky.' He pauses. 'It's when you forget to cough up eight million quid in duty that the Customs and Excise become a little upset.'

A young man in his late twenties takes the place of the police murderer on the other side of me. He brags that he's been banged up in six jails during the past ten years, so if I need a Cook's tour he's the best-qualified operator.

'Why have you been sent to six jails in ten years?' I enquire.

'No one wants me,' he admits. 'I've done over two thousand burglaries since the age of nineteen, and every time they let me out, I just start up again.'

'Isn't it time to give it up, and find something more worthwhile to do?' I ask naively.

'No chance,' he replies. 'Not while I'm making over two hundred grand a year, Jeff.'

After a time, I become sick of the catcalling, so leave the exercise yard and return to my cell, more and more disillusioned,

DAY 22

more and more cynical. I don't consider young people, who are first offenders and have been charged with minor offences, should be sent to establishments like this, where one in three will end up on drugs, and one in three will commit a far more serious offence once they've received tuition from the prison professors.

The next humiliation I have to endure is prisoners queuing up silently outside my cell door to get a look at me. No 'Hi, Jeff, how are you?' Just staring and pointing, as if I'm some kind of an animal at the zoo. I sit in my cage, relieved when at eight o'clock an officer slams the doors closed.

8.00 pm

I'm just about to start writing up what has happened to me today when Chris switches on the television. First we have half an hour of *EastEnders* followed by *Top Gear*, and then a documentary on Robbie Williams. Chris is clearly establishing his right to leave the TV on, with a programme he has selected, at a volume that suits him. Will he allow me to watch *Frasier* tomorrow?

I lie in bed on my thin mattress, my head resting on a rock-hard pillow, and think about Mary and the boys, aware that they too must be enduring their own private hell. I feel as low as I did during my first night at Belmarsh. I have no idea what time I finally fall asleep. I thought I had escaped from hell.

So much for purgatory.

DAY 23   FRIDAY 10 AUGUST 2001

5.49 am

Intermittent, fitful sleep, unaided by a rock-hard pillow, a cell-mate who snores and occasionally talks in his sleep; sadly, nothing of literary interest. Rise and write for two hours.

7.33 am

Cell-mate wakes and grunts. I carry on writing. He then jumps off the top bunk and goes to the lavatory in the corner of the cell. He has no inhibitions in front of me, but then he has been in prison for five years. I am determined never to go to the loo in my cell, while I'm still in a one-up, one-down, unless he is out.* I go on working as if nothing is happening. It's quite hard to distract me when I'm writing, but when I look up I see Chris standing there in the nude. His chest is almost completely covered with a tattoo of an eagle towering over a snake, which he tells me with pride he did himself with a tattoo gun. On the

---

*For hygiene reasons it's now against European law to have a lavatory in the cell, especially if it's also your eating place. The British ignore this rule, preferring to pay a heavy fine each year. There are several such rules the Prison Service ignores with impunity.

knuckles of his fingers on both hands are diamonds, hearts, spades and clubs, while on his shoulders he has a massive spider's web that creeps down his back. There's not much pink flesh left unmarked. He's a walking canvas.

8.00 am

The cell doors are unlocked so we can all go and have breakfast; one hour earlier than in Belmarsh. Chris and I walk down to the hotplate. At least the eggs have been boiled quite recently – like today. We're also given a half carton of semi-skimmed milk, which means that I can drop the long-life version from my weekly shopping list and spend the extra 79p on some other luxury, like marmalade.

9.40 am

Mr Newport pops his head round the cell door to announce that Mr Tinkler, the principal officer, would like a word with me. Even the language at Wayland is more conciliatory. When I leave my cell, he adds, 'It's down the corridor, second door on the left.'

When I enter Mr Tinkler's room, he stands up and ushers me into a chair on the other side of his desk as if he were my bank manager. His name is printed in silver letters on a triangular piece of wood, in case anyone should forget. Mr Tinkler resembles an old sea captain rather than a prison officer. He has weathered, lined skin and a neatly cut white beard. He's been in the service for over twenty years and I learn that he will be retiring next August. He asks me how I'm settling in – the most common question asked by an officer when meeting a prisoner for the first time. I tell him about the state of my room and the proclivities of my cell-mate. He listens attentively and, as there is little difference in our age, I detect some sympathy for my predicament. He tells me that as soon as my induction is over he plans to transfer me to a single cell on C block which houses mainly lifers. Mr Tinkler believes that I'll find the atmosphere there more settled, as I will be among a group of prisoners closer to my own age. I leave his office feeling considerably better than when I entered it.

10.01 am

I've only been back in my cell for a few minutes when Mr Newport pops his head round the door again. 'We're moving you to a cell down the corridor. Pack your belongings and follow me.' I hadn't really unpacked so this exercise doesn't take too long. The other cell also turns out to be a double, but once I'm inside Mr Newport whispers, 'We're hoping to leave you on your own.' Mr Tinkler's sympathy is translated into something far more tangible than mere words.

I slowly unpack my possessions from the regulation prison plastic bag for the seventh time in three weeks.

As I now have *two* small cupboards, I put all the prison clothes like shirts, socks, pants, gym kit, etc. in one, while I place my personal belongings in the other. I almost enjoy how long it takes to put my new home in order.

11.36 am

Mr Newport is back again. He's making his rounds, this time to deliver canteen lists to every cell. He has already warned me that if the computer hasn't transferred my surplus cash from Belmarsh I will be allowed an advance of only £5 this week. I quickly check the top of the list, to discover I'm in credit for

DAY 23

£20.46. This turns out to be my weekly allowance of £12.50 plus two payments from the education department at Belmarsh for my lecture on creative writing and two sessions at the workshop. I spend the next thirty minutes planning how to spend this windfall. I allow myself such luxuries as Gillette shaving foam, Robertson's marmalade and four bottles of Evian water.

12 noon

Lunch. On Fridays at Wayland lunch comes in a plastic bag: a packet of crisps, a bar of chocolate, a bread roll accompanied by a lettuce leaf and a sachet of salad cream. I can only wonder in which prison workshop and how long ago this meal was packed, because there are rarely sell-by dates on prison food. I return to my cell to find the canteen provisions have been deposited on the end of my bed in yet another plastic bag. I celebrate by thumbing my bread roll in half and spreading Robertson's Golden Shred all over it with the aid of my toothbrush handle. I pour myself a mug of Evian. Already the world is a better place.

12.40 pm

Part of the induction process is a private session with the prison chaplain. Mr John Framlington looks to me as if it's been some years since he's administered his own parish. He explains that he's a 'fill-in', as he shares the work with a younger man. I assure him that I will be attending the service on Sunday, but would like to know if it clashes with the RCs. He looks puzzled.

'No, we both use the same chapel. Father Christopher has so many parishes outside the prison to cover each Sunday he holds his service on a Saturday morning at ten thirty.' Mr Framlington is interested to discover why I wish to attend both services. I tell him about my daily diary, and my failure to hear Father Kevin's sermon while at Belmarsh. He sighs.

'You'll quickly find out that Father Christopher preaches a far better sermon than I do.'

2.40 pm

The first setback of the day. Mr Newport returns, the bearer of bad news. Six new prisoners have arrived this afternoon, and once again I will have to share. I learn later that there are indeed six new inductees but as the prison still has several empty beds there is no real need for me to share. However, there are several reporters hanging around outside the prison gates, so the authorities don't want to leave the press with the impression I might be receiving preferential treatment. Mr Newport claims he has selected a more suitable person to share with me. Perhaps this time it won't be a Stanley-knife stabber, just a machete murderer.

I transfer all my personal possessions out of one of the cupboards and stuff them into the other, along with the prison kit.

3.18 pm

My new room-mate appears carrying his plastic bag. He introduces himself as Jules (see plate section). He's thirty-five and has a five-year sentence for drug dealing. He's already been told that I don't smoke.

I watch him carefully as he starts to unpack, and I begin to relax. He has an unusual number of books, as well as an electric chessboard. I feel confident the evening viewing will not be a rerun of *Top of the Pops* and motorbike scrambling. At five to four I leave him to continue his unpacking while I make my way to the gym for another induction session.

3.55 pm

Twenty new inmates are escorted to the gym. There are no doors to be unlocked on our unimpeded journey to the other side of the building. I also notice that on the way we pass a library. I never even found the library at Belmarsh.

The gym is an even bigger shock. It's quite magnificent. Wayland has a full-size basketball court, which is fully equipped for badminton and tennis. The gym instructor asks us to take a seat on a bench where we're handed forms to fill in, giving such details as age, weight, height and sports we are interested in.

'My name is John Maiden,' he tells us, 'and I'm happy to be called John.' I never learnt the first name of any officer at Belmarsh. He tells us the different activities available: cricket, basketball, badminton, football, rugby and, inevitably, weight training. He then takes us into the next room, an area over-crowded with bars, dumb-bells and weights. Once again I'm disappointed to discover that there is only one treadmill, three rowing machines and no step machine. However, there are some very strange-looking bikes, the likes of which I've never seen before.

A gym orderly (a prisoner who has obviously been trained by Mr Maiden) takes us round the room and describes how to use each piece of equipment. He carries out the task most professionally, and should have no trouble finding a job once he leaves prison. I'm listening intently about bench pressing when I find Mr Maiden standing by my side.

'Are you still refereeing rugby?' he asks.

'No. I gave up about ten years ago,' I tell him. 'Once the laws started to change every season I just couldn't keep up. In any case I found that even if I only refereed veteran teams I couldn't keep up, quite literally.'

'Don't let knowledge of the laws worry you,' said Mr Maiden, 'we'll still be able to use you.'

The session ends with a look at the changing room, the shower facilities and, more importantly, clean lavatories. I'm issued with a plastic gym card and look forward to returning to my old training regime.

5.00 pm

Back in the cell, I find Jules sitting on the top bunk reading. I settle down to another session of writing before we're called for supper.

6.00 pm

I select the vegetarian pie and chips and am handed the obligatory yellow lollipop, which is identical to those we were given at Belmarsh. If it's the same company who makes and supplies them to every one of Her Majesty's prisons, that must be a contract worth having. Although it's only my third meal since I arrived, I think I've already spotted the power behind the hotplate. He's a man of about thirty-five, six foot three and must weigh around twenty-seven stone. As I pass him I ask if we could meet later. He nods in the manner of a man who knows that in the kingdom of the blind ... I can only hope that I've located Wayland's 'Del Boy'.

After supper we are allowed to be out of our cells for a couple of hours (Association) until we're banged up at eight.

What a contrast to Belmarsh. I use the time to roam around the corridors and familiarize myself with the layout. The main office is on the first landing and is the hub of the whole wing. From there everything is an offshoot. I also check where all the phones are situated, and when a prisoner comes off one he warns me, 'Never use the phone on the induction landing, Jeff, because the conversations are taped. Use this one. It's a screw-free line.'

I thank him and call Mary in Cambridge. She's relieved that I've rung as she has no way of contacting me, and can't come to see me until she's been sent a visiting order. I promise to put one in tomorrow's post, and then she may even be able to drive across next Tuesday or Wednesday. I remind her to bring some form of identification and that she mustn't try to pass anything over to me, not even a letter.

Mary then tells me that she's accepted an invitation to go on the *Today* programme with John Humphrys. She intends to ask Baroness Nicholson to withdraw her accusation that I stole money from the Kurds, so that I can be reinstated as a D-cat prisoner and quickly transferred to an open prison. I tell Mary that I consider this an unlikely scenario.

'She's not decent enough to consider such a Christian act,' I warn my wife.

'I'm sure you're right,' Mary replies, 'but I will be able to refer to Lynda Chalker's parliamentary reply on the subject and ask why Ms Nicholson wasn't in the House that day if she cares so much about the Kurds, or why had she not at least read the report in Hansard the following morning.' Mary adds that the BBC have told her that they accept I have no case to answer.

'When are you going on?'

'Next Wednesday or Thursday, so it's important I see you before then.'

I quickly agree as my units are running out. I then ask Mary to warn James that I'll phone him at the office at eleven tomorrow morning, and will call her again on Sunday evening. My units are now down to ten so I say a quick goodbye.*

I continue my exploration of the wing and discover that the main Association room and the servery/hotplate double up. The room is about thirty paces by twenty and has a full-size snooker table which is so popular that you have to book a week in advance. There is also a pool table and a table-tennis table, but no TV, as it would be redundant when there's one in every cell.

I'm walking back upstairs when I bump into the hotplate man. He introduces himself as Dale† and invites me to join him in his cell, telling me on the way that he's serving eight years for wounding with intent to endanger life. He leads me down a flight of stone steps onto the lower-ground floor. This is an area I would never have come across, as it's reserved for enhanced prisoners only – the chosen few who have proper jobs and are considered by the officers to be trustworthy. As you can't be granted enhanced status for at least three months, I will never enjoy such luxury, as I am hoping to be moved to a D-cat fairly quickly.

Although Dale's cell is exactly the same size as mine, there the similarity ends. His brick walls are in two tones of blue, and he has nine five-by-five-inch steel mirrors over his washbasin shaped in a large triangle. In our cell, Jules and I have one mirror between us. Dale also has two pillows, both soft, and an extra blanket. On the wall are photos of his twin sons, but no sign of a wife – just the centrefold of a couple of Chinese girls, Blu-tacked

---

* Each week you can buy two £2 phonecards comprising twenty units each. Each card lasts for about twenty minutes so I have to ration myself. Mary, James, William, Alison (my PA), my solicitor and, if there are any units over, friends. You quickly learn not to chatter.
† Also known as Big Mac.

above his bed. He pours me a Coca-Cola, my first since William and James visited me in Belmarsh, and asks if he can help in any way.

'In every way, I suspect. I would like a soft pillow, a fresh towel every day and my washing taken care of.'

'No problem,' he says, like a banker who can make an electronic transfer of a million dollars to New York by simply pressing a button – as long as you *have* a million dollars.

'Anything else? Phonecards, food, drink?'

'I could do with some more phonecards and several items from the canteen.'

'I can also solve that problem,' Dale says. 'Just write out a list of what you want and I'll have everything delivered to your cell.'

'But how do I pay you?'

'That's the easy part. Send in a postal order and ask for the money to be placed against my account. Just make sure the name Archer isn't involved, otherwise there's bound to be an investigation. I won't charge you double-bubble, just bubble and a half.'*

Three or four other prisoners stroll into Dale's cell, so he immediately changes the subject. Within minutes the atmosphere feels more like a club than a prison, as they all seem so relaxed in each other's company. Jimmy, who's serving a three-and-a-half year sentence for being an Ecstasy courier (carrying packages from one club to another), wants to know if I play cricket.

'The occasional charity match, about twice a year,' I admit.

'Good, then you'll be batting number three next week, against D wing.'

---

*Double-bubble: meaning certain debts have to be repaid twice over. This is an understood rule amongst prisoners.

'But I usually go in at number eleven,' I protest, 'and have been known to bat as high as number ten.'

'Then you'll be first wicket down at Wayland,' says Jimmy. 'By the way, we haven't won a match this year. Our two best batsmen got their D-cats at the beginning of the season and were transferred to Latchmere House in Richmond.'

After about an hour of their company, I become aware of the other big difference on the enhanced wing – the noise, or rather the lack of noise. You just don't hear the incessant stereos attempting to out-blare each other.

At five to eight I make my way back to my cell and am met on the stairs by an officer who tells me that I cannot visit the enhanced area again as it's off limits. 'And if you do, Archer,' he adds, 'I'll put you on report, which could mean a fortnight being added to your sentence.'

There's always someone who feels he has to prove how powerful he is, especially if he can show off in front of other prisoners – 'I put Archer in his place, didn't I?' In Belmarsh it was the young officer with his record bookings. I have a feeling I've just met Wayland's.

Back in my cell, I find Jules is playing chess against a phantom opponent on his electronic board. I settle down to write an account of the day. There are no letters to read as no one has yet discovered I'm in Wayland.

8.15 pm

Dale arrives with a soft pillow and an extra blanket. He's disappeared before I can thank him.

DAY 24   SATURDAY 11 AUGUST 2001

5.07 am

I've managed to sleep for six hours, thanks to Jules hanging a blanket from the top bunk, so that it keeps out the fluorescent arc lights that glare through the bars all night.* At 5.40 I place my feet on the linoleum floor and wait. Jules doesn't stir. So far no snoring or talking in his sleep. Last night Jules made an interesting observation about sleep: it's the only time when you're not in jail, and it cuts your sentence by a third. Is this the reason why so many prisoners spend so much time in bed? Dale adds that some of them are 'gouching out' after chasing the dragon. This can cause them to sleep for twelve to fourteen hours, and helps kill the weekend, as well as themselves.

8.15 am

The cell door is unlocked just as I'm coming to the end of my first writing session. During that time I've managed a little over two thousand words.

    I go downstairs to the hotplate hoping to pick up a carton of milk, only to be told by Dale that it's not available at the weekend.

---

* The lights are on all night to make sure you don't even think about escaping.

9.00 am

I'm first in the queue at the office, to pick up a VO for Mary. In a C-cat you're allowed one visit every two weeks. A prisoner can invite up to three adults and two children under the age of sixteen. The majority of prisoners are between the ages of nineteen and thirty, so a wife or partner plus a couple of young children would be the norm. As my children are twenty-nine and twenty-seven, it will be only Mary and the boys who I'll be seeing regularly.

10.00 am

I attend my first gym session. Each wing is allowed to send twenty inmates, so after my inability to get on the list at Belmarsh, I make sure that I'm at the starting gate on time.

The main gym is taken up with four badminton matches – like snooker it's a sport that is so popular in prison that you have to book a court a week in advance. The weight-training room next door is packed with heaving and pumping musclemen, and by the time I arrive, someone is already jogging on the one treadmill. I begin my programme with some light stretching before going on the rowing machine. I manage only 1,800 metres in ten minutes, compared with the usual 2,000 I do back in the gym on Albert Embankment. But at least that leaves me something to aim for. I manage a little light weight training before the running machine becomes free. I start at five miles an hour for six minutes to warm up, before moving up to eight miles an hour for another ten minutes. Just to give you an idea how feeble this is, Roger Bannister's four-minute mile in 1952 was at fifteen miles an hour, and I once saw Seb Coe do twelve miles an hour for ten minutes – hold your breath – at the age of forty.

DAY 24

And he was only warming up for a judo session. I end with ten minutes of stretching and a gentle warm down. Most of the prisoners walk into the gym and go straight on to the heavy weights without bothering to warm up. Later they wonder why they pull muscles and are then out of action for the next couple of weeks.

I return to my cell and try out the shower on our wing. The wash room has four showers which produce twice as many jets of water as those at Belmarsh. Also, when you press the button the water continues to flow for at least thirty seconds before you have to press it again. There are two young black lads already showering who, I notice, keep their boxer shorts on (I later learn this is because they're Muslims). However, one problem I still encounter is that I'm allowed only two small, thin towels (three by one foot) a week. If I intend to go to the gym five days a week, followed by a shower ... I'll have to speak to Dale about the problem.

11.30 am

I give James a call at the flat and ask him to send £100 in postal orders to Dale at Wayland so I can buy a razor, some shampoo, a dozen phonecards as well as some extra provisions. I also ask him to phone Griston Post Office and order *The Times* and *Telegraph* every day, Sundays included. James says he'll ask Alison to call them on Monday morning, because he's going on holiday and will be away for a couple of weeks. I'll miss him, even on the phone, and it won't be that long before Will has to return to America.

12.00 noon

I skip lunch because I need to start the second draft of today's script, and in any case, it looks quite inedible. I open a packet of crisps and bite into an apple while I continue writing.

2.00 pm

When the cell door is unlocked again at two o'clock, Dale is standing outside and says he's been given clearance to invite me down to the enhancement wing. The officer I bumped into yesterday must be off duty.

It's like entering a different world. We go straight to Dale's cell, and the first thing he asks me is if I play backgammon. He produces a magnificent leather board with large ivory counters. While I'm considering what to do with a six and a three, never a good opening throw, he points to a plastic bag under the bed. I look inside: a Gillette Mach3 razor, two packets of blades, a bar of Cusson's soap, some shaving foam, a bunch of bananas, a packet of cornflakes and five phonecards. I think it unwise to ask any questions. I thank Dale and hand him my next shopping list. I assure him funds are on the way. We shake hands on a bubble and a half. He'll supply whatever I need from the canteen and charge me an extra 50 per cent. The alternative is to be starved, unshaven or cut to ribbons by a prison razor. This service will also include extra towels, my laundry washed every Thursday, plus a soft pillow, all at an overall expense of around £30 a week.

We are once again joined by two other inmates, Darren (see plate section) and Jimmy (transporting Ecstasy). During the afternoon I play both of them at backgammon, win one and lose one, which seems acceptable to everyone present. Dale leaves us to check in for work as No. 1 on the hotplate, so we all move across to Darren's cell. During a game of backgammon I learn that Darren was caught selling cannabis, a part-time occupation, supplementing his regular job as a construction contractor. I ask him what he plans to do once he leaves prison in a year's time having completed three years of a six-year sentence. He admits he's not sure. I suspect, like so many inmates who can make fifty to a hundred thousand pounds a year selling drugs, he'll find it difficult to settle for a nine to five job.

Whenever he's contemplating his next move, I try to take in the surroundings. You can learn so much about a person from their cell. On the shelves are copies of the *Oxford Shorter Dictionary* (two volumes), the *Oxford Book of Quotations* (he tells me he tries to learn one a day) and a dozen novels that are clearly not on loan from the library. As the game progresses, he asks me if Rupert Brooke owned the Old Vicarage, or just lived there. I tell him that the great war poet only resided there while working on his fellowship dissertation at King's College.*

Jimmy tells me that they're plotting to have me moved down to the enhanced wing as soon as I've completed my induction. This is the best news I've had since arriving at Wayland. The cell door swings open, and Mr Thompson looks round.

'Ah,' he says, when he spots me. 'The governor wants a word.'†

I accompany Mr Thompson to Mr Carlton-Boyce's office.

---

* Brooke wrote to his mother begging her to buy the house while he was training at Betteshanger in the early days of the war. She did so, but not until after he'd died on a troop ship off the Greek coast in 1915. He is buried on the island of Skyros.

† The expression 'governor' does not mean that he or she is the senior officer in the prison. Most prisons have between three and five governors, in charge of different departments. The head of the prison is known as the No. 1 governor or the governing governor.

He's a man of about forty, perhaps forty-five. He welcomes me with a warm smile, and introduces me to the senior officer from C wing, which, he tells me, is where they plan to transfer me. I ask if they would consider me for the enhancement spur, but am told the decision has already been made. I've come to realize that once the machine has decided on something, it would be easier to turn the QEII around than try to get them to change their collective minds.

Mr Carlton-Boyce explains that he would quite happily move me to C wing today, but with so many press sniffing around outside, it mustn't look as if I am being given special treatment, so I have to be the last of my intake to be moved. No need to explain to him the problem of rap music and young prisoners hollering from window to window* all night, but, he repeats, the press interest is tying his hands.

4.00 pm

I return to my cell and continue writing. I've only managed a few pages when I'm interrupted by a knock on the cell door. It's a young man from across the corridor who looks to be in his early twenties.

'Can you write a letter for me?' he asks. No one ever introduces themselves or bothers with pleasantries.

'Yes, of course. Who is it to, and what do you want me to say?' I reply, turning to a blank page on my pad.

'I want to be moved to another prison,' he tells me.

'Don't we all?'

'What?'

'No, nothing, but why should they consider moving you?'

---

* Known as window warriors.

DAY 24

'I want to be nearer my mother, who's suffering from depression.' I nod. He tells me his name is Naz, and then gives me the name of the officer to whom he wishes to address the letter. He asks me to include the reason his request should be taken seriously. I pen the letter, reading each sentence out as I complete it. He signs along the bottom with a flourish. I can't read his signature, so I ask him to spell his name so I can print it in capitals underneath – then the officer in question will know who it's come from, I explain. I place the missive in an envelope, address it, and he seals it. Naz picks up the envelope, smiles and says, 'Thank you. If you want anything, just let me know.' I tell him I need a pair of flip-flops for the shower because I'm worried about catching verrucas. He looks anxiously at me.

'I was only joking,' I say, and wish him luck.

5.00 pm

Supper. I settle for a lump of cabbage and half a portion of chips, which is a normal portion in your world. The cabbage is floating around in water and reminds me of school meals, and why I never liked the vegetable in the first place. While I'm waiting in line, Jimmy tells me that he didn't enjoy his spell of serving behind the hotplate.

'Why not?' I ask.

'The inmates never stop complaining,' he adds.

'About the quality of the food?'

'No, about not giving them large enough portions, especially when it comes to chips.'

When I return to the cell, I find over a hundred letters stacked on the end of my bunk. Jules reminds me that at weekends we're banged up at around five thirty and will remain locked in our cells until eight fifteen the following morning. So

I'll certainly have enough time to read every one of them. Fourteen hours of incarceration, once again blamed on staff shortages. Unpleasant, but still a great improvement on Belmarsh. I say unpleasant only because when you've finished your meal, you're left with dirty, smelly plastic plates littering your tiny cell all night. It might be more sensible to leave the cell doors open for another twenty minutes so that prisoners can scrape the remains of their food into the dustbins at the end of each corridor and then wash their utensils in the sink. And don't forget that in many prisons there are three inmates to a cell with one lavatory.

I compromise, scrape my food into a plastic bag and then tie it up before dropping it in the waste-paper bin next to the lavatory. When I look out of my cell window I notice several prisoners are throwing the remains of their meal through the bars and out onto the grass.

Jules tells me that he's working on a letter to the principal officer (Mr Tinkler) about having his status changed from C-cat to D-cat. He asks if I will go through it with him. I don't tell him that I'm facing the same problem.

Jules is a model prisoner and deserves his enhanced status. He gained this while he was at Bedford where he became a Listener.* He's also quiet and considerate about my writing regime. He so obviously regrets his involvement with drugs, and is one of the few prisoners I've come across who I am convinced will never see the inside of a jail again. I do a small editorial job on his letter and suggest that we should go over the final draft tomorrow. I then spend the next couple of hours reading

---

* Selected prisoners are invited to become Listeners. They are trained by the Samaritans so that they can assist fellow inmates who are facing problems, some so depressed they even contemplate suicide.

through today's mail, which is just as supportive as the letters I received in Belmarsh. There is, however, one missive of a different nature that I feel I ought to share with you.

University College Hospital
London 1/8/01 4.30 pm

My dear Lord Archer
Many poets and writers have written much of their best work in prison, OW for one. However, I cannot conceive of you having to spend four miserable years in a maximum security prison. I spent 60 days in such a facility in Canada on a trumped-up charge of disturbing the peace.

I escaped by a most devious means.

I can arrange for your immediate release from bondage, however, only if you are willing to donate £15m to my charity foundation.

I can be contacted anytime at 020 7— If you would like some company, choose three non-criminal or white-collar offenders to join with you, for an appropriate amount.

Yours as an artist,

I am quite unable to read the signature. In the second post there is another letter in the same bold red hand:

1/8/01 5.05 pm

Dear Geofrey [sic]
After having sealed the letter to you I realized that I wrote £15m instead of £1.5m So just to reassure you, I'm not an idiot, I repeat my offer to spring you and a few other trustworthy buddies!

Yours in every greater art,

Again, I cannot read the signature.

DAY 25   SUNDAY 12 AUGUST 2001

5.56 am

Woken by voices in the corridor, two officers, one of them on a walkie-talkie. They open a cell door and take a prisoner away. I will find out the details when my door is unlocked in a couple of hours' time.

6.05 am

Write for two hours.

8.15 am

Breakfast. Sugar Puffs (prison issue), long-life milk (mine, because it's Sunday). Beans on burnt toast (prison's).

10.00 am

I go to the library for the first time and sign up. You are allowed to take out two books, a third if your official work is education. The library is about the same size as the weight-lifting room and, to be fair, just as well stocked. They have everything from Graham Greene to Stephen King, *I, Claudius* to Harry Potter.

However, although Forsyth, Grisham, Follett and Jilly Cooper are much in evidence, I can find none of my books on the shelves. I hope that's because they are all out on loan. Lifers often tell me they've read them all – slowly – and in some cases several times.

I take out a copy of *The Glass Bead Game* by Hermann Hesse, which I haven't read in years, and *Famous Trials* selected by John Mortimer. Naturally I have to fill in another form, and then my choices are stamped by the library orderly – a prisoner – to be returned by 26 August. I'm rather hoping to have moved on by then.

Kevin, the prisoner who stamps my library card, tells me that all my books were removed from the shelves the day they found out I was being transferred to Wayland.

'Why?' I ask.

'Direct order from the number one governor. It seems that Belmarsh informed her that the prisoners were stealing your books, and if they could then get you to sign them, the black-market price is a thousand pounds.'

I believe everything except the thousand pounds, which sounds like a tabloid figure.

10.30 am

I check my watch, leave the library and quickly make my way across to the chapel on the other side of the corridor. There is no officer standing by the entrance. It suddenly hits me that I haven't been searched since the day I arrived. I'm a couple of minutes late, and wonder if I've come to the wrong place, as there are only three other prisoners sitting in the pews, along with the chaplain. John Framlington is dressed in a long, black gown and black cape with crimson piping, and welcomes me with literally open arms.

The chapel is very impressive, with its wood-panelled walls and small oils depicting the life of Christ. The simple altar is covered in a cloth displaying a white cross with splashes of gold. There is also a large wooden cross hanging from the wall behind the altar. The seating consists of six rows of twenty wooden chairs set in a semicircle reminiscent of a small amphitheatre. I take a seat in the third row as a group of men and women all dressed in red T-shirts enters by the backdoor. They assemble their music on stands while a couple strap on guitars and a flautist practises a few notes. She's very pretty. I wonder if it's because it's my twenty-fifth day in prison. But that would be an ungallant thought. She is pretty.

By ten forty-five the congregation has swelled to seven, but we are still outnumbered by the nine-strong choir. The prisoners are all seated to the right of the altar while the choir is standing on the left. A man, who appears to be the group's leader, suggests we move across and join him on their side of the chapel. All seven of us dutifully obey. I've just worked out why the congregation at Belmarsh was over two hundred, week in and week out, while at Wayland it's down to seven. Here you are allowed to stroll around the buildings for long periods of time, so if you wish to make contact with someone from another wing, it's not all that difficult. In Belmarsh, chapel was a rare opportunity to catch up with a friend from another block, relay messages, pass on drugs and occasionally even pray.

The chaplain then walks up to the front, turns and welcomes us all. He begins by introducing Shine who, he tells us, are a local group that perform for several churches in the diocese.

We all join in the first hymn, 'He Who Would Valiant Be', and Shine turn out to be rather good. Despite our depleted numbers, the service still swings along. Once the chaplain has delivered the opening prayer, he comes and sits amongst the congregation. He doesn't conduct any other part of the service, as that has been left in the capable hands of the leader of Shine. Next we sing 'Amazing Grace', which is followed by a lesson from Luke, read by another member of the group. Following another hymn we are addressed by the leader of Shine. He takes his text from the first reading of the Good Samaritan. He talks about people who walk by on the other side when you are in any trouble. This time I do thank God for my family and friends, because so few of them have walked by on the other side.

The service ends with a blessing from the chaplain, who then thanks the group for giving up their time. I return to my cell and write notes on everything I have just experienced.

12.09 pm

I call Mary in Grantchester. How I miss my weekends with her, strolling around the garden at the Old Vicarage: the smell of the flowers and the grass, feeding the fish and watching students idly punting on the Cam. Mary briefs me on what line she intends to take on the *Today* programme, now that the Foreign Office and the KDP (Kurdish Democratic Party) have confirmed how the money for the Kurds was raised and distributed. I try to think how Ms Nicholson will spin herself out of this one.

Mary reminds me that she can't come to see me until she receives a VO. I confirm I sent her one yesterday. She goes on to tell me that her own book, *Photoconversion Volume One: Clean Electricity from Photovoltaics* (advance sales 1,229, price £110), has been well received by the academic world.

We finish by discussing family matters. Although I've come to the end of my twenty units, I don't tell her that I am in possession of another two phonecards as that might cause trouble for Dale, especially if the conversation is being taped. I promise to call her again on Tuesday, and we agree a time. Just in case you've forgotten, the calls are always one way: OUT.

My next call is to James, who is giving a lunch party for ten friends at our apartment in London. I do miss his cooking. He tells me who's sitting round my table and what they are eating: Roquefort, fig and walnut salad, spaghetti, and ice cream, followed by Brie, Stilton or Cheddar. This will be accompanied by an Australian red and a Californian white. I begin to salivate.

'Dinner,'* yells an officer, and I quickly return to the real world.

12.20 pm

Lunch: Chinese stir-fried vegetables (they may have been stirred, but they are still glued together), an apple, supplemented by a Mars bar (30p), and a glass of Evian. Guests: pre-selected.

1.00 pm

I join Dale on the enhanced wing. I grab Darren's *Sunday Times*, and read very slowly while Dale and Jimmy play backgammon. The lead story is the alleged rape of a girl in Essex by Neil and Christine Hamilton. This is more graphically described in Dale's *News of the World*, and the implausible story is memorable for Christine Hamilton's observation, 'If I wanted to do that sort of thing, it would be in Kensington or Chelsea, not Essex.'

We play several games of backgammon, during which time the assembled gathering questions me about the contest for the Tory party leadership. Darren (marijuana only) is a fan of Michael Portillo, and asks how I feel. I tell him that I think it

---

* In prison dinner is lunch, and tea is supper.

might have been wise of the 1922 Committee to let all three candidates who reached the second round – Clarke 59, Duncan Smith 54 and Portillo 53 – be presented to the party membership. Leaving Michael out is bound to create some bad feeling and may even cause trouble in the future. It's quite possible that the membership would have rejected Portillo in any case, but I feel that they should have been allowed the opportunity to do so.

Dale (wounding with intent) is a huge fan of Margaret Thatcher, while Jimmy (Ecstasy courier) voted for John Major. 'A decent bloke,' he says. It's sometimes hard to remember that I may be sitting in a room with an armed robber, a drug dealer, a million-pound fraudster, and heaven only knows who else. It's also worth mentioning that when it comes to their 'other world', they never discuss anything in front of me.

3.00 pm

Exercise: I take the long walk around the perimeter of the prison – about half a mile – and several inmates greet me in a more friendly fashion than they did on my first outing last Thursday. The first person to join me is a man who is obviously on drugs. Unlike William Keane – do you remember him from Belmarsh? – I can't tell which drug he's on just by looking at his skin. His name is Darrell, and he tells me that his original sentence was for ten years. His crime: cutting someone up in a pub with a broken bottle. He was nineteen at the time. I take a second look. He looks about forty.

'Then why are you still here?' I ask, assuming he will explain that he's serving a second or third sentence for another offence.

'Once I ended up in prison, I got hooked on drugs, didn't I?'

'Did you?'

'Yeah, and I'd never taken a drug before I came in. But when you're given a ten-year sentence and then banged up for twenty-two hours a day with prisoners who are already on skag, you sort of fall in with it, don't you? First I was caught smoking cannabis so the governor added twenty-eight days to my sentence.'

'Twenty-eight days for smoking cannabis? But . . .'

'I then tried cocaine and finally moved on to heroin. Every time I got caught, my sentence was lengthened. Mind you, I've been clean for over a year now, Jeff. I've had to be, otherwise I'm never going to get out of this fuckin' shithole, am I?'

'How long has it been?'

'Twenty-one years. I'm forty-one, and over half my sentence has been added because of being caught taking drugs while inside.'

I'm trying to take this in when we're joined by a burly older man of around my height, who looks Middle Eastern. Darrell slips quietly away, which I fear means trouble. The new man doesn't bother with any small talk.

'How would you like to make fifty grand a week while you're still in prison?'

'What do you have in mind?' I ask innocently, because he doesn't look like a publisher.

'I've got a lorry-load of drugs stuck on the Belgian border waiting to come into this country, but I'm a little short of cash at the moment. Put up fifty grand and you'll have a hundred by this time next week.' I quicken my pace and try to lose him, but within seconds he's caught me up. 'There would be no risk for you,' he adds, slightly out of breath. 'We take all the risk. In any case, no one could pin it on you, not while you're still in jail.'

I stop in my tracks and turn to face him. 'I hate drugs, and I detest even more those people who peddle them. If you ever try

307

to speak to me again, I will repeat this conversation, first to my solicitor and then to the governor. And don't imagine you can threaten me, because they would be only too happy to move me out of here, and my bet is your sentence would be doubled. Do I make myself clear?'

I have never seen a more frightened man in my life. What he didn't know was that I was even more terrified than he was. I couldn't forget the punishment meted out in Belmarsh for being a grass – hot water mixed with sugar thrown in your face – or the man with the four razor-blade scars administered in the shower. I quickly leave the exercise yard and go back to my cell, pull the door closed, and sit on the end of the bed, shaking.

4.00 pm

When Jules returns, I'm still shaking. I go off in search of Dale.

'I know that bastard,' says Dale. 'Just leave him to me.'

'What does that mean?' I ask.

'Don't ask.'

'I have to. I'm trying not to cause any trouble.'

'He won't trouble you again, that I guarantee.' He then raises his twenty-seven-stone frame from the end of the bed and departs.

4.30 pm

Association: I emerge from the enhanced wing with two Mars bars, having played a couple of games of backgammon with Darren. I become aware of the most incredible uproar emanating from the games room. Am I about to experience my first riot? I glance anxiously round the door to see a group of West Indians playing dominoes. Every time they place a domino on the table, it's slammed down as if a judge were trying to bring a rowdy courtroom to order. This is followed by screaming delight more normally associated with Lara scoring a century at Sabina Park. The officer on duty, Mr Nutbourne, and the other inmates playing snooker, pool and table tennis don't seem at all disturbed by this. I stroll across to join the dozen or so West Indians and decide to watch a couple of games. One of them looks up from the table, and shouts, 'You wanna try your luck, man?'

'Thank you,' I reply, and take a seat vacated by one of the players.

A West Indian with greying hair divides the dominoes between the four of us and we each end up with seven pieces. The player on my right is able to begin the game as he has a double six. He places his prize with a thump in the middle of the table, which is followed by shouts and screams from the assembled gathering. The game progresses for four rounds without any player failing to place a domino on the end of the line. During the next round the player on my left doesn't have a three or six, so passes and, as I have a six, I place my domino quietly on the table. I notice the brothers are becoming a little less noisy. By this time a large crowd has gathered round until only two of us are left with one domino; I have a five and a four, but it is my opponent's turn. If he's going to win, he has to hit, and hit now. The brothers fall almost silent. Can the player on my left thwart me and win the game? I pray for the second time that day. He has neither a four nor a one, and passes without a murmur. I try desperately to keep a poker face, while holding my last domino in the palm of my hand. A forest of black eyes are staring at me. I quietly place my four next to the four on the right-hand end and so much bedlam breaks out that even Mr Nutbourne decides to find out what's going on. I rise to leave.

'Another game, man? Another game?' they demand.

'How kind of you,' I say, 'but I must get back to my writing. It's been a pleasure to play you.' This is followed by much slapping of hands. I depart quickly, aware that if I were to play a second round, the myth would be shattered. Frankly I know nothing of the subtleties of the game, having just brought a new meaning to the phrase 'beginner's luck'.

5.45 pm

Supper. When I reach the hotplate, Dale takes my plastic bowl and, just as Tony always did at Belmarsh, decides what I shall be allowed to eat. He selects a vegetarian quiche, a few lettuce leaves carefully extracted from a large bowl and a tomato. I will no longer have to think about what to eat as long as Dale's on duty.

6.00 pm

Jules and I are banged up again until eight tomorrow morning. Fourteen hours in a cell seven paces by three, just in case you've forgotten. As it's Sunday, there are no letters awaiting me, so I just go over my script before returning to Hermann Hesse.

9.00 pm

Jules and I watch Meg Ryan and Kevin Kline in *French Kiss*, which has us both laughing, but then we are a captive audience.

10.54 pm

I settle my head on my new soft pillow. It isn't goose down, or even duck feather – just foam rubber – but I know luxury when I feel it.

DAY 26   MONDAY 13 AUGUST 2001

6.03 am

Yesterday's early morning commotion in the corridor turned out to be a prisoner needing medication and the assistance of a Listener. He had pressed the emergency call button. There's one in every cell next to the door which, when pressed, illuminates a small red light in the corridor, while another flashes up in the main office. It is known by the inmates as room service, although prison orders state that it must be used only in emergencies, otherwise you will be placed on report. I couldn't find out why the prisoner needed the help of a Listener, but as it was his first night at Wayland, it could have been for any number of reasons. Remembering my first night, I can only sympathize.

I write for two hours.

8.15 am

Breakfast. Sugar Puffs (mine), milk (theirs). One egg on a slice of toast (theirs), a second slice of toast (theirs), marmalade (mine).

10.00 am

Banged up for two hours, which I plan on using to work on the second draft of this morning's script. That's assuming there are no interruptions – there are two.

10.49 am

The cell door is unlocked by Mr Newport, who wants to talk to Jules about his application for a change of status from C-cat to D-cat. Jules explains that he has written his reasons in a letter so that they (the authorities) will have all the relevant details on record. Mr Newport glances over the two pages and promises to arrange an interview with Mr Stainthorpe, the classifications officer. The cell door is banged shut.

11.09 am

The cell door is opened a second time. On this occasion it's Mr Nutbourne, who says, 'Now tell me, Jeffrey,' (the first officer to call me by my Christian name) 'do you want the good news or the bad news?'

'You decide,' I suggest.

'You won't be going to C wing after all, because we're going to move you down to join your friends on the enhanced corridor.'

'So what's the bad news?' I ask.

'Unfortunately, a cell won't be available until 29 August, when the next prisoner on that corridor will have completed his sentence.'

'But you could still put me in a single cell on another part of the block.'

'Don't push your luck,' he says with a grin, before slamming the door closed.

DAY 26

12 noon

Lunch: soup (minestrone) and a piece of brown bread (fresh). Couldn't face the meat pie. Heaven knows what animal's inside it.

2.00 pm

Gym: I'm the first to set foot in the gym, only to find that the running machine has broken down. Damn, damn, damn.

I warm up and stretch for a few minutes before doing ten minutes on the rower. I manage 1,909 metres, a vast improvement on yesterday. A little light weight training before moving on to a bicycle, the like of which I have never seen before. I can't get the hang of it until Mr Maiden comes to my rescue and explains that once you've set the speed, the peddles just revolve until you stop them. He sets the pace at thirty kilometres per hour, and leaves me to get on with it. I sweat away for ten minutes, and then realize I don't know how to turn it off. I shout to Everett (GBH) for help – a black man who I sat next to during the dominoes encounter – but he just grins, or simply doesn't understand my predicament. When my screaming goes up a decibel, Mr Maiden finally comes to my rescue. He can't stop laughing as he shows me which button I have to press to bring the machine to a halt. It's marked STOP – in red. I fall off the bike, exhausted, which causes much mirth among the other prisoners, especially the dominoes players. I use the rest of my time lying on a rubber mat recovering.

As the prisoners begin to make their way back to their cells – no gates, no searches – I'm called to Mr Maiden's office. Once his door is closed and no other prisoner can overhear, he asks, 'Would you like to join the staff on Friday morning to assist with a special needs group from Dereham Adult Training Centre?'

'Of course I would,' I tell him.

'Jimmy is the only other prisoner who presently helps that group, so perhaps you should have a word with him.'

I thank Mr Maiden and return to my cell. I don't immediately take a shower as I am still sweating from the bicycle experience, so I use the time to call my PA, Alison. I tell her I need more A4 pads and pens because I'm currently writing two to three thousand words a day. I also need stamped envelopes addressed to her – large A4 size for the manuscript and slightly smaller ones so I can turn round my daily postbag.* Alison tells me that because of the sackfuls of letters I am receiving both in prison and at the office, as well as having to type two scripts at once, she's putting in even longer hours than when I was a free man.

'And to think that you were worried about losing your job if I were to end up in jail,' I remind her. 'Just wait until I get my hands back on my novel.† You'll be working weekends as well.'

Alison confirms that the last five chapters of *Belmarsh* have arrived safely, thanks to the cooperation of Roy, the censor. No such problem at Wayland, where you just drop your envelope in a postbox and off it goes. I remind her that I need the *Belmarsh* script back as soon as possible, to go over it once again before I let Jonathan Lloyd (my agent) read it for the first time. My final request is to be put through to Will.

'He's in Cambridge with Mary.'

Although I check to see how many units are left on the phonecard, I haven't needed to worry about the problem lately as Dale seems to be able to arrange an endless supply of them.

---

* You're not allowed stamps as they could be used for trading drugs, but you are permitted stamped addressed envelopes.
† Published in 2002 as *Sons of Fortune*.

315

I dial Cambridge and catch Mary, who is just leaving to chair a meeting at Addenbrooke's Hospital, where she is deputy chairman. After a few words, she passes me over to Will. He is full of news and tells me Mum has been preparing in her usual diligent way for the *Today* interview. Since he spoke to me last, Andy Bearpark, who covered Kurdish affairs at the Overseas Development Administration during the relevant time, confirms he has been contacted by KPMG regarding the audit. Will feels the police will be left with little choice but to complete their initial report quickly and reinstate my D-cat. I thank him, particularly for the support he's giving his mother. I then tell him that I've finished the Belmarsh section of the diaries and ask if he's found time to read the odd chapter.

'I just can't face it, Dad. It's bad enough that you're there.' I tell him that I have already decided that there will be three volumes of the prison diary: Hell, Purgatory and Heaven, with an epilogue called 'Back to Earth'. This at least makes him laugh. As I'm telling him this, Jimmy passes me in the corridor and I turn to ask if he could spare me a moment. He nods, and waits until I finish my conversation with Will.

Jimmy has also heard that I may be joining them on the enhanced wing, but wonders if Nutbourne's information came from on high.

'Exactly my thoughts,' I tell him. I then mention that Mr Maiden has invited me to join them in the gym on Friday morning to assist with the special needs group. I'm surprised by his reaction.

'You jammy bastard,' says Jimmy. 'I had to wait a couple of years before I was invited to join that shift, and you get asked after four days.' Funnily enough I hadn't thought of it as a perk, but simply as doing something worthwhile.

Jimmy invites me down to his cell for a drink, my only

chance of having a Diet Coke. We're joined by Jason, who spotted me in the corridor. Jason hands me a pair of slippers and a wash bag, which are normally only issued to enhanced prisoners.

'You jammy bastard,' repeats Jimmy, before he starts going on about his weight. Jimmy is six foot one, slim and athletic (see plate section). He trains every day in the gym and is known by the inmates as Brad Pitt.

'More like Arm Pitt,' says Jason.

Jimmy smiles and continues to grumble, 'I need to put on some weight.'

'I like you as you are, darling,' Jason replies.

I decide this is an ideal opportunity to ask them how drugs are smuggled into prison. Both throw out one-liners to my myriad questions, and between them continue my education on the subject.

Of the six major drugs – cannabis, speed, Ecstasy, cocaine, crack cocaine and heroin – only cannabis and heroin are in daily demand in most prisons. Each wing or block has a dealer, who in turn has runners who handle any new prisoners when they arrive on the induction wing. It's known as Drug Induction. This is usually carried out in the yard during the long exercise break each morning. The price ranges from double the street value to as much as a tenfold mark-up depending on supply and demand; even in prison free enterprise prevails. Payment can be made in several ways. The most common currency is phonecards or tobacco. You can also send in cash to be credited to the dealer's account, but most dealers don't care for that route, as even the dumbest officer can work out what they're up to. The preferred method is for the recipient of the drugs to arrange for a friend to send cash to the dealer's contact on the outside, usually his girlfriend, wife or partner. Just as there is a canteen list of prices taped to the wall outside the main office, so there is an accepted but, unprinted list, of available drugs in any prison. For example, the price of five joints of cannabis would work out at around £10 or five phonecards; a short line of cocaine would cost about £10, while heroin, a joey or a bag, which is about half a gram, can cost as much as £20.

Next we discuss the bigger problem of how to get the gear into prison. Jason tells me that there are several ways. The most obvious is via visits, but this is not common as the punishment for being caught usually fits the crime, for both the visitor and the prisoner. If you are caught, you automatically lose your visits and the use of phonecards. For most prisoners this is their only lifeline to the outside world. Few, other than desperate heroin addicts, are willing to sacrifice being able to see their family and friends once a fortnight or speak to them regularly on the phone. So most dealers revert to other safer methods because were they to be caught twice, they not only lose the right to a phonecard as well as a visit, but will be charged with the offence and can expect to have time added to their sentence.

'What are the other methods?' I ask.

'You can arrange to have gear thrown over the wall at a designated time so it can be picked up by a gardener or a litter collector. Helps to supplement their seven pounds a week wages,' Jason explains. 'But home leave or town visits are still the most common source of drugs coming in. A clever courier can earn some extra cash prior to being released.'

'Mind you,' adds Jimmy, 'if you're caught bringing gear in, not only do you lose all your privileges, but you can be transferred to an A-cat with time added to your sentence.'

'What about by post?' I ask.

'Sending in a ballpoint pen is a common method,' Jason says. 'You half fill the tube with heroin and leave the bottom half full of ink, so that when the screws remove the little cap on the bottom they can only see the ink. They could break the tube in half, but that might mean having to replace as many as a hundred biros a week. But the most common approach still involves brown envelopes and underneath stamps.'

'Envelopes?' I ask.

'Down the side of most large brown envelopes is a flap. If you lift it carefully you can place a line of heroin along the inside and carefully seal it back up again. When it comes in the post it looks like junk mail or a circular, but it could be hiding up to a hundred quid's worth of skag.'

'One prisoner went over the top recently,' says Jimmy. 'He'd been enhanced and put on the special wing. One of our privileges is that we can hang curtains in our cell. When his selected curtains arrived, prison staff found the seams were weighed down with heroin. The inmate was immediately locked up in segregation and lost all his privileges.'

'And did he also get time added to his sentence?'

'No,' Jason replies. 'He claimed that the curtains were sent in by his co-defendant from the original trial in an attempt to stitch him up.' I like the use of the words 'stitch him up' in this context. 'Not only did he get away with it,' continues Jimmy, 'but the co-defendant ended up being sentenced to five years. Both men were as guilty as sin, but neither of them ended up in jail for the crime they had committed,' Jimmy adds. Not the first time I've heard that.

'But you can also have your privileges taken away and time added if you're caught *taking* drugs,' Jason reminds me.

'True,' says Jimmy, 'but there are even ways around that. In 1994 the government brought in mandatory drug testing to catch prisoners who were taking illegal substances. But if you're on heroin, all you have to do is purchase a tube of smoker's toothpaste from the canteen and swallow a mouthful soon after you've taken the drug.'

'How does that help?' I ask.

'If they ask for a urine sample,' explains Darren, 'smoker's toothpaste will cloud it, and they have to wait another twenty-four hours before testing you again. By the time they conduct a second test, a couple of gallons of water will have cleared any trace of heroin out of your system. You may be up all night peeing, but you don't lose your privileges or have time added.'*

'But that's not possible with cannabis?' I ask.†

'No, cannabis remains in your bloodstream for at least a month. But it's still big business whatever the risk, and you can be fairly certain that the dealers never touch any drugs themselves. They all have their mules and their sellers. They end up only taking a small cut, and are rarely caught.'

'And some of them even manage to make more money inside prison than they did outside,' adds Jason.

The call for tea is bellowed down the corridor by an officer. I close my notepad, thank Jason for the slippers and wash bag, not to mention the tutorial, and return to my cell.

5.00 pm

Supper: vegetarian pie and two potatoes. If I become enhanced, I will be allowed to have my own plate plus a mug or cup sent in, not to mention curtains.

---

* Providing a contaminated urine sample is a *reportable* charge under prison rules.
† Cannabis can remain in the bloodstream for up to twenty-eight days. On arrival at a remand prison, you can be tested, but are likely to be given twenty-eight days' grace in order to clear your system out. However, if you are found to be positive on the twenty-ninth day, the prison adjudication system comes into force.

6.00 pm

Write for just over an hour.

7.15 pm

Watch Sue Barker and Roger Black sum up the World Athletics Championship, which has been a disaster for Britain. One gold for Jonathan Edwards in the triple jump and a bronze for Dean Macey in the decathlon. The worst result for Britain since the games began in 1983, and that was following such a successful Olympics in Sydney. I'm almost able to convince myself that I'm glad I was prevented from attending.

8.00 pm

Read through my letters. Just over a hundred today.

9.00 pm

Jules and I watch a modern version of *Great Expectations* with Robert De Niro and Gwyneth Paltrow. If I hadn't been in prison, I would have walked out after fifteen minutes.

I begin to read *Famous Trials* selected by John Mortimer. I start with Rattenbury and Stones, the problem of a younger man falling in love with an older woman. Now that's something I haven't experienced. I fall asleep around eleven.

DAY 27　　　　TUESDAY 14 AUGUST 2001

6.18 am

Overslept. After a night's rain, the sun is peeping through my four-bar window. I write for a couple of hours.

8.20 am

Breakfast: two Weetabix, one hard-boiled egg and a piece of toast.

10.56 am

I've been writing for about an hour when the cell door is opened; Mr Clarke tells me that as part of my induction I must attend a meeting with a representative from the BoV (Board of Visitors). Everything has an acronym nowadays.

Nine prisoners assemble in a waiting room opposite Mr Newport's office. There are eleven comfortable chairs set in a semicircle, and a low table in the middle of the room. If there had been a few out-of-date magazines scattered on the table, it could have passed for a GP's waiting room. We have to hang around for a few minutes before being joined by a man in his late fifties, who looks like a retired solicitor or bank manager. He's about five foot nine with greying hair and a warm smile. He wears an open-neck shirt and a pair of grey flannels. I suspect that the only other time he's this casually dressed is on a Sunday afternoon.

He introduces himself as Keith Flintcroft, and goes on to explain that the Board is made up of sixteen local people appointed by the Home Office. They are not paid, which gives them their independence.

'We can see the governor or any officer on request, and although we have no power, we do have considerable influence. Our main purpose,' he continues, 'is to deal with prisoners' complaints. However, our authority ends when it comes to an order of the governor. For example, we cannot stop a prisoner being placed in segregation, but we can make sure that we are supplied with details of the offence within a period of seventy-two hours.* We can also read any written material on a prisoner with the exception of their legal papers or medical records.'

Mr Flintcroft comes over as a thoroughly decent bloke, a man who obviously believes in giving service to the local community. Just like so many thousands of citizens up and down the country he expects little reward other than the satisfaction of doing a worthwhile job. I believe that if he felt a prisoner was getting a rough deal, he would, within the limits of his power, try to do something about it.

He ends his ten-minute chat by saying, 'You'll find that we spend a lot of our time roaming around the prison. You can't miss us because we wear these distinctive buff-coloured name

---

* Often, when a prisoner in segregation asks to see a member of the BoV, that request is not passed on for seventy-two hours, by which time any swelling or wound caused by fighting with an officer will be less obvious.

badges. So feel free to come and talk to us whenever you want to – in complete confidence. Now, are there any questions?'

To my surprise, there are none. Why doesn't anyone mention the state of the cells on the induction wing compared with the rest of the prison? Why, when there is a painter on each wing, who I observe working every day, isn't there one to spruce up the induction wing? Do they leave the wing in a filthy condition so that when inmates are moved to another part of the prison they'll feel it's an improvement, or is it that they just can't cope with the turnover of prisoners? Either way, I would like to tell Governor Kate Cawley (I've discovered the governor's name on a notice board, but haven't yet come across her) that it's degrading, and a blip in an otherwise well-run prison. Why are the induction prisoners locked up for such long hours while the rest of the inmates are given far more freedom? And why ... And then it hits me. I am the only person in that room who hasn't been through this process before, and the others either simply don't give a damn or can't see the point of it. They are mostly hardened criminals who just want to complete their sentence and have as easy a time as possible before returning to a life of crime. They believe that the likes of Mr Flintcroft will make absolutely no difference to their lives. I suspect that the likes of Mr Flintcroft have, over the years, made a great deal of difference to their lives, without their ever realizing or appreciating it.

Once Mr Flintcroft accepts that there are going to be no questions, we all file out and return to our cells. I stop and thank him for carrying out his thankless task.

12 noon

Mr Chapman tells me I have a large parcel in reception, which I can pick up after dinner (lunch).

12.15 pm

Lunch: spam fritters, two potatoes and a glass of Evian. HELP! I'm running out of Evian.

12.35 pm

I report to reception and collect my parcel, or what's left of it. It originally consisted of two books: Alan Clark's *Diaries*, and *The Diving Bell and the Butterfly* by Jean-Dominique Bauby, which has been sent in by Anton, one of James's closest friends. They're accompanied by a long letter about the latest bust-up with his girlfriend (I do love the young – only *their* problems exist) and, from Alison, a dozen writing pads, two packets of liquid-point pens and six books of first-class stamps. Mr Chapman explains that I can keep the long letter from Anton, but everything else will be placed in my box at reception and returned to me only when I'm transferred or released.

3.15 pm

I have become so accustomed to prison life that I not only remember to take my gym card, but also a towel and a bottle of water to my afternoon gym session. The running machine still isn't working, so I'm back to ten minutes on the rower (1,837 metres – not very impressive) followed by a light weight-training session and ten minutes on the bike, which I now know how to turn on and, more importantly, turn off.

Everett (GBH) leaves his 240-pound bench press, and asks if he can have a swig of my Evian. I nod, as I don't think there's much of an alternative. A moment later his black weight-lifting partner – taller and wider – strolls across and takes a swig without asking. By the time I've finished stretching, the bottle is empty.

Once I'm back on my wing I try to take a shower, but the door is locked. I look through the tiny window. It's all steamed up, and two prisoners are banging on the door trying to get out. I cannot believe that it is prison policy to lock them in and me out. I hang around for about ten minutes with a couple of other prisoners before an officer eventually appears. I tell him I'd like to have a shower.

'You've missed your chance.'

'I didn't have a chance,' I tell him. 'It's been locked for the past ten minutes.'

'I've only been away for a minute, maybe two,' he says.

'I've been standing here for nearly ten minutes,' I politely point out.

'If I say it's one minute, it's one minute,' he says.

I return to my cell. I now feel cold and sweaty. I sit down to write.

6.00 pm

Supper. A bowl of thick, oily soup is all I can face. Back in my cell I pour myself half a mug of blackcurrant juice. The only luxury left. At least I'm still losing weight.

6.30 pm

Exercise: I walk around the perimeter fence with Jimmy and Darren. Just their presence stops most inmates from giving me a hard time.

7.00 pm

I finally manage a shower. I then put on a prison tracksuit, grey and baggy, but comfortable. I decide to call Mary. There is a queue for the phone as this is the most popular time of day. When it's my turn, I dial the Old Vicarage only to find that the line is engaged.

I spot Dale hanging around in the corridor, obviously wanting to speak to me. He tells me that the money hasn't arrived. I assure him that if it isn't in the morning post, I'll chase it up. I try Mary again – still engaged. I go back to my cell and prepare my desk for an evening session. I check my watch. It's 7.55 pm. I'll only have one more chance. Back to the phone. I call Cambridge. Still engaged. I return to my cell to find an officer standing by the door. I'm banged up for another twelve hours.

8.00 pm

I read through today's script and then prepare outline notes for the first session tomorrow, to the accompaniment of two West Indians hollering at each other from cells on opposite sides of the wing. I remark to Jules that they seem to be shouting even louder than usual. He resignedly replies that there's not a lot you can do about window warriors. I wonder. Should I push my luck? I go over to the window and suggest in a polite but firm voice that they don't need to shout at each other. A black face appears at the opposite window. I wait for the usual diatribe.

'Sorry, Jeff,' he says, and continues the conversation in a normal voice. Well, you can only ask.

DAY 28   WEDNESDAY 15 AUGUST 2001

6.04 am

I wake, only to remember where I am.

8.15 am

Breakfast: when I go down to the hotplate to collect my meal, Dale gives me a nod to indicate that the money has arrived.

8.30 am

Phone Mary to be told that she's doing the *Today* programme with John Humphrys tomorrow morning and will be visiting me on Friday with Will. As James is on holiday, she suggests that the third place is taken by Jonathan Lloyd. He wants to discuss my new novel, *Sons of Fortune*, and the progress of the diary. As I am allowed only one visit a fortnight, this seems a sensible combination of business and pleasure, although I will miss not seeing James.

Phone Alison, who says she'll have finished typing *Volume One – Belmarsh: Hell* by Wednesday (70,000 words) and will post it to me immediately. She reminds me that from Monday she will be on holiday for two weeks. I need reminding. In prison you forget that normal people go on holiday.

When I return to my cell, I find David (whisky bootlegger) sweeping the corridor. I tell him about my water shortage. He offers me a large bottle of diet lemonade and a diet Robinsons blackcurrant juice in exchange for a £2 phonecard, which will give him a 43p profit. I accept, and we go off to his cell to complete the transaction. There is only one problem: you are not allowed to use phonecards for trading, because it might be thought you are a drug dealer. Each card has the prisoner's signature on the back of it, not unlike a credit card (see plate section).*

'No problem,' says David (he never swears). 'I can remove your name with Fairy Liquid and then replace it with mine.'

'How will you get hold of a bottle of Fairy Liquid?'

'I'm the wing cleaner.'

Silly question.

10.00 am

My pad-mate Jules has begun his education course today (life and social skills) so I have the cell to myself. I've been writing for only about thirty minutes when my door is unlocked and I'm told the prison probation officer wants to see me. I recall Tony's (absconding from Ford Open Prison) words when I was at Belmarsh: 'Don't act smart and find yourself on the wrong side of your probation officer, because they have considerable sway when it comes to deciding your parole date.'

I'm escorted to a private room, just a couple of doors away

---

* Some inmates sign their phonecards in pencil, as there is no prison rule against this. If there is a way around a regulation, a prisoner will find it.

from Mr Tinkler's office on the first-floor landing. I shake hands with a young lady who introduces herself as Lisa Dada. She is a blonde of about thirty and wearing a V-neck sweater that reveals she has just returned from holiday or spent a long weekend sitting in the sun. Like everyone else, she asks me how I am settling in. I tell her that I have no complaints other than the state of my cell, my rude introduction to rap music and window warriors.

Lisa begins by explaining that she has to see every prisoner, but there isn't much point in my case because her role doesn't kick in until six months before my parole.* 'And as I'm moving to Surrey in about two months' time,' she continues, 'to be nearer my husband who is a prison officer, you may well have moved to another establishment long before then, so I can't do much more than answer any questions you might have.'

'How did you meet your husband?' I ask.

'That's not the sort of question I meant,' she replies with a grin.

'He must be Nigerian.'

'What makes you think that?'

'Dada. It's an Igbo tribe name, the tribe of the leaders and warriors.'

She nods, and says, 'We met in prison in circumstances that sound as if they might have come from the pages of one of your novels.' I don't interrupt. 'I had a prisoner who was due to be released in the morning. The evening before, he was phoning his wife to arrange what time she should pick him up, but couldn't hear what she was saying because of the noise coming

---

*Parole: You are interviewed by a member of the Parole Board a few weeks before you have completed half your sentence, and their report can influence whether you should or should not be released.

from a TV in a nearby cell. He popped his head round the door and asked if the inmate could turn the volume down, and was told to "Fuck off". In a moment of anger he dropped the phone, walked into the cell and took a swing at the man. The inmate fell backwards onto the stone floor, cracked open his head and was dead before they could get him to a hospital. The first prison officer on the scene called for the assailant's probation officer, who happened to be me. We were married a year later.'

'What happened to the prisoner?' I ask.

'He was charged with manslaughter, pleaded guilty and was sentenced to three years. He served eighteen months. There was clearly no intent to murder. I know it sounds silly,' she adds, 'but until that moment, his record was unblemished.'

'So your husband is black. That can't have been easy for you, especially in prison.'

'No, it hasn't, but it helps me find a common thread with the dreadlocks.'*

'So what's it like being a thirty-something blonde probation officer?' I ask.

'It's not always easy,' she admits. 'Sixty per cent of the prisoners shout at me and tell me that I'm useless, while the other forty per cent burst into tears.'

'Burst into tears? That lot?' I say, thumbing towards the door.

'Oh, yes. I realize it's not a problem for you, but most of them spend their lives having to prove how macho they are, so when they come to see me it's the one chance they have to reveal their true feelings. Once they begin to talk about their families, their partners, children and friends, they often break down, suddenly aware that others might well be going through

---

*Dreadlocks is a term used by prisoners to describe a black man with long plaited hair.

an even more difficult time outside than they are locked up in here.'

'And the shouters, what do they imagine they're achieving?'

'Getting the rage out of their system. Such a disciplined regime creates pent-up emotions, and I'm often on the receiving end. I've experienced everything, including obscene language and explicit descriptions of what they'd like to do to me, while all the time staring at my breasts. One prisoner even unzipped his jeans and started masturbating. All that for twenty-one thousand a year.'

'So why do you do it?'

'I have the occasional success, perhaps one in ten, which makes it all seem worthwhile when you go home at night.'

'What's the worst part of your job?'

She pauses and thinks for a moment. 'Having to tell a prisoner that his wife or partner doesn't want him back just before they're due to be released.'

'I'm not sure I understand.'

'Many long-term prisoners phone their wives twice a week, and are even visited by them once a fortnight. But it's only when their sentence is drawing to a close and a probation officer has to visit the matrimonial home that the wife confesses she doesn't want her husband back. Usually because by then they are living with another man – sometimes their husband's best friend.'

'And they expect you to break the news?'

'Yes,' she replies. 'Because they can't face doing it themselves, even on the phone.'

'And is there any particular set of prisoners you don't like dealing with? The paedophiles, murderers, rapists, drug dealers, for example?'

'No, I can handle all of them,' she says. 'But the group I have no time for are the burglars.'

'Burglars?'

'They show neither remorse nor conscience. Even when they've stolen personal family heirlooms they tell you it's all right because the victim can claim it back on insurance.' She glances at her watch. 'I'm meant to be asking you some questions,' she pauses, 'not that the usual ones apply.'

'Try me,' I suggest. Lisa removes a sheet of paper from a file and reads out the listed questions.

'Are you married?, Are you living with your wife?, Have you any children?, Do you have any other children?, Are any of them in need of assistance or financial help?, Will you be returning to your family when you are released?, When you are released, do you have any income other than the ninety pounds the State provides for you?, Do you have somewhere to sleep on your first night out of prison?, Do you have a job to go to, with a guaranteed source of income?' She looks up. 'The purpose of the last question is to find out if you're likely to commit an offence within hours of leaving prison.'

'Why would anyone do that?' I ask.

'Because, for some of them, this is the only place that guarantees three meals a day, a bed and someone to talk to. You've got a good example on your wing. Out last month, back inside this month. Robbed an old lady of her bag and then immediately handed it back to her. He even hung around until the police arrived to make sure he was arrested.'

I think I know the prisoner she's referring to, and make a mental note to have a word with him. Our hour is drawing to a close, so I ask if she will stick with it.

'Yes. I've been in the service for ten years and, despite everything, it has its rewards. Mind you, it's changed a lot during the last decade. When I first joined, the motto emblazoned on our notepaper used to read, *Advise, Assist and Befriend.* Now it's

DAY 28

Enforcement, Rehabilitation and Public Protection; the result of a massive change in society, its new-found freedom and the citizen's demands for safety. The public doesn't begin to understand that at least thirty per cent of people in prison shouldn't be locked up at all, while seventy per cent, the professional criminals, will be in and out for the rest of their lives.'

There's a knock on the door. My hour's up, and we haven't even touched on the problem of drugs. Mr Chapman enters carrying two bundles of letters. Lisa looks surprised.

'That's only the first post,' Mr Chapman tells her.

'I can quite believe it,' she says. 'My parents send their best wishes. My father wanted you to sign one of his books, but I told him it would be most unprofessional.' I rise from my place. 'Good luck with your appeal,' she adds, as we shake hands. I thank her and return to my cell.

12 noon

Lunch: macaroni cheese and diet lemonade. I hate lemonade, so I spend some considerable time shaking the bottle in an effort to remove the bubbles. I have a considerable amount of time.

1.45 pm

Mr Chapman warns me that I will not be able to go to the gym this afternoon as I have to attend a CARAT (Counselling, Assessment, Referral, Advice and Through-care) meeting on drugs. This is another part of my induction. Despite the fact I've never touched a drug in my life, I can't afford to miss it. Otherwise I will never be moved from this filthy, dank, noisy wing. Naturally I comply.

2.00 pm

I try to pick up my books and notepads from reception only to be told by Mr Meanwell (a man who regularly reminds me 'Meanwell is my name, and mean well is my nature') that I can't have them because it's against prison regulations. All notepads and pens have to be purchased from the canteen and all books ordered through the library, who buy them direct from Waterstone's.

'But in Belmarsh they allowed me to have two notepads, two packets of pens and any number of books I required sent in, and they're a maximum-security prison.'

'I know,' says Meanwell with a smile. 'It's a damn silly rule, but there's nothing I can do about it.'

I thank him. Many of the senior officers know only too well what's sensible and what isn't, but are worried that if I receive what could be construed as special treatment it will be all over the tabloids the following morning. The rule is enforced because books, pads and pens are simply another way to smuggle in drugs. However, if I'm to go on writing, I'll have to purchase these items from the canteen, which means I'll need to cut down on Spam and Weetabix.

2.40 pm

I've been writing for about an hour when I am called to the CARAT meeting. Once again, eleven of us assemble in the room with the comfortable chairs. The CARAT representative is a young lady called Leah, who tells us that if we have any drug-related problems, she is there to advise and help. Leah reminds me of Mr Flintcroft, although she's pushing an even larger boulder up an even steeper hill.

DAY 28

I glance around the room at the other prisoners. Their faces are blank and resigned. I'm probably the only person present who has never taken a drug. The one comment Leah makes that catches the prisoners' attention is that if they were to have a period on D wing, the drug-free wing, it might even help with their parole. But before Leah can finish her sentence a ripple of laughter breaks out, and she admits that it's possible there are even more drugs on D wing than on A, B or C. Drug-free wings in most prisons have that reputation.*

When Leah comes to the end of her eight-minute discourse and invites questions, she is greeted with silence, the same silence Mr Flintcroft experienced.

I leave, feeling a little more cynical. Drugs are the biggest problem the Prison Service is currently facing, and not one prisoner has a question for the CARAT representative, let alone attempts to engage her in serious debate. However, I am relieved to observe that two inmates remain behind to have a private conversation with Leah.

6.00 pm

Kit change. Once a week you report to the laundry room for a change of sheets, pillowcases, towels and gym kit. I now have six towels and include four of them in my weekly change. They are all replaced, despite each prisoner only being allowed two. However, they won't replace my second pillowcase because you're allowed only one. I can't understand the logic of that.

You're meant to wash your own personal belongings, but I have already handed over that responsibility to Darren, who is

---

* This is yet another example of the implicit recognition by the Prison Service that over 70 per cent of inmates are on drugs.

the enhanced wing's laundry orderly. He picks up my bag of washing every Thursday, and returns it later that evening. He asks for no recompense. I must confess that the idea of washing my underpants in a sink shared with someone else's dirty cutlery isn't appealing.

6.30 pm

Supper. Unworthy of mention.

7.00 pm

Exercise. I walk round the perimeter of the yard with Darren and another inmate called Steve. Steve was convicted of conspiracy to murder. He is an accountant by profession, well spoken, intelligent and interesting company. His story turns out to be a fascinating one. He was a senior partner in a small successful firm of accountants. He fell in love with one of the other partners, who was already married to a colleague. One night, on his way home from work, Steve stopped at a pub he regularly frequented. He knew the barman well and told him that given half a chance he'd kill the bastard (meaning his girlfriend's husband). Steve thought nothing more of it until he received a phone call from the barman saying that for the right price it could be arranged. The phone call was being taped by the police, as were several others that followed. It was later revealed in court that the barman was already in trouble with the police and reported Steve in the hope that it would help have the charges against him dropped. It seems the key sentence that mattered was, 'Are you certain you want to go ahead with it?' which was repeated by the barman several times.

'Yes,' Steve always replied.

DAY 28

Steve and his girlfriend were arrested, pleaded guilty and were sentenced to seven years. She currently resides at Highpoint, while he has gone from A- to B- to C-cat status in a couple of years (record time), and is now living on the enhanced wing at Wayland with D-cat status. He doesn't want to move to an open prison because Wayland is near his home. He is also the prison's chief librarian. I have a feeling that you'll be hearing more about Steve in the future.

On the circuit round the perimeter we are joined by the prisoner I shared a cell with on my first night, Chris (stabbing with a Stanley knife). He tells me that the *News of the World* have been in touch with his mother and will be printing a story on Sunday. He tries to assure me that he has had no contact with them and his mother has said nothing.

'Then it will only be three pages,' I tell him.

When I return to my cell, Jules is looking worried. He's also heard that Chris will be featured in the *News of the World* this Sunday. Chris told him that a lot of his friends and associates don't even know he's in jail, and he doesn't want them to find out. He attends education classes twice a day and wants the chance to start a new life once he's been released. I just don't have the heart to tell him that the *News of the World* have absolutely no interest in his future.

10.00 pm

We watch the news. Still more August storms. At 10.30 Jules switches channels to *Ally McBeal* while I try unsuccessfully to sleep. I'm not sure which is more distracting, the TV in our cell, or the rap music emanating from the other side of the block.

DAY 29   THURSDAY 16 AUGUST 2001

5.50 am

I wake from a dream in which I had been using the most foul language when talking to Mary. I can't explain it. I write for a couple of hours.

8.00 am

I plug in Jules's radio so that I can hear Mary's interview with John Humphrys. I shave while the news is on, and become more and more nervous. It's always the same. I am very anxious when William screens one of the documentaries he's been working on, or James is running the 800 metres, and especially whenever Mary has to give a talk that lay people might expect to understand. She's first on after the news and handles all of John Humphrys' questions in that quiet academic way that could only impress an intelligent listener. But I can tell, even after her first reply, just how nervous she is. Once Mary has dealt with the Kurds and Baroness Nicholson, Humphrys moves on to the subject of how I'm getting on in jail. That was when Mary should have said, 'My agreement with you, Mr Humphrys, was to discuss only matters arising from the Kurds.' Once Mary failed

DAY 29

to point this out, he moved on to the trial, the appeal and the sentence. I had warned her that he would. He has no interest in keeping to any agreement made between her and the producer. And that's why he is such a sharp interviewer, as I know from past experience.

9.30 am

I call Mary, who feels she was dreadful and complains that John Humphrys broke the BBC's agreement and once the piece was over she told him so. What does he care? She then tells me that the CEO of the Red Cross, Sir Nicholas Young, was interviewed later, and was uncompromising when it came to any suggestion that one penny raised for the Kurds in the UK had not been accounted for. He went on to point out that I had nothing to do with either the collecting or distribution of any monies. I suggest to Mary that perhaps the time has come to sue Baroness Nicholson. Mary tells me that the lawyer's first priority is to have my D-cat reinstated so I can be moved to an open prison before we issue the writ. Good thinking.

'Don't waste any more of your units,' she says. 'See you tomorrow.'

9.50 am

Disaster. Darren reappears with my washing. All fresh and clean, but the dryer has broken down for the first time in living memory. I take the wet clothes back to my cell and hang the T-shirts on the end of the bed, my underwear from an open cupboard door and my socks over the single chair. The sun is shining, but not many of its rays are reaching through the bars and into my cell.

340

10.00 am

Today is the first day of the fourth test match against Australia, and Hussain is back as captain. He said that although we've lost the Ashes (3–0), English pride is now at stake. I write for an hour and then turn on the television at eleven to see who won the toss. It's been raining all morning. Of course it has; the match is at Headingley (Leeds). I switch off the television and return to my script.

11.40 am

I've been writing for over an hour when the cell door is unlocked. The governor would like a word. I go to the interview room and find Mr Carlton-Boyce and Mr Tinkler waiting for me.

Mr Carlton-Boyce looks embarrassed when he tries to explain why I can't have any writing pads and pens or Alan Clark's *Diaries*. I make a small protest but only so it's on the record. He then goes on to tell me that I will not be moving to C block after all. They've had a re-think, and I'll be joining the adults on the enhanced spur, but – and there is always a but in prison – as no one is being released until 29 August, I'll have to stay put until then.

I thank him, and ask if my room-mate Jules can be moved to a single cell, as I fear it can't be too long before the *News of the World* will do to him exactly what they've done to every other prisoner who has shared a cell with me. This shy, thoughtful man will end up being described as a drug baron, and he doesn't have any way of fighting back.

Governor Carlton-Boyce nods. Promises are never made in prison, but he does go as far as saying, 'The next thing on my agenda is cell dispersal, because we have eight more prisoners

341

coming in tomorrow.' I thank him and leave, aware that's about the biggest hint I'll get.

12 noon

Lunch. Dale passes me two little sealed boxes, rather than the usual single portion, and winks. I was down on today's menu for number three – vegetable stew – but when I get back to my cell, I discover the other box contains mushroom soup. So I linger over the soup followed by vegetable stew. It's not Le Caprice – but it's not Belmarsh either.

1.15 pm

I'm told that as part of my induction I must report to the education department and take a reading, writing and numeracy test. When I take my seat in the classroom and study the forms, it turns out to be exactly the same test as the one set at Belmarsh. Should I tell them that I took the papers only two weeks ago, or should I just get on with it? I can see the headline in the *Mirror*: Archer Refuses to Take Writing Test. It would be funny if it wasn't exactly what the *Mirror* would do.* I get on with it.

3.15 pm

Gym. It's circuit-training day, and I manage about half of the set programme – known as the dirty dozen. The youngsters are good, but the star turns out to be a forty-five-year-old gypsy,†

---

* If you want to study the details of the test, they're described in *Volume One – Belmarsh: Hell.*
† I later learn from an officer that it's politically incorrect to describe anyone as a gypsy nowadays. They prefer to be called travellers.

who is covered in tattoos, and serving an eleven-year sentence for drug dealing. He's called Minnie, and out-runs them, out-jumps them, out-lifts them, out-presses them, and isn't even breathing heavily at the end. He puts me to shame; I can only hope that the youngsters feel equally humiliated.

4.20 pm

I'm back in time for a shower. David (whisky bootlegger) is standing by my door. He tells me that he's written the outline for a novel and wants to know how to get in contact with a ghostwriter. This is usually a surrogate for *are you available?* I tell him exactly what I tell anyone else who writes to me on this subject (three or four letters a week): go to your local library, take out a copy of *The Writers' and Artists' Yearbook* and you'll find a section listing agents who handle ghostwriters. I assume that will keep him quiet for a few days.

4.41 pm

David returns clutching a copy of *The Writers' and Artists' Yearbook* and shows me a page of names. I glance down the list but none is familiar. I have come across only a handful of agents over the years – Debbie Owen, George Greenfield, Deborah Rodgers, Jonathan Lloyd and Ed Victor – but there must be at least another thousand I've never heard of. I suggest that as my agent is visiting me tomorrow, if he selects some names, I'll ask Jonathan if he knows any of them.

DAY 29

4.56 pm

David returns with the list of names written out on a single sheet of paper. He hands over a Diet Coke. He's what Simon Heffer would describe as 'a proper gent'.

6.00 pm

Supper. Vegetable pie, two boiled potatoes and a lump of petits pois, making *un seul pois*.

I switch on the TV. Australia are 241 for 3, and Ponting is 144 not out. Together with Waugh, they've put on 170. I switch off. Why did I ever switch on?

After supper, I go down to the Association room to find Dale (wounding with intent) and Jimmy (transporting Ecstasy tablets) playing snooker for a Mars bar.* It's the first time I've seen Jimmy beaten at anything, and what's more, he's being thrashed by a far superior player. It's a subject I know a little about as I was President of the World Snooker Association before I was convicted. Jimmy whispers in my ear, 'Dale beats everyone, but like any hungry animal, he has to be fed at least twice a day. We take it in turns to hand over a Mars bar. It's a cheap way of keeping him under control.' In case you've forgotten, Dale is six foot three and weighs twenty-seven stone.

After the game is over, the three of us join Darren in the exercise yard. Dale manages only one circuit before heading back in, exhausted, while the three of us carry on for the full forty-five minutes. During the second circuit, I tell them about Derek, who did the drawing of my cell (*Belmarsh*), and ask if

---

* The accepted tariff for almost all bets in prison is a Mars bar (30p).

they know of any artists in Wayland. Jimmy tells me that there is a brilliant (his word) artist on C block. I ask if he will introduce me.

'Be warned, he's weird,' says Jimmy, 'and can be very rude if he takes against you.'

I tell Jimmy that I've been dealing with artists for the past thirty-five years and I've never met one who could be described as normal. It's all part of their appeal.

'I feel like a drink,' says Darren as the evening sun continues to beat down on us. 'Know anyone who's got some hooch?' he asks Jimmy.

'Hooch?' I say. 'What's that?'

They both laugh, a laugh that suggests I still have much to learn. 'Every block,' says Darren, 'has a hotplate man, a cleaner, a tea-boy and a painter. They're all appointed by the screws and are paid around twelve pounds a week. Every block also has a drug dealer, a haircutter, a clothes-washer and a brewer. C block has the best brewer – for a two-pound phonecard, you can get half a litre of hooch.'

'But what's it made of?'

'The ingredients are normally yeast, sugar, water and orange juice. It's harder to produce during the summer months because you need the hot pipes that run through your cell to be boiling in order to ferment the brew, so it's almost impossible to get decent hooch in August.'

'What's it taste like?'

'Awful, but at least it's guaranteed to get you drunk,' says Jimmy. 'Which kills off a few more hours of your sentence, even if you wake up with one hell of a hangover.'

'If you're desperate,' Darren adds, 'fresh orange juice is still on the canteen list.'

'How does that help?'

'Just leave it on your window ledge in the sun for a few days, and you'll soon find out.'

'But where can you hide the hooch once you've made it?'

'We used to have the perfect hiding place,' Darren pauses, 'but unfortunately they discovered it.'

Jimmy smiles as I wait for an explanation. 'One Sunday morning,' Darren continues, 'the number one brewer on our spur was found roaming around inebriated. When breathalysed, he registered way above the limit. The drug squad were called in, and every cell on the spur was stripped bare, but no alcohol of any kind was discovered. His hiding place would have remained a mystery if a small fire hadn't broken out in the kitchen. An officer grabbed the nearest fire extinguisher and pointed it in the direction of the blaze, only to find that the flames leapt even higher. An immediate halt was called by the chef who fortunately understood the effects of ethanol, other-wise the prison might have been razed to the ground. A full enquiry was held, and three inmates were shipped out to differ-ent B-cats the following morning, "on suspicion of producing hooch".'

'In fact,' said Darren, 'It wasn't hooch they were guilty of brewing. This particular strain of neat alcohol had been made by filtering metal polish through six slices of bread into a plastic mug in the hope of removing any impurities.'

I feel sick, without even having to sample the brew.

Jimmy goes on to point out that not only are some inmates brighter than the officers, but they also have twenty-four hours every day to think up such schemes, while the screws have to get on with their job.

'But the best hooch I ever tasted,' said Darren, 'had a secret ingredient.'

'And what was that, may I ask?'

'Marmite. But once the screws caught on to how much yeast it contained, they took it off the canteen list.' He pauses. 'So now we just steal the yeast from the kitchen.'

'Damn,' I said. 'I like Marmite; it was on the Belmarsh canteen list.'

'I don't think that's a good enough reason, my lord, to be transferred back to Belmarsh,' says Darren. 'Mind you,' he adds, 'perhaps I should have a word with the governor, now it's known that you are partial to it.'

I kick him gently up the backside as an officer is passing in the opposite direction.

'Did you see that, Mr Chapman? Archer is bullying me.'

'I'll put him on report, and he'll be back in Belmarsh by the end of the week,' Mr Chapman promises.

We laugh as we continue on the perimeter circuit. However, I point out how easy it is to make an accusation, and how long it takes to refute it. It's been a month since Emma Nicholson appeared on *Newsnight* insinuating that I had stolen money intended for the Kurds, and it will probably be another month before the police confirm there is no case to answer.

'But just think about that for a minute, Jeffrey. If it hadn't been for that bitch Nicholson, you would never have met Jimmy and me, who have not only added greatly to your knowledge of prison life, but enabled a further volume to be written.'

7.30 pm

One of the officers says there's a package for me in the office. I'm puzzled as I've already had my mail for today, and registered letters are always opened in front of two officers, around eleven each morning. When I walk in, he makes a point of closing the office door before he hands over a copy of Alan Clark's *Diaries*, a pad and a book of stamps. Someone else who considers the regulations damned stupid.

He goes on to say that my wife will be searched when she visits the prison tomorrow. 'We're all embarrassed about it,' he adds, 'but it will be no worse than at an airport. But perhaps it might be wise to let her know. By the way, the press are still hanging about hoping to catch her when she arrives.' I thank him and leave.

8.00 pm

I read a few pages of the Clark *Diaries*, which I enjoy every bit as much a second time. I also enjoyed Alan's company, and will never forget a dinner party he gave at Saltwood just before the general election in 1997. Alan posed the question to his guests, 'What do you think the majority will be at the next election?' Most of the assembled gathering thought Labour would win by over a hundred.* The only dissenter was Michael Howard, who was Home Secretary at the time. He put up a bold defence of John Major's administration, and told his fellow guests that he felt it was still possible for the Conservatives to win the next election. Alan told him that if he really believed that, he was living in cloud cuckoo land. I don't know to this day if Michael was simply being loyal to the prime minister. Although I can tell you that, like John Major, he is one of those people who doesn't cross over to the other side of the road when you're in trouble.

---

* Selina Scott said that Labour would win by over 150, and she was closest to the final result.

10.00 pm

Suddenly feel very hungry – eat a bowl of cornflakes and a Mars bar. Check my clothes – still not dry. I don't bother with another of John Mortimer's great trials. Feel I have enough murderers surrounding me without having to read about them.

DAY 30   FRIDAY 17 AUGUST 2001

6.09 am

The first thing I notice when I wake is that my Mach3 razor has disappeared. The wash basin is next to the door. In future, after I've shaved, I'll have to hide it in my cupboard. It would have to be stolen on the day Mary is visiting me; I want to be clean shaven but I don't want to cut myself to ribbons with a prison razor. It also reminds me that, because I hadn't expected to be convicted, I've been wearing my Longines watch for the past month, and I must hand it over to my son during the visit this afternoon.

8.15 am

Breakfast. Before I go down to the hotplate, I extract a letter from yesterday's mail that is in Spanish. Dale has told me that one of the servers on the hotplate hails from Colombia, so he should be able to translate it for me. His name is Sergio, and he usually stands quietly on the end of the line, handing out the fruit. I pass the missive across to him, and ask if we could meet later. He nods, and hands me a banana in return.

9.00 am

Today's induction is education, once again held in the room with the comfy chairs. For the first time the other prisoners show some interest. Why? Because this is how they'll earn their weekly wage. The head of education introduces herself as Wendy. She must be in her fifties, has curly grey hair, wears a flowery blouse, white skirt and sensible shoes. She has the air of a headmistress.

Wendy wheels a little projector up to the front, and begins a slide show. Using the white brick wall as a backdrop, she shows us what her department has to offer. The first slide reveals five options:

Basic skills
English as an additional language
Social and life skills
Business skills
Art, craft and design

'Education,' Wendy points out, 'is part-time (one session a day), so you can only earn seven pounds thirty-five per week.' The other prisoners don't take a great deal of interest in this slide, but immediately perk up when the second chart flashes on to the wall. VT and CIT training courses:

Bricklaying
Plumbing
Electrical installation
Painting and decorating
Welding
Motor mechanics
Light vehicle body repair
Industrial cleaning
Computer application

The weekly pay for any one of these courses is also £7.35, but does give you a basic training for when you return to the outside world.

When the final slide comes up, most of the inmates begin licking their collective lips, because this offers not only real earning power, but a position of responsibility plus perks. The extra money guarantees a more substantial canteen list each week (extra tobacco) and even the opportunity to save something for when you are released. The slide reveals:

> Plastic recycling £10.15 per week
> Ration packing £9.35
> Gardening (one of the most sought-after jobs, with a long waiting list) £9.00
> General cleaner £6.70
> Works £8.50
> Kitchen £8.50
> Stores (very popular, longer waiting list than the MCC) £10.00
> Chapel £8.00
> Drug rehabilitation unit £6.70

Before she can turn back to face her audience, the questions come thick and fast. Wendy points out that most of these jobs already have waiting lists, even washing-up, as there are far more prisoners than jobs. Wendy handles the questions sympathetically, without giving anyone false hopes of being offered one of these more remunerative positions.

Her final task is to hand round more forms to be filled in. My fellow inmates grab them, and then take some time considering their options. I put a cross next to 'pottery' in the education box, but add that I would be happy to do a creative writing course, or teach other prisoners to read and write. Wendy has already pointed out that the education department is understaffed. However, she tells me that such an initiative would require the governor's approval, and she'll get back to me. I return to my cell.

11.00 am

I report to the gym to assist with the special needs group. They are about thirty in number, and I've been put in charge of four of them: Alex, Robbie, Les and Paul. Three head straight for the rowing machines, while Alex places himself firmly on the treadmill. He sets off at one mile an hour and, with coaxing and patience (something I don't have in abundance), he manages two miles an hour. I have rarely seen such delight on a competitor's face. This, for Alex, is his Olympic gold medal. I then suggest he moves on to the step machine while I try to tempt Paul off the rower and onto the running machine. I have to give him several demonstrations as to how it works before he'll even venture on, and when he finally does, we start him off at half a mile an hour. By using sign language – hands waving up and down – we increase his speed to one mile an hour. I next try to show him how to use the plus and minus buttons. He conquers this new skill by the time he's walked half a mile. While I teach him how to operate the machine, he teaches me to be patient. By the time he's done a mile, Paul has mastered the technique completely, and feels like a king. I feel pretty good too.

I look around the room and observe the other prisoners – murderers, drug barons, armed robbers and burglars, gaining just as much from the experience as their charges.

Our final session brings all the group together in the gym where we play a game that's a cross between cricket and football, called catchball. A plastic ball is bowled slowly along the ground to a child (I must remember that though they think like children, they are not), who kicks it in the air, and then takes a run. If they are caught, they're out, and someone else takes their place. One of the players, Robbie, catches almost everything, whether it flies above his head, at his feet, or straight at him. This is always greeted with yelps of delight.

By eleven thirty, we're all exhausted. The group are then ushered out of a special door at the side of the gym. The boys shake hands and the girls cuddle their favourite prisoner. Carl, a handsome West Indian, gets more cuddles than any of us (they see no colour, only kindness). As they leave to go home, they enquire how long you will be there, and thus I discover why prisoners with longer sentences are selected for this particular responsibility.* I make a bold attempt to escape with the group, who all laugh and point at me. When we reach the waiting bus, Mr Maiden finally calls me back.

12 noon

Lunch. I can't remember what I've just eaten because I'm glued to the morning papers. Mary is given rave reviews right across the board – dozens of column inches praising the way she handled John Humphrys.

Lord Longford's reported dying words, 'Free Jeffrey Archer', get a mention in almost every column. I didn't know Frank Longford well, but enjoyed his wife's reply to Roy Plomley on *Desert Island Discs*:

Plomley: 'Lady Longford, have you ever considered divorce?'

---

* Sex offenders who elect *not* to be placed on E wing but with the main prison population are never permitted to work with the special needs group.

Lady Longford: 'No, never. Murder several times, but divorce, never.'

I have a feeling Mary would have given roughly the same reply.

2.00 pm

I am watching the Australians leave the field – they were all out for 447 – when the cell door is unlocked and I'm told to report to the visitors' area. I switch off the TV and head out into the corridor. How unlike Belmarsh. I even have to ask the way. 'Take the same route as you would for the gym,' says Mr Chapman, 'but then turn right at the end of the corridor.'

When I arrive, the two duty officers don't strip search me, and show no interest in my watch, which is secreted under my shirtsleeve. For visits, all prisoners have to wear striped blue prison shirts and blue jeans.

The visitors' room is about the same size as the gym and is filled with seventy small round tables, each surrounded by four chairs – one red, three blue. The red chair and the table are bolted together so there is always a gap between you and your visitor. This is to prevent easy passing of illicit contraband. The prisoner sits in the red seat, with his back to the officers. In the middle of each table is a number. I'm fourteen. There is a tuck shop on the far side of the room where visitors can purchase non-alcoholic drinks, chocolate and crisps. The one prisoner trusted to handle cash in the shop is Steve (conspiracy to murder, librarian and accountant) – would-be murderer he may be, thief he is not. Once every prisoner has been seated, the visitors are allowed in.

I watch the different prisoners' wives, partners, girlfriends and children as they walk through the door and try to guess which table they'll go to. Wrong almost every time. Mary's about fifth through the gate. She is wearing a long white dress which shows off that glorious mop of dark hair. Will is only a pace behind, followed by my agent and close friend, Jonathan Lloyd. He and Will take a seat near the door, so that Mary and I can have a little time to ourselves.

Mary brings me up to date with what's happening at the Red Cross. Their CEO, Sir Nicholas Young, has been most supportive; no fence-sitter he. Because of his firm statements Mary feels confident that it won't be long before I am moved on to an open prison. She also feels that the Prison Service and the police have been put in an embarrassing position, and will fall back on claiming that they had no choice but to follow up Nicholson's accusation. The Red Cross may even consider taking legal action against her. The lawyers' advice is, if they do, we should remain on the sidelines. I agree. She beckons to Will who comes over to join us.

Will tells me that he's been monitoring everything, and although it's tough for me, they are both working daily on my behalf. I confess that there are times in the dead of night when you wonder if anyone is out there. But I realize when it comes to back-up, there can't be a prisoner alive with a more supportive family. When Will's completed his report, Jonathan is finally allowed to join us, while Will goes off to purchase six Diet Cokes and a bottle of Highland Spring. (Three of the Cokes are for me.)

Jonathan has travelled up to Wayland to discuss my latest novel. He also wants an update on the diaries. I'm able to tell him that Belmarsh is completed (70,000 words) although I still need to read it through once again, but hope to have it on his desk in about two weeks' time.

We discuss selling the newspaper rights separately, while allowing my publisher a 10 per cent topping right* on the three volumes, as they've been so good to me in the past. But we all agree that nothing should happen until we know the outcome of my appeal, both for conviction and sentence.

Once Jonathan feels his business is complete, he retires once again, so that I can spend the last half hour with Mary and Will. When we're alone, we recap on all that needs to be done before we meet again in a fortnight's time. At least I now have enough phonecards to keep in regular touch.

Steve comes across to clear our table – it's the first time Mary has met someone convicted of conspiracy to murder. This tall, elegant man 'looks more like a company secretary than a would-be murderer' is her only comment. 'You probably pass a murderer on the street once a week,' I suggest.

'Time for visitors to leave,' announces a voice behind me. I unstrap my Longines watch to exchange it for a twenty-dollar Swatch I purchased in a rash moment at Washington airport. Will is facing the two officers, who are seated on a little platform behind me. He nods, and we both put on our new watches.

'All visitors must now leave,' repeats the officer politely but firmly. We begin our long goodbyes and Mary is among the last to depart.

When I leave the room, the officer asks me to take off my shoes, which he checks carefully, but doesn't ask me to remove anything else, including my socks. He shows no interest in my watch and nods me through.

---

* After the final bid has come in, my publisher would be allowed to offer 10 per cent more and automatically be granted the rights.

DAY 30

4.17 pm

Back in my cell, I find my canteen order has been left on the end of the bed. Hip, hip, and my clothes are finally dry, hooray. As I unpack my wares, Dale arrives with back-up provisions.

6.00 pm

Supper. Beans and chips accompanied by a large mug of Volvic.

7.00 pm

Exercise. Dale joins Jimmy, Darren and me as we walk around the yard, and manages all three circuits. On the last one, he spots the artist he told me about yesterday. He is sitting in the far corner sketching a prisoner. An inmate is leaning up against the fence in what he assumes is a model's pose. We walk across to take a look. The drawing is excellent, but the artist immediately declares that he's not happy with the result. I've never known an artist say anything else. As he's more than fully occupied, we agree to meet tomorrow evening at the same time.

When I return to the wing, Sergio (hotplate, Colombian) asks me if I would like to join him in his cell on the enhanced spur. He's kindly translated the letter from the Spanish student; it seems that the young man has just finished a bachelor's degree and needs a loan if he's to consider going on to do a doctorate. I thank Sergio, and pen a note on the bottom of the letter, so that Alison can reply.

'Lock up,' bellows an officer. Just as I'm about to depart, Sergio asks, 'Can we talk again sometime, as there's something else I'd like to discuss with you?' I nod, wondering what this quiet Colombian can possibly want to see me about.

DAY 31   SATURDAY 18 AUGUST 2001

6.21 am

Had a bad night. There was an intake of young prisoners yesterday afternoon, and several of them turned out to be window warriors. They spent most of the night letting everyone know what they would like to do to Ms Webb, the young woman officer on night duty. Ms Webb is a charming, university-educated woman who is on the fast-track for promotion. Darren told me that whenever a new group of prisoners comes in, they spend the first twenty-four hours sorting out the 'pecking order'. At night, Wayland is just as uncivilized as Belmarsh, and the officers show no interest in doing anything about it. After all, the governor is sound asleep in her bed.

At Belmarsh I was moved into a single cell after four days. In Wayland I've been left for eleven days among men whose every second word is 'fuck', some of whom have been charged with murder, rape, grievous bodily harm and drug pushing. Let me make it clear: this is not the fault of the prison officers on the ground, but the senior management. There are prisoners who have been incarcerated in Wayland for some time and have never once seen the governor. I do not think that all the officers have met her. That's not what I call leadership.

359

DAY 31

One of yesterday's new intake thought it would be clever to slam my door closed just after an officer had unlocked it so that I could go to breakfast. He then ran up and down the corridor shouting, 'I locked Jeffrey Archer in, I locked Jeffrey Archer in.' Luckily, only a few of the prisoners are this moronic, but they still make everyone else's life unbearable.

8.15 am

Breakfast. One look at the lumpy, powdered scrambled egg and a tomato swimming in water and I'm off. As I leave, Sergio suggests we meet in his room at 10.30. I nod my agreement.

9.00 am

Saturday is a dreadful day in prison. It's the weekend and you think about what you and your family might have been doing together. However, because we are 'unlocked' during the day, but 'banged up' in the early evening, there is always a queue outside my cell door: prisoners wanting letters written, queries answered, or on the scrounge for phonecards and stamps. At least no one bothers to ask me for tobacco. So on a Saturday, my only chance of a clear two hours to write are between six and eight in the morning, and six and eight at night.

10.00 am

I call Chris Beetles at his gallery. It's the opening of his Cat Show, – these ones are in frames not cages – so I don't waste a lot of his time, and promise I'll call him back on Monday.

On my way back to the cell I pass Darren in the corridor and stop to ask him about Sergio, whose cell is three doors away from his.

'A real gentleman,' says Darren. 'Keeps himself to himself. In fact I don't know much more about him now than I did when he arrived at Wayland a year ago. He's a Colombian, but he's one of the few prisoners who never touches drugs. He doesn't even smoke. You'll like him.'

10.30 am

When I arrive at Sergio's cell he checks his watch as if he assumed I'd be on time. If the Archer theory is correct – namely that you can tell everything you need to know about a prisoner from his cell – then Sergio is a neat and tidy man who likes everything in its place. He offers me his chair, while he sits on the bed. His English is good, although not fluent, and it quickly becomes clear that he has no idea who I am, which helps considerably.

When I tell him I'm a writer, he looks interested. I promise to have one of my books (Spanish translation) sent in. An hour passes before he tells me anything about himself. He makes it clear, as if he wants the world to know, that Colombians fall into two categories: those who are involved in drugs and those who are not. He and his family come into the latter group, and he seems genuinely pleased when I tell him that I have an aversion to drugs that is bordering on the manic.

His family, he tells me, have no idea he's in jail.* In fact his weekly call to Bogotá accounts for almost his entire income. He's divorced with no children, so the only people he has to fool are his brother, his sister and his parents. They believe he has a responsible job with an import/export company in London. He

---

* Sergio is not his real name.

will return to Bogotá in five weeks' time. There is no need for him to purchase a plane ticket, as he will be deported. Were he ever to return to Britain, he would immediately be arrested, put back in jail, and would remain locked up until he had completed the other half of his eight-year sentence. He has no plans to come back, he tells me.

The conversation drifts from subject to subject, to see if we can find anything of mutual interest. He has a great knowledge of emeralds, coffee and bananas – three subjects of which I know virtually nothing, other than their colour. It's then I spot a photograph of him with, he tells me, his mother and sister. A huge smile comes over my face as he removes the picture from the shelf to allow me a closer look.

'Is that a Botero?' I ask, squinting at the painting behind his mother. He cannot hide his surprise that I should ever have heard of the maestro.

'Yes it is,' he says. 'My mother is a friend of Botero.'

I almost leap in the air, as I have long dreamed of adding a Botero to my art collection in London or my sculpture collection in Grantchester. In fact Chris Beetles and I travelled to Calabria two years ago to visit the great man at his foundry. Sergio quickly reveals that he knows a considerable amount about Latin American art, and names several other artists including Manzù, Rivera and Betancourt. He has met Botero, and his family are friends of Manzù. I tell him I would love to own one of their works, but both artists are way out of my price range, particularly Botero, who is considered to be the Picasso of South America. The French think so highly of him that they once held an exhibition of his sculptures along the Champs-Elysées; the first time a foreigner has been so honoured.

'It's just possible I could find one of his works at a price you could afford.'

'How is that possible?' I ask.

Sergio then explains to me at great length what he calls the 'Colombian mentality'.

'To start with, you have to accept that my countrymen only want to deal in cash. They do not trust banks, and do not believe in cheques, which is why they regularly alternate between being rich and penniless. When they are wealthy, they buy everything in sight – jewellery, yachts, cars, houses, paintings, women, anything; when they are poor they sell everything, and the women leave them. But Colombians have no fear of selling,' he continues, 'because they always believe that they will be rich again ... tomorrow, when they will buy back everything, even the women. I know a trader in Bogotá,' he continues, 'who bought a Botero for a million dollars, and five years later sold it for two hundred thousand cash. Give me time and I'll come up with a Botero at the right price,' he pauses, 'but I would expect something in return.'

Am I about to find out if Sergio is a con artist, or as Darren suggested, 'a real gentleman'?

'I have a problem,' he adds. 'I have been in jail for four years, and when I finish half my sentence I will be deported.' I'm trying to write notes as he speaks. 'I will be put on a plane without any presents for my three nephews and niece.' I don't interrupt. 'Would it be possible for you to get me three Manchester United shirts for the nephews – seven, ten and eleven years old – and a *Lion King* outfit for my eight-year-old niece?'

'Anything else?' I ask.

'Yes, I need a suitcase, because all I have is a HMP Wayland plastic bag, and,' he hesitates, 'I also need twenty pounds in phonecards so I can call Bogotá and not worry about being cut off.'

'Is that it?'

He hesitates once more. 'I would like one hundred pounds put in my prison account so I can pick up one or two things for my family at the airport. I don't want them to wonder why I don't have any presents for them.'

I consider his requests. For risk capital investment of around £200 I would have an outside chance of owning a Botero I can afford. I nod to show that I agree to his terms.

'If you do this for me,' he adds, 'I will tell you more. In fact I have already told you more in an hour than I have any other prisoner in four years.' He then writes down the name and address of a contact in London and says, 'Give her the suitcase, the T-shirts and the one hundred pounds, and she will send them on to me at Wayland. That way you won't be involved.'

11.44 am

I phone a friend who used to work in the T-shirt business, and pass on the order for Manchester United T-shirts and a *Lion King* outfit. He sounds intrigued, but doesn't ask any questions. I then call my driver at home and explain that the items are to be delivered to a flat in north London, along with £100 in cash. 'Consider it done,' he says.

11.51 am

I cross the corridor to Dale's room and tell him I need twenty pounds' worth of phonecards.

'Just like that, my lord?'

'Just like that,' I reply. 'Put it on my account and I'll have the money sent through to you.'

He opens a drawer and removes ten £2 cards and passes them across. 'You've wiped me out,' he says.

'Then get back to work, because I have a feeling I'm going to need even more next week.'

'Why? Are you calling America?'

'Right idea. Wrong continent.'

I leave Dale and return to Sergio's room. I hand over the ten phonecards and tell him that the other items will all have been delivered by this time tomorrow. He looks astonished.

'How fortunate that you are sent to this jail, just as I am leaving.'

I confess that I hadn't seen it quite that way, and remind him that we have a deal.

'One Botero, at a price you can afford, within a year,' he confirms. 'You'll have it by Christmas.'

When I leave him to return to my cell, I remember just how much I miss dealing, whether it's for £200 or £2 million. I once watched Jimmy Goldsmith bargaining for a backgammon board with a street trader in Mexico. It took him all of forty minutes, and he must have saved every penny of £10, but he just couldn't resist it.

12 noon

Lunch. I devour a plate of Princes ham (49p) surrounded by prison beans while I watch England avoid the follow on.*

2.00 pm

I head for the library – closed, followed by the gym – cancelled. So I'll have to settle for a forty-five-minute walk around the exercise yard.

---

* If you don't understand 'follow on', it would take a chapter to explain. Just be assured, it's not good.

DAY 31

3.00 pm

The man who was sketching the portrait of another prisoner yesterday is waiting for me as Darren, Jimmy and I walk out into the yard. He introduces himself as Shaun, but tells me that most inmates call him Sketch. I explain that I want a portrait of Dale (wounding with intent), Darren (marijuana only), Jimmy (Ecstasy courier), Steve (conspiracy to murder) and Jules (drug dealing) for the diary; a sort of montage. He looks excited by the commission, but warns me that he'll have to get on with it as he's due to be released in three weeks' time.

'Any hope of some colour?' I ask.

'Follow me,' he says. We troop across rough grass littered with rubbish and uneaten food to end up outside a cell window on the ground floor of C wing. I stare through the bars at paintings that cover almost all his wall space. There's even a couple on the bed. I'm left in no doubt that he's the right man for the job.

'How about a picture of the prison?' he suggests.

'Yes,' I tell him, 'especially if it's from your window, because I have an almost identical view two blocks over.' (See plate section.)

I then ask him how he would like to be paid. Shaun suggests that as he is leaving soon, it may be easier to send a cheque directly to his home, so his girlfriend can bank it. He says he'd like to think about a price overnight and discuss it with me during exercise tomorrow; I'm not allowed to visit his cell as he resides on another block so we can only talk through his barred window.*

---

*In theory, this is to prevent the movement of drugs from block to block, but I don't know why they bother, because every prisoner knows exactly which window to go to if they want a fix. Just as I go up to C wing, third window on the left, to view Shaun's pictures, some of the prisoners are, at this moment, queuing outside the next window to purchase their drugs.

5.00 pm

Supper: vegetable stir-fry and a mug of Volvic.

I've negotiated two art deals today, so I feel a little better. Because the library was closed and I have finished *The Glass Bead Game*, I have nothing new to read until it opens again tomorrow. I spend the rest of the evening writing about Sergio.

DAY 32   SUNDAY 19 AUGUST 2001

5.59 am

First peaceful night in weeks. Yesterday I visited the three prisoners with noisy stereos and the two inmates who go on shouting at each other all through the night. But not before I had been asked to do so by several other prisoners on the spur. I got two surprises: firstly, no one was willing to accompany me – they were all happy to point out which cells they were in, but no more than that. The second surprise was that all of the transgressors, without exception, responded favourably to my courteous request with either, 'Not me, gov,' or, 'Sorry, Jeff, I'll turn it down,' and in one case, 'I'll turn it off at nine, Jeff.' Interesting.

8.15 am

Breakfast. A prisoner in the queue for the hotplate asks me if I'm moving cells today.

'No,' I tell him. 'What makes you think that?'

'The name card outside your cell has disappeared, always the first sign that you're on the move.'

I laugh, and explain, 'It's been removed every day – a sort of talisman of my existence. I seem to be the only thing that doesn't move.'

When I reach the hotplate Dale gives a curt nod, a sign he needs to see me; Sergio also nods. I leave the hotplate empty-handed, bar a slice of toast and two appointments. I return to my cell and eat a bowl of my cornflakes with my milk.

9.15 am

Gym. The treadmill is not working again, so I start with the rower and manage 1,956 metres in ten minutes. I would have done better if I hadn't started chatting to the inmate on the next rower. All across his back is tattooed the word MONSTER, though, in truth, he's softly spoken and, whenever I've come across him in the corridor, friendly. I ask what his real name is.

'Martin,' he whispers, 'but only my mother calls me that. Everyone else calls me Monster.' He's managed 2,470 metres in ten minutes despite chatting to me.

He tells me that in January, when he arrived at Wayland, he weighed seventeen and a half stone. He is a taxi driver from Essex, and admits that it was easy to put on weight in that job. Now he tips the scales at thirteen stone five pounds, and his girlfriend has to visit him every two weeks just to make sure that she'll still recognize him when he's released. He was sentenced to three years for transporting cannabis from one Ilford club to another.

About a third of the men in this prison have been convicted of some crime connected with cannabis, and most of them will say, I repeat *say*, that they would never deal in hard drugs. In fact, Darren goes further and, snarling, adds that he would try to dissuade anyone who did. If cannabis were to be legalized – and for most of the well-rehearsed reasons, I remain unconvinced that it should – the price would fall by around 70 per cent, tax revenues would be enormous and prison numbers would drop overnight.

Many young prisoners complain, 'It's your lot who are smoking the stuff, Jeff. In ten years' time it won't even be considered a crime.' Jimmy admits that he couldn't meet the demand from his customers, and that he certainly never needed to do any pushing. Darren adds that although he and Jimmy covered roughly the same territory in Ipswich they hadn't come across each other until they ended up in jail, which will give you an idea of just how large the market is.

Just in case you've forgotten, I'm still in the gym. Monster leaves me to join Darren and Jimmy on the bench press, where he manages to pump ten reps of 250 pounds. I also turn to the weights where I achieve ten curls at 50 pounds. This is followed by a spell on the bicycle, where I break the world record by peddling three miles in twelve minutes and fifty-four seconds. Pity it's the world record for running.

Mr Maiden, the senior gym instructor, reintroduces me to the medicine ball, which I haven't come in contact with since I left school. I place the large leather object behind my head, raise my shoulders as in an ordinary sit-up, and then pass it up to him. He then drops it back on top of me. Simple, I think, until I reach my fifth attempt, by which time I'm exhausted and Mr Maiden is unable to hide his mirth at my discomfort. He knows only too well that I haven't done this exercise for over forty years, and what the result would be.

'We'll have you doing three sets of fifteen with a minute interval between sets before you're released,' he promises.

'I hope not,' I tell him, without explanation. I then carry out a fifteen-minute warm down and stretching as my trainer in London (Karen) would have demanded. At the end of the session

I am first at the gate, because I'll have to be in and out of the shower fairly quickly if I'm to get to the library before the doors are locked.

10.21 am

Jog to my cell, strip, shower, change, jog to the library. Still sweating, but nothing I can do about it. Steve (conspiracy to murder) is on duty behind the desk in his position as chief librarian. Because Steve's the senior Listener, he's allowed to wear his own clothes and is often mistaken for a member of staff. I return *Famous Trials* and take out *Twenty-one Short Stories* by Graham Greene.

10.30 am

Once I've left the library I walk straight across the corridor to the chapel and discover there are thirty worshippers in the congregation this week. From their dress, the majority must come from the local village. The black man sitting next to me, who was among the seven prisoners who attended last week, tells me it's the biggest turnout he's ever seen. This week a Methodist minister called Mary conducts the service, accompanied by an Anglican vicar called Val. Mary's sermon is topical. She talks about the World Athletics Championships and her feelings for those competitors who did not achieve what they had set out to do, but for many of them there will be another chance. I have now attended four consecutive church services, and the minister always pitches the message at what he or she imagines will be of interest to the inmates. Each time they have failed to treat us as if we might just be normal human beings. People who have not been to prison tend to fall into two categories. The majority who treat you as if you're a 'convict on the run' while the minority treat you as if you are in their front room.

After the blessing, we gather in an ante-room for coffee and biscuits with the locals. No need to describe them as they don't differ greatly from the kind of parishioners who attend church services up and down the country every Sunday morning. Average age double that of the prisoners. At twelve we are sent back to our cells. No search. Unaccompanied.

12 noon

Lunch. I haven't had a chance to speak to Dale or Sergio yet, so I fix appointments with Dale at 2 pm and Sergio at 3 pm. I leave the hotplate with a portion of macaroni liberally covered in cheese.

While we are waiting in the long queue, Darren tells me when it used to be almost all macaroni with little sign of any cheese. Nobody thought to comment about this, until it became clear that the allocation of cheese was becoming smaller and smaller as each week passed. Still no one did anything about it, until one week, when there was virtually no cheese, the officer on duty at last began to show some interest. The first thing he discovered was that the same cook had been on for the previous four Saturdays and Sundays, so the following weekend he kept an eye on that particular inmate. He quickly discovered that on Saturday night the prisoner in question was returning to his cell with a lump of cheese the size of a pillow (5kg). It was when three loaves of bread also went missing the same evening that the officer decided to report the incident to the governor. The following Saturday night a team of officers raided the prisoner's cell hoping to find out what he was up to. They discovered that he was running a very successful business producing Welsh rarebit, which, when toasted, was passed from cell to cell through the bars of his little window.

'And damn good they were,' adds Jimmy, licking his lips.

'How did he manage to toast them?' I demanded.

'On every wing there is a communal iron, which always ended up in Mario's cell on a Saturday evening,' explained Darren.

'How much did the chef charge?'

'For two nights' supply, a two-pound phonecard.'

'And how did they punish him?'

'The iron was confiscated, and Mario demoted to washer-up, with twenty-one days added to his sentence. But they had to reinstate him after a couple of months because so many inmates complained about the standard of cooking dropping during the weekends. So he was brought back, and after another six months they also forgot about the twenty-one-day added sentence.

'And what is Mario in for?' I ask.

'Tax evasion – three years – and the fraud squad needed to be just as sharp to discover what he was up to then,' says Darren as we leave the hotplate. I make a mental note to make sure I meet him.

2.00 pm

Dale wants to talk to me about my canteen list for next week and has set an upper limit of £20. 'Otherwise the screws will become suspicious,' he explains. £20 will be quite enough as I'm still credited each week with £12.50 from my own account. Dale's also solved my writing pad problem, because he's some-how got his hands on three A4 pads, for which he charges me £4. I would happily pay £10 as I'm down to twenty pages of my last pad, but this new supply should last me a month.

DAY 32

5.00 pm

I call Mary at Grantchester, but there is no reply. I try London but only get Alison's voice on the answer machine. I forgot she's away on holiday. In any case, it's Sunday.

5.45 pm

Supper. The ham looks good, but I'm down for the vegetarian dish and you can't change your mind once you've signed the weekly menu sheet. Dale thinks about giving me a slice, but as my bête noire is on duty behind the hotplate, he doesn't risk it. Every Sunday you are given a meal sheet which rotates on a four-week cycle (see opposite); you fill in your selection from a list posted outside the main office, giving the kitchen advance notice of how much they will have to order of each item. Can't complain about that.

6.00 pm

Banged up for the next fourteen hours. I begin *The Basement Room* by Graham Greene. His description of minor characters is breathtaking in its simplicity and the story, although complex, still demands that you turn the page. I consider it a reflection on the Nobel Committee, not Mr Greene, that he has never won the prize for literature.

Ch. 2.

INMATE PRE-SELECT MENU SHEET			

CELL NO	NAME		NUMBER
A2-49 .	ARCHER		FF8282

	MON	TUE	WED	THU	FRI	SAT	SUN
D	1	1	1	1	1	1	1
I	2	2	2	2	2	2	2
N	3	3	3	3	3	3	3
N	4	4	4	4	4	4	4
E	5	5	5	5	5	5	5
R	6	6	6	6	6		
	7	7	7	7	7		

	MON	TUE	WED	THU	FRI	SAT	SUN
T	1	1	1	1	1	1	1
	2	2	2	2	2	2	2
E	3	3	3	3	3	3	3
	4	4	4	4	4	4	4
A	5	5	5	5	5	5	5
	6	6	6	6	6	6	
	7	7	7	7	7	7	

WEEK NO: 9	DATE: AUGUST 19 2001

PLEASE CIRCLE ONE CHOICE FOR EACH MEAL FROM MENU AND
RETURN TO WING OFFICE BY WEDNESDAY LUNCH

INMATE'S SIGNATURE: Jeffrey Archer

cbs 6 February 1998

R3

DAY 33   MONDAY 20 AUGUST 2001

5.54 am

Wake and wonder how long it will take the police to close their file on the Kurds and allow me to be transferred to an open prison. I heard a story yesterday about a prisoner who wanted to do it the other way round. He put in an application to be transferred from a D-cat open prison to a C-cat – a more secure environment with a tougher regime. His reasons seem strange but, I'm told, are not uncommon.

He was serving a twenty-two-year sentence for murder. After five years, they moved him from an A-cat to a B-cat, which is a little more relaxed. After a further twelve years they transferred him to Wayland. At Wayland he became an enhanced prisoner with all the privileges that affords. He was also chief gardener, which allowed him to be out of his cell for most of the day and gave him an income of more than £30 a week. In his own world he wanted for nothing, and the governor considered him to be a model prisoner.

After twenty years he was granted D-cat status as part of his preparation for returning to the outside world. He was transferred to Ford Open Prison in Sussex to begin his rehabilitation.

He lasted at Ford for less than a month. One Saturday afternoon he absconded and turned himself in at the local police station a few hours later. He was arrested, charged with attempting to abscond and sent back to Wayland, where he remained until he had completed his sentence.*

The governor at the time couldn't resist asking him why he'd absconded. He replied that he couldn't handle the responsibility of making his own decisions. He also missed not having a proper job and the ordered discipline of the Wayland regime. But most of all he missed the high walls that surrounded the prison because they made him feel safe from all those people on the outside.

With less than six months to go before the end of his sentence, he was found in his cell with a piece of silver paper from a KitKat wrapper, a few grams of heroin and a lighted match.† He had even pressed the emergency button inside his cell to make certain that he was caught.

The governor wasn't sure what to do, because he knew only too well that the prisoner had never taken heroin in twenty years. Only six weeks were added to his sentence and he was released a few months later.

Within a month of leaving prison, he committed suicide.‡

---

* You can't escape from a D-cat, only abscond; a mistake the press continually make – because the word escape makes a better headline.

† The most ingenious method I came across for smoking heroin is to soak a Benson & Hedges packet in water and then separate the gold foil from the cardboard.

‡ Most suicides occur during the early stages of entering prison or soon after being released. Martin Narey, the Director General (now Commissioner for Correctional Services) spends a great deal of time telling the press how concerned he is about the number of suicides in prison – which incidentally have gone up every year during the past decade. What he doesn't tell you is how many suicides occur within a year of leaving prison, which is a far more damning indictment of the Prison Service's rehabilitation programme.

DAY 33

8.15 am

Breakfast. I have a Shredded Wheat and think of Ian Botham. This is doubly appropriate because it's twenty years ago this week that he scored 149 at Headingley and, with the assistance of Willis and Dilly, defeated Australia, despite England having to follow on. In today's match, Australia lead by 314, and I assume Adam Gilchrist will soon declare, as they've already won the series and England have only scored more than 300 in a final innings against Australia once in the last hundred years.

9.11 am

One of the prison chaplains visits me. She bears a message from Michael Adie, who until recently was the Bishop of Guild-ford. Michael and I first met in 1969 when he was Vicar of Louth and I was the Member of Parliament for that beautiful constituency.* He was a more natural friend for Mary, having gained a first-class honours degree in mathematics at Cam-bridge. Michael wants to visit me and has discovered that a bishop can see a prisoner without it affecting his quota of fort-nightly visits.

I suggest to Margaret, the prison chaplain, that for Michael to make the long journey to Norfolk is typical of his generous spirit, but it might be wiser to wait and find out which D-cat prison they are going to transfer me to. I feel sure it will be nearer London and he could then visit me there. She kindly agrees to relay that message back to him.

---

* We sat in the House of Lords together, and his contributions on a range of subjects were formidable.

12 noon

Lunch. When I reach the hotplate, Dale looks anxious and whispers that he has to see me urgently.

I return to my cell, flick on the television to find that England are 12 for 2 and an Australian victory now looks certain. All we can hope for now is a draw. The untutored Jules thinks England can still win. Bless him. After all, he has only taken to watching cricket because he's stuck in the same cell as me.

2.00 pm

Gym. I complete my usual programme and feel I'm just about back to the level of fitness I was before being sentenced. I leave the exercise room to check up on what's happening in the main hall, where I find a volleyball match in progress. So many prisoners want to join in that they are playing one team on and one team off. By the end of the game, I accept the fact that I can no longer hope to play at this level, and appoint myself referee. Within a minute, I've given a penalty point because a prisoner swears following one of my decisions. A near riot breaks out and it's several minutes before I can get the game started again. What then follows is a close, well-fought match without another swear word uttered. When I blow the final whistle, the players on both sides all turn to face me, and swear as one.

3.20 pm

After a shower, I sit in my tiny cell and watch England fight their way back to 107 for 2. Jules is still convinced England can win. Dale visits me in my cell soon after Jules has disappeared off to education. Dale warns me that he's been interviewed by a security officer. Although they have no proof, they are fairly sure that the five £20 postal orders he received last week came from me, and they've warned him that if any further monies materialize that cannot be accounted for, they'll set up a full enquiry. We both agree that payments will have to cease, and with it my weekly supplies. Help!

3.50 pm

The same officer interviews me thirty minutes later, saying he has reason to believe I have been sending money in to another prisoner. The officer could not have been more reasonable, and adds that if it occurs again, it could greatly harm my chances of regaining D-cat status. It is then that he asks me if I am being bullied and paying someone to protect me. I burst out laughing. The officer obviously feels that Dale, at six foot three and twenty-seven stone, is my paid minder.

I make it clear that no one is bullying me, and I don't require any protection, but if I do he will be the first person to hear about it. The last thing I need is to jeopardize my D-cat, or be beaten up.

I return to my cell to find England are 207 for 3 at tea and Butcher is playing out of his skin. Even McGrath is being regularly dispatched to all parts of the ground. Could Jules be right?

4.30 pm

Exercise. I go out into the yard every day now, not just because I need the exercise but to pick up stories from the prisoners on different wings. Many of them are professional criminals, while others are just stupid or lazy. The most dangerous and frightening are a combination of all three. However, a minority are bright; but for the circumstances of their upbringing many of them might well have held down responsible positions. Darren agrees with me, but pointing to an inmate a few paces ahead of us, adds, 'But not in his case.'

'Why?' I ask. 'Who's he?'

'That's Dumbo,' he says, but offers no further explanation until we have passed him and he is well out of earshot.

'In December last year,' Darren continues, 'Dumbo was unemployed and facing the prospect of a distinctly un-merry Christmas. His wife said she'd had enough, and told him to go out and get some money and she didn't care how. Dumbo disappeared off to the town's largest toy store, where he shoplifted a replica gun. He then walked across the road, held up the local chemist and departed with fourteen hundred pounds in cash. He returned home, handed over the money to his wife, confident that she would feel he'd done a good day's work. But after counting the notes, she told him that it wasn't enough and to go and get some more. Hold your breath,' said Darren, 'Dumbo once again leaves his home, returns to the high street, walks back into the same chemist shop with the intention of repeating the hold-up, only to find two police officers interviewing the proprietor. Dumbo was arrested on the spot, accompanied to the nearest police station, charged and later sentenced to eight years for robbery while in the possession of a firearm.'

No novelist would dare to consider such a plot.

5.15 pm

When I return to my cell, Jules is glued to the television. Butcher is still at the crease. We both watch as Jules's prediction comes true and England sweep to a famous victory – Butcher, having scored the winning run, is 173 not out. This is an innings he will not be the only person to remember for the rest of his life.

I feel I should point out that Jules is every bit as excited as I am. A convert. A week ago he couldn't understand a draw, let alone what a follow on was, now he can't wait for next Thursday to watch the fifth and final test. I do hope he doesn't expect them all to end like this.

5.45 pm

Supper. I'm tucking into my beans and chips when Mr Meanwell unlocks the cell door and asks to have a private word with me. He doesn't speak again until we are in his office and the door is closed.

'You were lucky to have got away with it this time, but don't do it again,' he warns me. 'If you do, it could hold up your D-cat for months. And if you're thinking of doing anything with Sergio, wait until he's completed his sentence.' I'm impressed by how well-informed Mr Meanwell is.*

---

*Most officers cultivate their own informers, but do not reveal to anyone, including other officers, who they are.

DAY 34   TUESDAY 21 AUGUST 2001

6.11 am

Slept well, write for two hours.

8.15 am

Breakfast. It's Rice Crispies again. It's taken me until the middle of the second week to work out that it's Shredded Wheat on Monday, Rice Crispies on Tuesday, cornflakes on Wednesday. Nothing changes. Everything is by rote.

10.00 am

My induction seems to have run its course. However, I remain on the induction wing as I wait for a single cell to become vacant. I am made aware of this because the cycle has begun again: a new group of prisoners is being seen by a member of the Board of Visitors. I peer through the little mesh window in the door; it's not Mr Flintcroft this time, but a lookalike.

DAY 34

10.15 am

Education. I pull on my newly supplied prison regulation heavy brown boots as I prepare for my first pottery lesson. Once I've left the spur I have to ask several officers and inmates the way to the Art Centre, which turns out to be on the other side of the prison.

When I finally locate it, the first person I see on entering the room is Shaun, who sits in the corner of the large square workshop working on an abstract pastel. He greets me with a smile. The next person I spot is a lady who I assume must be our tutor. She's around five foot six, dark-haired and dark-eyed with a warm smile. She introduces herself as Anne.

The first task Anne sets me is to read a pottery book and see if I come across any object I'd like to recreate. I try to tell her about my lack of talent in this area, but she just smiles. I begin to read the book as she moves on to Roger, a jolly West Indian (bank robber), who is doing a sculpture of the Virgin Mary. She then goes across to Terry (burglar), who is moulding his piece of clay into a lion. I am engrossed in my book when Anne returns, accompanied by a large lump of clay. She also has a thin wooden stick that looks like a knife without a handle, which is numbered four. She glances down at the page I've reached to see a head and shoulders figure of a man. With the help of the wooden knife, she carves chunks off the square putty to start forming the shoulders, and then leaves me to begin my first attempt at figurative sculpture.

As I turn my attention to the head and neck, I get into conversation with Shaun who is rubbing his fingers into the pastel to try and give his picture a blurred 'Turneresque' look. While he chats away about which artists influence him, I subtly try to steer the conversation off art and find out why he is in

384

prison, quite expecting him to claim that he's another victim of drugs.

'No, no, no,' he says. 'Forgery.' My ears prick up.

'Paintings?' I ask.

'No,' he replies. 'Much as I'd like to be a Keating or Elmyr Hory, it's more mundane than that – John Lewis gift vouchers.'

I laugh. 'So how were you caught?'

'I was grassed up by my mate who got nervous and turned Queen's evidence. He got off while I ended up with thirteen months in prison.'

'Thirteen months? That's a strange sentence.'

'I was given twelve months for the forgery and an extra month for not turning up to the first hearing.'

'How much did you get away with?' I ask casually.

'Can't tell you that,' he responds. 'But I admitted to a couple of grand.'

'And you'll be out in three weeks, so how long have you served?'

'Just over four months.'

'So you haven't that long to carry out my commission.'

He turns back to his sketch pad and flicks over a few pages. He reveals half a dozen sketches of five figures in different poses and asks which one I would prefer.

'Which one do *you* prefer?'

'Number three,' he says, placing his thumb on the sketch (see plate section). I nod my agreement as Anne reappears by my side.

'I see what you mean by lack of talent,' she says, and bursts out laughing at my feeble effort of a head and shoulders, which looks like a cross between ET and a Botero. Roger (bank robber) and Terry (burglar) come across to find out what's causing such merriment.

DAY 34

'You should have started with a pot, man,' says Roger, 'and not tried to advance so quickly.' He's already identified my biggest failing.

Without warning, two officers march in and begin to carry out a search. I assume it must be to check on the number of wooden knives and wire used for slicing the putty. But no, I'm told later it was for drugs. The workshops are evidently a common place for dealers to conduct their business.

On the way back to my cell I get lost again, but Shaun accompanies me to A wing and tells me that he has come up with a concept for the cover of *Wayland* (see plate section). I had always assumed that a graphic designer would do the cover of the book, but the idea of a fellow prisoner carrying out the commission is very appealing. I also admire Shaun's enterprise in spotting the opportunity. As we part at the T-junction between our two blocks, we agree to meet up during afternoon exercise to continue the discussion.

12 noon

Lunch. Dale's mushroom soup plus a vegetable fritter.

2.14 pm

I call my solicitor to try to find out the latest on the Simple Truth investigation. The police have been supplied with all our documents plus a detailed report from the Red Cross. Detective Chief Superintendent Perry, who's in charge of the case, is sympathetic, but says he must follow up all Baroness Nicholson's accusations. To DCS Perry a day is nothing; to me it's another fourteen hours locked in a cell.

5.00 pm

Supper: Chinese stir-fry and vegetables. An original recipe served up in one blob, and certainly not cooked by anyone who originated from the Orient.

6.00 pm

No evening gym because there is a cricket match between A and D blocks (the drug-free wing known as junkies' paradise).* I am going over my script for the day when Jimmy appears outside my cell door.

'You're batting at number five, my lord,' he says, looking down at his team sheet.

'What?' I say. 'The last game I played was for David Frost's eleven against the Lords Taverners and on that occasion I was clean bowled first ball.'

'Who was the bowler?' he asks.

'Imran Khan,' I reply.

'The Pakistani fast bowler?' he asks in disbelief.

'Yes, but he was bowling slow leg breaks at the time.'

'You're still batting number five. Report to the top corridor in five minutes.'

I change into a tracksuit, place a bottle top in the gap in my door† and run to the gate to find Darren waiting for me.

'Like the new Swatch,' he says. 'What happened to the Longines?'

---

* Many prisoners ask to go on the 'drug-free block' as it helps with their chances of early parole, while having no intention of coming off drugs.

† If you put a Robinsons bottle top in the gap where the bolt goes, you can leave your cell, push the door to, and it appears closed. When you return, you can pull it open without having to bother an officer. The officers turn a blind eye to this subterfuge – for obvious reasons.

I tell him of my illicit transfer of the watch to Will during the last family visit.

'The screws will have spotted it,' Darren assures me, 'and they would have been only too happy to see that particular watch leave the prison. Think of the trouble it would have caused them if someone had stolen it. Be warned, they don't miss much.'

'By the way,' adds Darren, 'one of the guys on our wing is being transferred tomorrow, so this may be your chance to get off the induction spur.'

My heart leaps at the news. I try to find out more details as we continue our stroll through a gate and out onto a large open field that is surrounded by a high fence topped with razor wire.*

Jimmy wins the toss and elects to bat. Now, for those of you who understand the game of cricket, HM prisons keep to a set of laws that even the MCC have no jurisdiction over. They may or may not give you a better insight into prison thinking:

(a) Both sides have ten overs each.

(b) Each over is nine balls and you never change ends.

(c) Each side must play five bowlers who can bowl two overs each, but not consecutively.

(d) There are no boundaries and you have to run every run.

(e) The side with the highest score is the winner.

(f) The umpire's decision is final.

While the other side takes to the field, Dale and Carl pad up for A block. I look in the equipment trolley, hoping I will find a box and a helmet. At the age of sixty-one I don't fancy facing a twenty-two-year-old West Indian bowler from Brixton who thinks it would be fun to put me in hospital with no fear of

---

* The use of razor wire is another example of the Prison Service breaking European law, preferring to pay a hefty fine each year.

388

being arrested for it. I can't believe my eyes: bats, pads, helmets, guards, boxes and gloves that are far superior to anything I've ever seen at any club game.

Our openers are both back in the pavilion by the end of the first over with the score at 6 for 2. We may well have first-class equipment, but I quickly discover that it does little for our standard of cricket. Our number four lasts for three balls so in the middle of the third over I find myself walking out to join Jimmy.

D Block boo me all the way to the crease, bringing a new meaning to the word 'sledging'. However, there is worse to come because the West Indian I referred to earlier is licking his lips in anticipation. Hell, he's fast, but he's so determined to kill me that accuracy is sacrificed and his nine-ball over is extended to thirteen, with four wides. After another couple of overs (don't forget, nine balls each), Jimmy and I advance happily on to 35 for 4. That is when my captain decides to try and launch the ball over the prison fence and ends up having his middle stump removed.

I fear neither Neville Cardus nor E. W. Swanton could have done justice to our progress from 35 for 4 to 39 all out. All you need to know is that the West Indian is back on for his second over, and during the next nine balls he takes five wickets at a cost of four runs. I leave the pitch 11 not out, having not faced a ball since my captain returned to the pavilion (bowlers don't change ends). But all is not lost because when A block takes to the field – thanks to our demon quickie Vincent (manslaughter) – three of our opponents are back in the pavilion by the end of the first over, for a total of only five runs.

The second bowler is *our* West Indian. He is robbed with two dropped catches and a plump LBW, or I felt so from cover point. When he comes off, D block have only reached 9 for 2, but then prison rules demand that we render up our third bowler. On his arrival, the game is quickly terminated as the ball is peppered ruthlessly around the pitch. D block reach the required total with no further loss of wickets and five overs to spare.

On the way back to our cells, the D block captain says, 'Not bad, Jeff, even though you played like a fucking public school cunt.' In prison you have to prove yourself every day.

Once we're back inside the block, I tell Jimmy that I may be joining him on the enhanced spur.

'I don't think so, Jeff,' he replies. 'The man who's leaving us is our wing cleaner, and I think they've offered his cell to David (whisky bootlegger), the cleaner on your wing.' My heart sinks. 'Your best bet is to move into David's cell, and stay there until another one comes free.'

8.00 pm

I return to my cell, but unfortunately there's no time for a shower before we're all banged up. I'm tired, sweaty, and even aching a little, having used muscles I don't normally press into action in the gym. I'm also hungry, so I open a tin of Princes ham (49p) and a packet of crisps (27p).

9.00 pm

Jules watches *The Bill*, while I continue to read Graham Greene's *The Man Within*. I fall asleep wondering if this is to be my last night in a double cell.

DAY 35   WEDNESDAY 22 AUGUST 2001

6.04 am

Wake. Fantasize about the possibility of a single cell. Write for two hours.

8.15 am

Breakfast. Cornflakes and one slice of toast. Dale is missing from behind the hotplate.

8.40 am

Spot Dale in the corridor. He tells me he's resigned from his job on the hotplate. He's sick of getting up thirty minutes before the rest of us just to be abused by inmates who never feel their portion of chips is large enough.

I see my name is chalked up on the blackboard outside the main office to report to the SO, Mr Meanwell. I go straight to the office. He has a registered letter for me, and slits it open. He extracts a two-sided typed missive which he hands over, but shows no interest in reading. While he checks inside the envelope for drugs, money, even stamps, I begin to read the letter, and after only a paragraph, pass it back to Mr Meanwell. When he peruses it, a look of disbelief comes over his face. The writer wants to borrow £10,000 to invest in 'an impossible to lose deal' and he's willing to split the profits fifty–fifty.

'How often do you get one of these?' he asks.

'Two or three times a week,' I confess, 'asking for sums for as little as fifty pounds right up to a million for yet another "impossible to lose deal".'

'By the way,' he says as he hands me the empty envelope, 'you may be moving today.' By the way, by the way, by the way – so casual for him, so important to me. 'One of the chaps on the enhanced spur is being transferred to a prison nearer his home and we're allocating his cell to an inmate who will take over his responsibilities as cleaner. Once that's been sorted out,' – Mr Meanwell is old enough still to include the word 'out' – 'we'll move you into his cell. I did think of sending you straight to the enhanced spur,' he admits, 'but there were two reasons not to. First, the spur needs a cleaner and you wouldn't be my first choice for that particular job, and second, I want you on the quieter side where it's not possible for other prisoners to peer through your window during exercise.'

Once I leave Mr Meanwell, I go in search of David (whisky bootlegger and spur cleaner). I find him attached to the industrial cleaner whirring around the floor of the induction corridor. He invites me along to his present cell on the first floor which, compared to my one up, one down on the induction wing, is the difference between Fawlty Towers and the Ritz.

11.00 am

Exercise. During the first circuit I'm asked by Chris (burglary) if I'll sponsor him for a half marathon in aid of the NSPCC. I agree to £1 a mile, as long as it comes out of my private finances and not my canteen account. Otherwise I'll be without food and bottled water for several weeks. He assures me that the authorities will allow that, so I sign up. He sticks with us for half a circuit, by which time I've learnt that he's the type of burglar our probation officer, Lisa Dada, so despises. He's twenty-seven years old and has spent eight of the last ten years in jail. He simply considers burglary a way of life. In fact, his parting words are, 'I'm out in six weeks' time, Jeff, but don't worry, your house is safe.' I realize those of you who have never been to jail may find this strange, but I now feel more sympathy for some of the murderers in Belmarsh than I do for professional burglars.

It was sometime later that I began to ponder on how he could run thirteen miles without occupying half the local constabulary to make sure he didn't escape. I'll ask him tomorrow.

Jason (conspiracy to blackmail) joins us on the second circuit and congratulates me on being moved to a single cell.

'It hasn't happened yet,' I remind him.

'No, but it will this afternoon.'

Prison has many similarities to the outside world. One is that you quickly discover who actually knows what's going on and who only picks up fag ends. Jason knows exactly what's happening.

'Of course, if you want to,' Jason adds, 'you can always get yourself transferred to another prison.'

'And how would I manage that?'

'Write yourself a note and drop it in the complaints box. You don't even have to sign it. It's known as "the grass box".'

'And what would I have to suggest?'

'Archer is offering me drugs and I can't resist much longer, or Archer is bullying me and I'm near breaking point. If they believe it, you'd be transferred the same day. In fact your feet wouldn't even touch the ground.'

12 noon

Lunch. The hotplate seems empty without the massive frame of Dale dominating proceedings. It looks as if Sergio has been promoted to No. 1 in his place, because he now stands next to the duty officer and hands out the dishes according to whether you're one, two, three (vegetarian) or four.

'Three,' Sergio says, without even glancing at the list, and then carefully selects my dish. The transfer of power has in no way affected me.

1.45 pm

Gym. The treadmill is working again so I'm almost able to carry out a full programme. With the new medicine ball exercise I'm up to fifteen, with a one-minute break, but after a further nine I'm exhausted and grateful when Mr Maiden blows the five-minute whistle so I can warm down. As we leave, everyone else picks up their assigned gym card before disappearing back to their cells. I no longer have a gym card. It's been stolen every day since I arrived, and the management have given up bothering to issue me with a new one.

3.30 pm

I come out of the shower to find Ms Webb waiting for me.

'When the induction wing is banged up at four o'clock,' she says, 'I'll leave your door open because we're going to move you across to number two cell on the far spur.'

I think about throwing my arms round Ms Webb, but as I only have a towel covering me, I feel sure she would put me on report, so I simply say, 'Thank you.'

Once I'm dressed, I place all my belongings into the Belmarsh plastic bag in preparation for the move to the other side of the block. I am packed and ready to leave long before four.

This will be my eighth move in five weeks.

4.06 pm

David (whisky bootlegger) is waiting for me in his old cell. It's typical of his good manners that he has left the room spotless. Now that I have an extra cupboard, it takes me nearly an hour to decide where everything should go. Although the cell remains the regulation five paces by three, it suddenly feels much larger when you no longer have to share the cramped space with another prisoner. No more having to keep out of someone else's way. No more television programmes I don't want to watch. No more having to check whose slippers you've put on, that you're using your own toothpaste, soap, even lavatory paper. No more ... There's a knock on the cell door and Darren, Jimmy, Sergio and Steve make an entrance.

'It's a house-warming party,' Darren explains, 'and, like any good party, we come bearing gifts.'

Sergio has three five-by-five-inch steel mirrors, the regulation size. He fixes them on the wall with prison toothpaste. I can now see my head and upper body for the first time in five weeks. Steve supplies – can you believe it – net curtains to hide my barred window, and at night tone down the glare of the fluorescent lights. Jimmy has brought all the paraphernalia needed – board, Blu-tack, etc. – to attach my family photos to the wall. And Darren demands a roll of drums before he will reveal his gift, because he's come up with every prisoner's dream: a plug. No longer will I have to shave in my cereal bowl.

'Anything else you require, my lord?' Steve enquires.

'I'm out of Evian.'

For the first time the visiting team admits defeat. A survey has been carried out and it's been discovered that I am the only prisoner on the block who purchases bottled water from the canteen.

'So, like the rest of us,' says Darren, 'if you want more water, you'll have to turn on the tap.'

'However,' adds Sergio, 'now that I'm number one on the hotplate,' he pauses, 'you will be able to have an extra carton of milk from time to time.'

What more could a man ask for?

7.00 pm

I read over today's script in my silent cell and when I've finished editing I place the six pages in one of my new drawers. Every ten days the sheets are transferred to a large brown envelope (30,000 words) and sent off to Alison to type up.

I settle down on my bed to watch *A Touch of Frost*. David Jason is as consistent as ever, but the script is too flimsy to sustain itself for two hours, so I switch off the television and, for the first time in ten days, also the light, climb into my single bed and sleep. Goodbye, window warriors, may I never hear from you again.

DAY 36   THURSDAY 23 AUGUST 2001

5.18 am

I wake, depressed about two matters. When I phoned Mary last night, she told me that the Red Cross have asked KPMG to audit the Simple Truth campaign, because some of their larger donors have been making waves and they want to close the subject once and for all. Tony Morton-Hooper wrote to the police, pointing out that this internal audit has nothing to do with my involvement with the campaign. Mary and Tony are doing everything they can to get the police to admit that the whole enquiry is a farce and that Ms Nicholson's accusations were made without a shred of evidence. Despite their efforts I have a feeling the police will not close their enquiry until they've considered his report, so it could now be months before my D-cat is reinstated.

I'm also depressed because the Tory party seems to have broken out into civil war, with Margaret Thatcher saying it will be a disaster if Ken Clarke wins, and John Major declaring that if IDS becomes leader we'll be in Opposition for another decade. Six years so far.

DAY 36

6.00 am

I write for two hours.

8.15 am

After breakfast, Darren picks up my laundry, and warns me that the tumble dryer is still not functioning.

9.00 am

Banged up for another two hours because the staff are having their fortnightly training session in the gym. I'm told their activities range from first-aid lessons to self-defence (secure and protect), from checking through the latest Home Office regulations to any race relations problems, plus fire training, HIV reports and likely suicide candidates. One good thing about all this is that the tax payer is saved having to fund my pottery class (£1.20).

11.00 am

I watch Nassar Hussain lose the toss for the fourteenth time in a row. I must ask Mary what the odds are against that.*

I walk out into the exercise yard just before the gates are closed at five past eleven. Jimmy points to Mario (not his real name) who is walking a few paces ahead of us. I hope you can recall Mario's scam. While working on the hotplate he stole almost all the cheese. He then made Welsh rarebit, at a phone-card for two, using an iron as the toaster. Mario was caught

---

* Mary tells me they are 1 in 2 to the power of 14, which is 1 in 16,384.

398

creaming off nearly half a million a year from his fashionable London restaurant without bothering to pay any tax on his windfall. Although I have never frequented Mario's establishment, I know it by reputation. There can be no doubt of the restaurant's success, because it was one of those rare places that do not accept credit cards – only cash or cheques.

While we stroll round the yard – Mario's not into power walking – he explains that approximately half of his income was in cash, the rest cheques or accounts. However, the taxman had no way of finding out what actual percentage was cash, until two tax inspectors visited the restaurant as diners. From careful observation they concluded that nearly half the customers were paying cash, whereas Mario's tax return showed a mere 10 per cent settled the bill this way. But how could they prove it? The inspectors paid cash themselves and requested a receipt. What they couldn't know was that Mario declared all the bills where the customer asked for a receipt, which he then entered in his books. Bills for which no receipts were given were destroyed and the cash then pocketed.

The taxmen couldn't become regular customers (their masters wouldn't allow such an extravagance) and were therefore unable to prove any wrongdoing. That was until a young, newly qualified accountant joined the Inland Revenue and came up with an ingenious idea as to how to ensnare Mario. The fresh-faced youth found out which laundry the restaurant used and over the next three months had the tablecloths and napkins counted. There were 40 per cent more tablecloths than bills and 38 per cent more napkins than customers.

Mario was arrested and charged with falsifying his accounts. He pleaded guilty and was sentenced to two years. He will be returning to his restaurant later this year having, in answer to customers' enquiries, taken a 'sabbatical' in his native Florence.

DAY 36

'They've got it all wrong, Jeffrey,' Mario says. 'The likes of you and me shouldn't be in jail mixing with all this riff-raff. They should have fined me a million pounds, not paid out thirty-five thousand to accommodate me for a year. My regulars are livid with the police, the courts and the Inland Revenue.' His final words are, 'By the way, Jeffrey, do you like buck rarebit?'

12 noon

Lunch. Among the many things Mario briefed me on was how to select the best daily dish from the weekly menu. You must only choose dishes that are made with fresh ingredients grown on the premises and not bought in. As from next week there will be variations from my usual vegetarian fare.

2.00 pm

I read the morning papers. Margaret and John have placed their cutlasses back in their sheaths and both have fallen silent – for the time being. The press are describing the leadership contest as the most acrimonious in living memory, and one from which the party may never recover. Reading this page a couple of years after the event will give us all the benefit of hindsight. Is it possible that the party that governed for the longest period of time during the twentieth century will not hold office in the twenty-first? Or will Tony Blair suddenly look fallible?

3.15 pm

Gym. It's the over-fifties' spinning session – nothing to do with politics. Don't kid yourself – it's agony. Forty-five minutes with an instructor shouting, 'On the straight', 'Up the slope', 'Hill climbing', 'Faster, faster'. I fall off the bike at four o'clock and Darren almost carries me back to my cell.

5.30 pm

Australia are 208 for 1 and looking as if they could score 700. I leave the cricket to get some loo paper from the store. This must be collected between 8.15–8.30 am or 5.30–6.00 pm; one roll per person, per week. As I come out of the store room, I notice my name is chalked up on the blackboard to see the SO. I go straight to Mr Meanwell's office. He has several registered letters for me, including one from some ladies in Northampton, who have sent me a lavender cake.

'I'm afraid you're not allowed to have it until you move prisons or have completed your sentence,' Mr Meanwell explains.

'Why not?' I ask.

'It could be laced with alcohol or drugs,' he tells me.

As I leave the SO's office, I spot a new prisoner with his right arm in a sling. I go over to have a chat: injuries usually mean stories. Was he in a fight? Was he hit by a prison officer? Did he fall or was he pushed? It turns out to be an attempted suicide. He shows me his wrist which displays three long, jagged scars forming a triangle which have been sewn up like a rough tear in a Turkish carpet. I stare for about a second at the crude, mauve scars before I have to turn away. Later, I'm relieved to discover that Jimmy reacted in the same way, though he tells me that if you really want to kill yourself, you don't cut across the artery.

'You only do that when you're looking for sympathy,' he adds, 'because the screws will always get there in time. But one long slash up the arm will sever the artery, and you'll die long before they can reach you.'

'Nevertheless,' I say, 'that's some cry for help.'

'Yes, his father had a heart attack last week, and he's just arrived back from the funeral.'

'How many suicides have there been at Wayland while you've been here?' I ask Jimmy.

'There was one about six weeks ago,' he replies. 'You'll always know when one takes place because we're banged up for the rest of the day. No one is allowed to leave their cell until the body has been removed from the prison. Then an initial report has to be written, and because so many officers become involved, including the governor, it never takes less than three hours. This prison's pretty good,' he adds. 'We only get about one suicide a year. In Norwich, where I began my sentence, it was far higher, more like one a month. We even had a prisoner sitting up on the roof with a noose round his neck, saying he'd jump unless the governor dealt with his complaint.'

'Did he jump?'

'No, they gave in and agreed to let him attend his mother's funeral.'

'But why didn't they agree to that in the first place?'

'Because last time they let him out, he flattened a screw with one punch and tried to escape.'

'So the governor gave in?'

'No, the governor refused to see him, but he did allow the prisoner to attend the funeral, double-cuffed.'

'Double-cuffed?'

'First they cross the prisoner's wrists before handcuffing him. Then they handcuff him to two officers with two separate pairs of handcuffs, one on either side.'

Thank God they didn't do that to me when I attended my mother's funeral.

It's an irony that an hour later, when going through my mail, I find a razor-blade paper attached to the top of one of my letters, with the message 'Just in case you've had enough.' The blade itself had been removed by an officer.

6.00 pm

Exercise. Shaun (forgery) has begun to work on an outline drawing of the montage. His first model is Dale (wounding with intent), who is standing on the grass in the sun, arms folded – not a natural model (see plate section). Dale scowls as we pass him, while a few of the other prisoners shout obscenities.

8.00 pm

Nothing worth watching on television, so I finish Graham Greene's *The Man Within*.

10.00 pm

I remove the newly washed clothes from all over my bed, where I had laid them out to dry. They are still wet so I hang them from every other available space – cupboard doors, the sink, my chair, even the curtain rail.

I fall asleep, still worrying about the KPMG report and how long it will take for the police to agree that there is no case to answer. By the time you read this, Wayland will be a thing of the past. But for now, it remains purgatory.

DAY 37   FRIDAY 24 AUGUST 2001

6.08 am

I draw my newly acquired curtains to allow the rising sun to enter my cell. I discovered during exercise yesterday evening that they used to belong to Dennis (VAT fraud). No one knows how much of the 17.5 per cent he retained for himself, but as he was sentenced to six years, we have to assume it was several millions.

Dennis applied for parole after two and a half years, having been a model prisoner. He heard nothing, so assumed that his request had been turned down. Yesterday, at 8 am, they opened his cell door and told him to pack his belongings. He was being released within the hour. The order had come from the Home Office the week before but, as his probation officer was on leave, no message had got through. Dennis had to borrow a phonecard – against prison regulations – to ask his wife to come and pick him up. He caught her just as she was leaving for work, otherwise he would have been standing outside the gates all day. That is how I inherited the fine net curtains which now adorn my cell, and when I leave they will be passed on to the new resident. I just hope I'm given a little more notice.

Jimmy was also let out yesterday, but only for the day. He

has just a few weeks left to serve before his release date, so they allow him out once a month on a town visit, from 9 am to 3 pm. This is part of the rehabilitation programme for any D-cat prisoner. Jimmy has been a D-cat, but resident in a C-cat prison, for over three months. He doesn't want to move to an open prison because he's coming to the end of his sentence and his family lives locally.

Yesterday Jimmy visited Dereham. He was accompanied by an officer who, for reasons that will become clear, I shall not name. At lunchtime the officer gave Jimmy a fiver to buy them both some fish and chips (Dereham prices) while he went to the bank to cash a cheque. Jimmy collected the fish and chips, strolled over to the National Westminster and waited outside for the officer. When he didn't appear, Jimmy began lunch without him. After the last chip had been devoured, Jimmy began to worry about what had happened to his guard. He went into the bank, but couldn't see him, so ran out and quickly headed towards Lloyds TSB, a hundred yards away. As he turned the corner, he saw the officer running down the street towards him, an anxious look on his face. The two men fell into each other's arms laughing; Jimmy didn't want to be accused of trying to escape only six weeks before his release date, and the officer would have been sacked for giving a prisoner money to assist in that escape. Jimmy told me later that he's never seen a more relieved man in his life.

'Where are my fish and chips?' demanded the officer, once he had recovered.

'I had to eat them, guv,' Jimmy explained, 'otherwise yours would have gone cold.' He handed over fifty pence change.

DAY 37

8.00 am

After breakfast I go in search of Stan (embezzler, £21,000, eighteen months), the spur painter. I ask him if he'd be kind enough to come and look at my cell and see if he can recommend any way of brightening it up. I tell him I hate the white door and the black square around the basin and the black floor skirting.

'I'll see what I can do,' he says, 'but I can't promise much. We only get colours that have been discontinued, or the ones no one else wants.'

9.00 am

Pottery. I fear this enterprise has proved to be a mistake. I simply don't have any talent with clay. I'm going to ask Wendy if I can be transferred to the library or education. The *Sun* told its readers yesterday that I had applied to take Dennis's (of curtain fame) job in the library. I didn't even know he worked in the library, but now the *Sun* has put the idea in my head, I'll ask Steve (conspiring to murder, head librarian) if there's a vacancy. Meanwhile I go off to pottery and waste two hours talking to Shaun (forgery). To be fair, it wasn't a complete waste of time because he brought me up to date on his progress with the book cover and the montage of prisoners (see plate section). I also discover more about his crime.

What I hadn't appreciated was that the forged John Lewis gift vouchers were not used simply to purchase articles from the store. Oh, no, Shaun is far brighter than that. He discovered that if you buy an item and present your gift voucher, the assistant will hand back the change in cash. Shaun also found out that if you purchase something for £1,000 (and he saw Chris Eubank buying a television with genuine vouchers) and return the item

406

an hour later, they don't reimburse you with vouchers. Once again, they hand over cash.

Armed with this information, Shaun acquired a map of England (kindly supplied by a helpful assistant) showing every John Lewis outlet in the country. He then began to travel the land, cashing vouchers in each town he passed through. He was finally caught when his co-conspirator panicked, went to the police and grassed on him (Shaun's words).

I wonder what Shaun will turn his mind to once he's released. I only mention this because when the conversation changed to the clash between Ken Clarke and Iain Duncan Smith, Shaun added a piece of knowledge to the euro debate which neither of the candidates seems to have grasped.

'Have you ever seen a euro note?' Shaun asked.

'No, I haven't,' I admitted.

'It's Monopoly money and will be quite easy to reproduce. From 1 January it will be legal tender in seventeen countries across Europe, and I'll bet most of the shops don't have any way of identifying a fake. Someone's going to make a fortune.'

I recall that Shaun has only three more weeks of his sentence to serve.

11.15 am

I return to my cell and find I have a beige door, a neat blue square around my basin and cream skirting. I go in search of Stan, and present him with a phonecard – value: £2; worth: inestimable.

DAY 37

11.30 am

I call Paula (Alison is on holiday) and discover to my great relief that the last ten days' text of this script have arrived. It doesn't bear thinking about having to rewrite those 30,000 words. You may well ask why I didn't make a copy. Because there isn't a copier available. Then why don't I hand the papers over to my wife after a visit? Because it's against the regulations. My only chance is to rely on the Post Office, and it hasn't let me down yet.

12 noon

Lunch. I mournfully watch the test match while eating my vegetable soup. Australia are piling on the runs at a rate of four an over.

3.00 pm

Exercise. Jimmy is chatting about his girlfriends, and don't forget this is a man who had three women come to see him at his last visit. At some time, he tells me, he's slept with all three of them – not at the same time, he's not kinky, just healthy – and what's more they didn't leave scratching each other's eyes out. Nevertheless, this brings me on to a taboo subject I haven't yet mentioned: sex or the lack of it – unless you are a homosexual. Darren reminds us that in Sweden and Holland they allow conjugal visits, which I can't see happening in this country for many years. The current solution is to put a notice on the message board (see opposite) and hope the problem will go away. It will be interesting to see which comes first: the legalization of cannabis or conjugal visits.

After two weeks of walking round the perimeter of Wayland

HM PRISON SERVICE

HMP Wayland

OFFENSIVE AND OBSCENE MATERIAL

STATEMENT OF POLICY

1. At HMP Wayland we feel that it is important that we provide an environment within which visitors, staff and prisoners are able to work and visit without being caused offence by the display of any material.

2. Our aim is to ensure that the dignity of all staff, visitors and prisoners is respected. It is the duty of all staff to help to ensure that our environment remains free from the display of potentially offensive material.

3. Therefore the public display of any material that is potentially offensive will not be permitted in any part of the Prison.

TYPES OF MATERIAL THAT WILL BE RESTRICTED:

4. Any sexually explicit material, eg magazines of a pornographic nature which are available from newsagents, will be allowed in possession but must not be on display.

5. "Page 3" type pictures can be placed on prisoners' noticeboards, but pictures showing full nudity cannot. Photographs, artwork and other material may be displayed on noticeboards providing it conforms to the criteria outlined above.

6. All managers have a duty to ensure that their areas remain free from the display of any potentially offensive material. This applies to all areas, including offices, rest rooms and other "staff only" areas.

prison, I can now spot evil, fear, helplessness and sadness at thirty paces. But even I am puzzled by a crouching man who always sits alone in the same place every day, huddled up against the fence. He can't be much more than thirty, perhaps thirty-five, and he rarely moves from his solitary position. I ask Darren about him.

'Tragic,' he says. 'Alistair is one of your lot – public school, followed by university, where he graduated as a heroin addict. If he doesn't kick the habit, he'll be in prison for the rest of his life.'

'How can that be possible?' I ask.

'Simple. He regularly gets caught injecting himself, and always ends up with a few more months being added to his sentence. In fact, even on the day he was sent down, he was found with a needle in his arm. Somehow, and it must have been before the judge passed sentence or soon after he was taken down, he managed to stuff a needle covered in cellophane, a plunger and ten grams of heroin wrapped in a condom up his backside. He then took a laxative so that he could empty his bowels as soon as he arrived at Belmarsh. Once they'd banged him up that evening – and don't forget there's a lavatory in every cell – he injected himself with heroin and passed out. At the nine o'clock flap check* the night officer found him lying on the floor with a needle stuck in his arm and several grams of heroin sprinkled on the floor beside him. He must be one of the few prisoners who has managed to have time added to his sentence before breakfast the following morning.'

I look at the tragic, hunched-up figure and wonder if prison is the right answer.

---

* A flap check is when the duty officer makes sure you are in your cell and have not escaped.

6.00 pm

Supper. I can't remember what I eat, but I do recall finding two extra cartons of milk on my window sill. Sergio is exercising his authority as the new No. 1 on the hotplate.

DAY 38   SATURDAY 25 AUGUST 2001

5.11 am

I wake and think about how I would be spending the August bank holiday weekend if I were not in prison. I also begin to consider whether there are any advantages to being in jail. Certainly, incarceration is something to be added to one's experiences, particularly as it has come at a period in life when I felt I was marking time. I've also had to stretch myself – unfortunate pun. But I've already reached a stage where I am gaining little from the experience. As I could be stuck here for a while longer, it might be wise to have an escape plan – escape of the mind.

I've already completed *Belmarsh: Hell,* and have penned 44,000 words of *Wayland: Purgatory.* I can't wait to get to heaven, whenever and wherever that might be.

8.15 am

'Buenos días,' I say to Sergio as he passes me a boiled egg and a slice of toast.

'Buenos días,' he repeats. *'Cómo estas tú?'*

I concentrate. *'Yo estoy bien, gracias.'*

'Bien, gracias, y tú?'

'Bien, gracias, y to?'

'No, tú, tú, tú.'

'Tú, tú, tú.'

'Bueno. We must meet later today,' Sergio adds, 'for another lesson.' At least ten prisoners standing in the queue, and three officers behind the hotplate, assume I am simply learning Spanish, as we have no wish for them to find out what we're really up to. But more of that later.

10.00 am

Gym. I complete a full programme for the first time since being convicted. I've lost over half a stone and feel a lot fitter. I'm about to take a shower when Mr King tells me that the governor wants a word. I've so far seen three people who claim the title of governor, and none of them has been Ms Cawley, the No. 1 governor. Am I about to meet her? No. On this occasion it's a Mr Greenacre, whom I've also never come across before. He informs me, 'You will be receiving a visit from a senior officer at Belmarsh' – surely they can't be sending me back there, is my first reaction – 'as they are investigating the theft of a chapter of your book.' You will recall that Trevor Kavanagh of the *Sun*, doyen of political editors, returned those stolen seven pages to Mary. He is well aware of the law of copyright.

It is clear that the culprit must have been an officer as no prisoners at Belmarsh have access to a photocopier. No one else could have unlocked my cell door, removed the script, photocopied and returned it and then sent a copy on to the *Sun*.

Of course, the deputy governor is only going through the motions. They have no way of finding out which officer was hoping to make a quick buck. The problem the Prison Service is facing is that Trevor will never reveal his source.

DAY 38

Back to the visitor from Belmarsh. Mr Greenacre tells me to expect a senior security officer to interview me on Tuesday morning, which means that, with luck, I'll miss pottery. I'll brief you fully next Tuesday.

11.00 am

Exercise. My legs are still aching from the gym session, so I find it quite hard to maintain the pace of Jimmy (twenty-nine) and Darren (thirty-five) as they march round the perimeter of the jail, but I'm damned if I'm going to admit it. They are chatting away about an unusual use of mirrors. Every cell has a five-by-five-inch steel mirror screwed to the wall. Jimmy is telling us about two West Indian prisoners who between them raised enough money to purchase a ghetto blaster and a pair of loud speakers. He describes how they went about arranging to listen to the same music in two different cells.

The first prisoner levered his thin steel mirror off the wall and inserted a coil of wire through one of the tiny holes in a corner. Every evening, after the nine o'clock flap check, he would slip the mirror under his door, then in one movement, slide it across the corridor until it reached the door opposite. After a few days, he could perform this skill as proficiently as any basketball player dunking a ball through a hoop.

The second prisoner then took the wire and attached it to his speaker so that both men could listen to the same music emanating from one source. Ingenious but – I'm told by anyone who lived within a mile of the jail – unnecessary, because on a still evening you could have danced to the music in Freiston town hall.

12 noon

Lunch. England are 200 for 3 and putting up a spirited fight. During the lunch interval I visit Sergio in his cell. He wastes no words, immediately informing me that he has spoken to his brother in Bogotá. He always sounds like a man who has only ten units left on his phonecard. Of course, he may turn out to be a con man who has no intention of trying to find a Botero.

In any case nothing can be done until Sergio has completed his sentence. He is due to be deported on 27 September, a month from today, by which time we expect to have worked out a plan to purchase a Botero. Win or lose, I'll keep you briefed.

3.00 pm

I have my hair cut by Matt (arson for insurance, failed to convince Cornhill or the jury, and was sentenced to three years). Matt has the reputation of being the best barber in the prison. In fact several prison officers also have their hair cut by him. In his last prison, while serving time for a previous offence, Matt enrolled on a hair-styling course, so now he's a semi-professional. He has all the proper equipment, and within moments of sitting on a chair in the corridor outside his cell, I'm in no doubt about his skill. I need to look neat and tidy for Friday, when Mary and William hope to visit me again. I haven't forgotten that Mary commented on the length of my hair when she last came to Wayland.

When Matt's finished the job he even produces a second mirror so I can see the back of my head. He's not Daniel Hersheson, but for ten units of a phonecard he's a pretty good imitation.

415

DAY 38

6.00 pm

At close of play England are 314 for 8 after a gritty 124 not out by Ramprakash assisted by Gough, who was clinging in there helping to avoid another follow on. The two of them enter the pavilion needing another 31 runs to make Australia bat again.

A couple of years ago Darren Gough asked me to conduct the auction at his London testimonial dinner at the Dorchester. As a huge fan of Darren's, I happily agreed. When the event finally materialized it fell in the middle of my trial. Mr Justice Potts made it clear to my silk that I should not honour the agreement, even though my name was already printed in the programme. After all, it might influence the jury into believing that I am a charitable man, and I suspect that was the last thing Mr Justice Potts would have wanted.

I'm feeling pretty low, so decide to use the other ten units left on my card to phone Mary. There's no response. I can't get in touch with William or James as they are both abroad. I sit on the end of my bed and recall the words of La Rochefoucauld: *Absence diminishes mediocre passions and increases great ones, as the wind extinguishes candles and fans fire.*

DAY 39　　　SUNDAY 26 AUGUST 2001

6.16 am

Sunday is always the longest day in prison. Wayland is short-staffed and there is nothing for inmates to do other than watch wall-to-wall television. In Belmarsh, chapel was a respite as it got you out of your cell, but in Wayland you're out of your cell without anything to keep you occupied. Mind you, I'd much rather be in Wayland than locked up in Belmarsh for twenty-two hours a day. I write for a couple of hours.

8.20 am

Breakfast. While I'm waiting in the queue for the hotplate, I get talking to a West Indian who is on my landing. He asks if he can have my *Times* and *Sunday Times* when I've finished with them. I agree to his request if, in return, he will show me how to clean my cell floor. I only mention this because the West Indians keep the cleanest cells. They are not satisfied with sweeping out the dust and dirt, but spend hours buffing up the linoleum floor until you can see your face in it. Although I shower, shave and put on fresh clothes every day, as well as make my bed and have everything in place before the cell door is opened at 8 am, I never look as smart or have as clean a cell as any of the West Indians on my spur.

DAY 39

9.30 am

On my way to the library I slip in behind a man who frightens me. He has an evil face and is one of those prisoners who is proud to describe himself as a career criminal. He is a burglar by profession, and I'm somewhat surprised to see him heading off towards the library with a pile of glossy, coffee-table books under his arm. I try to make out the titles on the spines while we're on the move: *The Encyclopaedia of Antiques*, *Know Your Antiques* and *Antiques in a Modern Market.*

'Are you interested in antiques?' I ask innocently.

'Yeah, I'm making a careful study of them.'

'Are you hoping to work in the antiques trade when you've completed your sentence?'

'I suppose you could say that,' he replies. 'I'm sick of nicking 'em only to find out they're fuckin' worthless. From now on I'll know what to fuckin' look for, won't I?'

You would think that after five weeks of mixing with criminals, night and day, I couldn't still be taken by surprise. It serves to remind me again of Lisa Dada's words about despising burglars, not to mention my own naivety.

10.00 am

In the library I get talking to an older prisoner called Ron (ABH). Most inmates tell me they never want to return to prison, especially the older ones who have served long sentences. But, time and again, they'll add the rider, 'That doesn't mean I won't, Jeff. Getting a job when you have a criminal record is virtually impossible, so you stay on the dole, until you slip back into a life of crime.'

It's a vicious circle for those who leave prison with their

418

statutory £90, NFA (no fixed abode) and little prospect of work. I don't know the answer, although I accept there is little you can do for people who are genuinely evil, and not much for those who are congenitally stupid. But the first-offence prisoners who want a second chance often leave prison only to find that for the rest of their lives the work door is slammed in their face.

I accept that perhaps only around 20 per cent of prisoners would be worth special treatment, but I would like to see someone come up with a solution for this particular group, especially the first-time offenders. And how many of you reading this diary can honestly say you've never committed a crime? For example:

(a) Smoked cannabis (5 million), crack cocaine (300,000), heroin (250,000)
(b) Stolen something – anything
(c) Fiddled your expenses
(d) Taken a bus or train and not paid for the ticket
(e) Not declared your full income to the taxman
(f) Been over the alcohol limit when driving
(g) Driven a vehicle without tax or insurance
(h) Brought in something from abroad and not paid import tax

I have recently discovered that those very people who commit such crimes often turn out to be the most sanctimonious hypocrites, including one leading newspaper editor. It's the truly honest people who go on treating one decently, as I've found from the thousands of letters I've received from the general public over the past few weeks.

DAY 39

10.45 am

Chapel. We're back to a congregation of eleven. The service is Holy Communion, and I'm not sure I care for the modern version. I must be getting old, or at least old-fashioned.

The service is conducted by John Framlington, resplendent in a long white robe to go with his white beard and head of white hair. He must be well into his seventies and he looks like a prophet. A local Salvation Army officer preaches the sermon, with the theme that we all make mistakes, but that does not mean that we cannot be saved. Once he has delivered his message, he joins John to dispense the bread and wine to his little flock. During the singing of the last hymn, John walks off down the aisle and disappears. We are all left literally standing, not quite sure what to do next. A female face peeps out from behind the organ, and decides to continue playing. This brave little gesture is rewarded by everyone repeating the last verse. When we've delivered the final line of '*O Blessed Jesu, Save Us*' John comes running back down the aisle. He turns to face his congregation, apologizes, blesses us and then disappears for a second time. He's a good man, and it's generous of him still to be giving his time every Sunday for such a motley crew as us.

11.45 am

When I return to my spur after chapel, I find that it has been 'locked off' and we are unable to get into our cells. A small crowd is gathering at the entrance of the spur, and I am informed by Darren that our cells are being searched for phonecards. It seems that one of the prisoners has shaved off the silver lining on the top of his card (see plate section) as this allows him to

420

have a longer period for each unit. Not a great crime you might consider, remembering that we're in a den of thieves. But what you won't realize is that the next person who makes a phone call will find that BT automatically retrieves those stolen units. Result: the next prisoner will be robbed blind.

The next inmate on the phone that morning turned out to be a voluble West Indian called Carl (GBH) who, when his last ten units were gobbled up in seconds, never stopped effing and blinding all the way to the PO's office. The spur was closed down in seconds, and Carl had unwittingly given the 'prison search team' an excuse to go through everyone's personal belongings.

When the gate to the cells is eventually unlocked, a team of three officers comes out carrying a sackful of swag. My bet is that the offending phonecard is not among their trophies, but several other illicit goods are. I return to my cell to find that nothing of mine has been touched. Even my script lies in exactly the same place as I left it. I take this as a compliment.

12 noon

Lunch. England have progressed to 40 for 1, but the ominously dark clouds that appear over Wayland are also, it seems, unpaid visitors at the Oval. I turn my attention to the Sunday papers. The *Sunday Mirror*, that bastion of accuracy, tells its readers that I defended myself from another inmate with a cricket bat. I gave you a full ball-by-ball summary of that match, and the only thing I tried to threaten – and not very successfully – was the ball. The article then goes on to say that I am paying protection money to a prisoner called Matthew McMahon. There is no inmate at Wayland called Matthew McMahon. They add that payment is made with £5 phonecards. There are no £5 phonecards. The funny thing is that some inmates are shocked by this:

they had assumed the papers reported accurately, and it wasn't until I took up residence that they realized how inaccurate the press can be.

2.00 pm

Exercise. We are allowed out for an hour, rather than forty-five minutes, which is a welcome bonus. As we walk round, I get teased by a lot of prisoners who say they are willing to protect me if I'll give them a £5 phonecard. Some ask how come you have a £5 phonecard when the rest of us only have £2 phonecards. Others add that I can hit them with my cricket bat whenever I want to. I confess that this wouldn't be so amusing if Jimmy and Darren were not accompanying me. Certainly, being the butt of everyone's humour inside, as well as outside, begins to tell on one. Jimmy has also read the story in the *Sunday Mirror* and what worries him is who to believe in the latest row between Ken Clarke and Iain Duncan Smith concerning immigration. I tell Jimmy that only one thing is certain: although the result of the leadership election will not be announced for another two weeks (12 September), 70 per cent of the 318,000 electorate have cast their votes, and I assure him that IDS* is already the next leader of the Tory party.

'Can I risk a bet on that?' asks Darren.

'Yes, if you can find anyone stupid enough to take your wager.'

'The spur bookie is offering 1–3 on Duncan Smith.'

'Those are still good odds, because you can't lose unless he drops down dead.'

---

* I note that he is now referred to as IDS by his supporters. I presume this is a desperate attempt to get over the next Tory leader having a double-barrelled name.

'The bookie or Iain Duncan Smith?' asks Jimmy.

'Either,' I reply.

'Good,' says Darren. 'Then I'll put three Mars bars on Duncan Smith as soon as we get back to the spur.'

4.00 pm

I visit Sergio in his cell to be given a lesson on emeralds. I'll let you know why later. Sergio takes his time telling me that emeralds are to Colombia what diamonds are to South Africa. When he's finished his tutorial, I ask him if it would be possible for his brother to find an emerald of the highest quality. He looks puzzled.

'What sort of price do you have in mind?' he asks.

'Around ten thousand dollars,' I tell him.

He nods. 'I'll see what I can do.' He looks at his watch and adds, 'I'll speak to my brother immediately.'

5.00 pm

Sunday supper is always a bag of crisps and a lemon mousse. However, this evening we are offered two lemon mousses because, I note, the sell-by date on the lid is 25 August.

7.00 pm

At last there's something worth watching on television. *Victoria and Albert* with a cast to kill for. Nigel Hawthorne, Diana Rigg, Peter Ustinov, Jonathan Pryce, David Suchet, John Wood and Richard Briers.

It only serves to remind me how much I miss live theatre, though at times I feel I'm getting enough drama at the Theatre Royal, Wayland.

DAY 40   MONDAY 27 AUGUST 2001

6.08 am

Forty days and forty nights, and, like Our Lord, I feel it's time to come out of the wilderness and get on with some work, despite the fact it's a bank holiday. I write for two hours.

8.15 am

Breakfast. Corn Pops (for a change), UHT milk, a slice of bread and marmalade. I stare at the golly on the jar. I read yesterday in one of the papers that he's no longer politically correct and will be replaced by a character created by Roald Dahl and illustrated by Quentin Blake. I like golly, he's been a friend for years. As a man without an ounce of prejudice in him, I am bound to say I think the world has gone mad.

9.00 am

I call Mary, who is furious with the Home Office. Winston Churchill has written to the Home Secretary, David Blunkett, asking why I'm still in a Category C jail, and Winston has received a reply from Stephen Harrison, David Blunkett's private secretary, suggesting that Lady Archer 'is satisfied that this is the best that can be hoped for'. Home Office officials obviously don't listen to the *Today* programme, or read any newspapers. It doesn't augur well for justice being done to those prisoners who do not have a supportive family. Mary will write to Martin Narey today and put the record straight. My solicitor has not yet received a reply from DCS Perry. Perhaps he's still on holiday. She's also written to the governor of Wayland – also no reply. Thank God I'm not locked up in Russia.

Now I'm no longer on the induction spur, I'm allowed to have my own plate, bowl and mug. Mary promises to dispatch all three today. I can't wait to be rid of the grey plastic set, even if they won't allow me to replace the plastic knife, fork and spoon. Mary tells me that the letters of support are still pouring in, and says she'll send a selection for me to read, plus a list of friends who want to visit me in prison. She confirms that she and William are hoping to visit me on Friday.

9.15 am

A block are playing C block at football, and Jimmy (captain of everything) asks if I'd like to be linesman, knowing it will get me out of my cell for at least an hour. How considerate, I tell him, but I don't know the rules, and I feel sure that there's more to it than just putting your flag in the air when the ball goes out. Fortunately, one of our reserves is fully proficient in the laws of the game, and runs up and down the line behind me, making me look quite competent.

The first player I have to adjudicate offside is Jimmy, who makes no protest and immediately raises his arm. The true character of a person cannot be hidden on a playing field.

By half-time we are two down. However, in the second half,

425

we pull one back and just before the final whistle, Carl (GBH, phonecard problem) thumps in a blinder from twenty yards to level the score. As he is in the next cell to me, I can expect several graphic replays in the corridor, with the yardage becoming longer by the day.

12.15 pm

Lunch: Toad-in-the-hole (vegetarian sausage) and peas.

3.00 pm

Exercise. We've managed about two circuits when Darren, Jimmy and I are joined by what can only be described as a gang of yobs, whose leader is a stockily built youth of about five foot six, with two rings in his nose and one in each ear. From what I can see of his neck, arms and chest, it doesn't look as if there's anywhere left on his body to needle another tattoo. As soon as he opens his mouth every other word is fucking-this and fucking-that. I'm no longer shocked by this, but I am surprised by the smell of alcohol on his breath. My usual approach when faced with this situation is to answer any question quietly and courteously. I've heard enough stories about prisoners being knifed in the yard over the slightest provocation to do otherwise. But as there are no questions, just abuse hurled at me and my wife, there's not much I can say in reply. Jimmy and Darren close in, not a good sign, but after another circuit, the young thug and his gang of four back off and go and sit against the fence and glare at us.

The Home Office could do worse than invite Darren to sit on one of their committees and advise them on prison policy. He is, after all, far better informed than Stephen Harrison, and therefore the Home Secretary. After a spell in Borstal, and two terms in prison, Darren would be a considerable asset to the drugs debate. He adds that when he was first sent to jail, some fifteen years ago, about 30 per cent of prisoners smoked cannabis and only about 10 per cent were on heroin.

'And today?' I ask.

'Around twenty to thirty per cent are still on cannabis, with approximately the same percentage, if not more, on heroin. And while the present regulations are in place, there's no hope of dealing with the problem. Only last week, a prisoner out on his first town visit returned with five hundred pounds' worth of heroin stuffed up his backside, and every addict in the prison knew about his cache within the hour. They were, if they could afford it, smoking and jabbing themselves all night.'

'But surely the prisoner in question, not to mention his customers, will be caught?'

'The drugs unit interviewed him the following morning. They couldn't prove anything, but it's the last town visit he'll make before he's released – on the grounds of "reasonable suspicion".'

'More fool him,' says Jimmy, who goes out on a town visit once a month. 'Some of them will do anything—' The group of yobs decide to rejoin us, so I have to face another barrage of abuse. I sometimes wish Mr Justice Potts could do just one circuit with me, but it's too late, my case was his last, and he was clearly determined to go out with a bang. When we're called back in, I'm not unhappy to return to the peace and safety of my cell.

DAY 40

4.07 pm

Sergio turns up to tell me the details of a conversation he's had with his brother in Bogotá.

'Tomorrow my brother will travel to the green mountains and select an emerald,' declares Sergio. He will then have it valued and insured. He will also send one gold necklace (18 carat). They sell at a tenth of the price they charge in England. I assure him that, if I decide to buy it, I will make a payment direct to his bank the day after he has been deported. This means he has to put a great deal of trust in me, which he seems happy to do. He accepts that the transaction cannot take place while both of us are still in jail. If he's successful, I'll have more confidence in his claim that he can produce a Botero at a sensible price.

5.00 pm

Darren and I play a couple of games of backgammon, and I'm thankful to have found something I can beat him at. He takes revenge by completing *The Times* crossword before supper.

6.00 pm

Supper: beans on toast and an extra lemon mousse stamped with yesterday's sell-by date.

7.00 pm

I watch the concluding episode of *Victoria and Albert*, every moment of which I thoroughly enjoy.

10.00 pm

Darren lends me his copy of *The Prisons Handbook* – a sort of Relais & Chateaux guide of jails in England and Wales. I accept Mr Meanwell's opinion that once my D-cat has been reinstated, I should apply for Spring Hill in Buckinghamshire, which is the best-located open prison for both London and Cambridge.

DAY 41 TUESDAY 28 AUGUST 2001

6.00 am

I write for two hours.

8.15 am

Breakfast. It's Shredded Wheat again. Eat one, save one.

9.00 am

Pottery. I take my new book, *Arts and Artists*, along to my class to while away the two-hour period. It doesn't seem to bother anyone that I'm not working on a sculpture as long as I'm studying some medium of art.

Shaun appears to be depressed, which could be nothing more than the melancholy of an artist lost in his thoughts. After an hour of painting, he opens his sketch book to reveal an excellent drawing of a Wayland landscape (fairly bleak) and another of a prison door. Then he confides why he is so low. Probation have decided not to let him out two months early on a tag because he failed to appear in court.* However, this two-

---

* The Probation Service can refuse tagging on the following grounds: a) reoffending whilst previously on bail; b) failing to appear in court; c) providing an unsatisfactory address.

month hold-up will pose some problems for both of us. The quality of the paper, pencils, pastels and oils that are available at Wayland are obviously not up to professional standards, so it may become necessary to enlist the help of a member of the art department to purchase the materials he needs. Shaun will have to select someone who believes in his talent, and more importantly, he needs to trust me enough to believe I will pay him back after he's been released in November. A member of staff tells me later that Shaun is the most talented prisoner they have come across since they started working in prisons. Our conversation is interrupted by a security officer who says I'm wanted in reception.

10.12 am

A senior officer from Belmarsh is waiting for me in the room with the comfortable chairs. The governor of Belmarsh has put her in charge of the investigation into the theft of seven pages of my diary. You will recall that Trevor Kavanagh, the *Sun's* political editor, handed the script over to Mary, who in turn passed the seven handwritten pages on to my lawyer.

The officer tells me that she has been in the Prison Service for nearly twenty years, and adds that she isn't on a whitewash expedition. She makes it clear from the outset that the seven pages of script could not have been stolen by a prisoner, as they wouldn't have had access to a photocopier. She goes even further and admits that they have narrowed the likely culprit down to one of two officers.

She then hands me a photocopy of my first seven pages, and after reading only a few lines I recall how distraught I was at Belmarsh. I confirm that I had written these pages when I was in the medical centre on my first day, but I have no way of knowing when they were removed or returned, or by whom. I only recall leaving the cell once in the first twenty-four hours, and that was for a forty-five-minute break in the exercise yard. She nods, as if she not only knows when I left my cell, but exactly how many minutes I was out of the room.

'You were then escorted across to B block to begin your induction. Did you have the script with you at the time?'

'Yes, I posted the pages to my PA every three or four days, but not before they were checked by Roy the censor, who I didn't meet until the third day, so it can't have been him.'

'No, it certainly wasn't Roy,' she replied, 'because the *Sun* received the material the following morning. And in any case, Roy's bright enough to understand the law of copyright. Whoever did this must have been surprised and disappointed that the *Sun* wouldn't touch it.'

She leaves after about an hour, promising to let me know the outcome of her investigation.*

12.15 pm

Lunch: vegetable soup and a chocolate wafer. Sergio slips me a banana.

2.00 pm

In order to make up my five lessons a week, I have to attend an education class on a Tuesday afternoon.

The Education Department is situated next to the library, and once I've signed in, I report to room one as instructed. I

---

* No member of the prison staff has ever reported back to me or my lawyers on the outcome of this enquiry.

enter a classroom containing twenty small desks set out in a U-shape facing a teacher. Her name is Ms Jocelyn Rimmington, and she looks as if she's been plucked straight out of an Evelyn Waugh novel. Her job is a difficult one, and I watch her carry it out with consummate skill and ingenuity. She has eight charges, including me. The prisoner she's talking to is learning basic English so he can take a plumbing exam. The inmate on his right is reading Chaucer as part of an A level course, and on his left is an inmate who is learning to read and write. The remaining four prisoners are preparing for GCSE English. Ms Rimmington moves slowly and methodically from desk to desk, answering each and every question thrown at her until she reaches me.

'Wendy tells me that you're in the middle of writing another book.'

'Yes, I am,' I reply.

'And she thinks the best thing would be for you to carry on with it, until we decide what to do with you.'

I don't demur; after all, what's the point of telling this charming lady that I would prefer to do something more productive. It's obvious that either Wendy Sergeant, who is head of the department, or those above her, lack the imagination of the education department at Belmarsh, who had me conducting a creative writing class before the end of my first week.

5.00 pm

Supper. I eat very little because the only gym session I can attend today is at six o'clock.

DAY 41

6.00 pm

Gym. Complete a full session, mainly because half the regulars are out playing football. Today is the final trial before they select the team for the first match on Sunday. As I cannot be present at Lord's for the one day final between Somerset and Leicestershire, I'll have to settle for Wayland versus RAF Methwold.

7.30 pm

After a long press, press, press-button shower, I return to the cell and dry myself with a mean little rough green towel. Sergio knocks on the door, walks in, plonks himself on the end of the bed and without any preamble, starts to give me another lecture on emeralds.

'Seventy per cent of the world's emeralds come from Colombia,' he proclaims. 'Over twenty thousand stones change hands in Bogotá every day. The emerald is second only in popularity and value to the diamond, and its size is measured in the same way (carat). The very finest stones,' he continues, 'are known as "drops of oil" because if you stare into the centre of the stone, you can see what appears to be just that. We must make sure that ours is at least four carats, and that the drop of oil is there for all to see.

'For one stone, the price can range according to quality,' continues Sergio, 'from a few hundred dollars to several millions.' He anticipates the stone his brother selects could be on its way to London as early as next week. Because Sergio went to the same school as the niece of the owner of 'the mountain', he hopes his brother will be able to deal direct, cutting out any middlemen. As his brother doesn't know that Sergio is ensconced in an English jail, I wonder why he isn't puzzled by the fact that he can't call back. I don't ask.

8.00 pm

Pottery followed by an interview with the lady from Belmarsh, followed by education, followed by the gym, followed by Sergio and his lecture on emeralds, interspersed with three writing sessions. I'm exhausted.

I fall asleep fully dressed during the *Ten O'Clock News*. When I wake, it's just after eleven. I undress, use the loo, climb into my tiny bed, and fall asleep a second time.

DAY 42   WEDNESDAY 29 AUGUST 2001

5.19 am

I have now undergone the same three-week induction cycle at HMP Wayland as I did at Belmarsh. My routine, compared with my life outside, is far more regimented, conforming to a daily pattern, and then a weekly one. So I have decided, as from today, to comment only on highlights, rather than simply repeat the numbing routine with which you must now be familiar.

6.00 am

I write for two hours and then eat the other Shredded Wheat covered in milk supplied by Sergio.

9.00 am

Paul, one of the tutors, brings in a set of slides to the art class, and gives us a lecture on the Impressionists. I am stunned that Shaun, such a talented artist, has never heard of Pissarro or Sisley. He also admits that he has visited a gallery only two or three times in his life. The slide show is so popular with the other prisoners that Paul promises to bring in examples of other artists next week when he will introduce us to Magritte, Rothko and Warhol, amongst others.

12 noon

After lunch, I go to the gym. When I've finished my programme, I jump on the scales to discover that I'm still losing weight – nearly a stone since I've been in prison. Just as I'm leaving, the football coach calls me into his office and asks if I would attend the first fixture of the season on Sunday, and write a match report for the prison magazine. I readily agree, only relieved he didn't invite me to play.

4.00 pm

Sergio joins me in my cell to tell me the latest on the emerald hunt before continuing with his tutorial. The majority of emeralds mined in Colombia come from one mountain that has been owned by the same family for generations. Most of the stones that come out of Colombia are exported to Japan, but Sergio is hoping, when he returns to Bogotá, to start diverting some of these gems to Europe. He is becoming more ambitious every day.

He also informs me that trading in emeralds is every bit as dangerous as dealing in drugs. Every day eight helicopters fly back and forth from the mountain to Bogotá airport with four armed guards on each and another twenty private police waiting for them on the runway. On the mountain there are 300 workers and 100 armed guards. A peasant (his description) can earn as much as $50,000 a year if, and he repeats if, he is lucky enough to dig up any high-quality gems.

'But what about theft?' I ask. 'How do they deal with that?'

'One or two of the workers are stupid enough to consider stealing the odd stone, but they quickly discover that there is no judge or jury on the mountain.'

'So how do they dispense justice?'

'Instantly,' he replies. 'One of the guards shoots the culprit in front of the other workers, who then bury him.'

'But you could swallow a stone, and then sell it in Bogotá, where you've already told me that twenty thousand emeralds change hands in the marketplace every day.'

'True,' Sergio replies. 'But you will still be caught, because the family has over a hundred spotters in the market, night and day. If a dealer ever traded with a thief, they would immediately be cut off from their source of supply. And in time the thief will have to return to the mountain if he hopes to go on trading. In any case, the workers know they will have a far higher standard of living than their fellow countrymen as long as they remain employed on the mountain.'

'But they could take the gems abroad and make a fortune?'

'Most peasants,' says Sergio, 'have never travelled further than the next village, and none of them speaks anything but mountain Spanish, which even I can't understand. Even the owner of the mountain can still only converse in his native tongue and would never consider leaving Colombia. It is only because of my four years in an English jail,' continues Sergio, 'that it's now possible for me to act as a go-between and consider the export business. And you now also have an advantage, Jeffrey, because your rivals cannot easily buy or sell paintings from Colombia.' I raise an eyebrow. 'I am being deported in four weeks' time, and can never return to Britain unless I am willing to risk completing the remaining four years of my sentence.'

'An enterprising dealer could always fly to Bogotá.'

'Not wise,' says Sergio. 'Fair-haired, blue-eyed people are not welcome in Bogotá, and especially not on the mountain.' He goes on to explain: 'It would be assumed that you are an American, and your chances of making it back to the airport would be about as good as a peasant caught stealing.' No wonder it's a closed market.

My tutorial comes to an end when an officer bellows, 'Lock up.' I run out of Sergio's cell to return to the real world, because I need the five minutes to join the queue and change my sheets, pillowcase, towels and gym kit. Don't forget it's Wednesday, and if you don't get to the laundry room before they close, you have to wait another week.

8.00 pm

When I get back to my cell I find a biography of *Oscar Wilde* by Sheridan Morley awaiting me on my bed. I had asked Steve (conspiracy to murder, chief librarian) to reserve this book for me. Nothing like a personal delivery service.

I become so engrossed in Wilde's life that I miss the *Ten O'Clock News*. I have reached Oscar's first trial by the time I put the book down. I must save the second trial for tomorrow night.

Not a bad day, but please don't think, even for one moment, that it's therefore been a good one.

DAY 43   THURSDAY 30 AUGUST 2001

8.45 am

I arrive for my pottery class to find it's been cancelled because the teacher hasn't turned up. Shaun tells me this is a regular occurrence, and he seems to be the only person who is disappointed because he was hoping to finish a painting. It gives me another couple of hours to write, while the other prisoners are happy to go off to the gym or their cells while still being paid £1.40.

10.45 am

I hear a cry of 'Library' bellowed down the corridor and, as I've just come to the end of another chapter of *Oscar Wilde*, decide to take a break and return *Arts and Artists*. I now know my way around the library and go straight to the art shelves. I select a book entitled *Legendary Gems* by Eric Bruton and add a novel by Robert Goddard.

When I return to my cell I find my laundry is waiting in a neat pile, washed and dried. I look up to see Darren standing on my chair, clipping up a new curtain rail.

'Let me warn you,' he says as he climbs back down off the chair, 'you can't hang yourself from a prison curtain rail.'

440

'I hadn't given the idea much thought, but why not?' I ask, opening my notebook.

'Because it just clips on, so if you attached a noose to the rail and then jumped off the chair, you'd land on the floor wrapped up in your curtain.'

'So how can I hang myself?' I demand.

'You should have done it at your remand prison,' Darren replies.

'I'm not sure I understand.'

'Most remand prisons are of a Victorian vintage, and have high-level barred windows making the job that much easier.'

'But I was only there for a few days.'

'There are more hangings in the first few days in jail than at any other time.'

'Why?'

'Often the psychological impact of entering prison for the first time causes deep depression, and that's when a prisoner sees suicide as the only way out.'

'So it's less common once you've been transferred?'

'Yes, but I knew a prisoner who still found an original way to kill himself.' I continue to scribble away. 'He was in a cell with a one-up and one-down, and when his room-mate went to work and he was left alone for the rest of the morning he stood the bed up on its end, so that the rail was about seven feet from the ground. He used his belt as a noose, and attached it to the top railing. He then climbed on top, placed his hands in the back of his jeans, rolled off the bed and hanged himself. On the table they found a letter from his girlfriend saying she couldn't wait for three years. If you want to kill yourself, you can always find a way,' Darren adds matter of factly. 'Each year the Prison Service publishes statistics on how many inmates commit suicide. There were ninety-two in 2001,' says Darren, just before he leaves to continue his rounds. 'However, what they don't tell you is how many people die, or commit suicide within six months of being released.' I slowly unpack my washing and stack it on the narrow shelves while I consider what Darren has just told me.

2.00 pm

After lunch I pick up *Legendary Gems* and turn to the chapter on emeralds. Everything Sergio has told me during the past ten days is verified by the author, which gives me more confidence in Sergio. However, two crucial questions remain: does Sergio have the right contacts and can he replace the middlemen? I am pleased to see that Laurence Graff warrants three mentions in the diamond chapter.

To date I haven't mentioned Laurence Graff (of Graff's of Bond Street, Madison Avenue and Monte Carlo), but I'm rather hoping he will agree to value the gem for me. Laurence and I first met at a charity function many years ago when I was the auctioneer. Since then he and his wife, Anne-Marie, have told me many stories about the diamond trade which have found their way into my books. It was Laurence who gave me the idea for the short story 'Cheap at Half the Price'.

3.00 pm

Jimmy rushes into my cell with a large grin on his face. He scowls at Darren's new curtain rail, immediately aware of who must have supplied it.

'I am the bearer of glad tidings,' he says. 'A prisoner on our spur will be leaving tomorrow morning, a week earlier than originally planned. He keeps the cleanest cell on the block. He's even decorated it, and best news of all, it's on the quiet side of the spur, so you'd better have a word with Meanwell before someone else grabs it.'

I'm just about to go off in search of Mr Meanwell, when Jimmy adds, 'He's off today, but he's back on tomorrow morning at 7.30, and don't forget you've got the special needs group at 8.45, so you'd better see him straight after breakfast.' Darren walks in, livid to find Jimmy sitting on the end of my bed. He's obviously picked up the same piece of information and had hoped to be the first to impart it.

'I think you'll find my information was as welcome as your curtain rail,' suggests Jimmy smugly.

'Only if his lordship ends up getting David's cell,' says Darren, well aware that I am playing them against each other. Still, like two children, they find the challenge irresistible.

7.00 pm

After supper, Sergio reveals good news. Having visited the mountain, his brother has selected a 4-carat emerald at a cost of $10,000.

'If my contact confirms that its shop value is twenty thousand, then I'll buy it,' I tell him. 'If not...' Sergio looks up and frowns. 'Purchase the emerald,' I continue, 'and have it sent to London. I'll need proper certification, but if my valuer says he can sell me a stone of the same quality at the same price or cheaper, it will all have been a waste of your time, and I'll return the stone to Colombia at my expense.'

'My whole reputation rests on this one stone?' Sergio asks.

'You've got it,' I tell him.

DAY 44   FRIDAY 31 AUGUST 2001

8.21 am

Breakfast. I eat my cereal out of a china bowl, my toast on a plate and drink my milk from a mug. Mary has selected the plate and bowl from the Bridgewater collection and the beaker – a garish object covered in the American stars and stripes – was a gift Will brought back from the States.

When I've finished my breakfast I fill my washbasin with hot water and Fairy Liquid, allowing my newly acquired treasures to soak while I go off in search of Mr Meanwell. The block's senior officer has been off for two days, so was unaware that David had been released six days early,* and that his cell on the enhanced wing has suddenly become available. He'll let me know what he's decided later today.

I return to my cell and find a gathering of West Indians in the corridor. They've come to say farewell to a prisoner who is leaving this morning, having served six years of a nine-year sentence for armed robbery – his first offence.

Most of you reading this will have already formed a picture

---

* This is often a result of police custody days being deducted from the prisoner's sentence.

444

of him in your mind, as I would have done only a couple of months ago. A young black thug who's better off locked up, and who will probably beat up some other innocent person the moment he's released and be back in prison within a year.

In fact, he is thirty-two years old, five foot eight, slim and good-looking. He was the one who politely asked if he could read my newspapers every evening. And he has used his six years productively. First to pass his GCSEs (five) and two years later A levels in English and History.

No sooner has he departed than Jules appears in the corridor carrying a plastic bag full of his worldly goods. He is taking over Steve's cell. He tells me that the past week has not been a happy one because he's had to share our old cell with a heroin addict who was injecting himself two, sometimes three times a day.

8.45 am

On Friday mornings the gym is taken over by the special needs group. They're an enthusiastic bunch who, despite their problems, bring a range of skills and boundless energy to everything they do. Les performs well on the rowing machine (1,000m in ten minutes), while Robbie enjoys lifting weights and Paul prefers to run. But when it comes to the game of catchball that we always play at the end of any session, Robbie can catch anything that comes his way. He could, and would, happily field in the slips for England.

All of them are chatterboxes, and demand answers to their endless questions. Do you have a father? Do you have a mother? Do you have any brothers or sisters? Are you married? Do you have any children? By the end of the hour's session, I am physically and mentally exhausted, and full of admiration

445

for their carer, Ann, who spends every waking moment with them.

At the end of the session, I watch them leave, chatting, laughing and – I hope – happier. There, but for the grace of God...

2.54 pm

Mr Nutbourne opens the cell door. 'You're moving again, Jeffrey,' he says. 'You've been allocated David's old cell on the enhanced spur.' He winks.

'Thank you,' I reply, and prepare for my ninth move in six weeks. The whole process takes less than an hour, because on this occasion I'm assisted by a local removal company: *Darren, Sergio and Jimmy Ltd.*

My new cell is on the ground floor with the enhanced prisoners. Number seventeen is opposite Darren's cell, who has Steve (conspiracy to murder and librarian) on one side, and Jimmy (Ecstasy courier, captain of everything) on the other. The officers describe it as the grown-up spur, and personally select who will be allowed to reside there. To have made it in three weeks is considered quite an achievement, although Darren managed it in four days.

The cells are exactly the same size as in any other part of the prison, but the table on which I'm now working is far larger (four feet by two). I also have an extra cupboard for my possessions, which seem to grow as each day passes, not unlike when you're on holiday.

5.00 pm

Once I've completed my move, I join Darren and Sergio for a walk in the exercise yard. I stop halfway round to watch Shaun sketching Dale. He is still proving to be a restless model, but despite this Shaun is producing a good likeness of him.

6.00 pm

After supper I call Mary (my new spur has a phone of its own, which any self-respecting estate agent would describe as 'an added amenity'). She's full of news, some good, some not so good. The police confirm that they will not be presenting their report on the Simple Truth until they've read the findings of the KPMG report. This won't be handed in to the Red Cross for at least another two, perhaps three weeks. Mary tells me that the police reply to Tony Morton-Hooper's letter was not unhelpful, and she hopes that once the KPMG report is finished, it will only be a matter of days before they move me to an open prison.

I use the remainder of my twenty units catching up with all things domestic, particularly what is happening at the Old Vicarage. When the phonecard flicks out, indicating I have only thirty seconds left, I promise to call again on Sunday. Don't forget, I no longer have an endless source of cards.

As soon as I replace the receiver, Sergio takes over the phone. He has the advantage of being able to hold a conversation in a language no one else on the spur can eavesdrop on, but the disadvantage of needing at least five phonecards every time he dials home.

DAY 44

6.50 pm

When Sergio has finished his call, he joins me in my cell. Now that we're on the same spur, it's no longer necessary for me to try and pretend I'm learning Spanish – he's just another prisoner from across the corridor.

Sergio's brother has selected four emeralds for consideration. He confirms they range in price from ten to fifteen thousand dollars. Once he has made the final choice, I will await a valuation from my expert. His brother claims that any one of the gems would retail on the London market at around $20,000. If this proves to be accurate, then I'll be happy to purchase the selected gem and give it to Mary as her Christmas present. Ah, you've finally discovered why I'm going to all this trouble.

8.15 pm

To my delight, I discover that our spur is unlocked first and banged up last, giving us an extra few minutes at each end of the day. What I enjoy most about being below stairs is the silence, or near silence, compared with the floor above. No rap music, no window warriors and no conversations shouted from one end of the corridor to the other. There is actually a feeling of community on this spur.

I don't bother to turn on the TV this evening as I am totally engrossed in Robert Goddard's *Caught in the Light*. I fall asleep fully dressed. It's been an exhausting day.

DAY 45   SATURDAY 1 SEPTEMBER 2001

8.15 am

The first day of a new month. After breakfast, I arrange with Locke (GBH), the spur painter, to have my new cell redecorated in his spare time. As the tariff has to be agreed in tobacco, and as I have no idea of the going rate, Darren (marijuana only) has agreed to act as my works manager for the transaction.

Once Locke has inspected my cell, he announces it will first need an undercoat of white, which will take him two, two-hour sessions. Darren agrees the price on a daily basis. Tomorrow he will add a coat of cream, and on Monday the cell door, the window ledge and frame plus the square around the wash basin will be painted beige. As far as I can work out, the painter will receive one pound's worth of Golden Virginia (his choice) a day. So the whole job will cost me £3 – which, Darren assures me, is the going rate. The paint, however, will be supplied by Her Majesty's tax payers. Please note that it was Margaret Thatcher who taught me never to say government; 'Governments don't pay taxes, Jeffrey, only tax payers do.'

Locke asks me to vacate my cell while the undercoat is being rolled on because once my bed, table and small cupboard have been pulled away from the walls and left in the centre of the room, there will only be enough space for one person.

I cross the corridor to join Sergio in his cell, where we hold a board meeting. Overnight, Sergio has typed out sixteen questions which he needs answered before he speaks to his brother again. For example: do I want to pay the full insurance cost? – Yes. Do I want the gold necklace to be 9, 14 or 18 carat? – 18 carat. Will I have to pay import tax when the chain and emerald land in London? – Don't know, but I'll find out.

Once Sergio has asked all his questions and written out the answers neatly in Spanish, we move onto item number two on the agenda.

I've received a letter from Chris Beetles, who has carried out considerable research into which South American artists have a worldwide market. He reports that Christie's and Sotheby's have two Latin American sales a year, both held in New York. With the exception of Botero, who has recently passed $2 million for an oil, only Lamand Tamayo regularly fetches $100,000 or more under the hammer. Sergio reads the letter slowly and places it in his file.

11.00 am

Exercise. It's Darren's turn to be sketched by Shaun, and he's proving a bit of a prima donna. He's a very private man who doesn't keep any photographs of himself. He's still grumbling about his participation as we walk out into the yard. We are greeted by Shaun, who is holding a large art pad in his right hand, and a couple of pencils in his left.

Darren reluctantly agrees to pose, but only on two conditions. That the drawing is carried out on the far side of the yard, where few inmates will see him during their perambulations. He also insists that if he doesn't like the result, he will be left out of the final montage. I don't have a lot of choice, so I

450

agree. I can only hope that Shaun will make such a good job of the preliminary sketch that Darren will be converted to the whole idea.

Jimmy and I go off for a circuit while Shaun begins his task. While we stroll round the perimeter, the talk among the inmates is only of football. England are playing Germany tonight, and Wayland are playing Methwold tomorrow. Some of the prisoners lying on the grass against the fence wish Jimmy, our captain, good luck, while another suggests that he couldn't score in a brothel.

By the end of the third circuit, a likeness is appearing on Shaun's sketch pad, but I have no way of knowing how Darren will react. He can be so perverse at times.

By the time we've completed two more circuits, the officers in the yard are beginning to herd us back to our blocks. We stop to look at Shaun's effort. Darren joins us to see the outline image for the first time. It's good, and he knows it. He nods his grudging approval, but finally gives the game away when, as we stroll back into A block, he asks, 'If that's only a sketch before Shaun does the final portrait, can I have it for my mother?' (See plate section.)

12 noon

Standing in the lunch queue I discover from Dumsday (who, Jimmy told me a few days earlier, had adopted an injured crow) that his crow died early this morning, despite his sitting up all night trying to feed it a boiled egg. I return to my cell and eat lunch standing in the middle of the room with the smell of fresh paint all around me. I survey my £3 investment. Locke has made a good start.

DAY 45

2.00 pm

The spur is getting worked up about the match this evening between England and Germany, which is a World Cup qualifying game. I am invited to pull the name of an England player out of a plastic cup, and should my selection score the first goal, I'll win nine Mars bars. I draw Gerard who, Jimmy assures me, has a good chance of scoring. I read in this morning's *Times* that England haven't won a match on German soil since 1965. But I don't pass on this information to a football-mad spur. I glance out of my window to see five rabbits eating the left-over food the prisoners have thrown out of their cell. As we are hemmed in behind a twenty-foot fine-meshed wire fence, I wonder how the rabbits get into the prison. I'll make enquiries.

6.00 pm

On a Saturday, we're banged up after supper but, as I've mentioned, the enhanced spur goes last so we can roam the corridors until six thirty – an extra thirty minutes. I check my TV listings in *The Times* to find that the football is on BBC 1, but clashes with Jane Austen's *Persuasion* on BBC 2. I elect to watch *Persuasion* while the rest of the spur settles down to follow the match. I'm confident that, if England score, the whole prison will let me know.

Just as Miss Elliot meets Captain Wentworth for the first time, the spur erupts with cheering and shouting. I quickly switch channels and watch a replay of Michael Owen scoring for England, which means I've lost a Mars bar. I switch back and continue my vigil with Miss Elliot who, because of her father's financial problems, has had to move from the family's magnificent country home to a smaller residence in Bath. I become deeply engrossed in the drama of lost love when there is another eruption of cheering. I switch over to find England have scored a second goal on the stroke of half-time. I discover that the score is 2–1 in England's favour, so I must have missed the German goal. It was obviously greeted by my fellow inmates in total silence.

I turn back to *Persuasion* to find that Captain Wentworth is flirting (the occasional glance) with our heroine, the one we want him to marry. There is another roar. I can't believe it, and switch across to find our other hero, Michael Owen, has scored again, and England are now leading three goals to one. No sooner have I switched back than there is a further roar, so I return to watch a replay of Owen completing his hat-trick, giving England an unbelievable 4–1 lead.

I flick over to Jane Austen and discover that the handsome Captain Wentworth could be about to marry the wrong girl, but then – an explosion – can it be true? I return to BBC 1 to find Heskey has scored for England and we now lead five goals to one with ten minutes to go. Quickly back to *Persuasion* where our hero and long-suffering heroine have become engaged. No suggestion of sex, not even a kiss. Long live Jane Austen.

10.00 pm

I finish the Robert Goddard book and then climb into my bed which is still in the middle of the room. I fall asleep to the smell of fresh paint and the sound of my fellow inmates reliving every one of those five England goals.

DAY 46   SUNDAY 2 SEPTEMBER 2001

10.00 am

After writing for a couple of hours and having breakfast, I report to the gym in my new capacity as football correspondent for the *Prison News*.

The Wayland team meet in the changing room where they are handed their kit: a light blue shirt, dark blue shorts, blue socks, shin pads and a pair of football boots. As with the cricket match last week, the team are far better equipped than most amateur club sides, and once again all at the tax payers' expense. All four blocks also have their own strip (A block's is yellow and black). I assume this is normal practice for every prison across the country.

Once the team has changed, and very smart they look, we're joined by our coach, Gary, who delivers an unusual team talk. Because the players have been selected from four different blocks and prisoners come and go every week, some of them haven't even met before. The first thing the eleven men and three subs have to do is to announce their names and the positions they'll be playing in. You may well consider that this is an insuperable barrier for any team, but not so, because the opposition also have several disadvantages to contend with. To start with, all of Wayland's fixtures are played at home – think about it – and the rival team are not allowed to bring along any supporters, especially not girlfriends. And when it comes to gamesmanship, our team are in a class of their own, and the officers are just as bad.

The opposition side are met at the gates by sniffer dogs before being searched. The players are then escorted to the changing rooms, accompanied by the boos of prisoners from all four blocks. And if that isn't enough to contend with, they then have to deal with our captain, Jimmy.

Now Jimmy is all charm and bonhomie as he accompanies the opposition side from the changing room onto the pitch. But he does consider it nothing less than his duty to inform the visitors that they should keep a wary eye on Preston, Wayland's main striker.

'Why?' asks the opposing team captain innocently.

'He's in for a double murder – chopped his parents' heads off while they were asleep.' Jimmy pauses. 'Even we don't like him. He's already got a twenty-five-year sentence, and as he's only done three, the occasional broken leg doesn't seem to worry him too much, especially as he's only likely to get a yellow card.'

The truth is that our main striker is in for breaking and entering (rather appropriate) but by the time Jimmy has reached the pitch, the Methwold team is convinced that if Hannibal Lecter were at Wayland he would be relegated to the subs bench.

The first half is a shambles; the ball goes up and down the pitch with little speed and even less purpose. Wayland are trying to get to know each other, while Methwold still aren't sure if they dare risk the occasional tackle. It's 0–0 when the whistle blows for half-time, and frankly no one deserved to score.

The second half is a complete contrast as I'm made aware of the other advantage Wayland has: fitness. All of our team spend at least an hour every day in the gym, rather than at the local pub, and it begins to show. The first goal is headed in by Carl (GBH), after an excellent cross by our 'double-murderer'. The second is scored by Dan (armed robbery), another of our strikers, and the third is added by Hitch (arson). We end up winning 3–0, which augurs well for the rest of the season. Perhaps we could even win the league cup this year. But it's back to disadvantages, because three of the team, including Jimmy, are due to be released before Christmas, and the side we will field at the end of the season will bear no resemblance to the one that lined up for the opening encounter.

Despite the team's glorious victory, some of the officers are irritated by the fact that they've been made to hang around until we return for a late lunch. With the exception of Mr Nutbourne, who makes sure that the team is fed, they can't wait to get us banged up and go off duty.

The relationship between officers and prisoners is always conducted on a tightrope which both sides walk every day. The officers on duty that Sunday morning unwisely miss an opportunity to make their own lives easier. A few words of praise and allowing an extra minute or two in the shower would have paid huge dividends in the long run. Instead, the victors return to their cells with shrivelled-up pieces of meat covered in cold gravy, unable to shower until we are unlocked again in two hours' time. Of course I understand that the prison is not run for the convenience of the prisoners, but here was an opportunity for the officers to make their own life easier in the long term. They botched it, with the exception of Mr Nutbourne, who will get far more cooperation and respect from the inmates in the future.

2.00 pm

Board meeting. Sergio has talked to his brother in Bogotá. The four emeralds that his brother initially selected have been short-listed to two and, along with a member of the family who owns the mountain, Sergio's brother will make the final selection tomorrow. He has also assured him that, whichever one they choose, the gem would retail at three times the price in a London shop. As for paintings, Sergio's school friend has told him that, through Sergio's mother, she has made an appointment with Botero's mother, and will report back by the end of the week. My heart leaps at the thought of finally owning a Botero.

4.00 pm

While I do a circuit with Jimmy, Shaun continues to draw Darren, who surprisingly now proves, unlike Dale, to be a still and patient model. I'm delighted with the preliminary sketches and, more importantly, so is Darren. While Shaun is sketching, I ask Darren about the rabbits. The rabbits, it seems, are no fools. They know when the prisoners are fed, and burrow under the fence to gather up the food thrown out of the windows by the inmates after lock-up. They are occasionally joined by a family of ducks. But, and there is always a but in prison, there is also a fox lurking around, who is even more cunning. He also enters under the fence after lock up, and catches the rabbits while they nibble the food dropped from the prisoners' table. The fox has also worked out that there is no such thing as 'The Wayland Hunt'.

I tell Shaun that I've spoken to Chris Beetles and hope that it will result in his being in receipt (I select the words carefully) of the highest quality drawing paper, chalks, watercolours and pencils, so that his final effort can't be blamed on his tools. He's delighted.

457

DAY 46

6.00 pm

Early lock up because of staff shortages. I will have to remain in my five paces by three cell for the next fourteen hours.

I start reading Jeeves. What a different world Bertie Wooster lived in. How would Bertie have coped with Wayland? I suppose Jeeves would have volunteered to take his place.*

---

*P. G. Wodehouse spent some time in a German jail during the Second World War. He was later accused of 'collaborating with the Germans' by the British press and then spent the rest of his life in America, which he considered exile.

DAY 47   MONDAY 3 SEPTEMBER 2001

5.43 am

I wake to the smell of fresh paint, so I feel I should bring you up to date on my redecoration programme. The white undercoat was finished yesterday, and while I was at pottery Locke (GBH, spur painter) added a coat of magnolia to the walls and beige to the door, window ledge and skirting board.

I have always liked brick as a medium, but I find the solid block of white a little unimaginative, so during pottery class this morning I'm going to suggest to Shaun that he might design a pattern for the walls, and then find out if Locke is willing to add 'interior decorator' to his portfolio. It may well cost me another couple of pounds, but I could then enter my cell for the Turner Prize.

9.00 am

During pottery class, Shaun begins to knock out a few ideas for a pattern on my walls, and very imaginative they are.

He then produces his sketch pad and shows me his latest ideas for the book cover. The first one is a cell door with eyes peeping through the little flap, while the second is a prisoner's card as displayed outside every cell. I wonder if he could somehow combine the two.*

12 noon

After lunch I make notes in preparation for a visit from William, James and David, my driver of fifteen years. Once I've done this I have to learn each of the headings by heart, as I'm not allowed to take anything into the visitors' room. I count how many topics need to be covered – William eight, James nine, David five. After that I'll have to rely on my memory.

1.30 pm

I shower and shave before putting on a new pair of jeans and a freshly ironed, blue-striped shirt. I have never been vain, but I am far too proud to allow the boys to see me looking unkempt – and wondering if prison has got the better of me.

2.00 pm

As I leave the cell to join my children, Locke strolls in. I haven't yet summoned up the courage to tell him about my idea for further redecoration, and I suspect I'll end up leaving the negotiations to my works manager, Darren.

When I arrive in the visitors' area, I am searched for the first time in over a week, but compared to Belmarsh this exercise is fairly cursory. I don't know if suspected drug addicts and dealers receive different treatment. I'm once again allocated table four-

---

* The cell card was eventually used on the back of *Volume One – Belmarsh: Hell.*

teen, where I take my place in the red chair, leaving the three blue chairs vacant. I look around the room that holds about seventy tables, but only five are occupied by prisoners. This is because of the breakdown of the prison computer, which has thrown the visiting schedule into chaos.

James is the first through the door, surprise, surprise, followed by William, then David. Once we have completed the hugs and greetings I explain that I wish to allocate the two hours judiciously. The first half hour I'll spend with William, the second with James and the third with David, before having the final half hour with all three of them.

While the other two disappear, Will updates me on the KPMG report and my D-cat reinstatement. Mary has been in touch with Gillian Shephard, currently my local MP, who has promised to contact the governor of Wayland and make it clear that once the police have dropped their enquiry, I ought to be moved on to an open prison as quickly as possible. Mind you, the Prison Service's idea of as quickly as possible . . .

Will also reports that he hopes to return to America in about three weeks as he has been offered several new commissions for documentaries. To his surprise, he's also been approached about some work in London.

While I try to recall my eight points, Will briefs me about his mother. Mary is holding up well in the circumstances, but he feels that she has probably been most affected by the whole experience.

I then ask if Will could do three things for me. First, give Chris Beetles £200 in order that Shaun will be in receipt of the art materials he needs. Second, select a bowl and plate from the Bridgewater collection and send them to Darren at Wayland, a man whose kindness I will never be able to repay properly. Finally, I ask if he will somehow get hold of my special Staedtler liquid pens, because— Will points to the tray in front of me, where I see he has slipped two behind a can of Diet Coke. I smile, but wonder if I can get the treasure back to my cell without it being confiscated.

Once I've completed my list, he brings me up to date on his social life. Ten minutes later he leaves me and James takes his place.

I spend some considerable time briefing James on Sergio's background, and explain how three weeks in prison, in such intense circumstances, is the equivalent of about three months on the outside. He nods, as he's well aware that this is only background before I broach the real subject. Having established Sergio's credentials, about which I tell him I have only my instinct to go on, we then discuss the subject of emeralds in great detail. I explain for an investment of $10,000, subject to valuation, we will acquire one emerald which will arrive in London later this week. If Sergio turns out to have been honest about the emerald, it might then be worth getting him to search for a Botero.

'If he doesn't manage to find any paintings,' I add, 'then the worse case scenario is that Mary will end up with a rather special Christmas present.'

Because James has inherited his mother's brains and my barrow-boy instincts, there's no need to repeat anything. We agree to speak again by phone towards the end of the week. I smile across at David and he joins us.

After a few preliminaries about his wife, Sue, and whether they had a good holiday, I can see he's nervous, which has always been David's way of telling me something is worrying him. I try to make it as easy as possible for both of us.

'Are you still thinking of emigrating to Australia?' I ask.

'No,' he replies, 'much as I'd like to, it's near impossible to get on the quota, unless you have a job to go to, or relatives already living there.'

'I suppose I'll have a better chance now I've been to prison,' I suggest, before adding, 'So what *are* you planning to do?'

'Sue and I are thinking of settling in Turkey. We've spent our last few holidays there, and we like the people, the climate and most of all the cost of living.'

'So when would you want to leave?'

'In a couple of months, if that's all right with you, boss?'

I smile and tell him that's just fine. We shake hands like old friends, because that's exactly what we are.

The four of us spend the last thirty minutes together swapping stories as if I wasn't in jail. I think I've made this observation before, but if your friends could be in prison with you, it would be almost bearable.

I place the pens Will smuggled in into my shirt pocket and just hope. I'm sorry to see the boys leave, and it's only their absence that reminds me just how much I love them. The officer who carries out the search checks my mouth, under my tongue, makes me take off my shoes, and then finishes with a Heathrow check. I escape – which means for the next week I'll be able to write with the implement of my choice.

5.00 pm

After supper I convene a board meeting in Sergio's cell. 'The ball is now in your court,' I tell him. 'You've selected the emerald, so we're about to discover if you're a serious player or a mountebank.' He has asked me to use one expression and one word every day that he won't have heard before. He immediately looks up mountebank in his Spanish/English dictionary.

DAY 47

He then stands and formally shakes my hand. 'The ball is now in my court,' he repeats, 'and you're about to find out that despite the circumstances in which we've met, I am not a mountebank.' I want to believe him.

DAY 48   TUESDAY 4 SEPTEMBER 2001

6.11 am

One of the interesting aspects of writing this diary during the day, and correcting the script of volume one in the evening, is being reminded just how horrendous an experience Belmarsh was.

9.00 am

Pottery. Paul gives us a lecture with slides on Rothko, Man Ray, Magritte and Andy Warhol. Several of the prisoners voice an opinion often heard about modern artists, only they put it more bluntly.

'That's fuckin' crap, why would anyone pay good money for that shit? My seven-year-old daughter could knock you up one of those.'

Neither of our tutors, Paul nor Anne, comments; both are professional artists and know only too well that if they could 'knock up one of those', they wouldn't be teaching in prison.

After the lecture Shaun presents me with a pattern for my cell wall – unquestionably influenced by Magritte. It's fun, but I wonder if Locke is capable of reproducing it. I'll have to discuss the problem with my *chef de chantier*, Darren. Will I really be allowed a sun and moon in my room?

DAY 48

2.00 pm

Education. Tuesday afternoon is a bit of a farce. I have to attend an education class to make up the statutory number of lessons required by a part-time worker – £6.50 a week – so end up sitting at the back of the classroom working on this script.

I've asked Wendy Sergeant (Head of the Education Department) if I can teach one lesson a week of creative writing, as I did at Belmarsh. Her latest comment on the subject is that the prisoners don't want another inmate teaching them. I find this unlikely because at least one inmate a day asks me to read and comment on something they've written, so I wonder what the truth really is. I won't bother Wendy again as it's obvious that someone else has made the decision, and she is simply carrying out instructions. In future I'll just sit at the back of the classroom and continue working for myself.

5.00 pm

Board meeting. Sergio reports that he's spoken to his brother again, and all the arrangements are in place. But he has an anxious look on his face.

'What's the problem?' I ask.

'I'm worried about my brother,' he explains. 'He's a civil servant, an academic, not used to the way business is carried out in Colombia. It must have taken a great deal of courage for him to travel to the mountain where no one would give a second thought to killing you for a thousand dollars. Now we want him to hand over ten thousand in cash and then transport the emerald to the airport without any protection.' Sergio pauses. 'I fear for his life.'

My first thought is that Sergio is trying to get off the hook now that he's leaving these shores in a few weeks' time.

'What are you suggesting?' I venture.

'Perhaps it would be wiser to wait until I return to Bogotá, then I can handle the problem personally. I fear for my brother's life,' he repeats.

Once Sergio is back in Bogotá I will have lost all contact with him, not to mention my £200. He has claimed many times during the past three weeks that several prisoners have offered to transfer money to his account in Bogotá in exchange for a regular supply of drugs, but he has always turned them down. Has he in fact accepted every payment? Is that account now in surplus thus guaranteeing him an easy life once he's back in Colombia? However, I feel I am left with no choice but to take the high road.

'If you're in any doubt about your brother's safety,' I tell him, 'let's postpone the sending of the emerald until you return to Bogotá.'

Sergio looks relieved. 'I'll call him tomorrow,' he says, 'and then I'll let you know our decision.'

I close the board meeting because, given the circumstances, there's not a lot more to discuss.

6.00 pm

Exercise. Shaun has finished his preliminary sketch of Darren, and is now making a further attempt at Dale.

As Jimmy and I proceed on our usual circuit (there isn't a lot of choice) we pass a group of three officers who are posted to keep an eye on us. One of them is a young, not unattractive, woman. Jimmy tells me that she has a 'bit of a thing' about Malcolm (ABH, punched a publican) who she will miss when he's transferred to his D-cat prison on Monday.

'The stories I could tell you about Malcolm,' says Jimmy.

'Yes, yes,' I say, my ears pricking up.

'No, no,' says Jimmy. 'I'm not saying a word about that man until I'm sure he's safely ensconced at Latchmere House. He flattened that publican with one punch.' He pauses. 'But ask me again next week.'

9.00 pm

I watch Ian Richardson on BBC 1 playing Dr Bell in a Conan Doyle drama described in *The Times* as the forerunner to Sherlock Holmes. I will never forget his portrayal of the chief whip in Michael Dobbs' excellent *House of Cards*. I've known seven chief whips in my time – Willie Whitelaw, Francis Pym, Humphrey Atkins, John Wakeham, Tim Renton, Peter Brooke, and Richard Ryder – but even their combined talents lacked the Machiavellian skills of Francis Urquhart, under whose gaze I certainly wouldn't have dared to miss a vote.

11.00 pm

I lie awake thinking about Sergio. Is he a liar, just another two-bit con man, or is he genuinely anxious about his brother's safety? Only time will tell.

DAY 49   WEDNESDAY 5 SEPTEMBER 2001

5.51 am

Locke has finished painting my cell, but is nervous about attempting the Magritte pattern Shaun has designed for the wall. Darren, as works manager, agrees that it's far too elaborate, and should be cut down to about half the original, and even then he's not sure I'll get away with it. But as Darren points out, the worst they can do is make us return the paintwork to its original colour – cost, £1. So it's agreed that while I'm away at pottery, the redecorating will begin, and then we'll have to wait and see how the spur officer reacts.

9.00 am

Pottery. Today the class settles down to do a still-life drawing. Anne, our tutor, and former Slade graduate, has taken a lot of trouble in gathering together objects of interest to make the drawing more of a challenge. She has set up in the centre of the room a small card table, and placed over it a cloth with a red and white diamond pattern. On the table she's placed an empty wine bottle, a green vase and a fruit bowl. In the bowl she's carefully arranged a bunch of grapes, a pineapple, three oranges,

469

two apples and a peach. Paul, one of our other tutors, has supplied a cheese board and a lump of Cheddar.

We all sit round the table in a circle and attempt to draw what we see in front of us. Keith (kidnapper), who is sitting next to me, will present the piece as part of his A-level submission. He understands both perspective and shading. I, on the other hand, do not. Anne helpfully points out – to everyone else's amusement – that my peach is bigger than my pineapple.

After an hour, we're given a ten-minute break, when most of the prisoners go off for a quick drag. Shaun and I disappear with Anne into her office to discuss some ideas for a prison landscape which I hope to include in this book. I take up as much of her time as possible, because I can't face another hour of still-life drawing. However, she seems keen to get back and see how the others are progressing.

Anne is a very easy-going person and I can't imagine her losing her temper. But when she walks back into the main room and sees the still-life table, she goes berserk. All that remains of the original offering is two apple cores, the top of a pineapple, three orange skins, a peach stone, a grape stalk with one grape attached and a cheese board with just a few morsels left on it. To be fair, what is left has been artistically arranged, and her pupils are studiously drawing the new composition.

I burst out laughing, and it is only moments before Anne joins in. I am happy to report that Keith's final effort was entered as part of his A level submission, and gained high marks for originality.

2.00 pm

Rugby. Over fifty prisoners turn out for the first training session of the season, which takes place on the main field adjacent to the football pitch. For an hour our coach, Andy Harley, puts us through passing and handling skills, and it soon becomes clear that several prisoners have never played the game before. For the last thirty minutes, the coach selects two sides for a game of touch rugby, which he asks me to referee. He tells me that I had refereed him some years before when a Newmarket XV visited Cambridge.

Because several of the prisoners didn't know the laws of the game, I had to be fairly liberal if I wasn't going to have to blow the whistle every few seconds for some minor infringement. However, I was left with little choice when a large black man threw the ball twenty yards forward, as if he were playing American football. I blew the whistle and awarded the blue side a penalty. He immediately bore down on me, shouting expletives, while the others stood around and watched. I paced ten yards towards his goal line, explaining that in rugby you can't swear at the referee. His language became riper, so I advanced another ten yards, by which time he had been joined by three of his mates who weren't much smaller. Two of the coaches ran quickly onto the field, and Mr Harley explained, 'Jeffrey is right. If you argue with the referee in rugby, it's automatically a penalty, and you'd better get used to it, because when we have our first match next week, a neutral ref will be even stricter.' Many of the prisoners looking on remained silent, as no one was sure what would happen next.

'Sorry, Jeff,' said the big black man, and added, 'it's just that we never played it like that in Brixton.' He then rejoined his team.

When I returned to the block, I went straight to the shower room, and a few minutes later was joined by Jimmy.

'I scored two goals,' he informs me, before adding, 'I've just heard about you and Big Nes.'

'Big Nes?'

'Yeah, Big Nes from Block C. I've managed to go a whole year without speaking to him.'

DAY 49

'Why?' I asked.

'He was Brixton heavyweight champion, and I once saw him knock a prisoner out with a single blow, and no one was sure what the poor bastard had done to annoy him.'

'Oh Christ,' I said, shaking under the shower, 'I'll never be able to go into the exercise yard again.'

'No, no,' said Jimmy, 'Big Nes is telling everyone you're his new friend.'

5.00 pm

I collect my supper from the hotplate, but Sergio avoids any eye contact.

As it's Wednesday, you have to change your sheets, blankets and towels after supper, so I was too preoccupied to go in search of him. Darren popped in while I was making up my bed to attach nine small mirrors to the wall using prison toothpaste as an adhesive. Regulations allow you only one five-by-five-inch mirror, so heaven knows how Darren got his hands on the other eight.

6.00 pm

I go in search of Sergio, and spot him on the phone. I return to my cell thinking he'll probably visit me once he's finished his call ... he doesn't.

10.00 pm

I'm exhausted and fall asleep fully dressed with the TV still on. Only later do I learn that it is an offence to fall asleep fully dressed, for which you can be put on report.

DAY 50   THURSDAY 6 SEPTEMBER 2001

6.57 am

The cell is at last finished and no longer smells of paint. Locke has run a day and a half over time, which is no more than one would expect from any self-respecting painter and decorator. Darren comes in to pick up my washing, sighs, and declares the new decor reminds him of a 1970s council house. He leaves with his nose in the air and several bundles of washing over his shoulder.

9.00 am

Pottery is cancelled as once a fortnight the prison officers carry out a session of in-house training, which means we're banged up for the rest of the morning. I attempt yesterday's *Times* crossword, and manage to complete three clues – quid, Turgenev and courtier. I can only improve.

12 noon

Lunch. When I go to pick up my meal from the hotplate, Sergio welcomes me with a broad grin, so I assume that after all

473

DAY 50

those phone calls he has some news. However, I won't have a chance to meet up with him until after I've returned from the gym.

2.00 pm

Gym. It's circuit day. I try to keep up with Minnie the traveller, and manage to do ten press-ups to his fifteen, and maintain the same ratio for sit-ups, bench presses, squats, pull ups and back raises, but let's face it, he's only forty-five and in the sixth year of an eleven-year sentence. He's hoping for parole next year.* At the end of the session, Minnie nods. He's a man of few words, and a nod is considered a remarkable gesture for someone he's only known for a month.

5.00 pm

Board meeting. Sergio begins by apologizing for not reporting back last night, but he had to call Bogotá six times and, in the process, went through nineteen phonecards (£38). To fund this, he had to sell his radio, a cassette player and an Adidas tracksuit. I hope I looked suitably guilty.

He tells me that the paperwork for the emerald is now complete (insurance, registration, authentication certificate, export licence and tax) and it's ready to be shipped. His brother, as you will recall, is a senior civil servant and therefore plays everything by the book. He has already told Sergio that he has no intention of losing his job over one small emerald. I feel even more guilty as I listen to the rest of Sergio's Colombian report...

------

* He was released in October 2002.

6.00 pm

Darren rushes into my cell. 'A problem,' he announces. Mr Meanwell has just witnessed him opening a registered parcel in reception. It turned out to be a plate and bowl sent in by my son Will. 'Prisoners are not allowed to send in gifts for other inmates, as it might be construed as a bribe, in exchange for drugs or protection.' Darren warns me that Mr Meanwell would be calling for me at some point, and perhaps it might be wiser if I were to go and 'bell the cat'. I shake my head. Meanwell is a wise old bird, and he'll work out that a plate and bowl doesn't constitute a bribe, and in any case, everyone is well aware of my views on drugs. He will also realize that I made no attempt to hide the gift. Will's name was printed all across the box, together with a compliment slip from my PA, which would allow Mr Meanwell to place the offending plate and bowl with the rest of my confiscated kit downstairs if he was at all suspicious. Like Nelson, Meanwell knows when to turn a blind eye.

6.15 pm

Exercise. It's the final evening outing. The nights are drawing in and we won't be allowed out again after six. I perambulate around the yard with Steve (not librarian Steve) who, because he's a D-cat prisoner, has spent the day out with his family. I ask him if he enjoyed the experience (9 am to 3 pm).

'Very much,' he replied, 'but only thanks to some help from the police.'

'The police?' I repeat.

He explains. One of the activities Steve most misses while he's in jail is a regular swim, so whenever he has a day release, he and the family go off to the local swimming pool. On this occasion they left their Ford in the municipal car park, and took the children to the pool. When they returned, his wife couldn't find her car keys, until one of the children spotted them on the back seat. Steve ran all the way to the nearest police station explaining his dilemma, exacerbated by the fact that if he failed to return to Wayland by three o'clock, he would automatically lose his D-cat status. The police happily broke into his car, and even phoned Wayland to confirm what happened. Steve arrived back at the front gate with ten minutes to spare.

DAY 51   FRIDAY 7 SEPTEMBER 2001

5.39 am

I have now been a resident of Wayland for a month, and Sergio will return to Colombia in a couple of weeks' time. So with a bit of luck he'll be deported around the same time as I'm being transferred to a D-cat. But will I also be in possession of an emerald?

9.00 am

Gym. Friday is special needs group, and my four new friends Alex, Robbie, Les and Paul shake hands with me as they come through the gate. Again all four display different talents during the training session. Les can now complete 1,650 metres on the rowing machine in ten minutes, but can only manage one mile an hour on the treadmill, whereas Paul can do five miles an hour on the running machine, but can't catch a ball. Robbie can catch anything, but hates all the machines, so only does weight training.

The instructors rightly tell us to play to their strengths, which results in much clapping and laughter, along with a huge sense of achievement.

DAY 51

Jimmy handles them better than anyone. He remembers all their names (over twenty came this morning) and they feel he's a real friend. He'd make a great PE teacher, but I have a feeling that once he's released the lure of easy money may be more attractive. He says he'll never deal in drugs again, but I wonder.

6.00 pm

Exercise. Cancelled because it's raining.

7.00 pm

Sergio calls his brother in Bogotá, but the line is engaged.

7.05 pm

Sergio comes to my cell and continues his tutorial on the history of Colombia. The political system is not unlike that of the United States with a president, vice-president, Senate and Congress. However, there are two big differences: the president and vice-president have to come from different parties, one conservative, one liberal – Colombia's idea of democracy – whereas in truth the president has all the power. The other big difference is that even a senator requires four bodyguards. Sergio tells me that one presidential candidate had forty bodyguards when he delivered a speech in Bogotá, and was still assassinated.

7.20 pm

Sergio tries his brother again. Still engaged.

7.23 pm

Sergio continues his lecture, explaining that the violence in his country makes it necessary for any presidential candidate to have an accommodation with the guerrillas or the Mafia or the army, or all three. We sometimes forget how fortunate we are in Britain. Our politicians only have to deal with the trade unions, the CBI – and Messrs Paxman and Humphreys.

7.35 pm

Sergio tries his brother again. Still engaged.

7.40 pm

According to Sergio, the civil service remains the only untainted profession. Although his brother is an adviser to several ministers, he doesn't need a bodyguard because it is accepted that he will never take a bribe from either the Mafia, the guerrillas or the army. The countryside, he assures me, is beautiful and the beaches that face both the Pacific and the Atlantic rival any that can be found in America or Europe. And as for the women . . .

DAY 52   SATURDAY 8 SEPTEMBER 2001

6.01 am

Since the age of twenty-six, I've been lucky enough to organize my own life, so having to follow the same routine day in and day out, weekends included, is enough to make one go stark raving bonkers. If I weren't writing this diary, and Sergio didn't exist, they would have had to put me in a straitjacket long before now and cart me off to the nearest asylum.

9.00 am

Gym. I put myself through a tough workout, and what makes it even tougher is that I'm surrounded by prisoners a third of my age. At the end of the session I climb onto the scales, to find I've put on a pound in the last week. I'll have to cut down on my chocolate intake. One of the many disadvantages of being locked up in a cell for hour upon hour is that sometimes you eat simply because there is nothing else to do (this is one of the reasons prisoners experiment with drugs, and addicts need a regular fix). In future I must show more self-control. If I don't buy it, I can't eat it.

Between each exercise, ten minutes on the treadmill, the

rower and the bicycle, I walk a complete circuit of the gym to get my breath back. By now I know most of the prisoners and the workouts they do, and usually acknowledge or encourage them as I stroll by. As I pass Jimmy he flexes his muscles, and describes himself as a gay icon; I'm seen by the other inmates as the geriatric icon.

Today I spot a six-foot-three West Indian of about twenty stone who's lifting massive weights on his own, so I stop to watch him.

'What are you fuckin' staring at?' he demands, once he's put the weights down.

'Just watching,' I reply.

'Then fuck off. I know you talk to everyone else, but you don't fuckin' talk to me.' I can't stop laughing, which doesn't seem to please him and has the officers on edge. 'Do you want your fuckin' head knocked off?' he asks.

'I don't think so, Ellis.' He looks surprised that I know his name. 'Not if you're hoping to be out of here in two weeks' time.' He looks even more surprised that I know when he's due to be released. He grunts, turns his back on me and lifts 210 kilos. In prison, what you know is every bit as important as who you know.

2.00 pm

As I cross the corridor to join Darren in his cell for a game of backgammon, I spot Sergio on the phone. He's holding a stack of £2 phonecards in his left hand; by now he must have traded everything he owns. Lately, his cell looks as if the bailiffs have paid a visit.

After three games, I return to my cell in possession of another Mars bar. If I am going to lose weight, I'm going to have to start losing at backgammon. I glance to my left to see Sergio furiously beckoning me.

'I need another phonecard,' he says desperately. I remove the one I always carry in the back pocket of my jeans and hand it over. He smiles. I return to my cell, sit at my desk and wait, sensing a board meeting is imminent.

2.34 pm

Sergio walks in, pushes the door to (if anyone enters your cell, officer or inmate, it's against regulations to lock yourself in) and turns on the TV – a sign that means he doesn't want to be overheard. He takes his usual place on the end of the bed, as befits the managing director. He opens his A4 pad.

'The stone takes off,' he checks his watch, 'in a couple of hours.' He can't resist a huge grin as he keeps me waiting. I nod. If I were to speak, it would only hold up the inevitable repetition of the entire conversation he and his brother have just held. And who can blame him? However, I'll skip the next forty minutes and give you a precis of what has caused such a big grin.

Sergio's brother has in fact completed all the paperwork and booked the tiny package onto a Lufthansa flight that leaves Bogotá for Heathrow via Frankfurt in two hours' time (10.30 am in Bogotá, 4.30 pm at Wayland). He has faxed all the relevant details to my office in London, so they'll know when and where to pick up the gem. Sergio pauses at this point and waits for some well-earned praise. He goes on to confirm that the emerald has come from the Muzo mining district, famous for the quality of its stones. It's 3.3 carats, and cost $9,000 (mountain price). Now all we can do is wait until I find out what value is placed on the emerald by my gemmologist. Sergio looks up from his notes, and adds that his brother would like confirmation that the fax has arrived in my office.

'Right now,' I ask, 'or when you've completed your report?' because I can see that he's only about halfway through the pages that are covered in his neat Spanish hand. He considers this for a moment, and then says, 'No, I'll finish first.'

'The second piece of news,' continues Sergio, turning another page, unable to suppress an even broader grin, 'is that Liana' – his former school friend – 'has tracked down four Boteros in private hands. In private hands,' he repeats with considerable emphasis. 'And they could be for sale. She will send the details to your office some time next week.' He checks his diary. 'That will give you twelve days to evaluate them. Evaluate,' he repeats. 'Is that the correct word?' I nod, impressed. 'By the time you have decided on a realistic price, I will be back in Colombia and can take over negotiations.' He closes the A4 pad.

'I'd better call my son,' I say, aware the ball is back in my court. 'Any units left on my phonecard?' I ask, returning to the real world.

3.17 pm

I call James on his mobile and ask where he is.

'In the car, Dad, but I'll be back at the flat in about fifteen minutes.' I put the phone down. Three units gone – mobiles gobble units. I return to my cell to tell Sergio I won't know if James has received the fax for another fifteen minutes. This gives Sergio enough time to repeat the highlights of his earlier triumph not unlike replays of Owen's hat-trick against Germany.

DAY 52

3.35 pm

I call Jamie at the flat and ask him if he's received the fax.

'Yes,' he replies, 'it arrived forty minutes ago.'

'And does it give you all the details you need?'

'Yes,' he replies.

I put the phone down. Sergio leaves me as he has to report for his job behind the hotplate. Although he too has to return to the real world, that grin just doesn't leave his face.

4.30 pm

Exercise. Darren and I are joined by Jason (conspiracy to black-mail) on our afternoon power walk. We pass Shaun who is sketching Jules, with whom I shared a cell for the first two weeks. He's now finished Darren and Dale and once he's completed Jules, he'll only have Jimmy to do, so he should have a full house by the end of the week.

'Why do I have this feeling,' asks Darren, 'that you consider the Prison Service has only one purpose, and that is to cater for your every need?'

'That's neither accurate nor fair,' I protest. 'I've tried to organize my entire life around the schedule the Prison Service demands. It makes it twice as difficult to carry out my usual routines, but it has put another perspective on the unforgiving minute.'

'I wish I could work the system,' says Jason. 'They had me in for an MDT (mandatory drugs test) this afternoon, à la Ann Widdecombe.'

'Will it prove positive?' I ask.

'No chance, I'm in the clear. What a nerve,' he adds, 'suggesting that it was "on the grounds of reasonable suspicion".'

'Knowing your past record,' says Darren – well aware that Jason occasionally dabbles in heroin – 'how can you be so confident you're in the clear?'

'Simple,' Jason replies. 'For the past three days I've been drinking more water than Jeffrey. I must have been up peeing at least seven times every night.'

5.40 pm

We're banged up for fourteen hours. After I've checked over the day's script, I turn to my letters. I am particularly touched by a missive from Gillian Shephard. She describes herself as 'your temporary MP'. She offers her support and goes on to point out that, 'No one can suggest I'm after your vote. After all, members of the House of Lords, convicted prisoners and lunatics are not entitled to a vote.' She concludes, 'There's only one category left for you to fulfil, Jeffrey.'

10.00 pm

I climb into bed and start to think about an aeroplane that's already halfway across the Atlantic on its way to Heathrow. In its massive hold there is a tiny package, no larger than an Oxo cube, and inside a tiny emerald that will either be on its way back to Bogotá in a few days' time, or hanging on my family's Christmas tree come December.

DAY 53   SUNDAY 9 SEPTEMBER 2001

5.39 am

The strangest thing happened last night, and I'm going to have to follow it up today. However, in order for you to be able to understand its significance, I'll first have to explain the layout of the enhanced spur on A block. The spur is L-shaped, with fourteen cells on each sprig. If I look out of the window to my left, I can see about five of the windows on the adjoining sprig.

Around eight yesterday evening, just after I'd finished writing for the day, I rose from my desk to draw the curtains, when I noticed a woman officer of about twenty-five years of age (I'd better not describe her in detail) chatting to a prisoner through his window. I wouldn't have given it a second thought – if she hadn't still been there an hour later ... now I'm unable to tell you any more at the moment, because I was banged up at five forty last night, and will not be let out until eight fifteen this morning. I shall then approach the oracle of all knowledge, Darren, and report back to you tomorrow. I have a feeling he'll know both the officer and the prisoner and – more importantly – be able to throw some light on their relationship.

486

9.00 am

Jimmy, Carl, Jules, Shane and I go across to the changing rooms for the football match against Lakenheath. After last Sunday's victory, and two good training sessions during the week, the team are buoyed up and ready for the encounter.

In my role as match reporter, I look around the benches and check to make sure I know the names of every team member. The players are becoming quite nervous, and start jumping up and down on the spot as they wait for the arrival of our coach to deliver his pep talk. Kevin Lloyd appears a few moments later, a look of despondency on his face.

'I'm sorry, lads,' he says, 'but the game's off.' A voluble groan goes round the changing room. 'Two of the opposition,' Kevin continues, 'failed to bring any form of ID with them, so we couldn't let them through the gates. I would have accepted credit cards, but they couldn't even supply those. I am sorry,' Kevin repeats, and there's no doubt he's as disappointed as we are.

While the others go off for a further training session, I have to return to my cell.

11.00 am

I call Mary, who brings me up to date on the reinstatement of my D-cat. 'KPMG's report is progressing slowly,' she tells me, 'and the police haven't even decided if they want to interview you.' Although the whole exercise is taking longer than she had anticipated, Mary says there is no reason to believe that they will find Ms Nicholson's accusations anything other than spurious.

I suggest that she goes ahead with the Christmas parties that we always hold in December and let Will and James act as co-hosts. I tell her to invite everyone who has stood firm and ignore the fair-weather friends (who have in fact turned out to be very small in number). I add that if I'm in a D-cat open prison by Christmas, I'll call up in the middle of the party and deliver a festive message over the intercom.

4.30 pm

I'm just about to leave for exercise when the spur officer tells me I'm required urgently in the SO's office. The word 'urgently' surprises me, as I haven't heard it used for the past seven weeks.

I join Mr King in his office, and am introduced to a female officer I've never seen before. Am I at last to meet the governor? No. The officer's name is Sue Maiden and she explains that she's part of the prison's security team. She then tells me that it has been reported to her that Ellis, who resides on B block, was abusive to me in the gym yesterday. I repeat exactly what took place. She then asks me if I want special protection.

'Certainly not,' I reply. 'That's the last thing I need.' She looks relieved.

'I had to ask,' she explains.

'That's all I need,' I repeat. 'You only have to read the story in the *Sunday Mirror* this morning about phonecards to see what the press would make of that.'

'Understood, but we'll still have to speak to Ellis.'

'Fine, but not at my request,' I make clear. She seems to accept this proviso, and I depart to find the barred gate that leads out on to the exercise yard has already been bolted, leaving me locked inside and unable to take my daily walk around the yard.

5.00 pm

I spend the forty minutes with Sergio in his cell. He tells me that there is only one recognized carrier willing to fly in and out of Bogotá, and then only on a Thursday, Saturday and Sunday. Sergio mentions that it's not easy to attract holidaymakers to a country where there are forty murders a day in the capital alone.

He uses the rest of exercise time to give me a geography lesson. I am shown in Darren's *Times* atlas (he's playing backgammon) where the emerald mountains are situated, as well as the extensive oil fields in the valleys to the east. I also discover that both the Andes and the Amazon make entrances and exits through Colombia.

6.00 pm

I drop into Darren's cell to have a blackcurrant cordial and watch him play a game of backgammon with Jimmy. He tells me that my meeting with the security officer was timed so that I wouldn't be able to go out into the exercise yard, as they felt it might be wise for me to cool it a little. Darren seems to know everything that's going on, and I take the opportunity to tell him about my nocturnal sightings.

Darren laughs. 'You're a peeping Tom,' he says. 'That has to be Malcolm. Macho Malcolm.'

'He's even more irresistible than me,' chips in Jimmy.

'Do I sense a good story for the diary?' I ask tentatively.

'Half a dozen,' says Darren, 'but not tonight because we're just about to be banged up.' He can't hide his pleasure at the thought of keeping me waiting for another few hours.

DAY 53

8.00 pm

Once I'm banged up, I start making extensive notes for my phone call to Alison, who returns from New Zealand tomorrow. I then turn to *Hamlet.* I am resolved to read, or reread, the entire works of Shakespeare – thirty-seven plays – by the time they transfer me to an open prison. If I succeed, I'll move on to the Sonnets.

After a couple of acts, I switch on the TV to watch the unforgettable John Le Mesurier in *Dad's Army*. What a distinguished career he had, making a virtue of letting other people take centre stage. Not something I've ever been good at.

DAY 54   MONDAY 10 SEPTEMBER 2001

5.51 am

Tomorrow and tomorrow and tomorrow . . .*

Tomorrow, I will need to book a call at seven in the evening with my son James, to find out if the emerald has arrived. I can't contact him today because on Monday we're banged up at five-thirty, and he'll still be at work in the City.

Tomorrow . . . Macho Malcolm leaves for his D-cat prison, and neither Darren nor Jimmy are willing to breathe a word about his sex life until he's off the premises. However, I *can* report that the woman officer who was spotted outside Malcolm's window was today seen walking down the corridor with him towards his cell. But this is the stuff of rumours; tomorrow I will be able to give you the facts as reported by Darren and Jimmy. However, Darren did let slip that three women were involved. He knows only too well such a hint will keep me intrigued for another night.

Tomorrow . . .

As for today, I rise a few minutes before six and write for two hours.

---

*When I originally wrote these words, I had no idea how portentous tomorrow would turn out to be.

DAY 54

9.00 am

Pottery. I take a grapefruit into art class, and an empty jar of marmalade for Keith (kidnapping) as part of another still life he's drawing for his A level course. Keith didn't even take up painting until he was sent to prison. When he comes up for parole in six months' time, he will leave, at the age of forty-six, with an A level. Much credit must go to Anne and Paul, who are every bit as proud of this achievement as Keith himself.

Keith tells me how sorry he was to read about my mother's death, and goes on to say that he was in prison when his wife died of breast cancer at the age of thirty-nine. He then adds the poignant comment, 'I shall not mourn her death until after I've been released.'

Shaun (forgery, artist) confirms that he's given up on Dale, and will now concentrate on Jules, Steve and Jimmy. We discuss how he'll deal with the arrival on Wednesday of his cache of special drawing paper, oils, chalks and pencils without the other prisoners becoming aware of what I'm up to. We don't want to get our smuggler into any trouble, and we certainly don't need any other inmates to feel envious.

Envy is even more prevalent in prisons than it is in the outside world, partly because all emotions are heightened in such a hot-house atmosphere, and partly because any little privilege afforded to one, however slight, seems so unfair to others who are not treated in the same way.

I spend the remainder of the class reading a book on the lives of the two great female Impressionists, Marie Laurencin and Berthe Morisot.

2.00 pm

Gym. Once again I complete my programme in the allocated hour. Just to give you an update on my progress, when I first arrived at Wayland four weeks ago, I managed 1,800 metres on the rowing machine, and today I passed 2,200 for the first time. When, and if, I ever get to a D-cat establishment, I can only hope they have a well-equipped gym.

3.42 pm

Mr Chapman unlocks my cell door to let me know that Mr Carlton-Boyce wants to see me.

Mr Carlton-Boyce, who seems to be the governor on my case, tells me that he can do nothing about the reinstatement of my D-cat until the police confirm that they will not be going ahead with any enquiry concerning the Simple Truth appeal.

'However,' he adds, 'once that confirmation comes through, we will transfer you to an open prison as quickly as possible. I am still receiving a pile of letters from the public every day,' he adds, 'but they just don't understand that my hands are tied.' I accept this, but point out that it's been six weeks, and the police haven't even interviewed me. He nods, and then asks me if I have any other problems. I say no, although I have a feeling he's referring to Ellis and the gym incident.

5.30 pm

I call Alison. I make an appointment to speak to Jonathan Lloyd, my agent, at five tomorrow and my son James at seven. I have to book 'time calls' because, as you will recall, no one can phone in.

DAY 54

5.45 pm

Banged up for another fourteen hours, so once I've gone over my script, I turn to my letters, one of which is from a journalist.

How flattering the press can be when they want something.

9.00 pm

I watch David Starkey present the first of an engrossing four-part series on the six wives of Henry VIII. I had no idea that Catherine of Aragon had been made regent and conducted a war against the Scots (Flodden 1513) while Henry was away fighting his own battles in France, or that they were married for over thirty years, and of course would have remained together until death if she had only produced a son. More please, Dr Starkey. I can't wait to learn about Anne Boleyn next week; even I know that she was the mother of Elizabeth I, but not a lot more.

10.00 pm

The lead story on the news is that John Prescott's retaliatory punch during the election campaign is to be referred to the CPS. Over the past few weeks several inmates have pointed out that they are serving sentences from six months to three years for punching someone after they had been attacked, so they're looking forward to the deputy prime minister joining us. I have little doubt that the CPS will sweep the whole incident under the carpet, I say when I raise the subject with Darren. 'They didn't in your case,' he remarks.

True, but it won't go unnoticed by the public that we can

expect two levels of justice in Britain as long as New Labour are in power. I just can't see Mr Prescott arriving at Belmarsh in two sweatboxes. Perhaps I do the CPS an injustice.

Tomorrow and tomorrow and tomorrow . . .

DAY 55   TUESDAY 11 SEPTEMBER 2001

5.39 am

I suspect that Tuesday September 11th 2001 will be etched on the memories of everyone in the free world as among the blackest days in history. But I shall still report it as it unfolded for me, in time sequence, although aware that my earlier reportage may appear frivolous.

9.40 am

Pottery is cancelled because Anne's car has broken down, so all the prisoners in the art class have to return to their cells (the first irony). Back on A block, everyone on my spur is shaking hands with Malcolm, who is about to be transferred to a D-cat. He comes to my cell to say farewell, and hopes that I will be joining him soon, as he knows Spring Hill is also my first choice.

'When are Group 4 collecting you?' I ask.

'They aren't,' he replies. 'Now I'm in a D-cat and past my FLED,* I can drive myself over to Aylesbury, and as long as I've checked in by three this afternoon, no one will give a damn.'

---

* FLED – Facility Licence Eligibility Date, one quarter of your sentence.

496

No sooner has Malcolm left the wing, than Jimmy slips into my cell. 'I'm ready to talk now,' he says.

Jimmy and Malcolm are both D-cats (Jimmy remains at Wayland because his home is nearby) and are the only two inmates at Wayland allowed to work outside the prison walls every day. Both of them have a job maintaining the grounds beyond the perimeter fence during the week, and at an animal sanctuary on Saturday mornings. The sanctuary is a voluntary project, which concentrates on helping animals in distress. The work ranges from assisting lame beasts to walk or birds to fly, to having to bury them when they die.

Every Saturday morning at the sanctuary, Jimmy and Malcolm join several volunteers from the local village. Among them one lady who has left Malcolm in no doubt how she feels about him – Malcolm has the rugged looks of a matinee idol, and possesses an inordinate amount of charm.

One of the tasks none of the volunteers relish is having to bury dead animals, and Percy the hedgehog was no exception. Everyone was surprised when the lady in question stepped forward and volunteered to bury Percy. Malcolm, gallant as ever, quickly agreed to accompany her into the forest that bordered the sanctuary.

Armed with spades, they disappeared into the thicket. Forty-five minutes later they reappeared but, Jimmy noticed, minus their spades.

'Where's your spade, mate?' demanded Jimmy.

'I knew there was something else we were meant to do,' Malcolm blurted out. They both charged back into the forest, and Malcolm returned only just in time to be escorted back to the prison.

Jimmy goes on to tell me that Malcolm left Wayland just in time, because one of the ladies who served behind the counter at family visits has also just signed up to join the group on Saturdays at the animal sanctuary. Not to mention the female officer who I saw standing outside his cell window for an hour two nights ago, who is now thinking of applying for a transfer . . .

'God knows,' says Jimmy, 'what Malcolm will get up to in a D-cat where the regime is far more relaxed.'

'Is he married?' I ask.

'Oh yeah,' Jimmy replies. 'Happily.'

1.17 pm

I am sitting on the end of my bed reading *The Times* when Darren bursts in without knocking – most unlike him.

'Switch on your TV,' he says without explanation, 'they're running it on every channel.'

Together we watch the horrors unfold in New York. I assume that the first plane must have been involved in some tragic accident, until we both witness a second jet flying into the other tower of the World Trade Center. To begin with, I feel the commentator's comparison with Pearl Harbor is somewhat exaggerated. But later, when I realize the full extent of the devastation and loss of life, I am less sure. The reporters have already moved on to asking, 'Who is responsible?'

Although I am mesmerized by this vile piece of history as it continues to unfold, prison timetables cannot be altered, whatever is taking place in the rest of the world. If I don't report to the gym by three fifteen, they will come in search of me.

3.15 pm

Much of the talk in the gym is of the carnage in New York and its consequences, although several of the prisoners continue their bench presses, oblivious to what's taking place in the outside world. As soon as the hour is up, I rush back to my cell to find that the Pentagon has been hit by a third domestic carrier, and a fourth commercial plane thought to have been heading for the White House has crashed just outside Pittsburgh.

4.30 pm

For several hours, I sit glued to the television. Among the snippets of news offered between the continual replays of the two planes crashing into the twin towers is a statement by William Hague; he has postponed the announcement of who will be the next leader of the Conservative Party as a mark of respect to the American people.

The prime minister cancels his speech to the TUC in Brighton and hurries back to Downing Street, where he makes a statement fully supporting President Bush, and describing terrorism as the new world evil.

7.00 pm

The sight of innocent people jumping out of those towers and the voices of passengers trapped on a domestic flight talking to their next of kin on mobile phones will be, for me, the enduring memory of this evil day. Calling my agent and my son James was to have been the highlight of my day. It now seems somewhat irrelevant.

DAY 56   WEDNESDAY 12 SEPTEMBER 2001

5.44 am

Yesterday was dominated by the news from America, and what retaliation George W. Bush might take.

Tony Blair seized the initiative by calling a press conference at No. 10 for 2 pm, which would be seen by the citizens of New York just as they were waking. I don't want to appear cynical but, at the end of the press conference, when the prime minister agreed to take questions, did you notice who he selected from a packed audience of journalists? The BBC (Andrew Marr), ITV (John Sergeant), CNN (Robin Oakley), Channel 4 (Eleanor Goodman), *The Times* (Philip Webster) and the *Sun* (Trevor Kavanagh). I sense Alastair Campbell's skills very much in evidence: only the major television companies and two Murdoch newspapers. However, to be fair, by recalling Parliament, Blair looks like the leading statesman in Europe, and that on the day when the Tory party are planning to announce their new leader.

9.00 am

Life goes on at Wayland, so I report to the art room for my pottery class. Our clandestine accomplice has successfully smuggled in the special materials that Shaun needs to complete his art work for this volume.

11.15 am

I call Alison at the office for an update. She tells me that the pressure has shifted onto KPMG to deliver an interim report, so as not to keep me waiting until they've completed the full investigation which apparently now includes some accusations Ms Nicholson has made against the Red Cross which have nothing to do with me. Can't spare any more units, as I have to speak to James tonight, so I say goodbye.

2.00 pm

Football. Wayland's match against RAF Marham is, to my surprise, still on. Not that I expect there would have been many fighter pilots in the visitors' team. We lose 4–3, despite Jimmy's scoring two goals. Three of our team receive red cards, so Wayland ended up with only eight players on the field, having led 3–2 at half-time. By the way, all three players deserved to be sent off.

As soon as I return to my cell, I switch on the TV.

4.00 pm

Most of the Muslim world are swearing allegiance to America, as they must all be fearful of retaliation. Yasser Arafat even gives blood to prove his solidarity with the citizens of New York. The prime minister continues to underline his support for the United States, as he considers the atrocities in New York to be an attack on the democratic world. I suspect he views this as his Falklands. Let's hope it's not his Vietnam.

DAY 56

6.00 pm

After supper Sergio convenes a board meeting. Item No. 1, he confirms that the suitcase and contents have been delivered to his friend in north London. Item No. 2. The emerald has arrived in London, with all the correct paperwork completed. Item No. 3. A colleague of his brother's will be flying into London on Saturday, bringing with him the gold necklace, a catalogue *raisonné* of Botero and four photos of Botero oils that are for sale. He pauses and waits for my reaction. I smile. It all sounds too good to be true.

7.00 pm

I phone James. He tells me that he's tired; he's just started his new job in the City. Because of the upheaval in the American market they expect him to be at his desk by 7 am, and he doesn't leave the office until after 7 pm. However, he confirms over the phone that the emerald has arrived, so out of curiosity I ask him what it looks like.

'It looks magnificient, Dad,' is his simple reply. 'But I've no idea if it's worth ten thousand dollars.'

'When are you hoping to see the expert?'

'Sometime this weekend.'

I don't ask any more questions as I wish to save my remaining units for Mary.

Quite a lot seems to be happening this weekend. Mary will visit Wayland on Friday. Liana will have news of the Botero paintings on Saturday. Sergio's friend flies into London on Sunday, by which time James should have a realistic valuation of the emerald. I only wish I could read Monday's diary now. Don't even think about it.

8.00 pm

All the news programmes are replaying footage from every angle of the American passenger jets flying into the twin towers of the World Trade Center in New York. All the commentators are in no doubt that the US will seek some form of revenge, once they can identify the culprit. Who can blame them? It's going to take a very big man to oversee this whole operation. President Kennedy proved to be such a man when he was faced with the Cuban crisis. I only hope that George W. Bush is of the same mettle.

DAY 57   THURSDAY 13 SEPTEMBER 2001

6.03 am

It was a clear cold night, and for the first time two flimsy blankets were not enough to keep me warm. I had to lie very still if I was not to freeze. It reminded me of being back at boarding school. As two blankets are the regulation issue, I shall have to speak to Darren about the problem. I'm pretty confident he will have a reserve stock.

8.15 am

I watch breakfast television while eating my cornflakes. The news coming out of Washington is that the State Department seems convinced that it was, as has already been widely reported, Osama bin Laden who orchestrated the terrorist attacks. We must now wait and see how George W. Bush plans to retaliate. The president's description of the terrorists as 'folks' hasn't filled the commentators with confidence. Rudy Giuliani, the Mayor of New York, on the other hand, is looking more like a world statesman every day. When the report switches from Washington to New York, I am surprised to observe a pall of smoke still hanging over the city. It's only when

THURSDAY 13 SEPTEMBER 2001

the cameras pan down onto the rubble that one is made fully aware of just how long it will be before that city's physical scars can be healed.

9.00 am

We're banged up for an hour owing to officers' staff training.

10.00 am

Pottery. I make my way quickly across to the art class as I need to see Shaun, and find out if he now has all the art materials he needs. I'm disappointed to find that he's not around, so I end up reading a book on the life of Picasso, studying in particular *Guernica* which he painted in support of his countrymen at the time of the Spanish Civil War. I know it's a masterpiece, but I desperately need someone like Brian Sewell to explain to me why.

2.00 pm

Gym. Completed my full programme, and feel fitter than I have done for years.

6.21 pm

Tagged onto the end of the news is an announcement that Iain Duncan Smith has been elected as the new leader of the Conservative Party. He won by a convincing margin of 155,935 (61 per cent) to 100,864 (39 per cent) for Kenneth Clarke. A far better turnout than I had expected. Having spent years trying to convince my party that we should trust our members to select the leader, the 79 per cent turnout gives me some satisfaction. However, I would have to agree with Michael Brown, a former Conservative MP who is now a journalist with the *Independent*: a year ago you could have got odds of a hundred to one against a man who hadn't served in either Margaret Thatcher's or John Major's governments – at any level – ending up as leader of the Tory party in 2001.

10.00 pm

I watch a special edition of *Question Time*, chaired by David Dimbleby. I only hope the audience wasn't a typical cross-section of British opinion, because I was horrified by how many people were happy to condemn the Americans, and seemed to have no sympathy for the innocent people who had lost their lives at the hands of terrorists.

My feelings went out to Philip Lader, the popular former American ambassador, as he found himself having to defend his country's foreign policy.

I fall asleep, angry.

DAY 58   FRIDAY 14 SEPTEMBER 2001

6.17 am

Today is one of those days when I particularly wish I were not in jail. I would like to be in the gallery of the House of Commons following the emergency debate on the atrocities in America, and attending the memorial service at St Paul's.

12 noon

Watching television this afternoon, I find myself agreeing with almost everything the prime minister says in his speech to the House. Iain Duncan Smith responds in a dignified way, leaving the PM in no doubt that the Opposition is, to quote IDS, 'shoulder to shoulder' on this issue. It is left to George Galloway and Tam Dalyell to express contrary views, which they sincerely hold. I suspect it would take a nuclear weapon to land on their constituencies – with Osama bin Laden's signature scribbled across it – before they would be willing to change their minds.

The service at St Paul's sees the British at their best and, like Diana, Princess of Wales' funeral, it strikes exactly the right note, not least by the service opening with the American national anthem and closing with our own.

DAY 58

I am pleased to see Phil Lader sitting amongst the congregation. But it is George Carey, the Archbishop of Canterbury, who rises to the occasion. He delivers an address that leaves no one in any doubt how he feels about the terrorists, but also expresses the view that this is a time for cool heads to make shrewd judgements, rather than macho remarks demanding immediate retaliation.

2.00 pm

Visit. Mary is among the first through the door into the visitors' room.

Her news is not good, and she doesn't try to pretend otherwise. KPMG are going at a snail's pace, making it clear that they have no interest in my plight, and will deliver their report when they are good and ready. They are hoping to interview me on Monday week, so it looks as if I'll be stuck at Wayland for at least another month. I feel sure that is not what Sir Nicholas Young, the CEO of the Red Cross, intended when he instigated an internal enquiry, even if it will delight Emma Nicholson. Mary has so obviously done everything she can to expedite matters, but, as she says, it's an accountant's duty to leave no piece of paper unturned.

We discuss our appeal. Mary describes it as *our* appeal, partly, I think, because she was so offended by Mr Justice Potts aiding and abetting Mrs Peppiatt when she was in the witness box, while in my view not affording Mary the same courtesy when she was put through a similar ordeal.

We talk about the boys, how admirably they are coping in the circumstances, and the fact that Will is desperate to see me before he returns to New York. Thank God he wasn't in Manhattan this week. Mary reports that my adopted sister, Elizabeth, is alive and well. Elizabeth had been at work in the city when she heard the explosion and looked out of her window to see the flames belching from the World Trade Center.

There is a restrained announcement over the intercom asking all visitors to leave. Where did the time go? I feel guilty about Mary. I've been unable to hide my disappointment about KPMG's lack of urgency. She couldn't have been more supportive during this terrible time in my life, and heaven knows what state I would be in without her love and friendship.

DAY 59   SATURDAY 15 SEPTEMBER 2001

9.00 am

I call David and ask him to drive to Sale in Cheshire on Monday and pick up a package which is being flown in from Colombia that morning.

10.00 am

No gym on Saturday, so I make sure I'm standing by the gate when exercise is called. To my surprise Dale is seated in the corner of the yard having his portrait finished. As I pass, he mumbles something about how much trouble he would have been in had he failed to show up two weekends in a row. When I return to my cell after forty-five minutes' hard walking, Darren tells me that we probably covered about three miles. I push open my heavy door to find my cell is spotless. The room has been swept, cleaned and the floor polished by Darren's latest recruit, all for £1. No problems with the minimum wage at Wayland, especially when you can only pay in Mars bars, tobacco or, if it's a big deal, a phonecard.

4.00 pm

Mr Meanwell calls me into his office to let me know that an envelope containing the rules of backgammon has been opened and sent down to reception. It will not be returned to me until I leave Wayland, as the item is on the prohibited list.

'How can the rules of backgammon be on the prohibited list?' I ask.

'The rules came in book form,' he explains, and shrugs his shoulders.

'If they had been in a magazine, could I have had them?' I enquire.

He nods.

6.00 pm

Early bang up. I channel hop so I can keep watching the latest news from Manhattan. I am moved by the sight of the New Yorkers on the streets applauding their firemen as they drive back and forth to the World Trade Center. Americans have a tremendous sense of patriotism and awareness of the country they belong to. It must have been the same in Britain during the last war.

DAY 60   SUNDAY 16 SEPTEMBER 2001

12 noon

Not a lot to report except Sergio is nervous about leaving. He will be deported in twelve days' time and we haven't yet received a valuation for the emerald. He's also waiting to hear about the second package which contains the gold necklace, and can't wait to see the photographs of the Boteros, as well as the catalogue *raisonné*.

I spend a long time reading the papers, and feel the coverage of all that has taken place in America this week elicited the very highest standards of journalism from the British press, not always the case on a Sunday.

DAY 61   MONDAY 17 SEPTEMBER 2001

6.19 am

The news is still all about New York, where Mayor Giuliani appears to be emulating his hero, Mayor La Guardia. Everything had gone wrong for Rudy Giuliani this year. He stood down from the Senate race against Hillary Clinton when he was diagnosed with cancer, and he then moved his mistress into Gracie Mansion to face the wrath of his popular wife and the Big Apple's press; in fact to quote the *New York Times,* 'he seems to have lost the plot'. And then, without warning, the city he loves is attacked by terrorists and all the talents boredom disguises suddenly return.

When I stood for Mayor of London, I spent a week in New York shadowing Giuliani as he went about his daily work, and quickly discovered that he has real power and a real budget to back it up. The truth is that Giuliani runs New York in a way Ken Livingstone can never hope to govern London. Tony Blair's dream of emulating the Americans with mayors in all our major cities would have been admirable, if only he allowed the mayor to be backed up with finance and executive power. Livingstone can huff and puff, but in the end only Blair can blow the house down.

DAY 61

9.00 am

Pottery. Out of boredom I begin, to Anne's surprise, to work on a flowerpot. Or that is what I've told my fellow inmates it's going to be. First you take the putty, run a circle of steel through it to cut off a smaller chunk and then roll it out to produce a long thin worm-like shape. You then twist the long thin worm into a circle and several long worms later all placed on top of each other and you have a pot, or that's the theory. An hour later I have a base and five long worms. The blessed release bell clangs.

11.30 am

I phone Alison to discover that the gold necklace, the book on Botero, the photographs of Botero oils and a sculpture have all arrived in Cheshire via Bogotá.

3.00 pm

Gym. Once again I manage 2,200 metres on the rower.

5.15 pm

Board meeting. Sergio has been on the phone to Bogotá for the past forty minutes. Armed with a dozen cards (£24) and the judicious use of an illegal pin number, he can now afford to spend an hour phoning Colombia. His brother is waiting to find out if I have any interest in the Boteros. I assure him that as soon as I've seen the photographs I will make a decision.

6.00 pm

I'm writing at my desk when I hear shouting and screaming in the corridor. I leave my cell to investigate, and see half a dozen prisoners standing outside a cell door at the far end of the corridor. I'm told by Darren that the occupant, Danny (burglar) will be released in the morning, and some of his friends wished to give him a farewell present. Half a dozen inmates have filled a black bin liner with water, and added tea bags, sugar, stale bread, butter and beans. They are now all peeing into it. They then empty the contents onto the hapless prisoner's bed just before we are due to be banged up. This ensures that he will have to spend his final night cleaning up the cell if he hopes to be released in the morning.

9.00 pm

Dr Starkey continues his excellent series on the six wives of Henry VIII. Tonight it's Anne Boleyn. Although Starkey spends the whole hour being fairly critical of the queen, one cannot but admire the lady's last sentiment before being beheaded. Her short speech was full of grace, with no fault placed at the door of Henry VIII. She can't have been all bad.

DAY 62   TUESDAY 18 SEPTEMBER 2001

6.00 am

It's been a week since the terrorists struck New York and Washington. It now seems unlikely that any more bodies will be rescued from beneath the rubble, although Mayor Giuliani is a long way off giving orders to stop the search while there's the slimmest hope that anyone might still be alive. He's lost so many firemen, policemen and city workers and was nearly killed himself that I can't see him calling off the search for at least another week; this despite the fact that nobody other than the closest of relatives believes that anyone else can have survived.

8.30 am

Danny, the prisoner who had his cell sacked last night, is now bidding farewell to everyone on the spur as he's due to be released within the hour. He seems to bear no grudges and I watch him shaking hands with Jimmy who tells me later that Danny was probably thankful that his departing gift wasn't physical, as it was on Mel's last night. Jimmy doesn't go into any detail but does admit that Mel had to spend his last few hours on the hospital wing.

516

9.00 am

Pottery. Carry on producing long worms for my pot, much to the amusement of the other prisoners, all of whom show far more promise than I do. Craig (GBH) is making a horse for his mother, Lloyd (drugs), a heart-shaped jewellery box for his girl-friend, Peter (burglary), another bowl for his aunt and Paul (murder), yet another Christ on the cross.

11.45 am

Call Alison. David's picked up the package from Sale and she has sent the Botero details plus photos to Sotheby's for a realistic valuation, with copies to me. She has also dispatched the Botero catalogue *raisonné* as a gift to the library. At least that way I will get to see the great artist's works rather than have the book confiscated and not returned until I am finally released. Alison has handed the necklace over to James, who awaits my instructions. Still no valuation on the emerald.

6.00 pm

Nothing else worth reporting today, except Jimmy (captain of everything) has just returned from town leave, and looks as if he's had sex. Sex is allowed when you're on town leave. How could they stop it? Jimmy has been out so much recently that he almost treats Wayland like a bed and breakfast motel. Still, to be fair, he'll only be with us for another three weeks. Will he leave Wayland before I do?

DAY 63   WEDNESDAY 19 SEPTEMBER 2001

6.04 am

Things American still dominate the news, as I feel sure they will
for some time to come. Tony Blair has seized the initiative and
flown to Berlin and Paris for talks with the chancellor and the
president. In *The Times* this morning Peter Riddell describes him
as having 'a good war', but the truth is that everyone is waiting
to find out what George W. Bush's response will be to the
Taliban's stonewalling.

9.00 am

Pottery. I finish my masterpiece. My tutor Anne asks the rest of
the class to gather round and help her decide what it is. Four
opt for a flowerpot, three an upside-down hat, and one inmate
feels I should have pressed on and produced an umbrella stand.

11.00 am

Another welcome flood of letters today, including one from John
Major and another from George Carey (see opposite). Both are
handwritten and full of understanding and kindness.

Lambeth Palace London SE1 7JU

Private   Sept 5th 2001

Dear Jeffrey

     Just a personal line, via Mary, to
say that Eileen and I are holding you and the
family up in our thoughts and prayers. What a time
you have been through — and what pain you and
the family have had to endure! All credit to you
all for the quiet dignity you have expressed!

     Jeffrey, you are surely proud of
Mary. She gave a brilliant interview on the Today
programme that was shown in the 10.00pm BBC
TV slot. Her attractive composure and articulate

defence was magnificent.

     Knowing you, you are putting the time
to very good use. 'Being in prison' is a relative
description. Freedom is primarily a personal
reality — and a person who is free in mind and
heart can transcend the limitations of time and
place and find God's grace where he / she is.

          Yours warmly

          George

WEEK COMMENCING

DAY	NO.	MENU CHOICE DINNER		QTY	NO.	MENU CHOICE TEA		QTY
MON	1	BEEF & ONION PIE	H	0	1	CHICKEN & MUSHROOM PIE		0
	2	CHICKEN SPRING ROLL		0	2	PASTA BOLOGNAISE	H	0
	3	MINESTRONE SOUP & BROWN BREAD	VG/LF	0	3	JAMAICAN RICE & PEAS	VG	0
	4	VEGETABLE SAUSAGE ROLL	V	0	4	VEGETABLE CHEESE GRILL	V	0
	5	CHICKEN ROLL SANDWICHES		0	5	HAM BAP - CRISPS - CHOCOLATE BAR		0
	6	CORNED BEEF SANDWICHES		0	6	CHEESE BAP - CRISPS - CHOCOLATE BAR	V	0
TUE	1	HAM & PINEAPPLE PIZZA		0	1	POACHED FISH - TOMATO & GARLIC SCE	LF	0
	2	BEEF & TOMATO SOUP - BREAD ROLL	H	0	2	STEAK & KIDNEY PIE	H	0
	3	VEGETABLE STEW & DUMPLING	VG/LF	0	3	VEGETABLE PASTA & SAUCE	VG/LF	0
	4	CHEESE & ONION FRITTER & BAP	V	0	4	CHEESE & ONION PIE	V	0
	5	CHEESE & PICKLE SANDWICHES	V	0	5	EGG MAYONNAISE SANDWICHES	V	0
	6	HAM SANDWICHES (BROWN BREAD)		0	6	CORNED BEEF SANDWICHES		0
WED	1	CORNISH PASTY		0	1	ROAST CHICKEN	H / LF	0
	2	BEEF BURGER & BAP	H	0	2	ROAST CHICKEN (non halal)	L/F	0
	3	VEGETABLE SAMOSA & CURRY SAUCE	V	0	3	VEGETABLE HOT POT	VG/LF	0
	4	TVP PASTA BOLAGNAISE	VG	0	4	VEGETABLE BURGER & BAP	V	0
	5	EGG MAYONNAISE SANDWICHES	V	0	5	TUNA SANDWICHES		0
	6	PORK LUNCHEON MEAT SANDWICHES		0	6	CHEESE SANDWICHES	V	0
		TVP - TEXTURED VEGETABLE PROTEIN						
THU	1	CHICKEN TIKKA PIE		0	1	SAVOURY MINCE BEEF & DUMPLING		0
	2	CHEESE & TOMATO PIZZA	V	0	2	RED PEA SOUP WITH SPINNERS (M/BEEF)	H	0
	3	VEGTABLE AND PASTA IN SAUCE	VG/LF	0	3	VEGETABLE CHILLI	VG/LF	0
	4	LENTIL SOUP & BREAD ROLL	V	0	4	VEGETARIAN SAUSAGE X2	VG	0
	5	CORNED BEEF & PICKLE SANDWICHES		0	5	CHICKEN ROLL SANDWICHES		0
	6	EGG MAYONNAISE SANDWICHES	V	0	6	CHEESE SANDWICHES	V	0
FRI	1	CHEESE BAP		0	1	FISH PORTION		0
	2	HAM BAP		0	2	JUMBO PORK SAUSAGE		0
	3	TURKEY BAP	LF	0	3	CHEESE & ONION SOUFFLE	V	0
	4	VEGAN FILLING BAP	VG	0	4	SAVOURY VEGETABLES	VG/LF	0
	5	VEGETABLE SOUP & BREAD ROLL L/F	V / VG	0	5	CHEESE & PICKLE SANDWICHES		0
		SERVED WITH CRISPS,YOGHURT,			6	EGG MAYONNAISE SANDWICHES	V	0
		FRUIT & CHOCOLATE BAR				NO. 6 BROWN BREAD		
SAT	1	CHILLI CON CARNE	H	0	1	SOUTHERN FRIED CHICKEN BURGER & BAP		0
	2	LIVER CASSEROLE		0	2	FISH FINGERS X4		0
	3	VEGETABLE PASTY		0	3	BBQ RICE & PEAS	VG/LF	0
	4	VEGETABLE CURRY	VG/LF	0	4	PORK LUNCHEON MEAT SANDWICHES		0
	5	CHEESE & TOMATO SANDWICHES	V	0	5	EGG MAYONNAISE SANDWICHES	V	0
SUN	1	ROAST BEEF &Y/SHIRE PUDD	LF	0	1	CHEESE X2 - BOILED EGG		0
	2	STEAK & KIDNEY PUDDING		0	2	CORNED BEEF X 2		0
	3	PORK CHOP		0	3	MEAT & POTATO PIE		0
	4	VEGETABLE STEW	VG/LF	0	4	CHEESE & ONION PASTY	V	0
	5	CREAMY VEGETABLE PIE	V	0	5	CHINESE VEGETABLES & SAUCE	VG	0

H	HALAL MEAT CHOICE	V	VEGETARIAN CHOICE
LF	LOW FAT / HEALTHY CHOICE	VG	VEGAN CHOICE

MON TEA CHOICE 3 AND THUR TEA CHOICE 2 WILL ALL BE HOT OR VERY HOT DISHES

SATURDAY, SUNDAY & MONDAY SWEET NOW CLASSED AS A SUPPER ISSUE, ALTHOUGH 2 SWEETS MAY BE ISSUE

ITEMS ON THIS MENU MARKED WITH AN ^ MAY CONTAIN
INGREDIENTS PRODUCED FROM GENETICALLY MODIFIED MAIZE OR SOYA

THE KITCHEN WILL TRY TO KEEP ALL MEALS AS THEY ARE ON THE MENU.
BUT IF FOR ANY REASON THE MEAL INDICATED CANNOT BE ISSUED A REPLACEMENT MEAL WILL BE ISSUED.

IF YOU DO NOT FILL IN YOUR SHEET YOU WILL BE GIVEN CHOICE NO 1

Mary tells me in her letter that she's been in touch with KPMG who are doing a very thorough job and refusing to be hurried. David Smith, one of their senior partners, plans to come and see me next Monday together with my solicitor. She feels, as I have nothing to hide, that I should agree to the meeting. I had never planned to do otherwise.

12 noon

Lunch. Every day you select a number from the lunch list (see opposite). I always choose the vegetarian option for reasons I have already explained. As I pass Mr Shepperson, he calls out two which turns out to be a beef burger. I point out politely that there must be some mistake. He immediately checks the master list to discover that the mistake is mine. I've circled two, not five. Result? No lunch today. He makes no attempt to offer me an alternative because all the dishes are pre-selected, he explains. In any case, that would set a precedent.

Carl (GBH, goal scorer) who serves the puddings on the end of the line, offers me a second orange and turning to Shepperson says, 'His lordship has never been the same since I introduced him to cannabis.' This is greeted by cheers from the waiting queue. Even Shepperson manages a smile.

6.00 pm

Supper. This time I circled the right number, vegetable hotpot, and, because Mr Chapman is on duty, I end up with two portions.

DAY 64 THURSDAY 20 SEPTEMBER 2001

5.59 am

During the past week George Bush has been criticized – mainly by journalists – for not being able to string a sentence together. But today he confounded his critics (me included) by delivering an elegant and moving speech to Congress. This was not only well written (I read the full text as reproduced in *The Times*), but the speech writer had caught his voice because he delivered the text with such assurance.

Meanwhile the prime minister's timing continues to be fault-less. He flew into New York following talks with Chirac in Paris and then was driven straight to Ground Zero. He was shown round the smouldering site by Mayor Guiliani, before attending a memorial service at St Patrick's.

I tune in four hours later to hear the president's speech to Congress only to find Mr Blair now sitting in the president's box – Mrs Bush on one side of him and Mayor Giuliani on the other. He's done more to strengthen the special relationship in one week than anyone since the days of Roosevelt and Churchill.

8.00 am

Mr Clegg arrives outside my door and stares into my cell. He informs me that the decor, as designed by Shaun, has not met with the governor's approval. The walls must be returned to their original colour by the end of the week. But as the governor hasn't been seen on A block, let alone my spur, in anyone's memory, this seems a little unlikely. However, I go in search of Locke . . .

11.30 am

In my post, among other things, is a catalogue from Sotheby's New York, for their Latin American sale last May. I walk across to Sergio's cell and it's my turn to give him a tutorial. I explain how an auction works, and what is meant by high and low estimates. On the right-hand side of each page is a reproduction of a painting or sculpture. On the left, the artist's name and any known provenance of the work.

We immediately check out the two oils, two sculptures and five drawings by Botero. A sculpture of a reclining woman had a low estimate of $175,000 and sold for $190,000. A vast sculpture of a nude woman had a low estimate of $400,000 but only managed $325,000, whereas an oil painting of a bowl of flowers which had a low estimate of $225,000, sold for $425,000. The five drawings, ranging in price from $15,000 to $25,000 failed to reach the hammer price and were BI (bought in) perhaps because the subject (bull fighting) would not have appealed to many Americans.

We then carefully check the photos of Boteros that arrived in the morning post and try to work out what their low estimate might be, and see if we can spot a bargain. There is a maquette

DAY 64

of a nude woman for which I'm willing to offer $10,000, two small oils, $25,000 and $35,000, a large smiling cat, $200,000, and a magnificent portrait entitled *The Card Players* (see plate section) which we settle on at $400,000, although the seller wants a million. My bids are all low, and although Sergio will offer the sellers cash, I doubt if we'll manage to pick up any of them as Botero is, after all, an established international name. However, as Sergio points out, although Christie's and Sotheby's have offices in Brazil, Mexico and Argentina, they have no presence in Colombia, which may provide us with a small edge in an overcrowded market. He also adds that September 11th may have caused prices to fall suddenly. We'll just have to wait and see if he's right.

When 'Lock up,' is bellowed out, I return to my cell.

10.30 pm

I fall asleep dreaming of *The Card Players*. I even know which wall I would hang it on in London.

DAY 65　　FRIDAY 21 SEPTEMBER 2001

6.11 am

George W. Bush and Tony Blair officially name Osama bin Laden as the man behind the terrorist attack on the twin towers in New York. Although ships and planes are spotted heading for the Gulf, no one seems to know when any retaliation is likely to take place.

Bush has warned the Taliban, give up bin Laden or we strike. The Taliban's response is that it would be an insult to Allah, but don't mention the fact that the leader of the Taliban is bin Laden's father-in-law. When Bush was told their response he appeared on TV offering $30 million for bin Laden, dead or alive. The moment I heard that I feared for the president's life.

9.00 am

Gym. Alex (special needs group) does three sets of ten sit-ups for the first time and, because he can't speak, gives me a thumbs-up sign, while Robbie and Les applaud him. They are as yet unaware that I will also expect them to begin sit-ups next week. One of the few experiences I shall miss when I leave Wayland (if I ever escape) will be these weekly sessions.

DAY 65

10.45 am

When I return from the gym the newspapers are on my bed. They are so full of news from both sides of the Atlantic that I don't discover until page eleven of *The Times* that the CPS are not going ahead with any assault charges against John Prescott. One or two of the inmates mutter about one rule for New Labour and another for the rest of us. A senior officer is even more appalled by the PM's flippant remark, 'Well, that's John, isn't it?' So much for, 'We'll deal with crime and the causes of crime.'

3.00 pm

Phone Mary, who tells me that the governor has sent all the Prison Service papers showing the stated reasons for my recategorization from D-cat to C-cat.* He wishes it to be known that it is not the Prison Service that is holding up my reinstatement.

She has other news, but not on the phone.

---

*Form RC1 (Adult Male Recategorization Form), dated 31 July 2001, states the reason as: 'Police investigation for allegation of misappropriation of money from the Kurdish Refugee Fund, as advised by the DCI (Detective Chief Inspector) of Police Advisers at HQ.'

DAY 66 SATURDAY 22 SEPTEMBER 2001

11.00 am

Gym. 2,116 metres on the rower in ten minutes; three miles on the running machine in twenty-five minutes fifty-two seconds; and six miles on the bike in ten minutes, making me feel about forty-five, until I see a West Indian replace me on the running machine and do twelve mph for twenty minutes. Still, he is a mere twenty-three.

1.15 pm

I call Chris at the gallery. He's unhappy about the Boteros because he has only black and white reproductions. I agree to do nothing until Sotheby's have authenticated them and come back with a low estimate.

7.00 pm

I call James. He's back in London and tells me that our expert has confirmed that the emerald was a good purchase for $10,000, although he isn't willing to place a value on it. I am relieved to discover that Sergio isn't a crook, and what's more, Mary will end up with a special Christmas present. I wonder where I'll be this Christmas?

DAY 67   SUNDAY 23 SEPTEMBER 2001

12.07 pm

Today is dominated by one incident worth recording in detail, and it all began while I was in my cell reading *The Times*.

I have already explained that during Association a group of West Indians play dominoes in the main room. The amount of noise that emanates from each move would lead one to believe that a heavyweight boxing contest was taking place, which is why a problem arises when a real incident occurs, because the uproar can hardly reach a higher pitch. However, this time the noise was accompanied by the ringing of bells and officers running from every direction towards the Association room. It was like being back in Belmarsh. By the time I made an entrance, the incident was well under control. However, several of the brothers still wished to give me their version of events.

It seems that one of the brothers had been moved from D to A block recently, ostensibly because he had been bullied. It seems that when he was out on a town visit to Norwich a couple of weeks ago, his mates gathered together a large sum of money so that he could pick up an order of drugs. A problem arose when he returned that night and didn't have any of the gear with him. His excuse was he didn't think he'd get the skag past the guards. However, he couldn't come up with a convincing explanation for not being able to return their cash. When he was found cowering in his cell with a cut below his eye and a broken nose, the unit officer quickly moved him across to our block and, they hoped, out of harm's way. However, during exercise yesterday the brothers on D block informed the brothers on A block how he'd stitched them up, and passed the responsibility of exacting revenge on to them.

Back to the Sunday afternoon game of dominoes, where a row broke out with the culprit. One of the players left the group, walked across to the snooker table, picked up a ball, turned round and hurled it at him. Amazingly, he hit the right man in the back of the head at thirty paces (there were eleven prisoners seated around the table at the time). The ball must have been propelled at about seventy-miles an hour, because it split the man's head open. The pitcher ended up in segregation, while the victim is on his way to the local hospital. Both will appear in front of the governor later this week.

The usual punishment would be twenty-eight days added to both men's sentences, which the governor can mete out without recourse to the courts and, in a case like this, an immediate transfer to different A- or B-cat establishments.

I go into great detail to describe this incident simply because those casually reading this diary might be left with an impression that life at Wayland is almost bearable. It isn't. You can never be sure from one moment to the next if your life is in danger. On this block alone there are a dozen murderers, countless thugs and drug addicts with whom I have to co-exist every day.

I'm not unhappy to see my door slammed shut tonight.

DAY 68   MONDAY 24 SEPTEMBER 2001

9.00 am

Legal visit. The governor of Wayland has generously waived the strict rule and allowed two partners of KPMG, David Smith and Alex Plavsic, to join my lawyers so that I can answer questions about the Simple Truth campaign and the accusations made against me by Baroness Nicholson. The five of us sit around a table in the visitors' room and, as the other four are dressed in suits, I feel a little out of place in my jeans and red and blue striped T-shirt.

David Smith is very formal and courteous, addressing me as Lord Archer – something I haven't experienced for the past seven weeks. When the junior partner starts to question me, it quickly becomes clear that they have been very diligent and thorough in their research. They admit they have found no evidence to suggest that I had anything to do with receiving any donations from the public or the distribution of any monies to the Kurds. However, they question me for some time about the make-up of the £57 million.

The Foreign Office has confirmed that it gave £10 million to the campaign, five of which went directly to the Red Cross, the other five to the United Nations. The ODA (Overseas

Development Administration) has also produced documents to show that it can account for a further £38,100,000.

Throughout the world, the Red Cross raised a sum in excess of £10 million at the time of the Simple Truth campaign. Several overseas societies were directly, or indirectly, involved with the concert held at Wembley, organized by Sir Paul Fox, Alan Yentob, Harvey Goldsmith and myself. This event was attended by Princess Diana and John Major, who was prime minister at the time. Mike Whitlam, the then director general, and John Gray, events director, were in charge of fundraising on behalf of the Red Cross. During that period we all seemed to work sixteen hours a day on the five-week campaign, and despite her claims about caring about the Kurds, I don't recall Baroness Nicholson's presence at any function during that time.

By the time you read this, KPMG's full report will have been published. The report will also cover the accusations Ms Nicholson made against that excellent organization – the Red Cross – whose people I watched this morning on TV, working at Ground Zero in New York, searching for bodies, and counselling those in distress. While on the other side of the world, they are on the borders of Afghanistan assisting a million refugees fleeing into Pakistan.

Before Mr Smith and Mr Plavsic leave, they assure me that they will be in touch with DCS Perry at Scotland Yard this afternoon to brief him on their findings. They still have more delving to do concerning Ms Nicholson's other accusations against the Red Cross, but as far as my involvement is concerned, their enquiries are complete.

Once the two accountants have left, Tony Morton-Hooper says he will call DCS Perry and request that my D-cat be reinstated immediately.

I brief Mr Tinkler (the principal officer) on the outcome of my meeting with KPMG and that an announcement is likely to be made in the next couple of days. He confirms that they have been ready to move me for some time, and they are only waiting for a call from the police.

I return to my cell aware that when KPMG finally announce their findings, and the police confirm that they have dropped their enquiries, that the press coverage will be about a hundredth of that created by Ms Nicholson the day after she had appeared on *Newsnight*.

DAY 69 TUESDAY 25 SEPTEMBER 2001

9.00 am

'Burglars.' This is the cry that goes up from fellow inmates when officers appear on the spur to begin a 'spin' – cell search.

I didn't get to pottery yesterday because of my legal visit, and it looks as if I'm going to miss it again today. We've just been told to stay in our cells, as a search is about to be conducted following the snooker hall incident on Sunday. I fail to see how a prisoner throwing a snooker ball at another inmate should result in the whole of A block being searched two days later. However, it's Shane (GBH, gym orderly) who tells me that when they 'spun' the assailant's cell, they found a nine-inch blade hidden under his mattress, and the governor has ordered a comprehensive search of the whole block.

Searching 112 cells takes the duty officers a little over two hours. Mr Shepperson and a colleague spend ten minutes in my cell only to discover that I have two more towels than I'm entitled to and a T-shirt that Sergio has given me because he's leaving on Thursday. They don't comment on these indiscretions as they are obviously looking for more important items.

As I hang around in my cell, I am amused to see the grass outside is littered with different objects that have been thrown

533

out of the windows since the shout of 'Burglars' went up. Apparently it's mainly drugs and other banned substances, but despite a further search amongst the rubbish, no other knives or blades are discovered.

When the 'spin' is over, I'm told that Nigel, (GBH, race relations rep, known as the Preacher – see plate section), has had a carpet removed from his cell, and Darren, two pots of sea-green paint. An officer confirms that no other knives were found on our spur which surprises Darren, although he won't tell me why.

The most common object removed from the cells turns out to be TV remote controls. For some inexplicable reason, remote controls are allowed only on D block (the drug-free block). Result? D blockers trade their remotes for drugs. Prison logic.

12 noon

Exercise. After half an hour of power walking in the fresh air, Darren and I return to the block. As he strolls back through the gate, his eyes light on his two pots of sea-green paint standing in the hallway. I'm afraid I can't resist it. I pick them both up and deposit them back in his cell. He immediately hides them in the dustbin room at the end of the corridor, explaining that should any officer discover they're missing, the first cell they would search would be his, and he could end up on report. If he hears nothing for twenty-four hours he'll feel it's safe to retrieve them. So much happens in prison every day, that it's not unlike a national newspaper. Yesterday's big story is quickly replaced by some new incident demanding the staff's immediate attention. Darren agrees it's the first time I've been able to do something for him.

6.00 pm

I call Will to confirm that he's still planning to visit me on Friday.

He tells me that DCS Perry is off sick and his deputy is unwilling to make a decision while he's away. So much for justice. I begin to think that I'll be in Wayland for the rest of my life.

DAY 70   WEDNESDAY 26 SEPTEMBER 2001

9.00 am

Pottery. It's Anne's birthday. She's amused by my flowerpot (we've all agreed now that it is to be thought of as a flowerpot) and says that it must be left to dry for two weeks before it can be placed in the kiln.

Another of the tutors has brought in a box of crayons for Shaun. When I leave the art room an hour later, I place the crayons in a plastic bag which, to my surprise, the officers don't bother to look inside. I then walk out onto the exercise yard and, in front of several other officers, stroll across to the window of Shaun's cell on C block and pass the crayons through the bars, dropping them on his bed. Only yesterday we were all searched for a knife. Today ... prison logic. I admit I'm only smuggling crayons, but you would have thought someone might have just checked.

2.00 pm

No gym because it's rugby practice. Mr Harley has selected a team of possibles v probables for the first match next week, which he asks me to referee.

The standard turns out to be far higher than I had expected. An Afro-Caribbean inmate picks up a ball that is passed to his toes at full speed and carves his way through a bunch of thugs and murderers to score a brilliant try under the posts. It augers well for next week.

When we return to the changing room the young man tells me that he's never played the game before. How much talent is there in this country that we just don't find out about, let alone nurture?

Another prisoner standing next to me in the shower is six foot nine, and was one of the second row forwards (surprise, surprise). He's more interested in talking about my trial, which he describes as a diabolical liberty. As I never discuss my case with other inmates, I only listen.

'I also got four years,' he said, 'for burglary – with five hundred and two, yeah, five hundred and two,' he repeats, 'other offences to be taken into consideration.'

DAY 71   THURSDAY 27 SEPTEMBER 2001

8.00 am

Sergio will be leaving for Heathrow within the hour. We agree that I will call him next Tuesday at 7 pm GMT, two o'clock in Bogotá. He tells me that there is at least £7 left on his BT phonecard, which ought to be enough for him to let me know that he has arrived safely and put in my offer for the Boteros. Could I really get *The Card Players* for $400,000?

9.00 am

Pottery. Shaun spends two hours, with two ten-minute breaks, drawing Jules's body – in a crouching position, and wearing his grey prison tracksuit. This is his best effort yet. He'll add the head next week. He now has only Steve (conspiracy to murder, library orderly) and Jimmy (Ecstasy and captain of everything) left to draw. However, as Steve rarely leaves the library, Jimmy is out all day working on the farm and Shaun is due to be released in four weeks' time, this may prove a close-run thing. I will not see the final montage until Shaun has presented his portfolio to my literary agent, Jonathan Lloyd.

3.30 pm

Exercise. As we circumnavigate the yard, Darren tells me about a prisoner who was transferred to Littlehey early this morning; the governor considered that his life might be in danger if he remained at Wayland. He had already been shipped out of Blunderstone Prison earlier this month when it was discovered that he was being beaten up on a regular basis.

'When he arrived here,' Darren continues, 'he claimed that he was in for punching a taxi driver, which few of us believed. It just didn't add up,' he added without further explanation. By now we've completed two circuits and I'm none the wiser as to what this is all about. But Darren is enjoying keeping me in suspense.

The unnamed prisoner lasted on C block for only a few days before they torched his cell, and set fire to all his belongings, so he was quickly moved to A block. But he lasted only one night before a delegation of prisoners paid a visit to the principal officer (Mr Tinkler), telling him that if the man was still on the block after the weekend, they could not be responsible for his safety.

'What is he in for?' I ask, unable to contain my curiosity.

'Ah, I see I still have your attention,' comments Darren, 'even if I haven't learnt to curtail your impatience.' He pauses dramatically. 'He has committed a crime for which his fellow prisoners would show no mercy.' Darren covers a few more yards before he adds, 'He kidnapped and raped a thirteen-year-old girl. So they've finally moved him to a prison where he will be safe, because he'll only be locked up with other nonces.'*

---

* Nonce – prison slang for not of normal criminal element.

DAY 71

6.00 pm

George W. Bush's first act of war is to sign an order freezing all accounts to which Osama bin Laden has access. It's being reported on the evening news that Clinton attempted to do the same thing when he was president but couldn't get Congress to back him.

Nothing worth watching on television, so I return to the works of Shakespeare. Tonight, *King Lear*. If only the Bard had experienced a few months in prison ...

DAY 72   FRIDAY 28 SEPTEMBER 2001

9.00 am

Gym. It's my weekly session with the special needs group. I now have my own little class – Alex, Robbie, Les and Paul. We begin on the rower before moving across to the running machine, and this week I ask them all to try sit-ups. A new challenge. Alex and Robbie manage ten, while Les and Paul find it difficult to do more than five. But at least they now have a weekly target.

12 noon

Lunch looks disgusting, so I don't bother. I have a visit today so I can supplement my diet from the canteen.

2.90 pm

Fortnightly visit. This Friday, my three visitors are my son Will and two of my dearest friends, Chris Beetles and Godfrey Barker. I've decided to allocate the first half hour to Will, followed by twenty minutes with Chris, then another twenty with Godfrey and then a final session with all three.

Will starts by telling me about a call he received during the journey to Wayland telling him that the KPMG accountants had just come out of a meeting with the police, and had left them in no doubt that I was never involved with the collecting or distribution of any Simple Truth money donated to the Red Cross. Will goes on to say that he can't believe I'll still be at Wayland this time next week.

Will's next piece of news is that he has a new girlfriend, but as he's returning to America on Thursday, he can't be sure if it's going anywhere. I'm disappointed. I can't wait to be a grand-father. The rest of Will's news is domestic, and after thirty minutes, he makes way for Chris.

Chris appears with a toasted cheese and tomato sandwich – quite the finest delicacy I've eaten for the past seventy days. I'm still not quite sure how he managed it.

I begin by briefing Chris on Shaun (forgery) and the sketches he's working on for this diary. As Shaun will be released in three weeks' time, I've asked him to visit Chris at the gallery and present his portfolio. Chris explains that there's a recognized fee for the reproduction of an artist's work, but if I want to purchase the originals, he will happily negotiate a fair price.

We go on to discuss Botero. Chris feels that as the great man has such an international following the chance of picking up a cheap original, even if Sergio *does* know Botero's mother, seems unlikely. I accept his judgment, but still feel it's possible Sergio might surprise us. Chris shrugs his shoulders. When he changes the subject to Tottenham Hotspur, I quickly replace him with Godfrey.

Godfrey brings me a second cheese and tomato sandwich, not toasted this time.

Godfrey is a distinguished art critic, academic and a friend of twenty years' standing. We discuss an important matter con-cerning Mr Justice Potts and a dinner Godfrey and his wife Ann attended a couple of years ago, when the judge made remarks about me which, if true, I believe should have disqualifed him from presiding over my case. Godfrey needs to check his diaries before he can confirm the exact evening the supper took place, and the reasons why Sir Humphrey made the remarks he did. Godfrey promises to keep Mary informed. Ann Barker serves on the Parole Board, and another member of the Parole Board was also present at the dinner. Thank God for friends who believe in justice.

The final session spent with all three of them is great fun, not least because Will brings me another cheese and tomato sandwich. I didn't have lunch, and now I needn't bother with supper. Godfrey tells me that he believes IDS can win the next election. Chris pours scorn on the idea, and is happy to stake a Mars bar on Blair, who he believes has hardly put a foot wrong since September 11th.

'Let's see what he looks like in a year's time,' counters Godfrey.

I can only wonder where I'll be in a year's time ...

The call for visitors to leave comes all too soon, and I am painfully reminded how much I enjoy the company of old friends.

When I leave to return to my cell, I am stopped and made to suffer the humiliation of a strip-search. Two junior officers obviously think it will be fun to tell their friends at the pub tonight that they made Lord Archer take all his clothes off. Good heavens, they discover I have a penis just like other inmates. It spoils what had been a better day. However, their pettiness is not typical of the majority of officers at Wayland.

DAY 72

6.00 pm

Jimmy is back from four days of home leave – this is allowed for non-parole prisoners who have served a third of their sentence. Jimmy's sentence was three and a half years, mine four. Mr Justice Potts understood the difference only too well.* Jimmy says he can't wait to get a good night's sleep. He's had sex with two women in the past forty-eight hours; one stupid but sexy, the other an undergraduate who likes telling her friends she's sleeping with a convict. He can't decide which of them to commit to when he's released in three weeks' time. Darren offers him sage advice: 'If you can't choose between them, neither can be right.'

10.00 pm

For the first time since September 11th the lead story on the *Ten O'Clock News* does not come from the other side of the Atlantic. It still involves terrorists, but this time the report comes from Northern Ireland. I wonder how long the problems of Osama bin Laden will remain paramount, as one can't help remembering that Saddam Hussein is still on the loose . . .

I switch off the news, and continue my Shakespearean marathon by turning to *Richard II.*

---

* If a prisoner is sentenced to less than four years, he is automatically released at the halfway stage, and now can also benefit from four and a half months' tagging. Thus a prisoner with three-and-a-half-year sentence will serve twenty-one months, with four-and-a-half months of that on tag. So he will be discharged from prison after sixteen-and-a-half months. If you are sentenced to four years and above, you have to complete at least half your sentence with no hope of a tag. That is why judges often pass sentences of three years and nine months. If Mr Justice Potts had sentenced me to three years and nine months, I would have been released six months earlier, and not have to endure stiff parole terms when released.

DAY 73   SATURDAY 29 SEPTEMBER 2001

9.00 am

Jimmy now wants to escape. He's due to be released in three weeks' time, but those four days on the outside have given him a taste for freedom. He has no intention of returning to jail. It was Jimmy's first offence, and he swears it will be his last.* I have come to admire the way the Prison Service, the probation officers and the parole board are able to assess which prisoners are likely to reoffend and which are not. They probably make mistakes, which will guarantee them unflattering headlines wishing they had chosen an easier profession. But let's at least be thankful someone's willing to do the job.

11.30 am

During exercise Darren tells me about a prisoner who's been shipped out this morning at short notice. It seems that he was fast becoming the No. 1 drug dealer for the prison, and was happy to exchange his wares – cannabis, cocaine and heroin – for phonecards or tobacco. However, a problem arose because the drug baron on C block was only willing to supply his stock

---

* Currently working on a building site in Ipswich.

for cash, paid into a private bank account on the outside. Let me remind you how this works. Prisoners will instruct a friend or relative during visits (they consider the phone or letters too risky) to place money into an account of an associate of the prison drug dealer, who then supplies the gear.

When the drug baron on C block found his customers were moving their business to the new boy on B block because he didn't require cash, something drastic needed to be done. Yesterday, while his rival was in the gym, he paid two other inmates (cleaners) on B block to torch his cell. Result, the prisoner whose cell was torched was immediately transferred to another gaol. This means that the drug baron on C block is able to continue his evil trade and will be released in a few weeks' time supported by a healthy bank balance.*

8.00 pm

There is rarely anything worth watching on TV on a Saturday night, so I finish off *Richard II* – or to be more accurate, an assassin finishes off the poor fellow. I last saw the play performed at the Barbican with Sam West in the title role. I had been looking forward to his Hamlet at Stratford, but it was not to be.

---

* In fact, he's now back on the outside acting as the supplier for the new drug baron on A block.

DAY 74   SUNDAY 30 SEPTEMBER 2001

8.00 am

I call Mary to be told that the police are dropping their enquiry
having not even bothered to interview me.* Mary is thinking of
writing to Baroness Nicholson and demanding an apology. I tell
her it's a waste of time as Nicholson has neither the grace nor
the decency to admit she made a false accusation. Ms Nicholson
is a wealthy woman. It would be a noble gesture on her part
were she to cover KPMG's costs, rather than leave the Red Cross
to foot the bill.

Mary goes on to discuss a conversation she's had with
Godfrey. He assured her that he is aware of the importance of
any affidavit he might sign, and the effect it would have on my
appeal. She also confirms that she is flying to Washington on
Thursday, and hopes that by the time she returns the following
Tuesday, I will have been moved to an open prison.

---

* Much later, I discover by means of making a 'subject access' request to the
Metropolitan Police under the Data Protection Act, that the enquiry was terminated because of 'the lack of evidence from the informant' (i.e. Nicholson). In
November, the police and Red Cross issued a joint press release stating that 'no
evidence had come to light in relation to these allegations'.

DAY 74

10.30 am

Chapel. The prison has appointed a new chaplain. His name is Nick Tivey and, from his accent, I can only assume he hails from somewhere in the north of these islands. He looks around thirty, and tells me that he's served in two parishes as a priest, before becoming a prison chaplain.

His sermon, or chat, to the inmates is very informal, and more effective for that. His theme is how Jesus despised the Pharaohs (bigwigs) and much preferred to mix with the sinners (us). Applause breaks out among his congregation of seventeen (nine black, eight white), which has doubled since I last attended chapel. He must be doing something right if it's only his second week.

8.00 pm

I begin to read *The Tempest* and am reminded of John Wood's consummate performance as Prospero at Stratford.

> We are such stuff
> As dreams are made on, and our little life
> Is rounded with a sleep

But not tonight, because Shane (GBH, gym orderly) has his TV full on while he watches the Sunday-night boxing. He likes to join in by offering his opinion on each bout, sometimes each punch, at the top of his voice. 'Prick' and 'wanker' are his more repeatable expletives. The boxing ends at 12.35 am, so I must have fallen asleep sometime after that.

DAY 75   MONDAY 1 OCTOBER 2001

8.15 am

I mention to Shane that he must have kept most of the spur awake until after one o'clock, to which he replies, 'Let's face it, Jeff, I'm a fuckin' yob, and you'll just have to fuckin' well learn to live with it.'

9.00 am

Pottery. One prisoner knocks the trunk off another inmate's elephant and all hell breaks loose. A lot of oaths are uttered as the two of them face up for a fight, while the lifers goad them on. Anne disappears into the next room, and it's some time before peace is restored. I discover later that both inmates involved are due to be released in a few weeks' time, and neither would have wanted their sentence extended. The lifers glower, disappointed by the lack of action.

When the atmosphere returns to near normal, I suggest to the two lads that perhaps they both owe Anne (our teacher) an apology. Two older prisoners, both lifers, look on to see how the youngsters will react. They immediately disappear into the next room and say sorry to Anne. She looks surprised. The lifers nod in my direction. I make no excuses for these two louts' behaviour, but how many of us realize just how lucky we are not to have been subjected to an upbringing where violence, bad language and crime are the norm?

3.00 pm

Three members of the Board of Visitors come to see me. They've heard I'm leaving in the near future, and I wanted a chance to chat to them. The BoV are all unpaid volunteers who give service without a great deal of thanks as both sides of the iron door are sceptical about their usefulness. Almost all the prisoners describe them as a complete waste of space, with the usual adjective attached. This isn't actually fair, because these volunteers have brought about many improvements to prison life over the years, and only last year convinced Jack Straw (Home Secretary at the time) to change his mind on a major decision that affected Wayland.

I suggest to them that perhaps they should appear more often in the exercise yard. Once prisoners get used to seeing them strolling around, they may well come up and have a chat, and that might give inmates more confidence in them. We then discuss several contentious issues, in particular, the daily gripe about being banged up early on a Saturday, Sunday and Monday, when we are incarcerated for fourteen hours at a stretch. They point out the problem of staff shortages. No one likes to admit that there are only four officers on our wing at weekends. Officers at Wayland are currently owed 4,000 hours of overtime between them, and I doubt if it's much different in any other prison.

DAY 76   TUESDAY 2 OCTOBER 2001

9.00 am

The new probation officer asks to see me. Once I've settled in his office, he explains that he's only going through the motions because if I move to a D-cat in the near future I won't be seeing him again. When he learns that I'm appealing against both conviction and sentence, the meeting comes to an abrupt halt, and I am sent back to my cell.

12 noon

I phone Alison to discover that Tony Morton-Hooper has faxed Mr Carlton-Boyce (governor in charge of movement) with my preferences for a D-cat:*

Latchmere House, Richmond
Spring Hill, Buckinghamshire
Ford, Sussex
Stamford Hill, Kent

---

* All inmates have the right to name the prison they would like to be transferred to, usually the one nearest to their family.

DAY 76

They all sound like minor public schools.

I know that they are unlikely to allow me to transfer to Latchmere House as I don't fulfil their criteria,* and Ford has already turned me down on the grounds that they couldn't handle the press interest. The inmates who have been to Stamford Hill tell me it's full of young crackheads who will drive me to an early grave. I expect therefore to end up at Spring Hill, which Mr Meanwell has recommended all along.

3.00 pm

The SO (senior officer) on duty calls me in for a private word. It seems that two prisoners on C block have complained to the governor that I was seen wearing a tracksuit top during exercise, a privilege enjoyed only by enhanced prisoners. He will therefore have to search my cell for the offending article, but he's rather busy at the moment, so he won't be able to do so for another thirty minutes.

The offending article is a cream Adidas top, bequeathed to me by Sergio on the day he was deported. I return to my cell and hand the top to Darren. After I've told him about the interview, he calls in Jimmy, and between them they give my cell a thorough going over. They also remove one bedside lamp, one tin opener and a yellow check blanket, all of which I have acquired during the past month, and am not entitled to unless enhanced.

The SO arrives thirty minutes later, accompanied by another officer and together they search my cell. They reappear fifteen minutes later, declaring my cell to be clean.

---

* Must have completed a quarter of your sentence, and therefore be eligible to work outside the prison.

I later learn that the two prisoners from C block who made the complaint are lifers – both in for murder. Envy in prisons is every bit as prevalent as it is on the outside.

7.00 pm

I call Sergio in Bogotá and take advantage of the £7 left on his phonecard. The news is not good. None of my bids for the Boteros has been accepted. Chris Beetles turned out to be right – knowing the artist's mother is of no significance when dealing with a painter of international reputation. 'Offer $500,000 for *The Card Players*,' is my immediate response. There is a long silence before Sergio admits, 'It's already been sold for $900,000.' Beep ... beep ... beep ... seconds to go. 'I'm sorry, Jeffrey, I'll keep trying to find you a ...'

I've never heard from Sergio since.

DAY 77   WEDNESDAY 3 OCTOBER 2001

8.15 am

As we wait to be called for breakfast, the talk among the prisoners in the corridor is all about Shane (GBH, gym orderly). They're fed up (not their actual words) with the incessant noise he makes late at night and first thing in the morning. I overhear that two or three of them are planning to beat him up in the shower room after he comes back from the rugby match this afternoon. I ask Darren if I ought to report this to Mr Tinkler.

'No,' he says adamantly. 'Mind your own fuckin' business and leave it to us. But when you next see Tinkler or Meanwell, you could mention what a fuckin' nuisance Shane's become. Most of us would like to see him moved back upstairs.' It's the first time Darren has sworn in front of me.

9.00 am

Pottery. Cancelled because I have to attend a meeting with Reg Walton, the sentence management officer. He seems a nice chap, if a little overburdened by it all. He explains that he has to fill in yet another form if I'm to advance to a D-cat.

'Be reinstated,' I explain firmly, giving him a brief run-down of how I ended up at Wayland. He nods, and begins to fill in the little boxes. Here we go again.

Drugs	no history
Violence	no history
Escape (risk)	low
Reoffend (risk)	low
Prison offences	none
Behaviour	stable
Self-inflicted harm (risk)	low
Offences in prison	none

Once he's filled in all the little boxes he stands up, shakes my hand and wishes me luck.

'My wife loves your books.' He pauses. 'Though I confess I've never read one.'

2.00 pm

I referee a rugby match between Wayland and a local RAF camp. It's our first game against a visiting team, and it shows. I play the advantage law as best I can to assist Wayland, but the RAF still end up winning 39–12.

4.10 pm

Mr Tinkler says that he needs to see me following my interview with Mr Walton. Steve tells me that he has never known the two meetings to take place on the same day, which he takes as a sign they will be moving me soon. I've come to learn what 'soon' means in prison, so I don't comment.

DAY 77

6.00 pm

Shane is roaming around the corridor in his dirty rugby kit, avoiding the shower room and being nice to everyone. He even walks across to my cell to congratulate me on how well I refereed the match (frankly, not that well). Darren later tells me that Monster (taxi driver, transporting cannabis) had warned him of his impending doom if he doesn't reform. Far more effective than a ticking-off from an officer.

8.00 pm

I finish *The Tempest* in peace. Shane has got the message, but for how long?

DAY 78   THURSDAY 4 OCTOBER 2001

8.20 am

Meeting with the PO, Mr Tinkler. He tells me that he's signed my D-cat forms, but they still have to be countersigned by my spur officer, Mr Clegg. Mr Tinkler leaves me in no doubt about how he feels the system has treated me. I accept that he and the uniformed staff have done everything in their power to make my incarceration in Wayland bearable, remembering that I was never meant to come here in the first place.

8.50 am

Carl (GBH, servery, goal every match) comes down to our spur to say goodbye. It's always interesting to see how the different prisoners react to someone who's being released. There are those who will be leaving themselves within weeks, even months, who hug him and shake him by the hand, while the long-termers look on sullenly with envy in their eyes.

My abiding memory of Carl will be the day I put on a smart pair of brown loafers when Mary came to visit me, and he said, 'I've got a pair just like those, Jeff. Did you get them in Harrods?'

'Yes,' I replied.

DAY 78

'So did I,' said Carl. 'But I'll bet you paid for yours.'

As Carl leaves, Mr Clarke comes onto the spur and wishes him luck. 'I feel sure we'll be seeing you again,' he adds.

9.00 am

Pottery. My pot, or however we think of it, is drying, so I watch Shaun add Jules's head to last week's shoulders. Jules is pleased with the result and wants the original to give to his mother, always an excellent sign. Normally Shaun would charge £5 or the equivalent in tobacco, but he explains to Jules that my publishers have to see all the sketches first. I promise that, once they have, Jules will be sent the original. (See plate section.)

Jules has already been enhanced, which affords him several privileges, including wearing his own clothes. He's recently come down to our spur to take over Danny's cell. He tells me that they've enrolled him as a Listener which, as I've already explained, is a big responsibility. His educational programme (A level English) is going well, and when he says, 'I won't be coming back once I've been released,' in his case, I believe him.

3.15 pm

Gym. Complete programme in one hour, steady or slight improvement almost every day.

6.30 pm

Mr Clegg takes me through my D-cat form and, as my spur officer, signs me off as a model prisoner. By that he means no drugs, no violence, no other charges since entering prison. The document will now be passed on to Mr King, who in turn will send it up to Mr Carlton-Boyce, who in turn . . .

Mr Clegg goes on to tell me that a prisoner has reported him for racism. Now whatever failings Mr Clegg might have, being a racist is not one of them. So when I return to the spur, I brief Nigel (GBH), known as Preacher (see plate section), who is the block's race relations representative. He tells me that he'll speak to Mr King and try to straighten things out.

8.00 pm

Mary has flown to Washington for the fiftieth birthday of a mutual friend, so I can't call her.

I begin *Henry IV, Part I*.

DAY 79   FRIDAY 5 OCTOBER 2001

9.00 am

My little special needs group are now breaking records every week. Alex is even joining in with catchball, which rounds off every session. Darren has promised to take them over once I depart, which is a relief, because he's almost as much of a martinet as I am.

11.00 am

Mr King tells me that my D-cat forms have been handed over to Mr Carlton-Boyce. He also adds that Nigel has been to see him about Mr Clegg, and made it clear that no other prisoner has ever described him as a racist. Mr King thanks me for my intervention, explaining that this sort of slur is hard to remove once it's been written up on an officer's report.

'Tell Ms Nicholson that,' I say in a moment of anger.

12 noon

Lunch. I have a small portion of beans and chips as it's canteen day. How can I hope to lose weight with a diet of beans and chips supplemented by Cadbury's Fruit and Nut plus crisps? I shall have to become the gym orderly at my next prison.

9.00 pm

The prime minister hints that the bombing of Afghanistan is about to begin. He adds that the ground war that will follow could continue beyond next summer. I can only wonder where I'll be next summer.

Manage Act IV of *Henry IV, Part I* before falling asleep.

'If I be not ashamed of my soldiers, I am a soused gurnet,' declares Falstaff. I have to look up gurnet.

DAY 80   SATURDAY 6 OCTOBER 2001

11.00 am

Governor Carlton-Boyce calls for me to confirm that my D-cat is going through the system. He asks if I have any preference as to which prison I would like to be moved to. It becomes clear he hasn't read Tony Morton-Hooper's letter. I explain that as my main residence is in London, any D-cat in that area would be fine, because then my family will find it easier to visit. We discuss Latchmere House, Spring Hill and Stamford Hill. He says he'll check on availability and let me know.

2.30 pm

Amazing Brookes cartoon of Osama bin Laden as a poisonous mushroom in *Nature Notes* on the back of today's *Times* (see plate section). I call Chris Beetles, who represents the cartoonist and ask if we should add it to the collection.

I have been putting together a cartoon collection – with Chris's help – for the past fifteen years, which I had intended to leave to the Palace of Westminster (Parliament). I'm even having second thoughts about that. The collection comprises around three hundred drawings, and includes works by Beerbohm,

Vicky, Gould, Kal, Searle, Furniss, Steadman and Scarfe, amongst many others. The collection also includes sixteen Brookes, but only nine hang in the flat. Chris feels we should remove Hague from the wall (an octopus surrounded by suckers) and replace him with bin Laden. The cartoonist keeps the odd gem for his private collection, so I may not be able to acquire it. Should you be wondering, black and white, £850, colour, £1,450. Chris points out that he hasn't yet seen the quintessential cartoon summing up the full horror of September 11th.

5.00 pm

Steve (conspiracy to murder, librarian) has just returned from the visits hall where he's been in charge of the shop. He tells me that they've had to stop selling Walkers crisps because one of the inmates opened a packet and pulled out a £20 note (the company's latest promotional scheme). The money was immediately impounded by a surveillance officer and credited to the prisoner's canteen account (no inmate is allowed to be in possession of money for obvious reasons). All boxes of Walkers have been replaced with Golden Wonder until this campaign is over.

DAY 81   SUNDAY 7 OCTOBER 2001

8.00 am

After writing for two hours I turn on the news to discover that the bombing of Afghanistan has begun in earnest. Forty strike aircraft and fifty cruise missiles (£750,000 each) have been deployed. David Frost interviews everyone from Kissinger to Clinton, but by 9.30 am we're none the wiser as to how the campaign is going.

11.00 am

Exercise. As Darren, Jimmy and I stroll round the yard we pass an officer I've never seen before because he's attached to another block. His name is Zac Carr, known as 'Z cars'. Jimmy tells me that he was temporarily suspended for allowing a prisoner to tattoo him. It's an offence for one prisoner to tattoo another, let alone an officer. Jimmy then describes how the prisoner (the best tattoo artist at Wayland) goes about his craft. I later ask Mr Nutbourne if the story is true. He nods and says, 'I could tell you many more stories about Z cars,' he pauses, smiles, and adds, 'but I won't.'

11.45 am

Nigel (GBH, race relations rep) walks into my cell to complain that black people aren't represented enough on TV. I sympathize with him and ask what he feels should be done about it.

'They ought to show *Crimewatch* seven nights a week,' he adds with a grin, 'because that would just about even it up.' Having got a rise out of me, he leaves. I continue writing.

8.00 pm

Patricia Routledge gives a moving performance in *Everyone's Nightmare*, the true story of a woman who was wrongly convicted of murdering her mother and spent four years in jail before her sentence was quashed. Once you've been convicted, it can take forever to prove your innocence.

DAY 82   MONDAY 8 OCTOBER 2001

11.00 am

All the papers have stories reporting that I'm about to be transferred to a D-cat. The *Daily Mail* mentions five possible prisons,
so that they can eventually tell their readers they got it right.
They didn't. None of them bother to say that the police have
dropped their enquiries. I suppose that would be asking too
much.

12 noon

The allies have bombed Kabul for a second night, but there is
still no news as to how effective the onslaught has been.

6.00 pm

Write for two hours, but am unable to concentrate because I
know Mary is on a flight back from New York. I won't be able to
speak to her until tomorrow morning as I'm already banged up.

8.00 pm

Mr Nutbourne comes to my cell to tell me that he's off on holiday to Cuba. He assumes I'll have been transferred by the time he returns and says that he's sorry to have met me in these circumstances, and wishes me well for the future.

DAY 83   TUESDAY 9 OCTOBER 2001

8.45 am

Mr King tells me as I collect my breakfast that I will not be going to Latchmere House, so they are now trying Spring Hill. As Mr Carlton-Boyce has not briefed me himself but left it to the duty officer, I fear this does not bode well.

11.00 am

Exercise. Darren and I are joined by a prisoner from Singapore, who wishes to remain anonymous. He tells us that he's inside for selling 'duff' heroin to a young girl, who later died in hospital. He was convicted of manslaughter and sentenced to four years. He just thought I ought to know.

5.00 pm

Jimmy has just come back from work and tells me that he saw a lifer being released this morning who had served over twenty years. He was accompanied by nine plastic bags and a double bed that he'd made in the workshop. But he has a problem. No one turned up to collect him, so they had to put him back in his cell overnight. Heaven knows what they did with the double bed.

DAY 84   WEDNESDAY 10 OCTOBER 2001

9.00 am

Pottery. Say farewell to Anne, as I'm fairly sure I won't be at Wayland this time next week. She promises to put my pot in the kiln, and then deliver it to Chris Beetles so that I can give it to Mary for Christmas.*

2.00 pm

Rugby. I referee a match against an army team from Bassing-bourne, which turns ugly in the last few minutes of the game. Shane (GBH and gym orderly) runs halfway down the pitch and thumps one of the visiting players. I realize I have no choice but to send him off. I blow my whistle and chase after him, but two officers run onto the field and drag him away before I can reach him. He's immediately banned from participating in any sport for two weeks. The army team beat us by 25–10, which wasn't too bad remembering that we played the second half with only fourteen players on the field. But then I was the referee.

---

* It shattered in the kiln. It's been that sort of year.

DAY 84

6.00 pm

I start reading *Twelfth Night*. I would happily exchange my present abode for a willow cabin.

DAY 85   THURSDAY 11 OCTOBER 2001

8.45 am

Governor Carlton-Boyce tells me that there is no room for me at Spring Hill, so they are now considering North Sea Camp near Boston, in Lincolnshire. I point out that it would be a round trip from London of 240 miles, and I'd never be able to see my family. Carlton-Boyce doesn't seem that interested and simply says, 'I'm just doing my job, and that's what I'm paid for.'

9.15 am

Mrs Wendy Sergeant (head of education) has heard that I'll be leaving imminently and asks to interview me for her PhD thesis on 'prison reform through education'. As I've only been in residence nine weeks, and she's served the Prison Service for eleven years, I'm not sure I have a great deal to offer her, other than to confirm her worst fears.

I tell her that I believe every prisoner should leave being able to read and write, and that the weekly pay for education ought to be at the same level as any job in the prison. In fact, I would go further and suggest that it would benefit society more if prisoners received a higher income for agreeing to

571

participate in education, rather than cleaning their spur, or serving chips.

Wendy tells me that she considers many people are unsuitable for prison and should not be mixing with hardened criminals. She will be suggesting in her thesis the use of halfway houses, especially as the prisons are equipped to handle only 62,500 inmates, with over 67,000 presently convicted.*

2.00 pm

I call Mary to warn her that I'm probably being transferred to a prison over a hundred miles away from London. She tells me that Ramona, my solicitor, has tried to phone Wayland, but the governor is refusing to take her calls, which seems in line with her apparent policy of remaining anonymous.

---

* Home Office statistics for September 2001.

DAY 86   FRIDAY 12 OCTOBER 2001

9.00 am

I turn up at the gym and wait for my little special needs group
to arrive. It will be the last time I'll work with them. Without
warning, two drug officers appear by the side of the running
machine and tell me that my name has come up on the computer for an MDT (Mandatory Drugs Test). Five names come up
every day so I can't complain if, after nine weeks, it's my turn.
I'm taken to the medical centre to join four other prisoners in a
waiting room. Two look distinctly furtive, while the other two
appear quite relaxed. When the officer puts his head round the
door he asks if anyone is ready. Like a greyhound in the slips, I
am through that gap before anyone else can reply.

Mr Kelvin Cross introduces himself and then proceeds to
read out my rights before asking me to sign a green form (see
overleaf). I ask – for research purposes – what would happen if I
refused to give a urine sample or sign the form.

'Twenty-eight days would automatically be added to your
sentence.'

I sign the form.

I disappear into the lavatory while one of the officers
watches me through a glass pane. After I have handed over my

MANDATORY DRUG TEST AUTHORISATION FORM

Prisoner Name: ...... ARCHER .... **Number:** ...FF 8282.

Test Reference Number:

283/01.

For allocation when sample is collected

1. The governor has authorised that in accordance with Section 16A of the Prison Act 1952 any prisoner may be required by a prison officer to provide a sample of urine for the purposes of testing for the presence of a controlled drug.

2. You are now required under the terms of Section 16A to provide a fresh and unadulterated sample of urine for testing for the presence of controlled drugs.

3. Authority for this requirement was given by: ...... Governer : ....

4. Reason for requirement: (only one box to be ticked)

   [✓] **Random test:** You have been selected for this test on a strictly random basis.

   [ ] **Reasonable suspicion:** You have been selected for this test because staff have reason to believe that you have misused drugs. This test has been approved by a senior manager.

   [ ] **Risk assessment:** You have been selected for this test because you are being considered for a privilege, or a job, where a high degree of trust is to be given to you.

   [ ] **Frequent test programme:** You have been selected for more frequent testing because of your previous history of drug misuse.

   [ ] **On reception:** You have been selected for testing on reception on a random basis.

5. The procedures used during the collection and testing of the sample have been designed to protect you and to ensure that there are no mistakes in the handling of your sample. At the end of the collection procedure you will be asked to sign a statement confirming that the urine sealed in the sample bottles for testing is fresh and your own.

6. Your sample will be split at the point of collection into separate containers which will be sealed in your presence. In the event of you disputing any positive test result, one of these containers will be available, for a period of up to 12 months, for you to arrange, if you so wish, for an independent analysis to be undertaken at your own expense.

7. You will be liable to be placed on report if you:

   (a) provide a positive sample;
   (b) refuse to provide a sample; or,
   (c) fail to provide a sample after 4 hours of the order to do so (or after 5 hours if the officer believes that you are experiencing real difficulty in providing a sample).

Consent to Medical disclosure

* (i) During the past 30 days I have not used any medication issued to me by Health Care.

Signature of Prisoner : ...... Jeffn Archo .... **Date:** 12· 10·01

* (ii) During the past 30 days I have used medication issued to me by Health Care. I understand that some medication issued by Health Care may affect the result of the test. I give my consent to the Medical Officer to provide details of this treatment to the prison authorities.

Signature of Prisoner : .... **Date:** ....

(*Delete as appropriate)

MDTA/2/97

PRISON SERVICE CHAIN OF CUSTODY PROCEDURE

Prisoner Name: ....Archer....   Number: FF 8282

RANDOM TESTING PROGRAMME

This form is to be used only for tests conducted as part of the MDT random programme
(i.e. where prisoners have been selected by the LIDS computer)

Test Reference Number: 283|01

Checklist for sample collection - tick boxes as you proceed. Refer to guidance notes if in doubt.

1. [✓] Only **One** sample collection kit present.
2. [✓] Check identity of prisoner. Complete details above and in sample collection register.
3. [✓] Carry out search and handwashing procedures. (No soap).
4. [✓] Show the prisoner that the collection cup and bottles are empty.
5. [✓] Ask prisoner to provide enough urine to be split **equally** between the two sample bottles.
6. [✓] *Take temperature using the temperature strip. If temperature is out of range (32-38C) (90-100F), make note in comment section and refer to guidance notes.*
7. [✓] Watched by prisoner, transfer urine **equally** between the two bottles. Fill each above 15ml line and below 30ml line. Press caps on securely.
8. [✓] Ask prisoner to initial and date both bottle seals.
9. [✓] Watched by prisoner, place a seal over each bottle cap.
10. [✓] Dispose of any surplus urine and the cup.
11. [✓] Pack two bottles in mailing container and then in chain of custody bag - **Do not seal bag.**
12. [✓] Watched by prisoner, fix barcode labels and enter test reference number on all copies of this form.
13. [✓] Ask the prisoner to sign and date the Prisoner's Declaration below.
14. [✓] Complete Chain of Custody Report, tear off and place in chain of custody bag facing outwards.
15. [✓] Seal bag, ask prisoner to initial bag where indicated.
16. [✓] Place sealed bag in secure refrigerator until ready for despatch to laboratory.
17. [✓] Allow prisoner to leave.

16526818

Prisoner Declaration

I confirm that
(i) I understand why I was required to provide the sample and what may happen if I fail to comply with this requirement;
(ii) the urine sample I have given was my own and freshly provided;
(iii) the sample was divided into two bottles and sealed in my presence with seals initialled and dated by me;
(iv) the seals used on these bottles carry a barcode identical to the barcode attached to this form.

Signature of prisoner .....Jeffrey Att ho....   Date 12.10.01

DAY 86

sample, I comment that there is no soap in the wash basin. Mr Cross explains that soap added to the urine sample would cloud it, and as a further test is not permitted again for another twenty-eight days, any drugs could have cleared themselves through your system. Can't argue with that either. By the time they've finished with me it's nearly eleven. I return to my cell and make notes on the MDT experience, only disappointed not to have been able to say goodbye to Alex, Robbie, Les and Paul.

1.00 pm

The news is full of riots in Pakistan, anthrax in New York and food parcels being dropped on the wrong villages in Afghanistan. I check my canteen list before spending the afternoon writing.

DAY 87   SATURDAY 13 OCTOBER 2001

2.00 pm

Visit. My son James and our mutual Kurdish friends Broosk and
Nadhim have driven up from London to see me. The talk is
mostly political, and they describe how it feels to live in London
during the present crisis. Nadhim adds that he attended the
Conservative Party conference in Blackpool (he's a councillor for
Wandsworth) and he couldn't help comparing the gathering
with his first conference in Brighton twenty years ago when
Margaret Thatcher was the prime minister.

'Same people,' he tells me, 'they're just twenty years older.'

'You included,' I remind him.

Nadhim's a great fan of IDS, but admits his conference
speech wasn't inspiring.

James is still enjoying his new job in the City and takes me
through a typical day. We then discuss my appeal which doesn't
now look as if it will be scheduled before the new year. The law
grinds slowly . . .

Broosk is full of news, having just landed two big contracts
to decorate large homes in London and Nice. I first met these
two young Kurds twelve years ago – 'Bean Kurd' and 'Lemon
Kurd' – when they helped me organize the Simple Truth campaign, and they have remained friends ever since.

DAY 87

8.00 pm

After a few games of backgammon with Darren and Jimmy I return to my cell to be banged up for another fourteen hours. I've become hooked on *Who Wants to be a Millionaire?*. I would have failed to make more than £2,000 this week because I didn't know the name of the actor who plays the barman in *EastEnders*. However, I was able to answer the £4,000 question, 'Who is the current leader of the Conservative Party? a) Michael Howard, b) David Davis, c) Iain Duncan Smith, d) Kenneth Clarke.' The father and son contestants picked David Davis. Hmm, I wonder if this is an omen or a prophecy?

DAY 88   SUNDAY 14 OCTOBER 2001

11.00 am

I'm called to the hospital wing to fill in some forms to confirm I'm fit to travel. When I return to the spur, Darren tells me it shows that I'm being transferred tomorrow. I find this hard to believe; surely Mr Carlton-Boyce would have warned me. I ask several officers, but as no one has informed them either, I assume Darren must be wrong.

2.30 pm

Exercise. I visit Shaun at his cell window, and talk through what work will be required for this diary just in case I am shipped out tomorrow: one watercolour of the prison, one pastel of a cell, plus drawings of Dale, Jimmy, Darren, Jules, Steve and Nigel. If I suddenly disappear, Shaun promises to deliver them to my agent just as soon as he's released.

DAY 89   MONDAY 15 OCTOBER 2001

8.15 am

Mr Newson arrives outside my cell door to tell me that the Group 4 van has arrived and is waiting for me in the yard. They are ready to transfer me to North Sea Camp. He seemed surprised that I haven't been warned. I dash upstairs to see Mr Tinkler in his office, who confirms the news, and adds that I must start packing immediately.

'And if I don't?'

'You'll be put on report and may have to stay here indefinitely, and not necessarily on the enhanced wing.'

So much for my so-called 'special treatment', as regularly reported in the press.

I try to say goodbye to as many inmates as possible – Darren, Jimmy, Dale, Nigel, Jason, Jules, Monster and Steve. Darren helps me pack my large plastic bag and then carries it down to the reception area for me. There are three other plastic bags awaiting me in reception. They are full of presents from the public – everything from Bibles to tea towels.

I thank Darren for his kindness and help over the past nine weeks. He smiles, and offers one last piece of advice.

'Once you've settled in North Sea Camp, contact Doug.* He's the hospital orderly, and can fix anything for you.' I try to thank Darren – inadequately.

The Group 4 guard who will accompany me to Lincolnshire introduces himself as Andrew and kindly carries two of the plastic bags out to the van, so I don't have to make several journeys. To my surprise, I'm to travel to my D-cat in a sweatbox, as if I were a rapist or a murderer. Andrew explains that he has to drop off another prisoner on the way, who is being transferred to a C-cat near Stamford.

'Why are you taking someone from one C-cat to another?' I enquire.

'We're having to move this particular prisoner every few days,' Andrew explains. 'He keeps telling everyone that he's a supporter of Osama bin Laden, and it seems that not every other prisoner is in favour of freedom of speech. However, it still remains our responsibility to keep him alive.'

On the journey to Stamford, the bin Laden supporter demands that the radio be turned up. Andrew tells him that it's quite loud enough already, for which I am grateful, as it's a long, slow trek across Norfolk and on to the plains of Lincolnshire.

I enjoy seeing tall trees and acres of green English country-side, even though it's through a glass darkly. We arrive at the 'bin Laden' prison, where my cohabitant departs. He's hand-cuffed and led away. I can just glimpse him through my little window. A round, colourful hat covers his head, and a black beard obscures most of his face.

We move off again, but it's another hour before I see a signpost: North Sea Camp, one mile. I begin to think about

---

* This also turned out to be good advice, as I took over Doug's job as hospital orderly, while at North Sea Camp.

starting all over again. I'm somewhat fearful. Belmarsh was hell, Wayland purgatory. Have I finally arrived in heaven?

When the van comes to a halt outside the prison, the first thing I notice is that there are no perimeter walls, no razor wire, no barred gates, no arc lights, no dogs, not even any sign of a prison officer. But when I step out of the van, I still feel the terror that gripped me on the first day at Belmarsh, and then again on my arrival at Wayland.

I walk into reception to be greeted by Regimental Sergeant Major Daff, Royal Marines (Rtd).

'We've been waiting for you for fuckin' months, Archer. What fuckin' took you so long?'

NORTH SEA CAMP

HEAVEN

CONTENTS

HEAVEN 587

BACK TO HELL 1017

Epilogue 1051

Postscript 1061

HEAVEN

DAY 89   MONDAY 15 OCTOBER 2001

2.30 pm

The signpost announces North Sea Camp, one mile. As we approach the entrance to the prison, the first thing that strikes me is that there are no electric gates, no high walls and no razor wire.

I am released from my sweat box and walk into reception, where I am greeted by an officer. Mr Daff has a jolly smile and a military air. He promises that after Wayland, this will be more like Butlins. 'In fact,' he adds, 'there's a Butlins just up the road in Skegness. The only difference is, they've got a wall around them.'

Here, Mr Daff explains, the walls are replaced by roll-calls – 7.30 am, 11.45 am, 3.30 pm, 8.15 pm and 10.00 pm, when I must present myself to the spur office: a whole new regime to become accustomed to.

While Mr Daff completes the paperwork, I unpack my HMP plastic bags. He barks that I will only be allowed to wear prison garb, so all my T-shirts are taken away and placed in a possessions box marked ARCHER FF8282.

Dean, a prison orderly helps me. Once all my belongings have been checked, he escorts me to my room – please note,

DAY 89

room, not cell. At NSC, prisoners have their own key, and there are no bars on the windows. So far so good.

However, I'm back to sharing with another prisoner. My room-mate is David. He doesn't turn the music down when I walk in, and a rolled-up cigarette doesn't leave his mouth. As I make my bed, David tells me that he's a lifer, whose original tariff was fifteen years. So far, he's served twenty-one because he's still considered a risk to the public, despite being in a D-cat prison. His original crime was murder – an attack on a waiter who leered at his wife.

4.00 pm

Dean (reception orderly) informs me that Mr Berlyn, one of the governors, wants to see me. He accompanies me to the governor's Portakabin, where I am once again welcomed with a warm smile. After a preliminary chat, Mr Berlyn says that he plans to place me in the education department. The governor then talks about the problem of NSC's being an open prison, and how they hope to handle the press. He ends by saying his door is always open to any prisoner should I need any help or assistance.

5.00 pm

Dean takes me off to supper in the canteen. The food looks far better than Wayland's, and it is served and eaten in a central hall, rather like at boarding school.

6.00 pm

Write for two hours, and feel exhausted. When I've finished, I walk across to join Doug in the hospital. He seems to have all the up-to-date gossip. He's obviously going to be invaluable as my deep throat. We sit and watch the evening news in comfortable chairs. Dean joins us a few minutes later, despite the fact that he is only hours away from being released. He says that my laundry has already been washed and returned to my room.

8.15 pm

I walk back to the north block and report to the duty officer for roll-call. Mr Hughes wears a peaked cap that resembles Mr Mackay's in *Porridge*, and he enjoys the comparison. He comes across as a fierce sergeant major type (twenty years in the army) but within moments I discover he's a complete softie. The inmates like and admire him; if he says he'll do something, he does it. If he can't, he tells you.

I return to my room and push myself to write for another hour, despite a smoke-filled room and loud music.

10.00 pm

Final roll-call. Fifteen minutes later I'm in bed and fast asleep, oblivious to David's smoke and music.

DAY 90   TUESDAY 16 OCTOBER 2001

5.30 am

Alsatians woke me at Belmarsh, at Wayland it was officers jangling keys as they made their early morning rounds, but as NSC is only 100 yards from the coastline, it's the constant squawk of seagulls that causes you to open your eyes. Later, much later, the muffled grunts of swine are added, as the largest group of residents at NSC are the pigs living on the 900-acre prison farm. I drape a pair of black boxer shorts over the light above my head to make sure David is not woken while I continue my writing routine. He doesn't stir. At seven-thirty I make my way to the shower room at the end of the corridor.

8.00 am

Dean accompanies me to breakfast: porridge from Monday to Friday, and cereal at weekends, he explains. I satisfy myself with a very hard-boiled egg and a couple of slices of burnt toast.

8.30 am

Induction. During the first week at NSC, a prisoner spends his time finding out how the place works, while the officers try to discover as much as possible about the new inmate. My first appointment is with Dr Walling, the prison doctor, who asks the usual questions about drugs, smoking, drinking, illnesses and allergies. After twenty minutes of prodding, breathing in, being weighed, and having my eyes, ears, teeth and heart checked, Dr Walling's only piece of advice is not to overdo it in the gym.

'Try not to forget you are sixty-one,' he reminds me.

As I leave the surgery, Doug, the hospital orderly a friend of Darren (Wayland, marijuana only), beckons me into the private ward. Doug is six foot, and about sixteen stone, with a full head of hair just beginning to grey, and I would guess is in his late forties. The ward has eight beds, one of which is Doug's, as someone has to be resident at night in case a prisoner is suddenly taken ill. But what a job; not only does Doug have a room the size of a penthouse suite, but he also has his own television, and his own bathroom. He tells me that he's in for tax evasion, but doesn't elaborate. Doug closes the door to his kingdom and confirms that medical orderly is the best job in the prison. However, he assures me that the second-best position at NSC is orderly at the sentence management unit (SMU). Doug whispers that the SMU job is coming up in just over four weeks' time when the present incumbent, Matthew, will be released. Mr New, the senior officer – equivalent to Mr Tinkler at Wayland – will make the final decision, but Doug will put in a good word for me. 'Whatever you do,' he adds, 'don't end up working on the farm. Winter's not far off, so if the food doesn't kill you, the farm will.' As I leave, he adds, 'Come and have a drink this evening.' (By that he means tea or coffee.) 'I'm allowed two guests from seven to ten, and you'd be welcome.' I thank him and, silently, my old mentor Darren. *Who you know* is just as important on the inside as it is on the outside.

DAY 90

10.30 am

My second induction meeting is to decide what job I'll do while I'm at NSC. I make my way to the sentence management unit, a building that was formerly the governor's house and is situated just a few yards from the front gate. The pathway leading up to the entrance is lined with tired red flowers. The light blue front door could do with a lick of paint; it looks as if it is regularly kicked open rather than pushed.

The first room I enter has the feel of a conservatory. It has a dozen wooden chairs, and a notice board covered in information leaflets. Four officers, including a Mr Gough, who looks like a prep school master, occupy the first room on the ground floor. As he ticks off my name, Mr Gough announces, in a broad Norfolk accent, that he will be speaking to all the new inductees once everyone has come across from their medical examination. But as Dr Walling is taking fifteen minutes with each new prisoner, we may be sitting around for some time. As I wait impatiently in the conservatory, I become aware how filthy the room is. At Wayland, the floors shone from their daily buffing, and if you stood still for more than a few moments, someone painted you.

Eventually, all seven new inductees turn up. Mr Gough welcomes us, and begins by saying that as most prisoners spend less than three months at NSC, the officers aim to make our time as civilized as possible while they prepare us for returning to the outside world. Mr Gough explains that at NSC anyone can abscond. It's all too easy as there are no walls to keep you in. 'But if you do decide to leave us, please remember to leave your room key on your pillow.' He's not joking.

He then tells us about a young man, who absconded sixteen hours before he was due to be released. He was picked up in

594

Boston the following morning and transferred to a C-cat, where he spent a further six weeks. Point taken.

Mr Gough takes us through the jobs that are available for all prisoners under the age of sixty, pointing out that over half the inmates work on the farm. The other half can enrol for education, or take on the usual jobs in the kitchen, or painting, gardening or as a cleaner.

Mr Gough ends by telling us that we all have to abide by a 'no drugs policy'. Refusing to sign the three documents stating you are not on drugs and will agree at any time to a voluntary drugs test will rule you out of becoming 'enhanced' in eight weeks' time. Enhancement allows you a further £5 a week to spend in the canteen, along with several other privileges. To a question, Mr Gough replies, 'Wearing your own clothes is not permitted in an open prison as it would make absconding that much easier.' However, I did notice that Doug (tax evasion) was wearing a green T-shirt and brown slacks held up by the most outrageous Walt Disney braces. There's always someone who finds a way round the system.

I happily sign all of Mr Gough's drug forms and am then sent upstairs to be interviewed by another officer. Mr Donnelly not only looks like a farmer, but is also dressed in green overalls and wearing Wellington boots. No wonder the place is so dirty. He appears keen for me to join him on the farm, but I explain (on Doug's advice) that I would like to be considered for Matthew's job as SMU orderly. He makes a note, and frowns.

12 noon

After ten weeks locked up in Wayland and always being handed a plate of food, I can't get used to helping myself. One of the kitchen staff laughs when I pass over my plate and expect to be served. 'A clear sign you've just arrived from a closed prison,' he remarks. 'Welcome to the real world, Jeff.'

After lunch, Dean takes me across to view the more secluded, quieter south block, which is at the far end of the prison and houses the older inmates.* Here, there is a totally different atmosphere.

Dean shows me an empty room, large by normal standards, about twenty by eight feet, with a window that looks out over the bleak North Sea. He explains that the whole spur is in the process of redecoration and is scheduled to reopen on Monday. In-cell electricity (ICE) will be added, and all rooms will eventually have a television. On our way back to the north block, an officer informs me that the principal officer, Mr New, wants to see me immediately. I'm nervous. What have I done wrong? Is he going to send me back to Wayland?

PO New is in his late forties, around five feet eleven, with a shock of thick white hair. He greets me with a warm smile. 'I hear you want to work at SMU?' he says, and before I can reply adds, 'You've got the job. As Matthew is leaving in four weeks' time, you'd better start straight away so there can be a smooth takeover.' I've hardly got the words thank you out before he continues, 'I hear you want to move to the south block, which I'm sure will be possible, and I'm also told you want to be transferred to Spring Hill, which,' he adds, 'will not be quite as easy, because they don't want you and the attendant publicity that goes with you.' My heart sinks. 'However,' he says, again before I can respond, 'if that's what you want, I'll have a word with my opposite number at Spring Hill and see if she can help.'

Once Mr New has completed his discourse, we go downstairs

---

* NSC has two blocks, north and south, with about 110 prisoners resident in each.

TUESDAY 16 OCTOBER 2001

to meet Matthew, the current orderly. Matthew is a shy young man, who has a lost, academic air about him. I can't imagine what he's doing in prison. Despite Mr New talking most of the time, Matthew manages to tell me what his responsibilities are, from making tea and coffee for the eleven occupants of the building, through to preparing induction files for every prisoner. He's out on a town leave tomorrow, so I will be thrown in at the deep end.

4.45 pm

Dean grabs my laundry bag and then accompanies me to supper, explaining that orderlies have the privilege of eating on their own thirty minutes ahead of all the other inmates.

'You get first choice of the food,' he adds, 'and as there are about a dozen of us,' (hospital, stores, reception, library, gym, education, chapel and gardens; it's quite a privilege). All this within twenty-four hours isn't going to make me popular.

597

DAY 91   WEDNESDAY 17 OCTOBER 2001

5.30 am

I wake a few minutes after five and go for a pee in the latrine at the end of the corridor. Have you noticed that when you're disoriented, or fearful, you don't go to the lavatory for some time? There must be a simple medical explanation for this. I didn't 'open my bowels' – to use the doctor's expression – for the first five days at Belmarsh, the first three days at Wayland and so far 'no-go' at NSC.

8.00 am

Dean turns up to take me to breakfast. I may not bother in future, as I don't eat porridge, and it's hardly worth the journey for a couple of slices of burnt toast. Dean warns me that the press are swarming all over the place, and large sums are being offered for a photo of me in prison uniform. Should they get a snap, they will be disappointed to find me strolling around in a T-shirt and jeans. No arrows, no number, no ball and chain.

8.45 am

At reception, I ask Mr Daff if it would be possible to have a clean T-shirt, as my wife is visiting me this afternoon.

'Where do you think you fuckin' are, Archer, fuckin' Harrods?'

9.00 am

As a new prisoner, I continue my induction course. My first meeting this morning is in the gym. We all assemble in a small Portacabin and watch a ten minute black-and-white video on safety at work. The instructor concentrates on lifting, as there are several jobs at NSC that require you to pick up heavy loads, not to mention numerous prisoners who will be pumping weights in the gym. Mr Masters, the senior gym officer, who has been at NSC for nineteen years, then gives us a guided tour of the gym and its facilities. It is not as large or well equipped as Wayland, but it does have three pieces of cardiovascular kit that will allow me to remain fit – a rowing machine, a step machine and a bicycle. The gym itself is just large enough to play basketball, whereas the weights room is about half the size of the one at Wayland. The gym is open every evening except Monday from 5.30 pm to 7.30 pm, so you don't have (grunt, grunt – the pigs are having breakfast) to complete the programme in a given hour. I hope to start this weekend, by which time I should have found my way around (grunt, grunt). Badminton is the most popular sport, and although NSC has a football team, the recent foot-and-mouth problems have played havoc when it comes to being allowed out onto the pitch (grunt, grunt).

9.30 am

Education. We all meet in the chapel. The education officer takes us through the various alternatives on offer. Most of the new inmates sit sulkily in their chairs, staring blankly at her. As I

599

have already been allocated a job as the SMU orderly, I listen in respectful silence, and once she's finished her talk, report back to my new job.

10.30 am

Matthew is away on a town visit today, but I quickly discover that the SMU job has three main responsibilities:

a) Making tea and coffee for the eleven staff who regularly work in the building, plus those who drop in to visit a colleague.

b) Preparing the files for new inductees so that the officers have all their details to hand: sentence, FLED (full licence eligibility date), home address, whether they have a home or job to go to, whether they have any money of their own, whether their family want them back.

c) Preparing prisoners' forms for visits, days out, weekend leave, work out and compassionate or sick leave.

It will also be part of my job to see that every prisoner is sent to the relevant officer, according to his needs. Mr Simpson, the resident probation officer tells me, 'I'll see anyone if I'm free, otherwise ask them to make an appointment,' allowing him to deal with those prisoners who have a genuine problem, and avoid those who stroll in to complain every other day.

11.45 am

I go to lunch with the other orderlies. The officer in charge of the kitchen, Wendy, tells me that NSC was commended for having the best food in the prison service. She says, 'You should try the meat and stop being a VIP [vegetarian in prison].' Wendy is a sort of pocket-sized Margaret Thatcher. Her kitchen is spotless, while her men slave away in their pristine white overalls leaving one in no doubt of their respect for her. I promise to try the meat in two weeks' time when I fill in my next menu voucher. (See overleaf.)

2.00 pm

Now I'm in a D-cat prison, I'm allowed one visit a week. After one-third of my sentence has been completed, other privileges will be added. Heaven knows what the press will make of my first town visit. However, all of this could change rapidly once my appeal has been heard. If your sentence is four years or more, you are only eligible for parole, whereas if it's less than four years, you will automatically be released after serving half your sentence, and if you've been a model prisoner, you can have another two months off while being tagged*

Back to today's visit. Two old friends, David Paterson and Tony Bloom, accompany Mary.

The three of them turn up twenty minutes late, which only emphasizes how dreadful the 250-mile round journey from London must be. Mary and I have thirty minutes on our own, and she tells me that my solicitors have approached Sir Sydney Kentridge QC to take over my appeal if it involves that Mr Justice Potts was prejudiced against me before the trial started. The one witness who could testify, Godfrey Barker, is now proving reluctant to come forward. He fears that his wife, who works at the Home Office, may lose her job. Mary feels he will do what is just. I feel he will vacillate and fall by the wayside. She is the optimist, I am the pessimist. It's usually the other way round.

---

* While tagged, you must remain at home between 7 pm and 7 am.

HM PRISON NORTH SEA CAMP

Week 2	Lunch Menu	Choice	Week 2	Dinner Menu	Choice
SUN.	1. Chicken Portions 2. Roast Pork & Stuffing * 3. Mushroom Pasta 4. Stuffed Pepper *H	1	SUN.	1. Fish Fingers *H 2. Beefburger * 3. Vegburger * 4. Egg Mayonnaise Sandwich *	3
MON.	1. Sausage Rolls *H 2. Fish Grills * 3. Vegetable Rolls * 4. Onion Bhajies *	2	MON.	1. Pork Curry & Rice H 2. Chicken & Sweetcorn Pie * 3. Veg Curry & Rice * 4. Veg Pie *	1
TUES.	1. Braised Sausage H 2. Cheese & Tomato Pizza * 3. Braised Veg Sausage * 4. Pilchard Sandwich H*	~~1~~ 2	TUES.	1. Beef Lasagne 2. Fish Fillets & Parsley Sauce H 3. Vegetable Lasagne * 4. Vegetable Pie *	2
WED.	1. Fish Fingers H* 2. Cheese & Onion Pie * 3. Faggots in Gravy 4. 4-Pack Cheese Sandwich *	2	WED.	1. Ham & Egg 2. Kidney Casserole H 3. Stir Fried Rice * 4. Vegetable Pie *	1
THURS.	1. Quiche Lorraine H 2. Cheeseburger * 3. Vegetarian Quiche * 4. Veg Cheeseburger *	3	THURS.	1. Chicken Meatballs in Tomato Sauce 2. Cottage Pie H 3. Veg Meatballs in Tomato Sauce * 4. Vegetarian Soya Pie *	2
FRI.	1. Shepherd's Pie H 2. Chicken Cutlets * 3. Veg Pie * 4. Onion Bhajies	4	FRI.	1. Liver, Sausage & Onions H 2. Chicken Fricassée & Rice * 3. Potato & Lentil Bake * 4. Veg Fricassée & Rice *	3
SAT.	1. Pork Hotpot H 2. Meat & Potato Pie * 3. Veg Hotpot * 4. Veg Pie	1	SAT.	1. Cornish Pasties 2. Welsh Rarebit 3. Vegetarian Pasty * 4. Vegburger *	3

You are responsible for returning your choices by Monday. Please hand to any staff on duty in the Kitchen. Print your name and number and sign the form. Failure to do so will result in you automatically being given a vegetarian meal. The Kitchen will endeavour to keep all meals as laid down on the menu. If, for any reason, the meal indicated cannot be issued, a replacement meal will be substituted. (H – Healthy Eating Option. * – Suitable for Muslims)

NAME: ARCHER   NUMBER: FF8282   SIGNATURE: Jeffrey Archer

During the visit, both Governor Berlyn, and PO New stroll around, talking to the families of the prisoners. How different from Wayland. Mr New tells us that NSC has now been dubbed 'the cushiest prison in England' (*Sun*), which he hopes will produce a better class of inmate in future; 'The best food in any prison' (*Daily Star*); I have 'the biggest room in the quietest block' (*Daily Mail*); and, 'he's the only one allowed to wear his own clothes' (*Daily Mirror*). Not one fact correct.

The hour and a half passes all too quickly, but at least I can now have a visitor every week. I can only wonder how many of my friends will be willing to make a seven-hour round trip to spend an hour and a half with me.

5.00 pm

Canteen. At Wayland, you filled in an order form and then your supplies were delivered to your cell. At NSC there is a small shop which you are allowed to visit twice a week between 5.30 pm and 7.30 pm so you can purchase what you need – razor blades, toothpaste, chocolate, water, blackcurrant juice and most important of all, phonecards. I also need a can of shaving foam as I still shave every day.

What a difference a D-cat makes.

6.00 pm

I go across to the kitchen for supper and join two prisoners seated at the far end of the room. I select them because of their age. One turns out to be an accountant, the other a retired insurance broker. They do not talk about their crimes. They tell me that they no longer work in the prison, but travel into Boston every morning by bus, and have to be back each afternoon by

DAY 91

five. They work at the local Red Cross shop, and earn £13.50 a week, which is credited to their canteen account. Some prisoners can earn as much as £200 a week, giving them a chance to save a considerable sum by the time they're released. This makes a lot more sense than turfing them out onto the street with the regulation £40 and no job to go to.

7.00 pm

I join Doug at the hospital for a blackcurrant juice, a McVitie's biscuit and the Channel 4 news. In Washington DC, Congress and the Senate were evacuated because of an anthrax scare. There seem to be so many ways of waging a modern war. Are we in the middle of the Third World War without realizing it?

8.15 pm

I return to the north block for roll-call to prove I have not absconded.* Doug assures me that it becomes a lot easier after the first couple of weeks, when the checks fall from six a day to four. My problem is that the final roll-call is at ten, and by then I've usually fallen asleep.

---

* You cannot escape from an open prison, only abscond. There are no walls, just a car barrier at the entrance and a public footpath at the back. Most prisoners who abscond do so in the first two weeks. Nine out of ten are back behind bars within forty-eight hours.

DAY 92   THURSDAY 18 OCTOBER 2001

6.00 am

Because so much is new to me, and so much unknown, I am still finding my way around.

Mr Hughes and Mr Jones, the officers in charge of the north block, try to deal quickly with prisoners' queries and, more important, attempt to get things 'sorted', making them popular with the other inmates. The two blocks resemble Second World War Nissen huts. The north block consists of a 100-yard corridor, with five spurs running off each side. Each corridor has nine rooms – you have your own key, and there are no bars on the windows.

Two prisoners share each room. My room-mate David is a lifer (murder), and has the largest room: not the usual five paces by three, but seven paces by three. I have already requested a transfer to the no-smoking spur on the south block, which tends to house the older, more mature prisoners. Despite the *News of the World* headline, 'Archer demands cell change', the no-smoking rule is every prisoner's right. However, Governor Berlyn is unhappy about my going across to the south block because it's next to a public footpath, which is currently populated by several journalists and photographers.

The corridor opposite mine has recently been designated a

DAY 92

no-smoking zone, and Mr Berlyn suggests I move across to one of the empty rooms on that spur. As the prison is presently low in numbers, I might even be left on my own. Every prisoner I have shared a cell with has either sold his story to the tabloids, or been subjected to front-page exposés – always exaggerated and never accurate.

8.30 am

My working day as SMU orderly is 8.30 am to 12, lunch, then 1 pm to 4.30 pm. I arrive expecting to find Matthew so he can begin the handover, but Mr Gough is the only person on parade. He has his head down, brow furrowed, staring at his computer. He makes the odd muttering sound to himself, before asking politely for a cup of tea.

9.00 am

Still no sign of Matthew. I read through the daily duties book, and discover that among my responsibilities are mopping the kitchen floor, sweeping all common areas, vacuuming the carpets and cleaning the two lavatories as well as the kitchen. Thankfully, the main occupation, and the only thing that will keep me from going insane, is dealing with prisoners' queries. By the time I've read the eight-page folder twice, there is still no sign of Matthew, which is beginning to look like a hanging offence.

If you are late for work, you are 'nicked', rare in a D-cat prison, because being put on report can result in loss of privileges – even being returned to a C-cat – according to the severity of your offence. Being caught taking drugs or absconding is an immediate recategorization offence. These privileges and punishments are in place to make sure everyone abides by the rules.

Mr New, the principal officer, arrives just as Mr Gough enters the room.

'Where's Matthew?' he asks.

I then observe the officers at their best, but the Prison Service at its most ineffective.

'That's why I came looking for you,' says Mr Gough. 'Matthew reported back late last night' – an offence that can have you transferred to a C-cat, because it's assumed that you've absconded – 'and he was put on report.' The atmosphere immediately changes. 'But I took him off.'

'Why?' asks Mr New, as he lights a cigarette.

'His father collapsed yesterday afternoon and was taken into Canterbury Hospital. He's been diagnosed with a brain tumour and the doctors think he may not survive the week.'

'Right,' says Mr New, stubbing out his cigarette, 'sign him up for a compassionate leave order, and let's get him off to Canterbury as quickly as possible.'

Mr New tells me that Matthew's mother died a year ago, having suffered from MS, and his grandmother a few weeks later. This all took place soon after he committed the offence that resulted in him being sent to prison for fifteen months.

Matthew walks in.

Mr New and Mr Gough could not have been more sympathetic. Forms are signed and countersigned with unusual speed, and Matthew is even allowed to use the office phone to arrange for his girlfriend to pick him up. A few minutes later, Governor Berlyn appears and agrees with Mr New that the boy (I think of Matthew as a boy because he's even younger than my son) must be shipped out as quickly as possible. Then the problems start to arise.

Matthew, who only has four weeks left to serve, doesn't know anyone in Canterbury, so he'll have to be locked up overnight in the local jail, despite his girlfriend and her mother staying at a hotel near the hospital. But worse, because Matthew is only allowed twenty-four hours compassionate leave, he will have to travel back from Canterbury and spend the second night at NSC, after which he will be released on Friday morning for weekend leave, when he need not return until Sunday evening. 'Why not just let the boy go and be with his father, and return on Sunday night?' I ask. Both Mr Berlyn and Mr New nod their agreement, but tell me that there is no way round the Home Office regulations.

10.30 am

Matthew's girlfriend arrives at the barrier, and he is driven quickly away. I pray that Matthew's father doesn't die while they are on the motorway. I recall with sadness learning that my mother was dying during my trial. Mr Justice Potts wouldn't allow me to leave the court to be with her, as he didn't accept the doctor's opinion that she only had a few hours to live. I eventually arrived at her bedside an hour or so before she died by which time she was past recognizing me.

11.00 am

Three prisoners who arrived yesterday check in for their induction talk. They pepper me with questions. I feel a bit of a fraud, trying to answer them, having only been around for forty-eight hours and still on induction myself. Mr Gough gives them the talk I heard two days ago. I hand out a booklet emphasizing his comments. A young prisoner whispers in my ear that he can't read. HELP. I tell him to come back and see me if he has any further problems.

12.15 pm

Mr New appears, and runs through my responsibilities. We open a large cupboard crammed full of forms and files, which he feels needs reorganizing. He lights up another cigarette.

2.00 pm

Mr Simpson, the probation officer, asks me to join him in his office on the first floor, as he wants to bring my case file up to date. He asks me if I saw a probation officer after being convicted.

'Yes, but only for a few minutes,' I tell him, 'while I was still at the Old Bailey.'

'Good,' he says, 'because that will show you're domiciled in London, and make it easier for you to be moved to Spring Hill.' He checks his computer and gives me the name of my probation officer. 'Drop her a line,' he advises, 'and tell her you want to be transferred.'

3.30 pm

Mr New joins me in the kitchen for another cigarette break. I learn that he's due to leave NSC in January, when he will be transferred to Norwich Prison as a governor, Grade 5.* He then produces all the necessary forms for my transfer. Although he'll speak to Mrs McKenzie-Howe, his opposite number at Spring Hill, he's not optimistic. Not only are they full, but it's a resettlement prison, and I don't need resettling; I'm not looking for a

---

* There are five grades of governor; the top man or woman is known as the governing governor. I still haven't met one.

job when I'm released, or a home and, as I have no financial problems, I just don't fit any of the usual categories.

5.00 pm

I go off to the canteen for supper, and again sit at a table with two older prisoners. They are both in for fraud; one was a local councillor (three and a half months), and the other an ostrich farmer. The latter promises to tell me all the details when he has more time. It's clear there's going to be no shortage of good stories. Belmarsh – murder and GBH; Wayland – drug barons and armed robbers. NSC is looking a little more sophisticated.

7.00 pm

I join Doug in the hospital. He has allowed me to store a bottle of blackcurrant juice and a couple of bottles of Evian in his fridge, so I'll always have my own supply. As Doug chats away, I learn a little more about his crime. He hates drug dealers, and considers his own incarceration a temporary inconvenience. In fact he plans a cruise to Australia just as soon as he's released. On 'the out' he runs a small transport company. He has a yard and seven lorries, and employs – still employs – twelve people. He spends half an hour a day on the phone keeping abreast of what's going on back at base.

Now to his crime; his export/import business was successful until a major client went bankrupt and renegued on a bill for £170,000, placing him under extreme pressure with his bank. He began to replenish his funds by illegally importing cigarettes from France. He received a two-year sentence for failing to pay customs and excise duty to the tune of £850,000.

DAY 93 FRIDAY 19 OCTOBER 2001

6.00 am

I write for two hours. Boxer shorts draped over the little light that beams down onto my desk ensure that I don't disturb David.

8.15 am

I prepare identity cards for the three new prisoners who arrived yesterday. As each officer comes in, I make them tea or coffee. In between, I continue to organize the filing system for inductees. I will still be one myself for another week.

When Mr New arrives, he leaves his copy of *The Times* in the kitchen, and retrieves it at six before going home.

I am slowly getting into a routine. I now meet new prisoners as they appear, and find out what their problems are before they see an officer. Often they've come to the wrong office, or simply don't have the right form. Many of them want to be interviewed for risk assessment, others need to see the governor, whose office is in the administration block on the other side of the prison. But the real problem is Mr New himself, because many prisoners believe that if their request doesn't have his imprimatur, it won't go any further. This is partly because he takes an interest in every prisoner, but mainly because he won't rush them. He can often take twenty minutes to listen to their problems when all that is needed is for a form to be signed, which results in four other prisoners having to sit in the waiting room until he's finished.

During any one day, about thirty prisoners visit SMU. I have to be careful not to overstep the mark, as inmates need to see me as fighting their corner, while the officers have to feel I'm helping to cut down their workload. I certainly need a greater mental stimulation than making cups of tea. But however much I take on, the pay remains 25p an hour, £8.50 a week.

12 noon

I pick up my lunch – vegetable pie and beans. No pudding. I take my tray back to the SMU and read *The Times*.

2.00 pm

A prisoner marches in and demands to be released on compassionate grounds because his mother is ill. Mr Downs, a shrewd, experienced officer, tells him that he'll send a probation officer round to see his mother, so that they can decide if he should be released. The prisoner slopes off without another word. Mr Downs immediately calls the probation officer in Leicester, just in case the prisoner does have a sick mother.

Bob (lifer) comes to see the psychiatrist, Christine. Bob is preparing for life outside once he's released, possibly next year, but before that can happen, he has to complete ten town visits without incident. Once he's achieved this, he will be allowed out at weekends unescorted. The authorities will then assess if he is ready to be released. Bob has been in prison for twenty-three years, having originally been sentenced to fifteen. But as Christine points out, however strongly she recommends his release, in the end it is always Home Office decision.

Christine joins me in the kitchen and tells me about a lifer who went out on his first town visit after twenty years. He was given £20 so he could get used to shopping in a supermarket. When he arrived at the cash till and was asked how he would like to pay, he ran out leaving the goods behind. He just couldn't cope with having to make a decision.

'We also have to prepare all lifers for survival cooking.' She adds, 'You have to remember that some prisoners have had three cooked meals a day for twenty years, and they've become so institutionalized they can't even boil an egg.'

The next lifer to see Christine is Mike. After twenty-two years in prison (he's forty-nine), Mike is also coming to the end of his sentence. He invites me to supper on Sunday night (chicken curry). He's determined to prove that he can not only take care of himself, but cook for others as well.

5.00 pm

I walk over to the canteen and join Ron the fraudster and Dave the ostrich farmer for cauliflower cheese. Ron declares that the food at NSC is as good as most motorway cafés. This is indeed a compliment to Wendy.

6.00 pm

Mr Hughes (my wing officer) informs me I can move across to room twelve in the no-smoking corridor.

When I locate the room I find it's filthy, and the only

furniture is a single unmade bed, a table and a chair. I despair. I am so pathetic at times like this.

In the opposite cell is a prisoner called Alan who is cleaning out his room, and asks if he can help. I enquire what he would charge to transform my room so that it looks like his.

'Four phonecards,' he says (£8).

'Three,' I counter. He agrees. I tell him I will return at eight-fifteen for roll-call and see how he's getting on.

8.15 pm

I check in for roll-call before going off to see my new quarters. Alan has taken on an assistant, and they are slaving away. While Alan scrubs the cupboards, the assistant is working on the walls. I tell them I'll return at ten and clear my debts. The only trouble is that I don't have any phonecards, and won't have before canteen on Wednesday. Doug comes to my rescue and takes over Darren's role of purveyor of essential goods.

Doug appears anxious. He tells me that his fourteen-year-old daughter has suffered an epileptic fit. He's being allowed to go home tomorrow and visit her.

We settle down to watch the evening film, and are joined by the senior security officer, Mr Hocking. He warns me that a *News of the World* journalist is roaming around the grounds but, with a bit of luck, will fall into the Wash. Just before he leaves, he asks Doug if he's on home leave tomorrow.

'Yes, I'm off to see my daughter, back by seven,' Doug confirms.

'Then we'll need someone to be on duty after sister leaves at one. We mustn't forget how many drugs there are in this building. Would you be willing to stand in as temporary hospital orderly, Jeffrey?' he asks.

'Yes, of course,' I reply.

10.00 pm

I return to the north block for roll-call, before checking my room. I don't recognize it. It's spotless. I thank Alan, who takes a seat on the corner of the bed

He tells me that he has a twelve-month sentence for receiving stolen goods. He owns two furniture shops, in Leicester whose turnover last year was a little over £500,000, showing him a profit of around £120,000. He has a wife and two children, and between them they're keeping the business ticking over until he has completed his sentence in four weeks' time. It's his first offence, and he certainly falls into that category of 'never again'.

10.45 pm

I spend my first night at NSC in my own room. No music, no smoke, no hassle.

DAY 94   SATURDAY 20 OCTOBER 2001

6.00 am

Weekends are deadly in a prison. Jules, my pad-mate at Wayland used to say the only time you're not in prison is when you're asleep. So over the weekend, a lot of prisoners just remain in bed. I'm lucky because I have my writing to occupy me.

8.00 am

I spot Matthew, who must have returned from Canterbury last night. His father is still in a coma, and he accompanies me to the office so he can phone the hospital. Although my official working week is Monday to Friday, it's not unusual for an officer to be on duty at SMU on a Saturday morning.

Mr Downs and Mr Gough are already at their desks, and after I've made them both a cup of tea, Matthew takes me through my official duties for any given day or week. If I were to stick to simply what was required, it would take me no more than a couple of hours each day.

Over a cup of tea (Bovril for me), Matthew tells me about his nightmare year.

Matthew is twenty-four, six foot one, slim, dark-haired and

616

handsome without being aware of it. He's highly intelligent, but also rather gauche, and totally out of place in prison. He read marine anthropology at Manchester University and will complete his PhD once he's released. I ask him if he's a digger or an academic. 'An academic,' he replies, without hesitation.

His first job after leaving university was as a volunteer at a museum in his home town. He was happy there, but soon decided he wanted to return to university. That was when his mother contracted MS and everything began to go badly wrong. After his mother was bedridden, he and his sister took it in turns to help around the house, so that his father could continue to work. All three found the extra workload a tremendous strain. One evening while at work in the museum, Matthew took home some ancient coins to study. I haven't used the word 'stole' because he returned all the coins a few days later. But the incident weighed so heavily on his conscience that he informed his supervisor. Matthew thought that would be the end of the matter. But someone decided to report the incident to the police. Matthew was arrested and charged with breach of trust. He pleaded guilty, and was assured by the police that they would not be pushing for a custodial sentence. His solicitor was also of the same opinion, advising Matthew that he would probably get a suspended sentence or a community service order. The judge gave him fifteen months.*

Matthew is a classic example of someone who should not have been sent to jail; a hundred hours of community service might serve some purpose, but this boy has spent the last three months with murderers, drug addicts and burglars. He won't turn to a life of crime, but how many less intelligent people might? It's a rotten system that allows such a person to end up in prison.

---

* Matthew will end up serving five and a half months.

DAY 94

My former secretary, Angie Peppiatt, stole thousands of pounds from me, and still hasn't been arrested. I feel for Matthew.

12 noon

Lunch today is just as bad as Belmarsh or Wayland. Matthew explains that Wendy is off. I must remember to eat only when Wendy is on duty.

2.00 pm

I report to the hospital and take over Doug's caretaker role, while he visits his daughter. I settle down with a glass of blackcurrant juice and Evian to watch England slaughter Ireland, and win the Grand Slam, the Triple Crown and ... after all, we are far superior on paper. Unfortunately, rugby is not played on paper but on pitches. Ireland hammer us 20–14, and return to the Emerald Isle with smiles on their faces.

I'm still sulking when a tall, handsome black man strolls in. His name is Clive. I only hope he's not ill, because if he is, I'm the last person he needs. He tells me that he's serving the last third of his sentence, and has just returned from a week's home leave – part of his rehabilitation programme.

Clive and I are the only two prisoners who have the privilege of visiting Doug in the evenings. I quickly discover why Doug enjoys Clive's company. He's bright, incisive and entertaining and, if it were not politically incorrect, I would describe him as sharp as a cartload of monkeys. Let me give you just one example of how he works the system.

During the week Clive works as a line manager for a fruit-packing company in Boston. He leaves the prison after breakfast at eight and doesn't return until seven in the evening. For this, he is paid £200 a week. So during the week, NSC is no more than a bed and breakfast, and the only day he has to spend in prison is Sunday. But Clive has a solution for that as well.

Two Sundays in every month he takes up his allocated town visits, while on the third Sunday he's allowed an overnight stay.

'But what about the fourth or fifth Sunday?' I ask.

'Religious exemption,' he explains.

'But why, when there's a chapel in the grounds?' I demand.

'*Your* chapel is in your grounds,' says Clive, 'because you're C of E. Not me,' he adds. 'I'm a Jehovah's Witness. I must visit my place of worship at least one Sunday in every month, and the nearest one just happens to be in Leicester.'

After a coffee, Clive invites me over to his room on the south block to play backgammon. His room turns out not to be five paces by three, or even seven by three. It's a little over ten paces by ten. In fact it's larger than my bedroom in London or Grantchester.

'How did you manage this?' I ask, as we settle down on opposite sides of the board.

'Well, it used to be a storeroom,' he explains, 'until I rehabilitated it.'

'But it could easily house four prisoners.'

'True,' says Clive, 'but remember I'm also the race relations representative, so they'll only allow black prisoners to share a room with me. There aren't that many black prisoners in D-cats,' he adds with a smile.

I hadn't noticed the sudden drop in the black population after leaving Wayland until Clive mentioned it. But I have seen a few at NSC, so I ask why they aren't allowed to room with him.

'They all start life on the north block, and that's where they stay,' he adds without explanation. He also beat me at backgammon – leaving me three Mars Bars light.

DAY 95   SUNDAY 21 OCTOBER 2001

6.00 am

Sunday is a day of rest, and if there's one thing you don't need in prison it's a day of rest.

8.00 am

SMU is open as Mr Downs is transferring files from his office to the administration block before taking up new responsibilities. Fifteen new prisoners arrived on Friday, giving me an excuse to prepare files and make up their identity cards.

North Sea Camp, whose capacity is 220, rarely has more than 170 inmates at any one time. As inmates have the right to be within fifty miles of their families, being stuck out on the east coast limits the catchment area. Two of the spurs are being refurbished at the moment, which shows the lack of pressure on accommodation.* The turnover at NSC is about fifteen prisoners a week. What I am about to reveal is common to all D-cat prisons, and by no means exclusive to NSC. On average, one prisoner absconds every week (unlawfully at large), the figures have a tendency to rise around Christmas and drop a little

---

* This is only true in D-cats – open prisons.

during the summer, so NSC loses around fifty prisoners a year; this explains the need for five roll-calls a day. Many absconders return within twenty-four hours, having thought better of it; they have twenty-eight days added to their sentence. A few, often foreigners, return to their countries and are never seen again. Quite recently, two Dutchmen absconded and were picked up by a speedboat, as the beach is only 100 yards out of bounds. They were back in Holland before the next roll-call.

Most absconders are quickly recaptured, many only getting as far as Boston, a mere six miles away. They are then transferred to a C-cat with its high walls and razor wire, and will never, under any circumstances, be allowed to return to an open prison, even if at some time in the future they are convicted of a minor offence. A few, very few, get clean away. But they must then spend every day looking over their shoulder.

There are even some cases of wives or girlfriends sending husbands or partners back to prison, and in one case a mother-in-law returning an errant prisoner to the front gate, declaring that she didn't want to see him again until he completed his sentence.

This is all relevant because of something that took place today.

When granted weekend leave, you must report back by seven o'clock on Sunday evening, and if you are even a minute late, you are placed on report. Yesterday, a wife was driving her husband back to the prison, when they became involved in a heated row. The wife stopped the car and dumped her husband on the roadside some thirty miles from the jail. He ran to the nearest phone box to let the prison know what had happened and a taxi was sent out to pick him up. He checked in over an hour late. Thirty pounds was deducted from his canteen account to pay for the taxi, and he's been placed on report.

DAY 95

2.00 pm

I go for a two-mile walk with Clive, who is spending a rare Sunday in prison. We discuss the morning papers. They have me variously working on the farm/in the hospital/cleaning the latrines/eating alone/lording it over everyone. However, nothing beats the *Mail on Sunday*, which produces a blurred photo of me proving that I have refused to wear prison clothes. This despite the fact that I'm wearing prison jeans and a grey prison sweatshirt in the photo.

After our walk, Clive and I play a few games of backgammon. He's in a different class to me, so I decide to take advantage of his superiority and turn each session into a tutorial.

6.00 pm

I write for two hours, and then sign in for roll-call with Mr Hughes.

9.00 pm

Doug, Clive and I watch a magnificent period drama set in Guildford and Cornwall in 1946. Mike (lifer) appears twenty minutes into the film, with a chicken curry in plastic containers – part of his cookery rehabilitation course. Doug serves it up on china plates – a real luxury in itself, even though we have to eat the meal with plastic knives and forks.

I eat the meal very slowly, and enjoy every morsel.

DAY 96 MONDAY 22 OCTOBER 2001

8.30 am

I've been at NSC for a week, and am beginning to feel that I know my way around.

I report to work at SMU. Matthew shows me how to make out an order form for any supplies that are needed for the office, which will then be sent to the stores, who should see that we have it the same day. We discover an outstanding order from 5 October for files and paper, marked urgent, and another for 15 October, marked very urgent. Inefficiency is endemic in parts of the Prison Service. Millions of pounds of taxpayers' money is wasted every year. The departments responsible for this differ from prison to prison, but to give you a small example: some years ago there was a prisoner at HMP Gartree who was a vicious killer and needed to be transferred from one cell to another, a distance of less than a hundred yards. Fifteen officers arrived to move him, an operation that took five minutes. All fifteen officers claimed four hours overtime. How do I know this? A senior officer who previously worked at Gartree told me.

DAY 96

12 noon

Matthew and I have lunch in the canteen with the other orderlies, and are joined by Roger (lifer, murdered his wife), who berated me about England losing to Ireland on Saturday.

'But you sound Welsh?' I venture.

'I am,' he replies, 'but I don't care who beats the English. It's one of the few pleasures I get in here.'

1.00 pm

Mr New arrives in the office, having spent the morning in court on a domestic matter. One has a tendency to forget that prison officers have problems of their own.

Matthew and I discuss how to improve office efficiency. I'd like to clear out every drawer and cupboard and start again. He agrees. We're about to begin, when the door opens and the governing governor walks in. Mr Lewis greets me with a warm, jovial smile. He asks Matthew to leave us and wastes no time with small talk.

'The press,' he tells me, 'are still camped at both ends of the prison.' And he adds that a prisoner has been caught with an expensive camera and long lens in his room. Mr Lewis has no idea which paper smuggled it in, or how much money was involved. The inmate concerned is already on his way to a C-cat, and will not be allowed to return to an open prison. Apparently several prisoners have complained about the press invading their privacy, and the governor has given his assurance that if a photograph of them appears in a national newspaper, they have legal recourse – a rule that doesn't seem to apply to me. We then discuss my move to Spring Hill before the governor calls Matthew back in. Mr Lewis grants him a further two days compassionate leave, which will allow Matthew to spend five days with his father. Mr Lewis appears to have combined compassion and common sense, while remaining inside the Home Office guidelines.

4.00 pm

Mr New arrives back in the office, anxious to know what the governor wanted to see me about. I don't mention the camera as Mr Lewis specifically asked me not to. I tell him that Mr Lewis intends to speak to the governor of Spring Hill, but he's leaving all the paperwork to him.

'It's been dealt with,' Mr New replies. 'I've already sent all the documents to my opposite number.'

4.30 pm

I ask Matthew, on a visit to his room in the south block, if he could redo the 'officers list of needs' presently listed on the back of the kitchen cabinet, so that it's as smart as the one Doug displays in the hospital. I glance up at Matthew's bookshelf: Pliny the Younger and Augustus Caesar. He asks me if I've read Herodotus.

'No,' I confess, 'I'm still circa 1774, currently reading about John Adams and the first Congress. I'll need a little longer sentence if I'm ever to get back to 484 BC.'

5.00 pm

I return to my room. I hate the north block. It's noisy, dirty and smelly (we're opposite the pig farm). I lock myself in and write for a couple of hours.

DAY 96

7.00 pm

I stroll across to Doug (tax avoidance) in the hospital. He allows me the use of his bathroom. Once I've had a bath and put on clean clothes, I feel almost human.

Clive (fraud) joins us after his day job in the fruit factory. He tells me that his fellow workers believe what they read about me in the *Sun* and the *Mirror*. I despair.

8.15 pm

I leave the hospital and return for roll-call before going back to my room to write for a couple hours. The tannoy keeps demanding that Jackson should report for roll-call. He's probably halfway to Boston by now.

10.00 pm

Final roll-call. Mr Hughes waves from the other end of the corridor to show my name has been ticked off. He's already worked out that I will be the last person to abscond. I certainly wouldn't get halfway to Boston before being spotted.

DAY 97   TUESDAY 23 OCTOBER 2001

6.03 am

All the lifers at NSC are coming to the end of their sentence and are being prepared to re-enter the outside world. The very fact that they have progressed from an A-cat, through B, C to D over a period of twenty years, is proof that they want a second chance.

One of the fascinating things about murderers – and we have a dozen or more at NSC – is that you cannot generalize about them. However, I have found that they roughly fall into two categories: those who are first offenders and unlikely to commit another crime, especially after twenty years in jail, and those who are evil and should be locked away in an A-cat for the rest of their lives.

Almost all the lifers at NSC fall into the former category; otherwise they would never have made it to an open prison. Bob, Chris, Mike and Roger are all now middle aged and harmless. This might seem strange to those reading this diary, but I feel none of the fear when I'm with them that I do with some of the young tearaways who only have a few weeks left to serve.

DAY 97

8.30 am

Matthew starts cleaning out the cupboard and drawers, while I concentrate on the new inductees. There are fifteen of them, and it's lunchtime before the last one has all his questions answered.

12 noon

Lunch is memorable only because Wendy says my menu sheet is missing. She suspects it's been stolen and will appear in one of the tabloids tomorrow. She supplies me with a new one, but asks me not to put my name on the top or sign it, just hand the sheet over to her.

2.00 pm

While clearing out the drawers, Matthew comes across a box of biros marked 1987, and a ledger with the initials GR and a crown above it. Two hours later, every shelf has been washed and scrubbed. All the documents we need for inductees are in neat piles, and we have three bin bags full of out-of-date material.

4.45 pm

I join Doug and Matthew for supper: vegetarian sausage and mash.

5.00 pm

Back in my room I write for two hours. Tomorrow I must – I repeat, must – go to the gym.

DAY 98　WEDNESDAY 24 OCTOBER 2001

8.30 am

Today is labour board. All inductees, having completed their other interviews, must now be allocated a job, otherwise they will receive no income. The board consists of two members from management (the farm and other activities) and a senior officer. Before any inductee faces the board I brief them on what to expect, as I went through the process only a week ago. I tell them it helps if they know what they want to do, and one of them, a bright young Asian called Ahmed, tells me he's after my job. Another, Mr Clarke, informs me that he's sixty-seven and wants a part-time cleaning job, perhaps a couple of hours a day. I immediately go upstairs and ask the board if he could be allocated to this office, which would allow me to concentrate on the weekly inductions and the several prisoners who pop in during the day to talk about their problems. They tell me they'll think about it.

12.15 pm

I return to the SMU after lunch to find a drugs officer in the kitchen. His black Labrador Jed is sniffing around. I melt into the background, and listen to a conversation he's having with Mr New. It seems there's going to be another clampdown on drugs. The drugs officer tells Mr New that last year, thirty-six visitors were found with drugs on them, two of them solicitors and one a barrister. I am so surprised by this that I later ask Mr New if he believes it. He nods. Ironically, the headline in today's *Times* is, 'Cannabis to be legalized?' I leave the office at 1.30 pm as I have a visit myself today.

2.00 pm

Alison, my PA, David, my driver, and Chris Beetles are sitting at a little square table in the visitors' room waiting for me. After we've picked up Diet Cokes and chocolate, mostly for me, we seem to chat about everything except prison; from Joseph my butler, who is in hospital, seriously injured after being knocked down by a bus on his way to work, and the 'folly' at the bottom of the garden in Grantchester being flooded, to how the public are responding to the events of 11 September.

Alison and I then go through my personal letters and the list of people who have asked to visit me at NSC. These weekly visits are a wonderful tonic, but they also serve to remind me just how much I miss my friends, holed up in this God-forsaken place.

4.00 pm

I return to the office, to find Mr New and a security officer, Mr Hayes, waiting to see me. The photographers just won't go away. One has even offered Mr Hayes £500 for the charity of his choice if I will agree to pose for a picture. I refuse, aware how much more will go into the journalist's pocket. It's against the law to take a photograph of a serving prisoner, not that that seems to bother any of the vultures currently hovering around. Both officers promise to do their best to keep them at bay. Mr New then tells me that a second camera has been found in an inmate's room, and the prisoner involved was transferred back to a closed prison this morning. I try to concentrate on my work.

7.00 pm

I visit the canteen to discover I have £18.50 in my account: £10 of my own money, and £8.50 added as my weekly wage. My Gillette blades alone cost £4.29, and two phonecards £4.00, so there's not a lot over for extras like toothpaste, soap, bottles of Evian water and perhaps even a bar of chocolate. I mention this only in passing lest any of you should imagine that I am, as the tabloids suggest, living the life of Riley.

7.15 pm

I stroll across to the hospital, and enjoy the fresh country air, even if the surroundings are rather bleak. Doug tells me that my application to Spring Hill is being processed. How does Doug know before Mr New? It turns out that he has a friend (inmate) who works in the administration block at Spring Hill.

I have a long, warm bath. Heaven.

DAY 99   THURSDAY 25 OCTOBER 2001

8.30 am

Mr Simpson (probation) and Mr Gough (induction officer) are the first to arrive in the office. They supply me with today's list of appointments. This has two advantages. I can process those inmates who have booked in, while dealing with the ones that just drop by on the off chance. Mr Clarke (crime not yet identified), our sixty-seven-year-old cleaner, also turns up on time. Matthew runs through his duties with him, while I make tea for the officers.

10.10 am

Mr Hocking (security officer) appears in the kitchen to let me know that a *Daily Mail* photographer (whose hair is longer than that of any of the inmates), has entrenched himself on a local farmer's land. He'll be able to take a picture whenever I return to the north block. Mr Hocking is going to seek the farmer's permission to eject him.

10.30 am

Mr Clarke has done a superb job; not only is the office spotless, but tomorrow he plans to get a grip on the waiting room – which presently resembles a 1947 GWR tea room.

12 noon

I have lunch with Malcolm (fraud and librarian orderly). He's quiet, well spoken and intelligent, and even in prison garb has the air of a professional man. What could he have done to end up here?

1.00 pm

Mr New appears, then disappears upstairs to join Mr Simpson, the probation officer. This afternoon they'll conduct interviews with three prisoners to discuss their sentence plans. That usually means that the inmate concerned only has a few months left to serve, so judgments have to be made on whether he is ready to take up work outside the prison, and if he is suitable for tagging.

The main factors in any decision are:

a) Is the prisoner likely to reoffend based on his past record?

b) Has he any record of violence?

c) Is he, or has he been, on drugs?

d) Has he completed all his town visits, and his week's leave, without incident?

Ticks in all those boxes means he can hope for early release, i.e. a two-year sentence becomes one year with an extra two months off for tagging. All three of today's applicants leave SMU with smiles on their faces.

DAY 99

2.20 pm

Mr Hocking returns, accompanied by a police officer. He tells me another camera has been found in an inmate's room. Once again, the prisoner concerned has been shipped off to a C-cat prison. The third in less than a week. No doubt whichever newspaper was responsible will try again. A few weeks of this, and I'll be the only prisoner still in residence.

4.30 pm

Mr Lewis the governing governor calls in to discuss the problem of lurking photographers. He asks me if I wish to return to Wayland.

'You must be joking,' are my exact words.

Mr New later explains that he only asked to protect the Prison Service, so that when a picture eventually appears in the press, I won't be able to suggest that I wasn't given the opportunity to return to closed conditions.

5.00 pm

Supper with Malcolm (fraud), Roger (murdered his wife), Martin (possession of a firearm which went off) and Matthew (breach of trust). All the talk is about an absconder who missed his girlfriend so much that he decided to leave us. He only had another nine weeks to go before his release date.

DAY 100   FRIDAY 26 OCTOBER 2001

A century of days in prison.

8.07 am

Breakfast. As it's Friday, we're offered weekend provisions: a plastic bag containing half a dozen tea bags, four sachets of sugar, some salt and pepper and a couple of pats of butter. Those of you who have read the previous two volumes of these diaries will recall my days in Belmarsh when I was on a chain gang, along with five other prisoners, putting tea bags into a plastic bag. Well, they've finally turned up at North Sea Camp. Prisoners do make useful contributions that can then be taken advantage of in other prisons, thus saving the taxpayer money, and giving inmates an occupation as well as a small weekly wage. For example, the tea towels in the kitchen were made in Dartmoor, the green bath towels in Liverpool, the brown sheets and pillow-cases at Holloway and my blankets at Durham.

Now don't forget the tea bags, because Doug has just told me over his eggs and bacon that a lifer has been shipped out to Lincoln Prison for being caught in possession of drugs. And where were they discovered? In his tea bags. Security staff raided his room this morning and found sixty tea bags containing cannabis, along with £40 in cash, which they consider proof that he was a dealer. But now for the ridiculous, sad, stupid, lunatic (choose your own word) aspect of this story – the prisoner in question was due for parole in eleven weeks' time. He will now spend the next eighteen months in a B-cat, before going on to a C-cat, probably for a couple of years, before being allowed to return to a D-cat in around four years' time. Doug adds that the security staff didn't know what he was up to, until another prisoner grassed on him.

'Why would anyone do that?' I ask.

'Probably to save their own skin,' Doug replies. 'Perhaps he was about to be shipped out for a lesser offence, so he offered them a bigger fish in exchange for a reprieve. It happens all the time.'

8.30 am

When I arrive at SMU, Mr Clarke is already standing by the door. He immediately sets about emptying the bins and mopping the kitchen floor. While we're working, I discover that it's his first offence, and he's serving a fifteen-month sentence for misappropriation of funds and is due to be released in March.

10.00 am

In the morning post there is a registered letter from my solicitors. I read the pages with trembling hands. My leave to appeal against conviction has been turned down. Only my leave to appeal against length of sentence has been granted. I can't describe how depressed I feel.

12 noon

Lunch. Doug nods in the direction of another prisoner who takes a seat at the next table. 'That's Roy,' he says, 'he's a burglar serving his fifteenth sentence. When the judge sentenced him this time to six months, he said, thank you, my Lord, I'll do that standing on my head.'

'Then I'll add a couple of months to help you get back on your feet,' replied the judge.

3.00 pm

I call my barrister, Nick Purnell QC. He feels we should still go for an appeal on conviction because three elements of our defence have been overlooked. How can Ted Francis be innocent if I am guilty? How can Mrs Peppiatt's evidence be relied upon when she confessed in the witness box to being a thief? How can I have perverted the course of justice, when the barrister representing the other side, Mr Shaw, said he had never considered the first diary date to be of any significance?

We also discuss the witness who could help me prove that Potts should never have taken the case. Nick warns me that Godfrey Barker is getting cold feet, and his wife claims she cannot remember the details.

5.30 pm

I see David (murder) in the corridor; he has a big grin on his face. He'll be spending tomorrow with his wife for the first time in two decades. He's very nervous about going out on his own, and tells me the sad story of a prisoner who went on a town visit for the first time in twenty-five years and was so frightened that

637

he climbed up a tree. The fire service had to be called out to rescue him. The police drove him back to prison, and he's never been out since.

6.00 pm

My evenings are now falling into a set pattern. I join Doug at six-thirty and have a bath, before watching the seven o'clock news on Channel 4.

8.15 pm

I report for roll-call, and then return to play a few games of backgammon with Clive.

10.00 pm

Final roll-call.

DAY 101   SATURDAY 27 OCTOBER 2001

8.07 am

There are some prisoners who prefer to remain in jail rather than be released: those who have become institutionalized and have no family, no friends, no money and no chance of a job. And then there is Rico.

Rico arrived at NSC from Lincoln Prison this morning. It's his fourth burglary offence and he's always welcomed back because he enjoys working on the farm. Rico particularly likes the pigs, and by the time he left, he knew them all by name. He even used to sleep with them at night – well, up until final roll-call. He has a single room, because no one is willing to share with him. That's one way of getting a single room.

9.00 am

I check in at SMU, but as there are no officers around I write for two hours.

11.00 am

I try to phone Mary at Grantchester, but because the flash flood has taken the phones out, all I get is a long burr.

DAY 101

12 noon

On the way to lunch, I pass Peter (lifer, arson), who is sweeping leaves from the road. Peter is a six-foot-four, eighteen-stone Hungarian who has served over thirty years for setting fire to a police station, although no one was killed.

I have lunch with Malcolm (fraud) who tells me that his wife has just been released from Holloway having completed a nine-month sentence for money laundering. The £750,000 he made was placed in her account without her knowledge (Malcolm's words) but she was also convicted. Malcolm asked to have her sentence added to his, but the judge declined.

Wives or partners are a crucial factor in a prisoner's survival. It's not too bad if the sentence is short, but even then the partner often suffers as much, if not more, being alone on the outside. In Mary's case, she is now living her life in a glare of publicity she never sought.

4.15 pm

There's a timid knock on the door. I open it to find a prisoner who wants to talk about writing a book (this occurs at least once a week). His name is Saman, and he's a Muslim Kurd. He is currently working on a book entitled *The History of Kurdistan*, and wonders if I'll read a few chapters. (Saman read engineering at a university in Kurdistan.) When he has completed his sentence, Saman wants to settle down in this country, but fears he may be deported.

'Why are you at NSC?' I ask him.

Saman tells me that he was convicted of causing death by dangerous driving, for which he was sentenced to three years. He's due to be released in December.

DAY 102   SUNDAY 28 OCTOBER 2001

6.00 am

Today's is my mother's birthday. She would have been eighty-nine.

8.15 am

After breakfast I read *The Sunday Times* in the library. Rules concerning newspapers differ from prison to prison, often without rhyme or reason. At Wayland the papers were delivered to your cell, but you can't have your own newspaper at NSC.

While I'm reading a long article on anthrax, another prisoner looks over his copy of the *News of the World*, and says, 'I'm glad to find out you're earning fifty quid a week, Jeff.' We both laugh. He knows only too well that orderlies are paid £8.50 a week, and only those prisoners who go out to work can earn more. Funnily enough, this sort of blatant invention or inaccuracy has made my fellow inmates more sympathetic.

10.00 am

Phone Mary in Grantchester and at last get a ringing tone. She's just got back from Munich, which she tells me went well. Not all the Germans are aware that her husband is a convict. Her book, *Clean Electricity from Photovoltaics*, was received by the conference with acclaim. After struggling for some years to complete volume one, she ended up selling 907 copies. Mind you, it is £110 a copy, and by scientific standards, that is a best-seller. I use up an entire phonecard (twenty units) getting myself up to date with all her news.

11.00 am

A message over the tannoy informs inmates that they can report to the drug centre for voluntarily testing. A negative result can help with parole or tagging applications. By the time I arrive, there's already a long queue. I stand behind Alan (fraud) who is being transferred to Spring Hill tomorrow. He says he'll write and let me know how the place compares to NSC and try and find out how my application is progressing.

I reach the head of the queue. Mr Vessey – he of the hatchet face who never smiles – points to a lavatory so I can give him a sample of urine in a little plastic bottle. He then places a filter into the bottle that will show, by five separate black lines, if I am positive or negative, for everything from cannabis to heroin. If two little black lines come up opposite each drug, then you're clear, if only one line appears, you've tested positive and will be up in front of the governor first thing in the morning.

An inmate three ahead of me tests positive for cannabis, and explodes when Mr Vessey says he'll be on report tomorrow. He storms out, mouthing expletives. Mr Vessey smiles. My own test comes up with only double lines, which is greeted with mock applause by those still waiting in the queue.

'And pour your piss down the drain, Archer,' says Mr Vessey.

'If you leave it hanging around, this lot would happily sell it to the *News of the World*.'

12 noon

Lunch. I'm joined by Brian (chapel orderly and organist). He was convicted of conspiracy to defraud an ostrich farming company of seven million pounds. His barrister convinced him that if he pleaded not guilty, a trial could take ten months, and if he were then found guilty he might end up with a six- or seven-year sentence. He advised Brian to plead guilty to a lesser charge, so that he would be sentenced to less than four years. He took the advice, and was sentenced to three years ten months. His two co-defendants decided on a trial and the jury found them not guilty. Brian considers that pleading guilty was the biggest mistake of his life.

2.00 pm

Write for two hours.

6.30 pm

I go to chapel to be joined by five other prisoners. Brian the ostrich man is playing the organ (very professionally). I take Holy Communion in memory of my mother, and can't help reflecting that it's my first sip of wine in three months. The vicar offers each of us a tiny plastic thimble of wine. It's only later that I work out why: some prisoners would attend the service just to drain the chalice.

The vicar, the Rev Johnson, is over seventy. A short, dapper man, he gives us a short, dapper sermon on why he is not quite sure about born-again Christians. We then pray for those Christians who were murdered while taking part in a church service in Pakistan.

Covering the wall behind the altar and part of the ceiling is a painting of the Last Supper. After the service, the vicar tells me that a former prisoner painted it, and each of the disciples was modelled on an inmate. He chuckles, 'Only Christ isn't a convict.'

DAY 103   MONDAY 29 OCTOBER 2001

6.11 am

I wake early and think about home. I have a little pottery model of the Old Vicarage on the table in front of me, along with a photograph of Mary and the boys, and another of a view of Parliament from our apartment in London; quite a contrast to the view from my little room on the north block. The sky is grey and threatening rain. That's the one thing I share with you.

8.15 am

Breakfast with Malcolm (fraud, chief librarian) and Roger (murder, twelve years so far). Malcolm is able to tell me more about the young man called Arnold who absconded last week. I recall him from his induction at SMU, a shy and nervous little creature. He was sharing a room with two of the most unpleasant men I've ever come across. One of them has been moved from prison to prison during the past seven months because of the disruption he causes wherever he goes, and the other is a heroin addict serving out the last months of his sentence. I have never given a moment's thought to absconding.

DAY 103

However, if I had to spend a single night with either of those men, I might have to reconsider my position.

8.30 am

Today I set myself the task of reorganizing the muddled and misleading notice board in the waiting room. Matthew and I spend the first thirty minutes taking down all thirty-seven notices, before deciding which are out of date, redundant or simply on the wrong notice board. Only sixteen survive. We then pin up five new neatly printed headings – drugs, education, leave, tagging and general information, before replacing the sixteen posters neatly in their correct columns. By lunchtime the waiting room is clean, thanks to Mr Clarke, and the notice board easy to understand, thanks to Matthew, although I think I've also earned my 25p an hour.

12 noon

I have to repeat that as far as prison food goes, NSC is outstanding. Wendy and Val (her assistant) set standards that I would not have thought possible in any institution that has only £1.27 per prisoner for three meals a day. Today I'm down for the pizza, but Wendy makes me try a spoonful of her lamb stew, because she doesn't approve of my being a VIP (vegetarian in prison). It's excellent, and perhaps next week I'll risk a couple of meat dishes.

2.30 pm

The turnover at NSC is continual. Last week fifteen inmates departed, one way or another: end of sentence – twelve, moved to another prison – two, absconded – one. So after only two

646

weeks, 20 per cent of the prison population has changed. Give me another month, and I'll be an old lag.

While I'm washing the teacups, Matthew tells me that his father has taken a turn for the worse, and the governor has pushed his compassionate leave forward by a day. He'll be off to Canterbury first thing in the morning, so he can be at his father's bedside for the next ten days. He doesn't complain about having to spend the ten nights in Canterbury Prison (B-cat), which can't be pleasant when your father is dying, and you don't have anyone to share your grief with.

4.30 pm

Another pile of letters awaits me when I return from work, among them missives from Chris de Burgh, Patrick Moore and Alan Coren. Alan's letter makes me laugh so much, rather than share snippets with you, I've decided to print it in full. (See overleaf.) All my life I have been graced with remarkable friends, who have tolerated my ups and downs, and this latest episode doesn't seem to have deterred them one iota.

5.00 pm

Tomorrow I'm going to the gym. I only write this to make sure I do.

6.00 pm

Write for two hours.

Alan Coren

---

26 October 2001

My dear Jeffrey:

Lots of forgivenesses to be begged. First off, forgive the typing, but not only is my longhand illegible, I should also be writing for some days, because I haven't picked up a pen for anything but cheques since about 1960. More important, try to forgive the fact that I haven't written before, but the truth is that I should so much have preferred to chat to you face to face (albeit chained to a radiator, or whatever the social protocols required) than to engage in the one-sided conversation of letters, so --- as you probably know --- I kept trying to get a visit, and kept being turned down. Most important of all, forgive me for not trying to spring you: I have spent a small fortune on grapnels, ropes, bolt-cutters, fake number-plates, one-way tickets to Sao Paolo, and drinks for large men from the Mile End Road with busted conks and tattooed knuckles, but whenever I managed to put all these elements together, there was always a clear night and a full moon.

Anyway, I gather from your office that it might now be possible to arrange a visit, once I and they have filled in all sorts of bumf, and you have been given enough notice to stick a jeroboam of Krug on ice and slip into a brocade dressing-gown and fez, so I shall set that in train forthwith --- if, of couurse, you agree. You are, by the way, bloody lucky not to be in that office now, these are bad days to be living at the top of a tall building next to MI6 and opposite the H of C --- and I speak as one who knows, having, as you'll spot from the letterhead, recently moved to a house in Regent's Park; where, from my top-floor study window as I type, I can see the Regent's Park Mosque 500 metres to my right, and the American Ambassador's residence 500 metres to my left. I am ground bloody zero right here: every time His Excellency's helicopter trrobs in, we rush down to the cellar. Could by anybody, or anything. Since even I don't know where Freiston is, I rather doubt that Osama bin Laden could find it, and you are further fortunate in the fact that, because every envelope to the clink is doubtless slit open, poked about in and generally vetted to the last square millimetre, if anybody's going to get anthrax, it won't be you.

Life goes on in London as normal: Anne and I have grown used to wearing our gas-masks in bed, though it's still a bit of a bugger waking up in the night and unthinkingly reaching for a bedside drink, so there's more nocturnal tumble-drying going on than there used to be. Giles and Victoria wish to be remembered to you, and want you to know that they're fine, and settling down well with their foster parents in Timbuktu, where they tell me they have made lots of new friends among the other evacuees, although HP sauce is proving dificult to find. Your beloved Conservative Party has elected a new leader, who may be seen every day at the doors of the Commons handing out his business cards to MPs and officials who would otherwise think we was someone who had turned up to flog them personal pension schemes.

2

Are you writing a book about chokey? *FF 8282* would make a terrific title, and since I am only one of countless hacks who envy you the opportunity to scribble away unencumbered by all the distractions that stop the rest of us from knocking out *Finnegan's Remembrance of War & Punishment*, I would, if I were you, seriously consider not going ahead with your appeal: giving up the chance of another couple of years at the typewriter could cost you millions.

All right --- if we must --- let's be serious for a moment: do you need anything, is there anything I can do, anyone I can see for you, all that? I know that you have truckloads of closer --- and far more influential --- friends than I, but because it's always on the cards that there may just be something you need that no-one else can come up with, I want you to know that I should do my very best to sort it out.

But if nothing else, do drop me the briefest of notes to let me know whether or not you'd like a visit. If you'd rather be left in peace, I should of course, understand. But it would be nice to meet for the odd laugh --- as if there could be any other kind of laugh, these days.

Anne joins me in sending you our very warmest wishes, Jeffrey. Bear up!

Yours ever,

Alan

DAY 103

8.15 pm

I sign in for roll-call. From tomorrow, as I will have completed my two weeks' induction, I need only sign in at 11 am, 4 pm and 8.15 pm. Because I'll be at work, in future, 8.15 pm will be the one time I have to appear in person. Doug says I will feel the difference immediately.

DAY 104   TUESDAY 30 OCTOBER 2001

6.01 am

Write for two hours. I've now completed 250,000 words since being incarcerated. Perhaps Alan Coren is right.

8.15 am

Ten new prisoners arrived yesterday. They will be seeing the doctor straight after breakfast before coming to SMU to be given their induction pack, and then be interviewed by the labour board. One by one they make an appearance. Some are cocky, know it all, seen it all, nothing to learn, while others are nervous and anxious, and full of desperate questions.

And then there's Michael Keane (lifer, fourteen years so far, aged thirty-nine).

Those of you who've been paying attention for the past 250,000 words will recall my twenty days at Belmarsh, where I met William Keane on the tea-bag chain gang. His brother Michael has the same Irish charm, wit and love of literature, but never forget that all seven Keane brothers have been in jail at the same time, costing the taxpayer a million pounds a year. Michael passes on William's best wishes, and adds that he heard

DAY 104

today that his sister has just been released from Holloway after serving nine months for a string of credit-card crimes. Michael is hoping for parole in March, and if Irish charm were enough, he'd make it, but unfortunately, the decision has to be ratified by the Home Office, who will only read his files, and never see him face to face. His fame among the Keanes is legendary, because when he was at Belmarsh – a high-security prison – he got as far as the first outer gate while emptying dustbins. The furthest anyone has managed while trying to escape from hell.

10.20 am

A scruffy, unshaven prisoner called Potts checks into SMU to confirm that he has a meeting with his solicitor this afternoon. I check my day sheet to see that his lawyer is booked in for three o'clock. Potts, who has just come off a three-hour shift in the kitchen, smiles.

'See you at three, Jeff.'

11.40 am

All ten inductees have been seen by the labour board, and are fixed up with jobs on the farm, in the kitchen or at the officers' mess. One, Kevin (six years for avoiding paying VAT), has opted for full-time education as he's in his final year of a law degree.

12 noon

Over lunch, Doug asks me if I've put in my takeaway order for the weekend. I realize I'm being set up, but happily play along. He then tells me the story of two previous inmates, Bruce and Roy, who were partners in crime.

Bruce quickly discovered that it was not only easy to abscond from NSC, but equally straightforward to return unobserved. So one night, he walked the six miles to Boston, purchased some fish and chips, stole a bicycle, rode back, hid the bike on the farm and went to bed. Thus began a thriving enterprise known as 'weekend orders'. His room-mate Roy would spend the week taking orders from the other prisoners for supper on Saturday night (the last meal every day is at five o'clock, so you can be a bit peckish by nine). Armed with the orders, Bruce would then cycle into Boston immediately after the eight-fifteen roll-call, visit the local fish and chip shop, McDonalds or KFC – not to mention the pub – and arrive back within the hour so he could drop off his orders and still be seen roaming round the corridors long before the 10 pm roll-call.

This dot-con service ran successfully for several months, in the best traditions of free enterprise. Unfortunately, there's always some dissatisfied customer who will grass, and one night two officers caught Bruce about a mile away from the prison, laden with food and drink. He was transferred to a C-cat the following morning. His room-mate Roy, aware it would only be a matter of days before he was implicated, absconded with all the cash and hasn't been seen since.

2.50 pm

Potts returns to SMU for the meeting with his solicitor. He has shaved, washed his hair and is wearing a clean, well-ironed shirt, and his shoes are shining. I have the unenviable task of telling him that his solicitor rang a few moments ago to cancel the appointment.

This is a message to all solicitors and barristers who deal with the incarcerated: your visit can be the most important event of the week, if not the month, so don't cancel lightly. Potts walks dejectedly back down the path, head bowed.

4.00 pm

Mr Hocking drops into SMU. He tells me that the whole of spur four on the north block (nine rooms) has just been searched, because an officer thought he heard a mobile phone ringing. Possession of a mobile phone is an offence that will ensure you are sent back to a C-cat the same day.

4.30 pm

Write for two hours, feel exhausted, but at least I no longer have to report for the 10 pm roll-call.

7.00 pm

I join Doug and Clive at the hospital. Clive tells me that the officers found nothing during this morning's search. Often 'hearing a mobile phone' is just an excuse to carry one out when they are actually trying to find something else. Doug chips in, 'Truth is, they were looking for another camera which the press have recently smuggled in. They even know the name of the prisoner involved, and as he's due to be released on Friday, they want to be sure he doesn't leave with a role of photos that would embarrass them.'

11.40 pm

Potts is rushed to Boston Hospital, having taken an overdose.

DAY 105 WEDNESDAY 31 OCTOBER 2001

6.23 am

I wake thinking about Potts. He reminds me how awful being incarcerated is, and why inmates forever live in hope. I later discover that Potts will be moved to Sudbury Prison, so that he can be near his wife and family. I know how he feels. I'm still waiting to hear from Spring Hill.

8.30 am

This morning we have a risk-assessment board. Four prisoners who are applying for early release on tag (HCD) are to appear before the deputy governor, Mr Leighton, and the senior probation officer, Mr Simpson. If a candidate has an unblemished record while in jail – never been put on a charge, never been involved with drugs – he is in with a chance. But the prime consideration is whether the prisoner is likely to reoffend. So if the inmate is in for burglary or credit-card fraud, his chances aren't that good.

During the next hour I take each of the four prisoners up to face the board. They leave twenty minutes later, two with smiles on their faces who want to shake me by the hand, and two who

DAY 105

barge past me, effing and blinding anyone who crosses their path.

11.11 am

Mr New has received a fax from Spring Hill, requesting three more documents and five more questions answered: a clearance release from the hospital to confirm I'm fit and well and not on any medication; my records from Belmarsh and Wayland to show I have never been put on report; and confirmation from NSC that I have not been put on a charge since I've been here. They also want to know if I intend to appeal against my sentence, and if so, will I be appearing in court. Mr New looks surprised when I say that I won't. There are two reasons for my decision. I never wish to spend another minute of my life in Belmarsh, which is where they transfer you if you are due to appear at the High Court, and I'm damned if I'll put my wife through the ordeal of facing the press outside the court as she arrives and departs.

11.30 am

At the hospital, sister checks over the forms from Spring Hill. Linda ticks all the little boxes and confirms I am remarkably fit – for my age, cheeky lady.

12 noon

Over lunch, Doug warns me that it still might be a couple of months before Spring Hill have a vacancy because it's the most popular prison in Britain, and in any case, they may not enjoy the attendant publicity that I would attract. Bell (a gym orderly) leans across and informs me, 'It's the best nick I've ever been to. I only moved here to be closer to my wife.'

3.52 pm

Mr New reappears clutching my blameless record from Belmarsh and Wayland.

At 4.04 he faxes Spring Hill with the eight pages they requested. He receives confirmation that they arrived at 4.09 pm. I'll keep you informed.

4.15 pm

The senior Listener, Brian (conspiracy to defraud an ostrich company), turns up at SMU. He asks if the backs of prisoners' identity cards can be redesigned, as they currently advertise the Samaritans and Crimestoppers. Brian points out that as no prisoner can dial an 0800 number the space would be better used informing new arrivals about the Listeners' scheme. He has a point.

5.00 pm

Write for two hours.

7.00 pm

Doug tells me that the governing governor, Mr Lewis, dropped into the hospital today as he'd read in the *News of the World* that I keep a secret store of chocolate biscuits in the fridge.

'Quite right,' Doug informed him, 'Jeffrey buys them from

657

the canteen every Thursday, and leaves a packet here for both of us which we have with my coffee and his Bovril.'

A week ago I told Linda that you could buy a jar of Marmite from the canteen, but not Bovril, which I much prefer. The following day a jar of Bovril appeared.

Prisoners break rules all the time, often without realizing it. Officers have to turn a blind eye; otherwise everyone would be on a charge every day of the week, and the prison service would grind to a halt. Of course there's a difference between Bovril and beer, between having an extra towel and a mobile phone, or a hardback book and a tea bag full of heroin. Most officers accept this and use their common sense.

8.26 pm

Two officers, Mr Spencer and Mr Hayes, join us in the hospital for a coffee break. We learn that eleven new prisoners came in this evening, and only seven will be released tomorrow, so the prison is nearly full. They also add that another prisoner has been placed in the segregation cell overnight and will be up in front of the governor tomorrow. He's likely to be on his way back to Lincoln Prison. It appears that a camera was found in his room, the third one in the past ten days. They also know which newspaper is involved.

DAY 106   THURSDAY 1 NOVEMBER 2001

6.19 am

In prison, you don't think about what can be achieved long term; all thoughts are short term. When is the next canteen so I can buy another phonecard? Can I change my job? Will I be enhanced? Can I move into a single room? At the moment the only thought on my mind is, can I get to Spring Hill? Not when, can. In prison *when* will only happens after *can* has been achieved.

8.30 am

Fifteen new prisoners in today, among them a Major Willis, who is sixty-four. I look forward to finding out what he's been up to.

Willis, Clarke (the cleaner) and myself do not *have* to work because we're all over sixty. But Willis makes it clear he's looking for a job, and the labour board allocate him to works (engineering).

DAY 106

9.30 am

Mr Hocking, the security officer, drops in for a cup of tea. He tells me that Braithwaite, who was found to have a camera in his room, is now on his way back to Lincoln. The newspaper involved was the *Mail on Sunday*. All the relevant papers have been sent to the local police, as an offence of aiding and abetting a prisoner may have been committed.

12.30 pm

I call Alison. Mary has been invited to Margaret and Denis Thatcher's golden wedding anniversary on 13 December. James will be making the long journey to visit me on Saturday.

7.15 pm

Doug tells me that his contact in the administration office at Spring Hill isn't sure if they'll have me. I'll bet that Doug finds out my fate long before any of the officers at NSC.

8.15 pm

A fight breaks out on spur six. It involves a tragic young man, who has been a heroin addict since the age of fourteen. He is due to be released tomorrow morning. Leaving ceremonies are common enough in prison, and an inmate's popularity can be gauged by his fellow prisoners' farewells on the night before he departs. This particular prisoner had a bucket of shit poured over his head, and his release papers burned in front of him. There's a lookout posted at the end of the spur, and the nearest officer is in the unit office at the far end of the corridor, reading a paper, so you can be sure the humiliation will continue until he begins his right rounds.

When I return to the hospital, I tell Doug the name of the prisoner involved. He expresses no surprise, and simply adds, 'That boy won't see the other side of forty.'

10.30 pm

Returning to my room, I pass Alan (selling stolen goods) in the corridor. He asks if he can leave a small wooden rocking horse in my room, as his is a little overcrowded with two inmates. He paid £20 for the toy (a postal order sent by someone on the outside to the wife of the prisoner who made it). It's a gift for his fourteen month old grandson.

As I write this diary, in front of me are several cards from well-wishers, a pottery model of the Old Vicarage, a photo of Mary and the boys and now a rocking horse.

Alan is due to be released in two weeks' time, and when he leaves, no excrement will be poured over his head. The prisoners will line up to shake hands with this thoroughly decent man.

DAY 107   FRIDAY 2 NOVEMBER 2001

6.19 am

Absconding is a D-cat phenomenon. It's almost impossible to escape from an A- or B-cat prison, and extremely difficult to do so even from a C-cat (Wayland, for example). In order for a prisoner to become eligible for D-cat status, he or she must be judged likely to complete their sentence without attempting to abscond. In practice, prisons are so overcrowded that C-cat establishments, which are desperate to empty their cells, often clear out prisoners who quite simply should not be sent to an open prison.

One intake of eleven such prisoners arrived from Lincoln last year and was down to seven before the final roll-call that night. I discovered today that because of the chronic shortage of staff, there are only five officers on duty at night, and two of them are on overtime, so absconding isn't too difficult.

Prisoners abscond for a hundred and one different reasons, but mainly because of outside family pressures: a wife who is having an affair, a partner who takes the children away or a death in the family that doesn't fulfil the criteria for compassionate leave. The true irony is that these prisoners are the ones mostly likely to be apprehended, because the first place they turn up at is the family abode and there waiting for them on the doorstep are a couple of local bobbies who then return them to closed conditions and a longer sentence.

Before I was sent to prison I would have said, 'Quite right, too, it's no more than they deserve.' However, after 106 days of an intense learning curve I now realize that each individual has to be judged on his own merits. I accept that they have to be punished, but it rarely falls neatly into black or white territory.

Then there's a completely different category of absconders – foreigners. They simply wish to get back to their country, aware that the British police have neither the time nor the resources to go looking for them.

For every Ronnie Biggs there are a hundred Ronnie Smalls.

Mr New tells me about two absconders who are part of North Sea Camp folklore. Some years ago Boston held a marathon in aid of a local cancer charity, and the selected route took the competitors across a public footpath running along the east side of the prison. One prisoner slipped out of the gym in his running kit, joined the passing athletes and has never been seen since.

The second story concerns a prisoner who had to make a court appearance on a second charge, while serving a six-year sentence for a previous conviction. When the jury returned to deliver their verdict, his guards were waiting for him downstairs in the cells. The jury delivered a verdict of not guilty on the second charge. The judge pronounced, 'You are free to leave the court.' And that's exactly what he did.

The reason I raise this subject is because Potts, who's had a bad week, absconded yesterday following his suicide attempt. It turns out that the final straw concerned the custody of his children – the subject he was going to raise with his solicitor.

DAY 107

8.15 am

After the frantic rush of events following the arrival of fifteen new prisoners yesterday, today is comparatively quiet. Allen (cannabis, six years) drops in to tell me that his weekend leave forms still haven't been processed, and it's this weekend. The duty officer Mr Hayes deals with it. Thomas (in charge of a gun that discharged) says his town visit form has not been authorized and asks how much longer he will have to wait to find out if he will be allowed out. Mr Hayes deals with it. Merry (embezzlement) arrives with still no word as to when Group 4 will be transporting him to Sudbury so that he can be nearer his family. Mr Hayes deals with it.

Mr Hayes is an unusual officer. He's not frightened of making decisions and standing by them. He also makes his own tea. When I asked him why, he simply replied, 'You're not here to serve me, but to complete your sentence. I don't need to be waited on.'

10.00 am

Mr Hocking and I agree it would be better for the press to take a photograph and then go away, leaving his little band of security officers to get on with their job.

I walk out of the SMU building and deliberately stop to chat to Peter (lifer, arson), who is sweeping leaves from the path. He keeps his back to the cameras. Three minutes later I return to the building and, true to form, the photographers all disappear.

12 noon

Major Willis comes to SMU to hand back his red induction folder. He tells me that he's sixty-four, first offence, GBH,

664

sentence one year, and that he'll be released in March. He was a major in the army, and after retiring, fell in love with a young Nigerian girl (a prostitute), whom he later married. She soon began to bully him, and to spend what little money he had. One day he could take no more, blew his top and stuck a kitchen knife in her. She reported him to the police. He will end up doing ten months (if he gets his tag), six of them at NSC.

He's puzzled as to why I got four years.

2.30 pm

A quiet afternoon. A fleeting visit from Mr Berlyn to check that I'm wearing a prison shirt as the press keep reporting that mine isn't regulation issue. He checks the blue and white HMP label, and leaves, satisfied.

9.00 pm

Fall asleep in front of the TV. Doug says I snore. I'm writing five hours a day, on top of a thirty-four-hour week, and I'm not even going to the gym.

DAY 108   SATURDAY 3 NOVEMBER 2001

I've written several times about the boredom of weekends, but something takes place today that turns the normal torpor into frantic activity.

8.50 am

The photographers have returned. They either missed getting a good shot yesterday, or work for the Sundays who want a 'today pic'. I agree with the deputy governor, Mr Berlyn, to do another walk on, walk off, in order to get rid of them once and for all. He seems grateful.

2.00 pm

I'm expecting a visit from my son James. When I enter the visitors' room I can't see him, but then spot someone waving at me. It turns out to be my son. He's grown a beard. I hate it, and tell him so, which is a bit rough, as he's just travelled 120 miles to see me.

James tells me that my legal team are concentrating their efforts on my appeal. Mr and Mrs Barker have confirmed that they heard the judge discussing me at a dinner party over a year before I was arrested. This could change my appeal.

5.00 pm

Doug and I are having tea in the hospital when Clive strolls in to announce that he's moving to another room.

'Why?' I ask, when he has the largest space in the prison.

'Because they're fitting electrics into all the other rooms.' I can't believe he'd give up his large abode in exchange for a TV. 'If you want to move in, Jeffrey, you'd better come over to the south block now.' We all go off in search of the duty officer, who approves the move. I spend the next two hours, assisted by Alan (selling stolen goods), transferring all my possessions from the north block to the south, while Clive moves into a little single room at the other end of the corridor.

I am now lodged in a room twenty-one by sixteen feet. Most prisoners assume I've paid Clive some vast sum of money to move out and make way for me, whereas the truth is that Clive wanted out. There is only one disadvantage. There always has to be a disadvantage. My new abode is next to the TV room, but as that's turned off at eleven each night, and I rarely leave Doug in the hospital before 10.30 pm, I don't think it will be a real problem.

I now have an interesting job, a better room, edible food and £8.50 a week. What more could a man ask for?

DAY 109   SUNDAY 4 NOVEMBER 2001

6.19 am

Write for two hours before I join Doug at the hospital. We watch David Frost, whose guests include Northern Ireland's Chief Constable of the Police Service Sir Ronnie Flanagan. While discussing the morning papers, Sir Ronnie says that it's an infringement of my privacy that the tabloid press are taking pictures of me while I'm in jail. The pictures are fine, but the articles border on the farcical.

A security officer later points out that two tabloids have by-lines attributed to women, and there hasn't been a female journalist or photographer seen by anyone at NSC during the past three weeks.

12 noon

Over lunch I sit opposite an inmate called Andy, who is a rare phenomenon in any jail as he previously served ten years – as a prison officer. He is now doing a seven-year sentence, having pleaded guilty to smuggling drugs into prison for an inmate. Andy tells me that the only reason he did so was because the inmate in question was threatening to have his daughter beaten up. She was married to an ex-prisoner.

'Did you fall for that one, Jeffrey?' I hear you ask. Yes, I did.

The police presented irrefutable evidence to the jury showing that Andy's daughter had been threatened, and asked the judge to take this into consideration when he passed sentence. Although Andy claims he didn't know what was in the packages, the final one he smuggled in, a box of Cadbury's Quality Street, contained four grams of pure heroin.

Had it been cannabis, he might have been sentenced to a year or eighteen months. If he hadn't confessed, he might have got away with a suspension. He tells me that he knew he would eventually be caught, and once he was called in for questioning, he wanted to get the whole thing off his chest.

Andy was initially sent to HMP Gartree (B-cat), with a new identity and a different offence on his charge sheet. He had to be moved the moment he was recognized by an old lag. From there he went to Swalesdale, where he lasted twenty-four hours. He was then moved on to Elmsley, a sex offenders' prison, where he lived on the same landing as Roy Whiting, who was convicted of the murder of Sarah Payne. Once he'd earned his D-cat, Andy came to NSC, where he'll complete his sentence.

The only other comment he makes, which I've heard repeated again and again and therefore consider worthy of mention, is, 'sex offenders live in far better conditions than any other prisoners.'

DAY 110   MONDAY 5 NOVEMBER 2001

8.28 am

When I was an MP I often heard the sentiment expressed that life should mean life. I am reminded of this because we have a lifers' board meeting at SMU today.

There are nine lifers at NSC and you can be fairly confident that if they've reached a D-cat, they won't consider absconding. In truth, they're all fairly harmless. Two of them go out each day to work in an old people's home, one in a library in Boston and another for the local Oxfam shop.

Linda, their probation officer, joins us for coffee during the morning break. She adds to the research I've pieced together over the past three months. I began my prison life at Belmarsh on a spur with twenty-three murderers. Lifers range from cold-blooded killers like Denis Nielsen, who pleaded guilty to murdering thirteen victims, down to Chris, who killed his wife in a fit of rage after finding her in bed with another man; he's already spent fourteen years regretting his loss of temper. Nielsen began his sentence, and will end it, in the highest security A-category facility. He is currently locked up in a SSU (a special security unit), a sort of prison within a prison. When he moves anywhere within the prison, he is always accompanied by at least two officers and a dog, and he is searched every time he

670

leaves his cell or returns to it. At night, he places all his clothes outside the cell door, and an officer hands them back to him the following morning. Nielsen told PO New on several occasions that it would have been better for everyone if they'd hanged him.

Now that the IRA terrorists are no longer locked up on the mainland, of the 1,800 murderers in custody, there are currently only seven SSU inmates.

Now Chris, who killed his wife, is at the other end of the scale. He's reached D-cat status after eleven years, and works in the kitchens. He therefore has access to several instruments with which he could kill or maim. Only yesterday, I watched him chopping up some meat – rather efficiently. He hopes that the parole board will agree to release him in eighteen months' time. During the past eleven years, he has moved from A-cat to D-cat via seventeen jails, three of them in one weekend when he was driven to Preston, Swalesdale and Whitemoor, only to find each time that they didn't have a cell for him.

All nine lifers at NSC will be interviewed today, so further reports can be sent to the Home Office to help decide if they are ready to return to the outside world. The Home Office will make the final decision; they are traditionally rather conservative and accept about 60 per cent of the board's recommendations. The board convenes at 9 am when Linda, the lifers' probation officer, is joined by the deputy governor, Mr Berlyn, a psychiatrist called Christine and the lifers' prison officer.

The first prisoner in front of the board is Peter, who set fire to a police station. He's so far served thirty-one years, and frankly is now a great helpless hunk of a man who has become so institutionalized that the parole board will probably have to transfer him straight to an old-peoples' home. Peter told me he has to serve at least another eighteen months before the board would be willing to consider his case. I don't think he'll ever be released, other than in a coffin.

The next to come in front of the board is Leon.

The biggest problem lifers face is their prison records. For the first ten years of their sentences, they can see no light at the end of the tunnel, so the threat of another twenty-eight days added to their sentence is hardly a deterrent. After ten years, Linda says there is often a sea change in a lifer's attitude that coincides with their move to a B-cat and then again when they reach a C-cat. This is even more pronounced when they finally arrive at a D-cat and can suddenly believe release is possible.

By the way, it's almost unknown for a lifer to abscond. Not only would they be returned to an A-cat closed prison, but its possible they never would be considered for parole again.

However, most of the lifers being interviewed today have led a fairly blameless existence for the past five years, although there are often scars, missing teeth and broken bones to remind them of their first ten years in an A-cat.

During the day, each of them goes meekly in to face the board. No swagger, no swearing, no attitude; that alone could set them back another year.

Leon is followed by Michael, then Chris, Roger, Bob, John, John and John (a coincidence not acceptable in a novel). At the end of the day, Linda comes out exhausted. By the way, they all adore her. She not only knows their life histories to the minutest detail, but also treats them as human beings.

4.00 pm

Only one other incident of note today – the appearance at SMU of a man who killed a woman in a road accident and was sentenced to three years for dangerous driving. He's a mild-mannered chap who asked me for help with his book on Kurdistan. Mr New tells me that he is going to be transferred to another jail. The husband of his victim lives in Boston and, as the inmate is coming up for his first town visit, the victim's husband has objected on the grounds that he might come across him in his daily life.

The inmate joins me after his meeting with Mr New. He's philosophical about the decision. He accepts that the victim's family have every right to ask for him to be moved. He's so clearly racked with guilt, and seems destined to relive this terrible incident for the rest of his life, that I find myself trying to comfort him. In truth, he's a different kind of lifer.

10.00 pm

It must be Guy Fawkes Day, because from my little window I can see fireworks exploding over Boston.

DAY 111   TUESDAY 6 NOVEMBER 2001

5.49 am

The big news in the camp today is that from 1 November, NSC is to become a resettlement prison. (No doubt you will have noticed that it's 6 November.) The change of status could spell survival for NSC, which has been under threat of closure for several years.

Resettlement means quite simply that once a prisoner has reached his FLED (facility licence eligibility date) – in my case July next year – he can take a job outside the prison working for fifty-five hours a week, not including travelling time. The whole atmosphere of the prison will change when inmates are translated into outmates. They will leave the prison every morning between seven and eight, and not return until seven in the evening.

Prisoners will be able to earn £150 to £200 a week, just as Clive does as a line manager for Exotic Foods. It will be interesting to see how quickly NSC implements the new Home Office directive.

8.30 am

Seven new arrivals at NSC today, who complete their induction talk and labour board by 11.21 am. My job as SMU orderly is now running smoothly, although Matthew tells me that an officer said that for the first week I made the worst cup of tea of any orderly in history. But now that I've worked out how to avoid tea leaves ending up in the mug, I need a fresh challenge.

2.30 pm

Mr New warns me that the prison is reaching full capacity, and they might have to put a second bed in my room. Not that they want anyone to share with me, after the *News of the World* covered three pages with the life history of my last unfortunate cell-mate. It's simply a gesture to prove to other inmates that my spacious abode is not a single dwelling.

5.00 pm

I write, or to be more accurate, work on the sixth draft of my latest novel *Sons of Fortune*.

7.00 pm

Doug and I watch Channel 4 news. Fighting breaks out in Stormont during David Trimble's press conference following his reappointment as First Minister. If what I am witnessing on television were to take place at NSC, they would all lose their privileges and be sent back to closed conditions.

Doug has a natural gift of timing, and waits until the end of the news before he drops his bombshell. The monthly prison committee meeting – made up in equal numbers of staff and prisoners – is to have its next get-together on Friday. The governor is chairman, and among the five prison representatives are Doug and Clive; two men who understand power, however limited. Doug tells me that the main item on the agenda will be resettlement, and he intends to apply to work at his haulage company in Cambridgeshire. His application fulfils the recommended criteria, as March is within the fifty-five-mile radius. It is also the job he will return to once he's released, relieving his wife of the pressure of running the company while he's been locked up.

But now for the consequences. His job as hospital orderly – the most sought-after position in the prison – will become available. He makes it clear that if I want the job, he will happily make a recommendation to Linda, who has already hinted that such an appointment would meet with her approval. This would mean my moving into the hospital, and although I'd be working seven days a week, there is an added advantage of a pay rise of £3.20 so, with my personal income of £10, I'd have over £20 a week to spend in the canteen.

But the biggest luxury of all would be sleeping in the hospital, which has an en-suite bathroom, a sixteen-inch TV and a fridge. It's too much to hope for, and might even tempt me to stay at NSC – well, at least until my FLED.

DAY 112   WEDNESDAY 7 NOVEMBER 2001

5.58 am

They call him Mick the Key. He arrived yesterday, and if he
hadn't been turned down for a job in the kitchens, I might
never have heard his story. Even now I'm not sure how much of
it I believe.

Originally sentenced to two years for breaking and entering, Mick is now serving his ninth year. They have only risked
moving him to a D-cat for his last twelve weeks. The reason is
simple. Mick likes escaping, or assisting others to escape, and he
has one particular gift that aids him in this enterprise. He only
needs to look at a key once and he can reproduce it. He first
commits the shape to memory, then draws the outline on a piece
of paper, before transferring that onto a bar of prison soap – the
first impression of the key. The next stage is to reproduce the
image in plastic, using prison knives or forks. He then covers
the newly minted key with thick paint he obtains from the
works department. The next day he has a key.

During his years in prison, Mick has been able to open not
only his own cell door, but also anyone else's. In fact, while he
was at Whitemoor, they closed the prison for twenty-four hours
because they had to change the locks on all 500 cells.

Getting out of prison is only half the enjoyment, this

charming Irishman tells me, 'Getting into kitchens, stores or even the governor's office adds to the quality of one's life. In fact,' he concludes, 'my greatest challenge was opening the hospital drugs cabinet in under an hour.' On that occasion, the officers knew who was responsible, but as nothing was missing (Mick says he's never taken a drug in his life), they could only charge him 'on suspicion', and were later unable to make the charge stick.

Some of the prison keys are too large and complicated to reproduce inside, so, undaunted, Mick joined the art class. He drew pictures of the skylines of New York, Dallas and Chicago before sending them home to his brother. It was some weeks before the innocent art teacher caught on. The security staff intercepted a package of keys brought into the prison by his sister. What a useful fellow Mick would have been in Colditz.

Mick tells me that he hopes to get a job in the kitchen, where he intends to be a good boy, as he wants to be released in twelve weeks' time.

'In any case,' he adds, 'it will do my reputation no good to escape from an open prison.'

The labour board turned down Mick's application to work in the kitchen; after all, there are several cupboards, cool rooms and fridges, all of which are locked, and for him, that would be too much of a temptation. He leaves SMU with a grin on his face.

'They've put me on the farm,' he declares. 'They're not worried about me breaking into a pigsty. By the way, Jeff, if you ever need to get into the governor's office and have a look at your files, just let me know.'

10.00 am

An extra bed has appeared in my room, because two of the spurs are temporarily out of service while they're being fitted for TVs. I found out today that prisoners are charged £1 a week for the hire of their TVs, and NSC will make an annual profit of £10,000 on this enterprise. At Wayland, I'm told it was £30,000. Free enterprise at its best. Still, the point of this entry is to let you know that I will soon be sharing my room with another prisoner.

2.40 pm

At Mr New's request, I join him in his office. He's just had a call from his opposite number at Spring Hill, who asked if I was aware that if transferred I would have to share a room.

'Yes,' I reply.

'And can they confirm that the principal reason for seeking a transfer is the inconvenience to your family of having a 250-mile round trip to visit you?'

'Yes,' I reply.

Mr New nods. 'I anticipated your answers. Although a decision has not yet been made, the first vacancy wouldn't be until 28 November.'

Suddenly it's crunch time. Would I rather stay at NSC as the hospital orderly, with my own room, TV, bathroom and fridge? Or move to Spring Hill and be nearer my family and friends? I'll need to discuss the problem with Mary.

5.00 pm

I return to my room to do a couple of hours writing; so far, no other occupant has appeared to claim the second bed.

DAY 112

6.42 pm

My new room-mate arrives, accompanied by two friends. His name is Eamon, and he seems pleasant enough. I leave him to settle in.

When I stroll into the hospital, Clive has a large grin on his face. He spent eleven months in that room without ever having to share it for one night. I couldn't even manage eleven days.

DAY 113   THURSDAY 8 NOVEMBER 2001

8.15 am

Breakfast. Wendy, the officer in charge of the kitchen, needs three new workers from this morning's labour board.

'But only yesterday you told me that you were overstaffed.'

'True,' she replies, hands on hips, 'but that was yesterday, and I had to sack three of the blighters this morning.'

'Why?' I ask hopefully.

'I knew you'd ask,' she replies, 'and only because you're bound to find out sooner or later, I'll tell you. I set three of them plucking chickens yesterday morning, and last night two of the birds went missing. I don't know who stole them, but in my kitchen I dispense summary justice, so all three were sacked.'

9.30 am

Eight new prisoners arrive for induction today, including my room-mate Eamon. It seems that he worked in the kitchen at his last prison, but 'on the out' is a builder by trade. He's due for release in January, and wants to work outside during the winter months to toughen himself up. Sounds logical to me, so I recommend that he opts for the farm.

DAY 113

10.00 am

Eamon gets his preferred job. I also find three new kitchen workers for Wendy, and the labour board is drinking coffee by 10.39 am. I need a new challenge.

12 noon

Lunch. I sit next to the new visits orderly, who tells me that 'on the out' he was a hairdresser in Leicester. He charged £27.50, but while he's in prison, he'll happily cut my hair once a month for a phonecard. Another problem solved.

2.30 pm

A fax has just been received from Spring Hill, requesting my latest sentence plan, which cannot be updated until I've served twenty-eight days at NSC. Sentence plans make up a part of every prisoner's record, and are an important element when it comes to consideration for parole. Sentence planning boards are held almost every afternoon and conducted by Mr New and Mr Simpson. I am due before the board on 20 November. Mr New immediately brings it forward a week to 12 November – next Monday, which would be my twenty-ninth day at NSC, and promises to fax the result through to Spring Hill that afternoon. I'll be interested to see what excuse they'll come up with next.

3.30 pm

Mr Berlyn (deputy governor) drops in to grumble about the prison being full for the first time in years and say that I'm to blame.

'How come?' I ask.

'Because,' he explains, 'the *News of the World* described NSC as the cushiest jail in Britain, so now every prisoner who qualifies for a D-cat wants to be sent here. It's one of the reasons I hope they take you at Spring Hill,' he continues, 'then we can pass that dubious accolade on to them. By the way,' he adds, 'don't get your hopes up about an early move, because someone up above [prison slang for the Home Office] is out to stop you.'

4.00 pm

John (lifer, murder) arrives in SMU, accompanied by a very attractive lady whom he introduces as his partner. This has me puzzled. If John murdered his wife, and has been in prison for the past fourteen years, how can he have a partner?

5.00 pm

I return to my room and write for two hours, relieved that Eamon doesn't make an appearance. I'm not sure if it's because he's with his friends from Derby, or is excessively considerate. This morning he told me he didn't mind my switching the light on at six o'clock.

'I'm in the building trade,' he explained, 'so I'm used to getting up at four-thirty.'

I feel I should add that he doesn't smoke, doesn't swear and is always well mannered. I still haven't found out why he's in prison.

683

DAY 113

7.15 pm

I find Doug and Clive at the hospital, heads down, poring over the new resettlement directive in preparation for tomorrow's facility meeting. Doug is determined to be the first prisoner out of the blocks, and if that should happen, then I might become the hospital orderly overnight. For the first time I look at the hospital in a different light, thinking about what changes I would make.

DAY 114   FRIDAY 9 NOVEMBER 2001

6.00 am

Before I went to sleep last night, I studied the latest Lords reform
bill, as set out in *The Times* and *Telegraph* by Phil Webster and
George Jones, those papers' respective political editors.

When I entered the Commons in 1969 at the age of twenty-
nine, I think I was the first elected MP not to have been eligible
for national service.* I mention this because, having won a
by-election in Louth, Lincolnshire, I experienced six months of
a 'fag-end' session of which almost every member had served
not only in the armed forces, but also in the Second World War,
with half a dozen having done so in the First World War. On the
back benches generals, admirals and air marshals – who could
add MC, DSO and DFC to the letters MP – were in abundance.
At lunch in the members' Dining Room, you might sit next to
Sir Fitzroy McLean, who was parachuted into Yugoslavia to assist
Tito, or Airey Neave, who escaped from Colditz.

In 1970, when Ted Heath became Prime Minister, Malcolm
Rifkind, Kenneth Clarke and Norman Lamont joined me – a new
breed of politician who would, in time, replace the amateurs of

---

* A two-year period of compulsory service in one of the branches of the armed
forces, which ceased to apply for anyone born after 1940.

685

the past. I use the word 'amateur' with respect and admiration, for many of these men had no desire to hold high office, considering Parliament an extension of the armed forces that allowed them to continue to serve their country.

When I entered the Lords in 1992, the House consisted of hereditary peers, life peers and working peers (I fell into the latter category). Peter Carrington (who was Foreign Secretary under Margaret Thatcher) is an example of an hereditary peer, the late Yehudi Menuhin of a life peer who rarely attended the House – why should he? And John Wakeham was a working peer and my first leader – a Cabinet minister appointed to the Lords to do a job of work.

A strange way to make up a second chamber, you may feel, and certainly undemocratic but, for all its failings, while I sat on the back benches I came to respect the skills, dedication and service the country received for such a small outlay. On the other side of that undemocratic coin were hereditary peers, and even some life peers, who never attended the House from one year to the next, while others, who contributed almost nothing, attended every day to ensure they received their daily allowance and expenses.

8.00 am

I learn a little more about John's (lifer) love life over breakfast. It seems John met his partner some six years ago when he was ensconced at Hillgrove, a C-cat prison. She had driven a couple of John's friends over to visit him. At that time John would only have been allowed a visit once a fortnight. On learning that a woman he had never seen in his life was sitting in the car park, he suggested she should join them. For the next few months, Jan continued to drive John's friends to his fortnightly visit, but it wasn't long before she was coming on her own. This love affair developed in the most restrictive and unpromising circumstances. Now John is in a D-cat, Jan can visit him once a week. It's their intention to get married, should he be granted his parole in eighteen months' time.

As you can imagine they still have several obstacles to overcome. John is fifty-one, and has served twenty-three years, and Jan is forty-eight, divorced and with three children by her first marriage. At some time between now and next March, Jan has to tell her three children, twenty-four, twenty-two and fifteen, that she has fallen in love with a murderer, and intends to marry him once he's released.

11.00 am

My name is bellowed out over the tannoy, and I am ordered to report to reception. Those stentorian tones could only come from Sergeant Major Daff (Daffodil to the inmates). I have several parcels to sign for, most of them books kindly sent in by the public; I am allowed to take them away only if I promise they'll end up in the library; also, two T-shirts for gym use only (he winks) and a box of Belgian truffles sent by a lady from Manchester. Now the rule on sweets is clear. Prisoners cannot have them, as they may be full of drugs, so they are passed on to the children who attend the gym on Thursdays for special needs classes (explain that one). I suggest that not many seven year olds will fully appreciate Belgian truffles, but perhaps Mrs Daff might like them (they've been married for forty years).

'No,' he replies sharply, 'that could be construed as a bribe.' Mr Daff suggests they're put in the raffle for the Samaritans' Ball in Boston. I agree. I have for many years admired the work of the Samaritans, and in prison they have unquestionably saved countless young lives.

687

DAY 114

4.00 pm

When I return to my room, I find Eamon preparing to move out and join his friends from Derby in the eight-room dormitory, so I'll be back on my own again. I take advantage of the time he's packing his HMP plastic bag to discover why he's in prison.

It seems that on the Saturday night of last year's Cup Final, Eamon and his friends got drunk at their local pub. A friend appeared and told them he had been beaten up by a rival gang and needed some help 'to teach the bastards a lesson'. Off went Eamon and his drunken mates armed with pool cues and anything else they could lay their hands on. They chased the rival gang back to their cars in the municipal car park next to the Crown Court, and a fierce battle followed – all of which was recorded on CCTV.

Five of them were charged with violent disorder and pleaded not guilty – one of them a member of Derby County football team. Their solicitor plea-bargained for the charge to be downgraded to affray. One look at the CCTV footage and they quickly changed their plea to guilty. They were each given ten months, and if they're granted tagging, will be released after only twelve weeks (five months minus two months tagging). Incidentally, the gang member who enlisted their help was the first to hear the sirens, and escaped moments before the police arrived.

DAY 115   SATURDAY 10 NOVEMBER 2001

6.38 am

There isn't a day that goes by when I don't wish I wasn't here. I miss my freedom, I miss my friends and above all I miss Mary and the boys.

There isn't a day that goes by when I don't curse Mr Justice Potts for what everyone saw as his prejudicial summing up to the jury, and his apparent delight at handing out such a draconian sentence.

There isn't a day that goes by when I don't wonder why the police haven't arrested Angie Peppiatt for embezzlement.

There isn't a day that goes by when I don't question how I can be guilty of perverting the course of justice while Ted Francis is not; either we are both guilty or both innocent.

I have been in jail for 115 days, and my anger and despair finally surface after a visit by a young man called Derek.

Derek knocks quietly on my door, and I take a break from writing to deal with his simple request for an autograph on the back of a picture of the girlfriend who has stood by him. I ask him about his sentence (most prisoners go into great detail, even though they know I'm writing a diary). Derek is spending three months in jail for stealing from his employers after issuing a personal cheque he knew he hadn't the funds to cover. He spent a month in Lincoln Prison, which the old lags tell me is even worse than Belmarsh. He adds that the magistrate's 'short, sharp shock' has enabled him to witness a violent beating in the shower, the injecting of heroin and language that he had no idea any human being resorted to.

'But,' he adds before leaving, 'you've been an example to me. Your good manners, your cheeriness and willingness to listen to anyone else's problems, have surprised everyone here.'

I can't tell him that I have no choice. It's all an act. I am hopelessly unhappy, dejected and broken. I smile when I am at my lowest, I laugh when I see no humour, I help others when I need help myself. I am alone. If I were to show any sign, even for a moment, of what I'm going through, I would have to read the details in some tabloid the following day. Everything I do is only a phone call away from a friendly journalist with an open cheque book. I don't know where I have found the strength to maintain this facade and never break down in anyone's presence.

I will manage it, even if it's only to defeat my enemies who would love to see me crumble. I am helped by the hundreds of letters that pour in every week from ordinary, decent members of the public; I am helped by my friends who remain loyal; I am helped by the love and support of Mary, Will and James.

I have no thoughts of revenge, or even any hope of justice, but God knows I will not give in.

DAY 116   SUNDAY 11 NOVEMBER 2001

8.05 am

I'm five minutes late for breakfast. Mr Hayes, a thoughtful and decent officer, takes me to one side and asks if I could be on time in future because otherwise some prisoners will complain that I'm getting special treatment.

9.00 am

Doug is out on town leave so that he can visit his family in March, and Linda (hospital matron) asks me if I'll act as 'keeper of the pills'. You need three qualifications for this responsibility:

1) non-smoker,

2) never been involved with drugs,

3) be able to read and write.

In a prison of 172 inmates, only seven prisoners fulfil all three criteria.

10.00 am

I write for two hours.

DAY 116

12.10 pm

Lunch. I'm on time.

1.15 pm

The governing governor, Mr Lewis, drops in to see Linda.

'Glad to catch you,' he says to me. 'I've had a letter from "Disgusted, Bexhill on Sea". She wants to know why you have a private swimming pool and are driven home in your Rolls Royce every Friday to spend the weekend with your family. I have disillusioned her on the first two points, and added that you are now working both Saturday and Sunday in the hospital at a rate of 25p an hour.'

2.00 pm

Mary visits me. It's wonderful to see her, although she looks drawn and tired. She brings me up to date on all my legal problems, including details of all the money that disappeared during the period Angie Peppiatt was my secretary. We also discuss whether I should issue a writ against Baroness Nicholson for her accusation that I stole millions from the Kurds, and how it's possible for Ted Francis to be innocent when I was found guilty of the same charge. Once she's completed the file on Mrs Peppiatt, it will be handed over to the police.

We finally discuss the dilemma as to whether I should remain at NSC and take over as hospital orderly. We decide I should still apply for Spring Hill.

6.00 pm

I read the only Sunday papers I can lay my hands on, the *Observer* and the *News of the World*. One too far to the left for me, the other too far to the right.

7.00 pm

Doug returns from a day out with his family, and I hand back my responsibility as 'keeper of the pills'. He's convinced that they're lining me up for the hospital job just as soon as he's granted leave to do outside work, which would take him out of the prison five days a week. I tell him that both Mary and I still feel it would be better if I could transfer to Spring Hill.

10.30 pm

Back to my room. The communal TV next door is showing some vampire film at full volume. Amazed by what the body learns to tolerate, I finally fall asleep.

DAY 117   MONDAY 12 NOVEMBER 2001

8.50 am

As each day passes, I tell myself that the stories will dry up and this diary with it. Well, not today, because Simon has just walked into SMU.

Simon works in the officers' mess, and although I see him every day I have not yet made his acquaintance. He's visiting SMU to check on an application he submitted to visit his mother in Doncaster. He has, I fear, been dealing with an officer ironically known as 'action man'. After six weeks and several 'apps', Simon has still heard nothing. After I've promised to follow this up, I casually ask him why he's in prison.

'I abducted my son,' he replies.

I perk up. I've not come across an abduction before.

Simon pleaded guilty to abducting ('rescuing' in his words) his five-year-old son for forty-seven days. He whisked him off to Cyprus, via France, Germany, Yugoslavia and Turkey. He did so, he explains, because after he'd left his wife, he discovered that his son was being physically abused by both his ex-wife and her new partner, a police detective sergeant. The judge didn't believe his story, and sentenced him to four years, as a warning to other

694

fathers not to take the law into their own hands. Fair enough, and indeed I found myself nodding.

A year later, his wife's new partner (the detective sergeant) was arrested and charged with ABH (actual bodily harm), and received a three-year sentence for, among other things, breaking the little boy's arm. Simon immediately appealed and returned to court to face the same judge. He pleaded not only extenuating circumstances, but added 'I told you so', to which the judge replied, 'It doesn't alter the fact that you broke the law, so you will complete your sentence.'

Ah, I hear you say, but he could have reported the man to the police and the social services. You try reporting a detective sergeant to the police. And Simon has files stacked up in his room filled with dozens of complaints to the social services with replies bordering on the ludicrous, 'We have looked into the matter very carefully and have no reason to believe...' Simon had to sell his home to pay the £70,000 legal bills, and is now incarcerated in NSC, penniless, and with no knowledge of where his only child is. My heart goes out to this man.

Would you have done the same thing for your child? If the answer is yes, then you're a criminal.

11.00 am

A call for me over the tannoy to report to reception. Sergeant Major Daff is on duty. He is happy to release my drug-free radio. It's a Sony three-band, sensible, plain and workmanlike. It will do the job and one only needs to look at the sturdy object to know it's been sent by Mary.

695

DAY 117

2.30 pm

A quiet afternoon, so Matthew gives me a lecture on Herodotus. He is rather pleased with himself, because he's come across a passage in book four of the *Histories* that could be the first known reference to sniffing cannabis (hemp). I reproduce the translation in full:

> And now for the vapour-bath. On a framework made up of three sticks, meeting at the top, they stretch pieces of woollen cloth, taking care to get the jams as perfect as they can, and inside this little tent, they place a dish with red-hot stones on it. They then take some hemp seed, enter the tent and throw the seed onto the hot stones. It immediately begins to smoke, giving off a vapour unsurpassed by any vapour bath one could find in Greece. The Scythians enjoy the experience so much that they howl with pleasure.

3.40 pm

Mr New and Mr Simpson interview me for my sentence plan. All the boxes are filled in with 'No History' (N/H) for drugs, violence, past offences, drink or mental disorder. In the remaining boxes, the words 'Low Risk' are entered for abscond, reoffend and bullying. The final box has to be filled in by my personnel officer. Mr New is kind enough to commend my efforts at SMU and my relationship with other prisoners.

The document is then signed by both officers and faxed to Spring Hill at 4.07 pm, and is acknowledged as received at 4.09 pm. Watch this space.

DAY 118   TUESDAY 13 NOVEMBER 2001

5.51 am

Write for two hours.

8.30 am

There are no new inductees today and therefore no labour board. Mr New will not be on duty until one o'clock, so Matthew and I have a quiet morning. He gives me a lecture on Alexander the Great.

12 noon

I phone Chris Beetles at his gallery. His annual *Illustrators' Catalogue* has arrived in the morning post. There is the usual selection of goodies: Vicky, Low, Brabazon, Scarfe, Shepard, Giles and Heath Robinson. However, it's a new artist who attracts my attention.

The first edition of *The Wind in the Willows* was illustrated by E. H. Shepard, and after his death for a short time by Heath Robinson. But a new version has recently been published, illustrated with the most delightful watercolours by Michael

Foreman, who is one of Britain's most respected illustrators. Original Shepards are now changing hands for as much as £100,000 and Heath Robinsons can fetch £10,000. So it was a pleasant surprise to find that Mr Foreman's works were around £500. I decide to select one or two for any future grandchildren.

So in anticipation I turn the pages and begin to choose a dozen or so for Mary to consider. I have to smile when I come to page 111: a picture of Toad in jail, being visited by the washer-woman. This is not only a must for a future grandchild, but should surely be this year's Christmas card. (See below.)

4.00 pm

An inmate called Fox asks me if it's true that I have a laptop in my room. I explain politely to him that I write all my manuscripts by hand, and have no idea how to use a computer. He looks surprised. I later learn from my old room-mate Eamon that there's a rumour going round that I have my own laptop and a mobile phone. Envy in prison is every bit as rife as it is 'on the out'.

5.00 pm

I receive a visit from David (fraud, eighteen months). He has received a long and fascinating letter from his former pad-mate Alan, who was transferred to Spring Hill a week ago. Alan confirms that his new abode is far more pleasant than NSC, and advises me to join him as quickly as possible. He doesn't seem to realize that the decision won't rest with me. However, there is one revealing sentence: 'An officer reported that they've been expecting Jeffrey for the past week, has he decided not to come?' David feels that they must have agreed to take me, and are only waiting for my sentence plan, which was faxed to them yesterday.

Incidentally, David (the recipient of the letter) was a school-master in Sleaford before he arrived at NSC via Belmarsh. Three of his former pupils are also residents; well, to be totally accurate, two – one has just absconded.

7.00 pm

Doug and I watch the tanks as they roll into Kabul while Bush and Blair try not to look triumphant.

DAY 118

10.30 pm

I'm back in my room, undressing, when a flash bulb goes off.* I quickly open my door and see an inmate running down the corridor. I chase after him, but he disappears out of the back door and into the night.

I return to my room, and a few moments later, an officer knocks on the door and lets himself in. He tells me that they know who it is, as several prisoners saw the culprit departing. So everyone will know who it was by this time tomorrow; yet another inmate who has been bribed by the press. The last three have been caught, lost their D-cat status, been shipped back to a B-cat and had time added to their sentence. I'm told the going rate for a photograph is £500. If they catch him, I'll let you know. If they don't, you'll have seen it in one of the national papers, captioned: 'EXCLUSIVE: Archer undressing in his cell'.

---

* The door to each inmate's room has a large glass panel in it, covered in wire mesh. On the outside is a green curtain to stop casual passers-by peering in. However, during the night, prison officers hold back the curtain to check you're in bed and haven't absconded.

DAY 119 WEDNESDAY 14 NOVEMBER 2001

8.15 am

As I walk over to breakfast from the south block, I pick up snippets of information about last night's incident. It turns out that the photographer was not a prisoner, but Wilkins, a former inmate who was released last Friday. He was recognized by several inmates, all of whom were puzzled as to what he was doing back inside the prison four days after he'd been released.

But here is the tragic aspect of the whole episode. Wilkins was in prison for driving without a licence, and served only twelve weeks of a six-month sentence. The penalty for entering a prison for illegal purposes carries a maximum sentence of ten years, or that's what it proclaims on the board in black and white as you enter NSC. And worse, you spend the entire term locked up in a B-cat, as you would be considered a high-escape risk. The last such charge at NSC was when a father brought in drugs for his son. He ended up with a three-year sentence.

I look forward to discovering which paper considers this behaviour a service to the public. I'm told that when they catch Wilkins, part of the bargaining over sentence will be if he is willing to inform the police who put him up to it.

DAY 119

2.30 pm

There's a call over the intercom for all officers to report to the gatehouse immediately. Matthew and I watch through the kitchen window as a dozen officers arrive at different speeds from every direction. They surround a television crew who, I later learn, are bizarrely trying to film a look-alike Jeffrey Archer holding up one of my books and claiming he's trying to escape. Mr New tells me he warned them that they were on government property and must leave immediately, to which the producer replied, 'You can't treat me like that, I'm with the BBC.' Can the BBC really have sunk to this level?

DAY 120 THURSDAY 15 NOVEMBER 2001

5.21 am

I'm up early because I have to report to the hospital by 7.30 am to take over my new responsibilities as Doug's stand-in, while he goes off on a three-day forklift truck-driving course. How this will help a man of fifty-three who runs his own haulage company with a two million pound turnover is beyond me. He doesn't seem to care about the irrelevance of it all, as long as he gets out of prison for three days.

I write for two hours.

7.30 am

I report to Linda at the hospital, and witness the morning sick parade. A score of prisoners are lined up to collect their medication, or to see if they can get off work for the day. If it's raining or freezing cold, the length of the queue doubles. Most farm workers would rather spend the day in the warm watching TV than picking Brussels sprouts or cleaning out the pigsties. Linda describes them as malingerers, and claims she can spot them at thirty paces. If I worked on the farm I might well join them.

DAY 120

Bill (fraud, farm worker) has had every disease, affliction and germ that's known to man. Today he's got diarrhoea and asks Linda for the day off work. He feels sure he'll be fine by tomorrow.

'Certainly,' says Linda, giving him her warmest smile. Bill smiles back in response. 'But,' she adds, 'I'm going to have to put you in the san [sanatorium] for the day.'

'Why?' asks Bill, looking surprised.

'I'll need to take a sample every thirty minutes,' she explains, 'before I can decide what medication to prescribe.' Bill reluctantly goes into the hospital, lies on one of the beds and looks hopefully in the direction of the television screen. 'Not a chance,' Linda tells him.

Once Linda has sorted out the genuinely ill from the trying-it-on brigade, I'm handed four lists of those she has sanctioned to be off work for the day. I deliver a copy to the south block unit office, the farm office, the north block, the gatehouse amd education before going to breakfast.

8.30 am

It's Matthew's last day at NSC and he's on the paper chase. He takes a double-sided printed form from department to department, the hospital, gym, canteen, stores and reception, to gather signatures authorizing his release tomorrow. He starts with Mr Simpson, the probation officer at SMU, and will end with the principal officer Mr New. He will then have to hand in this sheet of paper at reception tomorrow morning before he can finally be released. It's not unknown for a prisoner's release paper to disappear overnight, which can hold up an inmate's departure for several hours.

I'll miss Matthew, who, at the age of twenty-four, will be

returning to university to complete his PhD. He's taught me a great deal during the past five weeks. I've met over a thousand prisoners since I've been in jail, and he is one of a handful who I believe should never have been sent to prison. I wish him luck in the future; he's a fine young man.

12 noon

I drop into the hospital to see if sister needs me.

'Not at the moment,' says Linda, 'but as we're expecting seventeen new arrivals this afternoon, please come back around four, or when you see the sweat box driving through the front gate.'

'How's Bill?' I enquire.

'He lasted about forty minutes,' she replies dryly, 'but sadly failed to produce a specimen. I sent him back to the farm, but of course told him to return immediately should the problem arise again.'

2.00 pm

On returning to SMU I find a prisoner sitting in the waiting room, visibly shaking. His name is Moore. He tells me that he's been called off work for a meeting with two police officers who are travelling down from Derbyshire to interview him. He's completed seventeen months of a five-year sentence, and is anxious to know why they want to see him.

2.30 pm

The police haven't turned up. I go to check on Moore – to find he's a gibbering wreck.

DAY 120

2.53 pm

The two Derbyshire police officers arrive. They greet me with a smile and don't look at all ferocious. I take them up to an interview room on the first floor and offer them a cup of tea, using the opportunity to tell them that Moore is in a bit of a state. They assure me that it's only a routine enquiry, and he has nothing to be anxious about. I return downstairs and pass on this message; the shaking stops.

3.26 pm

Moore departs with a smile and a wave; I've never seen a more relieved man.

4.00 pm

The seventeen new prisoners arrive in a sweat box via Birmingham and Nottingham. I report to the hospital to check their blood pressure and note their weight and height. It's not easy to carry out my new responsibilities while all seventeen of them talk at once. What jobs are there? How much are you paid? Can I go to the canteen tonight? What time are roll-calls? Which is the best block? Can I make a phone call?

7.00 pm

Doug returns from his day on the fork-lift trucks. He's pleased to be doing the course because if he hopes to retain his HGV licence, he would still have to take it in a year's time. The course is costing him £340 but he'd be willing to pay that just to be allowed out for three days; 'In fact, I'd pay a lot more,' he says.

8.15 pm

After roll-call I take a bath before going over to the south block to say goodbye to Matthew. By the time I check in at the hospital at 7.30 am tomorrow morning he will be a free man. I do not envy him, because he should never have been sent to prison in the first place.

DAY 121   FRIDAY 16 NOVEMBER 2001

10.00 am

All seventeen new inmates are waiting in the conservatory for their introductory talk before they sign the pledge (on drugs). They're all chatting away, with one exception; he's sitting in the corner, head bowed, foot tapping, looking anxious. This could be for any number of reasons, but even though the officers keep a suicide watch during the first forty-eight hours of a prisoner's arrival, I still report my anxieties to Mr New. He tells me to bring the prisoner into his office but make it look routine.

When the man emerges forty minutes later, he is smiling. It turns out that X is a schedule A conviction, which usually means a sexual offence against a minor. However, X was sentenced to six months for lashing out at his son. He'll only serve twelve weeks, and the fact that he's in a D-cat prison shows there is no previous history of violence. However, if word got out that he's schedule A, other inmates would assume he's a paedophile. Mr New has advised the prisoner to say, if asked what he's in for, that he took a swipe at a guy who tried to jump a taxi queue. As he's only serving twelve weeks, it's just believable.

11.30 am

Storr marches into the building, waving a complaint form. Yesterday, after returning from a town visit, he failed a breathalyser test; yes, you can be breathalysed in prison without having driven – in fact walking is quite enough. Storr protested that he never drinks even 'on the out' and the real culprit is a bottle of mouthwash. Storr is sent back to the north block to retrieve the offending bottle, which has about an inch of red liquid left in the bottom. The label lists alcohol as one of several ingredients. After some discussion, Mr New decides Storr will be retested tomorrow morning. If the test proves negative, his explanation will be accepted.* He will then be subjected to regular random tests, and should one of them prove positive, he will be shipped back to his C-cat. Storr accepts this judgment, and leaves looking pleased with himself.

2.30 pm

I ask Mr New if there is any progress on my transfer to Spring Hill. He shakes his head.

4.00 pm

I report back to the hospital and carry out three more urine tests on the inductees we didn't get round to yesterday, measure their blood pressure and record their weight. Among them is a

---

* Mr New banned all mouthwashes from the canteen following a similar incident a year ago. As Storr purchased the bottle at his last prison, Mr New is issuing a new directive, that any new prisoners arriving at NSC with mouthwash will have the bottles confiscated.

DAY 121

prisoner called Blossom, who is returning to NSC for the third time in as many years.

'He's as good as gold,' says Linda. 'A gipsy, who, once convicted, never puts a foot wrong; he's always released as a model prisoner after serving half his sentence. But once he's left us, he's usually back within a year,' she adds.

10.30 pm

Television news footage reveals Kabul as it had been under the rule of the Taliban. Amongst the buildings filmed is Kabul jail, which makes NSC look like the Ritz; twenty men would have occupied my room with only three urine-stained, ragged mattresses between them.

I sleep soundly.

DAY 122   SATURDAY 17 NOVEMBER 2001

Anyone who's incarcerated wants their sentence to pass as quickly as possible. If you're fortunate enough to have an interesting job, as I have at SMU, that certainly helps kill Monday to Friday. That just leaves the other problem – the weekend. Once you've reached your FLED and can work outside the prison, have a town visit every week and a week out every month, I'm told the months fly by, but should I fail to win my appeal against length of sentence, none of this will kick in until July next year – another eight months. So boredom will become my greatest challenge.

I can write, but not for every hour of every day. With luck there's a rugby match to watch on Saturday afternoon, and a visitor to look forward to seeing on Sunday. So, for the record:

Saturday

6.00 am Write this diary for two hours.

8.15 am Breakfast.

9.00 am Read *The Times*, or any other paper available.

10.00 am Work on the sixth rewrite of *Sons of Fortune*.

12 noon Lunch.

2.00 pm Watch New Zealand beat Ireland 40–29 on BBC1.

DAY 122

4.00 pm   Watch Wales beat Tonga 51–7 on BBC2.

4.40 pm   Watch the highlights of England's record-breaking win of 134–0 against Romania on ITV.

6.00 pm   Continue to work on *Sons of Fortune* and run out of paper. My fault.

8.15 pm   Sign in for roll-call to prove I haven't absconded, or died of boredom.

8.30 pm   Join Doug in the hospital and watch a Danny de Vito/ Bette Midler film, followed by the news.

10.30 pm   Return to my room, go to bed and, despite the noise of *Match of the Day* coming from the TV room next door, fall asleep.

DAY 123   SUNDAY 18 NOVEMBER 2001

6.11 am

After five weeks at NSC, you must be as familiar with my daily
routine as I am so, as from today, I will refer only to highlights
or unusual incidents that I think might interest you.

2.00 pm

You will recall that I'm allowed one visit a week, and my visitors
today are Alan and Della Pascoe. I first met Alan when he was
an England schoolboy, and even the casual observer realized
that he was destined to be a star. He had a decade at the highest
level, and if that time hadn't clashed with Al Moses – the greatest
400m hurdler in history – Alan would have undoubtedly won
two Olympic gold medals, rather than two silvers. We only ran
against each other once in our careers; he was seventeen and I
was twenty-six. I prefer not to dwell on the result.

Although I had the privilege of watching Della run for her
country (Commonwealth gold medalist and world record holder),
we didn't meet until she married Alan, and our families have been
close ever since. They remain the sort of friends who don't run
round the track in the opposite direction when you've been disqualified.

DAY 124   MONDAY 19 NOVEMBER 2001

5.30 am

The noise of three heavy tractors harvesting acres and acres of Brussels sprouts wakes me. If I'm up every day by five-thirty, what time must the farm labourers rise to be on their tractor seats even before I stir?

8.15 am

Matthew, as you will remember, was released last Friday, and has been replaced in the SMU by Carl.

Carl is softly spoken and well mannered. He's the lead singer in the prison's rock band, and has the striking good looks required for someone who aspires to that calling: around five foot eleven, slim, with wavy fair hair. He tells me that he has a fifteen-year-old daughter born when he was twenty (he's not married), so he must be in his mid-thirties.

Carl arrives at eight-twenty, which is a good start, and as I run through our daily duties, he makes notes. Monday is usually quiet: no inductions or labour board, so I'm able to brief him fully on all personnel resident in the building and their responsibilities. He is a quick study, and also has all the women in the building coming into the kitchen on the flimsiest of excuses. In a week he'll have everything mastered and I'll be redundant.

Now of course you will want to know why this cross between Robbie Williams and Richard Branson is in prison. Simple answer, fraud. Carl took advances on property that he didn't own, or even properly represent. A more interesting aspect of Carl's case is that his co-defendant pleaded not guilty, while, on the advice of his barrister, Carl pleaded guilty. But there's still another twist to come. Because Carl had to wait for the outcome of his co-defendant's trial before he could be sentenced, he was released on bail for nine months, and during that time 'did a runner'. He disappeared off to Barcelona, found himself a job and tried to settle down. However, after only a few weeks, he decided he had to come back to England and, in his words, face the music.

Carl was a little surprised not to be arrested when he landed at Heathrow. He spent the weekend with a friend in Nottingham, and then handed himself in to the nearest police station. The policeman at the desk was so astonished that he didn't quite know what to do with him. Carl was charged later that day, and after spending a night in custody, was sentenced the following morning to three years. His co-defendant also received three years. His barrister says he would only have got two years if he hadn't broken bail and disappeared off to Barcelona. Carl is a model prisoner, so he will only serve sixteen months, half his sentence minus two months with a tag.

2.30 pm

Mr New phones Spring Hill to enquire about my transfer, but as there's no reply from Karen's office, he'll try again tomorrow. If I were back in my office, I'd try again at 3 pm, 4 pm and 5 pm,

DAY 124

but not in prison. Tomorrow will be just fine. After all, I'm not going anywhere.

5.00 pm

David (murder) arrives with all my clothes neatly laundered. Lifers have their own washing machine and iron. Jeeves of Pont Street would be proud of him. I hand over three Mars Bars, and my debt is paid.

6.00 pm

I need to buy a plug from the canteen (30p) because I keep leaving mine in the washbasin. I've lost four in the last four weeks. When I get to the front of the queue they're sold out. However, Doug tells me he has a drawer full of plugs – of course he does.

DAY 125   TUESDAY 20 NOVEMBER 2001

Many aspects of prison life are unbearable: boredom, confinement, missing family and friends. All of these might fade in time. But the two things I will never forget after I'm released will be the noise and the bad language.

When I returned to my room at 10 pm last night, the TV room next door was packed with screaming hooligans; the volume, for a repeat of the world heavyweight title fight between Lennox Lewis and Hasim Rahman, was so high that it reminded me of being back at Belmarsh when reggae music was blaring out from the adjacent cell. I was delighted to learn that Lennox Lewis had retained his title, but didn't need to hear every word the commentator said, or the accompanying cheers, screams and insults from a highly partisan crowd. In the end I gave up, went next door and asked if the volume could be turned down a little. I was greeted with a universal chorus of 'Fuck off!'

10.00 am

Sixteen new inductees turn up for labour board, all clutching their red folders. The message has spread: if you don't return your folders, you don't get a job, and therefore no wages.

717

DAY 125

Because the prison is so full at the moment, most of the good jobs – hospital, SMU, library, education, stores, officers' mess – are filled, leaving only kitchen, cleaners and the dreaded farm. Among the new intake is a PhD and an army officer. I fix it so that the PhD, who only has another five weeks to serve, will work in the stores, and the army officer will then take over from him. Only one of the new intake hasn't a clue what he wants to do, so he inevitably ends up on the farm.

11.00 am

I have already described the paper chase to you, so imagine my surprise when among the three prisoners to turn up this morning, clutching his release papers is Potts. Do you remember Potts? Solicitor didn't turn up, took an overdose? Well, he's fully recovered and went back to court for his appeal. However, he was half an hour late and the judge refused to hear his case, despite the fact that it was the Prison Service's fault that he wasn't on time. Here we are two weeks later and he's off tomorrow, even though he wasn't due for release until the middle of next year. As we are unable to have a lengthy conversation at SMU, I agree to visit him tonight and find out what caused this sudden reversal.

3.00 pm

The governor of Spring Hill (Mr Payne) calls to have a private chat with Mr New. He's concerned about the attendant publicity should he agree to my transfer. Mr New does everything he can to allay Mr Payne's anxieties, pointing out that once the tabloids had got their photograph, the press haven't been seen since. But Mr Payne points out that it didn't stop a series of stories appearing from 'insiders' and 'released prisoners' which, although pure fantasy doesn't help. Mr New tells him that I have settled in well, shared a room with another inmate and am a model prisoner. Mr Payne says he'll make a decision fairly quickly. I am not optimistic.

6.30 pm

I have been invited to attend a meeting of the Samaritans (from Boston) and the Listeners (prisoners). They meet about once a month in the hospital to exchange views and ideas. They only need me to sign some books for their Christmas bazaar. One of the ladies asks me if she can bring in some more books for signing from the Red Cross bookshop.

'Of course,' I tell her.

10.30 pm

There's a cowboy film on TV, so the noise is bearable – that is, until the final shoot-out begins.

DAY 126 WEDNESDAY 21 NOVEMBER 2001

6.18 am

The mystery of Potts's early release has been solved. A clerical error resulted in the judge thinking the case should be heard at 10 o'clock, while Potts was able to produce a piece of paper that requested his attendance in court at 10.30 am. The judge subsequently agreed to hear the appeal immediately and, having considered the facts, halved Potts's sentence. The governor called him out of work at the kitchen to pass on the news that he would be released this morning. The first really happy prisoner I've seen in months.

8.15 am

Twelve new inductees due today, and as always, if you look carefully through the list you'll find a story. Today it's Cormack. He was released just over six weeks ago on a tag (HDC) and is back, but only for eleven days.

Strict rules are applied when you are granted an HDC. You are released two months early with a tag placed around your ankle. You supply an address at which you will reside during those two months. You must have a home phone. You will be confined to that abode during certain hours, usually between seven in the evening and seven the following morning. You also agree in writing not to take drugs or drink.

Cormack is an unusual case, because he didn't break any of these rules. But yesterday morning he turned up at the local police station asking to be taken back into custody for the last eleven days because he was no longer welcome at the house he had designated for tagging.

'Wise man,' said Mr Simpson, the probation officer who recommended his early release. 'He kept to the letter of the law, and won't suffer as a consequence. If he'd attempted to spend the last eleven days somewhere else, he would have been arrested and returned to closed conditions.' Wise man indeed.

12 noon

Leon the PhD joins me for lunch. He's the new orderly in stores, which entitles him to eat early. He thanks me for helping him to secure the job. I discover over lunch that his doctorate is in meteorology. He tells me that there are not many job opportunities in his field, so once he's released he'll be looking for a teaching position; not easy when you have a prison record. Leon was sentenced to six months for driving without a licence, so will serve only twelve weeks. He tells me that this is not his biggest problem. He's engaged to a girl who has just left Birmingham University with a first-class honours degree, and like him, wants to be a teacher. So far, so good. But Leon is currently facing racial prejudice in reverse. She is a high-class Brahmin and even before Leon ended up in jail, her parents didn't consider he was good enough for their daughter. He explains that it is necessary to meet the father on three separate occasions before a daughter's hand can be granted in wedlock, and following that, you still have to meet the mother. All these ceremonies are conducted formally. Before he was sentenced, Leon had managed only one meeting with the father; now he is being refused a second or third meeting, and the mother is adamant that she will never allow him to enter the family home. Does his fiancée defy her parents and marry the man she loves, or does she obey her father and break off all contact? Seven of the twelve weeks have already passed, but Leon points out that it's not been easy to stay in touch while you're only allowed one visit a week, and two phonecards.

3.00 pm

Mr Berlyn (deputy governor) drops into SMU to ask me if I've invited any outsiders to come and hear my talk tomorrow night. To be honest, I'd forgotten that I'd agreed to the librarian's request to give a talk on writing a best-seller. I tell Mr Berlyn that I haven't invited anyone from inside – or outside – the prison.

He tells me that after reading about the 'event' in the local paper, members of the public have been calling in all day asking if they can attend.

Can they? I ask innocently. He doesn't bother to reply.

DAY 127   THURSDAY 22 NOVEMBER 2001

5.55 am

The problem of whether I should remain at NSC and become hospital orderly, or transfer to Spring Hill, has come to a head. Doug (VAT fraud and current hospital orderly) has been told by Mr Berlyn that if he applies for a job at Exotic Foods in Boston, who currently employ Clive (local council fraud and backgammon tutor), he would be granted the status of outside worker, which would take him out of the prison six days a week, even allowing him to use his own car to go back and forth to work.

If Doug is offered the job, then I will only do one more week as SMU orderly before passing on my responsibilities to Carl. I would then have to spend a week being trained by Doug in the hospital routines, so that I could take over the following Monday.

10.30 am

Eight new inductees today, and all seem relieved to be in an open prison, until it comes to job allocation. Once again, most prisoners end up on the farm, resulting in a lot of glum faces as they leave the building. Few of them want to spend their day with pigs, sheep and Brussels sprouts, remembering the tempera-

ture on the fens at this time of year is often below zero. One of
the prisoners, a West Indian called Wesley, used to warmer
climes, is so angry that he asks to be sent back to Ashwell, his
old C-cat prison. He says he'd be a lot happier locked up all day
with a wall to protect him from the wind. Mr Berlyn assures him
that if he still feels that way in a month's time, he'll happily send
him back.

5.00 pm

Early supper is, as I have explained, one of the orderlies' privileges, so I was surprised to see a table occupied by six inmates
I'd never seen before.

John (lifer, senior kitchen orderly) tells me that they're all
Muslims, and as Ramadan has just begun, they can only eat
between the hours of sunset and sunrise, which means they
cannot have breakfast or lunch with the other prisoners. That
doesn't explain why they're having dinner on their own, because
it's pitch black by five o'clock on a November evening and . . .

'Ah,' says John, 'good point, but you see the large tray
stacked with packets of milk and cornflakes? That's tomorrow's
breakfast, which they'll take back tonight and have in their
rooms around five tomorrow morning. If the other prisoners find
out about this, when they still have to come down to the dining
room whatever the weather, can you imagine how many complaints there would be?'

'Or conversions to Allah and the Muslim faith,' I suggest.

6.00 pm

I give my talk in the chapel on writing a best-seller. The audience
of twenty-six is made up of prisoners and staff. There are five

ladies in the front row I do not recognize, seventeen prisoners and four members of staff, including Mr Berlyn, Mr Gough and Ms Hampton, the librarian.

I enjoyed delivering a speech for the first time in three months, and although I've tackled the subject on numerous occasions in the past, it felt quite fresh after such a long layoff, and the questions were among the most searching I remember.

Two pounds was added to my canteen account.

7.00 pm

I call Mary and foolishly leave my phonecard in the slot. When I return three minutes later, it's disappeared. Let's face it, I am in prison.

7.30 pm

I pick up my letters from the unit office, thirty-two today, including one from Winston Churchill enclosing a book called *The Duel*, which covers the eighty-day struggle between his grandfather and Hitler in 1940. Among the other letters, nearly all from members of the public, is one from Jimmy.

You may recall Jimmy if you've read volume two of these diaries (*Purgatory*). He was the good-looking captain of football who had a three-year sentence for selling cannabis. He's been out for a month, and has a job working on a building site. It's long hours and well paid but, he admits, despite all the sport and daily gym visits while he was in prison, he had become soft after eighteen months of incarceration. He's only just beginning to get back into the work ethic. He assures me that he will never sell drugs again, and as he did not take them in the first place, he doesn't intend to start now. I want to believe him. He claims

725

to have sorted out his love life. He's living with the sexy one, and has ditched the intellectual one. As I now have an address and telephone number, I will give him a call over the weekend.

8.15 pm

After roll-call, Doug and I go through our strategy for a smooth changeover of jobs. However, if our plan is to work, he suggests we must make the officers on the labour board think that it's their idea.

DAY 128   FRIDAY 23 NOVEMBER 2001

8.10 am

John (murder, senior kitchen orderly) tells me over breakfast that two prisoners absconded last night. He reminds me of an incident a couple of weeks ago when Wendy sacked both of them from the kitchen for stealing chickens. A few days later she gave them a reprieve, only to sack them again the following day for stealing tins of tuna – not to eat but to trade for cannabis. They were then put on the farm, where it's quite hard to steal anything; the pigs are too heavy and the Brussels sprouts are not a trading commodity. However, last night the two prisoners were caught smoking cannabis in their room and placed on report. They should have been up in front of the governor this morning. It's just possible that they might have got away with a warning, but it's more likely they would have been shipped back to the dreaded Lincoln Prison – to sample all its Victorian facilities. They absconded before any decision could be taken.

12.08 pm

I am writing in my room when Carl knocks on the door. The Red Cross and KPMG have made a joint statement following

DAY 128

Baroness Nicholson's demand for an enquiry into what happened to the money raised for the Kurds. It's the lead item on the midday news, and I am delighted to have my name cleared.

12.20 pm

I call Alison at the office to find that Mary is at the House of Lords attending an energy resources meeting. Alison runs through the radio and television interview requests received by Mary, but she's decided only to issue this brief press statement.

PRESS RELEASE

LORD ARCHER AND THE SIMPLE TRUTH CAMPAIGN

My family and I are delighted, but not surprised, that KPMG's investigation into the Simple Truth campaign, spearheaded by Jeffrey in 1991, has confirmed that no funds were misappropriated by him or anyone else. We have known this from the outset. We are very proud of the work Jeffrey has done for Kurdish relief, the British Red Cross and many other good causes over the years. We hope that Baroness Nicholson, whose allegations have wasted much time and caused much unjustified distress, will accept KPMG's findings.

Mary Archer

1.00 pm

Lady Thatcher has come out saying she's not surprised by the outcome of the enquiry, which has dropped to the second item on the news following the death, at the age of ninety-two, of Dame Mary Whitehouse.

2.00 pm

Several of the officers are kind enough to comment on the outcome of the enquiry, but I've also fallen to second item with them. It seems that the two prisoners who absconded last night, Marley and Tom, were picked up early this morning by the police, only six miles from the prison. They were arrested, charged and transferred to Lincoln Prison. They will each have forty-two days added to their sentence and will never be allowed to apply for a D-cat status again, as they are now categorized as an escape risk.

5.00 pm

Slipped to third item on *Live at Five*, but as I have been exonerated, it's clearly not news. If I had embezzled the £57 million, or any part of it, I would have remained the lead item for a couple of days, and the prison would have been swarming with photographers waiting for my transfer to Lincoln.

Not one photographer in sight.

10.00 pm

A passing mention of the Red Cross statement on the ten o'clock news. I can see I shall have to abscond if I hope to make the headlines again.

10.30 pm

Irony. Eamon, my former room-mate, is now able to move in with his friend Shaun. They have been offered the room vacated by the two men who absconded.

DAY 129 SATURDAY 24 NOVEMBER 2001

4.00 am

A torch is flashed in my eyes, and I wake to see an officer checking if I'm in bed asleep and have not absconded. I'm no longer asleep.

7.17 am

I oversleep and only start writing just after seven.

10.00 am

The broadsheets all report the findings of the KPMG report. Several point out that none of this would have arisen if Baroness Nicholson, a former Tory MP turned Liberal peer, hadn't made her complaint to Sir John Stevens in the first place. I call Mary to discuss our next move, but there's no reply.

2.00 pm

I have a visit today from Doreen and Henry Miller. Doreen is a front-bench spokesman in the Lords having previously been a minister under John Major. She brings me up to date with news of the Upper House, and tells me that the latest Lords reform bill is detested on both sides of the chamber. The Bill ignores John Wakeham's excellent Royal Commission report, and doesn't placate the Labour party because not a large enough percentage of peers will be elected, and doesn't placate the Tory party because it removes all the remaining hereditary peers. 'It cannot,' Doreen assures me, 'reach the statute book in its present form, because it will meet with so much opposition in both Houses.'*

When Doreen and Henry leave, I don't know where the ninety minutes went.

4.00 pm

I call Mary, but the phone just rings and rings.

4.40 pm

Watch England beat South Africa 29–9 and despite the Irish hiccup, begin to believe we might be the best rugby team in the world. If I'm let out in time, I will travel to Australia to see the next world rugby cup.

7.00 pm

I call Mary. Still no reply.

8.15 pm

After checking in for roll-call I join Doug at the hospital to find four officers in the waiting room. One of them, Mr Harding,

---

* The government dropped the bill in March 2004.

is spattered with blood. Mr Hocking, the chief security officer, is taking a photograph of him. It turns out that Mr Hocking, acting on a tip-off, was informed that two inmates had disappeared into Boston to pick up some booze, so he and three other officers were lying in wait for them. However, when they were spotted returning, the first prisoner grabbed Mr Harding's heavy torch and hit him over the head, allowing his mate enough time to escape. The first prisoner was wrestled to the ground and hand-cuffed, and is now locked up in the segregation block. The second has still to reappear, although they know which prisoner it is. Even a cub reporter would realize there's an ongoing story here.

DAY 130   SUNDAY 25 NOVEMBER 2001

8.04 am

Phone Mary in Cambridge; no reply. Try London and only get the answering machine. Report to Linda at the hospital. Doug's away on a town leave (7 am to 7 pm) so I'm temporary keeper of the pills.

11.30 am

During lunch, I discover from one of the gym orderlies that they caught the second inmate who was trying to bring drink back into the prison. He'll be shipped out to Nottingham this afternoon.

Self-abuse is often one of the reasons they move offenders out so quickly. It's not unknown for a prisoner who is kept in lock-up overnight to cut his wrists or even break an arm, and then blame it on the officer who charged him. The prisoner can then claim he was attacked first, which means that he can't be moved until there has been a full enquiry. Mr Hocking took several photographs of both prisoners, which will make that course of action a little more difficult to explain.

DAY 130

12 noon

The morning papers are predicting that I'll soon be moved to Spring Hill so I can be nearer my family. One or two of them even suggest that I should never have been sent to Wayland or NSC in the first place simply on an allegation made by Ms Nicholson.

10.00 pm

After the news, I call Mary again, but there's still no reply.

DAY 131   MONDAY 26 NOVEMBER 2001

8.30 am

One of my duties at SMU is the distribution of bin liners. At eight-thirty every morning, two prisoners, Alf and Rod, check in for work and take away a bin liner each. This morning Alf demands ten. I will allow you a few seconds to fathom out why, because I couldn't.

I make a weekly order for provisions on a Friday, which is delivered on Monday, and always includes ten bin liners, so Alf is about to wipe out my entire stock in one day. I can't believe he's trading them and they are far too big for the small wastepaper baskets in his room, so I give in and ask why the sudden demand. Alf tells me that the director-general of the Prison Service, Martin Narey, is visiting NSC on Wednesday, and the governor wants the place smartened up for his inspection. Fair enough. However, if Mr Narey is half-intelligent, it won't take him long to realize that NSC is a neglected dump and short of money. If they show him the north or south block, he'll wonder if we have any cleaners as he holds his nose and steps gingerly through the rubbish. The visits room is a disgrace and extra-curricular activities almost non-existent. However, if he is only shown the canteen, gym, farm, hospital and SMU, he will leave with a favourable impression.

DAY 131

I'm told the real purpose for Mr Narey's visit is to discuss how this prison will prepare for resettlement status once the new governor takes over in January.

10.30 am

Mr Belford, a south block officer, pops in for a coffee. He tells me that the inmate who photographed me in my room failed to sell the one picture he managed to snap, because the negative came out so poorly.

11.00 am

Today's new inductees from Nottingham include a pupil barrister (ABH), a taxi driver (overcharging) and a farm labourer (theft from his employer). They all end up on the farm because the prison is overcrowded and there are no other jobs available.

6.00 pm

Canteen. I'm £13.50 in credit (I earn £8.50 a week, and can supplement that with £10 of my own money). I purchase two phonecards, three bottles of Evian, a packet of Gillette razor blades, a roll-on deodorant and a toothbrush, which cleans out my account. I'm not in desperate need of all these items, but it's my way of making sure I can't buy any more chocolate as I need to lose the half stone I've put on since arriving at NSC.

7.00 pm

I phone James at work. He tells me that Mary has been on the move for the past few days – Oundle, London and Cambridge, and then back to London this afternoon.*

I join Doug in the hospital. He is anticipating an interview with Exotic Foods on Wednesday or Thursday, and hopes to begin work next Monday, a week earlier than originally planned. He has already spoken to Mr Belford about a room on the south block, in the no-smoking spur, and to Mr Berlyn about his travel arrangements to Boston. However, there is a fly in the ointment, namely Linda, who feels Doug should train his successor for a week before he leaves.

7.10 pm

I call Chris Beetles' gallery and wish Chris luck for the opening of the illustrators' show. Mary is hoping to drop in and see the picture I've selected for this year's Christmas card. I ask him to pass on my love and tell her I'll ring Cambridge tomorrow evening. For the first time in thirty-five years, I haven't spoken to my wife in five days. Don't forget, she can't call me.

---

*I never phone Mary on her mobile because my two-pound phone card is gobbled up in moments.

DAY 132   TUESDAY 27 NOVEMBER 2001

6.11 am

One incident of huge significance took place today. In fact, it's a short story in its own right. However, as I write, I don't yet know, the ending. But to begin halfway through.

Do you recall Leon, the PhD who joined us about a week ago? He wants to marry an Indian girl of high caste, but her father and mother refuse to entertain the idea, and that was *before* he was sent to prison (driving without a licence, six months). Well, he reappeared at SMU at three o'clock this afternoon in what can only be described as an agitated state. Although we'd had ten new inductees and a labour board this morning, it was turning out to be a quiet afternoon. I sat Leon down in the kitchen while Carl made him a cup of tea. He was desperate to discover if he was going to be granted his HDC and be released early on a tag. The officer who deals with HDC was in her office, so I went upstairs to ask if she would see him.

Ten minutes later Leon reappears and says that a decision will be made tomorrow morning as to whether he can be released early.

'Well, that's another problem solved,' says Carl.

'No, it isn't,' says Leon, 'because if they don't grant my tag, it will be a disaster.'

Leon doesn't strike me as the sort of man who would use the world 'disaster' lightly, so I enquire why. He then briefs us on the latest complication in his love life.

His girlfriend's parents have found out that she plans to marry Leon as soon as he's released from prison on 6 December. She's even booked the register office. She told him over the phone last night that her parents have not only forbidden the match, but three men who she has never met have recently been selected as possible husbands and they will be flying in from India at the weekend. She must then select one of them before she and her intended bridegroom fly back to Calcutta to be married on 6 December.

I now fully understand Leon's desperation; I go in search of Mr Downs, a senior officer, who is a shrewd and caring man. I find him in the officers' room going over tomorrow's itinerary for the director-general's visit. I brief Mr Downs and he agrees to see Leon immediately.

After their meeting, Leon tells us that Mr Downs was most sympathetic and will report his worries direct to the governor. He has asked to see Leon again at eight o'clock tomorrow morning, one hour before the board meet to decide if he will be granted a tag. I had assumed that there would be nothing more to tell you until the outcome of that meeting. However ...

7.00 pm

I finally catch up with Mary, and forty minutes later have used up both my phonecards.

I go over to the hospital to have a bath, but before doing so tell Doug about Leon. I fail to reach the bathroom because he tells me he can remember a case where special dispensation was granted to allow an inmate to be married in the prison chapel.

'Why don't you ask the vicar about it?' he suggests.

'Because by then it will be too late,' I tell Doug, reminding him of the timetable of the board meeting at nine o'clock tomorrow morning, and the three gentlemen from India arriving in Sheffield over the weekend.

'But the Rev Derek Johnson is over at the chapel right now,' says Doug, 'it's the prison clergy's monthly meeting.'

I leave Doug and walk quickly over to the chapel. The orderly, John (ostrich fraud), tells me that the vicar has just left, but if I run to the gate I might still catch him. At sixty-one I'm past running fast, but I do jog, and hope that as the vicar is even older than I am I'll make it before he's driven off. When I arrive at the gate, his car is at the barrier waiting to be let out. I wave frantically. He parks the car and joins me in the gatehouse, where I tell him the whole story. Derek listens with immense sympathy and says that he can, in certain circumstances, marry the couple in the prison chapel, and he feels confident that the governor would agree, given the circumstances. He also adds that if the young lady needed to be put up overnight, he and Mrs Johnson could supply a room for her. I thank the vicar and return to the north block in search of Leon.

I find him in his room and impart my latest piece of news. He's delighted, and tells me that he's spoken to his fiancée again, and she's already arranged for the wedding to be held in a local register office as long as he's released early. If he isn't, we have at least come up with an alternative solution. Leon is thanking me profusely when I hear my name over the tannoy, 'Archer to report to the south block unit office immediately.'

I leave Leon to jog over to the south block and arrive at the unit office at one minute to nine. I had, for the first time, forgotten to check in for my eight-fifteen roll-call. If I'd arrived at one minute past nine, I would have been put on report and have lost my chance of being 'enhanced' for another eight weeks. Mr Belford, the duty officer, who knows nothing of my nocturnal efforts, bursts out laughing.

'I was so much looking forward to putting you on report, Jeffrey,' he says, 'but I was pretty sure you would come up with a good excuse as to what you were doing at eight-fifteen.'

'I was with the vicar,' I tell him.

DAY 133 WEDNESDAY 28 NOVEMBER 2001

9.50 am

Leon is sitting in the waiting room at SMU ready for his HDC ajudication with Mr Berlyn (deputy governor) and Mr Simpson (resident probation officer).

Leon called his fiancée again last night. The three suitors have arrived from India, and once Sunita has made her choice (and if she doesn't, her parents will decide for her) she will then be flown back to India to meet the man's parents. The couple will then return to England to prepare for a wedding on 6 December, the day before Leon will be released.

Sunita's plan is to take only hand luggage on the flight, so that when she returns, she will walk straight through customs while her parents wait to pick up their luggage from the baggage hall. Leon's brother will be waiting in the arrivals hall and drive her straight to Birmingham, where she and Leon will be married later that day.

If the board grants Leon his tagging, he will leave NSC at eight o'clock on the Saturday, and drive straight to Birmingham, and they will be man and wife before the family can work out where she's disappeared. Everything is riding on the result of Leon's interview with the board in a few minutes' time. Mr

Berlyn calls for Leon at ten-eleven and I escort him up to the interview room.

Carl and I run around the kitchen pretending to be busy. SMU is on full alert because Martin Narey, the director-general, arrived a few minutes ago.

10.32 am

Leon appears, almost in tears. The board have turned down his application. I fear he may abscond tonight and take the law into his own hands.

11.30 am

The Rev Derek Johnson drops in to tell us that he's met with the governor, who does not have the authority to sanction a wedding in the chapel. A prisoner must have at least nine months to serve before he can apply for such a privilege. He adds that no one has ever come across such an unusual set of circumstances.

Leon now can't do anything until seven o'clock this evening when he's arranged to phone his fiancée on her mobile. Before he leaves us, he adds two more pieces of information. First, his father, an extremely wealthy man, has offered a dowry of £500,000 to Sunita's family. Leon's mother is a Brahmini, but because his father is Irish, their son is unacceptable. One can only wonder how much the three suitors from India are offering as a dowry for this girl they have yet to meet. Second, Sunita's sister was subjected to the same drama two years ago, and is now going through a messy divorce. Carl and I agree to meet in Leon's room at 7.30 pm and plan his next move.

DAY 133

11.45 am

I leave for lunch a few minutes before the director-general is due to arrive at SMU. By the time I've finished my cauliflower cheese and gone back to the south block to make a couple of phone calls, Mr Narey has moved on to visit the lifers' quarters. I return to work at one o'clock.

5.00 pm

I drop in to see Doug, who confirms that Exotic Foods have agreed to interview him on Friday morning, and he is hoping to begin work with them on Monday week, so I could become hospital orderly in two weeks' time.

7.30 pm

Leon opens the door of his room to greet us with a warm smile. Sunita has escaped from Sheffield and has driven down to Portsmouth to stay with his brother and sister-in-law. She has purchased a new phone, as she is worried that her parents will hire a detective to trace her through the mobile Leon bought for her.

Leon removes a thick bundle of letters from his shelf.

'She writes twice a day,' he says.

I am delighted by the news, but suggest to Carl after we've left that it won't take a particularly bright private detective to work out Sunita might be staying with Leon's brother.

I have a feeling this saga is not yet over.

DAY 134 THURSDAY 29 NOVEMBER 2001

I have mentioned the worthwhile role played by the Samaritans who train selected prisoners as Listeners. At NSC they have taken this trust one stage further and set aside a room where a pre-programmed mobile phone has been provided for inmates who need to call the Samaritans.

This service has become very popular, as more and more prisoners claim to be in need of succour from the Samaritans; so much so that Mr New recently became suspicious. After one particularly long call, which was interspersed with laughter, he confiscated the phone and quickly discovered what the inmates had been up to. They had been removing the Sim card from inside the phone and replacing it with one of their own that had been smuggled in.

As of today, there will no longer be a dedicated room for the Samaritans, or a mobile phone.

11.00 am

This will be my last labour board if I am to join Doug in the hospital next week. I therefore suggest to Carl that he should take charge as if I wasn't there. During the rest of the morning, whenever a prisoner calls in with some problem, Carl handles it.

DAY 134

My only worry is that as Carl has another fifteen months to serve before he'll be eligible for a tag, he may become bored long before his sentence is up.

2.30 pm

Mr New calls Spring Hill to ask Mr Payne why my transfer is taking so long. He's told that Spring Hill is about to face a public enquiry as a consequence of something that happened before he became governor. Mr Payne fears that the press will be swarming all over the place and although he is quite willing to have me, he can't let me know his decision for at least another couple of weeks. I press Mr New for the details of what could possibly cause so much public interest but he refuses to discuss it. I wonder if it's simply a ploy to keep me from being transferred.*

7.00 pm

I visit Leon in the north block. He has just come off the phone to his fiancée, still safely ensconced in Portsmouth with Leon's brother. Sunita's three Indian suitors have returned home accompanied by her mother, leaving her father in Bradford. Sunita has rung her father who has agreed to meet Leon. But he still doesn't know that Leon is in jail and won't be released for another three weeks.

---

* No suggestion of a scandal at Spring Hill appeared in the national press during the next twelve months.

DAY 135   FRIDAY 30 NOVEMBER 2001

9.30 am

The best laid plans of mice and convicts.

I am making tea for Mr Simpson at SMU when the duty officer asks me to report to the hospital for a suicide watch. Doug has gone to Boston for his Exotic Foods interview, so they are short of an orderly.

Suicide watch is quite common in prison, and this is the second I've covered in three weeks. Linda and Gail have to judge whether the prisoner is genuinely considering taking his own life, or simply looking for tea and sympathy and a chance to sit and watch television.

I turn up at the hospital a few minutes later to find my charge is a man of about forty-five, squat, thick set, covered in tattoos, with several teeth missing. David is serving a six-year sentence for GBH. What puzzles me is that he is due to be released on 14 January, so he only has a few more weeks of his sentence to complete. All I'm expected to do is to keep an eye on him while Gail gets on with her other duties, which today include taking care of a prisoner who was injured after being thrown through a window at his previous jail.

David's first request is for a glass of water, which is no problem. He then disappears into the lavatory, and doesn't

747

reappear again for some time, when he requests another glass of water. No sooner has he gulped that down than the vicar arrives. He sits down next to David and asks if he can help. I ask David if he wants me to leave.

'No,' he says, but he would like another glass of water.

He then tells the vicar about the demons that visit him during the night, insisting that he must commit more crimes, and as he wants to go straight, he doesn't know what to do.

'Are you a practising member of any faith?' asks the Reverend.

'Yeah,' replies David, 'I believe in God and life after death, but I've never been sure which religion would be best for me.'

A long and thoughtful discussion follows after which David decides he's Church of England. The only thing of interest that comes out of the talk is that David wants to return to Nottingham jail, because he feels safer from the demons there, and more importantly they have a full-time psychiatrist who understands his problem. This also puzzles me. We have our own psychiatrist, Val, who is on duty at SMU this morning. Why would anyone want to leave NSC to return to a hell-hole like Nottingham?

Once the vicar has left, David disappears back into the lavatory and after another long period of time, returns and requests another glass of water.

Gail pops her head round the door to inform David that the governor has decided he can return to Nottingham, so he should go back to his room and pack his belongings. David looks happy for the first time. He drains the glass of water and gets up to leave. Are you also puzzled?

12 noon

Over lunch Dave (lifer), who after eighteen years has seen it all, tells me what David was really up to. Last night David was rumoured to be high on heroin, and feared having to take an MDT today. Had he failed that test, he would have had twenty-eight days added to his sentence and then been sent back to Nottingham. So we were treated to his little performance with the demons. Drinking gallons of water can flush heroin out of the system in twenty-four hours, and although David's still off to Nottingham, he avoided the added twenty-eight days. I'm so dim. I should have spotted it.

12.30 pm

Mr Lewis (the governing governor) has received a letter from the Shadow Home Secretary, Sir Brian Mawhinney, requesting to visit me.

1.15 pm

Disaster. Doug returns from his interview with Exotic Foods and tells me that they don't need him to start work until the middle of January. As he will be eligible for resettlement in February, and able to return to work with his own company, why should he bother? So he's decided to stay on as hospital orderly for the next couple of months.

My only hope now is the governor of Spring Hill.

DAY 136   SATURDAY 1 DECEMBER 2001

4.19 am

I lie awake for hours, plotting. Although I'm currently revising the sixth draft of *Sons of Fortune*, I've come up with a new idea for the ending, which will require some medical research. I will have to seek advice from Dr Walling.

10.40 am

It's just been officially announced that Mr Lewis will retire as governing governor on 1 January. I go over to the unit office and pick up a labour board change of job application form. If I'm not going to be hospital orderly I've decided to apply for his job. (See opposite).

12 noon

Doug tells me that he's going to try another ploy to get outside work. He has a friend in March who runs a small haulage company (three lorries), who will offer him a job as a driver. The only problem is that he doesn't work out of Boston, which is one of the current specifications for anyone who wishes to take up outside

CHANGE OF LABOUR REQUEST

NB. Eight weeks should elapse before submitting a request.

NO: FF 8782.	NAME: ARCHER		EDR: Up to you
PRESENT PARTY: Orderly SMU		REQUESTED PARTY: Governor of NSC	
HOW LONG ON PRESENT PARTY: Eight weeks Enhanced (just)			

REASON FOR REQUEST: I hear that the Governor of Leicester is unable to join due to stress, provable caused by the thought of taking care of me. I feel after eight weeks I am more than ready to take over from Mr Lewis.

Signed:

Fill in above and give it to Senior Officer i/c unit.

The RT Hon The Lord Archer of Weston-Super-Mare

1. PRESENT PARTY OFFICER'S COMMENTS: (Please return to SO i/c _____ unit)

Archer has all the necessary skills, oratory, written & organisational. He does however lack the freedom to represent NSM on a national level, which could hamper our fight to stay open. On the other hand his contacts more than balance this weakness. I therefore support this application.

Date: 1-12-01   Signed: ....Wilkinson..............

2. REQUESTED PARTY OFFICER'S COMMENTS: (Please return to SO i/c _____ unit)

Jeffrey has proved to be a first class orderly, although Mr Reeves has no opinion of him as a tea maker. He is good both the Officers and the other prisoners, showing remarkable skills & communication and presence which may disqualify him from the job of Governor. However he is willing to do the job for £8.40p per week

Date: Signed: .... CNSW Head of Res

3. LABOUR BOARD DECISION:

No order, over gratified.

Date: 1/12/2001   Signed: ....
(Head of Inmate Activities)

LPF030

DAY 136

employment. However, Doug's wife Wendy will meet the potential employer today and get him to send a fax offering Doug a job of driving loads from Boston back to March. We will have to wait and see if Mr Berlyn will sanction this. I refuse to get excited.

2.00 pm

I walk down to the football field and watch NSC play Witherton. We lose 5–0 so there's not a lot more to report, other than it was very cold standing on the touch line; the wind was blowing in off the next landmass to the east, which happens to be Russia.

7.00 pm

I sit in my room reading *This Week*, an excellent journal if you want an overall view of the week's events. It gives me a chance to bring myself up to date with the situation in Afghanistan, America and even NSC.

Under the heading, 'A Bad Week', it seems that a Jeffrey Archer look-alike is complaining about being regularly stopped by the police to make sure I haven't escaped. 'It's most unfair,' he protests, 'it's ruined my life.' The paper felt his protests would have been more convincing if he hadn't travelled down to NSC accompanied by a tabloid to have his photograph taken outside the prison.

9.00 pm

I visit Leon in his room on the north block. His fiancée has told her father that he is in Norway on business, and won't be returning to England until 21 December, the day he's released from prison.

DAY 137   SUNDAY 2 DECEMBER 2001

10.30 am

Leon's fiancée is visiting him today, and they'll use the ninety minutes to plan their wedding.

11.30 am

I join Doug at the hospital to read the morning papers. The *People* devote half a page to telling their readers that I am distraught because a prisoner has stolen my diary and I'll have to start again. I wouldn't be distraught. After 137 days and over 300,000 words, I'd be suicidal.

3.00 pm

Doug has just come off the phone with his wife and tells me that his friend is going to place an advertisement in the *Boston Target* this Wednesday, stating that he needs a driver to transport goods from Boston to March. Doug will apply for the job, and a fax will then be sent to Mr Berlyn the same day offering Doug an interview. If Mr Berlyn agrees, Doug will be offered the position the following day.

DAY 138   MONDAY 3 DECEMBER 2001

9.40 am

Mr New comes in cursing. It seems the prison is overcrowded and there are applicants from Nottingham, Lincoln, Wayland, Birmingham and Leicester who will have to be turned away because every bed is occupied. Apparently it's all my fault.

This would not be a problem for Spring Hill, because they always have a long waiting list, and can be very selective. At NSC it now means that if any inmate even *bends* the rules, he'll be sent back to the prison he came from, as three inmates discovered to their cost last week. This was not the case when there were dozens of empty beds.

10.50 am

I see Leon walking back from the gatehouse to the stores where he works, and leave the office to have a word with him. Yesterday's visit went well. 'But I have a feeling,' he adds, 'there's something she isn't telling me.'

I press him as to what this might be, but he says he doesn't know, or has he become wary about how much of his story will appear in this diary? He then asks me to change all the names. I agree and have done so.

2.15 pm

Doug gives me some good news. Mrs Tempest (principal officer in charge of resettlement) has assured him that if he gets an interview with another haulage company, she will accompany him, assuming they fulfil all the usual police and prison criteria. If they then offer him a job, she will recommend he starts immediately, and by that she means next Monday.

It's becoming clear to me that there are several officers (not all) who are determined that NSC will be given resettlement status, and not just remain a D-cat open prison. Should the Home Office agree to this, then several of the inmates will be allowed out during the day on CSV work and eventually progress to full-time jobs. It's clear that Doug is a test case, because he's an obvious candidate for outside work, and if they can get him started, the floodgates might well open and this prison's future would no longer be in doubt. So suddenly my fortunes could be reversed. Once again I envy the reader who can simply turn the pages to discover what happens next in my life.

4.00 pm

Mr Simpson (senior probation officer) has completed his interviews with the three inmates who are on sentence planning. He comes down to the kitchen for a glass of water.

Over the past six weeks, I've come to know Graham Simpson quite well, despite the fact that he's fairly reserved. I suppose it goes with the territory. He is a consummate professional, and wouldn't dream of discussing another prisoner, however good or bad their record. But he will answer general questions on the penal system, and after thirty years in the profession he has views that are worth listening to. I suspect that the majority of

755

people reading this diary would, in the case of lifers, lock them up and throw away the key, and in some cases, hang them. However . . .

All murderers are sentenced to ninety-nine years, but the judge will then set a tariff that can range from eight years to life. At NSC we have an inmate who is serving his thirty-second year in jail. There are over 1,800 prisoners in the UK doing life sentences, of whom only a tiny percentage ever reach a D-cat open prison. There are twenty-two lifers currently at NSC. After being sentenced, they begin their life in an A-cat and progress through to B and C, and finally arrive at a D-cat with the expectation of release. At NSC, of the twenty-two resident lifers, these tariffs are set from twelve years to Her Majesty's pleasure, and Mr Simpson confirms that although some will become eligible for release, they will never make it. The Home Office simply won't take the risk.

Mr Simpson explains that it's his responsibility to assess which of these prisoners should be considered for release, but he will always err on the side of caution because, however many successes you have 'on the out', it only takes one failure to hit the front pages.

Mr Simpson admits to one such failure – a man with no previous convictions, who had, until murdering his unfaithful wife, led a perfectly normal existence. He was sentenced to life imprisonment, with a tariff of twelve years. Once in prison, his model behaviour saw him progress quickly (by lifers' standards) from A, to B, to C, to NSC in under eight years. While at NSC his record remained unblemished, until he fell in love with a member of staff who had to resign her position, and look for another job. After twelve years he was released, and they were married shortly afterwards. The man found a good job, and settled down into the community. Three years later, on the anniversary of his first wife's murder, he killed his new spouse and then took his own life.

Mr Simpson sighs. 'There was nothing to suggest this would occur, and if he'd not been released, no lifer ever would be. The majority will never be a danger to the public as most murders are one-off crimes and first-time offences; 90 per cent of those released never commit another crime.'

It is possible for a lifer to be released after eight years, but the vast majority serve over twenty, and some never leave prison – other than in a coffin.

DAY 139   TUESDAY 4 DECEMBER 2001

8.57 am

Mr Clarke has been sacked and put on outside duties, while Carl has been sent back to the south block, and all because of a dishonest prison officer. I'll explain.

Mr Clarke is the cleaner at SMU and because he's sixty-seven years old, he only works mornings. It keeps him out of the cold, and gives him something to do rather than sit around in his room all day. You will all know from past reports that he carried out the job with a great deal of pride. Carl, whom I've been training to take over from me, will now only return to SMU when, and if, I become the hospital orderly. And why? An officer has been talking to the press to supplement his income, and among the things he's told them is that I have my own cleaner and a personal assistant. The governor has found it necessary to suspend the two jobs while an enquiry takes place. Mr New is livid, not so much about Carl, but because Mr Clarke has suffered as a direct result of an officer's 'unprofessional conduct'.

The detailed information given to the press has enabled the investigation to narrow the suspects down to two officers. The guessing game in the prison is which two – unfair, because it allows prisoners to put any officer they don't like in the frame.

10.00 am

Labour board. Carl is officially demoted to cleaner, but assured by Mr Berlyn that when my job becomes available, he will take over. Mr Clarke is now sweeping up leaves in the yard. Remember it's December.

12 noon

Over lunch Doug tells me that Mrs Tempest has suggested that his prospective employer come to the prison, where his credentials will be carefully checked, and he'll be questioned as to the job description, which entails driving a lorry from Boston to Birmingham to March and back every day. If all goes to plan, Doug will be able to begin work on Monday morning, I'll go to the hospital as orderly, Carl will move back into SMU and, if the prison shows an ounce of common sense, Mr Clarke will be reinstated as part-time cleaner.

2.00 pm

I spend the afternoon at SMU on my own. There are three prisoners up in front of the sentence planning board, and another who needs advice on HDC (tagging). As he can neither read nor write, I fill in all the forms for him.

Mr New arrives looking frustrated. Another crisis has arisen over prison beds: twelve of the rooms on the south block have no doors. He gives an order that they must be fitted immediately, which in prison terms means next Monday at the earliest.

DAY 139

6.00 pm

I'm called over the tannoy to report to reception. It can only be Mr Daff.

I arrive in front of the Regimental Sergeant Major to find he's on his own. Mr Daff tells me that he has decided to take early retirement because he doesn't like all the changes that are taking place in the Prison Service. 'Far too fuckin' soft,' he mutters under his breath. He adds that because I'm to be the next hospital orderly, I'll be allowed some of my personal belongings. He opens my box and lets me remove a tracksuit, a blanket, two pillowcases, a tablecloth and a dictionary. He fills in the necessary pink form and I sign for them. He then winks as he places them all in a black plastic bin liner. I depart with my swag.

10.00 pm

I leave the hospital, return to my room and settle down to read *The Diving Bell and the Butterfly*, which has been recommended by my son William.

DAY 140   WEDNESDAY 5 DECEMBER 2001

10.00 am

The punishment should fit the crime according to Mr W. S. Gilbert, and I have no quarrel with that. However, shouldn't all inmates be treated equally, whatever prison they are incarcerated in? Which brings me onto the subject of wages.

The practice at NSC is just plain stupid and, more important, unfair, because it discriminates in such a way as to be inexplicable to anyone. I have only become fully aware of the disparity because of my twice-weekly contact with the labour board, who not only arbitrarily allocate the jobs, but also decide on the wages. For example, as orderly to the sentence management unit, I am paid £8.50 a week. The library orderlies receive £9.40, the gym orderlies £11.90, reception orderlies £10.50, education orderlies £8.40 and the chapel orderly £9.10. However, a farm worker, who starts at eight in the morning and is out in the cold all day, gets £5.60, and a cleaner £7.20, whereas the prison barber, who only works from six to eight every evening, gets £10 a week.

It's no different in any other prison, but no one seems to give a damn.

Seven prisoners come through reception today. Two of them have been sent to NSC with only eleven and nine days left to serve. Why, when moving to a new prison is a disorientating, frightening and unpleasant experience?*

Why not appoint to the prison board carefully selected prisoners who could tell the Home Office one or two home truths? Here at NSC there are two inmates with PhDs, seven with BAs and several with professional qualifications, all of whom are as bright as any officer I've met, with the exception of Mr Gough, who is happy to discus Sisley, Vanburgh and John Quincy Adams rather than the latest prison regulations.

2.00 pm

Carl takes over from me at SMU because I have a theatre visit. By that I mean that the two people who are coming to see me today are the theatre director David Gilmore, and the producer Lee Menzies. David Gilmore (*Daisy Pulls it Off*) is just back from Australia, where he's been directing *Grease*, and Lee is about to put on *The Island* at the Old Vic.

Currently I'm an investor (angel) with both of them. *Grease*, which is on tour in the UK, has already not only returned my capital investment, but also shown a 50 per cent profit. This is not the norm, it's more often the other way round. I have 10 per cent of *The Island*, which hasn't yet opened. David Ian (who had to cancel his visit at the last minute) has several shows in production in which I have a share: *The King and I* (London and tour), *Chicago* (tour), *Grease* (tour), and he's now talking about a production of the successful Broadway musical, *The Producers*. Once David and Lee have brought me up to date on everything that's happening in the theatre world, we turn to a subject on which I feel they will be able to advise me.

---

* Because the last prison pays the expense of discharging a prisoner.

Mr Daff shouts out in his best Sergeant Major voice that it's time for visitors to leave. Where did the time go?

8.30 pm

Doug tells me that his wife visited him today. She confirmed that he will be offered the haulage job, and therefore I can become hospital orderly next week. I'm going to have to decide which course to take should Spring Hill offer me a transfer.

10.00 pm

Life may be awful, but after watching the ten o'clock news and seeing the conditions in the Greek jail where they've locked up eleven British plane spotters, I count my blessings.

DAY 141   THURSDAY 6 DECEMBER 2001

4.45 pm

After a day of no murders, no escapes, no one shipped out, I meet up with Doug for supper. We sit at a corner table and he brings me up to date on his interview for a job. Having applied to the advertisement in the *Boston Target*, Doug was interviewed in the presence of Ms Tempest. He was offered the job and begins work on Monday as a lorry driver. He will ferry a load of steel coils from Boston to Birmingham, to March, before returning to Boston. He must then report back to the prison by seven o'clock. The job will be for six days a week, and he'll be paid £5 an hour.

Just to recap, Doug is doing a four-and-a-half-year sentence for avoiding paying VAT on imported goods to the value of several millions. He's entitled, after serving a quarter of his sentence – if he's been a model prisoner, and he has – to seek outside employment. This is all part of the resettlement programme enjoyed only by prisoners who have reached D-cat status.

It works out well for everyone: NSC is getting prisoners out to work and in Doug they have someone who won't be a problem or break any rules. Although he has a PSV licence, he hasn't driven a lorry for several years, and says it will be like starting all over again. Still, it's better than being cooped up inside a prison all day.

DAY 142　　　FRIDAY 7 DECEMBER 2001

9.00 am

I'm asked to report to sister in the hospital for an interview. As I walk across from SMU, I have a moment's anxiety as I wonder if Linda is considering someone else for hospital orderly. These fears are assuaged by her opening comment when she says how delighted she is that I will be joining her. Linda's only worry is that I am keeping a diary. She stresses the confidentiality of prisoners' medical records. I agree to abide by this without reservation.

10.00 am

Mr New confirms that Mr Clarke (theft) has been reinstated as SMU cleaner. What a difference that will make. Carl can now concentrate on the real job of assisting the officers and prisoners and not have to worry whether the dustbins have been emptied.

2.00 pm

Do you recall the two prisoners who were caught returning from Boston laden with alcohol? One attacked an officer with a torch

DAY 142

so his friends could escape. The escapee, who managed to slip back to his room and thanks to a change of clothes supplied by a friend, got away with it because it wasn't possible to prove he'd ever been absent. Today, the same prisoner was found to have a roll-on deodorant in his room not sold at the canteen. He was shipped out to a B-cat in Liverpool this afternoon.

6.00 pm

I spend an hour signing 200 'Toad' Christmas cards.

8.15 pm

Doug is having second thoughts about giving up his job. The thought of driving eight hours a day for six days a week isn't looking quite so attractive.

10.00 pm

I return to my room and finish *The Diving Bell and the Butterfly* by the late Jean Dominique Bauby. It is, as my son suggested, quite brilliant. The author had a massive stroke and was left paralysed and speechless, only able to move one eyelid. And with that eyelid he mastered a letter code and dictated the book. Makes my problems seem pretty insignificant.

DAY 143   SATURDAY 8 DECEMBER 2001

8.00 am

Normally the weekends are a bore, but after a couple of hours editing *Sons of Fortune* I start moving my few worldly goods across to the hospital. Although I'm not moving in officially until tomorrow, Doug allows me to store some possessions under one of the hospital beds.

1.00 pm

Among today's letters are ones from Rosemary Leach and Stephanie Cole in reply to my fan mail following their performances in *Back Home*. Miss Leach, in a hand-written letter, fears she may have overacted, as the new 'in thing' is blandness and understatement. Miss Cole thought her own performance was a little too sentimental. I admire them for being so critical of themselves.

I receive seventy-two Christmas cards today, which lifts my spirits greatly. The officers have begun a book on how many cards I'll receive from the public: Mr Hart is down for 1,378, Mr New 1,290 and Mr Downs 2,007. I select three to be put on the ledge by my bed – a landscape by that magnificent Scottish

DAY 143

artist Joseph Farqueson, a Giles cartoon of Grandma and a Bellini painting of the Virgin Mother.

2.00 pm

Highlight of my day is a visit from Mary, James and Alison, who between them bring me up to date on all matters personal, office and legal. William returns from America next week, and, along with Mary and James, will come to see me on Christmas Eve. Mary will then fly off to Kenya and attend my nephew's wedding. Mary and I have always wanted to go on safari and see the big cats. Not this year.

DAY 144   SUNDAY 9 DECEMBER 2001

9.00 am

Doug has an 'away day' with his family in March, so I spend the morning covering for him at the hospital.

2.00 pm

A visit from two Conservative front bench spokesmen, Patrick McLoughlin MP, the party's deputy chief whip in the Commons, and Simon Burns MP, the number two under Liam Fox, who covers the health portfolio. They've been loyal friends over many years. I canvassed for both of them before they entered the House, Patrick in a famous by-election after Matthew Parris left the Commons, which he won by 100 votes, and Simon who took over Norman St John Stevas's seat in Chelmsford West where the Liberals had lowered Norman's majority from 5,471 in 1979 to 378 in 1983.

'If you felt the Conservatives might not be returned to power for fifteen years, would you look for another job?' I ask.

'No,' they both reply in unison. 'In any case,' Simon adds, 'I'm not qualified to do anything else.' Patrick nods his agreement. I'm not sure if he's agreeing that Simon couldn't do anything else, or that he falls into the same category.

DAY 144

We have a frank discussion about IDS. Both are pleased that he has managed to downgrade the debate on Europe within the party and concentrate on the health service, education and the social services. They accept that Blair is having a good war (Afghanistan), and although the disagreements with Brown are real, the British people don't seem to be that interested. Patrick feels that we could be back in power the election after next; Simon is not so optimistic.

'But,' he adds, 'if Brown takes over from Blair, we could win the next election.'

'What if someone takes over from IDS?' I ask.

Neither replies.

When they leave, I realize how much I miss the House and all things political.

10.15 pm

This is my last night on the south block. Despite a football match blaring from next door, I sleep soundly.

DAY 145   MONDAY 10 DECEMBER 2001

3.52 am

I wake early, so write for a couple of hours.

6.00 am

Pack up my final bits and pieces and go across to the hospital to join Doug, who's carrying out the same exercise in reverse.

7.30 am

I will describe my new daily routine before I tell you anything about my work at the hospital.

> *6.00 am* Rise, write until 7 am.
>
> *7.00 am* Bath and shave.
>
> *7.30 am* Sister arrives to take sick parade, which lasts until 8 am.
>
> *8.00 am* Deliver 'off work' slips to the north and south blocks, farm, works, education and the front gate.
>
> *8.20 am* Breakfast.

9–10.30 am	Doctor arrives to minister to patients until around ten-thirty, depending on number.
11.30 am	Sick parade until noon (collecting pills, etc.).
12.00	Lunch.
12.30 pm	Phone Alison at the office.
1–2.00 pm	Write.
3.00 pm	Prisoners arrive from Birmingham, Leicester, Wayland, Lincoln or Bedford, all C-cats, to join us at NSC. They first go to reception to register; after that their next port of call is the hospital, where sister signs them in and checks their medical records. You rarely get transferred to another prison if you're ill.

I check their blood pressure, their urine sample – for diabetes, not drugs; that is carried out in a separate building later – their height and weight, and pass this information onto sister so that it can be checked against their medical records.

4.30–5.00 pm	Sick parade. Linda, who began work at 7.30 am, leaves at 5 pm.
5.00 pm	Supper. If anyone falls ill at night, the duty officer can open up the surgery and dispense medication, although most are told they can wait until sick parade the following day. If it's serious, they're taken off to Pilgrim Hospital in Boston by taxi, which is fifteen minutes away.
5.30 pm	Write for a couple of hours.
7.45 pm	Call Mary and/or James and Will.
8.00 pm	Read or watch television; tonight, *Catherine the Great.* I'm joined by Doug and Clive (I'm allowed to have two other inmates in the hospital between 7 and 10.00 pm).

10.20 pm After watching the news, I settle down in a bed five inches wider than the one in my room on the south block and fall into a deep sleep. It is, as is suggested by the title of this book – compared with Belmarsh and Wayland – heaven.

DAY 146   TUESDAY 11 DECEMBER 2001

5.49 am

I am just about getting the hang of my daily routine. It's far more demanding than the work I carried out at SMU. I hope that Linda will be willing to teach me first aid, and more importantly give me a greater insight into the drugs problem in prisons.

7.25 am

I'm standing by the door waiting for Linda to arrive. I prepare her a coffee; one sweetener and a teaspoonful of milk in her pig mug. The five doctors all have their own mugs.

Linda has worked in the Prison Service for over ten years. She has three grown-up children, two sons and a daughter. She was married to a 'nurse tutor', Terry, who tragically died of skin cancer a couple of years ago at the age of fifty-three. She works long hours and the prisoners look on her much as I viewed my prep-school matron – a combination of mother, nurse and confidante. She has no time for shirkers, but couldn't be more sympathetic if you are genuinely ill.

8.15 am

After sick parade, I carry out my rounds to the different parts of the prison to let staff know who will be off work today, before going to breakfast. I ask John (lifer) what meat is in the sausage.

'It's always beef,' he replies, 'because there are so many Muslims in prisons nowadays, they never serve pork sausages.'

10.00 am

The hospital has a visit from a man called Alan, who's come to conduct a course on drug and alcohol abuse. He moves from prison to prison, advising and helping anyone who seeks his counsel. There are 150 such officers posted around the country, paid for by the taxpayer out of the NHS and the Home Office budgets.

Alan is saddened by how few prisoners take advantage of the service he offers. In Bradford alone, he estimates that 40 per cent of inmates below the age of thirty are on drugs, and another 30 per cent are addicted to alcohol. He shows me the reams of Home Office forms to be filled in every time he sees a prisoner. By the end of the morning, only two inmates out of 211 have bothered to turn up and see him.

11.00 am

I have a special visit from Sir Brian Mawhinney MP, an old friend whose constituency is about twenty miles south of NSC. As a former cabinet minister and Shadow Home Secretary, he has many questions about prisons, and as I have not entered the Palace of Westminster for the past six months, there are questions I'm equally keen for him to answer.

DAY 146

Brian stays for an hour, and after we stop going over past triumphs, we discuss present disasters. He fears that the Simon Burns scenario is realistic, a long time in the wilderness for the Conservatives, but 'Events, dear boy events, are still our biggest hope.' Brian runs over time, and I miss lunch – no complaints.

4.00 pm

Mr Hart passes on a message from my solicitors that my appeal papers have not been lodged at court. Panic. I passed them over to the security officer six weeks ago. Mr Hart calls Mr Hocking, who confirms that they were sent out on 29 October. Who's to blame?

5.00 pm

Canteen. Now that I'm enhanced, I have an extra £15 of my own money added to my account each week. With my hospital orderly pay of £11.70, it adds up to £26.70 a week. So I can now enjoy Cussons soap, SR toothpaste, Head and Shoulders shampoo, and even the occasional packet of McVitie's chocolate biscuits.

6.00 pm

I attend a rock concert tonight, performed by the 'Cons and Pros.' The standard is high, particularly Gordon (GBH) on the guitar, who sadly for the band will be released tomorrow.

8.00 pm

Doug returns from his second day at work. He has driven to Birmingham and Northampton in one day. He is exhausted, and fed up with his room-mate, who leaves the radio on all night. I'm in bed asleep by ten-thirty. You will discover the relevance of this tomorrow.

DAY 147 WEDNESDAY 12 DECEMBER 2001

2.08 am

The night security officer opens my door and shines his torch in my eyes. I don't get back to sleep for over an hour.

5.16 am

He does it again, so I get up and start writing.

8.07 am

On my journey around the prison this morning handing out 'off-work' slips, I have to drop into the farm. It's freezing and a lot of the inmates are claiming to have colds. I bump into the farm manager, Mr Donnelly, a charming man who I came to know from my days at the SMU when he sat on the labour board. He introduces me to Blossom, a beautiful creature.

Blossom weighs in at twenty-six stone, and has a broken nose and four stubby, fat hairy legs. She is lucky to be alive. Blossom is the prisoners' favourite pig, so when her turn came for slaughter, the inmates hid her in a haystack. When Mr Donnelly was unable to find Blossom that morning she was granted a week's reprieve. Blossom reappeared the next day, but mysteriously disappeared again when the lorry turned up the following week. Once again Mr Donnelly searched for her, and once again he failed to find her. The inmates knew that it couldn't be long before Blossom's hiding place was discovered, so they put in an application to the governor to buy her, so that she could spend the rest of her days at NSC in peace. Mr Donnelly was so moved by the prisoners' concern that he lifted the death penalty and allowed Blossom to retire. The happy pet now roams around the farm, behaving literally like a pig in clover. (See below.)

Blossom and his friend Blossom

DAY 147

8.30 am

On my way back to the hospital after breakfast, I sense something different, and realize that Peter (lifer, arson) is not on the road sweeping the leaves as he does every morning. A security officer explains that Peter is out on a town leave in Boston; the first occasion he's left prison in thirty-one years. I'll try to have a word with him as soon as he returns, so that I can capture his first impressions of freedom.

9.00 am

The new inductees report to the doctor for their medical checkup. I now feel I'm settling into a routine as hospital orderly.

12 noon

Call Mary to assure her that the courts have now located my papers, and to wish her luck with our Christmas party tomorrow night. She will also be attending Denis and Margaret Thatcher's fiftieth wedding anniversary at the East India Club earlier in the evening. She promises to call me and let me know how they both went. No, I remind her, I can only call you.

4.08 pm

An announcement over the tannoy instructs me to report to reception. I arrive to be told by Sergeant Major Daff that I have been sent two Christmas cakes – one from Mrs Gerald Scarfe, better known as Jane Asher, with a card, from which I reproduce only the final sentence:

I'm baking you a cake for Christmas with a hacksaw and file inside.

See you soon, love Jane

– and one from a ladies' group in Middleton. As no prisoner is allowed to receive any foodstuffs in case they contain alcohol or drugs, Mr Daff agrees that one can go to the local retirement home, and the other to the special needs children. So it's all right for the children to be stoned out of their minds and the old-age pensioners to be drugged up to the eyeballs, but not me.

'It's Home Office regulations,' explains Mr Daff.

5.00 pm

I spot Peter (lifer, arson) coming up the drive. He looks in a bit of a daze, so I invite him to join me in the hospital for coffee and biscuits. We chat for nearly an hour.

The biggest shock for Peter on leaving prison for the first time in over thirty years was the number of 'coffin dodgers' (old people) that were on the streets of Boston doing their Christmas shopping. In 1969, the life expectancy for a man was sixty-eight years and for a woman seventy-three; it's now seventy-six and eighty-one respectively. Peter also considered many of the young women dressed 'very tarty', but he did admit that he couldn't stop staring at them. Peter, who is six foot four inches tall and weighs eighteen stone, was surprised that he no longer stands out in a crowd, as he would have done thirty-one years ago. When he visited Safeways supermarket, it was the first time he'd seen a trolley; in the past he had only been served at a counter and used a shopping basket. And as for money, he knows of course about decimalization, but when he last purchased something from a shop there were 240 pennies in a pound, half-crowns, ten shilling notes and the guinea was still of blessed memory.

Peter was totally baffled by pelican crossings and was frightened to walk across one. However the experience he most disliked was having to use a changing room to try on clothes behind a curtain, while members of the public walked past him – particularly female assistants who didn't mind drawing back the curtain to see how he was getting on. He was amazed that he could try on a shirt and then not have to purchase it.

I suspect that the process of rehabilitation – accompanied town visits (six in all), unaccompanied town visits, weekend home visits, week visits, CSV work, followed by a job in the community – will take him at least another three to four years, by which time Peter will qualify for his old-age pension. I can only wonder if he will ever rejoin the real world and not simply be moved from one institution to another.

10.00 pm

I listen to the ten o'clock news. Roy Whiting has been given life imprisonment for the murder of Sarah Payne. Once the sentence has been passed, we discover that Whiting had already been convicted some years ago for abducting a child, and sexually abusing a minor. His sentence on that occasion? Four years.

DAY 148   THURSDAY 13 DECEMBER 2001

6.00 am

Orderlies are the prison's school prefects. They're given their jobs because they can be trusted. In return, they're expected to work for these privileges, such as eating together in a small group, and in my case having a single room with a television.

There are over a dozen orderlies in all. Yesterday both reception orderlies were sacked, leaving two much sought-after vacancies.

Martin, the senior of the two reception orderlies, was due to be discharged this morning, two months early, on tag (HCD). The only restriction was that he must remain in his place of residence between the hours of 7 pm and 7 am. Martin had already completed the 'paper chase', which had to be carried out the day before release. Unfortunately, before departing this morning he decided to take with him a brand-new prison-issue denim top and jeans, and several shirts. A blue and white striped prison shirt apparently sells at around a hundred pounds on the outside, especially if it has the letters NSC on the pocket.

When the theft was discovered, he was immediately sacked and, more sadly, so was the other orderly, Barry, whose only crime was that he wouldn't grass on Martin. It's rough justice when the only way to keep your job is to grass on your mate

DAY 148

when you know what the consequences will be for that person – not to mention how the other inmates will treat you in the future. We will find out the punishment tomorrow when both men will be up in front of the governor.

2.00 pm

I am disappointed to receive a letter from William Payne, the governor of Spring Hill, turning down my application for transfer. His reasons for rejecting me are shown in his letter reproduced here. (See opposite.) I feel I should point out that the last five inmates from NSC who have applied to Spring Hill have all been accepted. It's not worth appealing, because I've long given up expecting any justice whenever the Home Office is involved.

3.00 pm

Six new inductees: four on short sentences ranging from three weeks to nine months, and two lifers who, for the past sixteen years, have been banged up for twenty-two hours a day. They are walking around the perimeters of the prison (no walls) in a daze, and can't understand why they're not being ordered back to their cells. Linda tells me that lifers often report at the end of the first week with foot-sores and colds, and take far longer to adapt to open conditions.

One of the short-termers from Nottingham who's been placed in the no-smoking spur on the south block that has mostly more mature CSV workers who only return to the prison at night – tells me with a wry smile that he couldn't sleep last night because it was so quiet.

HM Prisons
Grendon & Springhill
Grendon Underwood
Aylesbury
Bucks HP18 0TL
Telephone   01296 770301
Fax   01296 770756
E mail   governorpayne@hotmail.com

INVESTORS IN PEOPLE

Mr J Archer FF8282
HMP North Sea Camp
Frieston
Boston
Lincs
PE22 0QX

Ref: 103/2001

Date: 10 December 2001

Dear Mr Archer,

APPLICATION TO TRANSFER TO SPRING HILL

Thank you for your application to transfer to HMP Spring Hill.

I have considered your application carefully. You requested a transfer in order that you may receive visits from your family more easily than you can at North Sea Camp. While Spring Hill would be suitable, there are currently more vacancies at HMP Hollesley Bay,*near Woodbridge in Suffolk which is within easy reach of Cambridge and commuting distance of London. For this reason I am refusing your request to transfer to Spring Hill.

The Governor of Hollesley Bay has confirmed that he is able to offer you a place should you wish to request a transfer to that establishment. I hope this provides a positive alternative to you.

Yours sincerely,

William Payne.

William Payne
Governor

cc: Colin New, HMP North Sea Camp
    Karen Mackenzie-Howe, HMP Spring Hill

---

* Hollesley Bay is further away from Cambridge than North Sea Camp.

DAY 148

6.00 pm

A visit from Mr Hocking. I'm no longer to dispose of personal papers, letters, envelopes or notes in the dustbin outside the hospital, as a prisoner was caught rifling through the contents last night. In future I must hand them to a security officer, who will shred them. NSC does not want to repeat the Belmarsh debacle, where an officer stole a chapter of my book and tried to sell it to the *Sun*.

8.00 pm

I sit in my palace and hold court with Doug, Clive and Carl, or at least that's how it feels after Belmarsh and Wayland.

In London, Mary is hosting our Christmas party.

DAY 149   FRIDAY 14 DECEMBER 2001

10.00 am

Today is judgment day. Three prisoners are up in front of the governor. Inmates take a morbid interest in the outcome of any adjudication as it's a yardstick for discovering what they can hope to get away with.

Martin, the reception orderly who pleaded guilty to attempting to steal prison clothes on the day he was due to be released, has his tagging privileges removed, and seven days added to his sentence. So for the sake of a pair of jeans and a few prison shirts, Martin will remain at NSC until a couple of weeks before Easter, rather than spending Christmas at home with his wife and family. Added to this, the sixty-seven days will not be spent in the warmth of reception as an orderly, but on the farm in the deep mid-winter cleaning out the pig pens.

Barry is next up. His crime was not grassing on Martin. Although Martin stated clearly at the adjudication that Barry was not party to the offence, he also loses his orderly job, and returns to the farm as a shepherd. For the governor to expect him to 'grass' on his friend (I even doubt if they were friends) seems to me a little rough.

Finding competent replacements will not be easy. The rumour is that Peter (lifer, just had his first day out after thirty-one years) has been offered the job as the next step in his rehabilitation. Peter tells me that he doesn't want to be an orderly, and is happy to continue sweeping up leaves.

The third prisoner in front of the governor this morning is Ali, a man serving three months for theft. Ali has refused to work on the farm and locked himself in his room. For this act of defiance, he has four days added to his sentence. This may not sound excessive, and in normal circumstances I don't think he could complain, as it's the statutory sentence for refusing to work. However, the four days are Christmas Eve, Christmas Day, Boxing Day and 27 December.

Ali arrives in the hospital moments after the adjudication and bursts into tears. The governor decides that I should be punished as well, because Linda puts me in charge of him. It's ten-forty and the governor wants Ali back on the farm by this afternoon. Fortunately, England are playing India. It's the second day of the Test, and Ali knows his cricket. We settle down in the hospital ward to watch the final session of the day. Sachin Tendulkar is at the crease so Ali stops crying. By lunchtime (end of play in Madras), Tendulkar has scored 123 and Ali's tears have turned to smiles.

He's back on the farm at one o'clock.

3.00 pm

Seven new prisoners in from Nottingham today, and as we only released three this morning, our numbers reach 211; our capacity is 220. The weekly turnover at NSC is about 20 per cent, and I'm told it always peaks at this time of year. I'm also informed by one of the lifers that there are more absconders over Christmas, many of whom give themselves up on Boxing Day evening. The governor's attitude is simple; if they return to the gate and apologize, they have twenty-eight days added to their sentence; if they wait until they're picked up by the police, then in addition to the added twenty-eight days, they're shipped out to a B-cat the following morning.

4.00 pm

Linda asks me to take two blood samples down to the gate, so they can be sent to Pilgrim Hospital. On the three-hundred-yard walk, I become distracted by a new idea for how the twins discover their identity in *Sons of Fortune*. When I arrive at the gate, the blood samples are no longer in the plastic packet, and must have fallen out en route. I run for the first time in weeks. I don't want to lose my job, and end up working on the farm. I see Jim (gym orderly) running towards me – he's found the samples on the side of the path. I thank him between puffs – he's saved me from my first reportable offence. Actually, I think I should confess at this stage that some weeks ago I picked up a penny from the path and have kept the tiny coin in my jeans pocket, feeling a slight defiance in possessing cash. I put the samples back in their plastic packet and hand them in at the gate.

Incidentally, the other gym orderly Bell is also the NSC goalkeeper. He used to be at Spring Hill, but asked for a transfer to be nearer his wife. NSC needed a goalkeeper, so the transfer only took four days. Thanks to this little piece of subterfuge we're now on a winning streak. However, I have to report that the goalkeeper's wife has run off with his best friend, which may account for Bell being sent off last week. We lost 5–0.

DAY 150   SATURDAY 15 DECEMBER 2001

7.30 am

I now have to work seven days a week, as there's a surgery on Saturday and Sunday. It's a small price to pay for all the other privileges of being hospital orderly.

Not many patients today, eleven in all, but then there's no work to skive off on a Saturday morning. Sister leaves at ten-thirty and I have the rest of the day to myself, unless there's an emergency.

11.00 am

Spend a couple of hours editing *Sons of Fortune*, and only take breaks for lunch, and later to watch the prison football match.

2.00 pm

The football manager and coach is a senior officer called Mr Masters. He's proud of his team, but when it comes to abusing the referee, he's as bad as any other football fan. Today he's linesman, and should be supporting the ref, not to mention the other linesman. But both receive a tirade of abuse, as Mr Masters feels able to give his opinion on an offside decision even though he's a hundred yards away from the offence, and the linesman on the other side of the pitch is standing opposite the offending player. To be fair, his enthusiasm rubs off on the rest of the team, and we win a scrappy game 2–0.

DAY 151   SUNDAY 16 DECEMBER 2001

7.30 am

Only five inmates turn up for early morning surgery. Linda explains that although the prison has a photographic club, woodwork shop, library, gym and chapel, a lot of the prisoners spend the weekend in bed, rising only to eat or watch a football match on TV. It seems such a waste of their lives.

2.00 pm

My visitors today are Malcolm and Edith Rifkind. Malcolm and I entered the House around the same time, and have remained friends ever since. Malcolm is one of those rare animals in politics who has few enemies. He was Secretary of State for Defence and Foreign Secretary under John Major, and I can't help reflecting how no profession other than politics happily divests itself of its most able people when they are at their peak. It's the equivalent of dropping Beckham or Wilkinson at the age of twenty-five. Still, that's the prerogative of the electorate, and one of the few disadvantages of living in a democracy.

Malcolm and his wife Edith want to know all about prison life, while I wish to hear all the latest gossip from Westminster.

Malcolm makes one political comment that will remain fixed in my memory: 'If in 1979 the electorate had offered us a contract for eighteen years, we would have happily signed it, so we can't complain if we now have to spend a few years in the wilderness.' He and Edith have travelled up from London to see me, and they will now drive on to Edinburgh. I cannot emphasize often enough how much I appreciate the kindness of friends.

8.00 pm

Mr Baker drops in for coffee and a chat. The officers' mess is closed over the weekend, so the hospital is the natural pit stop. He tells me that one prisoner has absconded, while another, on returning from his town visit, was so drunk that he had to be helped out of his wife's car. That will be his last town visit for several months. And here's the rub, it was his first day out of prison for six years.

DAY 152   MONDAY 17 DECEMBER 2001

8.50 am

'Papa to Hotel, Papa to Hotel, how do you read me?'

This is PO New's call sign to Linda, and I'm bound to say that the hospital is the nearest I'm going to get to a hotel while I remain incarcerated in one of Her Majesty's establishments.

It's a freezing morning in this flat, open part of Lincolnshire, so there's a long queue for the doctor. First in line are those on the paper chase, due for release tomorrow. The second group comprises those facing adjudication – one caught injecting heroin, a second in possession of money (£20) and finally the inmate who came back drunk last night. The doctor declares all three fit, and can see no medical reason that might be used as mitigating circumstances in their defence. The heroin addict is subsequently transferred back to Lincoln. The prisoner found with £20 in his room claims that he just forgot to hand it in when he returned from a town visit, so ends up with seven days added. The drunk gets twenty-one days added to his sentence, and no further town visits until further notice. He is also warned that next time, it's back to a B-cat.

Those in the third group – by far the largest – are either genuinely ill or don't feel like working on the farm at below-zero

794

temperatures. Most are told to return to work immediately or they will be put on report and come up in front of the governor.

2.00 pm

I phone Mary, who has some interesting news. I feel I should point out that Mr Justice Potts claimed at the end of my trial that this is, 'As serious an offence of perjury as I have had experience of and as I have been able to find in the books'.

A Reader in Law at the University of Buckingham has been checking sentencing for those convicted of perjury. She has discovered that, in the period 1991–2000, 1,024 people were charged with this offence in the United Kingdom. Of the 830 convicted, just under 400 received no custodial sentence at all, while in the case of 410, the sentence was eighteen months or less. Only four people were given a four-year sentence upheld on appeal. One of these framed an innocent man, who served thirty-one months of a seventeen year sentence for a crime he did not commit; the second stood trial twice for a murder of which he was acquitted, but was later convicted of perjury during those trials. The other two were for false declarations related to marriage as part of a large-scale immigration racket.

7.17 pm

There's a knock on my door, and as the hospital is out of bounds after six o'clock unless it's an emergency, I assume it's an officer. It isn't. It's a jolly West Indian called Wright. He's always cheerful, and never complains about anything except the weather.

'Hi, Jeff, I think I've broken my finger.'

I study his hand as if I had more than a first-aid badge from my days as a Boy Scout in the 1950s. I suggest we visit his unit officer. Mr Cole is unsympathetic, but finally agrees Wright should be taken to the Pilgrim Hospital. Wright reports back an hour later with his finger in a splint.

'By the way,' I ask, 'how did you break your finger?'

'Slammed it in a door, didn't I.'

'Strange,' I say, 'because I think I've just seen the door walking around, and it's got a black eye.'

DAY 153   TUESDAY 18 DECEMBER 2001

10.00 am

In my mailbag is a registered letter from the court of appeal. I print it in full. (See overleaf.) The prison authorities or the courts seem to have been dilatory, as my appeal may be put off until February, rather than held in December. The experts on the subject of appeals, and by that I mean my fellow inmates, tell me that the usual period of time between receiving the above letter and learning the date of one's appeal is around three weeks. It's then another ten days before the appeal itself.

Among my other letters is one from Dame Edna, enquiring about the dress code when she visits NSC.

12 noon

Brian (attempt to defraud an ostrich company) thanks me for a box of new paperbacks that have arrived at the Red Cross office in Boston, sent by my publisher.

1.00 pm

My new job as hospital orderly means I've had to adjust my writing regime. I now write between the hours of 6 and 7 am,

797

COURT
SERVICE

All letters should be addressed to

THE REGISTRAR

JEFFREY HOWARD ARCHER
HMP NORTH SEA CAMP
FREISTON
BOSTON
LINCS
PE22 0QX

THE COURT SERVICE

Criminal Appeal Office
Royal Courts of Justice,
Strand, London, WC2A 2LL
Telephone: 020 7947 7082 (Direct line)
            0207 7947 6014 (Enquiries)
(Direct line - between 9.00am and 5.00pm)
Fax: 020 7947 6900   DX 44450 STRAND
Minicom: 020 7947 7594

Date: 12 December 2001

Your ref: FF8282

Our ref: 200104555S2

Dear Sir/Madam,

Regina v JEFFREY HOWARD ARCHER

I acknowledge receipt of the form seeking to renew your application for leave to appeal against conviction.

In due course our List Office will set a date for your application to be considered by the Full Court of Appeal. You will be aware that since leave to appeal was refused, you are not entitled to Legal Aid for counsel to represent you in relation to the application(s). Accordingly, unless you have already informed this office of a different arrangement, the List Office will presume that the matter is to be fixed for consideration without a legal representative to appear on your behalf.

Please note that if your renewal was not filed within the specified time limits and an extension of time to renew is required, the Court will consider that application first. If an extension of time is refused, the matter will be finished and the Court will not go on to consider the main application for leave to appeal.

It is most important for you to be aware that your application(s) may be listed for hearing at very short notice. If, therefore, you have already made private arrangements for legal advisers to represent you or if you make such arrangements before the hearing date, you must inform this office <u>immediately</u>, supplying details of their name(s), address(es) and telephone number(s). You should also ensure that they are aware of any date fixed for consideration of your application(s).

Yours faithfully

Jushna Chowdhury.

Mrs Jushna Chowdhury
For Registrar
A copy of this letter is being sent for information purposes to;
The Governor, HMP NORTH SEA CAMP
MICHCON DE REYA, Solicitors

1 and 3 pm, and 5 and 7 pm. During the weekends, I can fit in an extra hour each day, which means I'm currently managing about thirty-seven hours of writing a week.

6.00 pm

I visit the canteen to purchase soap, razor blades, chocolate, Evian and phonecards, otherwise I'll be dirty, unshaven, unfed and unwatered over Christmas, not to mention uncontactable. The officer on duty checks my balance, and finds I'm only £1.20 in credit. Help!

DAY 154   WEDNESDAY 19 DECEMBER 2001

9.00 am

'Archer to report to reception immediately, Archer to report to reception immediately.'

Now Mr Daff has retired, I'm not allowed the same amount of latitude as in the past.

I've received five parcels today. The first is a book by Iris Murdoch, *The Sea, The Sea*, kindly sent in by a lady from Dumfries. As I read it some years ago when Ms Murdoch won the Booker Prize, I donate it to the library. The second is a silver bottle opener – not much use to an inmate as we're not allowed to drink – but a kind gesture nevertheless. I ask if I can give it to Linda. No, but it can be put in the old-age pensioners' raffle. The third is a Parker pen. Can I give it to Linda? No, but it can be put in the old-age pensioners' raffle. The fourth is a teddy bear from Dorset. I don't bother to ask, I just agree to donate it to the old-age pensioners' raffle. The fifth is a large tube, which, when opened, reveals fifteen posters from the Chris Beetles Gallery, which I've been eagerly awaiting for over a week. I explain that it's a gift to the hospital, so there's no point in putting it in store for me because the hospital will get it just as soon as I am released. This time *they* agree to let me take it away. Result: one out of five.

2.00 pm

I happily spend a couple of hours, assisted by Carl and a box of Blu-Tack, fixing prints by Albert Goodwin, Ronald Searle, Heath Robinson, Emmett, Geraldine Girvan, Paul Riley and Ray Ellis to the hospital walls. With over 900 Christmas cards littered around the beds, the ward has been transformed into an art gallery. (See opposite.)

5.00 pm

I return to the canteen. I'm only £2.50 in credit, whereas I calculate I should have around £18. It's the nearest I get to losing my temper, and it's only when the officer in charge says he's been trying to get the system changed for the past year that I calm down, remembering that it's not his fault. He makes a note of the discrepancy on the computer. I thank him and return to the hospital. I have no reason to complain; I've got the best job in the prison and the best room, and am allowed to write five hours a day. Shut up, Archer.

6.00 pm

I attend the carol service at six-thirty, where I read one of the lessons. Luke 2, verses eight to twenty. As I dislike the modern text, the vicar has allowed me to read from the King James version.

The chapel is packed long before the service is due to begin and the organ is played with great verve and considerable improvisation by Brian (ostrich fraud). The vicar's wife, three officers and four inmates read the lessons. I follow Mr New, and Mr Hughes follows me. We all enjoy a relaxed service of carols

and lessons, and afterwards there is the added bonus of mince pies and coffee, which might explain the large turnout.

After the service, Brian introduces me to Maria, who's in charge of the Red Cross shop in Boston. She has brought along my box of paperbacks and asks if I would be willing to sign them. I happily agree.

DAY 155   THURSDAY 20 DECEMBER 2001

7.30 am

Record numbers report sick with near freezing conditions outside.

11.00 am

The last inmate to see the doctor is a patient called Robinson. He's shaking and trying in vain to keep warm. I've been in prison long enough now to spot a heroin addict at thirty paces. While he waits for his appointment, Robinson confides that he's desperately trying to kick the habit, and has put himself on a compulsory urine test every morning. He's thirty-two years old, and has been in and out of prison for the past fourteen years.

'I'm lucky to be alive,' he says. 'After I got nicked this time, I took the rap and let me mate get off in exchange for a promise he'd send me ten quid a week while I'm inside.'

The 'friend' died a few weeks later after injecting himself from a contaminated batch of heroin.

'If the deal had been the other way round,' Robinson suggests, 'I'd be the dead man.'

12.30 pm

Over lunch I discuss the drug problem in prisons with the two gym orderlies, both of whom abhor the habit. I am shocked – can I still be shocked? – when Jim (burglary, antiques only) tells me that 30 per cent of the inmates at NSC are on heroin. But more depressing still, when Jim was here eight years ago for a previous offence, he says only a handful of the inmates were on drugs. What will it be like in ten years' time?

1.00 pm

As I walk back from lunch, I see Brian and John, the CSV Red Cross workers, heading towards me. They've both been taken off the job and confined to the prison while an enquiry is being conducted. Maria, who runs the Red Cross shop in Boston, has been accused of smuggling contraband (twelve paperbacks) into the prison. Apparently she should have informed the gate staff of her request to have the books autographed by me. Brian tells me they left her in tears, and I am bound to say that what started out as a simple goodwill gesture has ended in turmoil; the Red Cross have been removed as participants in the CSV scheme, and Brian and John have lost their jobs. I resolve to find out if there is more to it – prison has taught me not to automatically take something on trust – and if there isn't, to try to right this injustice.

8.00 pm

Carl suggests we watch *Midnight Express*, a sure way of reminding ourselves just how lucky we all are. And to think Turkey wants to be a full member of the European Union.

DAY 156   FRIDAY 21 DECEMBER 2001

9.00 am

Dr Walling is on duty today. He's full of good cheer, and brings
Christmas presents for Linda and myself. Linda gets a box of
Ferrero Rocher chocolates, and he presents me with a bottle
of Scotch. Linda quickly grabs the bottle, explaining that it's
against prison rules to offer prisoners alcohol. If I'd been caught
with a bottle of whisky (actually I don't drink spirits) I would
have lost my job, and possibly have been sent to a B-cat with
added days. Dr Walling looks suitably embarrassed.

12.00 pm

Simon (abduction of his son, mess orderly) drops in to deliver
Linda's sandwich lunch. While I make her a coffee, Simon tells
me he's moving room today. His room-mate, a married man with
two children, asked him last night if he'd ever considered being
bisexual. Simon tells me that he jumped out of bed, got dressed,
left the room and demanded to be moved, as he didn't want to
be locked up with, in his words, 'a raving faggot'.

8.00 pm

I watch *Great Artists* on BBC 2. The subject is Breughel, and all the little Breughels.

10.00 pm

Fall asleep in my chair, exhausted. It must be the combination of writing and hospital duties. Can't complain though, as the days are passing far more quickly.

DAY 157   SATURDAY 22 DECEMBER 2001

9.00 am

Prison life is like a game of cricket; every day you discover a new way of getting out.

The doctor has to pass as fit this morning an inmate by the name of Hal (cat burglar, six months) before he goes up in front of the governor. Last night Hal left the prison and walked into Boston. He dropped into one of the local pubs, had a pint and then purchased a bottle of vodka, a bottle of rum and a six-pack of Fosters. Hal didn't feel like walking the six miles back, so he decided to thumb a lift to the prison. Mr Blackman, one of our younger officers, obliged and happily escorted Hal back, confiscated the contraband and booked him into the segregation block. Hal was due to be released in January, but I fear it's now looking more like February. It turns out that he also suggested to Mr Blackman that if he dropped him off half a mile from the prison, he could keep the bounty. Nice try, Hal.

Among the other inmates who will appear in front of the governor this morning is Simon (abducting his son), but only for a warning. It appears he's been telling anyone who will listen that his cell-mate is 'a raving faggot'. The governor will order him to stop using such inflammatory language otherwise he will lose his job as mess orderly.

I chat to the cat burglar as he waits to see the doctor. Hal says he doesn't care that much what the governor decides. His partner has left him, his mother won't speak to him and he hasn't seen his father in years. When he gets out, he doesn't have anywhere to stay overnight, and only has £37 to his name. He says he needs a job that will earn him enough money to ensure that he doesn't have to revert to stealing again.

I ask him, 'How much is enough?'

'Two hundred quid,' he replies. 'Then I'd have a chance of finding some digs and getting a job.'

11.00 am

Mr Lewis drops into the hospital to wish Linda a happy Christmas. While I'm making him a coffee, he complains that I've thrown away the hospital ashtray, so he can't enjoy a cigar. I reluctantly supply an old saucer. He tells me that he was surprised by the Spring Hill decision and, looking round the hospital, says point-edly, 'If they suggest Hollesley Bay, don't even consider it.'

2.50 pm

Mary and William turn up almost an hour late for their visit because of the snow and ice that caused long hold-ups on the A1. My time with them is cut down to forty minutes.

It's Mary's birthday, and she's wearing the emerald that Sergio purchased for me from the Green Mountains after he returned to Columbia.* I wanted to also give her the pot I made at Wayland, but they told me it shattered in the kiln.

We chat about her forthcoming trip to Kenya for her

---

* See *Volume II – Wayland: Purgatory.*

nephew's wedding. She'll be away for the first ten days of January, but as my appeal won't be heard until mid-February, this isn't a problem. She hopes to see Sir Sidney Kentridge and Godfrey Barker before she leaves. If Godfrey signs an affidavit confirming that Mr Justice Potts discussed me adversely at a dinner party they both attended a year before my arrest, I could be out of here in a few weeks' time. Will isn't optimistic. He feels Godfrey will feel compromised because his wife works for the parole board. As Godfrey has sent me a Christmas card, I can only hope Will's wrong.

Surely justice and truth matter to such a man. We shall soon find out.

DAY 158   SUNDAY 23 DECEMBER 2001

8.35 am

The *Sunday Telegraph* reports that I've written a 300,000-word novel entitled *Sons of Fortune* during the *short* time I've been in prison. It might seem short to them, but it's been 158 days for me.

I actually wrote the first three drafts of the novel before my conviction. I had planned to drive from Boston (Connecticut) to Newhaven via Hartford, where the book is set, and research the final points before Mr Justice Potts intervened. I ended up spending the month of August not in the US, but in Belmarsh writing the first diary.

9.00 am

Five inmates' names are called over the tannoy. They are told to report to the doctor, which means they've been charged and will later be up in front of the governor for adjudication: two for smoking cannabis, one for being drunk, one for secreting £25 in a cigarette tin, and finally Hal, who you will recall thumbed a lift back from Boston, while in possession of a bottle of vodka, a bottle of rum and a six-pack of Fosters. Hal did point out to me that it's a twelve-mile round trip to Boston and back to NSC, and

DAY 158

it was 2 degrees below zero. I don't think the governor will consider these to be mitigating circumstances!

Hal loses all privileges, and has twenty-one days added to his sentence.

11.00 am

The governor, Mr Lewis, who has only a few days to go before retirement, pops into the hospital to check on the end of year audit, or was it just to enjoy a cup of coffee with Linda and a cigar during his morning break? As he's leaving, I ask him to tell me a story.

'What about my memoirs?' he protests, but then recounts an anecdote from his time as governor of Oxford Prison: two brothers were charged with a burglary, but the elder did not feel his younger brother would be able to cope with a spell in jail, so he took the rap and was sentenced to six months. As it turned out, the younger brother couldn't cope with being 'on the out' without his elder brother, so he stole a ladder, climbed over the prison wall and broke *into* jail. No one was any the wiser until roll-call that night, when the duty officer reported that they had one more prisoner than was on the manifest. The younger brother was arrested and charged with breaking into a prison. He got three months, and ended up sharing a cell with his brother.

Mr Lewis went on to tell me about two prisoners who escaped from Oxford Crown Court while handcuffed to each other. They ran down the street pursued by the police, but when they came to a zebra crossing, one decided to cross the road while the other kept on going. The handcuffs that bound them together collided with the Belisha beacon at full speed, and they swung round and knocked each other out.

DAY 159   CHRISTMAS EVE

Today is a nightmare for security. First there are the truly stupid inmates who abscond sometime during the morning and then return to the prison on Boxing Day evening. If they are also drunk, they are allowed to sleep it off, with twenty-eight days added to their sentence. Second are the group who slip out to Boston and arrive back with provisions and food. As long as they remain in their rooms and cause no trouble, the officers turn a blind eye. Should they cause any trouble, they also get twenty-eight days. This is known as 'Nelson time', and occurs only at Christmas.

It must seem madness to you, but when you have 211 inmates and only 5 officers on duty, it's no more than common sense. Why aren't there more officers on duty? Because the service is understaffed and underpaid. The average prison officer is paid £17,000 a year, and this year's pay rise was 1.8 per cent. Why not send the offenders back to a closed prison? Because they are all already overcrowded (67,500 in Britain) and if you did, the D-cats would be empty. Then cut down on D-cats? If you did that, you would never rehabilitate anyone. Prisoners in a D-cat used to be released at 8 am (with the exception of lifers) on Christmas Eve and had to return to prison before 8 pm on Boxing Day. But Michael Howard put a stop to that when he

DAY 159

became Home Secretary. This little break was more for the staff than the prisoners.

7.30 am

Dave (murder) is among the walking wounded, and comes to surgery doubled up with stomach cramps. Sister gives him painkillers that contain certain opiates. She then has to make out a separate form, which I take across to security because if Dave were to have an MDT he would show up positive. Sister is especially vigilant in these cases, looking out for those prisoners who fake the pain in order to get the drugs, especially when they know they're about to be tested for heroin. In Dave's case, there is no doubt that he's in real pain, and any case, he's been a model prisoner since the day he arrived at NSC. He's desperate to impress the parole board and be released as soon as possible. He's already served twenty-one years, and his wife says she can't wait much longer.

9.00 am

Despite its being Christmas Eve, one inmate will not be able to avoid a nicking because he has pushed his luck a little too far. During an MDT, he attempted to exchange a tube of someone else's urine for his while he was in the loo. It turns out that he got this drug-free sample from another prisoner in exchange for a Mars Bar.

11.00 am

Sue from accounts drops into the hospital to tell me that my private money has run out, and that's why my canteen account only showed £1.20 in credit. Had she let me know a week ago, I could have asked Mary to top it up. However, Sue explains that she is not allowed to let a prisoner know that his money is running low, and can only inform him if he asks directly for his account balance. The reason is that most inmates are penniless, and don't need to be continually reminded of that fact. Fair enough.

8.00 pm

Doug returns from the canteen laden with goodies, and tells me that an inmate has just been nicked for ordering a taxi to take him on a round trip to Boston. The cab company phoned the prison, so two officers were waiting when the inmate returned. He was caught in possession of forty-eight cans of lager and one bottle each of whisky, vodka and brandy. He also had six packets of fish and chips, a melon, a carton of strawberries, a pot of cream and a box of jellied eels.

The prisoner begged to be placed in the segregation cell overnight in case the inmates who had lost their 'Christmas cheer' thought he'd sold the goodies to someone else. The duty officer duly obliged, but he'll still be up in front of the governor on Boxing Day.

DAY 160   CHRISTMAS DAY

Christmas Day for those who are incarcerated can be summed up in one word: dreadful. I have learned during the last 159 days as a prisoner how perverse reality is.

I go to work today, as every other day, and am grateful for something to do. At the seven-thirty surgery, only six prisoners report for sick parade; you have to be really ill to get up at 7.30 am on Christmas morning and troop across to the hospital when the temperature on the east coast is minus two degrees.

At eight-fifteen I go to breakfast, and even though it's eggs, bacon and sausage served by the officers (Mr Hocking, Mr Camplin, Mr Baker and Mr Gough), only around forty of the two hundred inmates bother to turn up.

On returning to the hospital, Linda and I unload bags of food from her car so I can hold a tea party for my friends this afternoon. She also gives me a present, which is wrapped in Christmas paper. I open it very slowly, trying to anticipate what it might be. Inside a neat little box is a china mug, with a black cat grinning at me. Now I have my own mug, and will no longer have to decide between a Campbell's Soup giveaway and a plain white object with a chip when I have my morning Bovril.

10.00 am

Linda leaves me in charge of the hospital while she attends the governor's Christmas party. Frankly, if over half the prisoners weren't still in bed asleep, I could arrange for them all to abscond. When the tabloids claim I have privileges that the other prisoners do not have, in one respect they are right; I am lucky to be able to carry on with the job I do on the outside. While everyone else tries to kill time, I settle down to write for a couple of hours.

12 noon

Lunch is excellent, and once again served by the officers, and shared with a half dozen old-age pensioners from the local village; tomato soup, followed by turkey, chipolatas, roast potatoes and stuffing, with as much gravy as will go on the plate. I don't allow myself the Christmas pudding – several officers have kindly commented on the fact that I'm putting on weight (nine pounds in nine weeks).

After lunch I walk over to the south block and phone Mary and the boys. All things considered they sound pretty cheerful, but I can't hide the fact that I miss them. My wife is fifty-seven, my boys twenty-nine and twenty-seven, and today I'm surrounded by men sitting in their rooms staring at photographs of young children anywhere from six months to fifteen years old. Yes, they deserve to be incarcerated if they committed a crime, but we should remember it is Christmas Day, and it's not their families who are guilty.

As I walk back through the block, I notice that those not in the TV room or on the phone are just lying on their beds willing the day to pass. I have so much food in my fridge that I invite a dozen inmates over to join me in the hospital.

They all turn up, without exception. We watch *The Great Escape* (somewhat ironic) and enjoy Linda's feast – pork pies, crisps, sausage rolls, shortbread biscuits, KitKats and, most popular of all with my fellow inmates, a chunk of my Cheddar cheese. This is accompanied not by Krug, but a choice of lemonade, Evian water, tea, coffee or Ribena.

They laugh, they chat, they watch the film, and when they leave, David (fraud, schoolmaster) pays me a compliment I have never received at any of my champagne and shepherd's pie parties. 'Thank you for getting rid of the afternoon so pleasantly.'

DAY 161   BOXING DAY

7.30 am

For those prisoners who do not return to work, Boxing Day is almost worse than Christmas Day. Very few inmates attend surgery this morning, and certainly none of them have any illness worth reporting.

8.15 am

Over breakfast, I learn another terrible consequence of the drug culture in prisons. Jim (antiques only), the gym orderly, tells me that inmates who are addicted to heroin often die within a few months of leaving prison. The reason? The heroin they take in jail is always weaker because the dealers add other substances such as caster sugar, talc or flour. So when they are released, they are immediately exposed to a purer substance, which the body can no longer tolerate. Result? They end up dying of an overdose.

11.00 am

The governor drops in to see Linda, and gives me a Christmas present and a birthday present for Mary, neither of which he's allowed to do, as it could compromise him should I ever come up in front of him on report. However, as it's only a few days before he retires, I suppose he feels this is unlikely.

It turns out that the governor is a collector of farthings, and he gives Mary a farthing dated 1944 and I receive one dated 1940 – our respective years of birth. I am touched. He also brings in three volumes of *The World's Greatest Paintings: Selected Masterpieces*, published in 1934 and edited by T. Leman Hare, for me to read over Christmas. He understands what turns me on.

The three volumes are fascinating at several levels, not least because of the one hundred pictures, almost all of them would be in an equivalent compilation circa 2002. The paintings include da Vinci's *Mona Lisa*, Bellini's *Portrait of the Doge Lorendano*, Rembrandt's *Mother*, Landseer's *Shoeing the Bay Mare* (wonderful) and Yeames' *When Did You Last See Your Father?* However, in this 1934 volume, there is no mention of the Impressionists; no examples of Monet, Manet, Van Gogh or even Cézanne. Velasquez is described as the greatest Spanish painter of all time, with Murillo in second place. I wonder if Professor Hare had even heard of Picasso in 1934, and where he would place him in the lexicon of Spanish artists in 2002.

There are only two artists I have never come across before: John MacWhiter and Millet – not Jean-Francois Millet, but an American, Francis David Millet. 'On the out' I visit Tate Britain regularly – I live opposite, on the other side of the river – but I don't remember seeing either MacWhiter's *June in the Austrian Tyrol* (magnificent), or Millet's *Between Two Fires*. I hope Sir Nicholas Serota has them on display, because Tate Britain will be among the first places I visit once I'm released.

In his foreword, Professor Hare writes something that, in my opinion, is even more relevant today than it was in 1934:

There is so much nonsense spoken and written about art today that the average man is, naturally, inclined to be shy of the whole subject, and suspicious of those who practise the Arts. He thinks, if this mass of contradiction and confusing jargon is the result of the love of Art, he had better do without Art altogether. There is no mystery about Art, but there is mystification without end, evolved by certain critics who love to pose as superior persons. Such writers put forward the theory that the enjoyment of fine arts is reserved for a select and exclusive minority, meaning of course, themselves and their disciples. No greater error could be propounded than this, which is a comparatively modern fallacy and one which is so dangerous that if persisted, it must in time bring into contempt everything and everyone connected with Art.

1934.
2002. No comment.

1.00 pm

Linda shuts up shop for the day and goes home for a well-earned rest. She has been on duty for the past nineteen days without a break.

9.00 pm

I confess that, by prison standards, I am in heaven. But I feel I ought to let you know I'm still desperate to get back to earth.

DAY 162   THURSDAY 27 DECEMBER 2001

10.00 am

Governor Lewis has received a call from Sir Brian Mawhinney, and although he can't divulge any details, he suspects the Shadow Home Secretary will be in touch with Mary who in turn will brief me. Mystery.

The governor sips his tea. 'As I'm leaving shortly, I'm going to tell you a story about a present member of staff who must remain anonymous. The officer concerned had a day off, and in the evening he and his wife went to their local for a drink. When they left the pub later, the officer saw a man trying to get his car started, but it sounded as if the battery was flat. The officer asked if he could help by giving a push. The driver said thank you and the officer pushed him out of the car park. The ignition caught, and the driver gave a toot of thanks as he disappeared over the horizon.

When the officer concerned returned to work the following morning, he learned that one of the inmates had absconded. The prisoner had even managed to steal a car from a local pub with the help of an obliging member of the public, who had given him a push start.'

'It can't be true,' I protest. 'Surely he recognized the prisoner?' (To be fair, there are over two hundred inmates at NSC and the turnover is often twenty to thirty a week.)

'You'd think so,' replied the governor, 'especially as the inmate was the only West Indian on the camp.'* He laughs. 'The officer concerned might have even lived it down if it weren't for the fact that neither the prisoner nor the stolen car has been seen since.'

---

* In Belmarsh, around 70 per cent of the inmates were black, in Wayland 30 per cent, and currently at NSC we have four black prisoners out of 207. I'm not sure what this proves: possibly there might be more black prisoners involved in violent crime than in fraud.

DAY 163   FRIDAY 28 DECEMBER 2001

11.07 am

Whenever there's a serious injury in prison, the immediate question always asked is, 'Was another prisoner involved?' So when Linda and I are called over to the north block to check on an inmate who is thought to have broken his leg after slipping on the floor, Linda's first question is, 'Who pushed him?'

By the time we arrive the duty officers, Mr Hughes and Mr Jones, are present, and they are satisfied Ron has had a genuine accident. However, there are several touches of irony in this particular case. The inmate involved is serving a six-week sentence, and is due to be released next Thursday. Last year he broke his left leg in a motorbike accident. This time he has managed to break his right leg, and several of the pins in his left have been dislodged. Linda confirms that an officer must accompany him to hospital; although how he'd abscond with two broken legs is beyond me – and why would he want to try, six days before he's due to be released? However, regulations are regulations.

Normally you can't be released from prison unless you have been given a clean bill of health by the duty doctor, and in Ron's case it will be at least six weeks before the plaster comes off.

'We'll let him go,' Linda says, 'but only if a family member picks him up next Thursday and also agrees to take responsibility for him.'

'And if no one does?' I ask.

'Then he'll stay here until he's fully recovered.'

DAY 164   SATURDAY 29 DECEMBER 2001

2.00 pm

Mary, William and James visit me. We talk mainly of the legal issues surrounding my trial and appeal. The topic of conversation then turns to Baroness Nicholson. Mary has written to her asking for an apology.

Mary is off to Kenya with her sister Janet on Monday, a journey she has wanted to make for some years because of her love of cats, whatever their size.

What happened to our ninety minutes together?

6.00 pm

I'm in my final writing session for the day when there's a knock on the door. This usually means that a prisoner has a headache and needs some paracetamol, which I am allowed to dispense as long as the inmate has a note from the duty officer. If it's something more serious, then his unit officer has to be consulted. I open my door and smile up at an inmate, who looks pretty healthy to me.

'Have you got any condoms, Jeff?' he asks.

'No,' I tell him, aware that Linda keeps a supply for prisoners going on weekend leave, or just about to be released, but even then she only gives them out very sparingly. 'If you report to surgery at seven-thirty tomorrow morning, Linda will . . .'

'It'll be too late by then,' he says. I look surprised. 'It's just that my sister visited me this afternoon and she hasn't got enough money to get home. A few of the lads are willing to pay her ten quid for a blow job, which usually ends up with them going the whole way and ending up paying twenty.'

All of which begs several questions when possession of money in a prison is illegal. Is this an indoor or outdoor activity (it's minus two degrees outside) and is she really his sister?

'Sorry, I can't help,' is my only response, and after he has disappeared into the night. I try hard to concentrate on my writing.

DAY 165   SUNDAY 30 DECEMBER 2001

7.30 am

The security officer on duty today enjoys his job, but never feels fulfilled until he's put someone on a charge. Mr Vessey rushes into surgery to see sister. During the night he's found fourteen empty bottles of vodka at the bottom of the skip by the entrance to the prison. A whispered conversation ensues, not that it takes a lot of imagination to realize that he's asking if any inmates checked into surgery this morning 'a little worse for wear'. Moments later, he rushes off to the south block.

In fact, very few inmates were on sick parade this morning as most of them are sleeping in, or sleeping it off, and the ones that appeared were genuinely ill. He will be disappointed.

10.00 am

During the morning we have visits from Mr Lewis and Mr Berlyn, the new deputy governor, who join Linda for coffee. Mr Hocking is the next to arrive, with the news that five inmates have failed the breathalyser test. Two of them are CSV workers, who could lose all their privileges. For example, they could be put back to work on the farm for the rest of their sentence.* Mr Hocking tells me he doubts if the punishment will be that draconian, but the warning will be clear for the future.

Why would anyone risk losing so much for a couple of vodkas?

12 noon

Linda leaves at midday so I spend four of the next six hours editing *Belmarsh*, volume one of these diaries.

7.00 pm

During the evening I read *Here is New York* by E. B. White, which Will gave me for Christmas. One paragraph towards the end of the essay is eerily prophetic.

> The subtlest change in New York is something people don't speak much about, but that is in everyone's mind. The city, for the first time in its long history, is destructible. A single flight of planes, no bigger than a wedge of geese, can quickly end this island fantasy, burn the towers, crumble the bridges, turn the underground passages into lethal chambers, cremate the millions. The intimation of mortality is part of New York now; in the sound of jets overhead, in the black headlines of the latest edition.

This was written in 1949, and the author died in 1985.

---

* An inmate who completes a quarter of his sentence and proves to be a model prisoner is eligible for outside work. First he must complete two town visits without incident. The next step is to apply for Community Service Volunteers work (CSV), perhaps in an old people's home or an Oxfam shop. Once he's completed a month of CSV without incident, he can move on to a wage-earning job, making perhaps £200–£250 a week. This gives a prisoner the chance to send money back to his wife or partner, and to build up some savings to fall back on once released.

DAY 166   NEW YEAR'S EVE 2001

11.00 am

Four new prisoners arrive at the hospital from Nottingham, looking lost and a little disorientated. I'm surprised that Group 4 has deposited them before lunch as they don't usually arrive until around four in the afternoon.

'It's New Year's Eve,' explains Linda. 'They'll all want to be home by four.'

12 noon

Linda checks her books and tells me that NSC had a turnover of just over a thousand prisoners during 2001, so after eleven weeks, I'm already something of an old lag.

6.00 pm

Mary and I usually invite eight guests to dinner at the Old Vicarage on New Year's Eve. This year I'll have to settle for a KitKat, a glass of Ribena and hope that Doug and Clive are able to join me.

DAY 167   NEW YEAR'S DAY 2002

6.00 am

The camp is silent, so I begin to go over volume one of these diaries. Reading through those early days when I was so distressed, I can't believe how much I have made myself forget. And this has become even more pronounced since my appointment as hospital orderly, where I have everything except freedom and the daily company of my wife, family and friends; a punishment in itself, but not purgatory and certainly not hell.

10.00 am

Mr New drops into the hospital to say his farewells. He leaves NSC tonight and will, on 8 January, change his uniform for a suit, when he becomes a governor at Norwich Prison. He's taught me a great deal about good and evil during the past three months.

6.00 pm

I miss my wife, I miss my family and I miss my friends. The biggest enemy I have to contend with is boredom, and it's a killer.

DAY 167

For many prisoners, it's the time when they first experiment with drugs. To begin with, drugs are offered by the dealers for nothing, and when they demand more, in exchange for a phonecard and an ounce of tobacco or cash, and finally, when they're hooked, they'll give anything for a fix – including their life.

Tonight, the Lincolnshire constabulary informed sister that a former prisoner called Cole, who left NSC six weeks ago, has been found under a hedge in a quiet country lane.

He died from an overdose.

Happy New Year.

DAY 168   WEDNESDAY 2 JANUARY 2002

6.00 am

I continue to edit *A Prison Diary Volume One – Belmarsh: Hell.*

10.00 am

Mr Berlyn drops in to tell me that he already has plans for my CSV work should my sentence be reduced, and this even before the date of my appeal is known. He wants me to work in an old-age pensioners' home, as it will be out of sight of the press. He also feels I would benefit from the experience. I had hoped to work in the Red Cross shop in Boston, but Mr Berlyn has discounted that option after Maria brought in, without permission, some books for me to sign before Christmas to raise money for their Afghanistan appeal. The Rev Derek Johnson, the prison chaplain, has been to see him to plead their case, explaining that he is in the forgiveness and rehabilitation business. Mr Berlyn's immediate retort was, 'I'm in the punishment and retribution business.' He must have meant of prisoners; I can't believe he wishes to punish a hard-working, decent woman trying to run a Red Cross shop.

DAY 168

4.50 pm

Linda looks very tired. She's worked twenty-one of the last twenty-four days. She tells me that she's going to apply for a job in Boston. My only selfish thought is that I hope she doesn't leave before I do.

8.00 pm

Doug turns up at the hospital for his nightly bath and to watch television. He's now settled into his job as a driver, which keeps him out of the prison between the hours of 8 am and 7 pm. I wonder if, for prisoners like Doug, it wouldn't be better to rethink the tagging system, so he could give up his bed for a more worthy candidate.

DAY 169　　THURSDAY 3 JANUARY 2002

7.30 am

Morning surgery is packed with inmates who want to sign up for acupuncture. You must report to hospital between 7.30 and 8 am in order to be booked in for an eleven o'clock appointment. Linda and Gail are both fully qualified, and 'on the out' acupuncture could cost up to £40 a session. To an inmate, it's free of charge, as are all prescriptions.

The purpose of acupuncture in prison is twofold: to release stress, and to wean you off smoking. Linda and Gail have had several worthwhile results in the past. One inmate has dropped from sixty cigarettes a day to three after only a month on the course. Other prisoners, who are suffering from stress, rely on it, and any prisoner who turns up for a second session can be described as serious.

However, back to the present. Eight inmates suspiciously arrive in a group, and sign up for the eleven o'clock session. They all by coincidence reside in the south block and work on the farm, which means that they'll miss most of the morning's work and still be fully paid.

At eight o'clock Linda calls Mr Donnelly on the farm to let him know that the morning's acupuncture session is so oversubscribed (two regular applicants, one from education and one unemployed) so she'll take the eight from the farm at four o'clock this afternoon. This means that they'll have to complete their day's work before reporting to the hospital. It will be interesting to see how many of them turn up.

9.00 am

Young Ron (both legs broken) hobbles in to see the doctor. He's on the paper chase and has to be cleared as fit and free of any problems before he can be released at 8 am tomorrow. After the hospital, he still has to visit the gym, stores, SMU, education, unit office and reception. How will they go about signing out a man with two broken legs as fit to face the world? Linda comes to the rescue, phones each department and then signs on their behalf. Problem solved.

9.15 am

When Dr Walling has finished ministering to his patients, he joins me in the ward. We discuss the drug problem in Boston, sleepy Boston, (population of around 54,000).

Recently Dr Walling's car was broken into. All the usual things were stolen – radio, tapes, briefcase – but he was devastated by the loss of a box of photographic slides that he has built up over a period of thirty years. Because he hadn't duplicated them, they were irreplaceable, and the theft took place only days before he was due to deliver a series of lectures in America. Assuming that it was a drug-related theft (cash needed for a quick fix), Dr Walling visited the houses of Boston's three established drug barons. He left a note saying that he needed the slides urgently and would pay a reward of £100 if they were returned.

The slides turned up the following day.

The true significance of this tale is that a leading doctor knows who the town's drug barons are, and yet the police seem powerless to put such men behind bars. Dr Walling explains that it's the old problem of 'Mr Big' never getting his hands dirty. He arranges for the drugs to be smuggled into the country before being sold to a dealer. Mr Big also employs runners to distribute the drugs, free of charge, mainly to children as they leave school unaccompanied, so that long before they reach university or take a job, they're hooked. And that, I repeat, is in Boston, not Chelsea or Brixton.

What will Britain be like in ten years' time, twenty years, thirty, if the police estimate that 40 per cent of all crime *today* is drug-related?

4.00 pm

No one from the farm turns up for acupuncture.

7.37 pm

Carl rushes in, breathless, to say a prisoner has collapsed on the south block. Linda went home two hours ago, so I run out of the hospital, to find Mr Belford and Mr Harman a few yards ahead of me.

When we arrive at the prisoner's door, we find the inmate gasping for breath. I recognize him immediately from his visit to Dr Walling this morning. I feel helpless as he lies doubled-up, clutching his stomach, but fortunately an ambulance arrives within minutes. A paramedic places a mask over the inmate's face, and then asks him some routine questions, all of which I am able to answer on his behalf – name of doctor, last visit to surgery, nature of complaint and medication given. I'm also able to tell them his blood pressure, 145/78. They rush him to the Pilgrim Hospital, and as he failed his recent risk assessment, Mr Harman has to travel with him.

As Mr Harman is now off the manifest, we are probably down to five officers on duty tonight, to watch over 211 prisoners.

DAY 170   FRIDAY 4 JANUARY 2002

5.00 am

I finish editing *Belmarsh*, and post it back to my publishers.

8.00 am

I leave the hospital to carry out my morning rounds. This has three purposes: first, to let each department head know which inmates are off work, second, in case of a fire, to identify who is where, and third, if someone fails to show up for roll-call, to check if they've absconded.

En route to the farm I bump into Blossom, who had one of the pigs named after him. (See photo page 193.) Blossom is a traveller, or a gipsy as we used to describe them before it became politically incorrect. Blossom tells me that he's just dug a lamb out of the ice. It seems it got its hindquarters stuck in some mud which froze overnight, so the poor animal couldn't move.

'You've saved the animal's life,' I tell Blossom.

'No,' he says, 'he's going to be slaughtered today, so he'll soon be on the menu as frozen cutlets.'

DAY 170

12 noon

I pick up my post from the south block. Although most of the messages continue along the same theme, one, sent from a Frank and Lurline in Wynnum, Australia is worthy of a mention, if only because of the envelope. It was addressed thus:

> Lord Jeffrey Archer
> Jailed for telling a fib
> Somewhere in England.

It is dated Christmas Day, and has taken only nine days to reach me in deepest Lincolnshire.

2.30 pm

The main administration block has been sealed off. Gail tells me that she can't get into the building to carry out any paperwork and she doesn't know why. This is only interesting because it's an area that is off-limits to inmates.

Over the past few months, money and valuables have gone missing. Mr Berlyn is determined to catch the culprit. It turns out to be a fruitless exercise, because, despite a thorough search, the £20 that was stolen from someone's purse doesn't materialize. Mr Hocking, the security officer in charge of the operation, found the whole exercise distasteful as it involved investigating his colleagues. I have a feeling he knows who the guilty party is, but certainly isn't going to tell me. My deep throat, a prisoner of long standing, tells me the name of the suspect. For those readers with the mind of a detective, she doesn't get a mention in this diary.

DAY 171   SATURDAY 5 JANUARY 2002

7.30 am

A prisoner from the south block checks into surgery with a groin injury. Linda is sufficiently worried about his condition to have him taken to the local hospital without delay. Meanwhile she dresses his wounds and gives him some painkillers. He never once says please or thank you. This attitude would be true of over half the inmates, and nearer 70 per cent of those under thirty. Although it's a generalization, I have become aware that those without manners are also the work shy amongst the prison population.

2.30 pm

Among the thousands of letters I've received since I've been incarcerated, several are from charities that continue to ask for donations, signed books and memorabilia, and occasionally for a doodle, drawing, poem or even a painting. Despite my life-long love of art, the good Lord decided to place a pen in my hand, not a paintbrush. But I found an alternative when I came across Darren, an education orderly. Darren has already designed several imaginative posters and signs for the hospital. The latest charity request is that I should produce a sunflower, *in any medium*. I came up with an idea which Darren produces. (See overleaf.)

DAY 172   SUNDAY 6 JANUARY 2002

8.00 am

As it's Twelfth Night, I spend a couple of hours taking down my Christmas cards (1,712), and packing them up so I can hand them over to Will when he visits me this afternoon.

10.30 am

Linda tells me that a nurse at the Pilgrim Hospital phoned urgently about the prisoner with the groin injury. An officer is dispatched immediately to keep an eye on him until he's safely back in his room at NSC. Not a bad idea to get yourself transferred to the local hospital if you plan to escape, but it's not that bright to ask a nurse where the exits are.

2.00 pm

Will visits me, accompanied by my Christmas present. Neither he nor James have heard a word from their mother since she landed in Kenya. Will reassures me by suggesting she's either having a good time, or she's been eaten by a lion.

DAY 172

8.00 pm

Doug arrives at the hospital with the news that five prisoners who were out on a town leave have failed to return. As none of them are murderers, only the local police will be alerted. If a murderer absconds, the Home Office has to brief the national press within twenty-four hours.

DAY 173   MONDAY 7 JANUARY 2002

North Sea Camp has been told to increase its bed space. Now that almost every room has a TV set, the large television rooms can be converted into three dormitories, giving the prison another thirteen beds. I don't think this will go a long way to solving the problem of overcrowding in prisons.

11.00 am

When Mr Berlyn drops into the hospital, Linda tells him that she's applying for a job at the coroner's office in Boston. He assures me later that he doesn't believe she'll ever leave. He seems surprised, and frowns when I tell him that she's already completed an application form.

He then reveals that, of the five prisoners who failed to check back in by seven the previous evening, two turned up late and will be in front of the governor this morning, two were caught drunk in an amusement arcade in Skegness and have already been shipped out to Lincoln, where they'll complete their sentence with a further twenty-eight days added, and one is still on the run.

'It can't be worth it,' I declare when discussing the absconders with Jim (antiques only) over lunch.

DAY 173

'It may not be worth it for you, Jeffrey, but we don't know their domestic situation. Has the wife run away with his best mate? Are the children OK? Are they all being turfed out of their home? Are they...'

I agree with Jim. I can't begin to imagine such problems.

DAY 174   TUESDAY 8 JANUARY 2002

10.00 am

HM PRISON SERVICE

RACE RELATIONS POLICY STATEMENT

The Prison Service is committed to racial equality. Improper discrimination on the basis of colour, race, nationality, ethnic or national origins or religion, is unacceptable, as is any racially abusive or insulting language or behaviour on the part of any member of staff, prisoner or visitor, and neither will be tolerated.*

This statement is publicly displayed in every prison in England, and I must admit that I have never witnessed an officer showing any racial prejudice at any time. On the contrary, I have witnessed several prisoners play the race card to their advantage.

'You're only saying that because I'm black...'

'You're picking on me because I'm a Muslim...'

Unfortunately, I've not seen a black or Asian officer at either Wayland or North Sea Camp, otherwise I might have tried, 'You're only picking on me because I'm white...'

Can you name one country on earth that has a race relations

---

* Interesting grammatical error.

847

policy to protect the whites? Certainly not Zimbabwe, which is in the headlines again today. I mention this only because a circular was sent to all departments today, which clearly shows how seriously the Prison Service takes minority rights.

12 noon

Mr Belford drops into the hospital and reports a conversation he heard between two elderly ladies standing at a bus stop in Boston:

First lady: 'Did you see Jeffrey Archer in the pub last night?'
Second lady: 'No, I thought he was in jail.'
First lady: 'No, he's down at our local almost every night, drinking pint after pint, before he's driven back to the prison by his chauffeur in a Rolls Royce.'
Second lady: 'It's a disgrace.'

The officer pointed out to the ladies that I have never once left the NSC since the day I arrived, and I don't drink.

'That's what you think,' came back the immediate reply.

DAY 175   WEDNESDAY 9 JANUARY 2002

5.14 am

I wake and consider the future.

Everything rests on the result of my appeal. I currently have a four-year sentence. In present circumstances, assuming I remain a model prisoner, I'll serve two, subject to my parole board report being positive, which means I will be released on 19 July 2003. However, I am appealing against sentence and conviction, and if my conviction is overturned, then I'll be released the same day. If not, all will depend on my sentence being reduced. If the three appeal judges were to lower my sentence from four years to three, I would no longer be subject to the parole board, and would be eligible for automatic release in eighteen months. If my record remains unblemished, I will be released on a tag two months before that, after sixteen months – on 17 November 2002. Ten months' time. If the appeal court judges reduce my sentence to two years, I will be released on 17 May, which is only another four months. If my sentence is reduced to the common length for perjury, i.e. eighteen months, I will be released on 17 March – in six weeks' time.

Perhaps now you can understand why I am so anxious about my appeal, and wait daily to hear from the courts when I will appear before them.

DAY 175

10.00 am

A trainee nurse joins us. Simon will spend three weeks at NSC on secondment from the Pilgrim Hospital. He will quickly discover that prisoners are treated far better than the general public. At seven, you can pick up your paracetamol, aspirins, lozenges, mouthwash and prescribed medication. At nine, you can see the doctor, and you never have to wait for more than twenty minutes. At eleven, if you are stressed or want to give up smoking or come off drugs, you can attend an acupuncture course. At twelve, you can come back and get some more medication. At two-thirty you can attend a talk on giving up smoking; nicotine patches are handed out when the talk is over. At four-thirty you can come back for more medication. After 5 pm, the orderly can supply aspirin or paracetamol to any prisoner who has a slip from an officer. If you are seriously ill, an ambulance will have you tucked up in the Pilgrim Hospital within the hour.

In any one day, a determined prisoner can spend hundreds of pounds of taxpayers' money, whereas in truth, I doubt if 10 per cent of them would visit a doctor 'on the out' and certainly wouldn't go to a chemist if it meant parting with a penny of their own cash. So what, our new intern will learn is that if you are ill, it's better to be in prison than an infirm old-age pensioner or a sick child.

DAY 176   THURSDAY 10 JANUARY 2002

1.15 pm

Although the fire alarm is tested every day at one o'clock, today it sounds for a second time at one-fifteen. Security are carrying out a full-scale fire drill.

All staff, prison officers and inmates have to report to the farmyard, where we line up in separate pens. I go to the one marked hospital, and join Linda, Gail and Simon. On my left is north block one, on my right the lifers' unit – a score of murderers gathered together.

Everyone from the governor to the most recently arrived inmate is on parade. We wait to be checked off by Mr Hocking, the senior security officer. It's the first time I've seen the whole community in one place, and it highlights how disproportionate the numbers of staff are to prisoners. This is fine in a D-cat where everything is based on trust, but would be impossible in closed conditions. If you had a fire drill in an A- or B-cat, you could only hope to carry it out spur by spur, in a C-cat perhaps block by block, unless you wanted a riot on your hands or a mass escape.

DAY 176

1.45 pm

Two hundred and eleven prisoners, and thirty-eight staff (including clerical) return to work.

8.00 pm

I watch *Raiders of the Lost Ark*. The last time I saw this film was with my two sons – Will was then nine and James seven. It was produced by one of my oldest friends, Frank Marshall.*

---

* Frank flew from LA to London to appear in my trial to deny a statement by Angie Peppiatt that I had been in Rome with a mistress when in fact I had been with Frank attending the World Athletics Championships. Not that I think Mr Justice Potts gave a damn, as by then he had already made up his mind that I was guilty.

DAY 177 FRIDAY 11 JANUARY 2002

6.03 am

I'd like to bring you up to date on a couple of matters you may wish to have resolved.

Six prisoners have absconded in the past ten days, and I have already accounted for five of them. But not McGeekin. McGeekin had a town visit, which allowed him to leave the prison at eight in the morning, as long as he reported back to the gate by seven the same night. He did not return, so the matter was placed in police hands. 'He's already back in custody,' the gate officer was informed by the local desk sergeant. He'd reported to his nearest police station and told them he wanted to be sent back to HMP Wayland in Norfolk, rather than return to North Sea Camp.

It's not uncommon for an inmate to want to return to the more regulated life of a closed prison. Some will even tell you they feel safer with a wall around them. Lifers in particular often find the regime of an open prison impossible to come to terms with. After fifteen years of being banged up, often for twenty-two hours a day, they just can't handle so much freedom. Within hours of arriving, they will apply to be sent back, but are told to give it a month, and if they then still feel the same way, to put in a transfer application.

Frankly they'd have to drag me back to Wayland and I'd abscond rather than return to Belmarsh.

DAY 178   SATURDAY 12 JANUARY 2002

10.00 am

The hospital bath plug has been stolen which is a bit of a mystery, because it's the only bath in the prison available to inmates, so the plug can't be of much use to anyone else. However, I have a reserve one, which makes me king, because I am now 'controller of the bath plug'. I will still have to make an application for a new one, which will mean filling in three forms and probably waiting three months.

2.00 pm

The camp is playing football against the local league leaders. When our team runs out onto the pitch, I hardly recognize any of them. Mr Masters, gym officer and coach, points out that the rapid turnover of inmates has meant he's put fifty-four players on the pitch since the opening match of the season. That's something even Man United couldn't handle. Added to this is the fact that our star goalkeeper, Bell, has been suspended for one match after using foul and abusive language when the referee awarded a penalty to the opposition. He was a little unlucky that an FA official was assessing the referee that afternoon, and therefore the ref couldn't pretend not to have heard Bell. Indeed they could have heard, 'Get some glasses, you fuckin' muppet,' in the centre of Boston.

Our reserve goalkeeper is Carl (fraud), the SMU orderly who took over from me and comes over most evenings to watch TV in the hospital. He gamely agreed to stand in for the one fixture, while Bell watches from the sidelines.

I felt it nothing less than my duty to turn up and support the team in such dire circumstances. I left at half time, when we were trailing 7–1, just after our prison reporter, Major Willis (stabbed his wife with a kitchen knife – two years), told me that the *Boston Standard* had given him so little space to report the match that he would only be able to list the names of the scorers. I was also amused by his chivvying from the touchline: 'Well played, Harry,' 'Good tackle, David,' and 'Super shot, Reg,' as if he were a house master addressing the 3rd XI of a minor public school.

5.00 pm

I join Carl for supper, but he doesn't look too happy.

'What was the final score?' I ask.

'We had a better second half,' he offers.

'So what was the final score?' I repeat.

'15–3.'

The only man who has a big smile on his face is the suspended Bell, whose position as 'first choice goalkeeper' remains secure.

DAY 179   SUNDAY 13 JANUARY 2002

11.00 am

Once Linda has closed the surgery for the morning, I settle down to read *The Sunday Times*. The lead story is about Prince Harry, and the revelation in the *News of the World* that he's tried marijuana and has also been involved in heavy drinking, despite the fact that he's still under age. Some of us are old enough to remember the shocking revelation that Prince Charles was caught drinking cherry brandy when he was still at Gordonstoun.

2.00 pm

My visitors this week are Stephan Shakespeare, my former chief of staff for the London mayoral campaign, Robert Halfon, senior adviser to Oliver Letwin MP, the Shadow Home Secretary, and my son Will.

The general view is that IDS is doing better than expected. I warn them that if the inmates and the prison staff are anything to go by most people simply don't know who he is.

Will tells me that he won't be returning to the States until after the appeal. He also reports that Godfrey Barker has had a change of heart and is no longer willing to help and may even

DAY 179

leave the country rather than be forced to give evidence about the dinner party conversation that took place with Mr Justice Potts. His wife Anne has said she will divorce him if he does.*

8.00 pm

A lifer has absconded. He was out on an unaccompanied town visit and didn't return for check-in by 7 pm. If he's still absent in twenty-four hours' time, the Home Office will release the name and his record to the press. When a young hooligan escapes, it rarely makes even the local paper, but the public has a right to know if a murderer is on the loose.

Doug fills me in on the background. It seems that the inmate failed an MDT (heroin) a few weeks ago and was moved out of the lifers' unit back onto the north block. The result of his latest test last week is also expected to be positive. As this will be a second offence, he would automatically be transferred back to a B-cat, and have at least another eighteen months added to his sentence. This is a man who began with a twelve-year tariff, and has already served seventeen years.

If he'd been a model prisoner, he could have been released five years ago.

---

* Mr and Mrs Barker are now separated. Mrs Barker stood down from the parole board in September 2001.

DAY 180   MONDAY 14 JANUARY 2002

9.00 am

When the doctor arrives each morning, he first signs the discharge papers of any prisoner due to be released. He then signs applications for a five-day leave, showing a clean bill of health. His next task is to see all the new prisoners who have just arrived from another jail. Finally, the doctor handles 'nickings': prisoners who have been put on a charge, and again must be passed fit both mentally and physically before punishment can be administered. Once all these inmates have been dealt with, the doctor moves onto the genuinely sick.

Today we have three 'nickings'. Two are commonplace, but the third even took the governor by surprise. The first was for swearing at an officer, and that has to be pretty extreme for the prisoner to end up in front of the governor. The second was an inmate found to have £20 in his room. The first ended up with four days added to his sentence, the second seven days, but the third . . .

All prisoners out on town leave have to report back to the gate sober before 7 pm. This particular inmate was a few minutes late and was, to quote the gate officer, legless. Out there you can be breathalysed if you're driving, in here we are when we're walking.

When charged with being drunk, the prisoner claimed that he'd swallowed half a bottle of mouthwash thirty minutes before returning to the prison. It is true that a bottle of mouthwash contains alcohol, and it will register on the breathalyser at 0.5 per cent. The trouble was that the breathalyser was showing 3.5 per cent. Next, they checked his medical records, and as the prisoner had not visited the surgery for over a month, and never requested a mouthwash, he was asked to explain why he suddenly drank half a bottle.

'Because I was giving my partner a blow job,' he replied.

When the officer recovered from this revelation, he thumbed through the rule book and came up with a winner. 'Did you sign the trust agreement for prisoners who are on a town visit?' he asked innocently.

'Yes,' came back the immediate reply.

'And who did you select as the person who would be responsible for you at all times?'

'My mother,' the prisoner replied.

'And did your mother witness the action you have just described?'

The inmate paused for a moment, pleaded guilty, and had twenty-eight days added to his sentence.

11.00 am

Linda leaves the hospital and walks across to reception, where two prisoners have just been taken from their rooms without warning, as they are to be shipped out to Lincoln (B-cat). They have both failed an MDT and came up positive for heroin.

Prisoners are never given any warning they are on the move in case they decide to abscond rather than be transferred back to closed conditions.

DAY 181   TUESDAY 15 JANUARY 2002

9.00 am

The Derby Five are on the paper chase, and each of them comes to the hospital to say goodbye. Eamon, who shared a room with me for a short time, is particularly friendly and says he hopes we will meet again. I nod.

5.00 pm

Over supper I sit next to John (murder) who makes an interesting point about Chris (murder) who is still on the run. If he's managed to escape to certain European countries (Sweden, Portugal or Italy) whose governments do not approve of our tariff system for lifers, it's possible that the authorities in that country may turn a blind eye, especially after the Home Office announced today that they did not consider Chris to be a danger to the public.

8.30 pm

I'm going over today's script when an inmate staggers into the hospital. He's sweating profusely, and badly out of breath.

I take his blood pressure, 176/109, and immediately brief the unit officer, but not until I've taken my own (130/76) to check the machine is not faulty.

Mr Downs (who replaced Mr New as PO) is on duty and I tell him that Gail has been keeping an eye on this patient for the past four days, and told me that if the monitor went over 105 again, he was to be taken straight to Pilgrim Hospital for a full check-up.

'It's not quite that easy,' explains Mr Downs. 'I've only got five officers on duty tonight, and this inmate hasn't been risk assessed, so one of us would have to accompany him.'

Mr Downs sighs, phones for a taxi, and instructs an officer to travel with the inmate to Pilgrim Hospital (cost £20).

That means tonight we have 191 prisoners being guarded by four officers – one of them a young woman who's recently joined the service.

Good night.

DAY 182   WEDNESDAY 16 JANUARY 2002

10.00 am

Martin, the inmate who lost two months for attempting to steal some prison clothes on the morning he was due to be released, has had another twenty-five days added to his sentence, this time for being caught with marijuana in his room. He was originally due to leave NSC on 14 December, and now he won't be released until 14 March. At this rate I might even get out before him.

It's not uncommon for inmates to end up serving a longer period than their original sentence. However it will take Martin a number of 'knock backs' before he can beat a prisoner in Wayland (*A Prison Diary*, Volume II) who started with a three-year sentence for possession of heroin and is still a resident of that establishment eight years later.

3.00 pm

Among the new inductees are a policeman and a man who was sentenced to five years for attempting to kill his mother-in-law. The rest are in for the usual tariff – burglary, driving offences, drugs, drugs and drugs. Still, I sense one or two stories among this lot.

DAY 182

7.00 pm

I have a visit from Keith (class B drugs), which is a bit of a surprise as he was on the paper chase last Monday, and should have been discharged yesterday. I can't believe he's committed another crime in the last twenty-four hours. No. It turns out that the parole board, having informed the prison that he could be released on Monday, have now told him he must wait until one or two more pieces of paper are signed. Why couldn't they tell him that last Monday rather than unnecessarily raise his hopes?

I tell Keith about a prisoner who was transferred from Leicester yesterday and is being returned to that prison today. The authorities forgot to send all his parole details. The man travelled to NSC in a sweat box, spent the night here, and now has to go back to Leicester Prison. By the way, we expect him to return to NSC next week. This bureaucratic incompetence will be paid for out of taxpayers' money.

DAY 183   THURSDAY 17 JANUARY 2002

After a month of being hospital orderly, I have my work schedule mastered.

5.00–7.00 am Write first draft of previous day's events.

7.00–7.30 am Draw curtains, make bed, put on kettle, shave, bathe and dress.

Prepare lists and make coffee for Linda – dash of milk, one sweetener.

7.30–8.00 am Surgery, usually twenty to thirty inmates who collect prescriptions or need to make an appointment to see the doctor at nine.

8.00–8.30 am Deliver slips for absentees from work to the farm, the works, stores, mess, education department, north and south blocks and the gate.

8.30–8.45 am Breakfast in the dining room.

9.00–10.30 am Doctor's surgery.

11.00 am Acupuncture, usually three or four inmates.

11.10–11.40 am Read this morning's draft of this diary.

11.50 am Wake up patients having acupuncture; Linda removes needles.

12 noon Lunch.

12.40 pm	Phone Alison at the penthouse, and collect my mail from south unit office.
1.00–3.00 pm	Continue second draft of yesterday's work.
3.00–4.00 pm	Check in arrivals from other prisons. Give short introductory talk, then take their blood pressure and weight, and carry out diabetes test (urine).
4.30–4.50 pm	Evening surgery. Those inmates who ordered prescriptions this morning can pick them up as they'll have been collected from a chemist in Boston during the afternoon.
4.50 pm	Linda leaves for the day.
5.00 pm	Supper.
5.30–7.00 pm	Final writing session, totalling nearly six hours in all.
7.00 pm	Unlock the end room for use by outside personnel, e.g. Listeners, Jehovah's Witnesses, drug and alcohol counselling sessions and prison committees.
7.10–8.00 pm	Read through the day's mail, make annotated notes and post to Alison.
8.00–10.00 pm	Doug and Carl join me for a coffee, to chat or watch a film on TV.
10.30 pm	Read until I feel sleepy.

The hospital orderly has the longest and most irregular hours of any prisoner. It's seven days a week. On Saturday and Sunday after Linda and Gail have left I sweep the hospital ward, lobby, lavatory and bathroom before mopping throughout. (Although I can't remember when I last did any domestic chores, I find the work therapeutic. I wouldn't, however, go so far as saying I enjoy it.)

866

I then check my supplies, and restock the cupboards. If I'm short of anything, I make out an order form for the stores (memo pads, lavatory paper and today for a new vacuum cleaner – the old one has finally given up).

Some prisoners tell me that they would rather work in the kitchen or the officers' mess because they get more food. I'd rather be in the hospital, and have a bath and a good night's sleep.

DAY 184 FRIDAY 18 JANUARY 2002

5.26 am

The night security guard has just walked in and tells me with a smile that I can abscond. I put my pen down and ask why.

'We've got one too many on the manifest.'

'How did that happen?' I ask.

'A lad who was released yesterday arrived home and no one wanted him, so he crept back in last night and dossed down in his old room.'

'So what did you do?' I ask.

'Marched him back to the gate and threw him out for a second time.'

I feel sorry for a man who has nowhere to go, and can only wonder how long it will be before he reoffends.

8.00 am

I bump into Keith ('knowingly concerned' with a class B drug) on his way back from breakfast. He must still be waiting for his missing papers to be signed before they can release him. You might be – as I was – puzzled by what his charge means.

Keith ran a small transport company, and one of his lorries

had been fitted with spare fuel tanks. When the driver came through customs, the spare fuel tanks were found to contain 249 kilos of marijuana. Keith was sentenced to nine years.

Whenever a judge passes a sentence on drugs, there's a tariff according to the class of the drug – A, B or C. Also relevant is whether you are considered to be 'in possession of' or a supplier, and the amount involved.

Drugs' classification:

Class A   heroin, ecstasy, cocaine, opiates

Class B   cannabis (marijuana) (now Class C), amphetamines

Class C   anabolic steroids, keratin, amyl nitrite (poppers)

Here's a rough guide to the *maximum* penalties:

Class A	possession, seven years (fine or both)	supplier, life (fine or both)
Class B	possession, five years	supplier, fourteen years
Class C	possession, two years	supplier, five years

Many of the inmates feel unjustly treated when sentences can vary so much from court to court, and as over 50 per cent of prisoners are in on drug-related charges, comparisons are made all the time. A few admit to having got off lightly, while most feel hard done by.

5.00 pm

The man who was sentenced to five years for attempting to murder his mother-in-law turns out to be another unusual case. This particular inmate hit his mother-in-law when she refused to allow him access to visit his children. She collapsed and was taken to hospital. As she didn't die, and the police didn't have

proof that he intended to murder her, the charge was dropped
to aggravated burglary and he was sentenced to five years. It
would take a trained legal mind to understand how the second
charge came about. The prisoner explains that when he went in
search of his children, he entered his mother-in-law's house
when she had not invited him in – and this offence is aggravated
burglary.

DAY 185   SATURDAY 19 JANUARY 2002

2.00 pm

I was hoping to see Mary, Will and James today, but the authorities have decreed that I've used up all my visits for this month, and therefore can't see them until the beginning of February.

3.00 pm

This week's football match has also been cancelled, so once again I come face to face with the prisoner's biggest enemy, boredom.

DAY 186   SUNDAY 20 JANUARY 2002

10.51 am

Mr Hart (an old-fashioned socialist) visits the hospital to tell me that there's a double-page spread about me in the *News of the World*. It seems that Eamon (one of the Derby Five) is the latest former inmate to take his thirty pieces of silver and tell the world what it's like to share a room with Jeff.

I am surprised how many prisoners visit me today to tell me what they think of Eamon. Strange phrases like 'broken the code', 'not the done thing' come from men who are in for murder and GBH. After Belmarsh, Fletch, Tony, Del Boy and Billy said nothing, while Darren, Jimmy, Jules and Sketch from Wayland also kept their counsel. Here at NSC, I trust Doug, Carl, Jim, Clive and Matthew. And they would have stories to tell.

4.00 pm

I've started a prison tea club as I love to entertain whatever the circumstances. Admittedly it would have been impossible at Belmarsh or Wayland, but as I now reside in the hospital, I am even able to send out invitations. Membership is confined to those over the age of forty.

My guests are invited to attend 'Club Hospital' on Sunday between the hours of 4 pm and 6 pm. They will be served tea, coffee, biscuits and scones supplied by Linda. The current membership is around a dozen, and includes David (fraud, schoolmaster), John (fraud, accountant), John (fraud, business-man), Keith (knowingly in possession of drugs), Brian (ostrich farm and chapel organist), Doug (importing cigarettes), the Major (stabbed his wife), the Captain (theft, drummed out of the regiment), Malcolm (fraud) and Carl (fraud).

The talk is not of prison life, but what's going on in the outside world. Whether the IRA should be given rooms in Parliament, whether Bin Laden is dead or alive, the state of the NHS and the latest from the Test Match in India. All of my guests keep to the club rules. They remove their shoes and put on slippers as they enter the hospital, and no smoking or swearing is tolerated. Two of them will be leaving us next week, Keith will have served five years, and Brian nearly three. We raise a cup to them and wish them luck. Carl and David stay behind to help me with the washing-up.

DAY 187   MONDAY 21 JANUARY 2002

7.30 am

I'm becoming aware of the hospital regulars: five prisoners who turn up every morning between 7.30 and 8 am to collect their medication. I couldn't work out why these five need the same medication for something most of us would recover from in a few days. Sister has her suspicions, but if a prisoner complains of toothache, muscle sprain or arthritis, they are entitled to medications that are opiate based – for example codeine, co-codamol or dextropropoxyphene. These will show up as positive on any drugs test, and if a prisoner has been on them every day for a month, they can then claim, 'It's my medication, guv.' However, if an inmate tests positive for heroin, the hospital will take a blood sample and seek medical advice as to whether his daily medication would have registered that high. Several prisoners have discovered that such an element of doubt often works in their favour. Doug tells me that some addicts return to their rooms, flush the pills down the lavatory and then take their daily dose of heroin.

11.20 am

A lifer called Bob (twelve years, murder) is due to appear in front of the parole board next week. He's coming to the end of his tariff, and the Home Office usually recommends that the prisoner serves at least another two years before they will consider release. This decision has recently been taken out of the hands of the Home Office and passed to the parole board. Bob received a letter from the board this morning informing him he will be released next Thursday.

Try to imagine serving twelve years (think what age you were twelve years ago) and now assume that you will have to do another two years, but then you're told you will be released on Thursday.

The man is walking around in a daze, not least because he fell off a ladder yesterday and now has his ankle in a cast. What a way to start your re-entry back to Earth.

DAY 188   TUESDAY 22 JANUARY 2002

11.00 am

Andrew Pierce of *The Times* has got hold of the story that Libby
Purves will be interviewing Mary tomorrow. The BBC must have
leaked it, but I can't complain because the piece reads well, even
if Mr Pierce is under the illusion that NSC is in Cambridgeshire.
I only wish it were.

4.00 pm

Among my afternoon post is a Valentine's card, which is a bit
like getting a Christmas card in November, one proposal of
marriage, one offer of a film part (Field Marshal Haig), a request
to front a twelve-part television series and an invitation to give
an after-dinner speech in Sydney next September. Do they know
something I don't?

8.00 pm

An officer drops in from his night rounds for a coffee. He tells
me an alarming story about an event that took place at his last
prison.

It's universally accepted among prisoners that if one particular officer has got it in for you, there's nothing you can do about it. You can go through the complaints procedure, but even if you're in the right, officers will always back each other up if a colleague is in trouble. I could fill a book with such instances. I have experienced this myself at such a petty level that I have not considered the incident worth recording. On that occasion, the governor personally apologized, but still advised me not to put in a complaint.

However, back to a prisoner from the north block who did have the temerity to put in a written complaint about a particular officer. On this occasion, I can only agree with the prisoner that the officer concerned is a bully. Nevertheless, after a lengthy enquiry (everything in prison is lengthy) the officer was cleared of any misdemeanour, but that didn't stop him seeking revenge.

The inmate in question was serving a five-year sentence, and at the time he entered prison was having an affair that his wife didn't know about, and to add to the complication, the affair was with another man. The prisoner would have a visit from one of them each fortnight, while writing to both of them during the week. The rule in closed prisons is that you leave your letters unsealed in the unit office, so they can be read by the duty officer to check if you're still involved in any criminal activity, or asking for drugs to be sent in. When the prisoner left his two letters in the unit office, the officer on duty was the same man he had made a complaint about to the governor. The officer read both the love letters, and yes, you've guessed it, switched them and sealed the envelopes and with it, the fate of the prisoner.

How do I know this to be true? Because the officer involved has just told me, and is happy to tell anyone he considers a threat.

877

DAY 189   WEDNESDAY 23 JANUARY 2002

9.00 am

Mary is on *Midweek* with Libby Purves.

12.15 pm

I call Mary. She's off to lunch with Ken Howard RA and other artistic luminaries.

2.00 pm

My visitors today are Michael Portillo and Alan Jones (Australia's John Humphrys). I must first make my position clear on Michael's leadership bid. I would have wanted him to follow John Major as leader of the party. I would also have voted for him to follow William Hague, though I would have been torn if Malcolm Rifkind had won back his Edinburgh seat.

It is a robust visit, and it serves to remind me how much I miss the cut and thrust of Westminster, stuck as I am in the coldest and most remote corner of Lincolnshire. Michael tells us about one or two changes he would have made had he been elected leader. We need our own 'Clause 4' he suggests, which

Tony Blair so brilliantly turned into an important issue, despite it being of no real significance. Michael also feels that the party's parliamentary candidates should be selected from the centre, taking power away from the constituencies. It also worries him how few women and member of minority groups end up on the Conservative benches. He points out that at the last election, the party only added one new woman to its ranks, at a time when the Labour party have over fifty.

'Not much of an advertisement for the new, all-inclusive, modern party,' he adds.

'But how would you have handled the European issue?' ask Alan.

Michael is about to reply when that red-hot socialist (local Labour councillor) Officer Hart tells us that our time is up.

Politics is not so overburdened with talent that the Conservatives can survive without Portillo, Rifkind, Hague, Clarke and Redwood, all playing important roles, especially while we're in opposition.

When the two men left I was buzzing. An hour later I wanted to abscond.

5.00 pm

I call Mary. She has just left the chambers of Julian Malins QC, and is going to dinner with Leo Rothschild.

DAY 191   FRIDAY 25 JANUARY 2002

8.15 am

I'm called out of breakfast over the tannoy and instructed to return to the hospital immediately. Five new prisoners came in last night after Gail had gone home. She needs all the preliminaries carried out (heart rate, weight, height) before Dr Walling arrives at nine. One of the new intake announces with considerable pride that although this is his fifth offence, it's his first visit to NSC.

10.30 am

Once surgery is over, Dr Walling joins me for a coffee on the ward. 'One of them was a nightmare,' he says, as if I wasn't 'one of them'. He doesn't tell me which of the twenty patients he was referring to, and I don't enquire. However, his next sentence did take me by surprise. 'I needed to take a blood sample and couldn't find a vein in his arms or legs, so I ended up injecting his penis. He's not even half your age, Jeffrey, but you'll outlive him.'

2.00 pm

The new vacuum cleaner has arrived. This is a big event in my life.

4.00 pm

I call Mary at Grantchester. She has several pieces of news; Brian Mawhinney has received a reply to his letter to Sir John Stevens, the commissioner of the Metropolitan Police, asking why I lost my D-cat and was sent to Wayland. A report on the circumstances surrounding that decision has been requested, and will be forwarded to Brian as soon as the commissioner receives it.

Mary's next piece of news is devastating.

Back in 1999, Julian Mallins had kindly sent a note he had retained in his files (see overleaf), sent to him by Geoffrey Shaw, junior to Michael Hill for the defence in the libel trial. In the note, Shaw asks Julian for my two diaries for 1986 (an A4 diary and an Economist diary) 'in case Michael asks to look at them'. Julian passed the diaries to Shaw and Hill for inspection, and told Mary he is pretty sure that they would have gone through them thoroughly – and clearly found nothing worthy of comment in them, since they were not an issue in the libel trial. Julian added that it would be 'absolute rubbish' to suggest that the *Star*'s lawyers could not have examined these two diaries (which Angela Peppiatt had claimed in the criminal trial were almost entirely blank) in court for other entries.

Later Julian wrote to Mary: 'English law in 1986 was not an ass. If it had been Michael Hill's suggestion that the alibi evidence was all true, except for the date, neither Lord Archer in the witness box nor the judge, still less Lord Alexander nor I,

881

Twenty morning

Dear Julian,

Could you have Mr. Archer's
diaries in court in case Michael
asks to look at them?

I wanted to ask you
this last night. I'm sorry I
forgot to do so!

Love

Geoffrey Shaw

could have objected to Michael Hill going through the rest of the diary to find the same dinner date with the same companion at the same restaurant but on another date.'

None of us had known anything of Peppiatt's pocket diary for 1986, in which she noted both her own and my engagements, kept as her own property for over ten years, but produced in court as my 'true' diary for that year.

Mary also tells me that she has written to Godfrey Barker about his earlier reference to dining with Mr Justice Potts some time before the trial, when the judge might have made disparaging remarks about me. She now fears Godfrey will disappear the moment the date of the appeal is announced.

DAY 192   SATURDAY 26 JANUARY 2002

10.00 am

I weigh myself. Yuk. I'm fourteen stone two pounds. Yuk. I lost eleven pounds during my three weeks at Belmarsh, falling to twelve stone seven pounds. At Wayland I put that eleven pounds back on in ten weeks, despite being in the gym every day. At NSC the food is better, but because of my job I don't have time to go to the gym (poor excuse). On Monday I must stop eating chocolate and return to the gym. I am determined to leave the prison, whenever, around twelve stone eight pounds.

1.00 pm

I have a visit from an inmate who was sentenced to three months, which means he'll serve around five or six weeks. His crime? The theft of £120 while in a position of trust. He was a policeman. I am not going into much detail about his crime, as I'm more interested in the problems a police officer faces when being sent to jail. He's remarkably frank.

On his arrival, he was placed in the north block, and within minutes recognized a drug dealer he'd arrested in the past. He reported this to Mr Hughes, the unit officer, and was immediately placed in segregation overnight. The duty governor had to make a decision the following morning as to which one to ship out. He chose the drug dealer, as he had recently proved positive for an MDT. The policeman was put back on the north block, given a job in the kitchen and told to keep his head down. That was a week ago. So far no one else has recognized him, but he still has two weeks to serve.

Incidentally, he was originally charged with stealing £1,000, which, by the time the case came to court, had dwindled to £120. However, that was three years ago, and during that time he was suspended on full pay (a little over £60,000).

The police and Prison Service don't seem to care how much taxpayers' money they spend. If either service were a private company, they would be declared bankrupt within a year. I'm not suggesting he shouldn't have been charged, but I am saying it ought not to have cost over £100,000 and taken three years to discover if he'd stolen £120.

2.00 pm

I stand in the drizzle watching the prison football team do a little better than last week. However, one of our best strikers, Jean-Noel, is called off when Mr Masters (our coach) receives a call over the intercom to say that Jean-Noel has a young lady waiting for him in the visits hall. He runs off the pitch, quickly showers and changes, and joins his girlfriend.

At the time we are 1–0 in the lead. We lose 5–1.

5.00 pm

At tea I felt I had to chastise Jean-Noel for getting his priorities wrong and letting the team down. After all, surely the match was more important than seeing his girlfriend, and in any case, how could he forget that she was coming? He laughed, and explained that they'd had a row during the week, and she told him she wouldn't be turning up. She did, and we lost.

6.00 pm

Another pile of letters awaits me in the hospital, including a long handwritten missive from John Major, who among other things mentions that he's heard that I'm writing a prison diary. He suggests that reporting the facts will be both interesting and informative, but he also wants to hear about my personal feelings on the issues and the people involved. He adds that he's not surprised that the public have been so supportive; he says he got far more sympathy and backing when he lost an election than when he won one.

DAY 193   SUNDAY 27 JANUARY 2002

4.00 pm

The members of Club Hospital meet for tea and biscuits. However, as Brian (ostrich farm), Keith (knowingly, etc.) and John (fraud) were released this week, and David (fraud) and Malcolm (fraud) are on town leave, our little band of miscreants has dwindled to five. We discuss whether we should ask anyone else to join the club, as if we were all attending a Conservative committee meeting; and let's face it the Conservative party seem to be suffering from a similar problem. Some of them have been released, and several more are on temporary leave. But just like prison, one must wonder just how many will in time return.

6.00 pm

I spend a quiet evening reading and bringing the diary up to date.

DAY 194   MONDAY 28 JANUARY 2002

12.45 am

The duty night officer wakes me and asks for an ice pack. I take one out of the fridge and ask if he needs any help.

'No,' he says without explanation, and dashes off.

2.15 am

The same officer wakes me again when he returns accompanied by a prisoner called Davis who has a large swelling on his forehead and cuts over his face. Mr Hayes explains that the inmate has been in a fight, and the window in his door has shattered, leaving glass all over the floor. The prisoner can't remain in his room, because if he were to be injured by a piece of broken glass he could sue the Prison Service for negligence (can you believe it?).

While we make up his bed Davis tells me that the other prisoner involved in the fight was his cell-mate Smith (one of eleven Smiths currently at NSC), who has now been moved to the south block. They have shared a pad for eight months, a sort of forced marriage. Smith, who works in education, often needs to borrow cigarettes. Davis got sick of this and refused to hand over his tobacco, so Smith took a swipe at him. Davis claims he didn't retaliate, as he'd recently been up on a charge of taking marijuana and didn't need to be 'nicked' again. Once Smith had calmed down, Davis decided to leave the room. As he opened the door, Smith picked up a table leg that had broken off during the fight, and took a swipe at Davis – hence the shattered glass and the cuts and bruises.

It doesn't add up, and I feel sure Davis will have refined his story by the time he comes up in front of the governor. Mind you, I'd like to hear Smith's version of what took place.

9.00 am

Both prisoners involved in last night's fracas have to be passed as fit before they come up for adjudication at ten o'clock. They sit chatting to each other like bosom buddies in the corner of the waiting room.

12 noon

Over lunch I learn that the two fighting inmates have both had a fortnight's wages deducted from their pay packets to cover the damage they caused to the furniture and the broken window in their room. They also have had seven days added to their sentence. This is significant for Smith, because he was due to be released in two weeks' time. I'm told the reason they didn't get a tougher punishment was because both apologized to the governor and then to each other. They left almost holding hands.

DAY 194

7.00 pm

I go off to the canteen to buy some Oxo cubes, Evian water, two phonecards and a tin of Princes ham. No chocolate.

Mr Blackman (the officer on duty) asks me if I want a Valentine card and produces a large selection for me to consider. They are all about a foot high in size and contain some of the worst rhyming couplets I have ever come across; more interesting is that there are just as many cards for men as for women. I obviously don't mask my surprise because Mr Blackman sighs and says, 'If I didn't supply them in equal numbers, I'd be accused of discrimination.'

DAY 195   TUESDAY 29 JANUARY 2002

9.00 am

Ten new prisoners who arrived from Leicester last night are waiting to see the doctor. While they sit around, one of them boasts that he can always beat any drugs test, even fool the breathalyser. Although Lee is well aware I'm writing a diary, he's still quite willing to reveal his secrets. Lee is in his mid-twenties, good looking and well built. However, after one look at the inside of his arm, there's no doubt that he's on drugs, and heaven knows what state he'll be in in ten years' time.

'How can you beat an MDT?' I ask.

'Easy,' he says, and produces a tiny bar of soap from his jeans pocket – the kind you find in the washbasin of any small hotel. He breaks the soap in half, puts it in his mouth and begins to suck it as if it were a hard-boiled sweet.

'What difference does that make?' I enquire.

'If I'm tested in the next few hours, my urine sample will be so cloudy that they won't be able to charge me, and they're not allowed to test me again for another twenty-eight days. By then I will have had enough time to wash everything out of my system. I can even go on taking heroin up until the twenty-fourth day; it's only cannabis that takes a month to clear out of the blood stream.'

'But that can't apply to the breathalyser?'

'No,' he says, laughing, 'but I've got two ways of beating the breathalyser.' He produces three pennies from another pocket and begins to suck them. After a few moments he removes them and claims that the copper neutralizes the alcohol, and it therefore won't register.

'But what happens if the police don't give you enough time to put the coins in your mouth?'

'I can still beat them,' says Lee, 'using my special breathing technique.' Every prisoner in the waiting room is now hanging on his every word, and when the next patient is called in to see the doctor, he doesn't move, for fear of missing the final instalment.

'When the police hand you the machine to blow into,' Lee continues, aware of his captive audience, 'you pump out your chest, but you don't take a deep breath. For the next four seconds you blow in very little air, until the machine registers orange. You hand back the machine and gasp as if you've given everything. You'll get away with it because green is negative and orange is still clear. It's only the red you have to worry about, and they can't charge you once you've registered orange. And,' he goes on, 'if your eyes are blurred or vacant, I also have a way of getting over that problem. There's a product you can buy over the counter from any chemist called Z1 which was developed for clubbers to stop their eyes getting irritated by smoke. A combination of the copper, careful breathing and Z1, and you'll never be charged.'

11.00 am

One of the inmates has been put on suicide watch. He's a lad of twenty-one, five foot five, seven and a half stone and terrified of his own shadow. He's in for driving while disqualified, and will be released in two weeks' time.

He turns up at eleven to collect two new sheets and hands over two in a plastic bag because he wet them last night. While I go off to the cupboard to collect new sheets, he walks around in small circles, muttering to himself.

Gail can't be sure if it's all an act, because he's currently working on the farm and some prisoners will go to any lengths to get themselves off that detail. In fact, when he learns that he will be granted a change of job, he smiles for the first time. However, Gail can't afford to take any risks so she writes out a detailed report for the unit officer.

Suicide watch in this particular case means that an officer (Mr Jones) will have to check on the inmate every hour until all concerned are confident he is back to normal. This usually takes two to three days. I'll keep you informed.

7.00 pm

Doug has the flu and Carl is at singing practice with the 'cons and pros,' so I'm on my own for the evening.

I read a paper on the effects of heroin on children, written by Dr Simon Wills. I never imagined that Dr Wills would replace Freddie Forsyth as my bedtime reading.

DAY 196   WEDNESDAY 30 JANUARY 2002

9.00 am

Two new inductees arrive from Nottingham (A-cat). A young man serving four months for a driving offence tells me that on his block at Nottingham they had three suicides in three weeks, and all of them prisoners who had not yet been convicted.

The other inmate nods and tells me that he was made to share a cell with a man who was injecting himself with vinegar because he couldn't afford heroin.

DAY 197   THURSDAY 31 JANUARY 2002

10.00 am

Mr Lewis drops in to see Linda, as it's his last official day as governor. He's handed in his keys, handcuffs, whistle, torch, identity card and everything else that denoted his position of authority. An experience he obviously didn't enjoy. He jokes about suddenly becoming aware of afternoon television, and endless advertisements for comfortable chairs that move with the press of a button, beds that change shape when you turn over and baths that you can easily get out of.

Mr Lewis smiles, says goodbye and we shake hands. I suspect that we will never meet again as we both head towards the world of zimmer frames.

11.00 am

Mr McQuity, the National Health inspector, pays a visit to NSC, and leaves Linda in no doubt that he's well satisfied with the way she is running the prison hospital.

DAY 197

2.30 pm

The press is full of stories about the problems the Prison Service is facing because of overcrowding. There are currently a maximum of 71,000 bed spaces, and just over 70,000 of them are taken up. The Home Secretary David Blunkett has the choice of releasing people early or building more prisons. He's just announced that tagging will be extended from two months to three, with effect from 1 April. This would get me out three months early if, on appeal, my sentence is lowered by even a day.

4.00 pm

Among this afternoon's inductees is a prisoner from Lincoln who has only three weeks left to serve. He hasn't stopped complaining since the moment he arrived. He's demanding a single room with a TV, and a bed-board because he suffers from a bad back. All prisoners start life at NSC in a double room, and there are several inmates who have been around for some months and still don't have a TV. And as for the bed-board, all four are out at the moment.

Within an hour of leaving the hospital, the inmate was discovered lying on his back in the car park next to the governor's car. When Mr Leighton was called to deal with the problem, he said he could see no reason why the prisoner shouldn't sleep in the car park and drove away. The inmate returned to his allocated room within the hour. He's been no trouble since.

DAY 198   FRIDAY 1 FEBRUARY 2002

9.00 am

Among those on the paper chase today is a young man who has not yet celebrated his thirtieth birthday, but has been to jail *eighteen* times. He's a small-time burglar, who has – and this is the important point – no fear of prison. For him it's a temporary inconvenience in his chosen career. Because he has no record of violence or involvement with drugs, he's rarely sentenced to more than six months. He spends a few days in an A-cat, before being transferred to a D-cat, open prison. NSC provides him with three meals a day, a room and the company of fellow professionals. When he leaves, he will go on stealing until he is caught again. He will then be arrested, sentenced and return to NSC, the nearest D-cat to his home in Boston.* He earns between fifty and a hundred thousand a year (no taxes), according to how many months he spends 'on the out' in any particular year.

Mr Hocking (head of security) tells me that this young man has a long way to go before he can beat Greville the cat burglar, who left NSC last year at the age of sixty-three, declaring he now had enough to retire on. During a full-time career of crime,

---

* He was very distressed to learn last year that the Home Office was considering closing the prison.

897

Greville was sentenced on thirty-one occasions (not a record) and preferred NSC, where he was always appointed as reception orderly within days of checking back in. So professional was he at his chosen occupation that if there was a burglary in his area, with absolutely no trace of entry, fingerprints or any other clues, the local police immediately paid a visit to Greville's home. Greville has since retired to a seaside bungalow to live off his profits, and tend his garden. And thereby hangs another tale, which Mr Hocking swears is true.

Greville was the prime suspect when some valuable coins went missing from a local museum. A few days later, the police received an anonymous tip-off reporting that Greville had been seen burying something in the garden. A team of police arrived within the hour and started digging; they were there for five days, but found nothing.

Greville later wrote and thanked the chief constable for the excellent job his men had done in turning over his soil, particularly for the way they'd left everything so neat and tidy.

2.30 pm

I have my hair cut by the excellent prison barber, Gary (half a phonecard). I want to look smart for my visitors on Sunday.

3.00 pm

Friday is kit change day for every inmate. The hospital has its own allocated time because we require twenty new towels, six sheets, twelve pillowcases and several different items of cleaning equipment every week. While the chief orderly, Mark (armed robbery, ten years), selects a better class of towel for the hospital, he tells me about an inmate who has just come in for his weekly change of clothes.

This particular prisoner works on the farm, and never takes his clothes off from one week to the next, not even when he goes to bed. He has a double room to himself because, surprise, surprise, no one is willing to share a pad with him. Mark wonders if he does it just to make sure he ends up with a single room. I find it hard to believe anyone would be willing to suffer that amount of discomfort just to ensure they were left alone.

Before you ask, because I did, the Prison Service cannot force him to wash or shave. It would violate his human rights.

DAY 199   SATURDAY 2 FEBRUARY 2002

9.24 am

Mr Berlyn drops by. He's agreed to Linda's suggestion that a drug specialist visit the prison to give me an insight into the problems currently faced by young children in schools. But Mr Berlyn goes one step further and tells me about an officer from Stocken Prison who regularly visits schools in East Anglia to tell schoolchildren why they wouldn't want to end up in prison, and it may be possible for me, once I've passed my FLED, to accompany him and learn about drugs first-hand. If my sentence is cut, I would be allowed to visit schools immediately, rather than going through the whole learning process after my appeal.

11.00 am

Sister is just about to close surgery, when a very depressed-looking inmate hobbles in.

'I've caught the crabs,' he says, his hand cupped around the top of his trousers.

Sister unlocks the door to the surgery and lets him in. He looks anxious, and Linda appears concerned. He slowly unzips his jeans, in obvious pain, and places his hands inside. Linda and

900

I stare as he slowly uncups his hands to reveal two small, live crabs, which he passes across to Linda. She recoils, while I burst out laughing, aware that we will be the butt of prison humour for some weeks to come.

'Oh my God,' says Linda, as she stares down at his unzipped jeans, 'I don't like the look of that. I think I'll have to take a blood sample.'

The inmate rushes out of the door, his jeans falling around his knees. Honour restored, except that he has the last laugh, because it's the hospital orderly (me) who ends up taking the two crabs back down to the sea.

2.00 pm

An inmate was caught in the visitors' car park in possession of two grammes of heroin. On the outside, two grammes of heroin have a street value of £80. Inside prison, each gramme will be converted into ten points, and each point will be made into three sales. Each sale will be one-third heroin and two-thirds crushed paracetamol, which can be picked up any day from the hospital by a prisoner simply claiming to have a headache. Each sale is worth £5, so the dealer ends up with £300 for two grammes, almost four times the market price.

Some dealers are happy to remain in prison because they can make more money inside than they do 'on the out'. The inmate concerned claims a man who was visiting another prisoner handed him a packet in the car park. The head of security is aware who the visitor was, but can't charge him because he wasn't caught in the act. He also knows which prisoner the heroin was destined for, but he's also in the clear because he never received it.

DAY 200   SUNDAY 3 FEBRUARY 2002

5.00 am

I rise early and write for two hours.

2.00 pm

My visitors today are my son Will and Chris Beetles. Will takes me through the preparations for my appeal on sentence, which are almost complete as both pieces of research on perjury and an attempt to pervert the course of justice show that eighteen months would historically be a high tariff for a first offender. Chris brings me up to date on everything that's happening in the art world.

4.00 pm

At Club Hospital's Sunday afternoon tea party, David (fraud, schoolmaster) reveals that Brian (ostrich farm fraud) and John (fraud) are both having trouble since being released. Brian is waking in the middle of the night, sweating because he's frightened he won't make it back in time for the 7 pm check-in and John is stressed because he hasn't been able to find a job.

6.00 pm

Once the club members have left, I settle down to make myself some supper. In a large soup bowl (a gift from William), I place the contents of a tin of Princes ham, two packets of Walkers crisps and an Oxo cube; hot water is then poured on top. What a combination. I eat while reading *Street Drugs* by Andrew Tyler, which is my set text for the week.

The food is wonderful, the book harrowing.

DAY 201   MONDAY 4 FEBRUARY 2002

9.00 am

A young lad from the north block, who only has two weeks to serve of a three-month sentence, has been found in his room with his head in a noose made from a sheet hanging from the end of his bed. The slightly built lad, who must be about twenty-one, reminds me of the boy having sand kicked into his face in those Charles Atlas advertisements I saw when I was a child. He is taken to the hospital to be interviewed by Mr Berlyn, Dr Harris and sister behind closed doors. He's certain to be placed on red suicide watch, with an officer checking on him every thirty minutes.

Mr Berlyn tells me that they've never had a suicide at NSC because if a prisoner is that desperate, he usually absconds. The real problem arises in closed prisons from which there is no escape. There were seventy-three suicides in prisons last year and not one of them was at a D-cat.

Just as Mr Berlyn leaves, the lad who wets his bed reappears with a black bag containing two more sheets. I supply him with two clean sheets and he leaves looking even more helpless than the suicide case; you'd never think this was a men's prison.

904

2.00 pm

I watch four videos on the subject of heroin. I'm slowly gaining more knowledge about drugs through reading, videos and my day-to-day work as hospital orderly, but I still have no first-hand experience. I go over to see David in the CARAT (Counselling, Assessment, Referral, Advice, Through-care) office. He is willing to let me attend one of his drug counselling sessions, as long as the other participants agree, because I'll be the only one who isn't currently, and never has been, an addict.

6.00 pm

I attend the drug rehab discussion in the CARAT office. David asks the five other inmates if any of them object to my presence. They all seem pleased that I've taken the trouble to attend.

David opens the discussion by asking if they feel that once they are released they'll be able to resist going back on drugs, and in particular heroin. One of them is adamant that he will never touch a drug again. His relationship with those he loves has been ruined, and he wonders if anyone will ever be willing to employ him. He tells the group that he had reached the stage where he would steal from anyone, including his own family, to make sure he got his fix, and just before he was arrested, he needed four fixes a day to satisfy his addiction.

The next participant says that his only thought on waking was how to get his first fix. Once he'd begged, borrowed or stolen the £20 needed, he'd go in search of a dealer. As soon as he'd got his half gramme of heroin, he'd run back to his house and, often with his wife and two children in the next room, he would place the powder in a large tablespoon, to which he would add water and the juice from any citrus fruit. He would then stir the mixture until he had a thick brown liquid, which he would pour onto a piece of aluminium foil and then warm it with a match. He would then sniff it up through a straw. One of the inmates butts in and adds that he preferred to smoke it. However, all of them agree that the biggest kick came when you injected it. The lad from Scarborough then lifts the sleeve of his denim jacket and his trouser leg, and declares, 'That gets difficult when there are no veins left to inject.'

The one who so far hasn't said a word chips in for the first time. He tells us that he's been off heroin for five weeks and still can't sleep, and what makes it worse is that his room-mate snores all through the night. The dealer jumps in. 'You'll start getting to sleep after about eight weeks, and then it gets better and better each day until you're back to normal.'

I ask what he means by that.

'Once you're an addict, you don't need a fix to make you feel good, you need one just so you can return to normal. That's when you become a "smack head" – in between fixes you start shaking, and the worse you are the more desperate you become to return to normal. And, Jeff,' he adds, 'if you're planning to talk about the problem in schools, you should start with the eleven year olds, because by fourteen, it's too late. In Scarborough, good-looking, well-brought-up, well-educated fourteen-year-old girls approach me all the time for their daily fix.'

The last person to participate is another dealer, who claims he only dealt because the profits allowed him to finance his own drug addiction. From eight in the morning to ten at night, his mobile would ring with a non-stop flow of requests from customers. He assures me that he's never needed to solicit anyone. He tells the group that he's been off heroin for nearly seven months, and will never deal in, or take drugs, again. I don't feel that confident after he adds that he can earn £1,000 a day as a seller. He ends the session with a statement that takes me – but no one else in the room – by surprise. 'Nearly all my friends are in jail or dead.'

He's thirty-one years old.

DAY 202   TUESDAY 5 FEBRUARY 2002

7.00 am

I put my pen down after a couple of hours of writing to switch on the *Today* programme. Britain is in the middle of a rail strike. There's no station at North Sea Camp.

9.00 am

Two of the inmates who attended last night's drugs counselling meeting are up on a 'nicking'. Once the doctor has pronounced them fit, they will attend an adjudication chaired by Governor Leighton. One of them tested positive for cannabis on his latest MDT, and adds ruefully that he expects to be shipped out to a B-cat prison later today. Now I know why he hardly spoke at yesterday's meeting. He also looks as if he didn't sleep last night.

1.00 pm

The newspapers are full of stories about David Blunkett's proposed prison reforms, which seem no more than common sense. Anyone with a non-custodial sentence for a non-violent first offence will be placed on immediate tagging, with weekend custody, and possibly having to report to a police station every evening. For lesser offences, they would be tagged immediately, with a curfew of 7 pm to 7 am. A second offence and they would be sent to prison.

As of 1 February, the prison population stood at 67,978 and the prediction is that already overcrowded prisons will be under additional pressure following Lord Chief Justice Woolf's recent pronouncement on mobile phone muggers.

4.00 pm

Three more manuscripts arrive in the post today with letters asking if I could critique them. Four publishers have turned one down; another says his wife, who is his sternest critic, thinks it's first class, and the final one seeks my advice on vanity publishers.*

4.20 pm

One of today's inductees is a Mr T. Blair. He has been sentenced to six months for disturbing the peace, but with remission and tagging, expects to be released after only eight weeks. The other Mr T. Blair looks set to serve at least eight years.

4.37 pm

I still marvel at what prisoners will have the nerve to ask sister for. Today, one inmate has demanded a bottle of aftershave because he has a skin problem. I'm about to burst out laughing,

---

* So-called vanity publishers are only too happy to publish your book – if, along with the script, you enclose a cheque for £3,000.

when Linda hands him a bottle and he leaves without another word.

'Why can't he buy one in the canteen?' I ask.

'You can't buy aftershave in the canteen,' Linda reminds me, 'it contains alcohol, and several inmates would happily drink it.'

'But you've just given . . .'

'Non-alcoholic aftershave supplied especially for prison hospitals. On your day of release,' Linda reminds me, 'any prisoner can demand a free needle to inject himself with heroin, as well as a packet of condoms.'

DAY 203   WEDNESDAY 6 FEBRUARY 2002

9.00 am

I can't believe how stupid some people can be.

On Monday I attended a CARAT meeting where one of the participants told everyone present that he had given up drugs. On Tuesday the same man comes up in front of the governor for failing an MDT for cannabis. Seven days were added to his sentence, and he told me he considered himself lucky not to be shipped out. Last night the same man was caught on his way back from Boston in possession of a plastic bag full of drugs that included cannabis and heroin. He was locked up in the segregation cell overnight, and will be shipped out this morning to a B-cat with a further twenty-one days added to his sentence.

His stupidity is not the only aspect of this incident worth considering. If he'd been caught with such an assignment of drugs 'on the out' he would have been sentenced to at least seven years, but as his sentence is already fourteen, he gets away with twenty-one days added. It's just another pointer to the drugs problem this country is currently facing.

11.00 am

Mary has a piece in *Peterborough* that she came across on the Web. It makes me laugh so much it's simply better to reproduce it rather than attempt any precis. (See below.)

Woman of substance

Lady Archer's sense of humour is alive and well. The fragrant chemist has just submitted a "hazardous materials data sheet" to the *Chemistry at Cambridge* newsletter. "**Element**: woman. **Symbol**: Wo. **Discoverer**: Adam. **Atomic mass**: accepted as 55kg but known to vary from 45kg to 225kg. **Occurrence**: found in large quantities in urban areas, with trace elements in outlying regions. **Physical properties**: boils at absolutely nothing, freezes for no apparent reason. Melts if given special treatment, bitter if used incorrectly. **Chemical properties**: affinity to gold, silver, platinum and all precious stones. The most powerful money-reducing agent known to man. **Common use**: highly ornamental, especially in sports cars. Can be a very effective cleaning agent. **Hazards**: highly dangerous except in experienced hands. Illegal to possess more than one, although several can be maintained at different locations as long as specimens do not come into direct contact with each other."

The *Telegraph* also publishes the results of a poll on Mr Blunkett's recent pronouncements that non-violent, first-offence prisoners should be able, where possible, to continue their work while reporting into jails in the evenings and at weekends; 83 per cent say 'keep them locked up', while only 12 per cent feel the Home Secretary is right to consider legislation along these more realistic lines. I must confess that before I'd been to prison, I would have been among the 83 per cent.

7.00 pm

I phone Mary, who tells me before I can get beyond 'Hello' that Baroness Nicholson has finally issued a statement in which she offers a grudging apology. (See below.)

Baroness Nicholson wishes to make it quite clear that at no time did she intend to suggest that Lord Archer had personally misappropriated money raised by the Simple Truth appeal. Indeed, it had not occurred to her to think that it might have been possible for Lord Archer to gain access to funds raised by the British Red Cross. If the inference was drawn that she was accusing Lord Archer of having stolen Simple Truth money from the British Red Cross, she regrets the misunderstanding and regrets any upset that may have been caused to Lord Archer's family.

DAY 204   THURSDAY 7 FEBRUARY 2002

9.00 am

Mr Berlyn strides in at a brisk pace. After a few minutes ensconced with sister in her office, he emerges to tell me that the Home Office has issued an 'overcrowding' draft, as all the prisons in the north of England are fully occupied. Result: we will be getting ten new inmates today, and will be 'surplus to our manifest' of 213. Here at NSC we are already seeing those overcrowding statistics translated into reality.

Mr Berlyn has directed that two inmates will have to be billeted in the hospital overnight. I fear I will be experiencing a lot of this during the next few weeks, and I may without warning have to share heaven with some other sinners. However, as six inmates are being released tomorrow, this might be only temporary.

12.07 pm

Linda and Gail charge out of the hospital carrying an oxygen cylinder and two first-aid boxes. All I'm told is that a staff member has fallen off a ladder. On the intercom it's announced that all security officers must report to the south block immediately. It's like being back in an A-cat where this was a daily

914

occurrence. Prisoners tell me that in Nottingham ambulances were more common than Black Marias.

A few minutes later Linda and Gail return with a shaven-headed officer covered in blood. It seems that he leaned back while climbing a ladder and overbalanced, landing on the concrete below. No prisoner was involved.

I quickly discover that a small head wound can spurt so much blood that it appears far worse than it is. When Linda has finished cleaning up her patient and I've given him a cup of tea (only the English), he's smiling and making light of the whole episode. But Linda still wants to dispatch him to the Pilgrim Hospital for stitches to the scalp wound, and both she as hospital sister, and Mr Hocking, head of security, have to fill in countless forms, showing that no prisoner was responsible.

6.00 pm

I read another chapter of *Street Drugs*, this time to learn more about crack cocaine, its properties and its consequences. It's quite difficult not to accept the argument that some young people, having experimented with one drug and got a kick out of it, might wish to progress to another, simply to discover if the sensation is even more exciting.

10.00 pm

Only one of the extra two inmates allocated to spend the night in the hospital appears at my door, a blanket and sheet under his arm. It seems they found a bed for the other arrival. He's very quiet, despite the fact that he's being released tomorrow. He slips into bcd and simply says, 'Goodnight, Jeff.'

Am I that frightening?

DAY 205   FRIDAY 8 FEBRUARY 2002

5.30 am

'What do you think you're doing, you fucking dickhead?'

I'm about to explain to my overnight companion that I write for a couple of hours every morning, but when I turn to face him, I realize he's still fast asleep. It's the first occasion someone's sworn in front of me for a long time, even in their sleep, and it brings back memories of Belmarsh and Wayland. I continue writing until seven, when I have to wake him.

'Morning, Jeff,' he says.

By the time I emerged from the bathroom, he's disappeared – his sheets and pillowcases folded neatly at the end of the bed. By now he'll be in reception, signing his discharge papers, and by eight-thirty will be on his way, a free man.*

2.00 pm

Our two new inductees today are somewhat unusual, and not just because they're both lifers (we now have 23 lifers out of 210 occupants). The first one tells me that he's been in jail for

_____

* The prison is entitled to keep you until midnight on the day of your release, but you're usually off the premises by nine o'clock.

twenty-three years and he's only thirty-nine. The second one limps into the hospital and spends a considerable time with sister behind closed doors.

Later, when I take his blood pressure and check his weight, he tells me that he's already served fourteen years, and two years ago he contracted encephalitis. Once I've filled in his chart and handed it to Linda, I look up encephalitis in the medical dictionary. Poor fellow. Life imprisonment he may deserve, encephalitis he does not.

DAY 206   SATURDAY 9 FEBRUARY 2002

2.00 pm

Mary and James visit me today, and it's far from being a social event. Mary even has a written agenda. I do adore her.

On the domestic front, she has purchased a small Victorian mirror for the hall, and seeks my approval. She goes on to tell me that Baroness Nicholson has written saying that she wants to end the feud, claiming that she never intended anyone to think that I had misappropriated any funds in the first place. In which case, how did I end up in a cell three paces by five, banged up for fourteen hours a day at Wayland, if the police and Prison Service misunderstood her?*

As for the prejudice of Mr Justice Potts, it remains to be seen whether Godfrey Barker is still willing to make a witness statement. He has confirmed, on many occasions, in the presence of

---

* Baroness Nicholson wrote to Sir John Stevens, Commissioner of the Metropolitan Police, in July 2001, demanding 'an investigation into the involvement of Jeffrey Archer in funds raised and spent through the Simple Truth Appeal'. This precipitated not only a police enquiry, but a lengthy and expensive investigation by KPMG on behalf of the Red Cross. Baroness Nicholson's insinuation that I had stolen money from the Appeal was irresponsible and wholly without foundation, and on 23 January 2002, the police closed their enquiry 'in view of ... the lack of any evidence from the informant'.

several witnesses, that Potts, at a dinner party he and his wife attended, railed against me for some considerable time.

4.00 pm

When my name is called over the tannoy to report to reception, I assume that James has left something for me at the gate. I've been expecting a dozen *West Wing* tapes that will first have to go to the library before I can take them out. My gift turns out to be eight tapes, twelve CDs and three DVDs, not from James, but from an anonymous member of the public, so I can't even write to thank them.

Someone else has sent seven books of first-class stamps and a packet of stamped envelopes, after hearing how many letters I'm receiving every day. Mr Garley, the duty officer, explains that I can't have the stamps (could be exchanged for drugs), but I can have the stamped envelopes (prison logic). Shouldn't the rule be universal to all prisons? At Belmarsh, a category A prison, stamps are permitted. I make no comment. It's not Mr Garley's fault, and he can't do anything about it.

DAY 207   SUNDAY 10 FEBRUARY 2002

7.21 am

Gail is angry. She's recently bought a smart new dark green Peugeot, which she parks outside the hospital. Yesterday, one of the prisoners put matchsticks in her locks, so that when she tried to open the door, she pushed the matchstick further in and jammed the lock.

4.00 pm

Club Hospital meets for tea and biscuits. One of our new members, who has only been with us for a month, will be released tomorrow. He was charged with road rage and sentenced to three months. He will have spent six weeks in prison. I've watched him carefully at our get-togethers and as he goes about his business around the prison. He is well educated, well mannered and looks quite incapable of swatting a fly.

He tells the group that he stopped his car to go to the aid of a woman who was being attacked, but for his troubles, got punched to the ground by what turned out to be her boyfriend. The two of them then drove off. He returned home, but was later arrested for road rage as the woman bore witness that *he* attacked her. Had he gone to the police station first and reported them for assault, the other man would now be in jail, not him. He has lost his job with the pharmaceutical company he's been with for twenty-one years, and is worried about getting another one now he has a criminal record. His wife has stuck by him, and she hopes that one of his old firm's rivals will want to take advantage of his expertise.* This brings me onto the subject of wives.

Of the seven married Club members present today, two of their wives have had to sell their homes and move to smaller houses in another area; two have had to go out to work full time while trying to bring up children (three in one case, two in the other), and the other two have received divorce petitions while in jail. I'm the seventh.

I make no excuse for the crimes committed, but I feel it bears repeating that it's often the wives who suffer even more than the husbands – for them there is no rehabilitation programme.

---

*He later wrote to tell me that his old firm took him back the day he was released, and treated the six weeks absence as holiday on full pay.

DAY 208   MONDAY 11 FEBRUARY 2002

9.00 am

One of the prisoners waiting to be seen by Dr Walling this morning is a regular attendee. Today he somehow managed to get a nail stuck in his head. It only grazed the surface of his skull, but produced a lot of blood. Once Gail has cleaned and bandaged him up, he asks, 'Could I have rust on the brain?'

2.00 pm

The prison is jam-packed; 211 at lock up last night. Two inmates have been released this morning, and three new prisoners arrived this afternoon from Leicester. They couldn't be more different. One is eighteen, and serving a six-week sentence for a road-traffic offence. He has only two more weeks to serve before taking up a place at Leicester University in September to read mathematics. The second is around twenty-four – he is doing six months for punching someone in a pub. He requests counselling for his drink problem; drink is considered by the prison authorities to be just as much a drug as cannabis or heroin. The third is serving six years for GBH, a year of which he spent in Belmarsh.

6.00 pm

I attend the weekly CARAT meeting, but one of the prisoners objects to my presence, so I leave immediately.

The drugs counsellor tells me later that because I've never been an addict myself and am writing a diary, he doesn't feel free to express himself while I'm there – fair enough.

I settle down to read the latest booklet on the subject of addiction, *Is Your Child on Drugs?* No, thank God. However, it's a fascinating read. It is not uncommon for a child to start smoking at seven – eleven is the norm – so it's no surprise that some children are hooked on heroin by the age of fourteen.

DAY 209   TUESDAY 12 FEBRUARY 2002

9.00 am

We have a full surgery this morning: three for release, two for a week's temporary release and eleven with imagined or real illnesses. Dr Allwood, a thorough and conscientious man, always takes his time. In fact, after forty minutes, one of the inmates in the waiting room complains about how long he's taking. Gail leaps out of the surgery and tells the prisoner that her husband visited his GP last week and had to sit around for three hours, and that was after having to wait a week before he could make an appointment. The inmate snarls.

Chris, a lifer (murdered his wife), rolls up his sleeve and shows me a faded scar on the inside of his arm. 'I did that,' he says, thrusting it under the gaze of the complaining prisoner, who looks surprised. 'Yeah,' he continues, 'stabbed in the middle of the night by my pad-mate, wasn't I, and when I pressed the emergency button no screws came to help me because I was on the top floor.' Chris now has the full attention of the rest of the surgery. 'No doctor at Gartree to come to my aid, so I sewed it up myself.' I look at his faded scar in disbelief, but Gail nods to confirm she's seen many examples of amateur stitching over the years.

'Just a needle and thread was all I needed,' he adds.

10.40 am

Mr Berlyn marches into the hospital and says he needs an urgent word with me. We go into the ward. He has been in touch with Mr Le Sage at HMP Stocken about my accompanying him when he gives his talk to schools on the problems of young people becoming involved in drugs and ending up in prison. The good news is that Mr Le Sage is looking for a new prisoner to assist him, and has agreed to travel up to NSC next Monday to talk about the possibility of my working alongside him. This is the best news I've had since being appointed hospital orderly.

Escaping the confines of NSC, visiting schools and feeling I'm doing something worthwhile must be the next step on this particular journey. I thank Mr Berlyn and once again have something to look forward to. Next Monday.

3.00 pm

Only two new inductees today because the prison is full. When I check my board, I note one of them is called Blackburn. We already have a Blackburn, I tell the young lad sitting in front of me.

'Yeah, that's my dad,' he says. 'He was my co-defendant.' I smell a story. 'You'll never believe what we're in for, Jeff,' he adds. I remain silent. 'We were caught stealing Lion Bars, and got three and a half years.'

'That sounds a bit rough,' I venture foolishly.

'Yeah, well, I have to admit, Jeff, it was forty-six tons of 'em with a street value of nearly two hundred grand.'

'But how do you fence chocolate bars?'

He laughs. 'We already had a buyer.'

'At what price?'

'Forty grand.'

'So how did you get caught?'

'One of the night watchmen who was part of our team grassed us up, didn't he.'

'Why?'

'He was up for a minor charge of burglary and did a deal with the scum.'

'Did he get off?'

'Yeah, they dropped the charge, didn't they, but nicked him for somethin' else a couple of months later and then they banged him up in the Scrubs ... with my father.'

4.07 pm

Mr Hocking drops in to say that he's pleased I might be going out to assist a prison officer with his drugs talk. He's already informed the governor that I am not considered a security risk. He's only been with me a couple of minutes when his radio intercom asks him to report back to the security office immediately.

'We've had another one,' are the only words I clearly hear. I look suitably inquisitive.

'We've got a serial informer,' he explains, 'he writes every day telling us who the drug dealers are and where we'll find the next drop. So far he's been on the button every time.'

'Do you know who the informer is?' I ask.

'No idea, don't want to know,' he replies. 'All I can tell you is that the handwriting is the same every time.'

DAY 210   WEDNESDAY 13 FEBRUARY 2002

5.43 am

I dreamed last night about a lovely man called John Bromley – Brommers to his friends – who died of cancer a few days ago. I had the privilege of working with him – you didn't work *for* John, even though he was the head of ITV's sport. He had an amazing gift of making even the tea lady feel part of the team. If you had a love of sport, good humour, fine wine and beautiful women, he was quite simply the best company a man could ask for. I predict that his memorial service will be as well attended as any prime minister's. I only hope I'm out in time to be there.

9.30 am

A beautiful black Labrador called Bessie saunters into the hospital accompanied by two officers from the drug squad. I am told to wait in the lobby while Bessie goes about her work. Through the closed door, I can hear her padding around sniffing for drugs among my personal possessions. If Bessie can read, she'll find several books, pamphlets and papers on drugs, but until you can fail an MDT for Ribena, Bovril or Evian, not much else.

The other prisoners sitting in the lobby waiting to see the

DAY 210

doctor can't mask their surprise. A few moments later, the door is opened and Bessie reappears, and as she passes by, ignores me – a good sign, because if Bessie starts to sniff you, you're in trouble. If she licks you, you'll be up on a charge. I ought to be pleased, but when I return to the ward, Bessie's paw-prints are everywhere, and I scrubbed the floor only yesterday.

11.00 am

Mr Hocking explains that the drug search had a purpose. They are about to make a big swoop, following another tip-off, and he wanted the other inmates to see that I was not exempt from being searched. By now everyone in the prison will know, and some might even wonder if I'm about to be shipped out. I suspect the real search will take place later today.

3.00 pm

I have a legal visit from my solicitors Tony Morton Hooper and Lord Mishcon, now aged eighty-four – it's kind of him to endure the seven-hour round trip. We spend the next two hours preparing for the upcoming appeal, not that a date has yet been fixed.

6.00 pm

Doug tells me that we are to have a new governing governor called Mr Beaumont. As he was governor of Leicester Prison, there will be a lot of inmates who can brief us about him.

DAY 211   THURSDAY 14 FEBRUARY 2002

8.15 am

I no longer have breakfast in the main hall because Linda supplies me with a box of cornflakes once a week and a half pint of milk every day. Today she added a new luxury – a banana.

9.00 am

One of the prisoners in surgery this morning needs a weekend leave form signed by the doctor, to show he is fit to be out of prison. Yesterday his leave was revoked because he drew out a large sum of money from his canteen account, leaving a balance of only £3.72. You cannot take weekend leave unless you have at least £4 in your account. It is assumed that if you empty your account, then you're probably going to abscond. This seems unlikely in this case as the prisoner has only two weeks of his sentence left.

Mr Berlyn shows some common sense, allows the prisoner to put 28p back into the account and signs his weekend leave pass.

DAY 211

12 noon

Lunch in the canteen. Potato bake and cabbage, followed by sponge cake covered, and I mean covered, in custard. I never eat the second course, but take it, because Carl can always eat two portions.

3.00 pm

Dr Harris is on duty and his first responsibility is to sign the discharge papers for eight prisoners who will be released tomorrow. All of them have been granted tagging status, which allows them to leave two months early as long as they remain in their homes between the hours of 7 pm and 7 am. These hours can be flexible if it affects their job.

When I first arrived at NSC and worked as the orderly in the sentence management unit, the tagging board of Mr Berlyn and Mr Simpson used to agree to about 50 per cent of those eligible for this privilege. Now all eight are granted on the same day,* including a twenty-three-year-old who's already been to prison four times. Lee admits that he was shocked when the board granted him tagging status, as his offence was punching someone on the nose in a pub brawl and in any case he looks upon prison as a way of life. In fact, his last comment to Linda before leaving us was, 'See you towards the end of the year, if not before.' He turns to me and adds, 'Let's hope you're out by then, Jeff.'

---

* Caused by the problem of overcrowding.

4.15 pm

I sweep out the ward and mop the floor. On alternate days I vacuum Linda's little office removing Bessie's paw prints. All very therapeutic.

5.00 pm

I call Mary. She thanks me for the flowers that I asked Alison to send her yesterday. She then brings me up to date on Angie Peppiatt and Mr Justice Potts.

5.30 pm

I collect my post. Eleven Valentine cards, which I display in the ward for all to see, plus several letters, including one from John Major and another from Billy Connolly.

Many years ago when John was Chancellor of the Exchequer, I asked him to open the extension to our new folly at the Old Vicarage at our annual summer party. John described the building as 'Mary's second folly'. Billy spoke next and immediately closed it.

DAY 212　　　FRIDAY 15 FEBRUARY 2002

5.23 am

I've only just worked out why it's the same five inmates who appear at the front of the queue every morning for medication; Linda as hospital sister will only allow them one day's supply of drugs, whereas in a surgery 'on the out', she would prescribe enough for a week, and in some cases even a month. Why, you may ask.

a) If a prisoner were given a month's supply he might well take it all on one day.

b) He could also trade his medication for other drugs.*

c) They could be lost or stolen.

Result, we have a long queue every morning for one day's supply of medication, so they will all be back tomorrow.

---

* The analgesic the inmates most commonly ask for is Kapake which is a mixture of paracetamol and codeine. The reason is that codeine will show up in MDT as an opiate, and thus disguise illegal opiates. The user can then protest, 'But I'm taking Kapake which the doctor prescribed.' Prison doctors are now trying to limit the use of Kapake and diazepam when a prisoner has a record of taking drugs.

7.30 am

Mr Beaumont the new governor has hit the ground running. He's demanded that his office be repainted and all the furniture be replaced, and it all has to be completed by the time he gets back from a visit to the Home Office tomorrow.

8.30 am

Mr Vessey, a security officer, marches into the hospital. His appearance usually means that a prisoner is about to be nicked for some offence. I can't think of any offence I've committed recently, other than being in possession of a bottle of Ribena (smuggled in by Doug). Mr Vessey, who never makes any attempt to be friendly, asks me to accompany him, and takes considerable pleasure in marching me out of the hospital and across the camp. Several prisoners stare in disbelief. He eventually tells me my name has come up on the computer for a random MDT test.

He escorts me into a Portacabin, where I am locked in a room with five other prisoners. Three of them look relaxed and are happily chatting, while the other two are silent, twitchy and look distinctly nervous. A few minutes later I hear a key turning in the lock and another officer joins us.

Four of us came up on the computer for a random test, while two others are here on 'reasonable suspicion'. The serial grasser has undoubtedly offered up their names. The officer then reads his authority to carry out such a test (see overleaf) before asking who would like to be tested first.

I stand up and follow him into an adjoining room. The procedure is then explained to me (see page 349), and I am requested to sign a form saying I agree to the test. I am then

MANDATORY DRUG TEST AUTHORISATION FORM

Prisoner Name: .... *ARCHER* .... Number: FF 8282 ......

> Test Reference Number:
>
> NS 33/01
>
> *For allocation when sample is collected*

1. The governor has authorised that in accordance with Section 16A of the Prison Act 1952 any prisoner may be required by a prison officer to provide a sample of urine for the purposes of testing for the presence of a controlled drug.

2. You are now required under the terms of Section 16A to provide a fresh and unadulterated sample of urine for testing for the presence of controlled drugs.

3. Authority for this requirement was given by: .... GOVERNOR. ....

4. Reason for requirement: (only one box to be ticked)

   [✓] **Random test:** You have been selected for this test on a strictly random basis.

   [ ] **Reasonable suspicion:** You have been selected for this test because staff have reason to believe that you have misused drugs. This test has been approved by a senior manager.

   [ ] **Risk assessment:** You have been selected for this test because you are being considered for a privilege, or a job, where a high degree of trust is to be given to you.

   [ ] **Frequent test programme:** You have been selected for more frequent testing because of your previous history of drug misuse.

   [ ] **On reception:** You have been selected for testing on reception on a random basis.

5. The procedures used during the collection and testing of the sample have been designed to protect you and to ensure that there are no mistakes in the handling of your sample. At the end of the collection procedure you will be asked to sign a statement confirming that the urine sealed in the sample bottles for testing is fresh and your own.

6. Your sample will be split at the point of collection into separate containers which will be sealed in your presence. In the event of you disputing any positive test result, one of these containers will be available, for a period of up to 12 months, for you to arrange, if you so wish, for an independent analysis to be undertaken at your own expense.

7. You will be liable to be placed on report if you:

   (a) provide a positive sample;
   (b) refuse to provide a sample; or,
   (c) fail to provide a sample after 4 hours of the order to do so (or after 5 hours if the officer believes that you are experiencing real difficulty in providing a sample).

Consent to Medical disclosure

* (i) During the past 30 days I have not used any medication issued to me by Health Care.

Signature of Prisoner : .... Date: 15 . 2 . 02 . ....

PRISON SERVICE CHAIN OF CUSTODY PROCEDURE

Prisoner Name: .... ARCHER .... Number: ..FF.8282...

RANDOM TESTING PROGRAMME

This form is to be used only for tests conducted as part of the MDT random programme
(i.e. where prisoners have been selected by the LIDS computer)

Test Reference Number: .NS.33/01..

Checklist for sample collection - tick boxes as you proceed. Refer to guidance notes if in doubt.

1 [✓] Only **One** sample collection kit present.
2 [✓] Check identity of prisoner. Complete details above and in sample collection register.
3 [✓] Carry out search and handwashing procedures. (No soap).
4 [✓] Show the prisoner that the collection cup and bottles are empty.
5 [✓] Ask prisoner to provide enough urine to be split **equally** between the two sample bottles.
6 [✓] *Take temperature using the temperature strip. If temperature is out of range (32-38C) (90-100F), make note in comment section and refer to guidance notes.*
7 [✓] **Watched by prisoner**, transfer urine **equally** between the two bottles. Fill each **above 15ml line and below 30ml line. Press caps on securely.**
8 [✓] Ask prisoner to initial and date both bottle seals.
9 [✓] **Watched by prisoner**, place a seal over each bottle cap.
10 [✓] Dispose of any surplus urine and the cup.
11 [✓] Pack two bottles in mailing container and then in chain of custody bag - **Do not seal bag.**
12 [✓] **Watched by prisoner**, fix barcode labels and enter test reference number on all copies of this form.
13 [✓] Ask the prisoner to sign and date the Prisoner's Declaration below.
14 [✓] Complete Chain of Custody Report, tear off and place in chain of custody bag facing outwards.
15 [✓] Seal bag, ask prisoner to initial bag where indicated.
16 [✓] Place sealed bag in secure refrigerator until ready for despatch to laboratory.
17 [✓] Allow prisoner to leave.

Prisoner Declaration

I confirm that (i)   I understand why I was required to provide the sample and what may happen if I fail to comply with this requirement;
(ii) the urine sample I have given was my own and freshly provided;
(iii) the sample was divided into two bottles and sealed in my presence with seals initialled and dated by me;
(iv) the seals used on these bottles carry a barcode identical to the barcode attached to this form.

Signature of prisoner .... *[signature]* .... Date ..15 . 2 .02..

asked to strip and put on a dressing gown. Mr Vessey hands me a plastic beaker, and asks me to go to the lavatory next door and fill it with at least 60 ml of urine. Having managed this, I hand the beaker back to Mr Vessey, who unseals two plastic tubes in my presence and then pours half the urine into each tube. After I have initialled both, he seals them and places them in a plastic bag, which he also seals. The bag is then deposited in the fridge. He points out that my name is not on the bag, only my number, FF8282.

Having completed this procedure, I sign another form to

confirm that I am satisfied with the way the test has been conducted. I am then released to return to the hospital.

Despite this being a humiliating experience, it's one I thoroughly approve of. Although I've never got on with Mr Vessey, he is a professional who cannot hide his contempt for anyone involved in drugs, especially the dealers.

9.00 am

One of the inmates up in front of the governor this morning has been charged with illegal possession of marijuana – but with a difference. When his room was raided they found him trying to swallow a small plastic packet. They wrestled him to the ground and extracted the evidence from his mouth. Had he swallowed the contents, they would not have been able to charge him. The packet was one of those we supply from the hospital containing six paracetamol pills. This one had an ounce of marijuana inside, and the inmate ended up with seven days added to his sentence.

3.00 pm

Mr Hocking appears in the hospital carrying a large attaché case and disappears into Linda's office. A few minutes later they both come out and join me on the ward. The large plastic case is placed on a hospital bed and opened to reveal a drugs kit: twenty-one square plastic containers embedded in foam rubber show the many different drugs currently on the market. For the first time I see heroin, crack cocaine, ecstasy tablets, amphetamines and marijuana in every form.

Linda and Mr Hocking deliver an introductory talk that they give to any prison officer on how to recognize the different drugs and the way they can be taken. Mr Berlyn and his security team are obviously determined that I will be properly briefed before I am allowed to accompany Mr Le Sage when we visit schools.

It's fascinating at my age (sixty-one) to be studying a new subject as if I were a first-year undergraduate.

5.00 pm

The new governor, Mr Beaumont, is making a tour of the camp and spends seven minutes in the hospital – a flying visit. He has heard the hospital is efficiently run by Linda and Gail, and as long as that continues to be the case, gives them the impression that he will not be interfering.

DAY 213   SATURDAY 16 FEBRUARY 2002

8.45 am

Yesterday I was frog-marched off to do an MDT. Today there's an announcement over the tannoy that there are voluntary drugs tests for those with surnames beginning A–E. These are known as dip tests, because once again you pee into a plastic beaker, but this time the officer in charge dips a little stick into the beaker and moments later is able to give you a result.

I walk across to the Portakabin, supply another 60ml of urine and I'm immediately cleared, which makes yesterday's test somewhat redundant.

I later learn that one of the Bs came up positive, and he had to call his wife to let her know that he won't be allowed out on a town visit this weekend. As it was a voluntary test, I can't work out why he agreed to be tested.

10.00 am

Surgery is always slow at the weekend because the majority of inmates who appear with various complaints during the week in the hope that they will get off work remain in bed, while all those who are fit never visit us in the first place.

938

11.00 am

Carl and an inmate called Jason who is only with us for two weeks (motoring offence) turn up at the hospital. Together we remove all the beds from the ward and push them into the corridor, before giving the hospital a spring clean.

Jason tells me that 'on the out' he's a painter and decorator, and could repaint the ward during his two-week incarceration. I shall speak to the governor on Monday, because at £8.20 a week this would be quite a bargain. You may well ask why Carl and Jason helped me with the spring clean. Boredom. The spring clean killed a morning for all of us.

2.00 pm

I watch the prison football team lose 7–2, and witness two more pieces of unbelievable stupidity by fellow inmates. Our goalkeeper, who was sent off by the same referee the last time we played, shouts obscenities at him again, and is surprised when he's booked. I fear he will be back in prison within months of being released. But worse, our centre forward is a prisoner who's just come out of the Pilgrim Hospital after a groin injury, and has been told to rest for six weeks. He will undoubtedly appear at surgery on Monday expecting sympathy. It's no wonder the NHS is in such crisis if patients behave so irresponsibly after being given expert advice.

DAY 214   SUNDAY 17 FEBRUARY 2002

6.01 am

If I had been given the same sentence as Jonathan Aitken, I would have been released today. Jonathan was sentenced to eighteen months, and because he was a model prisoner, only had to serve seven (half minus two months on tag). Tomorrow I will not be returning home to my wife and family because Mr Justice Potts sentenced me to four years. Instead I will be meeting Mark Le Sage, an officer from Stocken Prison who visits schools in Lincolnshire, warning children of the consequences of taking drugs.

I will remain at NSC until I know the result of my appeal, but for the first time in seven months (since my mother's funeral) I will be able to leave the prison and return to the outside world.

DAY 215　　MONDAY 18 FEBRUARY 2002

10.00 am

Mr Le Sage does not turn up for our meeting.

The governor of HMP Stocken has decided that they should not have to bear the cost of my accompanying Mr Le Sage on any school visit, as it would no longer be a voluntary activity that Mr Le Sage would normally pursue in his off-duty time.

As so often is the case in prisons, someone will look for a reason for *not* doing something rather than trying to make a good idea work. I cannot pretend that I've become so used to this negative attitude that I am not disappointed. Mr Berlyn is also unable to mask his anger, and seems determined not to be thwarted by this setback. He has decided that NSC will send its own officer (Mr Hocking) as my escort, so that I might still attend Mark Le Sage's lectures. As I won't know if this suggestion will be vetoed until Mr Berlyn has spoken to the Stocken's governor, I will continue in my role as hospital orderly.

11.30 am

Alan Purser, the prison drugs counsellor, comes across to the hospital to give me a copy of *The Management of Drug Misuse in*

DAY 215

Prisons by Dr Celia Grummitt. Dr Grummitt will become my new bedtime companion.

4.00 pm

Mr Vessey has charged Chris (lifer, murder) and David (lifer, murder) with being on the farm in possession of four potatoes and a cabbage. In normal circumstances this would have caused little interest, even in our self-contained world. However, this will be the new governor's first adjudication, which we all await with bated breath.

DAY 216 TUESDAY 19 FEBRUARY 2002

10.00 am

Mr Beaumont dismissed the charges against Chris and David as a farm worker came forward to say he'd given them permission to take the potatoes and the cabbage.

2.07 pm

As part of my preparation for talking to children about the dangers and consequences of drugs, I have a visit from a police officer attached to the Lincolnshire drug squad. Her name is Karen Brooks. She's an attractive, thirty-five-year-old blonde, and single mother of two. I mention this only to show that she is normal. Karen has currently served two and a half years of a four-year assignment attached to the drug squad, having been a member of the force for the past fourteen years: hardly the TV image of your everyday drug officer.

She gives me a tutorial lasting just over an hour, and perhaps her most frightening reply to my endless questions – and she is brutally honest – is that she has asked to be transferred to other duties as she can no longer take the day-to-day strain of working with drug addicts.

Karen admits that although she enjoys her job, she wishes she'd never volunteered for the drugs unit in the first place, because the mental scars will remain with her for the rest of her life.

Her son, aged twelve, is a pupil at one of the most successful schools in Lincolnshire, and has already been offered drugs by a fourteen-year-old. This is not a deprived school in the East End of London, but a first-class school in Lincolnshire.

Karen then tells a story that brings her almost to tears. She once arrested a twelve-year-old girl from a middle-class, professional family for shoplifting a pair of socks from Woolworth's. The girl's parents were horrified and assured Karen it wouldn't happen again. Two years later the girl was arrested for stealing from a lingerie shop, and was put on probation. When they next met, the girl was seventeen, going on forty. Three years of experimentation with marijuana, cocaine, ecstasy and heroin, and a relationship with a twenty-year-old drug dealer, had taken their toll. The girl died last month at the age of eighteen. The dealer is still alive – and still dealing.

As Karen gets ready to leave, I ask her how many officers are attached to the drug squad.

'Five,' she replies, 'which means that only about 10 per cent of our time is proactive, while the other 90 per cent is reactive.' She says that she'll visit me again in two weeks' time.

6.30 am

Yesterday I read Celia Grummitt's pamphlet on the misuse of drugs in prisons and the following facts bear repeating:

a) Seven million people in Britain take drugs on a regular basis (this docs not include alcohol or cigarettes).

b) Sixteen million people in Britain smoke cigarettes.

c) Drug-related problems are currently costing the NHS, the police service, the Prison Service, the social services, the probation service and courts – the country – eighteen *billion* pounds a year.

d) If Britain did not have a drug problem, and by that I mean abuse of Class A drugs such as heroin and crack cocaine, we could close 25 per cent of our jails, and there would be no waiting lists on the NHS.

e) In 1975, fewer than 10,000 people were taking heroin. Today it's 220,000, and for those of you who have never had to worry about your children, just think about your grandchildren.

DAY 231   WEDNESDAY 6 MARCH 2002

10.00 am

Mark Le Sage, the young prison officer from HMP Stocken, visits me at the hospital. He's been in the Prison Service for the past twelve years, and for the last eight, has spent many hours as a volunteer addressing schools in the Norfolk area.

Mr Berlyn joins us, as it was his idea that I should attend a couple of Mark's talks before I venture out on my own. As I have not yet passed my FLED, I'll have to be accompanied by Mr Hocking, who has also agreed to carry out this task in his own time, as NSC do not have the funds to cover the extra expense (£14 an hour). Mr Berlyn says that he'll write to the governor of HMP Stocken today, as Mr Le Sage comes under his jurisdiction.

11.00 am

Blossom (traveller, see page 193) is at the High Court today for his appeal. He's currently serving a five-and-a-half-year sentence for stealing cars and caravans. He's grown his beard even longer, as he's hoping that the judge will think he's a lot older than he is, and therefore shorten his sentence. He intends to shave the beard off as soon as he returns this evening.

6.00 pm

Blossom returns from his appeal and announces that a year has been knocked off his sentence. It had nothing to do with the length of his beard, because he was only in the dock for a couple of minutes and the judge hardly gave him a second look. He had clearly read all the relevant papers long before Blossom showed up.

7.00 pm

Blossom has already shaved off the beard.

The other interesting piece of information to come out of Blossom's visit to the High Court was that three cannabis dealers had their sentences halved from seven to three and a half years. A sign of things to come?

DAY 234   SATURDAY 9 MARCH 2002

8.00 am

Blossom comes in to see sister. He's in a dreadful state. His wife has written to let him know that his oldest son (aged twenty-nine) is on heroin. He asks me to fill out a form so that he can apply for compassionate leave. He tells me that he's already got hold of a pair of handcuffs and he plans to chain the boy to a water pipe until he comes off the drug. He's quite serious.

Linda tells him firmly that his plan is neither legal or practical, nor of much value to his son.

6.00 pm

Blossom has been granted two days compassionate leave. He is such a strange mixture of high moral values and low life. He's quite happy to steal caravans and cars, which has been the reason for several of his family ending up in prison, but is devastated when he discovers his son is on heroin. This is a man who has been married for thirty-six years, has eleven children and countless grandchildren, and until now, none of his offspring has ever been involved in drugs.

DAY 235　　　SUNDAY 10 MARCH 2002

2.00 pm

My visitors today are Ed Streator, the former US minister to the Court of St James's and later American ambassador to NATO, and Quentin Davies MP, who is currently Shadow Secretary of State for Northern Ireland. The ninety minutes fly by, as both men have so much to tell me about what's happening where you all are.

I had forgotten that Quentin was PPS to Kenneth Baker when he was Home Secretary. During that period, he developed strong views on the reform of our penal system after becoming aware of the drug problem both inside and outside of prison. He talks with refreshing frankness and honesty about both subjects.

Ed adds a view from the other side of the Atlantic, and when we debate smoking cannabis he reminds me that California has recently passed a law to prevent anyone under the age of twenty-one purchasing tobacco, let alone cannabis. In fact, he adds, in California it's virtually illegal to smoke anywhere except in your own home. Quentin suggests that if tobacco was discovered today, cigarettes would be illegal – possession two years, tobacconists five years.

DAY 235

4.00 pm

Stephen is the latest member to join Club Hospital (Sundays, 4 pm to 6 pm). He's currently serving a two-year sentence for theft, perverting the course of justice and false accounting. But there are several twists.

He is a former captain in the Adjutant General's Corps, and after being court-martialled, was sent to Colchester Prison (an army establishment) for the first month. But because his sentence was more than twenty-eight days, he was automatically transferred into the prison system to complete his term.

And now for the second twist. A European Court ruling has recently determined that the armed forces disciplinary system is invalid, and all prisoners serving a sentence resulting from a court martial must be released.

Not only might Stephen be set free, but he will also be entitled to £60,000 in compensation, as well as being reinstated as a captain. Our masters in The Hague have decided that you should not be arrested, charged, tried and convicted *by your peers*.

Stephen tells me that there are 600 such prisoners currently in British jails, and he hopes to learn the outcome of this ruling in the next few weeks.

The final twist – just before he was arrested, Stephen received a letter from his commanding officer to tell him that he was being considered for promotion to major.

DAY 236   MONDAY 11 MARCH 2002

9.00 am

A man comes into surgery whom I despise.

Drink drivers are the staple diet of NSC. Of the 220 prisoners currently resident, around 20 per cent have been sentenced with driving offences. Sadly, Tony is not untypical.

Tony is in his early fifties, the father of five children by four women. He currently lives with another woman on a caravan park in Scunthorpe. He pleaded guilty to his latest charge, of driving whilst being disqualified and uninsured (surely the time has come for all motorists to display – as they do in France – an insurance disc, as well as a road fund licence). For this, his latest offence, Tony was sentenced to twelve months, which in real terms means that if he is granted a tagging facility, he will be released after four. Now here is the rub: during the past twenty years, he has been charged with twelve similar offences, and sent to jail on seven separate occasions. He's been banned from driving for four years, and happily tells anyone who will listen that as soon as they release him he'll be back behind the wheel.

It gets worse. He's currently employed by a local garage as a second-hand car dealer, and therefore has access to a variety of vehicles, and admits he likes to get 'tanked-up' at the pub across the road once he's closed a sale. He displays no remorse, and has no fear of returning to prison. He considers NSC to provide a slightly higher standard of living than the one he currently enjoys on a Scunthorpe caravan park.

Perhaps the time has come to change the offence for those who are regularly convicted of drink driving to one of 'potential manslaughter', carrying with it a custodial sentence of four years in a closed prison, and treat such people like any other violent criminals.

12 noon

Alison tells me that the BBC has been in touch about a programme on best-selling authors called *Reading the Decades*. While accepting the fact that I can't appear on camera, they ask if I could do a telephone interview. They already have contributions from King, Grisham, Le Carre, Forsyth, Cooper and Rowling. I ask Governor Leighton for a view, and he says that he'll seek advice from the Home Office.*

4.00 pm

Mr Beaumont sent a circular to all the officers at NSC a few days before he arrived which I obtained recently. It gives you a flavour of the man. (See opposite.) I can't believe his secretary ever checked the piece for grammatical mistakes. Even an eleven-year-old would have spotted the error in the last line. I can't wait to meet him.

---

* Mr Leighton is unable to make the decision himself. He reports back the following day that the BBC had already been in touch with the Home Office, and they have been turned down.

STAFF INFORMATION NOTICE NO. 62/2002
(Not to be displayed in inmate areas)

APPOINTMENT OF NEW GOVERNOR
NORTH SEA CAMP

The following message has been received from Keith Beaumont, who has been appointed as Governor of North Sea Camp with effect from Monday, 18 March 2002:

"**By now you will all know that I am appointed as your new Governor and I have no doubt that there are a thousand and one opinions as to why I am coming to North Sea Camp and why I have left Nottingham. The truth is very simple. I am coming to North Sea Camp to take over as its Governor and to help develop it for the future. The new units give it a chance to re-emphasise and re-focus itself so that it can establish itself as a place of excellence.**

This will require hard work from us all but, as you have already demonstrated so far, keeping North Sea Camp open was not just about staying there but about offering reasons why the place should remain open and demonstrate that to one and all. This you have clearly done in order to get the new development.

I have no doubt equally, that you have heard much rumour, some of it true, some of it malicious, about my person, about my styles and about how I like to operate. Again, I am an honest person who believes in honesty and together we will be able to move forward.

I look forward to the chance of working with you and trust, over the months to come, we will get to know one and other well."

KEITH BEAUMONT
Governor designate

New Units = Quick Build this next 3 months for one or two blocks holding 40 inmates!

R LEIGHTON
Acting Governor

13 March 2002

DAY 238   WEDNESDAY 13 MARCH 2002

7.22 am

Gail rushes in, slightly flushed. She's been door-stepped by a woman from the *News of the World* who has discovered (from an inmate) that she's leaving NSC to take up another post. The journalist is looking for stories and asked, 'Are you leaving because of Archer?'

Gail replied that I am working as a hospital orderly, and that I take the job very seriously, am popular with both the officers and the other prisoners and am learning about drugs and their relevance in prison. Gail innocently asked how much they would pay for a story, to which the journalist replied a couple of thousand pounds – more if it was a big story that would show Archer in a bad light.

10.11 am

I am called in for a voluntary drugs test. You can refuse, but should you do so your privileges – town visits, canteen cash and weekend leave – are likely to be rescinded. I discover that two prisoners have come up positive, one for amphetamines, the other for cannabis.

954

By the end of the morning, that number had risen to five; all will appear in front of the governor for adjudication tomorrow.

12 noon

An officer comes into the hospital and tells me that he once worked on the sex offenders' unit at Whitemoor Prison and he could tell me enough stories to fill another volume.

'Give me an example,' I ask, topping up his coffee.

He pauses for a moment. 'We once had a young prisoner on B block who used to keep a budgerigar in his cell, and the little bird became the most important thing in his life. Another prisoner living on the same wing, sensing the lad's vulnerability, threatened to kill the budgie unless he gave him a blow job. The prisoner reluctantly agreed. Within days, the first prisoner had become a prostitute, and the second his pimp. The pimp would charge two phonecards for the prisoner to give a blow job and three to be buggered. The pimp ended up making a hundred pounds a week, and the budgie survived. That was until an inmate grassed on him in the hope that the pimp would be transferred to another prison and he could take over his lucrative position. Both prisoners were moved to separate establishments the following day.

That morning the budgie was strangled.'

DAY 247   FRIDAY 22 MARCH 2002

Governor Berlyn comes to the hospital this morning and tells me that despite his efforts, I will not be allowed to accompany Mark Le Sage whenever he addresses school on the problem of drugs. The governor of HMP Stocken has told Mr Le Sage that he will not permit such excursions even if an NSC security officer accompanies me.

The nation is currently in the grip of a massive drug epidemic, with children of twelve being offered heroin in our playgrounds. As part of my rehabilitation, I have volunteered to visit schools in the Lincolnshire area and talk to them about the problem. To date I have had assistance from the local police drug squad, the Lincolnshire education authority and the medical team at NSC, lead by Dr Walling. So I can only wonder why the governor of Stocken would want to stop such a worthwhile project.

Perhaps the Home Office knows the answer?

DAY 249   SUNDAY 24 MARCH 2002

4.00 pm

It's been a week for visitors: last Sunday, Henry Togna and David Watson, Monday, Gilly Gray QC, Wednesday, Lords Hayhoe and Denham – Bertie, my old Chief Whip.

So now I'm up to date on the Lords reform bill, foxhunting and the state of Margaret Thatcher's health. Not to mention the euro, and when the planned referendum might or might not be.

I put an idea to Bertie on the Lords reform bill, when to my horror he withdrew from an inside pocket, a small memo recorder. I glance over to the desk to see the duty officers chatting to each other. I was relieved when Bertie put the recorder back in his pocket. We don't need another member of the House of Lords as a resident of North Sea Camp.

DAY 250   MONDAY 25 MARCH 2002

10.00 am

The papers are full of stories about the model Naomi Campbell, who has been awarded £3,500 against the *Daily Mirror* and its then editor, Piers Morgan, for breaching her privacy. However, the judge also states that she had deliberately lied when in the witness box.

Norman Tebbit has asked through the press if she will be tried for perjury, or do these laws only apply to Conservative politicians?

4.00 pm

Mr Belford comes to the hospital clutching the results of my MDT. (See opposite.)

6.00 pm

Peter (arson, set fire to a police station) has so far served thirty-one years; you may recall that I earlier reported his first town visit. This morning, two officers arrived outside his room and took him down to the segregation cells, which can only mean one thing: he's going to be shipped out to a closed prison today.

958

HM PRISON SERVICE

H M PRISON NORTH SEA CAMP

MANDATORY DRUG TEST

NAME: ARCHER   **NUMBER:** FF8282   **LOCATION:** HOSP.

I am pleased to inform you that the urine sample you gave under the Mandatory Drug Test Programme has tested **negative** and no further action will be taken.

You will, however, still be liable to be tested again, if need be, at a later date.

DRUG TEST CO-ORDINATOR   DATE: 20 / 2 / 02.

I suspect that one trip to Boston will be the last time he ever sees the outside world.

When I first came to NSC some months ago, Peter swept the main road that runs from the gate through to the office block; some 300 yards away. With a six-foot-four-inch frame, Peter had a presence you could not easily avoid, but zero social skills, and thirty-one years in prison (twenty-eight of them behind bars) ensured that it was never going to be easy for him to settle.

Every morning he would break away from his sweeping and open car doors for members of the female staff. He would then engage them in long conversations. Harmless enough, you may say, but several of the younger girls felt harassed and didn't complain for fear it might harm Peter's parole prospects. Unfortunately, these episodes continued, despite several warnings from officers. Governor Berlyn, who is in charge of the lifers, was left with little choice but to take action to allay the staff's fears.

He took Peter off his job as a road sweeper and asked him to be a reception orderly. Peter made the tea and helped officers with minor tasks. It was beyond him. He lasted a fortnight. They next moved Peter to the officers' mess, to assist with cleaning and occasional serving. He lasted ten days before being transferred to the farm as a shepherd, where he survived less than a week before being sent to the kitchen. This was no more successful, and he has ended up in segregation prior to being moved back to the B-cat.

Peter is in his sixties, and has no hope of returning to a D-cat in under five years, if ever. This case highlights a bigger issue. Don't we have some duty to a human being other than to lock him up for the rest of his life? Peter failed to come to terms with the system, so the system has failed him.

When I am eventually released, I am going to be asked so many questions to which I do not know the answer.

DAY 257   MONDAY 1 APRIL 2002

10.30 am

I listen to an announcement over the tannoy.

'Anyone wanting to assist with the special needs group trip to Skegness, please report to the bus at the front gate.' The word 'please' should have given it away. Prison officers rarely, if ever, say please. However, two inmates still report to the gate in the hope of boarding the non-existent bus to Skegness.

The April Fool prank played on me took a different form. Mr Hewitt, the head of the works department, purchased a jigsaw puzzle of the House of Lords at a car-boot sale, and told me he expected me to finish it by the end of the week as part of my anger management programme.

It took me two hours just to finish the border. I intend to draft in all the members of Club Hospital to assist me with this 1,000-piece monster.

DAY 262   SATURDAY 6 APRIL 2002

Dr Susan Edwards, Reader of Law at Buckingham University, has completed her independent study showing the harshness of my four-year sentence.*

> Jeffrey Archer, former deputy chairman of the Conservative party and best-selling author, was convicted of perjury and perverting the course of justice arising from a libel action over whether he spent a particular night with a Monica Coghlan, for which, following a 'not guilty' plea, he received a prison sentence of four years. As Jeffrey Archer's prison sentence is the longest passed in any case of civil perjury and the sentence length is comparable to prison sentences passed in the gravest cases of criminal perjury including murder and police corruption it requires some rather more detailed consideration.

Gilbert Gray QC has already warned Mary that he'll be able to predict the outcome of my appeal as soon as he knows the make-up of the three-judge panel. What a dreadful condemnation of British justice – that my future will not be decided on whether I'm innocent or guilty, but on who judges me.

---

* The full report was published in the *Criminal Law Review* of August 2003.

DAY 265 TUESDAY 9 APRIL 2002

NSC, like most prisons in Britain, is badly understaffed. We have over 200 inmates, and only 27 full-time officers, meaning that there are never more than 12 officers on duty at any one time. The following advertisement appears in several local papers *every week*, and elicits few replies. (See overleaf.)

I'm told it's no different for any of the other 137 prisons in Britain. It's hardly an appealing career, other than for the truly dedicated believers in justice – or someone not quite tall enough to get into the police force.

INVESTOR IN PEOPLE

HM PRISON SERVICE

POSITIVE ABOUT DISABLED PEOPLE

HMP NORTH SEA CAMP
OPERATIONAL SUPPORT GRADE VACANCIES

HM Prison North Sea Camp has vacancies for operational support grades (OSG). The posts will involve the supervision of prisoners: applicants should be able to communicate clearly and effectively and want to be an effective part of the prisoner rehabilitation process. Duties may include security, working in the gate lodge, driving escorts, switchboard, canteen and stores.

Hours:	39 hours per week
Annual leave:	22 days a year rising to 25 after one year
Salary:	starts at £12,651 rising annually to the maximum of the grade by annual increments A full clean driving licence is essential A PSV licence would be an advantage but is not essential

Application forms may be obtained from the Boston Job Centre, West Street, Boston, Lincs. Tel: (01205) 883000.

For further information please contact Mrs Carole Pattinson in the personnel office at North Sea Camp. Tel (01205) 760481 ext 2 28.

Application forms should be returned to the Boston Job Centre by Friday, 22 March, 2002.

Applicants will be required to declare whether they are a member of a group or organisation which the Prison Service considers to be racist.

The Prison Service is an equal opportunities employer. We welcome applications from candidates regardless of ethnic origin, religious belief, gender, sexual orientation, disability or any other relevant factor. Members of the ethnic minorities are currently under-represented at North Sea Camp and applications from them would be welcome. All applications will be considered and appointments made on merit.

DAY 268   FRIDAY 12 APRIL 2002

9.07 am

Dr Walling arrives a few minutes late. When Stephen Sherbourne (Margaret Thatcher's former political secretary) visited me, I told him that if you reported sick between 7.30 and 8 am any morning, Monday to Friday, you were guaranteed to see a doctor at nine o'clock the same day.

Stephen asked if I could think of a crime for which he would be sentenced to two weeks, so he could get all his medical problems sorted out.

11.11 am

MURDERER WEDS PRISON PSYCHIATRIST is the sort of headline one might expect to read in the *Sun*.

Today Andy, a lifer who has served twelve years, has been granted a week's leave. He has been a model prisoner and expects to be released some time next year. While he was in his previous prison, Ashwell, part of his rehabilitation course included regular meetings with the prison psychiatrist, and as the months passed, they struck up a relationship. I think it right to point out at this stage that Andy is thirty-five, six foot one, with the dark swarthy looks of an Italian film star. When he was transferred to NSC, the psychiatrist visited him regularly. A report of her visit was passed back to her own prison, and she subsequently had to resign from the service. She found a new job in Loughborough and her relationship with Andy continued to blossom. Today they were married at a ceremony in Boston attended by five officers and nine prisoners.

NSC currently has twenty-three resident murderers, and I think I've met every one of them. Three of them, including Andy, are among the gentlest people I have ever come across.

3.30 pm

One of the inmates is refusing to take an MDT. It's well known that he's a heroin addict, and has found yet another way to beat the system. If he refuses to take the test, the governor can only add twenty-eight days to his sentence, whereas if he agrees to take it and then proves positive for heroin, he could be sentenced to fifty-six extra days and even be shipped out to a B-cat. However, Mr Vessey points out that should he refuse a second time, they can ship him out the same day.

The new chapel orderly committed an unusual crime. 'On the out' he was an accounts executive for a well-known furniture company. He became head of the complaints department, whose responsibility it was to ensure that when customers returned goods they received a refund and the article was returned to the store's seconds department.

One Christmas, the chapel orderly purchased a sofa for his mother, but she didn't like it. He returned the sofa and applied for a refund, giving his own name and address. The money was refunded quite legally. It was then that the man realized that only he and the computer were aware of the transaction. Using a false name but his own address, he authorized and presented a bogus claim and the computer happily credited his account. By changing the name every time, he could make a claim once a week, and during the following year, he supplemented his income by over £200,000. The chapel orderly and his girlfriend (she unwittingly) lived in comfort, as he became more and more confident, upping the sums on a weekly basis, and even giving himself a bonus over the Christmas rush.

So how was he caught? A secretary mistakenly opened a random file on her computer, and was surprised by what she found – how could 127 people living at the same address all require a refund for 127 different pieces of furniture they'd ordered over the past year?

The accounts executive pleaded guilty and was sentenced to three years. He is now the chapel orderly at NSC.

As part of his rehabilitation into society, one of the lifers (Malcolm, armed robbery) has just started an outside job as a cleaner at Haven High School.

The first day turned out to be a bit of a culture shock when he discovered how mature and self-confident modern young women have become. He repeated a conversation he'd had this morning with a fourteen-year-old who approached him in the corridor.

'Are you a convict?'

'Yes, I am.'

'What are you in for?'

'Armed robbery.'

'How many years have you served?'

'Fourteen.'

'Fourteen years without sex?' the girl said in mock disbelief.

'Yes,' he repeated, to which the girl lifted up her skirt, and said, 'Well you must be up for it.'

Malcolm ran out of the building. Had she reported him for even talking about sex, he probably would have been transferred back to a B-cat the same day.

DAY 287   WEDNESDAY 1 MAY 2002

10.30 am

Strange goings-on in the camp today. Tony, a well-known drug dealer, has collapsed after taking an overdose only hours before he's due to be released. What kind of problems can he have on the outside, that he considers suicide a better way out than the front gate?

Tony has been a regular at the hospital over the past few weeks, so there's no way of knowing if he's been storing up pills, and how many he swallowed today. Rather than wait for an ambulance, Tony's been rushed into the Pilgrim Hospital in the prison mini-bus, accompanied by two officers. I'll know more tonight.

6.00 pm

Tony has just returned to the camp to spend his final night in jail. They pumped out his stomach, so he'll still leave us at 8 am tomorrow. But how long will he survive on the outside?

7.08 pm

I have just returned from an hour's walk around the playing field with the intention of watching Hendry vs. Doherty in the quarter-final of the World Championship snooker,* when there's a knock on my door.

It's Tony clutching a letter that he wants me to hand to sister, but he asks me to read it first. It's a two-sided handwritten missive, apologizing for his behaviour over the past few weeks, and thanking sister for her kindness and understanding. I promise to give it to her tomorrow morning. Tony is just about to leave when I ask him if he'd be willing to answer a few questions about drugs. I quite expect him to tell me what I can do with myself, using the usual prison vernacular, but to my surprise he takes a seat in the waiting room and says, 'Ask me anything you want, Jeff. I don't give a fuck, I'm out of here first thing in the morning.'

During the next hour, I ask him question after question, all of which he answers with a brutal frankness.

'Did you try to commit suicide?'

'No, I just OD'd.'

'How often do you take heroin?'

'While I've been here, usually four times a day. When I wake in the morning, just after dinner, then again after tea and just before I go to bed.'

'Do you inject it, sniff it or smoke it?'

'Smoke it,' Tony replies. 'Only fuckin' morons inject it. I've seen too many crack-heads get HIV or hepatitis B by injecting themselves with someone else's needle. While I've been in jail,

---

* I was president of the World Snooker Association until I was arrested, when the board asked me to resign. Two other bodies expelled me, the Royal Society of Arts and the MCC.

I've seen needles used by a hundred different inmates. Don't forget, Jeff, 235,000 people in Britain are regular heroin users, and if you consider their families, over a million people must be involved. Heroin costs the NHS three billion a year.'

'How do you get the heroin into prison?'

'There are several ways, but the most common is to pick it up from a dealer when you're out on a weekend leave, and then pack a couple of ounces in a condom and stuff it up your rectum. No officer enjoys checking up there.'

'A couple of ounces?'

'That was all I could afford this time. My record "on the out" was coming back from Holland with seven ounces of marijuana.'

'How much would that be worth?'

'If it's pure, the best, you could be talking around a hundred grand.'

'So when you bring the drugs back into the prison, are they just for you?'

'No, no, no, I have to pay my supplier "on the out". I'm only a dealer. Dealers are either kings or pawns. I'm a pawn. A king rarely takes drugs, just brings them in from abroad and distributes them among his pawns, most of whom only deal so they can satisfy their own craving.'

'So how many of the two hundred inmates at NSC are on heroin?'

He pauses to consider the question. 'Thirty-nine that I'm aware of,' he says.

'But that's around twenty-five per cent.'

'Yeah,' he replies, matter-of-factly.

'How do you pay back the king dealer while you're on the inside?'

'Easy,' says Tony. 'I only sell to those inmates who have

someone on the outside who will hand over cash direct to my dealer. I never supply until the money has been received.'

'But that could take days, and if you're in the grip of a craving . . .'

'It only takes one phone call, and an hour later I check with the dealer and if he's received the cash, then I supply.'

'If you were on the outside and not a dealer, how much would you need to cover your own addiction?'

'Three hundred quid a day.'

'But that's a hundred thousand pounds a year – cash.'

'Yeah, but as a dealer I can earn twice that, and still get my fix four times a day.'

Tony goes on to talk about his fears after he's released tomorrow morning. His parents will come to pick him up at eight o'clock. They believe he's kicked the habit following a spell in special prison in Devon, where they weaned him off heroin for fifteen months. But, once he was considered cured, they transferred him to a D-cat, in this case NSC, where it was 'in his face', and within weeks he was addicted again.

'I won't live to see fifty,' Tony says. 'I'll have been in jail for over half my life.' He pauses. 'I wish I'd never taken that first freebie when I was fifteen. You'll pass ten of us in the street every day, Jeff, and you won't have been aware. Perhaps you will from now on.'

Tony left the hospital at 7.28 pm.

I handed his letter to sister the following morning.

DAY 294   WEDNESDAY 8 MAY 2002

9.00 am

Today's list of new inductees to see the doctor includes Patel, Patel, Patel and Patel. It's hard to believe that there isn't a story there somewhere. When the prisoners appear, it soon becomes clear we are dealing with a father and three sons. I later discover that the mother is also in jail at Holloway; all five were charged with the same offence.

The Patels are Sikhs, and have very strong family values, so that when they discovered that their daughter/sister was earning her living as a prostitute, they formed a plan to kidnap her (the law's views)/ rescue her (the Patel family's value). The first part of this plan was not too difficult to carry out for a bright, reasonably determined team of Sikhs – they simply bundled the girl into a car and whisked her off to the family home. However the pimp/ lover/friend – I can't be sure which – set out to *rescue* her, so that she could be put back to work. Unfortunately for him, he had not taken into account the resolution of the Patel family, so he ended up with a broken arm and nose after being beaten up.

The pimp reported the incident to the police, which resulted in the father and three brothers being sentenced to two years for kidnapping and ABH, and the mother to eighteen months as an accomplice. All five went to jail, while the daughter was set free to continue to ply her trade. As a novelist, I can come up with a dozen scenarios as to what might happen when the Patel family are all released in 2003.

10.30 am

Among the prisoners who will be released today is Daryl, who is serving twelve months for burglary. He has been a model prisoner, no sign of any drugs, never on report, and whenever he visits the hospital, he's always courteous and considerate, so I was not surprised he had been granted his tag and would be leaving us after only four months. Once the doctor has checked him out and signed him off, Daryl thanks sister and shakes hands with me.

'Good luck,' I offer, and add, 'I hope we never meet again,' – the traditional goodbye to those you consider unlikely to reoffend. Imagine my surprise when I learned this evening that Daryl was back in jail. It happened thus.

He was driven to Boston station on the prison bus, where he was handed a rail voucher for Manchester and £40 in cash. Every prisoner who is not picked up at the front gate is given a travel voucher and £40 if they have a known address to go to. If they are of no fixed abode (NFA) they are handed £90, and the address of a hostel in the area they are heading for. After fourteen days, if they have been unable to find a job they can go on the social service register and collect unemployment benefit. Back to Daryl.

He boarded the train at Boston, but had to change at Birmingham to catch another train to Manchester. During the stopover at Birmingham, he picked up some fish and chips before making his way over to platform six. But as the train was not due to arrive for a few minutes he popped into W. H. Smith and picked up a magazine to read on the journey. The magazine rack is situated next to the bookshelf, and his eye lighted on the A section. He left a few moments later with a magazine and three paperbacks by the same author. He was about to board the train when a station policeman arrested him for shoplifting.

When the police learned that Daryl had been released from jail that morning on a tag, he was immediately taken to Gartree Prison in Leicestershire, where he will spend the next two months completing his sentence, and whatever period of time is added because of the shoplifting.

Daryl, however, does not hold the record for being back in custody the quickest following his release. Mr Belford assures me that that distinction belongs to Fingers Danny of Pentonville.

Danny was released from Pentonville at 8 am on a cold November morning. Clutching his £90, he headed off on foot to Islington, not in search of the nearest hostel, but the nearest Sainsbury's. He arrived just as they were opening the front doors. He proceeded to fill a trolley with products, and then walked slowly out of the shop without making any attempt to pay. When the store detective approached him on the pavement, Danny made a dash for it, but not too quickly.

Danny was arrested, and appeared in front of the magistrate at ten o'clock that morning. He pleaded guilty. Before sentence was passed, Danny threw in a few choice observations concerning the magistrate's bald head, his lack of charisma and his doubtful parentage, ensuring that he was back in his cell at Pentonville by midday.

However, the difference between Danny and Daryl is that the Irishman had planned the whole operation weeks before he was released. After all, it was November, and where else could Danny be guaranteed a bed in a warm cell, three meals a day and the companionship of his friends during the festive season?

He put his £90 release money in his canteen account.

DAY 311   SATURDAY 25 MAY 2002

Three inmates absconded yesterday; it's an hour to Boston on foot, about an hour and a half to Skegness. The first, Slater (GBH) had a six-year sentence and had only been at NSC for four days. Even more inexplicable is the fact that he was due for parole in September, and having been transferred to a D-cat, could expect to have been released. Slater was rearrested four hours after departing and taken off to HMP Lincoln, a B-cat, where he will spend the rest of his sentence – two more years plus twenty-eight days for absconding. Madness.

I am informed by an officer that the second inmate, Benson (ABH), was anticipating a positive MDT back from the Home Office, and as it was his second offence in three months, the governor would have been left with little choice but to ship him out to a B-cat. So he shipped himself out. He was picked up in Boston early this morning, and is now on his way to Nottingham (A-cat) with twenty-eight days added to his sentence.

The third inmate, Blagdon (pub stabbing), is a more interesting case. He was due out in July, having already served nine years. He walked into a police station this morning, and gave himself up after being on the run for only seven hours. He is also now safely locked up in an A-cat. However, in Blagdon's case, he never intended to make good his escape. His cell-mate tells me that he didn't think he could handle the outside world after nine years in jail – eight of them in closed conditions (banged up for twenty-two hours a day) – so now he'll return to those conditions for at least a further five years, at the end of which he will have to come up with another way of making sure he isn't set free, because he'll never return to a D-cat.

10.00 am

Every day this week, an inmate called Jenkins has been popping into hospital to ask me how many new inductees we were expecting that day, and added 'Are any of them from HMP Lincoln?' I assumed Jenkins was hoping that one of his mates was being transferred to NSC. On the contrary, he is fearful of the imminent arrival of an old enemy.

Yesterday morning the hospital manifest showed that six prisoners were due in from Lincoln, and when Jenkins studied the list of names, he visibly paled before quickly leaving the hospital. That was the last I saw of him, because he missed the 11.45 am roll-call. Three hours later he gave himself up at a local police station. He was arrested and shipped off to Lincoln.

I sat next to Jenkins's room-mate at lunch, who was only too happy to tell me that Jenkins had been sleeping with the wife of another prisoner called Owen whenever he was out on a fortnightly town leave. He went on to tell me that Owen (manslaughter) had recently found out that his wife was being unfaithful, and she had even told him the name of her lover. Owen, who had just been given D-cat status after eight years in jail, immediately applied to be sent to NSC and is due to arrive this afternoon. Now I understand why Jenkins absconded.

2.00 pm

A group of five prisoners arrive from Lincoln, but Owen is not among them. When they walk through the door, I report to sister that we seem to have lost one.

'Oh yes, Owen,' she says, looking down at her list. 'He committed some minor offence this morning and had his D-cat status taken away. So he'll be remaining at Lincoln for the foreseeable future.'

DAY 313   MONDAY 27 MAY 2002

9.07 am

A letter from the High Court informs me that my appeal date is set for Monday 22 July – in eight weeks' time.

10.07 am

A prisoner called Morris arrived this morning. He is thirty-six years old and serving a four-year sentence for credit-card fraud. Morris has stolen over £500,000 since leaving school, and shows no remorse. He tells me with considerable pride that he still has just under £100,000 in cash safely stashed away, and that he and his co-defendant lead 'the good life'. They share a large flat in London, drive a Mercedes, enjoy a wardrobe full of designer clothes and only stay at the best hotels. They fly first class, and work even while on holiday. He is a career criminal for whom prison is a temporary inconvenience, and as the authorities always transfer him to a D-cat within three weeks of being sent down, not *that* much of an inconvenience.

Morris has been found guilty of fraud four times in the last ten years, and received sentences of six months, eight months, twelve months and four years. However, he will have served less than three years in all by the time he's released next January.

In 2003, he anticipates that he and his partner will have cleared over a million pounds in cash, and if they are caught, he will be happy to return to NSC.

In Dickens's time Morris would have been known as 'a dip'. While the artful dodger stole handkerchiefs and fob watches, Morris purloins credit cards. His usual method is to book into a four-star hotel which is holding a large weekend conference. He then works the bars at night when many of the customers have had a little too much to drink. After a good weekend, he can leave the hotel in possession of a dozen or more credit cards. By Sunday evening, he's sitting in first class on a plane to Vienna (one card gone) where he books into a five-star hotel (second card). He then hires a car, not with a credit card, but with cash, because he needs to travel across Europe without being apprehended. He will then drive from Vienna to Rome, spending all the way, before returning to England in a car loaded with goods. He and his partner then take a short rest, before repeating the whole exercise.

Morris has several pseudonyms, and tells me that he can pick up a false passport for as little as a thousand pounds. He intends to spend another ten years rising to the top of his profession before he retires to warmer climes.

'It's a beautiful way of life,' he says. 'I can tell you more, Jeffrey.'

But I don't want to hear any more.

11.45 am

A prisoner comes in asking to see the doctor urgently. I explain that he left about an hour ago, and sister is over at the administration block, but he could see the doctor tomorrow. He looks anxious, so I ask if I can help.

'I've just come back from home leave,' he explains, 'and while I was out, I had unprotected sex, and I'd like to check that I haven't caught anything.'

'Did you know the girl?' I ask.

'I didn't know any of them,' he replies.

'Any of them?'

'Yes, there were seven.'

When I later tell sister, she doesn't bat an eyelid, just makes an appointment for him to see the doctor.

12 noon

Among the new receptions today is a prisoner called Mitchell (drink driving, three months). While I'm checking his blood pressure, he tells me he hasn't been back to NSC since 1968, when it was a detention centre.

'It's changed a bit since then,' he adds. 'Mind you, the hospital was still here. But before you saw the doctor, they hosed you down and shaved your head with a blunt razor, to make sure you didn't have fleas.'

'How about the food?' I ask.

'Bread and water for the first fortnight, and if you spoke during meals an officer called Raybold banged your head against the wall.'

I had to smile because I know one or two officers who'd still like to.

2.30 pm

The director-general, Martin Narey, has issued a directive requiring all prison officers to address inmates with the prefix Mr.

When an officer bellows across the car park, 'Get your

fuckin' arse over here, Archer,' I courteously point out to her that she must have missed the director-general's missive.

'I don't give a fuck about the director-general,' she replies, 'I'll fuckin' well call you what I like.'

One prisoner found an unusual way around this problem a few years ago. He changed his name by deed poll to Mister Rogers, but then he did have a twenty-year sentence.

3.00 pm

If you work outside the prison, you can earn up to £300 a week, which allows you to send money back to your wife, partner and family, which you certainly can't do on the amount you are paid working inside. An added bonus is that some companies offer full-time work on release to any prisoner who has proved himself while in their employ.

Once you're qualified to work outside, you must first complete a month of CSV (Community Service Volunteer) work, partly as retribution, and also to prove you are both fit and safe to work in the community. Once this has been completed, you can then spend the rest of your sentence working outside, so that when you're released, in the best scenario, it's a seamless progression. In the worst . . .

Mike was only a few weeks away from that seamless progression when two prison officers turned up at his place of work, and accompanied him back to NSC. It seems that a young lady who worked at the same factory could do nothing to deter his unrequited advances. Her mother also worked there, and reported him to the management. The management, quite rightly, were not willing to condemn the prisoner simply on the mother's word, and carried out their own investigation. A few days later they sent a full report to the prison governor.

DAY 313

Mike has subsequently been shipped out of NSC back to Lincoln Prison, a tough B-cat. He was only a few weeks away from parole, and the factory had already offered him a full-time job on release. He has now lost his D-cat status, lost his job, lost his income and possibly lost any chance of parole.

I am reminded of Robin Williams's classic remark: 'God gave man a penis and a brain, but not enough blood to work both at the same time.'

DAY 314   TUESDAY 28 MAY 2002

Few prisoners turn down the opportunity to have weekly visits, or the chance to be tagged and released two months early. Gary is the rare exception.

Gary was sentenced to two years for theft of a motor vehicle (BMW), and because of good behaviour will only serve twelve months. But why does no one visit him, and why won't he take up his two-month tagging option and serve only ten months?

None of Gary's family or friends knows that he is in prison. His mother believes that he is working with his friend Dave on a one-year contract on an oil rig in Mexican waters. When he arrived in Mexico, Dave sent Gary a large selection of Mexican scenic postcards. Gary pens a weekly card to his mother, sends it back to his friend Dave in Mexico, who then stamps it and forwards the missive to England.

Gary will be released next week, and seems to have got away with his little subterfuge, because Dave will fly back from Mexico on the same day, when they will meet up at Heathrow and return to Wolverhampton together. During the journey, Dave will brief Gary on what it's like to work and live on a Mexican oil rig.

Now that's what I call a friend.

DAY 316   THURSDAY 29 MAY 2002

North Sea Camp has five doctors who work a rota, and one of them, Dr Harris, is also responsible for the misuse of substances unit in Boston. Dr Harris arrives at the hospital today, accompanied by a male nurse. Nigel, who is in his early thirties and is dressed in a black T-shirt, blue jeans, with a ring in his ear, has come to visit me because he is currently working with young people aged twelve to nineteen who have a heroin problem. I can see why they would feel at ease with him.

Nigel explains that he can only work with youngsters who want to work with him. He listens to their questions, offers answers, but never judges. They've had enough of their parents telling them to grow up, behave themselves and find a job. He outlines the bare statistics – they are terrifying.

There are currently 220,000 heroin addicts in Britain, of which only 3,000 (11 per cent) are involved in some form of detox programme. One of the problems, Nigel explains, is that if you apply to your local GP for a place on one of these programmes, the wait can be anything up to six weeks, by which time 'the client' has often given up trying to come off the drug. The irony is that if you end up in prison, you will be put on a detox programme the following day. Nigel knows of several addicts who commit a crime hoping to be sent to jail so that they can wean themselves off drugs. Nigel works directly with a small group of seven addicts, although he reminds me, 'You can't save anyone; you can only help those who want to help themselves.'

He then guides me through the problems the young are facing today. They start experimenting with cannabis or sniffing solvents, then progress to ecstasy and cocaine, followed by crack cocaine, ending up on heroin. He knows several seventeen year olds who have experienced the full gamut. He adds ruefully that if the letter of the law were adhered to, seven million Britons would be in jail for smoking cannabis, as possession currently has a two-year tariff. A gramme of an A-class drug costs about £40. This explains the massive rise in street crime over the past decade, especially among the young.

The danger is not just the drugs, but also the needles. Often, drug users live in communes and share the same needles. This is the group that ends up with HIV and hepatitis B and C.

Today, for example, Nigel has appointments with two girls addicted to heroin, one aged nineteen and the other seventeen, who both want to begin a detox programme. His biggest problem is their boyfriends, who are not only responsible for them being on drugs in the first place, but are also their suppliers, so the last thing they want is for their girlfriends to be cured of the craving. Nigel tells me that there is only a 50–50 chance they will even turn up for the appointment. And if they do, addicts on average make seven attempts to come off heroin before they succeed.

Nigel's responsibility is to refer his cases to a specialist GP so that they can be registered for a detox programme. He fears that too many addicts go directly to their own GP, who often pre- scribes the wrong remedy to cure them.

Nigel displays no cynicism as he takes me through a typical day in his life, and reminds me that he's not officially funded, something he hopes the NHS will sort out in the near future. He suddenly brings the problem down to a local level, highlighting the national malaise. Nigel has seven heroin addicts on his books, in a county that has 10,000 on the drug. It's not a chip, not a dent, not even a scratch, on the overall surface.

Nigel leaves me to keep his appointment with a seventeen-year-old boy who has, for the past four years, been visiting caravan sites so that he can feed his addiction; he cuts the rubber hose and sniffs calor gas. He's not even breaking the law, other than by damaging property.

2.00 pm

Gail is searching for a bed-board for a new inmate with a back problem. There are twelve boards out there somewhere. The problem is that once you've allocated them, you never get them back, because when an inmate is released, the last thing on his mind is returning a bed-board.

Gail calls the south block unit, only to discover that a replacement officer from Lincoln is holding the fort. She throws her hands in the air in despair, but nevertheless tells him about her problem. By cross-referencing with the prisoners' files, she can check those who are in genuine need, and those who have just come into possession of a bed-board by default. To her surprise, the officer returns an hour later accompanied by seven of the offending bed-boards.

I offer him a cup of coffee and quickly discover that his whole life is equally well organized. He tells me about work at Lincoln, and one sentence stops me in my tracks.

'I've developed a system that ensures I only have to work five months a year.'

The officer has been in the Prison Service for just over seven years, and has, along with five other colleagues, developed an

988

on-off work schedule so he only needs to be on duty for five months a year for his £23,000 salary. He assures me that the system is carried out in most jails with slight variations. He would be happy to work extra hours if he could get paid overtime, but currently few prisons can afford the extra expense except for accompanied visits (hospitals, court or transfer). This is the bit where you have to concentrate. Officers work the following shifts:

Shift A: the early shift, 7.30–12.30 or Shift B: a main shift (day), 7.30–5.30.

Shift C: the late shift, 1.30–8.30 or Shift D: the evening shift, 5.00–9.00.

Shift E: a main shift (night), 9.00–7.00.

The officer and his colleagues swap shifts around and, as there is no overtime, they take time off in lieu. Every officer should work thirty-nine hours per week, but if they swap shifts with colleagues, they can end up doing A+C or B+D or D+E, and that way notch up nearly seventy hours per week, while another colleague takes the week off. Add to this the twenty-eight days holiday entitlement per year, and they need work only five months while taking off seven. Three of his colleagues also have part-time jobs, 'on the out' and the officer assures me that a large percentage of junior officers supplement their income this way.

I can only assume this does not come as a surprise to Martin Narey, currently the director-general of the Prison Service. I'm bound to say if my secretary, housekeeper, agent, accountant, publisher or doctor took seven months per year to do another job, I would either reorganize the system or replace them.

DAY 320   MONDAY 3 JUNE 2002

As from today, the Home Office have recategorized NSC as a resettlement prison. In future all prisoners having served one quarter of their sentence and passed their FLED will be eligible to move into one of the recently built blocks and start working outside the prison. The thinking behind this is that by allowing prisoners to earn a living, they will be less likely to reoffend when released. Two new blocks (Portakabins) of forty rooms have been constructed on the playing fields near the gate for this purpose. From today, sixty-two prisoners will be eligible to leave NSC from 7.30 am, and need not return until 7 pm.

But, and there are always buts in prison, Mr Berlyn has posted a notice in both new blocks, making it clear that this is to be considered a privilege, and anyone who fails to keep to the guidelines will be suspended and put to work on the farm at £5.60 a week.*

---

* Two prisoners absconded during their first week at work. Both were caught and transferred to a B-cat in Nottingham. Two were found in a pub and are back working on the farm; while three were sacked for inappropriate behaviour – unwanted advances to the female staff. And that was in the first week.

DAY 325   FRIDAY 7 JUNE 2002

Mr Beaumont (the governing governor) has just marched into the hospital, accompanied by Mr Berlyn. Dr Walling, David and I are watching England play Argentina in the World Cup, and Beckham has just scored from a penalty to put us in the lead. I assume they had heard the cheering and popped in to find out the score. However, they don't even glance at the screen. One look in my direction, and they both stride out again.

I learn later that the governor had received a call from Reuters asking him to confirm that I had committed suicide.

Not while we're in the lead against Argentina.

11.00 am

An officer drops in and tells me over coffee that there is disquiet among the officers and staff that sex offenders will in future make up a considerable percentage of our inmates. Officers fear the atmosphere may change from the relaxed state we currently enjoy to one of constant tension, as regular offenders despise paedophiles. It is even possible that one or two of the more violent inhabitants might take it upon themselves to administer their own form of justice.*

---

* Most sex offenders, when housed in an open prison, are given a cover story should anyone ask what they are in for.

DAY 325

The officer goes on to tell me that a murderer at Gartree shared a cell with a prisoner who was allegedly in for burglary. But the lifer discovered from another prisoner, who had been in a previous jail with his cell-mate, that he was in fact a sex offender who had raped his nine-year-old daughter.

At roll-call the following morning, the lifer reported to the main office. His statement was simple and explicit. He had stabbed his cell-mate to death and left him on his bed. The lifer was immediately placed in solitary confinement, charged and later given another life sentence. The judge added that on this occasion, life meant the rest of his life.

6.00 pm

I umpire this evening's cricket match between NSC and a local school. I give the opening batsman from the visiting side out, caught and bowled. When I see the look of surprise on the batsman's face, I immediately feel anxious, because the bowler had taken the catch as he ran in front of me. Have I made a mistake? The batsman is already heading towards the pavilion (a small wooden hut) when Mo (murder, terrorist), who is fielding at silly mid-on, looks at me and says, 'It was a bump-ball, Jeff.' I call the opening batsman back and apologize for my mistake as the rest of the team applaud Mo's sportsmanship.

The visiting team go on to win, thanks to a fine innings from the opening batsman. Funny old world.

It's been a tense day as I wait to discover how much longer I'll have to remain here. My appeal against conviction took Mr Justice Rose two minutes to dismiss, which was no more than my counsel, Nick Purnell QC, had predicted. The appeal against sentence was granted by Mr Justice Brown, so we had all felt more confident that Mr Justice Rose would knock off at least a year, possibly two, allowing me to return home this evening.

At 5.07 pm, Mr Hocking walks slowly into the hospital, looking grim. As senior security officer, he had already set in motion a plan to have me off the premises before the press could arrive. He told me that Alison had rung to say that my sentence had not been cut, even by a day. Although Mr Purnell addressed the judges for over two hours, Mr Justice Rose returned to the court one minute and forty-eight seconds after Nick sat down, and read out a prepared statement that he must have written some days before. Mr Justice Rose could at least have had the courtesy to tell Mr Purnell not to bother, as he'd already made up his mind and wasn't interested in any new evidence.

So much for British justice.

The press are curious to know why Mary didn't appear in court to hear my appeal. She was being interviewed for the chairmanship of Addenbrooke's Hospital at 1 pm, and the date had been fixed for some weeks.

I had told her that under no circumstances was she to request a change of dates, as this was clearly the most important interview of her life. Addenbrooke's, attached umbilically to Cambridge University, is one of the country's leading teaching hospitals. It has a budget of some £250 million per year, and nearly 1,000 doctors and 2,500 nurses. Mary has been vice-chairman for the past two years, and on the board for eight, and although she is up against a formidable shortlist I still feel she's in with a good chance.

We spent over an hour on the phone (until I ran out of phonecards) considering the likely questions that might come up. I want Mary to get this chairmanship job more than I want to be released from jail; otherwise I would spend the rest of my life feeling that I was the reason she failed.

I call Mary to confirm that she will be coming to pick me up on Saturday and take me out on my first town visit, a precursor to home leave. I don't get a chance to ask any questions because everything is overshadowed by the news that she has been appointed chairman of Addenbrooke's.

I'm so delighted that I can't remember why I called.

DAY 373　　　　FRIDAY 26 JULY 2002

There has never been a suicide at NSC, despite the fact that there were seventy-three suicides in British jails last year.

Today an inmate made two attempts to take his life. First he tried to cut his wrist, and after being rushed to the Pilgrim Hospital and patched up, he attempted to hang himself. He failed.

He's a young man who recently lost his mother, and last week his girlfriend sent him a 'Dear John' letter. I later learned that during his trial he took 106 paracetamol tablets and although they pumped his body out, he has irreversibly damaged his liver. His crime, by the way, was shoplifting, for which he received six months, and will serve three at most.

However, one good thing came out of it. The Listeners, who have been requesting a room for counselling for some time, were allocated one this morning.

DAY 374   SATURDAY 27 JULY 2002

7.00 am

They have turned off the central heating today, which is all you need to know about the way North Sea Camp is run.

10.00 am

My first day out of jail for a year.

Mary picks me up and, as the press are waiting at the gatehouse, we avoid Boston. We end up in a field of cows, eating a picnic. Heaven, even if the press do get the inevitable picture.*

Over a lunch of turkey and ham salad, followed by Cheddar cheese helped down with a Diet Coke, Mary and I discuss her new responsibilities as chairman of Addenbrooke's Hospital.

After a drive around the countryside, Mary takes me back to NSC just after five, as she is flying to Japan tomorrow, to address a conference.

On your first town visit, you're not allowed beyond the environs of Boston (ten miles) and must return to the camp by

---

* They did. It was published in the *Sunday Mirror* the next day. (See overleaf.)

DAY 374

7 pm. Next week, assuming I've broken none of the rules, strayed beyond the ten-mile limit, had a drink or committed a crime (shoplifting the most common), I will be allowed to travel an 'as the crow flies' distance of fifty-five miles, which takes in Cambridge and Grantchester.

On returning to the hospital, I decide to pick up a phone-card and call Mary to thank her for all she's doing. I go to the drawer by my bed to discover that my phonecards are missing. It's a few minutes before I can accept that a fellow inmate has broken into the hospital and stolen all my phonecards (eight, worth £16). Don't forget that I earn £11.70 a week. But when I check the window opposite my bed, I notice that it's not on its usual notch. So now I know how the thief got in.

I'll have to borrow a couple of cards from David, two from Stephen and two from Tony if I'm going to survive the coming week.

NICE DAY OUT

Strolling Archer gets first taste of freedom

PICTURE EXCLUSIVE

DAY 377   TUESDAY 30 JULY 2002

8.00 am

This morning, four of the Highpoint prisoners were put in a van and shipped out to Lincoln (B-cat) accompanied by six officers and a driver. Just before leaving NSC, one of the prisoners attacked an officer. The governor has made it clear that he will no longer accept prisoners from that establishment.

9.00 am

Five HM Prisons Inspectors arrive unannounced at the front gate. Mr Beaumont (the governing governor) is on holiday in Wales, but rushes back to the camp, along with several other staff.

During the next three days I come across all five inspectors, and am impressed by how quickly they identify the good, the bad and the simply indifferent. They single out the kitchen and the hospital – both run by women – for high praise.

However, the governor wasn't around to hear their final report, as he had gone back to Wales.

As I have completed my first town visit without incident, I am now entitled to travel to Cambridge (within a fifty-five-mile radius of NSC). (See below.) Mary is in Japan attending a conference, and Will is working at the Kennedy Center, in Washington DC, so I spend the day with James.

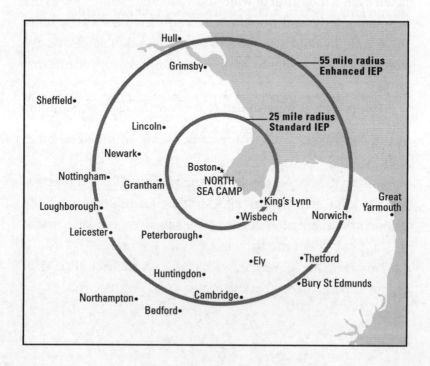

As we drive into Grantchester, I yearn to see the Old Vicarage. I spend the first hour strolling around the slightly overgrown garden – our gardener has been on holiday for a couple of weeks – admiring the flowers, the lake full of koi carp, and the sculptures that adorn the lawn.

James prepares lunch, and after reading the Sunday papers I settle down to slivers of melon with Parma ham, followed by spaghetti bolognaise (my choice) and a Diet Coke. We would normally have a glass of red wine, but not for another year. After a cheese board – I am only interested in the Cheddar – we once again stroll round the garden on a cloudless day, before returning to the house to watch the Commonwealth Games. What a triumph for Manchester.

I leave at 5 o'clock, as I have to report back before 7 pm, when I will be breathalysed and searched. Any sign that I had taken even a mouthful of wine and I would forfeit my job as the hospital orderly, and would not be considered for a CSV job in the future. I would also have to return to a double cell on the north block and be put to work on the farm. Can anyone be that stupid?

Two prisoners were shown to be over the limit on returning this evening. They both lost all their privileges.

DAY 384

TUESDAY 6 AUGUST 2002

All prisoners who have passed their FLED are eligible to work in the outside community as long as they are within twelve months of their parole date (mine is 19 July 2003). A prisoner can then work outside the camp between the hours of 7 am and 7 pm for five days a week, and even have a sixth day of training. Once accepted for the resettlement programme, a prisoner moves into one of the residential blocks located near the gate (single rooms) and is allowed to wear his own clothes at all times. You can also drive your own car to work and have a mobile phone (which cannot be taken out of the car).

The purpose of the resettlement programme is to help prisoners help themselves by earning a living wage (£150–£250 a week). If you are financially independent, these rules do not apply. However, you are still able to work for a voluntary or charitable organization and the prison will pay you £12.50 per week (current salary as a hospital orderly, £11.60 per week).

Governor Berlyn (head of resettlement) has already turned down my application to work for Dr Walling at the Parkside clinic as a trainee nurse. He gives two reasons for his decision: some of the camp staff are patients at the clinic, and Dr Walling, as head of the practice, is technically a member of staff, and therefore not permitted to employ me. However, Mr Berlyn has received a letter from a Mr Moreno at the Theatre Royal Lincoln, who has offered me a job assisting with the theatre's community programme. Mr Berlyn will accompany me to Lincoln next Tuesday for an interview. The Theatre Royal Lincoln falls into the category of a charitable organization as it is subsidized by the Lincolnshire County Council.

DAY 386   THURSDAY 8 AUGUST 2002

8.00 am

Some wit has pinned up on the notice board outside the stores, 'If it fits, hand it back.'

It seems that over twenty pads (cells) have been broken into during the past two weeks, and more than two hundred phonecards have been stolen. The old lags tell me that it has to be a crack-head if he was desperate enough to break into the hospital. By the end of the week, the thief has broken into the chapel and the canteen (shop).

Some inmates are claiming they know the culprit.

6.00 pm

A prisoner who recently arrived from Highpoint says he's going to beat me up before he's released. This threat was made during my morning rounds in front of a group of his mates. He must be around thirty and is in for GBH.

I confess to feeling frightened for the first time in months.

DAY 387　　　　FRIDAY 9 AUGUST 2002

8.00 am

This morning the same prisoner turns up at the hospital. I try to look calm. He apologizes for what he said yesterday, claiming that it was a joke and I obviously misunderstood him. 'I would never do anything to harm you Jeff.' I suspect he's worried that his threat may reach the ears of an officer, which would result in his being shipped out to a B-cat. Bullying is considered to be a worse crime than taking drugs. I nod, and he quickly leaves the hospital.

6.00 pm

David (post-office robbery) tells me that the prisoner from Highpoint who threatened me had a visit from Jim (robbery, antiques only), Mo (terrorist) and Big Al (GBH) in the middle of the night. They explained what would happen to him if Jeff came to any harm, or words to that effect.

I'm touched that three inmates whom I do not know that well feel strongly enough to watch my back.

I gave Big Al out LBW in last week's cricket match, and he hasn't stopped grumbling since.

DAY 391   TUESDAY 13 AUGUST 2002

Mr Berlyn drives me over to Lincoln for an interview with Chris Moreno and Chris Colby, the owner and director of the Theatre Royal Lincoln.

Both men could not have been more welcoming and kind. They make it clear to Mr Berlyn that they need 'volunteers' and would welcome other prisoners to join me. Mr Berlyn seems satisfied that a real job of work exists, and that I could be of some service to the community. He says he will recommend that I start work on Monday.

DAY 393   THURSDAY 15 AUGUST 2002

2.00 pm

A prisoner called Hugh attacks an officer in the north block. She arrives in hospital with a broken cheekbone. Hugh is immediately transferred to Lincoln Prison and will be charged with assault. The officer tells Linda that she will be claiming compensation, and expects to be off work for at least four months.

5.30 pm

'Lucky Ball' arrives at NSC – the man who claimed to have won the lottery and proceeded to spend his non-existent winnings.

7.00 pm

It's my last day as hospital orderly. Stephen (two years, VAT fraud, £160,000) takes my place. I will continue as Saturday orderly so I can keep my daily bath privileges, when Stephen will have the day off.

DAY 396　　　　SUNDAY 18 AUGUST 2002

8.00 am

Jim (gym orderly) drives me to Cambridge so I can spend the day at home with James. Mary is still in Japan. James and I buy four new koi carp from the local garden centre. Freedom is underrated.

5.00 pm

I drive Mary's car back to the camp and leave it in the prison car park. This will be the vehicle I use to get myself to Lincoln and back each day. I decided not to drive my BMW 720 as it would cause all sorts of problems, with the press, the prison staff and the other prisoners. While I'm driving, I feel a little like Toad in his motor on the open road.

DAY 397   MONDAY 19 AUGUST 2002

9.00 am

I began work at the Theatre Royal Lincoln today and enjoy wearing a shirt and tie for the first time in a year. Couldn't find a parking place and arrived a few minutes late. Over a hundred journalists, photographers and cameramen are waiting for me.

The first thing I notice is that my little office has bars on the window.

When I walk in the street during my lunch break, the public are kind and considerate. Find it hard to leave at five, grab a meal and be back by seven.

I reach NSC with three minutes to spare. If I'd failed to make it on time, I would have lost all my privileges on the first day, and probably been put to work on the farm.

DAY 424   SUNDAY 15 SEPTEMBER 2002

I can now leave the prison every Sunday and travel to Grantchester to be with Mary and the family for the day.

Today, my fourth Sunday, Mary and I have been invited to
lunch with Gillian and Tom Shephard and a few of their friends
at their home in Thetford. As Thetford is on the way back to
NSC, and within the fifty-five-mile radius of NSC, we decide to
take separate cars so I can return to prison after lunch.*

We leave the Old Vicarage at 12.15 pm.†

---

*See map page 414.
† I had no idea how important this lunch would turn out to be on the evening I
wrote these words.

DAY 434 WEDNESDAY 25 SEPTEMBER 2002

Five idyllic weeks working at the Theatre Royal. *Annie* goes into rehearsal with Su Pollard, Mark Wynter and Louise English. I've been in charge of the children and in particular their accommodation needs, as they go on tour around the country. After the terrible events in Soham, Mr Moreno is adamant that their safety must be paramount. I spend hours organizing where the young girls and their chaperones will stay in each town.

Today, I attend the 2.30 pm dress rehearsal of *Annie* at the Liberal Club and leave the cast after Chris Colby has run through his notes.* I wish them all luck and depart a few minutes before six. I now feel not only part of the team, but that I'm doing a worthwhile job.

I arrive back in Boston at six and go to the Eagles restaurant for what I didn't then know was to be my last steak and kidney pie.

On my arrival back at the camp, Mr Elsen, a senior officer, asks me to accompany him to the governor's office. I am desperately trying to think what I can possibly have done wrong. Mr Beaumont, the governor, and Mr Berlyn, the deputy governor,

---

* When I first entered the Liberal Club, an elderly gentlemen remarked, 'Prison is one thing, Jeff, but the Liberal Club?'

are sitting waiting for me. The governor wastes no time and asks me if, on Sunday 15th, I stopped on the way back to the camp to have lunch with Gillian Shephard MP.

'Yes,' I reply without hesitation, as I don't consider Gillian or any of her other guests to be criminals.

Mr Beaumont tells me that I have breached my licence by leaving my home in Cambridge. This, despite the fact that I remained within the permitted radius of the prison, had been with my wife, hadn't drunk anything stronger than apple juice and returned to NSC well in time.

Without offering me the chance to give an explanation, I am marched to the segregation block, and not even allowed to make a phone call.

The cold, bleak room, five paces by three, has just a thin mattress on the floor against one wall, a steel washbasin and an open lavatory.

DAY 435 THURSDAY 26 SEPTEMBER 2002

5.00 am

I have not slept for one second of the ten hours I have been locked in this cell.

8.00 am

My first visitor is Dr Razzak who assures me that she will inform the governor I should not be moved on medical grounds.*

10.00 am

I have a visit from Mr Forman (chairman of the IMB, the prison's Independent Monitoring Board), who assures me that I will not be moved if my only offence was having lunch with Gillian Shephard.

11.30 am

I am escorted to adjudication. It quickly becomes clear that all decisions are being made in London by Mr Narey, the director-general of the Prison Service. Once I realize this, I accept there is no hope of justice.

---

* I assume that Mr Beaumont was given Dr Razzak's advice. If so, he ignored it.

Mr Beaumont tells me that as a result of this breach of licence, I am being transferred to B-cat Lincoln Prison, despite the fact that I have, until now, had an exemplary record, and have never once been placed on report. He adds that I have embarrassed the Prison Service, following a press story. The paper accused me of drinking champagne at a Tory bash.

'Which paper?' I ask innocently.

'The *Sun*,' says Mr Beaumont, thus revealing which paper Mr Narey reads each morning, and which editorials help him make his decisions.

At North Sea Camp last week, a prisoner who arrived back late and drunk was stripped of all privileges for a month; another, who brought vodka into the camp, was grounded for a month. Only last week, an NSC inmate nicknamed Ginger went on home leave and returned three days late. His excuse was that his girlfriend had held him captive (this provoked a mixture of envy and hilarity among other inmates). His only punishment was confinement to NSC for a short period. Several former inmates have since contacted my wife pointing out that they regularly visited friends and in-laws on their home leave days, as well as taking their children on outings to the park or swimming pool, and it was never once suggested this was against the regulations.

I was given no opportunity to appeal.

I learn later that Dr Walling (the prison's senior doctor) protested about my being put in segregation and moved to Lincoln Prison. Dr Walling told me that he was warned that if he made his feelings public, his days at NSC would be numbered.

3.45 pm

One officer, Mr Masters, is so appalled by the judgement that he comes to the side of the Group 4 van to shake my hand.

30 April 2004

Dear Mr Wragg

INVESTIGATION INTO THE CONDUCT OF MR KEITH BEAUMONT

I understand that you are leading an investigation into the conduct of Mr Keith Beaumont as Governing Governor of HMP North Sea Camp.

As you may be aware, I was an inmate in North Sea Camp from October 2001 until September 2002, when I was summarily transferred to HMP Lincoln by Mr Beaumont.

It is clearly essential that I give evidence to your enquiry about these matters, of which I made contemporaneous records. I can make myself available for this purpose at any time. I can be contacted during the working week at the above number, and over the weekend on 01223 840213.

Yours sincerely

Jeffrey Archer

Jeffrey Archer

cc   Mr Phil Wheatley, Director-General of the Prison Service[*]

---

[*] I received a fax from Mr Wragg a week later turning down my request.

On 18 April 2004, Mr Beaumont was suspended from his duties until a full enquiry could investigate his conduct as governor of NSC.

On 30 April 2004, I wrote to Mr Wragg, the chairman of the tribunal, asking to be allowed to give evidence. (See above.)

BACK TO HELL

4.19 pm

The Group 4 sweat box drives through the gates of HMP Lincoln just after 4 pm. Lincoln Prison is less than a mile from the Theatre Royal, but may as well be a thousand miles away.

I am escorted into reception to be met by a Mr Fuller. He seems mystified as to what I am doing here. He checks through my plastic bags and allows me to keep my shaving kit and a pair of trainers. The rest, he assures me, will be returned when I'm transferred to another prison, or released. He fills in several forms, a process that takes over an hour, while I hang around in a dirty smoke-filled corridor, trying to take in what has happened during the past twenty hours. When the last form has been completed, another officer escorts me to a double cell in the notorious A wing.

When I enter the main block, I face the usual jeering and foul language. We come to a halt outside cell fourteen. The massive iron door is unlocked, and then slammed behind me. My new cell-mate looks up from his bed, smiles and introduces himself as Jason. While I unpack what's left of my belongings and make up my bed, Jason tells me that he's in for GBH. He found a man in bed with his wife, and thrashed him to within an inch of his life.

'I wish I'd gone the extra inch,' he adds.

His sentence is four years.

Jason continues to chat as I lie on my hard mattress and stare up at the green ceiling. He tells me that he's trying to get back together with his wife. He will be seeing her for the first time since his conviction (ten weeks ago) at a visit on Saturday. I also learn that Jason served ten years in the airforce, winning three medals in the Gulf, and was the RAF's light heavyweight boxing champion. He left the forces with an exemplary record, which he feels may have helped to get his charge reduced from attempted murder to GBH.

I fall asleep, but only because I haven't slept for thirty-nine hours.

DAY 436   FRIDAY 27 SEPTEMBER 2002

I wake to the words, 'Fuck all screws,' echoing through the air from the floor above.

I haven't eaten for two days, and force down a slice of bread and an out-of-date lemon sorbet.

When they let me out of the cell (forty-five minutes a day), I phone Mary. An inmate from the landing above spits on me, and then bursts out laughing.

Despite the fact that the officers are friendly and sympathetic, I have never been more depressed in my life. I know that if I had a twenty-five-year sentence I would kill myself. There have been three attempted suicides at Lincoln this week. One succeeded – a lad of twenty-two, not yet sentenced.

Jason tells me that he's heard I am to be moved to C wing. He says that it's cleaner and each cell has a television but, and there's always a 'but' in prison, I'll have to work in the kitchen. If that's the case, I'll be stuck on A wing for however long I'm left in here. Jason passes over his newspaper. The *Mirror* gives a fair report of my lunch with Gillian and Tom Shephard; no one suggests I drank any alcohol. *The Times* adds that Martin Narey has said it will not be long before I'm moved. It cheers me up – a little, and then I recall the reality of 'not long' in prison. The press in general consider I've been hard done by,

DAY 436

and the *Daily Mail* is in no doubt that the Home Secretary's fingerprints are all over the decision to take revenge on me. I lie on my bed for hour after hour, wondering if I will ever be free.

DAY 437   SATURDAY 28 SEPTEMBER 2002

12 noon

I'm standing in line for lunch wondering if anything will be edible. I spot an apple. I must remember to write to Wendy and congratulate her on the standard of the food at North Sea Camp. A prisoner, three ahead of me in the queue, gruffly asks for some rice. The server slams a ladle-full down on his tin tray.

'Is that all I fuckin' get?' asks the inmate, to which the server replies, 'Move along, you fuckin' muppet.' The prisoner drops his tray on the floor, charges round to the back of the counter and punches the server on the nose. In the ensuing fight, the server crashes his heavy ladle over the other prisoner's head and blood spurts across the food. The rest of the queue form a ring around the two combatants. Prisoners never join in someone else's quarrel, only too aware of the consequences, but it doesn't stop them jeering and cheering, some even taking bets. The fight continues for over a minute before an alarm goes off, bringing officers running from every direction.

By the time the officers arrive, there's blood everywhere. It takes five of them to drag the two men apart. The two combatants are then frogmarched off to segregation.*

---

*One officer pushes the prisoner's head down, while another keeps his legs

DAY 437

5.00 pm

I'm not eating the prison food. Once again, I have to rely on chocolate biscuits and blackcurrant juice. And once again I have a supply problem, which was taken care of at Belmarsh by 'Del Boy'. I quickly discover Lincoln's equivalent, Devon.

Devon is the spur's senior cleaner. He tells me with considerable pride that he is forty-one, has five children by three different women and already has five grandchildren. I tell him my needs. He smiles; the smile of a man who can deliver.

Within the hour, I have a second pillow, a blanket, two bottles of water, a KitKat and a copy of yesterday's *Times*. By the way, like Del Boy, Devon is West Indian. As Devon is on remand, he's allowed far longer out of his cell than a convicted prisoner. He's been charged with attacking a rival drug dealer with a machete (GBH). He cut off the man's right arm, so he's not all that optimistic about the outcome of his forthcoming trial. 'After all,' he says, flashing a smile, 'they've still got his arm, haven't they.' He pauses. 'I only wish it had been his head.' I return to my cell, feeling sick.

6.00 pm

I find it difficult to adjust to being banged up again for twenty-two hours a day, but imagine my surprise when, during association – that forty-five-minute break when you are allowed out of your cell – I bump into Clive. Do you remember Clive? He used to come to the hospital in the evening at North Sea Camp and play backgammon with me, and he nearly always won. Well,

---

bent; this is known as being 'bent up' or 'twisted up'. In the rule book it's described as 'control and restraint'.

he's back on remand, this time charged with money laundering. As we walk around the yard, he tells me what's been happening in his life since we last met.

It seems that after being released from NSC, Clive formed a company that sold mobile phones to the Arabs, who paid for them with cash. He then distributed the cash to different banks right around the globe, while keeping 10 per cent for himself.

'Why's that illegal?' I ask.

'There never were any phones in the first place,' he admits.

Clive seems confident that they won't be able to prove money laundering, but may get him for failure to pay VAT.*

During association, I phone Mary. While she's briefing me on Narey's attempts on radio and television to defend his decision to send me to Lincoln, another fight breaks out. I watch as two more prisoners are dragged away. Mary goes on to tell me that Narey is backtracking as fast as he can, and the Home Office is nowhere to be seen. The commentators seem convinced that I will be transferred back to a D-cat fairly quickly. It can't be too soon, I tell her, this place is full of violent, drug-addicted thugs. I can only admire the way the officers keep the lid on such a boiling cauldron.†

While I roam around association with Jason, he points at three Lithuanians who are standing alone in the far corner.

'They're on remand awaiting trial for murder,' he tells me. 'Even the officers are fearful of them.' Devon joins us, and adds that they are hit men for the Russian mafia and were sent to

---

*I am pleased to learn that David, the friendly schoolmaster at NSC who joined Clive's company on leaving prison, quickly realized what he was up to, and resigned.
† There was a riot the week after I left, and seventeen inmates ended up in hospital.

DAY 437

England to carry out an execution. They have been charged with killing three of their countrymen, chopping them up into little pieces, putting them through a mincer and then feeding them to dogs.

DAY 438   SUNDAY 29 SEPTEMBER 2002

11.00 am

The cell door is opened and an officer escorts me to the chapel: anything to get out of my cell. After all, the chapel is the largest room in the prison. The service is Holy Communion with the added pleasure of singing by choristers from Lincoln Cathedral. They number seventeen, the congregation thirteen.

I sit next to a man who has been on A block for the past ten weeks. He's fifty-three years old, serving a two-year sentence. It's his first offence, and he has no history of drugs or violence.

The Home Secretary can have no idea of the damage he's causing to such people by forcing them to mix in vile conditions with murderers, thugs and drug addicts. Such men should be sent to a D-cat the day they are sentenced.*

12 noon

I go to the library and select three books, the maximum allowed. I spend the next twenty hours in my cell, reading.

---

* I wrote this in *A Prison Diary Volume One – Belmarsh: Hell*, and the Home Office have shown scant interest. There aren't any votes in prisons.

DAY 438

10.00 pm

I end the day with Alfred Hitchcock's *Stories To Be Read With The Doors Locked.* Somewhat ironic.

DAY 439   MONDAY 30 SEPTEMBER 2002

6.00 am

Over the past few days I have been writing furiously, but I have just had my work confiscated by the deputy governor – so much for freedom of speech. He made it clear that his orders to prevent me from sending out any written material came from the Home Office direct. I rewrite my day, and have this copy smuggled out – not too difficult with nearly a hundred prisoners on remand who leave the prison to attend court every day.

8.00 am

After breakfast, I'm confined to my cell and the company of Jason for the next eight hours.

6.00 pm

Mr Marsh, a senior officer, who has a rare gift for keeping things under control, opens the cell door and tells me I have a meeting with the area manager.* I am escorted to a private room, and

---

* An area manager is senior to a governor, and can have as many as fifty prisons under his remit. He reports directly to the deputy director-general.

introduced to Mr Spurr and Ms Stamp. Mr Spurr explains that he has been given the responsibility of investigating my case. As I have received some 600 letters during the past four days (every one of them retained), every one of them expressing outrage at the director-general's judgment, this doesn't come as a great surprise.

Mr Spurr's intelligent questions lead me to believe that he is genuinely interested in putting right an injustice. I tell him and Ms Stamp exactly what happened.

On Friday 27 September, the Prison Service announced that 'further serious allegations' had been made against me. It turned out these related to a lunch I had attended on Wednesday 25 September in Zucchini's Restaurant, Lincoln (which is near the Theatre Royal) with Mr Paul Hocking, then a Senior Security Officer at North Sea Camp, and PC Karen Brooks of the Lincolnshire Constabulary.

I explained to Mr Spurr that the sole purpose of the lunch as far as I was concerned was so that I could describe what I had seen of the drug culture permeating British prisons to PC Brooks, who had by then returned to work with the Lincolnshire Police Drug Squad. After all, I'd had several meetings with Hocking and or Brooks in the past on the subject of drugs. I did not know that prison officers are not supposed to eat meals with prisoners, nor is there any reason I should have known this. Moreover, when a senior officer asks a prisoner to attend a meeting, even in a social context, a wise prisoner does not query the officer's right to do so.

As for SO Hocking, I have been distressed to learn that he was summarily forced to resign from the Prison Service on 27 September under the threat of losing his pension if he did not do so*. PC Karen Brooks was more fortunate in her employers. Her role was

---

*Since Mr Beaumont's suspension, Mr Hocking has addressed the tribunal, and made it clear that he was forced to resign by Beaumont, with the threat of being sacked. But who bullied Mr Beaumont?

investigated comprehensively by Chief Inspector Gossage and Sergeant Kent of the Lincolnshire Police, and she remains with the force. Chief Inspector Gossage and Sergeant Kent interviewed me during their later investigation of the same lunch, and made it very clear that they thought the Prison Service had acted hastily and disproportionately in transferring me to HMP Lincoln.

As Mr Spurr leaves, he assures me that he will complete his report as quickly as possible, although he still has several other people to interview. He repeats that he is interested in seeing justice being done for any prisoner who has been unfairly treated.

It was some time later that the *Daily Mail* reported that the Home Secretary had bullied Mr Narey into the decision to have me moved to HMP Lincoln.

The sequence of events, so far as I am able to establish them, are as follows. The *Sun* newspaper telephoned Martin Narey's office on the evening of Wednesday 25 September and the following day published a highly coloured account of the Gillian Shephard lunch. This provoked the Home Secretary to send an extraordinary fax (see overleaf) to Martin Narey demanding that the latter take 'immediate and decisive disciplinary action' against me. Narey, who had previously stood up against the press's attempts to portray my treatment as privileged, buckled and instructed Mr Beaumont to transfer me forthwith to Lincoln. Narey also went on a number of TV and radio programmes to criticize me in highly personal terms in what the *Independent on Sunday* described as 'an unprecedented attack on an individual prisoner', especially in the light of later pious assertions that the Prison Service is 'unable to discuss individual prisoners in detail with third parties'.

Mr Beaumont found himself in even more difficulty: he had not asked me about the Zucchini lunch, so he could hardly

PRIVATE & CONFIDENTIAL

FROM: Home Secretary
Queen Anne's Gate

DATE: 26 September 2002

MARTIN NAREY

Dear Martin

I would be grateful if you would report personally to me on the two incidents you are investigating in relation to Jeffrey Archer.

If either of these incidents are true, I expect you to take immediate and decisive disciplinary action.

I am sick and tired of reading Jeffrey Archer stories about the cushy conditions in which he was placed, the freedom he has been given, the opportunity to do whatever he likes, and the snook that he is cocking at all of us.

Best wishes

[signature]

DAVID BLUNKETT

make that the basis of an order to transfer me. In the event, the Notice of Transfer which he signed stated simply: 'Following serious allegations reported in the media and confirmed by yourself that on 15 September 2002, you attended a dinner party rather than spend the day on a Community Visit in Cambridge with your wife, it is not appropriate for you to remain at HMP North Sea Camp any longer.'

My licence did *not* restrict me to my home in Grantchester while on release. But, an e-mail was circulated within the Home Office which stated: '*The prison* [HMP North Sea Camp] *had granted JA home leave but his licence conditions stipulated that he should not go anywhere else but home. In light of this, he has breached his licence conditions, and will face adjudication.*' At that time, the copy of my master passbook (a record retained by the prison which records all a prisoner's releases on temporary licence) contained no such stipulation, nor did I ever face adjudication in respect of any breach of such a stipulation.

Mr Spurr later said in a letter he was 'unable to locate' my master passbook when he conducted his investigation into my transfer, a fact which he acknowledged as 'regrettable'. One has to wonder why and how this passbook disappeared. However, Mr Narey told me to stop writing to him on the subject as the matter was closed.

DAY 440   TUESDAY 1 OCTOBER 2002

6.00 am

A frequent complaint among prison officers and inmates –
with which I have some sympathy – is that paedophiles and
sex offenders are treated more leniently, and live in far more
palatable surroundings, than the rest of us.

On arriving at Lincoln you are immediately placed on A
wing, described quite rightly by the tabloids as a Victorian hell-
hole. But if you are a convicted sex offender, you go straight to
E wing, a modern accommodation block of smart, single cells,
each with its own television. E wing also has table tennis and
pool tables and a bowling green.

During the past few days, I have been subjected to segregation, transferred to Lincoln, placed in A block with murderers,
violent criminals and drug dealers, in a cell any self-respecting
rat would desert, offered food I am unable to eat and I have to
share my cell with a man who thrashed someone to within an
inch of their life. All this for having lunch with the Rt Hon
Gillian Shephard in the company of my wife when on my way
back to NSC from Grantchester.

Sex offenders can survive in an open prison because the
other inmates are on 'trust' and don't want to risk being sent
back to a B-cat or have their sentences extended. However, these

rules do not apply in a closed prison. An officer recently reported to me the worst case he had come across during his thirty years in the Prison Service. If you are at all squeamish, turn to the next page, because I confess I found this very difficult to write.

The prisoner concerned was charged and convicted of having sex with his five-year-old daughter. During the trial, it was revealed that not only did the defendant rape her, but in order for penetration to take place he had to cut his daughter's vagina with a razor blade.

I know I couldn't have killed the man, but I suspect I would have turned a blind eye while someone else did.

10.34 am

I have a visit from a Portuguese prisoner called Juan. He warns me that some inmates were seen in my cell during association while I was on the phone. It seems that they were hoping to get their hands on some personal memento to sell to the press.

English is Juan's second language, and I have not come across a prisoner with a better command of our native tongue; and I doubt if there is another inmate on A block who has a neater hand – myself included. He is, incidentally, quietly spoken and well mannered. He wrote me a thank you letter for giving him a glass of blackcurrant juice. I must try and find out why he is in prison.

11.17 am

An officer (Mr Brighten) unlocks my door and tells me that he needs a form filled in so that I can work in the kitchen. To begin with, I assume it's a joke, and then become painfully aware that he's serious. Surely the staff can't have missed that I've hardly

DAY 440

eaten a thing since the day I arrived, and now they want to put me where the food is prepared? I tell him politely, but firmly, that I have no desire to work in the kitchen.

3.11 pm

I look up at my little window, inches from the ceiling, and think of Oscar Wilde. This must be the nearest I've been to living in conditions described so vividly by the great playwright while he was serving a two-year sentence in Reading jail.

> I never saw a man who looked
> With such a wistful eye
> Upon that little tent of blue
> Which prisoners call the sky.

5.15 pm

Mr Brighten returns to tell me that I will be placed on report if I refuse to work in the kitchen. I agree to work in the kitchen.

DAY 443   FRIDAY 4 OCTOBER 2002

The end of the second longest week in my life.

Jason (GBH) has received a movement order to transfer him to HMP Stocken in Rutland (C-cat) later this morning. He's 'gutted' as he hoped to be sent directly to a D-cat. However, a conviction for violence will have prevented this. By the way, he and his wife did agree to get back together, and she will now visit him every Saturday.

10.00 am

An officer unlocks my cell door and bellows, 'Gym.' Twenty or thirty of us form a line by the barred gate at the far end of the brick-walled, windowless room. A few minutes later we are escorted down long, bleak, echoing corridors, with much unlocking and locking of several heavy gates as we make our slow progress to the gym situated on the other side of the prison.

We are taken to a changing room, where I put on a singlet and shorts. Clive (money laundering) and I enter the spacious gym. We warm up with a game of paddle tennis, and he sees me off in a few minutes. I move on to do a thousand metres on the rowing machine in five minutes, and end up with a little light weight training. When an officer bellows, 'Five more minutes,'

DAY 443

I check my weight. Twelve stone twelve pounds. I've lost six pounds in six days. I join my fellow inmates in the shower room and have my first press-button shower for a year, bringing back more unpleasant memories of Belmarsh.

As we are all escorted back to A block by Mr Lewis, the senior gym officer, we pass E Wing (paedophiles) and not one of the inmates even looks in the direction of the staring faces. Why? Because we are accompanied by an officer. Prisoners are warned that any abuse (shouting, foul language) will be treated as a disciplinary matter, with the loss of daily gym rights as punishment. When you're locked up for twenty-two hours a day, that's incentive enough to remain silent, whatever your thoughts.

5.00 pm

The cell door is unlocked, and my new pad-mate enters carrying the inevitable plastic bag. Jason is replaced by Phil, an amiable, good-looking – despite the scar on his face – twenty-eight-year-old.

He has been put in my cell because he doesn't smoke, which is very rare in jail. Phil talks a great deal, and tells me that he wants to return to work in the kitchen. He certainly seems to know his way round the prison, which turns out to be because he's paid several visits to Lincoln during the past ten years.

He is only too happy to tell me the finer details of his record.

Offence	Age	Length of Sentence	Time Served
ABH	17	18 months	13½ months
armed robbery (post office)	19	4½ years	3 years 2 months
credit card fraud, deception	22	21 months	11 months
driving while disqualified	25	6 months	3 months

driving without a licence	25	4 months	2 months
drink driving	25	community service	80 hours
ABH (car crash, assaulted the other driver)	26	6 months	3 months
common assault (his wife)	27	5 months	10 weeks
Total	28	9½ years	6 years 1 month

Twenty-eight other offences were taken into consideration before the judge passed sentence on Phil this morning.

Phil tells me, 'Never again.' He now has a happy family life – I don't ask how he explains his latest conviction – and a good job to go back to. He can earn £500 a week laying concrete and doesn't need another spell in jail. Phil admits that his problem is a short fuse.

'Strike a match and I explode,' he adds, laughing.

5.40 pm

Mr Brighten unlocks the cell door to inform me that I start work in the kitchen tomorrow at eight o'clock. He slams the door closed before I can comment.

6.00 pm

My cell door is unlocked again and Phil and I, along with three others, are escorted to the hospital. I'm told that I have to take a drugs test before I'm allowed to work in the kitchen. Despite the fact that I don't want to work in the kitchen, Phil tells me that five prisoners apply every day because the work is so popular. Phil and I pass the urine test to show we are drug free, and the duty officer tells us to report to the kitchen by eight. The other three fail.

DAY 443

6.40 pm

During association I phone my agent, Jonathan Lloyd. He goes over the details of tomorrow's announcement of the publication of volume one of these diaries. I congratulate him on how well the secret has been kept. Not one newspaper has picked up that *A Prison Diary by FF8282* will be published tomorrow. This is quite an achievement remembering that at least twenty people must have known at Macmillan and ten or more at the *Daily Mail.*

DAY 444   SATURDAY 5 OCTOBER 2002

5.52 am

This is my tenth day of incarceration at Lincoln.

6.01 am

The publication of *A Prison Diary Volume One – Belmarsh: Hell,* is the lead item on the news. The facts are fairly reported. No one seems to think that the Home Office will try to prevent the publication. However, the director-general is checking to see if I have broken any prison rules. Mr Narey is particularly exercised by the mention of other prisoners' names. I have only referred to prisoners' surnames when they are major characters in the diary, and only then when their permission has been granted.*

A representative of the Prison Officers' Association said on the *Today* programme that as I hid in my room all day, I wouldn't have anything worthwhile to say about prisons. Perhaps it might have been wiser for him to open his mouth after he's read the

---

*Two years and two prison diaries later, and I have not received one letter of complaint from a prisoner or prison officer about the diaries despite receiving some 16,000 letters in the last three years.

DAY 444

book, when he would have discovered how well his colleagues come out of my experience.

7.32 am

My cell door is unlocked so I can be transferred from A to J wing. This is considered a privilege for that select group who work in the kitchen. The cells are a lot cleaner, and also have televisions. My new companion is a grown-up non-smoker called Stephen (age thirty-nine), who is number one in the kitchen.

Stephen is serving a seven-year sentence for smuggling one and a half tons of cannabis into Britain. He is an intelligent man, who runs both the wing and the kitchen with a combination of charm and example.

8.00 am

A group of fourteen prisoners is escorted to the kitchens. Only two of the five who reported for drugs testing yesterday evening are still in the group.

I am put to work in the vegetable room to assist a young twenty-three-year-old called Lee, who is so good at his job – chopping potatoes, slicing onions, grating cheese and mashing swedes – that I become his incompetent assistant. My lack of expertise doesn't seem to worry him.

The officer in charge of the kitchen, Mr Tasker, turns out to be one of the most decent and professional men I have dealt with since being incarcerated. His kitchen is like Singapore airport: you could eat off the floor. He goes to great pains to point out to me that he only has £1.27 per prisoner to deliver three meals a day. In the circumstances, what he and his staff manage to achieve is nothing less than a miracle.

DAY 445   SUNDAY 6 OCTOBER 2002

11.14 am

On this, my eleventh day, I have a second visit from Mr Spurr
and his colleague Ms Stamp.

They say they wish to tidy up a few minor points. I'm
impressed by Mr Spurr's grasp of what's going on at North Sea
Camp, and once again he gives the impression of being
concerned.

He leaves promising that he will be able to tell me the
outcome of his enquiry on Friday.

DAY 450   FRIDAY 11 OCTOBER 2002

7.30 am

A particularly officious, ill-mannered officer unlocks my cell door and thrusts some papers at me. He tells me with considerable pleasure that I will be on a charge at 4 o'clock this afternoon.

I read the papers several times. I don't have a lot more to do. It seems that by publishing *A Prison Diary* I have broken prison Rule 51 Para 23, in 'naming staff such that they could be identified', contrary to SO 5 Para 34 (9) (d).

8.10 am

On leaving my cell to go to work in the kitchen, I am surprised to find Mr Spurr and Ms Stamp awaiting me. I am escorted into a side room. Mr Spurr tells me that he has completed his enquiry, and I will be transferred to Hollesley Bay (D-cat) some time next week. Do you recall Governor Lewis's words, 'Whatever you do, don't end up in Hollesley Bay...'?

10.30 am

I take a break from peeling the spuds, not that I can pretend to have done that many. I notice that Mr Tasker is sitting in his office reading the *Daily Mail*. He beckons me in, and tells me to close the door.

'I've just been reading about your time at Belmarsh,' he says, jabbing a finger at the centre pages, 'and I see you're suggesting that seventy per cent of prisoners are on drugs and as many as thirty per cent could be on heroin.' He looks up, gives me a pained expression and then adds, 'You're wrong.'

I don't comment, expecting him to dismiss my claims, and remind me of the official statistics always parroted by the Home Office whenever the question of drugs is raised.

'Which would you say is the most popular job in the prison?' Mr Tasker asks, folding his newspaper.

'The kitchen, without question,' I reply, 'and for all the obvious reasons.'

'You're right,' he says. 'Every day, at least five inmates apply to work in the kitchen.' He pauses, sips his coffee and adds, 'Did you take a drugs test yesterday?'

'Yes,' I reply, 'along with four others.'

'And how many of you were invited to work in the kitchen?'

'Just Phil and me,' I reply.

'Correct, but what you don't know is that I'm entitled to have twenty-one prisoners working in the kitchen, but currently employ only seventeen.' He takes another sip of his coffee. 'I have never managed to fill all the vacancies during the last ten years, despite the fact that we never have fewer than seven hundred inmates.' Mr Tasker rises from his seat. 'Now I'm no mathematician,' he says, 'but I think you'll find that seventeen out of seven hundred does not come to thirty per cent.'

DAY 450

3.00 pm

The same officious, ill-mannered lout who unlocked my cell door this morning returns to pick me up from the kitchen and escort me to segregation. This time I am only left there for about forty minutes before being hauled up in front of Mr Peacock, the governing governor. Mr Peacock sits at the top of the table with the deputy governor on his right and my wing officer on his left. The thug stands behind me in case I might try to escape. The governor reads out the charge and asks if I wish to plead guilty or not guilty.

'I'm not sure,' I reply. 'I'm not clear what offence I've committed.'

I am then shown the prison rules in full. I express some surprise, saying that I handed over every page of *Belmarsh: Hell* to the prison censor, and he kindly posted them on to my secretary, and at no time did he suggest I was committing any offence. The governor looks suitably embarrassed when I ask him to write down every word I have said. He does so.

Mr Peacock points out that every inmate has access to a copy of the prison rules in the library. 'Yes, but anyone who reads my diary,' – he has a copy of *Belmarsh* on the table in front of him – 'would know that I wasn't allowed to visit the library, or have access to education while at Belmarsh.' I direct him to the passage on the relevant page. At least he has the grace to smile, adding that ignorance of the law is no excuse.

Mr Peacock then calls for my wing officer to make his report. 'Archer FF8282, works in the kitchen and is a polite, well-mannered prisoner, with no history of drugs or violence.' The governor also writes these words down, before clearing his throat and pronouncing sentence.

'Loss of all privileges for fourteen days, and of canteen during the same period,' the governor pauses, 'to be suspended for six months.'

I rise, thank him and leave. I have a feeling he'll be only too happy to see the back of me. But more important, the decision has been made not to remove my D-cat status, thus proving that they had no reason to send me here in the first place.

It was to be another six days before my transfer to Hollesley Bay in Suffolk, and even that simple exercise they managed to botch.

DAY 457   FRIDAY 18 OCTOBER 2002

6.00 am

I rise and pack my belongings into an HMP plastic bag as I
prepare for my next move, not unlike one does when leaving a
no-star motel at the end of a rainy holiday. While I'm gathering my possessions together, I chat to my pad-mate, Stephen
(marijuana, seven years), who tells me that he's been granted his
D-cat status, and hopes it will not be long before they transfer
him to North Sea Camp.

7.00 am

The cell doors on our wing are unlocked to allow Stephen and
his crew to be escorted to the kitchens and begin the day's work.
I try inadequately to thank him for his kindness and help during
the past ten days, while wishing him luck for a speedy transfer.

8.07 am

The cell door is thrown open for the last time, to reveal a young
officer standing in the doorway. Without a word, he escorts me
to reception. It's a protracted journey, as I have to drag along

two large, heavy plastic bags, and however many times I stop, the officer makes no attempt to help me.

When we finally reach reception, I'm placed in the inevitable waiting room. From time to time, I'm called to the counter by Mr Fuller so that I can sign forms and check through the contents of another six plastic bags that have been kept under lock and key. These are filled with gifts – mainly books – sent in by the public during the past three weeks. I sort out those that can be donated to the library (including nine Bibles) and still end up with four full bags, which will have to travel with me to Suffolk.

It's another thirty minutes before the final form is completed and I am cleared to depart for my next destination. Meanwhile, back to the waiting room.

10.19 am

Two young officers from Group 4 appear in the corridor. They are to accompany me and two other inmates from this hell-hole – not that the devils' keepers have been unkind. In fact, with one loutish exception, they have been supportive and friendly.

The Group 4 officers help me with my endless plastic bags, before I am locked into a tiny cubicle in another sweat box. I sit cramped up in silence awaiting a 'movement order'.

11.49 am

The electric gates swing slowly open, and the van eases out onto the main road. I stare from my darkened window to see several photographers snapping away. All they'll get is a blacked-out window.

I remain hunched up in my little box, despite the fact that as a D-cat prisoner I am entitled to have my wife drive me to

DAY 457

Hollesley Bay in the family car. But once again, the Home Office has put a stop to that.

For the next five hours, I am cooped up with two stale sandwiches and a bottle of water as we trundle through four counties on the endless journey to somewhere on the Suffolk coast.

3.19 pm

The van finally arrives at Hollesley Bay, and comes to a halt outside a squat brick building. The three of us step outside, to be escorted into reception. More form filling and more bag checking – decisions to be made about what we can and cannot possess.

While my plastic bags are being checked, the duty officer inadvertently gives it all away with an innocent remark. 'It's the first time I've checked anyone in from Lincoln.' And worse, the other two prisoners who came with me have only two weeks and three weeks respectively to serve before they complete their sentences; this despite the fact that their homes are in north Yorkshire. They have been uprooted because the Home Office is prepared to mess around with their lives just to make sure I couldn't travel by car.

When all the red tape is completed, I am accompanied to the north block by another officer, who dumps me in a single room.

Once again I begin to unpack. Once again, I will have to find my feet. Once again, I will be put through induction. Once again, I will have to suffer the endless jibes and sullen stares, never lowering my guard. Once again, I will have to find a job.

Once again . . .

EPILOGUE

For the past fourteen months, I have been writing two thousand words a day, nearly a million in all, which has resulted in three published diaries.

Although Hollesley Bay turned out to be quite different from North Sea Camp, it was not dissimilar enough to warrant a fourth diary. However, there is one significant difference worthy of mention. Hollesley Bay is an open prison, not a resettlement establishment. It was clearly selected to ensure that I couldn't work outside. After I had completed my induction, the director of Genesis, a Mencap project in Ipswich, offered me a job. His request was rejected by Mr Jones, the prison governor, despite there being three other inmates working at Genesis at that time. I appealed to the Prison Ombudsman about this blatant discrimination, but he said he didn't have the authority to reverse the governor's decision.

I reluctantly settled for the position of library orderly, with a remit from Mr Jones to 'get more prisoners reading'. Thirty-two books were taken out in my first week as library orderly, one hundred and ninety one in my last, eight months later.

However, as the library was only open to prisoners between 12.30 and 1.30, and 6 and 7 pm, I was left with countless hours to occupy myself. It doesn't take that long to replace on the shelves the twenty or thirty books returned each day. I could have occupied those lifeless hours writing a fourth diary, but as I have explained, I felt it would have achieved little.

During those first few months of incarceration at Hollesley Bay, I edited *A Prison Diary Volume Two – Wayland: Purgatory*, and had it smuggled out on a weekly basis by a prisoner who was working in Ipswich. But even that demanding exercise did not fully occupy my time.

My next venture was to write nine short stories based on tales that I had picked up from all four prisons. This collection will be published in 2005 under the title *Cat of Nine Tales*. Unfortunately, even this endeavour, with its several rewrites, only occupied me through to Christmas, leaving me another six months to kill before I was due to be released.

It was the death of an old friend that spurred me into action, and once again gave my life some purpose ...

A few months before my trial began, I had lunch at Mosimann's with Chris Brasher and a mutual friend, John Bryant. The purpose of the lunch, and Chris always had a purpose, was first to persuade me that I should run in the London marathon and attempt to break the world record for the amount raised for charity by an individual in this event (£1,166,212) and second, that I should write my first screenplay.

While the marathon was postponed by events, I suddenly found myself with time on my hands to write a screenplay. Chris Brasher also knew the subject he wanted me to tackle, and proceeded to tell me the story of George Mallory, an Englishman who in 1924, climbed to within 800 feet of the summit of Everest, dressed in a three-piece tweed suit, with a coiled rope over one shoulder, a fifty-five-pound pack on his back, and carrying an ice axe in one hand and a rolled umbrella in the other.

At 12.50 pm on 17 July 1924 (Ascension Day), he and his young companion Sandy Irvine were enveloped in clouds and never seen again.

Was Mallory the first man to conquer Everest?

It was the untimely death of Chris Brasher that brought the memory of that lunch flooding back.

I resolved to put into action his second suggestion.

DAY 725　　　MONDAY 21 JULY 2003

5.09 am

I had a good night's sleep and rose early to take a shower. I pack my bags, so that no time will be wasted once the tannoy calls me across to reception.

I am touched by how many prisoners come to my room this morning, to shake me by the hand and wish me luck. However, it is not true, as one tabloid suggested, that I was given a guard of honour as I left the prison.

7.00 am

My last prison breakfast – cornflakes and milk. I can't help looking at my watch every few minutes.

8.09 am

I am called to reception where – no surprise – there is a new bundle of forms to be signed before I can be released.

At last, my release papers are completed by Mr Swivenbank, and he doesn't try to hide a grin as he hands over my regulation £40. I place the notes in the charity box on the counter, shake hands with both officers and depart, with the seventh draft of a screenplay, tucked under my arm, and in my pocket a CD of a song that was performed by The Seven Deadly Sins at my farewell party last night. (See overleaf.)

Will is sitting in my car parked outside the back door, waiting for me. He drives us slowly through the phalanx of journalists who litter both sides of the road. Just as we accelerate away and I think we've escaped them, we spot a Sky TV news helicopter hovering above us, as well as three motorbikes with cameramen glued to the back seats, and another five cars behind them, in close pursuit. Will never once exceeded the speed limit on the journey home to Cambridge.

On arrival back at the Old Vicarage, Mary dashes out to greet me, and I make a short press statement:

Press Release: Embargoed until midnight, Sunday 20 July 2003

Statement by Jeffrey Archer

I want to thank my wife Mary and my sons, William and James, for their unwavering and unstinting support during this unhappy period in my life.

I should also like to thank the many friends who took the trouble to visit me in prison, as well as countless members of the public who sent letters, cards and gifts.

I shall not be giving any interviews for the foreseeable future.

However, I have accepted an invitation to address the Howard League for Penal Reform's conference at New College Oxford in September, and several requests to do charity auctions in the run up to Christmas.

* * *

JEFFREY

(to the tune of 'Daniel' by Elton John)

Jeffrey is leaving today down the lane
I can see the paparazzi, flashing away in vain;
Oh, and I can see Jeffrey waving goodbye;
God, it looks like Jeffrey might have a teardrop in his eye.

Oh, ooh, Jeffrey our brother, bet you're glad to be free;
Now you can tell the world what you think of Narey.
You did time well, it's now your time to tell;
Jeffrey, you're a star, go on, son, give 'em hell.

I have not given an interview to the press, or appeared on radio or television, since.

During the last year, I have addressed a dozen or so organizations since speaking to the Howard League, including the Disraelian Society, Trinity College Oxford, the Thirty Club, the Hawks club and the Criminal Law Solicitors' Association.

I have also conducted twenty charity auctions, raising just over a million pounds, and run the Flora London marathon (5 hrs 26 mins) where I was overtaken by a camel, a phone box, a cake and a girl walking.

Most of my spare time has been taken up with carrying out research for my next novel – and continuing to work on the screenplay of *Mallory: Walking Off the Map*.

POSTSCRIPT

Many people have asked me during the past year if there are any particular prison reforms I would urge the Home Office to implement.

I believe that there are three changes the Home Secretary could put in place at little extra cost that would be of great benefit to the public.

1) During a trial, defendants should be categorized A, B, C or D. This would allow first offenders, with no history of violence or drugs, to be sent directly to an open prison, where they would be less likely to come into contact with professional criminals, violent thugs and drug addicts.

2) The punishment for smoking marijuana in prison should *not* be the same as for those prisoners who take heroin.

   This would stop a number of social marijuana smokers turning to heroin simply because marijuana remains in the bloodstream for twenty-eight days, while heroin can be flushed out in twenty-four hours by drinking pints of water, thus avoiding any adverse MDT result.

3) Payment to inmates for all jobs throughout the Prison Service should be universal and standardized, including payment to those who opt to do education.

   If prisoners knew it was just as financially rewarding to

learn to read and write, to take a GCSE or even a degree, perhaps they would not only sign up, but be less likely to reoffend once they've been released.

If these three recommendations were to be taken up, I would feel that my two years in prison were not entirely without purpose.